STRUCTURAL ECONOMETRIC MODELS

ADVANCES IN ECONOMETRICS

Series Editors: Juan Carlos Escanciano,
Thomas B. Fomby, R. Carter Hill,
Eric Hillebrand, David Jacho-Chávez,
Ivan Jeliazkov, Daniel L. Millimet,
and Rodney Strachan

Recent Volumes:

Volume 20B: Econometric Analysis of Financial and Economic Time Series – Edited by Dek Terrell and Thomas B. Fomby

Volume 21: Modelling and Evaluating Treatment Effects in Econometrics – Edited by Daniel L. Millimet, Jeffrey A. Smith and Edward Vytlacil

Volume 22: Econometrics and Risk Management – Edited by Jean-Pierre Fouque, Thomas B. Fomby and Knut Solna

Volume 23: Bayesian Econometrics – Edited by Siddhartha Chib, Gary Koop, Bill Griffiths and Dek Terrell

Volume 24: Measurement Error: Consequences, Applications and Solutions – Edited by Jane Binner, David Edgerton and Thomas Elger

Volume 25: Nonparametric Econometric Methods – Edited by Qi Li and Jeffrey S. Racine

Volume 26: Maximum Simulated Likelihood Methods and Applications – Edited by R. Carter Hill and William Greene

Volume 27A: Missing Data Methods: Cross-Sectional Methods and Applications – Edited by David M. Drukker

Volume 27B: Missing Data Methods: Time-Series Methods and Applications – Edited by David M. Drukker

Volume 28: DSGE Models in Macroeconomics: Estimation, Evaluation and New Developments – Edited by Nathan Balke, Fabio Canova, Fabio Milani and Mark Wynne

Volume 29: Essays in Honor of Jerry Hausman – Edited by Badi H. Baltagi, Whitney Newey, Hal White and R. Carter Hill

Volume 30: 30th Anniversary Edition – Edited by Dek Terrell and Daniel Millmet

ADVANCES IN ECONOMETRICS VOLUME 31

STRUCTURAL ECONOMETRIC MODELS

EDITED BY

EUGENE CHOO
University of Calgary, Calgary, Canada

MATTHEW SHUM
California Institute of Technology, Pasadena, CA, USA

Emerald

United Kingdom – North America – Japan
India – Malaysia – China

Emerald Group Publishing Limited
Howard House, Wagon Lane, Bingley BD16 1WA, UK

First edition 2013

British Library Cataloguing in Publication Data
A catalogue record for this book is available from the British Library

ISBN: 978-1-78350-052-9
ISSN: 0731-9053 (Series)

CONTENTS

LIST OF CONTRIBUTORS

Victor Aguirregabiria	Department of Economics, University of Toronto, Toronto, ON, Canada
Peter Arcidiacono	Department of Economics, Duke University, Durham, NC, USA
Patrick Bayer	Department of Economics, Duke University, Durham, NC, USA
Federico A. Bugni	Department of Economics, Duke University, Durham, NC, USA
Jiawei Chen	Department of Economics, University of California-Irvine, Irvine, CA, USA
Eugene Choo	Department of Economics, University of Calgary, Calgary, Canada
Federico Echenique	Division of Humanities and Social Sciences, California Institute of Technology, Pasadena, CA, USA
Alfred Galichon	Department of Economics, Sciences Po, Paris, France
Bryan S. Graham	Department of Economics, University of California-Berkeley, Berkeley, CA, USA
Yingyao Hu	Department of Economics, Johns Hopkins University, Baltimore, MD, USA
Jonathan James	California Polytechnic State University, San Luis Obispo, CA, USA
Ivana Komunjer	Department of Economics, University of California-San Diego, La Jolla, CA, USA
SangMok Lee	Department of Economics, University of Pennsylvania, Philadelphia, PA, USA

Arvind Magesan	Department of Economics, University of Calgary, Calgary, Canada
Matthew Shum	Division of Humanities and Social Sciences, California Institute of Technology, Pasadena, CA, USA
Shannon Seitz	Analysis Group, Inc., Boston, MA, USA
Wei Tan	Hanqing Institute of Economics and Finance, Renmin University of China, Beijing, China
Migiwa Tanaka	Department of Economics, University of Toronto, Toronto, ON, Canada
Kosuke Uetake	School of Management, Yale University, New Haven, CT, USA
Yasutora Watanabe	Department of Management and Strategy, Kellogg School of Management, Northwestern University, Evanston, IL, USA

INTRODUCTION

This volume of Advances in Econometrics series focuses on recent developments in the use of structural econometric models in empirical economics. Structural econometric models has recently gained popularity in a diverse set of fields in economics. These models explicit combines formal economic modeling with statistical theories to describe data. The articles in this volume are divided in to three broad groups. The first part looks at recent developments in the estimation of dynamic discrete choice models. This includes using new estimation methods for these models based on Euler equations, estimation using sieve approximation of high dimensional state space, the identification of Markov dynamic games with persistent unobserved state variables. The second part looks at recent advances in the area empirical matching models. The articles in this section look at developing estimators for matching models based on stability conditions, estimating matching surplus functions using generalized entropy functions, and solving for the fixed point in the Choo–Siow matching model using a contraction mapping formulation. While the issue of incomplete, or partial identification of model parameters is touched upon in some of the foregoing articles, two articles focus on this issue, in the context of testing for monotone comparative statics in models with multiple equilibria, and estimation of supermodular games under the restrictions that players' strategies be rationalizable. The last group of four articles looks at empirical applications using structural econometric models. Two application applies matching models to solve endogenous matching to the loan spread equation and to endogenize marriage in the collective model of intrahousehold allocation. Other applications examine market power of condominium developers in the Japanese housing market in the 1990s, and cigarette firms' repsonses to the U.S. government's anti-smoking policies.

The volume begins with "Euler Equations for the Estimation of Dynamic Discrete Choice Structural Models," by Victor Aguirregabiria and Arvind Magesan, that proposes a two-step method based on moment conditions that involve payoffs and choice probabilities at only two periods. The main advantages of this method are that: it does not require approximation of value functions; choice probabilities should be estimated at only states observed in the sample; and it can be applied to nonstationary models using very short panels. The article includes examples for the derivation of this discrete type of Euler equations, and presents an empirical application to illustrate the method.

The article entitled "Approximating High-Dimensional Dynamic Models: Sieve Value Function Iteration" introduces a method for approximating the value function of high-dimensional dynamic models based on sieves. Peter Arcidiacono, Patrick Bayer, Federico A. Bugni, and Jonathan James establish (a) consistency, (b) rates of convergence, and (c) bounds on the error of approximation. The method can be embedded in an estimation routine without affecting the consistency of the estimates of the model's parameters. Monte Carlo evidence shows that the method can successfully be used to approximate models that would otherwise be infeasible to compute, suggesting that these techniques may substantially broaden the class of models that can be solved and estimated.

In "Identifying Dynamic Games with Serially Correlated Unobservables," Yingyao Hu and Matthew Shum consider the nonparametric identification of Markov dynamic games models in which each firm has its own unobserved state variable, which is persistent over time. These models have been the basis for much of the recent empirical applications of dynamic game models. The authors provide conditions under which the joint Markov equilibrium process of the firms' observed and unobserved variables can be nonparametrically identified from data. For stationary continuous action games, they show that only three observations of the observed component are required to identify the equilibrium Markov process of the dynamic game. When agents' choice variables are discrete, but the unobserved state variables are continuous, four observations are required.

The second part of the volume begins with "Partial Identification in Two-Sided Matching Models." In this article Federico Echenique, SangMok Lee, and Matthew Shum propose a methodology for estimating preference parameters in matching models. The proposed estimator applies to repeated observations of matchings among a fixed group of individuals, and is based on stability conditions in the matching models. Transferable utility (TU) and nontransferable utility (NTU) models are considered. In both cases, the stability conditions yield moment inequalities which can be taken to the data. The preference parameters are partially identified. The article presents an empirical application to aggregate marriage markets.

Alfred Galichon's article on "Identification of Matching Complementarities: A Geometric Viewpoint" deals with the identification of matching complementarities interpreted from a geometric viewpoint. A geometric formulation of the problem of identification of the matching surplus function is provided. Geometrically, optimal assignments lie on the boundary of the set of assignments, while the assignments observed in the data are usually on the interior of that set. Galichon shows how the estimation problem can be solved by the introduction of a generalized entropy function over the set of matchings. The effect of this addition is to attain interior points, allowing one to rationalize assignments that are empirically observed.

Bryan S. Graham's article on "Comparative Static and Computational Methods for an Empirical One-to-One Transferable Utility Matching Model" shows that the equilibrium distribution of matches associated with the empirical transferable utility (TU) one-to-one Choo-Siow matching model corresponds to the fixed point of a contraction mapping. The contraction mapping representation suggests to new approach to estimation of these models, based on computation of the equilibrium. He further derives comparative static results, some in closed-form, showing how the match distribution varies with match surplus and the marginal distributions of agent types.

In "A Test for Monotone Comparative Statics," Federico Echenique and Ivana Komunjer design an econometric test for a class of models that may have multiple equilibria. It exploits the property that the extreme quantiles of the dependent variable increase monotonically with the explanatory variables. The test is an asymptotic "chi-bar squared" test for order restrictions on intermediate quantiles. Key features of the approach are: (1) no need to estimate the underlying nonparametric model relating the dependent and explanatory variables to the latent disturbances; (2) few assumptions on the cardinality, location, or probabilities over equilibria. The test avoids the need to specify an equilibrium selection rule.Structural models often possess multiple equilibria.

In their article titled "Estimating Supermodular Games using Rationalizable Strategies," Kosuke Uetake and Yasutora Watanabe propose a set-estimation approach to supermodular games using the restrictons of rationalizable strategies. The set of rationalizable strategies of a supermodular game forms a complete lattice, and is bounded below and above by two extremal Nash equilibria. They use a well-known algorithm to compute the two extremal equilibria, and then construct moment inequalities for set estimation of the supermodular game. Finally, they conduct Monte Carlo experiments to illustrate how the estimated confidence sets vary in response to changes in the data generating process.

Finally, the volume concludes with several articles with substantial applications of the models presented in earlier articles. In "Estimation of the Loan Spread Equation with Endogenous Bank-Firm Matching," Jiawei Chen estimates the loan spread equation taking into account the endogenous matching between banks and firms in the loan market. To overcome the endogeneity problem, Chen supplements the loan spread equation with a two-sided matching model and estimate them jointly. He finds that medium-sized banks and firms tend to be the most attractive partners, and that liquidity is also a consideration in choosing partners. Furthermore, banks with higher monitoring ability charge higher spreads, and firms that are more leveraged or less liquid are charged higher spreads.

Eugene Choo and Shannon Seitz contribute a article on "The Collective Marriage Matching Model: Identification, Estimation and Testing." They develop and estimate an empirical collective model with endogenous marriage formation, participation, and family labor supply. Intra-household transfers arise endogenously as the transfers that clear the marriage market. The intra-household allocation can be recovered from observations on marriage decisions. Introducing the marriage market in the collective model allows us to independently estimate transfers from labor supplies and from marriage decisions. They estimate a semi-parametric version of the model using 1980, 1990, and 2000 U.S. Census data. Estimates of the model using marriage data are much more consistent with the theoretical predictions than estimates derived from labor supply.

Migiwa Tanaka's article on "Deflation in Durable Goods Markets: an Empirical Model of the Tokyo Condominium Market" addresses an empirical puzzle in the Japanese housing market. Throughout the 1990s, the supply of new condominiums in Tokyo significantly increased while prices persistently fell. Tanaka's article investigates whether the market power of condominium developers is a factor in explaining the outcome in this market and whether there is a relationship between production cost trend and the degree of market power that the developers were able to exercise. In order to respond to these questions, she constructs and structurally estimates a dynamic durable goods oligopoly model of the condominium market. She finds that the data provide no evidence that firms in the primary market have substantial market power in this industry. Moreover, the counterfactual experiment provides evidence that inflationary and deflationary expectations on production cost trends have asymmetric effects to the market power of condominium producers. The increase in their markup when cost inflation is anticipated is significantly higher than the decrease in the markup when the same magnitude of cost deflation is anticipated.

Wei Tan's concluding article is a "Dynamic Analysis of the U.S. Cigarette Market and Antismoking Policies." Tan constructs a dynamic oligopoly model of the cigarette industry is developed to study the responses of firms to various antismoking policies and to estimate the implications for the policy efficacy. The structural parameters are estimated using a combination of micro and macro level data and firms optimal price and advertising strategies are solved as a Markov Perfect Nash Equilibrium. The simulation results show that tobacco tax increase reduces both the overall smoking rate and the youth smoking rate, while advertising restrictions may increase the youth smoking rate. Firms' responses strengthen the impact of antismoking policies in the short run.

Eugene Choo
Matthew Shum
Editors

PART I
STRUCTURAL DYNAMIC MODELS

EULER EQUATIONS FOR THE ESTIMATION OF DYNAMIC DISCRETE CHOICE STRUCTURAL MODELS

Victor Aguirregabiria and Arvind Magesan

ABSTRACT

We derive marginal conditions of optimality (i.e., Euler equations) for a general class of Dynamic Discrete Choice *(*DDC*) structural models. These conditions can be used to estimate structural parameters in these models without having to solve for approximate value functions. This result extends to discrete choice models the* GMM-Euler equation *approach proposed by Hansen and Singleton (1982) for the estimation of dynamic continuous decision models. We first show that DDC models can be represented as models of continuous choice where the decision variable is a vector of choice probabilities. We then prove that the marginal conditions of optimality and the envelope conditions required to construct Euler equations are also satisfied in* DDC *models. The GMM estimation of these Euler equations avoids the curse of dimensionality associated to the computation of value functions and the explicit integration over the space of state variables. We present an empirical application and compare*

Structural Econometric Models
Advances in Econometrics, Volume 31, 3–44

ISSN: 0731-9053/doi:10.1108/S0731-9053(2013)0000032001

estimates using the GMM-Euler equations method with those from maximum likelihood and two-step methods.

Keywords: Dynamic discrete choice structural models; Euler equations; choice probabilities

JEL classifications: C35; C51; C61

INTRODUCTION

The estimation of *Dynamic Discrete Choice* (*DDC*) *structural models* requires the computation of expectations (value functions) defined as integrals or summations over the space of state variables. In most empirical applications, the range of variation of the vector of state variables is continuous or discrete with a very large number of values. In these cases the exact solution of expectations or value functions is an intractable problem. To deal with this dimensionality problem, applied researchers use approximation techniques such as discretization, Monte Carlo simulation, polynomials, sieves, neural networks, etc.[1] These approximation techniques are needed not only in full-solution estimation techniques but also in any two-step or sequential estimation method that requires the computation of value functions.[2] Replacing *true* expected values with approximations introduces an approximation error, and this error induces a statistical bias in the estimation of the parameter of interests. Though there is a rich literature on the asymptotic properties of these simulation-based estimators,[3] little is known about how to measure this *approximation-induced estimation bias* for a given finite sample.[4]

In this context, the main contribution of this article is in the derivation of marginal conditions of optimality (Euler equations) for a general class of *DDC* models. We show that these Euler equations provide moment conditions that can be used to estimate structural parameters without solving or approximating value functions. The estimator based on these Euler equations is not subject to bias induced by the approximation of value functions. Our result extends to discrete choice models the *GMM-Euler equation* approach that Hansen and Singleton (1982) proposed for the estimation of dynamic models with continuous decision variables. The *GMM-Euler equation* approach has been applied extensively to the estimation of dynamic structural models with continuous decision variables, such as problems of household consumption, savings, and portfolio choices, or firm investment decisions, among others. The conventional wisdom was that this method could not be applied to discrete choice models because, obviously, there are not marginal conditions of optimality with respect to discrete choice variables. In this article, we show that the optimal decision rule in a dynamic (or static) discrete choice model can be derived from a decision problem where the choice variables are probabilities that have continuous support. Using this representation of a discrete choice model, we obtain Euler equations by combining marginal conditions of optimality and Envelope Theorem conditions in a similar way as in dynamic models with continuous decision variables. Just as in the Hansen–Singleton approach, these Euler equations can be used to construct moment conditions and to estimate the structural parameters of the model by GMM without having to evaluate/approximate value functions.

Our derivation of Euler equations for DDC models extends previous work by Hotz and Miller (1993), Aguirregabiria and Mira (2002), and Arcidiacono and Miller (2011). These papers derive representations of optimal decision rules using *Conditional Choice Probabilities* (CCPs) and show how these representations can be applied to estimate DDC models using simple two-step methods that provide substantial computational savings relative to full-solution methods. In these papers, we can distinguish three different types of CCP representations of optimal decisions rules: (1) the *present-value* representation which consists of using CCPs to obtain a closed-form expression for the expected and discounted stream of future payoffs associated with each choice alternative; (2) the *terminal-state* representation which applies only to optimal stopping problems with a terminal state; and (3) the *finite-dependence* representation which was introduced by Arcidiacono and Miller (2011) and applies to a particular class of DDC models with the finite dependence property.[5]

Our article presents a new CCP representation that we call *CCP-Euler-equation* representation. This representation has several advantages over the previous ones. The *present-value representation* is the CCP approach more commonly used in empirical applications because it can be applied to a general class of DDC models. However, that representation requires the computation of present values and therefore it is subject to the curse of dimensionality and to biases induced by approximation error (e.g., discretization, Monte Carlo simulation). The *terminal-state*, the *finite-dependence*, and the CCP-Euler-equation representations do not involve the computation of present values, or even the estimation of CCPs at every possible state, and this implies substantial computational savings as well as avoiding biases induced by approximation errors. Furthermore, relative to *terminal-state* and *finite-dependence* representations, our *Euler equation* applies to a general class of DDC models. We can derive Euler equations for any DDC model where the unobservables satisfy the conditions of additive separability (AS) in the payoff function, and conditional independence (CI) in the transition of the state variables.

The estimation based on the moment conditions provided by the *Euler equation*, or *terminal-state*, or *finite-dependence* representations imply an efficiency loss relative to estimation based on *present-value* representation. As shown by Aguirregabiria and Mira (2002, Proposition 4), the two-step pseudo maximum likelihood (PML) estimator based on the CCP *present-value* representation is asymptotically efficient (equivalent to the maximum likelihood (ML) estimator). However, this efficiency property is not shared by the other CCP representations. Therefore, there is a trade-off in the choice between CCP estimators based on Euler equations and on present-value representations. The present-value representation is the best choice in models that do not require approximation methods. However, in models with large state spaces that require approximation methods, the Euler equations CCP estimator can provide more accurate estimates.

We present an empirical application where we estimate a model of firm investment. We compare estimates using CCP Euler equations, CCP present-value, and ML methods.

EULER EQUATIONS IN DYNAMIC DECISION MODELS

Dynamic Decision Model

Time is discrete and indexed by t. Every period t, an agent chooses an action a_t within the set of feasible actions $\mathcal{A}$ that, for the moment, can be either a continuous or a discrete choice set. The agent makes this decision to maximize his expected intertemporal payoff $\mathbb{E}_t\left[\sum_{j=0}^{T-t} \beta^j \Pi_t(a_{t+j}, s_{t+j})\right]$, where $\beta \in (0,1)$ is the discount factor, T is the time horizon that can be finite or infinite, $\Pi_t(.)$ is the one-period payoff function at period t, and s_t is the vector of state variables at period t. These state variables follow a controlled Markov process, and the transition probability density function at period t is $f_t(s_{t+1}|a_t, s_t)$. By Bellman's principle of optimality, the sequence of value functions $\{V_t(.) : t \geq 1\}$ can be obtained using the recursive expression:

$$V_t(s_t) = \max_{a_t \in A} \left\{ \Pi_t(a_t, s_t) + \beta \int V_{t+1}(s_{t+1}) f_t(s_{t+1} \mid a_t, s_t)\, ds_{t+1} \right\} \tag{1}$$

The sequence of optimal decision rules $\{\alpha_t^*(.) : t \geq 1$ are defined as the argmax in $a_t \in \mathcal{A}$ of the expression within brackets in Eq. (1).

Suppose that the primitives of the model $\{\Pi_t, f_t, \beta\}$ can be characterized in terms of vector of structural parameters θ. The researcher has panel data for N agents (e.g., individuals, firms) over $\tilde{T}$ periods of time, with information on agents' actions and a subset of the state variables. The estimation problem is to use these data to consistently estimate the vector of parameters θ. In this section, we first describe this approach in the context of continuous-choice models, as proposed in the seminal work by Hansen and Singleton (1982). Second, we show how a general class of discrete choice models can be represented as continuous choice models where the decision variable is a vector of choice probabilities. Finally, we show that it is possible to construct Euler equations using this alternative representation of discrete choice models, and that these Euler equations can be used to construct moment conditions and a GMM estimator of the structural parameters θ.

Euler Equations in Dynamic Continuous Decision Models

Suppose that the decision a_t is a vector of continuous variables in the K dimensional Euclidean space: $a_t \in \mathcal{A} \subseteq \mathbb{R}^K$. The vector of state variables $s_t \equiv (y_t, z_t)$ contains both *exogenous* (z_t) and *endogenous* (y_t) variables. Exogenous state variables follow a stochastic process that does not depend on the agent's actions $\{a_t\}$, for example, the price of capital in a model of firm investment under the assumption that firms are price takers in the capital market. In contrast, the evolution over time of the endogenous state variables, y_t, depends on the agent's actions, for example, the stock of capital in a model of firm investment. More precisely, the transition probability function of the state variables is

$$f_t(s_{t+1} | a_t, s_t) = 1\{y_{t+1} = Y(a_t, s_t, z_{t+1})\}\, f_t^z(z_{t+1} | z_t) \tag{2}$$

where $1\{.\}$ is the indicator function, $Y(.)$ is a vector-valued function that represents the transition rule of the endogenous state variables, and f_t^z is the transition density function for the exogenous state variables. For the derivation of Euler equations in a continuous decision model, it is convenient to represent the transition rule of the endogenous state variables using the expression $1\{y_{t+1} = Y(a_t, \mathbf{s}_t, z_{t+1})\}$. This expression establishes that y_{t+1} is a deterministic function of $(a_t, \mathbf{s}_t, z_{t+1})$. However, this structure allows for a stochastic transition in the endogenous state variables because z_{t+1} is an argument of function $Y(.)$.[6] The following assumption provides sufficient conditions for the derivation of Euler equations in dynamic continuous decision models.

Assumption EE-Continuous. (A) The payoff function Π_t and the transition function $Y(.)$ are continuously differentiable in all their arguments. (B) a_t and y_t are both vectors in the K-dimension Euclidean space and for any value of $(a_t, \mathbf{s}_t, z_{t+1})$ we have that

$$\frac{\partial Y(a_t, \mathbf{s}_t, z_{t+1})}{\partial y_t'} = H(a_t, \mathbf{s}_t) \frac{\partial Y(a_t, \mathbf{s}_t, z_{t+1})}{\partial a_t'} \tag{3}$$

where $H(a_t, \mathbf{s}_t)$ is a $K \times K$ matrix.

For the derivation of the Euler equations, we consider the following *constrained optimization problem*. We want to find the decisions rules at periods t and $t+1$ that maximize the one-period-forward expected profit $\Pi_t + \beta\, \mathbb{E}_t(\Pi_{t+1})$ under the constraint that the probability distribution of the endogenous state variables y_{t+2} conditional on $\mathbf{s}_t$ implied by the new decision rules $\alpha_t(.)$ and $\alpha_{t+1}(.)$ is identical to that distribution under the optimal decision rules of our original DP problem, $\alpha_t^*(.)$ and $\alpha_{t+1}^*(.)$. By construction, this optimization problem depends on payoffs at periods t and $t+1$ only, and not on payoffs at $t+2$ and beyond. And by definition of optimal decision rules, we have that $\alpha_t^*(.)$ and $\alpha_{t+1}^*(.)$ should be the optimal solutions to this constrained optimization problem. For a given value of the state variables $\mathbf{s}_t$, we can represent this constrained optimization problem as

$$\begin{array}{l} \max_{\{a_t, a_{t+1}\} \in \mathcal{A}^2} \left\{ \Pi_t(a_t, \mathbf{s}_t) + \beta \int \Pi_{t+1}(a_{t+1}, Y(a_t, \mathbf{s}_t, z_{t+1}), z_{t+1})\, f_t^z(z_{t+1}|z_t) dz_{t+1} \right\} \\ \text{subject to: } Y(a_{t+1}, Y(a_t, \mathbf{s}_t, z_{t+1}), z_{t+1}, z_{t+2}) = \kappa_{t+2}^*(\mathbf{s}_t, z_{t+1}, z_{t+2}) \end{array} \tag{4}$$

where $Y(a_{t+1}, Y(a_t, \mathbf{s}_t, z_{t+1}), z_{t+1}, z_{t+2})$ represents the realization of y_{t+2} under arbitrary choice (a_t, a_{t+1}), and $\kappa_{t+2}^*(\mathbf{s}_t, z_{t+1}, z_{t+2})$ is a function that represents the realization of y_{t+2} under the optimal decision rules $\alpha_t^*(\mathbf{s}_t)$ and $\alpha_{t+1}^*(\mathbf{s}_{t+1})$, and it does not depend on (a_t, a_{t+1}). This constrained optimization problem can be solved using the Lagrangian method. It is possible to show that the optimal solution should satisfy the following marginal condition of optimality:[7]

$$\mathbb{E}_t\left(\frac{\partial \Pi_t}{\partial a_t'} + \beta\left[\frac{\partial \Pi_{t+1}}{\partial y_{t+1}'} - H(a_{t+1}, s_{t+1})\frac{\partial \Pi_{t+1}}{\partial a_{t+1}'}\right]\frac{\partial Y_{t+1}}{\partial a_t'}\right) = 0 \tag{5}$$

where $\mathbb{E}_t(.)$ represents the expectation over the distribution of $\{a_{t+1}, s_{t+1}\}$ conditional on (a_t, s_t). This system of equations is the *Euler equations* of the model.

Example 1. (*Optimal consumption and portfolio choice*; Hansen & Singleton, 1982). The vector of decision variables is $(c_t, q_{1t}, q_{2t}, \ldots, q_{Jt})$ where c_t represents the individual's consumption expenditure, and q_{jt} denotes the number of shares of asset/security j that the individual holds in his portfolio at period t. The utility function depends only on consumption, that is, $\Pi_t(a_t, s_t) = U_t(c_t)$. The consumer's budget constraint establishes that $c_t + \sum_{j=1}^{J} r_{jt}q_{jt} \leq w_t + \sum_{j=1}^{J} r_{jt}$, where w_t is labor earnings, and r_{jt} is the price of asset j at time t. Given that the budget constraint is satisfied with equality, we can write the utility function as $\Pi_t(a_t, s_t) = U_t\left(w_t - \sum_{j=1}^{J} r_{jt}[q_{jt} - q_{jt-1}]\right)$, and the decision problem can be represented in terms of the decision variables $a_t = (q_{1t}, q_{2t}, \ldots, q_{Jt})$. The vector of exogenous state variables is $z_t = (w_t, r_{1t}, r_{2t}, \ldots, r_{Jt})$, and the vector of endogenous state variables consists of the individual's asset holdings at $t-1$, $y_t = (q_{1t-1}, q_{2t-1}, \ldots, q_{Jt-1})$. Therefore, the transition rule of the endogenous state variables is trivial, that is, $y_{t+1} = a_t$, such that $\partial Y_{t+1}/\partial y_t' = 0$, $\partial Y_{t+1}/\partial a_t' = I$, and the matrix $H(a_t, s_t)$ is a matrix of zeros. Also, given the form of the utility function, we have that $\partial \Pi_t/\partial q_{jt} = -U_t'(c_t)r_{jt}$ and $\partial \Pi_t/\partial q_{jt-1} = U_t'(c_t)r_{jt}$. Plugging these expression in the general formula (5), we obtain the following system of Euler equations: for any asset $j = 1, 2, \ldots, J$:

$$\mathbb{E}_t\left(U_t'(c_t)r_{jt} - \beta U_{t+1}'(c_{t+1})r_{jt+1}\right) = 0 \tag{6}$$

Random Utility Model as a Continuous Optimization Problem

Before considering DDC models, in this section we describe how the optimal decision rule in a static discrete choice model can be represented using marginal conditions of optimality in an optimization problem where decision variables are (choice) probabilities. Later, we apply this result in our derivation of Euler equations in DDC models.

Consider the following *Additive Random Utility Model* (ARUM) (McFadden, 1981). The set of feasible choices $\mathcal{A}$ is discrete and finite and it includes $J+1$ choice alternatives: $\mathcal{A}=\{0,1,\ldots,J\}$. Let $a\in\mathcal{A}$ represent the agent's choice. The payoff function has the following structure:

$$\Pi(a,\varepsilon)=\pi(a)+\varepsilon(a) \tag{7}$$

where $\pi(.)$ is a real valued function, and $\varepsilon\equiv\{\varepsilon(0),\ \varepsilon(1),\ldots,\varepsilon(J)\}$ is a vector of exogenous variables affecting the agent's payoff. The vector ε has a cumulative distribution function (CDF) G that is absolutely continuous with respect to Lebesgue measure, strictly increasing and continuously differentiable in all its arguments, and with finite means. The agent observes ε and chooses the action a that maximizes his payoff $\pi(a)+\varepsilon(a)$. The optimal decision rule of this model is a function $\alpha^*(\varepsilon)$ from the state space $\mathbb{R}^{J+1}$ into the action space $\mathcal{A}$ such that: $\alpha^*(\varepsilon)=\text{argmax}_{a\in\mathcal{A}}\{\pi(a)+\varepsilon(a)\}$. By the AS of the ε's, this optimal decision rule can be written as follows: for any $a\in\mathcal{A}$

$$\left\{\alpha^*(\varepsilon)=a\right\} \quad \text{iff} \quad \left\{\varepsilon(j)-\varepsilon(a)\leq\pi(a)-\pi(j) \ \text{ for any } j\neq a\right\} \tag{8}$$

Given this form of the optimal decision rule, we can restrict our analysis to decision rules with the following threshold form: $\left\{\alpha(\varepsilon)=a\right\}$ if and only if $\{\varepsilon(j)-\varepsilon(a)\leq\mu(a)-\mu(j)$ for any $j\neq a\}$, where $\mu(a)$ is an arbitrary real valued function. We can represent decision rules within this class using a CCP function $P(a)$, that is the decision rule integrated over the vector of random variables ε, that is, $P(a)\equiv\int 1\left\{\alpha(\varepsilon)=a\right\}G(\varepsilon)d\varepsilon$. Therefore, we have that

$$\begin{aligned} P(a)= & \int 1\left\{\varepsilon(j)-\varepsilon(a)\leq\mu(a)-\mu(j) \ \text{ for any } j\neq a\right\} \\ & dG(\varepsilon)=\tilde{G}_a(\mu(a)-\mu(j) : \text{for any } j\neq a) \end{aligned} \tag{9}$$

where $1\{.\}$ is the indicator function, and $\tilde{G}_a$ is the CDF of the vector $\{\varepsilon(j)-\varepsilon(a)$: for any $j\neq a\}$.

Lemma 1 establishes that in an ARUM we can represent decision rules using a vector of CCPs $\mathbf{P}\equiv\{P(1),P(2),\ldots,P(J)\}$ in the J-dimension simplex.

Lemma 1. (McFadden, 1981). Consider an ARUM where the distribution of ε is G that is absolutely continuous with respect to Lebesgue measure, strictly increasing and continuously differentiable in all its arguments. *Let* $\alpha(.)$ be a discrete-valued function from $\mathbb{R}^{J+1}$ into $\mathcal{A} = \{0, 1, ..., J\}$; let $\mathbf{m} \equiv \{\mu(1), \mu(2), ..., \mu(J)\}$ be a vector in the J-dimension Euclidean space, and consider the normalization $\mu(0) = 0$; and let $\mathbf{P} \equiv \{P(1), P(2), ..., P(J)\}$ be a vector in the J-dimension simplex $\mathcal{S}$. We can say that $\alpha(.)$, μ, and $\mathbf{P}$ represent the same decision rule in the ARUM if and only if the following conditions hold:

$$\alpha(\varepsilon) = \sum_{a=0}^{J} a 1\{\varepsilon(j) - \varepsilon(a) \leq \mu(a) - \mu(j) \text{ for any } j \neq a\} \tag{10}$$

and for any $a \in \mathcal{A}$

$$P(a) = \tilde{G}_a(\mu(a) - \mu(j)\text{: for any } j \neq a) \tag{11}$$

where $\tilde{G}_a$ is the CDF of the vector $\{\varepsilon(j) - \varepsilon(a)\text{: for any } j \neq a\}$.

Lemma 2 establishes the invertibility of the relationship between the vector of CCPs $\mathbf{P}$ and the vector of threshold values μ.

Lemma 2. (Hotz & Miller, 1993) Let $\tilde{\mathbf{G}}(.)$ be the vector-valued mapping $\{\tilde{G}_1(.), \tilde{G}_2(.), ..., \tilde{G}_J(.)\}$ from $\mathbb{R}^J$ into $\mathcal{S}$. Under the conditions of Lemma 1, the mapping $\tilde{\mathbf{G}}(.)$ is invertible everywhere. We represent the inverse mapping as $\tilde{G}^{-1}(.)$.

Given an arbitrary decision rule, represented in terms $\alpha(.)$, or μ, or $\mathbf{P}$, let Π^e be the expected payoff before the realization of the vector ε if the agent behaves according to this arbitrary decision rule. By definition

$$\Pi^e \equiv \int \{\pi(\alpha(\varepsilon)) + \varepsilon(\alpha(\varepsilon))\} dG(\varepsilon) = \mathbb{E}[\pi(\alpha(\varepsilon)) + \varepsilon(\alpha(\varepsilon))] \tag{12}$$

where the expectation $\mathbb{E}(.)$ is over the distribution of ε. By Lemmas 1–2, we can represent this expected payoff as a function either of $\alpha(.)$, or μ, or $\mathbf{P}$. For our analysis, it is most convenient to represent it as a function of CCPs, that is, $\Pi^e(\mathbf{P})$. Given its definition, this expected payoff function can be written as

$$\Pi^e(\mathbf{P}) = \sum_{a=0}^{J} P(a)\{\pi(a) + e(a, \mathbf{P})\} = \pi(0) + e(0, \mathbf{P}) + \sum_{a=1}^{J} P(a)\{\pi(a) - \pi(0) + e(a, \mathbf{P}) - e(0, \mathbf{P})\} \tag{13}$$

where $e(a,\mathbf{P})$ is defined as the expected value of $\varepsilon(a)$ conditional on alternative a being chosen under decision rule $\alpha(\varepsilon)$. That is, $e(a,\mathbf{P}) \equiv \mathbb{E}(\varepsilon(a) \mid \alpha(\varepsilon)=a)$, and as a function of $\mathbf{P}$ we have that

$$e(a,\mathbf{P}) = \mathbb{E}\left(\varepsilon(a) \mid \varepsilon(j) - \varepsilon(a) \leq \tilde{G}^{-1}(a,\mathbf{P}) - \tilde{G}^{-1}(j,\mathbf{P}) \text{ for any } j \neq a\right) \tag{14}$$

The conditions of the ARUM imply that functions $e(a,\mathbf{P})$ and $\Pi^e(\mathbf{P})$ are continuously differentiable with respect to $\mathbf{P}$ everywhere on the simplex $\mathcal{S}$. Therefore, this expected payoff function $\Pi^e(\mathbf{P})$ has a maximum on $\mathcal{S}$. We can define $\mathbf{P}^*$ as the vector of CCPs that maximizes this expected payoff function:

$$\mathbf{P}^* = \underset{\mathbf{P} \in \mathcal{S}}{\operatorname{argmax}} \left\{\Pi^e(\mathbf{P})\right\} \tag{15}$$

Then, we have two representations of the ARUM, and two apparently different decision problems. On the one hand, we have the discrete choice model with the optimal decision rule $\alpha^*(.)$ in Eq. (8) that maximizes the payoff $\pi(a)+\varepsilon(a)$ after ε is realized and known to the agent. We denote this as the ex-post decision problem to emphasize that the decision is *after* the realization of ε is known to the agent. Associated to α^*, we have its corresponding CCP, that we can represent as $\mathbf{P}^{\alpha^*}$, that is equal to $\tilde{\mathbf{G}}(\tilde{\pi})$ where $\tilde{\pi}$ is the vector of differential payoffs $\{\tilde{\pi}(a) \equiv \pi(a) - \pi(0)$: for any $a \neq 0$. For econometric analysis of ARUM, we are interested in the $\mathbf{P}^{\alpha^*}$ representation because these are CCPs from the point of view of the econometrician (who does not observe ε) describing the behavior of an agent who knows π and ε and maximizes his payoff. On the other hand, we have the optimization problem represented by Eq. (15) where the agent chooses the vector of CCPs $\mathbf{P}$ to maximize his ex-ante expected payoff Π^e before the realization of ε. In principle, this second optimization problem is not the one the ARUM assumes the individual is solving. In the ARUM we assume that the individual makes his choice after observing the realization of the vector of ε's. Proposition 1 establishes that these two optimization problems are equivalent, that the choice probabilities $\mathbf{P}^{\alpha^*}$ and $\mathbf{P}^*$ are the same, and that $\mathbf{P}^*$ can be described in terms of the marginal conditions of optimality associated to the continuous optimization problem in Eq. (15).

Proposition 1. Let $\mathbf{P}^{\alpha^*}$ be the vector of CCPs associated with the optimal decision rule α^* in the discrete decision problem (8), and let $\mathbf{P}^*$ be the vector of CCPs that solves the continuous optimization problem (15). Then, (i) the vectors $\mathbf{P}^{\alpha^*}$ and $\mathbf{P}^*$ are the same; and (ii) $\mathbf{P}^*$ satisfies the marginal conditions of optimality $\partial \Pi^e(\mathbf{P}^*)/\partial P(a)=0$ for any $a>0$, and the marginal expected payoff $\partial \Pi^e(\mathbf{P})/\partial P(a)$ has the following form:

$$\frac{\partial \Pi^e(\mathbf{P})}{\partial P(a)} = \pi(a) - \pi(0) + e(a,\mathbf{P}) - e(0,\mathbf{P}) + \sum_{j=0}^{J} P(j)\frac{\partial e(j,\mathbf{P})}{\partial P(a)} \tag{16}$$

Proof in the appendix.

Proposition 1 establishes a characterization of the optimal decision rule in terms of marginal conditions of optimality with respect to CCPs. In the third section, we show that these conditions can be used to construct moment conditions and a two-step estimator of the structural parameters.

Example 2. (*Multinomial logit*). Suppose that the unobservable variables $\varepsilon(a)$ are i.i.d. with an extreme value type 1 distribution. For this distribution, the function $e(a,\mathbf{P})$ has the following simple form: $e(a,\mathbf{P})= \gamma - \ln P(a)$, where γ is Euler's constant (see the appendix to Chapter 2 in Anderson, de Palma, and Thisse (1992), for a derivation of this property). Plugging this expression into Eq. (16), we get the following marginal condition of optimality:

$$\frac{\partial \Pi^e(\mathbf{P}^*)}{\partial P(a)} = \pi(a) - \pi(0) - \ln P^*(a) + \ln P^*(0) = 0 \tag{17}$$

because in this model, for any a, the term $\sum_{j=0}^{J} P(j)\,[\partial e(j,\mathbf{P})/\partial P(a)]$ is zero.[8]

Example 3. (*Binary probit model*). Suppose that the decision model is binary, $\mathcal{A}=\{0,1\}$, and $\varepsilon(0)$ and $\varepsilon(1)$ are independently and identically distributed with a normal distribution with zero mean and variance σ^2. Let $\phi(.)$ and $\Phi(.)$ denote the density and the CDFs for the standard normal, respectively, and let $\Phi^{-1}(.)$ be the inverse function of Φ. Given this distribution, it is possible to show that $e(0,P(1))=\frac{\sigma}{\sqrt{2}}\frac{\phi(\Phi^{-1}[1-P(1)])}{1-P(1)}$, and $e(1,P(1))=\frac{\sigma}{\sqrt{2}}\frac{\phi(\Phi^{-1}[P(1)])}{P(1)}$. Using these expressions, we have that[9]

$$\begin{aligned}\frac{\partial e(0,P(1))}{\partial P(1)} &= \frac{\sigma}{\sqrt{2}}\left[\frac{-\Phi^{-1}(1-P(1))}{1-P(1)} + \frac{\phi(\Phi^{-1}[P(1)])}{[1-P(1)]^2}\right]\\ \frac{\partial e(1,P(1))}{\partial P(1)} &= \frac{\sigma}{\sqrt{2}}\left[\frac{-\Phi^{-1}(P(1))}{P(1)} - \frac{\phi(\Phi^{-1}[P(1)])}{P(1)^2}\right]\end{aligned} \tag{18}$$

Solving these expressions into the first order condition in Eq. (16) and taking into account that by symmetry of the Normal distribution

$\Phi^{-1}(1 - P(1)) = -\Phi^{-1}(P(1))$, we get the following marginal condition of optimality:

$$\frac{\partial \Pi^e(\mathbf{P}^*)}{\partial P(1)} = \pi(1) - \pi(0) - \sqrt{2}\sigma\, \Phi^{-1}(P(1)) = 0 \tag{19}$$

Euler Equations in Dynamic Discrete Choice Models

Consider the dynamic decision model in section "Dynamic Decision Model" but suppose now that the set of feasible actions is discrete and finite: $\mathcal{A} = \{0, 1, \ldots, J\}$. There are two sets of state variables: $\boldsymbol{s}_t = (\boldsymbol{x}_t, \varepsilon_t)$, where $\boldsymbol{x}_t$ is the vector of state variables observable to the researcher, and ε_t represents the unobservables for the researcher. The set of observable state variables $\boldsymbol{x}_t$ itself is comprised by two types of state variables, exogenous variables z_t and endogenous variables y_t. They are distinguished by the fact that the transition probability of the endogenous variables depends on the action a_t, while the transition probability of the exogenous variables does not depend on a_t. The vector of unobservables satisfies the assumptions of AS and CI (Rust, 1994).

Additive Separability (AS): The one-period payoff function is additively separable in the unobservables: $\Pi_t(a_t, \boldsymbol{s}_t) = \pi_t(a_t, \boldsymbol{x}_t) + \varepsilon_t(a_t)$, *where* $\varepsilon_t \equiv \{\varepsilon_t(a) : a \in \mathcal{A}\}$ *is a vector of unobservable random variables.*

Conditional Independence (CI): The transition probability (density) function of the state variables factors as: $f_t(\boldsymbol{s}_{t+1} | a_t, \boldsymbol{s}_t) = f_{xt}(\boldsymbol{x}_{t+1} | a_t, \boldsymbol{x}_t)\, dG(\varepsilon_{t+1})$, *where* $G(.)$ *is the CDF of* ε_t *which is absolutely continuous with respect to Lebesgue measure, strictly increasing and continuously differentiable in all its arguments, and with finite means.*

Under these assumptions the optimal decision rules $\alpha_t^*(\boldsymbol{x}_t, \varepsilon_t)$ have the following form:

$$\left\{\alpha_t^*(\boldsymbol{x}_t, \varepsilon_t) = a\right\} \quad \text{iff} \quad \left\{\varepsilon_t(j) - \varepsilon_t(a) \leq v_t(a, \boldsymbol{x}_t) - v_t(j, \boldsymbol{x}_t) \text{ for any } j \neq a\right\} \tag{20}$$

where $v_t(a, \boldsymbol{x}_t)$ is the conditional-choice value function that is defined as $v_t(a, \boldsymbol{x}_t) \equiv \pi_t(a, \boldsymbol{x}_t) + \beta \int_{\boldsymbol{x}_{t+1}} \overline{V}_{t+1}(\boldsymbol{x}_{t+1})\, f_{xt}(\boldsymbol{x}_{t+1} | a, \boldsymbol{x}_t) d\boldsymbol{x}_{t+1}$, and $\overline{V}_t(\boldsymbol{x}_t)$ is the *integrated value function*, $\overline{V}_t(\boldsymbol{x}_t) \equiv \int_{\varepsilon_t} V_t(\boldsymbol{x}_t, \varepsilon_t)\, dG(\varepsilon_t)$. Furthermore, the integrated value function satisfies the following integrated Bellman equation:

$$\overline{V}_t(\boldsymbol{x}_t) = \int_{\varepsilon_t} \max_{a_t \in \mathcal{A}} \left\{ \pi_t(a_t, \boldsymbol{x}_t) + \varepsilon_t(a_t) + \beta \int \overline{V}_{t+1}(\boldsymbol{x}_{t+1}) f_{xt}(\boldsymbol{x}_{t+1} | a, \boldsymbol{x}_t)\, d\boldsymbol{x}_{t+1} \right\} dG_t(\varepsilon_t) \tag{21}$$

We can restrict our analysis to decision rules $\alpha_t(\boldsymbol{x}_t, \varepsilon_t)$ with the following "threshold" structure: $\{\alpha_t(\boldsymbol{x}_t, \varepsilon_t) = a\}$ if and only if $\{\varepsilon_t(j) - \varepsilon_t(a) \leq \mu_t(a, \boldsymbol{x}_t) - \mu_t(j, \boldsymbol{x}_t)$ for any $j \neq a\}$, where $\mu_t(a, \boldsymbol{x}_t)$ is an arbitrary real valued function. As in the ARUM, we can represent decision rules using a discrete valued function $\alpha_t(\boldsymbol{x}_t, \varepsilon_t)$, a real valued function $\mu_t(a, \boldsymbol{x}_t)$, or a probability valued function $P_t(a \mid \boldsymbol{x}_t)$.

$$
\begin{aligned}
P_t(a|\boldsymbol{x}_t) &\equiv \int 1\{\alpha_t(\boldsymbol{x}_t, \varepsilon_t) = a\} G_t(\varepsilon_t)\, d\varepsilon_t \\
&= \tilde{G}_a\big(\mu_t(a, \boldsymbol{x}_t) - \mu_t(j, \boldsymbol{x}_t): \text{for any } j \neq 0,\ a\big)
\end{aligned}
\tag{22}
$$

where $\tilde{G}_a$ has the same interpretation as in the ARUM, that is, the CDF of the vector $\{\varepsilon(j) - \varepsilon(a)\ :\ \text{for any } j \neq a\}$. Lemmas 1 and 2 from the ARUM extend to this DDC model (Proposition 1 in Hotz & Miller, 1993). In particular, at every period t, there is a one-to-one relationship between the vector of value differences $\tilde{\mu}_t(\boldsymbol{x}_t) \equiv \{\mu_t(a, \boldsymbol{x}_t) - \mu_t(0, \boldsymbol{x}_t): a > 0$ and the vector of CCPs $\mathbf{P}_t(\boldsymbol{x}_t) \equiv \{P_t(a|\boldsymbol{x}_t) : a \neq 0$. We represent this mapping as $\mathbf{P}_t(\boldsymbol{x}_t) = \tilde{G}(\tilde{\mu}_t(\boldsymbol{x}_t))$, and the corresponding inverse mapping as $\tilde{\mu}_t(\boldsymbol{x}_t) = \tilde{G}^{-1}(\mathbf{P}_t(\boldsymbol{x}_t))$.

Given an arbitrary sequence of decision rules, represented in terms of either $\alpha \equiv \{\alpha_t(.) : t \geq 1\}$, or $\tilde{\mu} \equiv \{\tilde{\mu}_t(.) : t \geq 1\}$, or $\mathbf{P} \equiv \{\mathbf{P}_t(.) : t \geq 1\}$, let $W_t^e(\boldsymbol{x}_t)$ be the expected intertemporal payoff function at period t before the realization of the vector ε_t if the agent behaves according to this arbitrary sequence of decision rules. By definition

$$
\begin{aligned}
W_t^e(\boldsymbol{x}_t) &\equiv \mathbb{E}\left(\sum_{r=0}^{T-t} \beta^r [\pi_{t+r}(\alpha_{t+r}(\boldsymbol{x}_{t+r}, \varepsilon_{t+r}), \boldsymbol{x}_{t+r}) + \varepsilon_{t+r}(\alpha_{t+r}(\boldsymbol{x}_{t+r}, \varepsilon_{t+r}))] \mid \boldsymbol{x}_t \right) \\
&= \mathbb{E}\left[\pi_t(\alpha_t(\boldsymbol{x}_t, \varepsilon_t), \boldsymbol{x}_t) + \varepsilon_t(\alpha_t(\boldsymbol{x}_t, \varepsilon_t)) + \beta \int W_{t+1}^e(\boldsymbol{x}_{t+1}) f_{xt}(\boldsymbol{x}_{t+1} | \alpha_t(\boldsymbol{x}_t, \varepsilon_t), \boldsymbol{x}_t) d\boldsymbol{x}_{t+1} \right]
\end{aligned}
\tag{23}
$$

We denote $W_t^e(\boldsymbol{x}_t)$ as the *valuation function* to distinguish it from the optimal value function and to emphasize that $W_t^e(\boldsymbol{x}_t)$ provides the valuation of any arbitrary decision rule. We are interested in the representation of this valuation function as a function of CCPs. Therefore, we use the notation $W_t^e(\boldsymbol{x}_t, \mathbf{P}_t, \mathbf{P}_{t'>t})$. Given its definition, this function can be written using the recursive formula:

$$
\begin{aligned}
W_t^e(\boldsymbol{x}_t, \mathbf{P}_t, \mathbf{P}_{t'>t}) = \Pi_t^e(\boldsymbol{x}_t, \mathbf{P}_t) + \beta \int & W_{t+1}^e(\boldsymbol{x}_{t+1}, \mathbf{P}_{t+1}, \mathbf{P}_{t'>t+1}) \\
& \times f_t^e(y_{t+1} | \boldsymbol{x}_t, \mathbf{P}_t) f_z(z_{t+1} \mid z_t) d\boldsymbol{x}_{t+1}
\end{aligned}
\tag{24}
$$

where $\Pi_t^e(\boldsymbol{x}_t, \mathbf{P}_t)$ is the expected one-period profit $\sum_{a=0}^{J} P_t(a|\boldsymbol{x}_t)[\pi_t(a,\boldsymbol{x}_t) + e_t(a, \mathbf{P}_t(\boldsymbol{x}_t))]$; $e_t(a, \mathbf{P}_t(\boldsymbol{x}_t))$ has the same definition as in the static model, that is, it is the expected value of $\varepsilon_t(a)$ conditional on alternative a being chosen under decision rule $\alpha_t(\boldsymbol{x}_t, \varepsilon_t)$[10]; and $f_t^e(y_{t+1}|\boldsymbol{x}_t, \mathbf{P}_t)$ is the transition probability of the endogenous state variables y induced by the CCP function $\mathbf{P}_t(\boldsymbol{x}_t)$, that is, $\sum_{a=0}^{J} P_t(a|\boldsymbol{x}_t) f_{yt}(y_{t+1}|a, \boldsymbol{x}_t)$.

The valuation function $W_t^e(\boldsymbol{x}_t, \mathbf{P}_t, \mathbf{P}_{t'>t})$ is continuously differentiable with respect to the choice probabilities over the simplex. Then, we can define $\mathbf{P}^*$ as the sequence of CCP functions $\{\mathbf{P}_t^*(x) : t \geq 1,\ x \in \mathcal{X}\}$ such that for any (t,x) the vector of CCPs $\mathbf{P}_t^*(x)$ maximizes the values $W_t^e(x, \mathbf{P}_t, \mathbf{P}_{t'>t})$ given that future CCPs $\mathbf{P}_{t'>t}$ are fixed at their values in $\mathbf{P}^*$.

$$\mathbf{P}_t^*(x) = \arg\max_{\mathbf{P}_t(x) \in \mathcal{S}} \left\{ W_t^e\left(x, \mathbf{P}_t, \mathbf{P}_{t'>t}^*\right) \right\} \tag{25}$$

As in the ARUM, we have apparently two different optimal CCP functions. We have the CCP functions associated with the sequence of optimal decision rules $\alpha_t^*(.)$, that we represent as $\{\mathbf{P}_t^{\alpha^*} : t \geq 1\}$. And we have sequence of CCP functions $\{\mathbf{P}_t^* : t \geq 1\}$ defined in Eq. (25). Proposition 2 establishes that the two sequences of CCPs are the same one, and that these probabilities satisfy the marginal conditions of optimality associated to the continuous optimization problem in Eq. (25).

Proposition 2. Let $\{\mathbf{P}_t^{\alpha^*} : t \geq 1\}$ be the sequence of CCP functions associated with the sequence of optimal decision rules $\{\alpha_t^* : t \geq 1\}$ as defined in the DDC problem (20), and let $\{\mathbf{P}_t^* : t \geq 1\}$ be sequence of CCP functions that solves the continuous optimization problem (25). Then, for every (t,x): (i) the vectors $\mathbf{P}_t^{\alpha^*}(x)$ and $\mathbf{P}_t^*(x)$ are the same; and (ii) $\mathbf{P}_t^*(x)$ satisfies the marginal conditions of optimality

$$\frac{\partial W_t^e\left(x, \mathbf{P}_t^*, \mathbf{P}_{t'>t}^*\right)}{\partial P_t(a|x)} = 0 \tag{26}$$

for any $a > 0$, and the marginal value $\partial W_t / \partial P_t$ has the following form:

$$\begin{aligned}\frac{\partial W_t^e}{\partial P_t(a|x)} &= v_t(a, \boldsymbol{x}_t, \mathbf{P}_{t'>t}) - v_t(0, \boldsymbol{x}_t, \mathbf{P}_{t'>t}) + e_t(a, \mathbf{P}_t(x)) - e_t(0, \mathbf{P}_t(x)) \\ &+ \sum_{j=0}^{J} P_t(j|x) \frac{\partial e_t(j, \mathbf{P}_t(x))}{\partial P_t(a|x)}\end{aligned} \tag{27}$$

where $v_t(a, \boldsymbol{x}_t, \mathbf{P}_{t'>t})$ is the conditional-choice value function $\pi_t(a, \boldsymbol{x}_t) + \beta \int W_{t+1}(\boldsymbol{x}_{t+1}, \mathbf{P}_{t+1}, \mathbf{P}_{t'>t+1}) f_t(\boldsymbol{x}_{t+1}|a, \boldsymbol{x}_t)\, d\boldsymbol{x}_{t+1}$.

Proof in the appendix.

Proposition 2 shows that we can treat the DDC model as a dynamic continuous optimization problem where optimal choices, in the form of choice probabilities, satisfy marginal conditions of optimality. Nevertheless, the marginal conditions of optimality in Eq. (27) involve value functions. We are looking for conditions of optimality in the spirit of Euler equations that involve only payoff functions at two consecutive periods, t and $t+1$. To obtain these conditions, we construct a constrained optimization problem similar to the one for the derivation of Euler equations in section "Euler Equations in Dynamic Continuous Decision Models".

By Bellman's principle, the optimal choice probabilities at periods t and $t+1$ come from the solution to the optimization problem $\max_{\mathbf{P}_t, \mathbf{P}_{t+1}} \times W_t^e(x, \mathbf{P}_t, \mathbf{P}_{t+1}, \mathbf{P}^*_{t'>t+1})$, where we have fixed at its optimum the individual's behavior at any period after $t+1$, $\mathbf{P}^*_{t'>t+1}$. In general, the CCPs $\mathbf{P}_t$ and $\mathbf{P}_{t+1}$ affect the distribution of the state variables at periods after $t+1$ such that the optimality conditions of the problem $\max_{\mathbf{P}_t, \mathbf{P}_{t+1}} \times W_t^e(x, \mathbf{P}_t, \mathbf{P}_{t+1}, \mathbf{P}^*_{t'>t+1})$ involve payoff functions and state variables at every period in the future. Instead, suppose that we consider a similar optimization problem but where we now impose the constraint that the probability distribution of the endogenous state variables at $t+2$ should be the one implied by the optimal CCPs at periods t and $t+1$. Since $(\mathbf{P}^*_t, \mathbf{P}^*_{t+1})$ satisfy this constraint, it is clear that these CCPs represent also the unique solution to this constrained optimization problem. That is

$$\{\mathbf{P}^*_t(x), \mathbf{P}^*_{t+1}\} = \arg \max_{\{\mathbf{P}_t(x), \mathbf{P}_{t+1}\}} \Delta_t = \left\{ W_t^e(x, \mathbf{P}_t, \mathbf{P}_{t+1}, \mathbf{P}^*_{t'>t+1}) - W_t^e(x, \mathbf{P}^*_t, \mathbf{P}^*_{t+1}, \mathbf{P}^*_{t'>t+1}) \right\}$$

$$\text{subject to:} f^e_{t\to t+2}(.|x, \mathbf{P}_t, \mathbf{P}_{t+1}) = f^e_{t\to t+2}(.|x, \mathbf{P}^*_t, \mathbf{P}^*_{t+1}) \tag{28}$$

where we use function $f^e_{t\to t+2}(.|x, \mathbf{P}_t, \mathbf{P}_{t+1})$ to represent the distribution of y_{t+2} conditional on $\boldsymbol{x}_t = x$ and induced by the CCPs $\mathbf{P}_t(x)$ and $\mathbf{P}_{t+1}$, that can be written as

$$f_{t\to t+2}(y_{t+2}|\boldsymbol{x}_t, \mathbf{P}_t, \mathbf{P}_{t+1}) = \int f^e_{t+1}(y_{t+2}|\boldsymbol{x}_{t+1}, \mathbf{P}_{t+1})\ f^e_t(y_{t+1}|\boldsymbol{x}_t, \mathbf{P}_t)\ f_z(z_{t+1}|z_t) d\boldsymbol{x}_{t+1} \tag{29}$$

and, as defined above, $f_t^e(.|x, \mathbf{P}_t)$ is the one-period-forward transition probability of the endogenous state variables y induced by the CCP function $\mathbf{P}_t(x)$, that is, $\sum_{a=0}^{J} P_t(a|\boldsymbol{x}_t)\ f_t(y_{t+1}|a, \boldsymbol{x}_t)$.

By the definition of the valuation function W_t^e, we have that

$$W_t^e(\boldsymbol{x}_t, \mathbf{P}) = \Pi_t^e(\boldsymbol{x}_t, \mathbf{P}_t) + \beta \int \Pi_{t+1}^e(\boldsymbol{x}_{t+1}, \mathbf{P}_{t+1}) f_t^e(y_{t+1}|\boldsymbol{x}_t, \mathbf{P}_t) f_z(z_{t+1}|z_t) d\boldsymbol{x}_{t+1}$$
$$+ \beta^2 \int W_{t+2}^e(\boldsymbol{x}_{t+2}, \mathbf{P}_{t'>t+1}) f_{t\to t+2}(y_{t+2}|\boldsymbol{x}_t, \mathbf{P}_t, \mathbf{P}_{t+1})\ f_z(z_{t+2}|z_t) d\boldsymbol{x}_{t+2} \tag{30}$$

The last term in this expression is exactly the same for $W_t^e(x, \mathbf{P}_t, \mathbf{P}_{t+1}, \mathbf{P}_{t'>t+1}^*)$ and for $W_t^e(x, \mathbf{P}_t^*, \mathbf{P}_{t+1}^*, \mathbf{P}_{t'>t+1}^*)$ because we have the same function W_{t+2}^e and because we restrict the distribution of y_{t+2} to be the same. Therefore, subject to this constraint we have that Δ_t is equal to $\Pi_t^e(x, \mathbf{P}_t) + \beta \int \Pi_{t+1}^e(\boldsymbol{x}_{t+1}, \mathbf{P}_{t+1}) f_t^e(\boldsymbol{x}_{t+1}|x, \mathbf{P}_t) d\boldsymbol{x}_{t+1}$, and the optimal CCPs at periods t and $t+1$ solve the following optimization problem:

$$\{\mathbf{P}_t^*(x), \mathbf{P}_{t+1}^*\} = \arg \max_{\{\mathbf{P}_t(x), \mathbf{P}_{t+1}\}} \Delta_t$$
$$= \left\{ \Pi_t^e(x, \mathbf{P}_t) + \beta \int \Pi_{t+1}^e(\boldsymbol{x}_{t+1}, \mathbf{P}_{t+1}) f_t^e(\boldsymbol{x}_{t+1}|x, \mathbf{P}_t) d\boldsymbol{x}_{t+1} \right\}$$
$$\text{subject to}: f_{t\to t+2}^e(.|x, \mathbf{P}_t, \mathbf{P}_{t+1}) = f_{t\to t+2}^e(.|x, \mathbf{P}_t^*, \mathbf{P}_{t+1}^*) \tag{31}$$

Suppose that the space of the vector of endogenous state variables $\mathcal{Y}$ is discrete and finite. Therefore, the set of restrictions on $f_{t\to t+2}^e \times (y_{t+2}|x, \mathbf{P}_t, \mathbf{P}_{t+1})$ in the constrained optimization problem (31) includes at most $|\mathcal{Y}| - 1$ restrictions, where $|\mathcal{Y}|$ is the number of points in the support set $\mathcal{Y}$. Therefore, the number of Lagrange multipliers, and the matrix that we have to invert to get these multipliers is of at most as large as $|\mathcal{Y}| - 1$. In fact, in many models, the number of Lagrange multipliers that we must solve for can be much smaller than the dimension of the vector of endogenous state variables. This is because in many models the transition probability of the endogenous state variable is such that, given the state variable at period t, the state variable at period $t+2$ can take only a limited and small number of possible values. We present several examples below.

Let $\mathcal{Y}_{+s}(\boldsymbol{x}_t)$ be the set of values that the endogenous state variables can reach with positive probability s periods in the future given that the state today is $\boldsymbol{x}_t$. To be precise, $\mathcal{Y}_{+s}(\boldsymbol{x}_t)$ includes all these possible values except one of them because we can represent the probability distribution of y_{t+s}

using the probabilities of each possible value except one. Let $\lambda_t(\mathbf{x}_t) = \{\lambda_t(y_{t+2}|\mathbf{x}_t) : y_{t+2} \in \mathcal{Y}_{+2}(\mathbf{x}_t)\}$ be the $|\mathcal{Y}_{+2}(\mathbf{x}_t)| \times 1$ vector of Lagrange multipliers associated to this set of restrictions. The Lagrangian function for this optimization problem is

$$\mathcal{L}_t(\mathbf{P}_t(\mathbf{x}_t), \mathbf{P}_{t+1}) = \Pi_t^e(x, \mathbf{P}_t) + \beta \sum_{\mathbf{x}_{t+1}} \Pi_{t+1}^e(\mathbf{x}_{t+1}, \mathbf{P}_{t+1}) f_t^e(y_{t+1} \mid \mathbf{x}_t, \mathbf{P}_t) f_z(z_{t+1}|z_t)$$
$$- \sum_{y_{t+2}} \lambda_t(y_{t+2}|\mathbf{x}_t) \left[\sum_{\mathbf{x}_{t+1}} f_{t+1}^e(y_{t+2}|\mathbf{x}_{t+1}, \mathbf{P}_{t+1}) f_t^e(y_{t+1}|\mathbf{x}_t, \mathbf{P}_t) f_z(z_{t+1}|z_t) \right] \quad (32)$$

Given this Lagrangian function, we can derive the first order conditions of optimality with respect to $\mathbf{P}_t(\mathbf{x}_t)$ and $\mathbf{P}_{t+1}$ and combine these conditions to obtain Euler equations.

Proposition 3. The marginal conditions for the maximization of the Lagrangian function in Eq. (32) imply the following Euler equations. For every value of $\mathbf{x}_t$:

$$\frac{\partial \Pi_t^e}{\partial P_t(a|\mathbf{x}_t)} + \beta \sum_{\mathbf{x}_{t+1}} \left[\Pi_{t+1}^e(\mathbf{x}_{t+1}) - \mathbf{m}(\mathbf{x}_{t+1})' \frac{\partial \mathbf{\Pi}_{t+1}^e(z_{t+1})}{\partial \mathbf{P}_{t+1}(z_{t+1})} \right] \tilde{f}_t(y_{t+1}|a, \mathbf{x}_t) f_z(z_{t+1}|z_t) = 0 \quad (33)$$

where $\tilde{f}_t(y_{t+1}|a,\mathbf{x}_t) \equiv f_t(y_{t+1}|a,\mathbf{x}_t) - f_t(y_{t+1}|0,\mathbf{x}_t)$; $\partial \mathbf{\Pi}_{t+1}^e(z_{t+1})/\partial \mathbf{P}_{t+1}(z_{t+1})$ is a column vector with dimension $J|\mathcal{Y}_{+1}(\mathbf{x}_t)| \times 1$ that contains the partial derivatives $\{\partial \Pi_{t+1}^e(y_{t+1}, z_{t+1})/\partial P_{t+1}(a|y_{t+1}, z_{t+1})\}$ for every action $a>0$ and every value $y_{t+1} \in \mathcal{Y}_{+1}(\mathbf{x}_t)$ that can be reach from $\mathbf{x}_t$, and fixed value for z_{t+1}; and $\mathbf{m}(\mathbf{x}_{t+1})$ is a $J|\mathcal{Y}_{+1}(\mathbf{x}_t)| \times 1$ vector such that $\mathbf{m}(\mathbf{x}_{t+1}) \equiv \mathbf{f}_{t+1}^e(x_{t+1})'[\tilde{\mathbf{F}}_{t+1}(z_{t+1})'\tilde{\mathbf{F}}_{t+1}(z_{t+1})]^{-1}\tilde{\mathbf{F}}_{t+1}(z_{t+1})'$ where $\mathbf{f}_{t+1}^e(\mathbf{x}_{t+1})$ is the vector of transition probabilities $\{f_{t+1}^e(y_{t+2}|\mathbf{x}_{t+1}) : y_{t+2} \in \mathcal{Y}_{+2}(\mathbf{x}_t)\}$, and $\tilde{\mathbf{F}}_{t+1}(z_{t+1})$ is matrix with dimension $J|\mathcal{Y}_{+1}(\mathbf{x}_t)| \times |\mathcal{Y}_{+2}(\mathbf{x}_t)|$ that contains the probabilities $\tilde{f}_{t+1}(y_{t+2}|a,\mathbf{x}_{t+1})$ for every $y_{t+2} \in \mathcal{Y}_{+2}(\mathbf{x}_t)$, every $y_{t+1} \in \mathcal{Y}_{+1}(\mathbf{x}_t)$, and every action $a>0$, with fixed z_{t+1}.

Proof in the appendix.

Proposition 3 shows that in general we can derive marginal conditional of optimality that involve only payoffs and states at two consecutive periods. The derivation of this Euler equation, described in the appendix, is based on the combination of the Lagrangian conditions $\partial \mathcal{L}_t/\partial P_t(a|\mathbf{x}_t) = 0$

and $\partial\mathcal{L}_t/\partial P_{t+1}(a|\boldsymbol{x}_{t+1})=0$. Using the group of conditions $\partial\mathcal{L}_t/\partial P_{t+1}(a|\boldsymbol{x}_{t+1})=0$ we can solve for the vector of Lagrange multipliers as $[\tilde{\mathbf{F}}_{t+1}(z_{t+1})'\tilde{\mathbf{F}}_{t+1}(z_{t+1})]^{-1}\tilde{\mathbf{F}}_{t+1}(z_{t+1})'\partial\boldsymbol{\Pi}^e_{t+1}(z_{t+1})/\partial\mathbf{P}_{t+1}(z_{t+1})$ and then we can plug this solution into the first Lagrangian conditions, $\partial\mathcal{L}_t/\partial P_t(a|\boldsymbol{x}_t)=0$. This provides the expression for the Euler equation in (33). The main computational cost in the derivation of this expression comes from inverting the matrices $[\tilde{\mathbf{F}}_{t+1}(z_{t+1})'\tilde{\mathbf{F}}_{t+1}(z_{t+1})]$. The dimension of these matrices is $|\mathcal{Y}_{+2}(\boldsymbol{x}_t)|\times|\mathcal{Y}_{+2}(\boldsymbol{x}_t)|$, where $\mathcal{Y}_{+2}(\boldsymbol{x}_t)$ is the set of possible values that the endogenous state variable y_{t+2} can take given $\boldsymbol{x}_t$. In most applications, the number of elements in the set $\mathcal{Y}_{+2}(\boldsymbol{x}_t)$ is substantially smaller that the whole number of values in the space of the endogenous state variable, and several orders of magnitude smaller than the dimension of the complete state space that includes the exogenous state variables. This property implies very substantial computational savings in the estimation of the model. We now provide some examples of models where the form of the Euler equations is particularly simple. In these examples, we have simple closed form expressions for the Lagrange multipliers. These examples correspond to models that are commonly estimated in applications of DDC models.

Example 4. (*Dynamic binary choice model of entry and exit*). Consider a binary decision model, $\mathcal{A}=\{0,1\}$, where a_t is the indicator of being active in a market or in some particular activity. The endogenous state variable y_t is the lagged value of the decision variable, $y_t=a_{t-1}$, and it represents whether the agent was active at previous period. The vector of state variables is then $\boldsymbol{x}_t=(y_t,z_t)$ where z_t are exogenous state variables. Suppose that $\varepsilon_t(0)$ and $\varepsilon_t(1)$ are extreme value type 1 distributed with dispersion parameter σ_ε. In this model, the one-period expected payoff function is $\Pi^e_t(\boldsymbol{x}_t,P_t)=P_t(0|\boldsymbol{x}_t)\,[\pi(0,\boldsymbol{x}_t)-\sigma_\varepsilon\ln P_t(0|\boldsymbol{x}_t)]+P_t(1|\boldsymbol{x}_t)\,[\pi(1,\boldsymbol{x}_t)-\sigma_\varepsilon\ln P_t(1|\boldsymbol{x}_t)]$. The transition of the endogenous state variable induced by the CCP is the CCP itself, that is, $f^e_t(y_{t+1}|\boldsymbol{x}_t,P_t)=P_t(y_{t+1}|\boldsymbol{x}_t)$. Therefore, we can write the Δ_t function in the constrained optimization problem as

$$\Delta_t=\Pi^e_t(\boldsymbol{x}_t,P_t)+\beta\sum_{z_{t+1}}f_z(z_{t+1}|z_t)\,[P_t(0|\boldsymbol{x}_t)\Pi^e_{t+1}(0,z_{t+1},P_{t+1})$$
$$+P_t(1|\boldsymbol{x}_t)\,\Pi^e_{t+1}(1,z_{t+1},P_{t+1})] \quad (34)$$

Given $\boldsymbol{x}_t$, the state variable y_{t+2} can take two values, 0 or 1. Therefore, there is only one free probability in $f^e_{t\to t+2}$ and one restriction in the Lagrangian problem. This probability is

$$f^{e}_{t\to t+2}(1|\boldsymbol{x}_t, P_t, \mathbf{P}_{t+1}) = \sum_{z_{t+1}} f_z(z_{t+1}|z_t)\,[P_t(0|\boldsymbol{x}_t)P_{t+1}(1|0,\, z_{t+1}) + P_t(1|\boldsymbol{x}_t)P_{t+1}(1|1,\, z_{t+1})] \tag{35}$$

Let $\lambda(\boldsymbol{x}_t)$ be the Lagrange multiplier for this restriction. For a given $\boldsymbol{x}_t$, the free probabilities that enter in the Lagrangian problem are $P_t(1|\boldsymbol{x}_t)$, $P_{t+1}(1|0,\, z_{t+1})$, and $P_{t+1}(1|1, z_{t+1})$ for any possible value of z_{t+1} in the support set $\mathcal{Z}$. The first order condition for the maximization of the Lagrangian with respect to $P_t(1|\boldsymbol{x}_t)$ is

$$\frac{\partial \Pi^e_t}{\partial P_t(1|\boldsymbol{x}_t)} + \beta \sum_{z_{t+1}} [\Pi^e_{t+1}(1) - \Pi^e_{t+1}(0) - \lambda(\boldsymbol{x}_t)\{P_{t+1}(1|1, z_{t+1}) - P_{t+1}(1|0, z_{t+1})\}]\, f_z(z_{t+1}|z_t) = 0 \tag{36}$$

The marginal condition with respect to one of the probabilities $P_{t+1}(1|\boldsymbol{x}_{t+1})$ (for a given value of $\boldsymbol{x}_{t+1}$) is $\beta \frac{\partial \Pi^e_{t+1}(0, z_{t+1}, P_{t+1})}{\partial P_{t+1}(1|0, z_{t+1})} = \beta \frac{\partial \Pi^e_{t+1}(1, z_{t+1}, P_{t+1})}{\partial P_{t+1}(1|1, z_{t+1})} = \lambda(\boldsymbol{x}_t)$. Substituting the marginal condition with respect to $P_{t+1}(1|\boldsymbol{x}_{t+1})$ into the marginal condition with respect to $P_t(1|\boldsymbol{x}_t)$ we get the Euler equation:

$$\frac{\partial \Pi^e_t}{\partial P_t(1|\boldsymbol{x}_t)} + \beta \mathbb{E}_t \left(\Pi^e_{t+1}(1, z_{t+1}) - \Pi^e_{t+1}(0, z_{t+1})\right) + \beta \mathbb{E}_t \left(P_{t+1}(1|0, z_{t+1}) \frac{\partial \Pi^e_{t+1}(0, z_{t+1}, P_{t+1})}{\partial P_{t+1}(1|0, z_{t+1})} - P_{t+1}(1|1, z_{t+1}) \frac{\partial \Pi^e_{t+1}(1, z_{t+1}, P_{t+1})}{\partial P_{t+1}(1|1, z_{t+1})} \right) = 0 \tag{37}$$

where we use $\mathbb{E}_t(.)$ to represent in a compact form the expectation over the distribution of $f_z(z_{t+1}|z_t)$. Finally, for the logit version of this model and as shown in Example 2, the marginal expected profit $\partial \Pi^e_t / \partial P_t(1|\boldsymbol{x}_t)$ is equal to $\pi(1, \boldsymbol{x}_t) - \pi_t(0, \boldsymbol{x}_t) - \sigma_\varepsilon(\ln P_t(1|\boldsymbol{x}_t) - \ln P_t(0|\boldsymbol{x}_t))$. Taking this into account and operating in the Euler equation, we can obtain this simpler formula for this Euler equation:

$$\left[\pi(1, y_t, z_t) - \pi(0, y_t, z_t) - \sigma_\varepsilon \ln\left(\frac{P_t(1|y_t, z_t)}{P_t(0|y_t, z_t)}\right)\right] + \beta \mathbb{E}_t \left[\pi(1, 1, z_{t+1}) - \pi_t(1, 0, z_{t+1}) - \sigma_\varepsilon \ln\left(\frac{P_{t+1}(1|1, z_{t+1})}{P_{t+1}(1|0, z_{t+1})}\right)\right] = 0 \tag{38}$$

Example 5. (*Machine replacement model*). Consider a model where the binary choice variable a_t is the indicator for a firm's decision to replace an old machine or equipment by a new one. The endogenous state variable y_t is the age of the "old" machine that takes discrete values $\{1, 2, \ldots\}$ and it follows the transition rule $y_{t+1} = 1 + (1 - a_t)y_t$, that is, if the firm replaces the machine at period t (i.e., $a_t = 1$), then at period $t+1$ it has a brand new machine with $y_{t+1} = 1$, otherwise the firm continues with the old machine that at $t+1$ will be one period older. Given y_t, we have that y_{t+1} can take only two values, $y_{t+1} \in \{1, y_t + 1\}$. Thus, the Δ_t function is

$$\Delta_t = \Pi_t^e(\mathbf{x}_t) + \beta \sum_{z_{t+1}} f_z(z_{t+1}|z_t)[P_t(0|\mathbf{x}_t)\Pi_{t+1}^e(y_t + 1, z_{t+1}) + P_t(1|\mathbf{x}_t)\Pi_{t+1}^e(1, z_{t+1})] \tag{39}$$

Given y_t, we have that y_{t+2} can take only three values, $y_{t+1} \in \{1, 2, y_t + 1\}$. There are only two free probabilities in the distribution of $f_{t\to t+2}^e(y_{t+2}|\mathbf{x}_t)$. Without loss of generality, we use the probabilities $f_{t\to t+2}^e(1|\mathbf{x}_t)$ and $f_{t\to t+2}^e(2|\mathbf{x}_t)$ to construct the Lagrange function. These probabilities have the following form:

$$\begin{aligned} f_{t\to t+2}^e(1|\mathbf{x}_t) &= \sum_{z_{t+1}} f_z(z_{t+1}|z_t)[P_t(0|\mathbf{x}_t)P_{t+1}(1|y_t + 1, z_{t+1}) \\ &\quad + P_t(1|\mathbf{x}_t)P_{t+1}(1|1, z_{t+1})] \\ f_{t\to t+2}^e(2|\mathbf{x}_t) &= P_t(1|\mathbf{x}_t)\sum_{z_{t+1}} f_z(z_{t+1}|z_t)P_{t+1}(0|1, z_{t+1}) \end{aligned} \tag{40}$$

The Lagrangian function depends on the CCPs $P_t(1|\mathbf{x}_t)$, $P_{t+1}(1|1, z_{t+1})$, and $P_{t+1}(1|y_t + 1, z_{t+1})$. The Lagrangian optimality condition with respect to $P_t(1|\mathbf{x}_t)$ is

$$\begin{aligned} &\frac{\partial \Pi_t^e}{\partial P_t(1|\mathbf{x}_t)} + \beta \sum_{z_{t+1}} f_z(z_{t+1}|z_t)\left[\Pi_{t+1}^e(1, z_{t+1}) - \Pi_{t+1}^e(y_t + 1, z_{t+1})\right] \\ &\quad - \lambda(1)\sum_{z_{t+1}} f_z(z_{t+1}|z_t)[P_{t+1}(1|1, z_{t+1}) - P_{t+1}(1|y_t + 1, z_{t+1})] \\ &\quad - \lambda(2)\sum_{z_{t+1}} f_z(z_{t+1}|z_t)P_{t+1}(0|1, z_{t+1}) = 0 \end{aligned} \tag{41}$$

And the Lagrangian conditions with respect to $P_{t+1}(1|1, z_{t+1})$ and $P_{t+1}(1|y_t + 1, z_{t+1})$ are $\beta \frac{\partial \Pi_{t+1}^e(1, z_{t+1})}{\partial P_{t+1}(1|1, z_{t+1})} - \lambda(1) + \lambda(2) = 0$, and $\beta \frac{\partial \Pi_{t+1}^e(y_t + 1, z_{t+1})}{\partial P_{t+1}(1|y_t + 1, z_{t+1})} -$

$\lambda(1)=0$, respectively. We can use the second set of conditions to solve trivially for the Lagrange multipliers, and then plug in the expression for this multipliers in the first set of Lagrangian conditions. We obtain the Euler equation:

$$\frac{\partial \Pi_t^e}{\partial P_t(1|\boldsymbol{x}_t)} + \beta \mathbb{E}_t\left[\Pi_{t+1}^e(1, z_{t+1}) - \Pi_{t+1}^e(y_t+1, z_{t+1})\right]$$
$$+\beta \mathbb{E}_t\left[\frac{\partial \Pi_{t+1}^e(1, z_{t+1})}{\partial P_{t+1}(1|1, z t+1)} P_{t+1}(0|1, z_{t+1}) - \frac{\partial \Pi_{t+1}^e(y_t+1, z_{t+1})}{\partial P_{t+1}(1|y_t+1, z_{t+1})} P_{t+1}(0|y_t+1, z_{t+1})\right] = 0 \tag{42}$$

Finally, taking into account that for the logit specification of the unobservables the marginal expected profit $\partial \Pi_t^e / \partial P_t(1|\boldsymbol{x}_t)$ is equal to $\pi(1, \boldsymbol{x}_t) - \pi(0, \boldsymbol{x}_t) - \sigma_\varepsilon[\ln\, P_t(1|\boldsymbol{x}_t) - \ln P_t(0|\boldsymbol{x}_t)]$, and operating in the previous expression, it is possible to obtain the following Euler equation:

$$\left[\pi(1, y_t, z_t) - \pi(0, y_t, z_t) - \sigma_\varepsilon \ln\left(\frac{P_t(1|y_t, z_t)}{P_t(0|y_t, z_t)}\right)\right]$$
$$+\beta \mathbb{E}_t\left[\pi(1, 1, z_{t+1}) - \pi(1, y_t+1, z_{t+1}) - \sigma_\varepsilon \ln\left(\frac{P_{t+1}(1|1, z_{t+1})}{P_{t+1}(1|y_t+1, z_{t+1})}\right)\right] = 0 \tag{43}$$

Relationship between Euler Equations and Other CCP Representations

Our derivation of Euler equations for DDC models above is related to previous work by Hotz and Miller (1993), Aguirregabiria and Mira (2002), and Arcidiacono and Miller (2011). These papers derive representations of optimal decision rules using CCPs and show how these representations can be applied to estimate DDC models using simple two-step methods that provide substantial computational savings relative to full-solution methods. In these previous papers, we can distinguish three different types of CCP representations of optimal decisions rules: (1) the *present-value* representation; (2) the *terminal-state* representation; and (3) the *finite-dependence* representation.

The *present-value* representation consists of using CCPs to obtain an expression for the expected and discounted stream of future payoffs associated with each choice alternative. In general, given CCPs, the valuation function $W_t^e(x, \mathbf{P})$ can be obtained recursively using its definition, $W_t^e(\boldsymbol{x}_t, \mathbf{P}) = \Pi_t^e(\boldsymbol{x}_t, \mathbf{P}) + \beta \int W_{t+1}^e(\boldsymbol{x}_{t+1}, \mathbf{P}) f_t^e(\boldsymbol{x}_{t+1} | \boldsymbol{x}_t, \mathbf{P})\, d\boldsymbol{x}_{t+1}$. And given this valuation function we can construct the agent's optimal decision rule (or best response) at period t given that he believes that in the future he will behave according to the CCPs in the vector $\mathbf{P}$. This *present-value* representation is the CCP approach more commonly used in empirical applications because it can be applied to a general class of DDC models. However, this representation requires the computation of present values and therefore it is subject to the curse of dimensionality. In applications with large state spaces, this approach can be implemented only if it is combined with an approximation method such as the discretization of the state space, or Monte Carlo simulation (e.g., Bajari et al., 2007; Hotz et al., 1994). In general, these approximation methods introduce a bias in parameter estimates.

The *terminal-state* representation was introduced by Hotz and Miller (1993) and it applies only to optimal stopping problems with a terminal state. The *finite-dependence* representation was introduced by Arcidiacono and Miller (2011) and applies to a particular class of DDC models with the finite dependence property. A DDC model has the finite dependence property if given two values of the decision variable at period t and their respective paths of the state variables after this period, there is always a finite period $t' > t$ (with probability one) where the state variables in the two paths take the same value. The *terminal-state* and the *finite-dependence* CCP representations do not involve the computation of present values, or even the estimation of CCPs at every possible state. This implies substantial computational savings as well as avoiding biases induced by approximation errors.

The system of *Euler equations* that we have derived in Proposition 3 can be seen also as a CCP representation of the optimal decision rule in a DDC model. Our representation shares all the computational advantages of the *terminal-state* and *finite-dependence* representations. However, in contrast to the *terminal-state* and *finite-dependence*, our Euler equation representation applies to a general class of DDC models. We can derive Euler equations for any DDC model where the unobservables satisfy the conditions of AS in the payoff function, and CI in the transition of the state variables.

GMM ESTIMATION OF EULER EQUATIONS

Suppose that the researcher has panel data of N agents over $\tilde{T}$ periods of time, where he observes agents' actions $\{a_{it}: i = 1, 2, \ldots, N;\ t = 1, 2, \ldots, \tilde{T}\}$, and a subvector x of the state variables, $\{x_{it}: i=1, 2, \ldots, N; t=1, 2, \ldots, T\}$. The number of agents N is large, and the number of time periods is typically short. The researcher is interested in using this sample to estimate the structural parameters of the model, θ. We describe here the GMM estimation of these structural parameters using moment restrictions from the Euler equations derived in section "Euler Equations in Dynamic Decision Models."

GMM Estimation of Euler Equations in Continuous Decision Models

The GMM estimation of the structural parameters is based on the combination of the Euler equation(s) in (5), the assumption of rational expectations, and some assumptions on the unobservable state variables (Hansen & Singleton, 1982). For the unobservables, this literature has considered the following type of assumption.

Assumption GMM-EE continuous decision. (A) The partial derivatives of the payoff function are $\partial\Pi(a_t, \mathbf{s}_t)/\partial a_t = \pi_a(a_t, \mathbf{x}_t)$ and $\partial\Pi(a_t, \mathbf{s}_t)/\partial y_t = \pi_y(a_t, \mathbf{x}_t) + \varepsilon_t$, where $\pi_a(a_t, \mathbf{x}_t)$ and $\pi_y(a_t, \mathbf{x}_t)$ are known functions to the researcher up to a vector of parameters θ, and ε_t is a vector of unobservables with zero means, not serially correlated, and mean independent of $(\mathbf{x}_t, \mathbf{x}_{t-1}, a_{t-1})$ such that $\mathbb{E}(\varepsilon_{t+1}|\mathbf{x}_{t+1}, \mathbf{x}_t, a_t) = 0$. (B) The partial derivatives of the transition rule, $\partial Y_{t+1}/\partial a_t'$ and $\partial Y_{t+1}/\partial y_t'$, and the matrix $H(a_t, \mathbf{s}_t)$ do not depend on unobserved variables, that is, $\partial Y_{t+1}/\partial a_t' = Y_a(a_t, \mathbf{x}_t)$, $\partial Y_{t+1}/\partial y_t' = Y_y(a_t, \mathbf{x}_t)$, and $H(a_t, \mathbf{s}_t) = H(a_t, \mathbf{x}_t)$.

Under these conditions, the Euler equation implies the following orthogonality condition in terms only of observable variables $\{a, x\}$ and structural parameters θ: $\mathbb{E}(\omega(a_t, \mathbf{x}_t, a_{t+1}, \mathbf{x}_{t+1}; \theta)|\mathbf{x}_t) = 0$, where

$$\begin{aligned}\omega(a_t, \mathbf{x}_t, a_{t+1}, \mathbf{x}_{t+1}; \theta) \equiv \pi_a(a_t, \mathbf{x}_t; \theta) + \beta[\pi_y(a_{t+1}, \mathbf{x}_{t+1}; \theta) \\ - H(a_{t+1}, \mathbf{x}_{t+1}; \theta)\pi_a(a_{t+1}, \mathbf{x}_{t+1}; \theta)]Y_a(a_t, \mathbf{x}_t; \theta) \qquad (44)\end{aligned}$$

The GMM estimator $\hat{\theta}_N$ is defined as the value of θ that minimizes the criterion function $m_N(\theta)'\Omega_N m_N(\theta)$, where $m_N(\theta) \equiv \{m_{N,1}(\theta), m_{N,2}(\theta), \ldots, m_{N,T-1}(\theta)\}$ is the vector of sample moments

$$m_{N,t}(\theta) = \frac{1}{N}\sum_{i-1}^{N} Z(x_{it})\omega(a_{it}, x_{it}, a_{it+1}, x_{it+1}; \theta) \qquad (45)$$

and $Z(x_{it})$ is a vector of instruments (i.e., known functions of the observable state variables at period t).

The GMM-Euler equation approach for dynamic models with continuous decision variables has been extended to models with corner solutions and censored decision variables (Aguirregabiria, 1997; Cooper, Haltiwanger, & Willis, 2010; Pakes, 1994), and to dynamic games (Berry & Pakes, 2000).[11]

GMM Estimation of Static Random Utility Models

Consider the ARUM in section "Random Utility Model as a Continuous Optimization Problem." Now, the deterministic component of the utility function for agent i is $\pi(a_i, x_i; \theta)$, where x_i is a vector of exogenous characteristics of agent i and of the environment which are observable to the researcher, and θ is a vector of structural parameters. Given a random sample of N individuals with information on $\{a_i, x_i\}$, the marginal conditions of optimality in Eq. (16) can be used to construct a *semiparametric two-step GMM estimator* of the structural parameters. The first step consists in the nonparametric estimation of the CCPs $P(a|x) \equiv \Pr(a_{it} = a|x_{it} = x)$. Let $\hat{\mathbf{P}}_N \equiv \{\hat{P}(a|x_i)\}$ be a vector of nonparametric estimates of CCPs for any choice alternative a and any value of x_i in the sample. For instance, $\hat{P}_t(a|x)$ can be a kernel (Nadaraya–Watson) estimator of the regression between $1\{a_i = a\}$ and x_i. In the second step, the vector of parameters θ is estimated using the following GMM estimator:

$$\hat{\theta}_N = \arg\min_{\theta \in \Theta} m'_N(\theta, \hat{\mathbf{P}}_N) \Omega_N m_N(\theta, \hat{\mathbf{P}}_N) \tag{46}$$

where $m_N(\theta, \mathbf{P}) \equiv \{m_{N,1}(\theta, \mathbf{P}), m_{N,2}(\theta, \mathbf{P}), \ldots, m_{N,J}(\theta, \mathbf{P})\}$ is the vector of sample moments, with

$$m_{N,a}(\theta, \mathbf{P}) = \frac{1}{N} \sum_{i=1}^{N} Z_i \left[\pi(a, x_i; \theta) - \pi(0, x_i; \theta) + e(a, x_i, P) \right. \\ \left. - e(0, x_i, P) + \sum_{j=0}^{J} P(j|x_i) \frac{\partial e(j, x_i, P)}{\partial P(a|x_i)} \right] \tag{47}$$

This two-step semiparametric estimator is root-N consistent and asymptotically normal under mild regularity conditions (see Theorems 8.1 and 8.2 in Newey & McFadden, 1994). The variance matrix of this estimator can be estimated using the semiparametric method in Newey (1994), or as recently shown by Ackerberg, Chen, and Hahn (2012) using a computationally simpler parametric-like method as in Newey (1984).

GMM Estimation of Euler Equations in DDC Models

The Euler equations that we have derived for DDC model implies the following orthogonality conditions: $\mathbb{E}(\xi(a_t, \boldsymbol{x}_t, \boldsymbol{x}_{t+1}; P_t, P_{t+1}, \theta)|a_t, \boldsymbol{x}_t) = 0$, where

$$\xi(a_t, \boldsymbol{x}_t, \boldsymbol{x}_{t+1}; P_t, P_{t+1}, \theta) \equiv \frac{\partial \Pi_t^e}{\partial P_t(a_t|\boldsymbol{x}_t)} + \beta\left[\Pi_{t+1}^e(\boldsymbol{x}_{t+1}) - \mathbf{m}(x_{t+1})' \frac{\partial \boldsymbol{\Pi}_{t+1}^e(z_{t+1})}{\partial \mathbf{P}_{t+1}(z_{t+1})}\right] \frac{\tilde{f}_t(y_{t+1}|a_t, \boldsymbol{x}_t)}{f_t(y_{t+1}|a_t, \boldsymbol{x}_t)} \tag{48}$$

Note that this orthogonality condition comes from the Euler equation (33) in Proposition 3, but we have made two changes. First, we have included the expectation $\mathbb{E}(.|a_t, \boldsymbol{x}_t)$ that replaces the sum $\sum_{x_{t+1}}$ and the distribution of $\boldsymbol{x}_{t+1}$ conditional on $(a_t, \boldsymbol{x}_t)$, that is, $f_t(y_{t+1}|a_t, \boldsymbol{x}_t)\ f_z(z_{t+1}|z_t)$. And second, the Euler equation applies to any hypothetical choice, a, at period t, but in the orthogonality condition $\mathbb{E}(\xi(a_t, \boldsymbol{x}_t, \boldsymbol{x}_{t+1}; P_t, P_{t+1}, \theta)|a_t, \boldsymbol{x}_t) = 0$ we consider only the actual/observed choice a_t.

Given these conditions, we can construct a consistent an asymptotically normal estimator of θ using a semiparametric two-step GMM similar to the one described above for the static model. For simplicity, suppose that the sample includes only two periods, t and $t+1$. Let $\hat{\mathbf{P}}_{t,N}$ and $\hat{\mathbf{P}}_{t+1,N}$ be vectors with the nonparametric estimates of $\{P_t(a|\boldsymbol{x}_t)\}$ and $\{P_{t+1}(a|\boldsymbol{x}_{t+1})\}$, respectively at any value of $\boldsymbol{x}_t$ and $\boldsymbol{x}_{t+1}$ observed in the sample. Note that we do not need to estimate CCPs at states which are not observed in the sample. In the second step, the GMM estimator of θ is

$$\hat{\theta}_N = \arg\min_{\theta \in \Theta} m_N'\left(\theta, \hat{\mathbf{P}}_{t,N}, \hat{\mathbf{P}}_{t+1,N}\right) \Omega_N m_N\left(\theta, \hat{\mathbf{P}}_{t,N}, \hat{\mathbf{P}}_{t+1,N}\right) \tag{49}$$

where $m_N(\theta, \mathbf{P}_t, \mathbf{P}_{t+1})$ is the vector of sample moments:

$$m_N(\theta, \mathbf{P}_t, \mathbf{P}_{t+1}) = \frac{1}{N}\sum_{i=1}^{N} Z(a_{it}, x_{it})\xi(a_{it}, x_{it}, x_{it+1}; P_{it}, P_{it+1}, \theta) \tag{50}$$

$Z(a_{it}, x_{it})$ is a vector of instruments, that is, known functions of the observable decision and state variables at period t. As in the case of the static ARUM, this semiparametric two-step GMM estimator is consistent and asymptotically normal under mild regularity conditions.

Relationship with Other CCP Estimators

The estimation based on the moment conditions provided by the *Euler equation*, or *terminal-state*, or *finite-dependence* representations imply an efficiency loss relative to estimation based on *present-value* representation. As shown by Aguirregabiria and Mira (2002, Proposition 4), the two-step PML estimator based on the CCP *present-value* representation is asymptotically efficient (equivalent to the ML estimator). This efficiency property is not shared by the other CCP representations. Therefore, there is a trade-off in the choice between CCP estimators based on Euler equations and on present-value representations. The present-value representation is the best choice in models that do not require approximation methods. However, in models with large state spaces that require approximation methods, the Euler equations CCP estimator can provide more accurate estimates.

AN APPLICATION

This section presents an application of the Euler equations-GMM method to a binary choice model of firm investment. More specifically, we consider the problem of a dairy farmer who has to decide when to replace a dairy cow by a new heifer. The cow replacement model that we consider here is an example of asset or "machine" replacement model.[12] We estimate this model using data on dairy cow replacement decisions and milk production using a two-step PML estimator and the ML estimator, and compare these estimates to those of the Euler equations-GMM method.

Model

Consider a farmer that produces and sells milk using dairy cows. The farm can be conceptualized as a plant with a fixed number of stalls n, one for each dairy cow. We index time by t and stalls by i. In our model, one period of time is a lactation period of 13 months. Farmer profits at period t is the sum of profits across the stalls, $\sum_{i=1}^{n} \Pi_{it}$ where Π_{it} is the profit from stall i at period t, minus the fixed cost of operating a farm with n stalls/cows, $FC_t(n)$. In this application, we take the size of a farm, n, as exogenously given. Furthermore, profits are separable across stalls and we can view the problem as maximization of profit from an individual stall.

The farmer decides when (after which lactation period) to replace the existing cow by a new heifer. Let $a_{it} \in \{0, 1\}$ be the indicator for this replacement decision: $a_{it} = 1$ means that the existing cow is replaced at the end of the current lactation period. The profit from stall i at period t is

$$\Pi_{it} = \begin{cases} p_t^M M(y_{it}, \omega_{it}) - C(y_{it}) + \varepsilon_{it}(0) & \text{if} \quad a_{it} = 0 \\ p_t^M M(y_{it}, \omega_{it}) - C(y_{it}) - R(y_{it}, p_t^H) + \varepsilon_{it}(1) & \text{if} \quad a_{it} = 1 \end{cases} \tag{51}$$

$M(y_{it}, \omega_{it})$ is the production of milk of the cow in stall i at period t, where $y_{it} \in \{1, 2, ..., y^{\max}\}$ is the current cow's age or lactation number, and ω_{it} is a cow-stall idiosyncratic productivity. p_t^M is the market price of milk. $C(y_{it})$ is the maintenance cost that may depend on the age of the cow. $R(y_{it}, p_t^H)$ is the net cost of replacing the existing cow by a new heifer. This net cost is equal to the market price of a new heifer, p_t^H, plus some adjustment/transaction costs, minus the market value of the retired cow. This market value depends on the quality of the meat, and this quality depends on the age of the retired cow but not on her milk productivity. In what follows we assume that the prices p_t^M and p_t^H are constants and as such, do not constitute part of the vector of state variables. So the vector of observable state variables is $x_{it} = (y_{it}, \omega_{it})$ where y_{it} is the endogenous state variable, and $z_{it} = \omega_{it}$ is the vector of endogenous state variable.

The estimations that we present below are based on the following specification on the functions $C(.)$ and $R(.)$: $C(y_{it}) = \theta_C y_{it}$, and $R(y_{it}) = \theta_R$. That is, the maintenance cost of a cow is linear in the cow's age, and the replacement cost is fixed over time.[13] While the productivity shock ω_{it} is unobservable to the econometrician, as we show below, under some assumptions it can be recovered by estimation of the milk production function, $m_{it} = M(y_{it}, \omega_{it})$, where m_{it} is the amount of milk, in liters, produced by the cow in stall i at period t. The transition probability function for the productivity shock ω_{it} is

$$\Pr(\omega_{i,t+1} | \omega_{it}, a_{it}) = \begin{cases} p_\omega(\omega_{i,t+1} | \omega_{it}) & \text{if} \quad a_{it} = 0 \\ p_\omega^0(\omega_{i,t+1}) & \text{if} \quad a_{it} = 1 \end{cases} \tag{52}$$

An important feature of this transition probability is that the productivity of a new heifer is independent of the productivity of the retired cow. Once we have recovered ω_{it}, the transition function for the productivity shock can be identified from the data. The transition rule for the cow age is trivial: $y_{i,t+1} = 1 + (1 - a_{it})y_{it}$. The unobservables $\varepsilon_{it}(0)$ and $\varepsilon_{it}(1)$ are assumed i.i.d. over i and over t with type 1 extreme value distribution with dispersion parameter σ_{ε}.

Data

The dataset comes from Miranda and Schnitkey (1995). It contains information on the replacement decision, age and milk production of cows from five Ohio dairy farms over the period 1986–1992. There are 2,340 observations from a total of 1,103 cows: 103 cows from farmer 1; 187 cows from farmer 2; 365 from farmer 3; 282 from farmer 4; and 166 cows from the last farmer. The data were provided by these five farmers through the Dairy Herd Improvement Association.

Here we use the sample of cows which entered in the production process before 1987. The reason for this selection is that for these initial cohorts we have complete lifetime histories for every cow, while for the later cohorts we have censored durations. Our working sample consists of 357 cows and 783 observations.

Table 1. Descriptive Statistics (Working Sample: 357 Cows with Complete Spells).

		Cow Lactation Period (Age)				
		1	2	3	4	5
Distribution of cows (%) by age of replacement		113 (31.7%)	126 (35.3%)	68 (19.0%)	37 (10.4%)	13 (3.6%)
Hazard rate for the replacement decision		0.317	0.516	0.571	0.740	1.000
Mean Milk Production (thousand pounds) by age (row) and age at replacement (column)	1	14.90	18.13	18.76	18.42	16.85
	2	–	17.42	19.80	20.46	19.40
	3	–	–	20.06	23.74	22.28
	4	–	–	–	20.07	21.60
	5	–	–	–	–	16.99

In Table 1 we provide some basic descriptive statistics from our working sample. The hazard rate for the replacement decision increases monotonically with the age of the cow. Average milk production (per cow and period) presents an inverted-U shape pattern both with respect to the current age of the cow and with respect to the age of the cow at the moment of replacement. This evidence is consistent with a causal effect of age of milk output but also with a selection effect, that is, more productive cows tend to be replaced at older ages.

Estimation

In this section we estimate the structural parameters of the profit function using our Euler equations method, as well as two more standard methods for estimation of DDC models, the two-step PML method and ML method for illustrative purposes.

Estimation of Milk Production Function

Regardless of the method we use to estimate the structural parameters in the cost functions, we first estimate the milk production function, $m_{it} = M(y_{it}, \omega_{it})$, outside the dynamic programming problem. We consider a specification for milk production that is nonparametric in age, and log-additive in the productivity shock ω_{it}:

$$\ln(m_{it}) = \sum_{j=1}^{y^{\max}} \alpha_j 1\{y_{it} = j\} + \omega_{it} \tag{53}$$

A potentially important issue in the estimation of this production function is that we expect age y_{it} to be positively correlated with the productivity shock ω_{it}. Less productive cows are replaced at early ages, and high productivity cows at later ages. Therefore, OLS estimates of α will not have a causal interpretation, as the age of the cow y_{it} is positively correlated with unobserved productivity ω_{it}. Specifically, we would expect that $E[\omega_{it}|y_{it}]$ is increasing in y_{it} as more productive cows survive longer than less productive ones. This would tend to bias downward the α's at early ages and upward bias the α's at old ages.[14]

To overcome this endogeneity problem, we consider the following approach. First, note that if the productivity shock were not serially correlated, there would be no endogeneity problem because age is a predetermined variable which is not correlated with an unanticipated shock at period t. Therefore, if we can transform the production function such that the unobservable is not serially correlated, then the unobservable in the production function will not be correlated with age. Note that the productivity shock ω_{it} is cow specific and is not transferred to another cow in the same stall. Therefore, if the age of the cow is 1, we have that ω_{it} is not correlated with $1\{y_{it}=1\}$. That is,

$$\alpha_1 = \mathbb{E}[\ln(m_{it})|y_{it}=1] \tag{54}$$

and we can estimate consistently α_1 using the frequency estimator $[\sum_{i,t} 1\{y_{it}=1\} \ln(m_{it})]/[\sum_{i,t} 1\{y_{it}=1\}]$. For ages greater than 1, we assume that ω_{it} follows an AR(1) process, $\omega_{it} = \rho\ \omega_{it-1} + \xi_{it}$, where ξ_{it} is an i.i.d. shock. Then, we can transform the production function to obtain the following sequence of equations. For $y_{it} \geq 2$

$$\ln(m_{it}) = \rho \ln(m_{it-1}) + \sum_{j=2}^{y^H} \gamma_j 1\{y_{it}=j\} + \xi_{it} \tag{55}$$

where $\gamma_j \equiv \alpha_j - \rho\ \alpha_{j-1}$. OLS estimation of this equation provides consistent estimates of ρ and $\gamma's$. Finally, using these estimates and the estimator of α_1, we obtain consistent estimates of ρ and $\alpha's$. We can also iterate in this procedure to obtain Cochrane–Orcutt FGLS estimator.

Table 2. Estimation of Milk Production Function (Working Sample: 357 Cows with Complete Spells).

Explanatory Variables	Estimates (Standard Errors)		
	Not controlling for selection	Controlling for selection	
		γ parameters	α parameters
$\ln(m_{it-1})$	–	0.636 (0.048)	
1{Age = 1}	2.823 (0.011)	–	2.823 (0.010)
1{Age = 2}	2.905 (0.014)	1.068 (0.139)	2.863 (0.014)
1{Age = 3}	3.047 (0.019)	1.150 (0.144)	2.971 (0.020)
1{Age = 4}	3.001 (0.030)	1.004 (0.152)	2.894 (0.030)
1{Age = 5}	2.809 (0.059)	0.862 (0.155)	2.702 (0.057)
R^2	0.13	0.364	
Number of observations	783	426	

Table 2 presents estimates of the production function. In column 1 we provide OLS estimates of Eq. (53) in levels. Column 2 presents OLS estimates of semi-difference transformed Eq. (55). And column 3, provides the estimates of the α parameters implied by the estimates in column 2, where their standard errors have been obtained using the delta method. The comparison of the estimates in columns 1 and 3 is fully consistent with the bias we expected. In column 1 we ignore the tendency for more productive cows to survive longer and we estimate a larger effect of age on milk production than when we do account for this in column 3. The difference is particularly large when the cow is age 4 or 5.

Structural Estimation of Payoff Parameters

We now proceed to the estimation of the structural parameters in the maintenance cost, replacement cost/value, and variance of ε, that is, $\boldsymbol{\theta}=\{\sigma_\varepsilon, \theta_C, \theta_R\}$. We begin by deriving the Euler equations of this model. This Euler equations correspond to the ones in the machine replacement model in Example 5 above. That is,

$$\left[\pi(1, y_t, \omega_t) - \pi(0, y_t, \omega_t) - \sigma_\varepsilon \ \ln\left(\frac{P(1|y_t, \omega_t)}{P(0|y_t, \omega_t)}\right)\right]$$
$$+\beta\mathbb{E}_t\left[\pi(1, 1, \omega_{t+1}) - \pi(1, y_t+1, \omega_{t+1}) - \sigma_\varepsilon \ \ln\left(\frac{P(1|1, \omega_{t+1})}{P(1|y_t+1, \omega_{t+1})}\right)\right] = 0 \tag{56}$$

where we have imposed the restriction that the model is stationary such as the functions $\pi(.)$ and $P(.)$ are time-invariant. Using our parameterization of the payoff function, we have that $\pi(1, y_t, \omega_t) - \pi(0, y_t, \omega_t) = -\theta_R$, and $\pi(1, 1, \omega_{t+1}) - \pi(1, y_t+1, \omega_{t+1}) = [p^M M(1, \omega_{t+1}) - p^M M(y_t+1, \omega_{t+1})] + \theta_C y_t$, such that we can get the following simple formula for this Euler equation:

$$\mathbb{E}_t\left(\tilde{M}_{t+1} - \theta_R + \theta_C \beta y_t + \sigma_\varepsilon \tilde{e}_{t+1}\right) = 0 \tag{57}$$

where $\tilde{M}_{t+1} \equiv \beta p^M[M(1,\omega_{t+1}) - M(y_t+1,\omega_{t+1})]$, and $\tilde{e}_{t+1} \equiv [\ln P(0|\boldsymbol{x}_t) + \beta \ln P(1|y_t+1,\omega_{t+1})] - [\ln P(1|\boldsymbol{x}_t) + \beta \ln P(1|1,\omega_{t+1})]$. We estimate $\boldsymbol{\theta}=\{\sigma_\varepsilon, \theta_C, \theta_R\}$ using a GMM estimator based on the moment conditions $\mathbb{E}_t(Z_t \{\tilde{M}_{t+1} - \theta_R + \theta_C y_t + \sigma_\varepsilon \tilde{e}_{t+1}\})$ where the vector of instruments Z_t is $\{1, y_t, \omega_t\ M(1,\omega_t) - M(y_t+1,\omega_t), \ln P(0|\boldsymbol{x}_t) - \ln P(1|\boldsymbol{x}_t), \ln P(1|y_t+1,\omega_t) - \ln P(1|1,\omega_t)\}'$.

Table 3. Estimation of Maintenance Cost and Replacement Cost Parameters (Working Sample: 357 Cows with Complete Spells).

Structural Parameters	Estimates			
	Two-Step PML	MLE	GMM-Euler equation	
			1-step	2-step (Opt. Wei. matrix)
Dispersion of unobs. σ_ε	0.296 (0.035)	0.288 (0.031)	0.133 (0.042)	0.138 (0.038)
Maintenance cost θ_C	0.136 (0.029)	0.131 (0.029)	0.103 (0.035)	0.105 (0.031)
Replacement cost θ_R	0.363 (0.085)	0.342 (0.079)	0.209 (0.087)	0.241 (0.085)
Number of observations	770	770	770	770
Pseudo R^2	0.707	0.707		

Table 3 presents estimates of these structural parameters using GMM-Euler equations, and using two other standard methods of estimation, the two-step PML (see Aguirregabiria & Mira, 2002), and the ML estimator. We use the nested pseudo likelihood (NPL) method of Aguirregabiria and Mira (2002) to obtain the ML estimates.[15] For these PML and ML estimations, we discretize the state variable ω_{it} in 201 values using a uniform grid in the interval $[-5\hat{\sigma}_\omega, 5\hat{\sigma}_\omega]$. The two-step PML and the MLE are very similar both in terms of point estimates and standard errors. Note that these estimators are asymptotically equivalent (Proposition 4, Aguirregabiria & Mira, 2002). However, in small samples and with large state spaces the finite sample properties of these estimators can be very different, and more specifically the two-step PML can have a substantially larger small sample bias (Kasahara & Shimotsu, 2008). In this application, it seems that the dimension of the state space is small relative to the sample size such that the initial nonparametric estimates of CCPs are precise enough, and the finite sample bias of the two-step PML is also small.

Table 3 presents two different GMM estimates based on the Euler equations: a 1-step GMM estimator where the weighting matrix is $(\sum_{i,t} Z_{it} Z_{it}')^{-1}$, and 2-step GMM estimator using the optimal weighting matrix. Both GMM estimates are substantially different to the MLE estimates, but the optimal GMM estimator is closer. A possible simple explanation for the difference between the GMM-EE and the MLE estimates is that the GMM estimates is asymptotically less efficient, that is, it is not using the optimal set of instruments. Other possible factor that may generate differences between these estimates is that the GMM estimator is not invariant to normalizations. In particular, we can get quite different estimates of $\boldsymbol{\theta} = \{\sigma_\varepsilon, \theta_C, \theta_R\}$ if we use a GMM estimator under the normalization that the coefficient of $\tilde{M}_{t+1}$ is equal to one (i.e., using moment conditions $\mathbb{E}(Z_t\{\tilde{M}_{t+1} - \theta_R + \theta_C \beta y_t + \sigma_\varepsilon \tilde{e}_{t+1}\}) = 0$) and if we use a GMM estimator under the normalization that the coefficient of $\tilde{e}_{t+1}$ is equal to one (i.e., using moment conditions $\mathbb{E}(Z_t\{(1/\sigma_\varepsilon)\tilde{M}_{t+1} - (\theta_R/\sigma_\varepsilon) + (\theta_C/\sigma_\varepsilon)\ \beta y_t + \tilde{e}_{t+1}\}) = 0)$. While the first normalization seems more "natural" because our parameters of interest appear linearly in the moment conditions, the second normalization is "closer" the moment conditions implied by the likelihood equations and MLE. We plan to explore this issue and obtain GMM-EE estimates under alternative normalizations.

The estimates of the structural parameters in Table 3 are measured in thousands of dollars. For comparison, it is helpful to take into account that the sample mean of the annual revenue generated by a cow's milk production is \$150,000. According to the ML estimates, the cost of replacing a cow by a new heifer is \$34,200 (i.e., 22.8% of a cow's annual revenue), and maintenance cost increases every lactation period by \$13,100 (i.e., 8.7% of annual revenue). There is very significant unobserved heterogeneity in the cow replacement decision, as the standard deviation of these unobservables is equal \$28,800.

Fig. 1 displays the predicted probability of replacement by age of the cow (replacement probability at age 5 is 1). The probabilities are

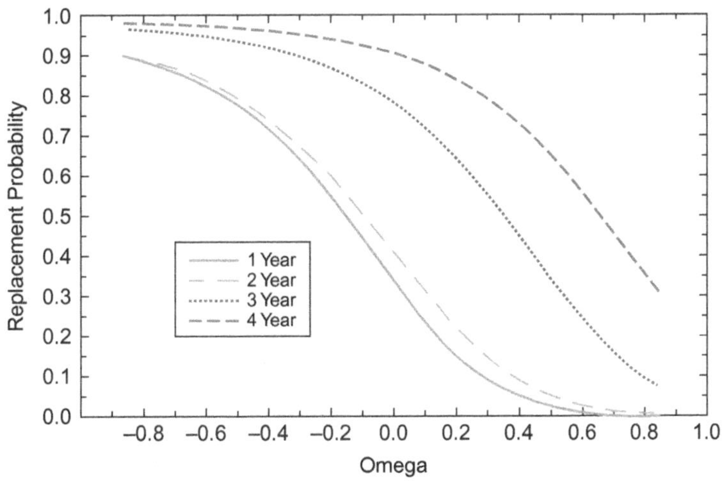

Fig. 1. Predicted probability of replacement.

constructed using the ML estimates. The results suggest that at any age, replacement is less likely the more productive the cow, and that for any given productivity older cows are more likely to be replaced. There is an especially large increase in the probability of replacement going from age 2 to age 3.

Because its simplicity, this empirical application provides a helpful framework for a first look at the estimation of DDC models using GMM-Euler equations. However, it is important to note that the small state space also implies that this example cannot show the advantages of this estimation method in terms of reducing the bias induced by the approximation of value functions in large state spaces. To investigate this issue, in our future work we plan to extend this application to include additional continuous state variables (i.e., price of milk, and the cost of a new heifer). We also plan to implement Monte Carlo experiments.

CONCLUSIONS

This article deals with the estimation of DDC structural models. We show that we can represent the DDC model as a continuous choice model where the decision variables are choice probabilities. Using this representation of the discrete choice model, we derive marginal conditions of optimality (Euler equations) for a general class DDC structural models, and based on these conditions we show that the structural parameters in the model can be estimated without solving or approximating value functions. This result generalizes the *GMM-Euler equation* approach proposed in the seminal work of Hansen and Singleton (1982) for the estimation of dynamic continuous decision models to the case of discrete choice models. The main advantage of this approach, relative to other estimation methods in the literature, is that the estimator is not subject to biases induced by the errors in the approximation of value functions.

NOTES

1. See Rust (1996) and the recent book by Powell (2007) for a survey of numerical approximation methods in the solution of dynamic programming problems. See also Geweke (1996) and Geweke and Keane (2001) for excellent surveys on integration methods in economics and econometrics with particular attention to dynamic structural models.

2. The Nested Fixed Point algorithm (NFXP) (Rust, 1987; Wolpin, 1984) is a commonly used full-solution method for the estimation of single-agent dynamic structural models. The Nested Pseudo Likelihood (NPL) method (Aguirregabiria & Mira, 2002, 2007) and the method of Mathematical Programming with Equilibrium Constraints (MPEC) (Su & Judd, 2012) are other full-solution methods. Two-step and sequential estimation methods include Conditional Choice Probabilities (CCP) (Hotz & Miller, 1993), K-step Pseudo Maximum Likelihood (Aguirregabiria & Mira, 2002, 2007), Asymptotic Least Squares (Pesendorfer & Schmidt-Dengler, 2008), and their simulated-based estimation versions (Bajari, Benkard, & Levin, 2007; Hotz et al., 1994).

3. Lerman and Manski (1981), McFadden (1989), and Pakes and Pollard (1989) are seminal works in this literature. See Gourieroux and Monfort (1993, 1997) Hajivassiliou and Ruud (1994), and Stern (1997) for excellent surveys.

4. In empirical applications, the most common approach to measure the importance of this bias is local sensitivity analysis. The parameter that represents the degree of accuracy of the approximation (e.g., the number of Monte Carlo simulations, the order of the polynomial, the number of grid points) is changed marginally around a selected value and the different estimations are compared. This approach may have low power to detect approximation-error-induced bias, especially when the approximation is poor and these biases can be very large.

5. A DDC model has the finite dependence property if given two values of the decision variable at period t and their respective paths of the state variables after this period, there is always a finite period $t' > t$ (with probability one) where the state variables in the two paths take the same value.

6. This representation is more general than it may look like because the vector of exogenous state variables in z_{t+1} can include any i.i.d. stochastic element that affects the transition rule of the endogenous state variables y. To see this, suppose that the transition probability of y_{t+1} is stochastic conditional on $(z_{t+1}, a_t, \mathbf{s}_t)$ such that $y_{t+1} = Y(\xi_{t+1}, z_{t+1}, a_t, \mathbf{s}_t)$ where ξ_{t+1} is a random variable that is unknown at period t and is i.i.d. over time. We can expand the vector of exogenous state variables to include ξ such that the new vector is $z_t^* \equiv (z_t, \xi_t)$. Then, $f^*(y_{t+1}, z_{t+1}^* | a_t, y_t, z_t^*) = f^{y*}(y_{t+1} | z_{t+1}^*, a_t, y_t, z_t^*) f^{z^*}(z_{t+1}^* | z_t^*)$ and by construction $f^{y*}(y_{t+1} | z_{t+1}^*, a_t, y_t, z_t^*) = 1\{y_{t+1} = Y(\xi_{t+1}, z_{t+1}, a_t, \mathbf{s}_t)\}$.

7. See Section 9.5 in Stokey, Lucas, and Prescott (1989) and Section 4 in Rust (1992).

8. Note that $\sum_{j=0}^{J} P(j)[\partial e(j, \mathbf{P}) / \partial P(a)]$ is equal to $P(a)[-1/P(a)] + P(0)[1/P(0)] = 0$.

9. For the derivation of these expressions, it is useful to take into account that $\phi'(z) = -z\phi(z)$ and $d\Phi^{-1}(P)/dP = 1/\phi(\Phi^{-1}(P))$.

10. Therefore, we also have that $e_t(a, \mathbf{P}_t(\boldsymbol{x}_t))$ is equal to $\mathbb{E}(\varepsilon_t(a) | \varepsilon_t(j) - \varepsilon_t(a) \leq \tilde{G}^{-1}(a, \mathbf{P}_t(\boldsymbol{x}_t)) - \tilde{G}^{-1}(j, \mathbf{P}_t(\boldsymbol{x}_t))$ for any $j \neq a)$.

11. The paper by Cooper et al. (2010) is "Euler Equation Estimation for Discrete Choice Models: A Capital Accumulation Application." However, that paper deals with the estimation of models with continuous but censored decision variables, and not with pure discrete choice models.

12. Dynamic structural models of machine replacement have been estimated before by Rust (1987), Sturm (1991), Das (1992), Kennet (1994), Rust and Rothwell (1995), Adda and Cooper (2000), Cho (2011), and Kasahara (2009), among others.

13. The latter may seem a strong assumption, but given that almost every cow in our sample is sold in the first few years of its life, the assumption may not be so strong over the range of ages observed in the data.

14. The nature of this type of bias is very similar to the one in the estimation of the effect of firm-age in a production function of manufacturing firms, or in the estimation of the effect of firm-specific experience in a wage equation.

15. In the context of single agent DDC models with a globally concave pseudo likelihood, the NPL operator is a contraction such that it always converges to its unique fixed point (Kasahara and Shimotsu) and this fixed point is the MLE (Aguirregabiria & Mira, 2002). In this application the NPL algorithm converged to the MLE after seven iterations using a convergence criterion of $\|\hat{\theta}_k - \hat{\theta}_{k-1}\| < 10^{-6}$.

ACKNOWLEDGMENT

We thank Peter Arcidiacono, Aureo de Paula, Bob Miller, Pedro Mira, Whitney Newey, Andriy Norets, and an anonymous referee for their comments and suggestions.

REFERENCES

Ackerberg, D., Chen, X., & Hahn, J. (2012). A practical asymptotic variance estimator for two-step semiparametric estimators. *The Review of Economics and Statistics*, *94*(2), 481–498.

Adda, J., & Cooper, R. (2000). Balladurette and Juppette: A discrete analysis of scrapping subsidies. *Journal of Political Economy*, *108*, 778–806.

Aguirregabiria, V. (1997). Estimation of dynamic programming models with censored decision variables. *Investigaciones Economicas*, *21*(2), 167–208.

Aguirregabiria, V., & Mira, P. (2002). Swapping the nested fixed point algorithm: A class of estimators for discrete Markov decision models. *Econometrica*, *70*, 1519–1543.

Aguirregabiria, V., & Mira, P. (2007). Sequential estimation of dynamic discrete games. *Econometrica*, *75*, 1–53.

Anderson, S., De Palma, A., & Thisse, J.-F. (1992). *Discrete choice theory of product differentiation*. Cambridge, MA, USA: MIT Press.

Arcidiacono, P., & Miller, R. (2011). CCP estimation of dynamic discrete choice models with unobserved heterogeneity. *Econometrica*, *79*, 1823–1867.

Bajari, P., Benkard, L., & Levin, J. (2007). Estimating dynamic models of imperfect competition. *Econometrica*, *75*, 1331–1370.

Berry, S., & Pakes, A. (2000). *Estimation from the optimality conditions for dynamic controls*. Manuscript, Department of Economics, Yale University.

Cho, S. (2011). An empirical model of mainframe computer investment. *Journal of Applied Econometrics*, *26*(1), 122–150.

Cooper, R., Haltiwanger, J., & Willis, J. (2010). *Euler equation estimation for discrete choice models: A capital accumulation application.* NBER Working Paper No. 15675. NBER, Cambridge, MA, USA.

Das, M. (1992). A micro-econometric model of capital utilization and retirement: The case of the cement industry. *Review of Economic Studies, 59*, 277–297.

Geweke, J. (1996). Monte Carlo simulation and numerical integration. In H. Amman, D. Kendrick, & J. Rust (Eds.), *Handbook of computational economics* (pp. 731–800). Amsterdam: North-Holland. Chap. 15.

Geweke, J., & Keane., M. (2001). Computationally intensive methods for integration in econometrics. In J. J. Heckman & E. E. Leamer (Eds.), *Handbook of econometrics* (1st ed., Vol. 5, pp. 3463–3568). Amsterdam, The Netherlands: Elsevier. Chap. 56.

Gourieroux, C., & Monfort, A. (1993). Simulation-based inference: A survey with special reference to panel data models. *Journal of Econometrics, 59*(1), 5–33.

Gourieroux, C., & Monfort, A. (1997). *Simulation-based econometric methods.* Oxford University Press, Oxford, UK.

Hajivassiliou, V., & Ruud, P. (1994). Classical estimation methods for LDV models using simulation. In D. McFadden & R. Engle (Eds.), *The handbook of econometrics* (Vol. 4). Amsterdam: North-Holland.

Hansen, L. P., & Singleton, K. J. (1982). Generalized instrumental variables estimation of nonlinear rational expectations models. *Econometrica, 50*, 1269–1286.

Hotz, J., & Miller, R. A. (1993). Conditional choice probabilities and the estimation of dynamic models. *Review of Economic Studies, 60*, 497–529.

Hotz, J., Miller, R. A., Sanders, S., & Smith, J. (1994). A simulation estimator for dynamic models of discrete choice. *Review of Economic Studies, 61*, 265–89.

Kasahara, H. (2009). Temporary increases in tariffs and investment: The Chilean case. *Journal of Business and Economic Statistics, 27*(1), 113–127.

Kasahara, H., & Shimotsu, K. (2008). Pseudo-likelihood estimation and bootstrap inference for structural discrete Markov decision models. *Journal of Econometrics, 146*(1), 92–106.

Kennet, M. (1994). A structural model of aircraft engine maintenance. *Journal of Applied Econometrics, 9*, 351–368.

Lerman, S., & Manski, C. (1981). On the use of simulated frequencies to approximate choice probabilities. In C. Manski & D. McFadden (Eds.), *Structural analysis of discrete data with econometric applications.* Cambridge, MA: MIT Press.

McFadden, D. (1981). Econometric models of probabilistic choice. In C. Manski & D. McFadden (Eds.), *Structural analysis of discrete data with econometric applications.* Cambridge, MA: MIT Press.

McFadden, D. (1989). A method of simulated moments for estimation of discrete response models without numerical integration. *Econometrica, 57*(5), 995–1026.

Miranda, M., & Schnitkey, G. (1995). An empirical model of asset replacement in dairy production. *Journal of Applied Econometrics, 10*, S41–S55.

Newey, W. K. (1984). A method of moments interpretation of sequential estimators. *Economics Letters, 14*, 201–206.

Newey, W. K. (1994). The asymptotic variance of semiparametric estimators. *Econometrica, 62*, 1349–1382.

Newey, W. K., & McFadden, D. F. (1994). Large sample estimation and hypothesis testing. In R. F. Engle III & D. F. McFadden (Eds.), *The handbook of econometrics* (Vol. 4). Amsterdam: North-Holland.

Pakes, A. (1994). Dynamic structural models, problems and prospects. In C. Sims (Ed.), *Advances in econometrics. Sixth world congress.* Cambridge, UK: Cambridge University Press.

Pakes, A., & Pollard, D. (1989). Simulation and the asymptotics of optimization estimators. *Econometrica, 57*(5), 1027–1057.

Pesendorfer, M., & Schmidt-Dengler. (2008). Asymptotic least squares estimators for dynamic games. *The Review of Economic Studies.*

Powell, W. B. (2007). *Approximate dynamic programming: Solving the curses of dimensionality* (Vol. 703). New York, NY, USA: Wiley-Interscience.

Rust, J. (1987). Optimal replacement of GMC bus engines: An empirical model of Harold Zurcher. *Econometrica, 55*, 999–1033.

Rust, J. (1992). *Do people behave according to Bellman's principle of optimality?* Working Paper No. E-92–10, The Hoover Institute, Stanford University.

Rust, J. (1994). Structural estimation of Markov decision processes. In R. E. Engle & McFadden (Eds.), *Handbook of econometrics* (Vol. 4). Amsterdam, The Netherlands: North-Holland.

Rust, J. (1996). Numerical dynamic programming in economics. In *Handbook of computational economics* (Vol. 1, pp. 619–729). North-Holland, Amsterdam, The Netherlands.

Rust, J., & Rothwell, G. (1995). Optimal response to a shift in regulatory regime: The case of the US nuclear power industry. *Journal of Applied Econometrics, 10*, S75–S118.

Stern, S. (1997). Simulation-based estimation. *Journal of Economic Literature, 35*, 2006–2039.

Stokey, N., Lucas, R., & Prescott, E. (1989). *Recursive methods in economic dynamics.* Cambridge, MA, USA: Harvard University Press.

Sturm, R. (1991). *A structural economic model of operating cycle management in European nuclear power plants.* Manuscript, RAND Corporation.

Su, C.-L., & Judd, K. (2012). Constrained optimization approaches to estimation of structural models. *Econometrica, 80*(5), 2213–2230.

Wolpin, K. (1984). An estimable dynamic stochastic model of fertility and child mortality. *Journal of Political Economy, 92*, 852–874.

APPENDIX

Proof of Proposition 1.

Part (i). Let $\Pi(\alpha,\varepsilon)$ be the ex-post payoff function associated with a decision rule α, such that $\Pi(\alpha,\varepsilon)=\sum_{a=0}^{J}1\{\alpha(\varepsilon)=a\}[\pi(a)+\varepsilon(a)]$. By Lemmas 1−2, there is a one-to-one relationship between $\mathbf{P}$ and α. Given this relationship, we can represent the ex-post payoff function associated with a decision rule α using the following function of $\mathbf{P}$:

$$\Pi(\mathbf{P},\varepsilon)\equiv\sum_{a=0}^{J}1\left\{\varepsilon(j)-\varepsilon(a)\leq\tilde{G}^{-1}(a,\mathbf{P})-\tilde{G}^{-1}(j,\mathbf{P})\ \text{for any}\ j\neq a\right\}[\pi(a)+\varepsilon(a)] \tag{A.1}$$

Given that α^* maximizes $\Pi(\alpha,\varepsilon)$ for every possible value of ε, then by construction, $\mathbf{P}^{\alpha^*}$ maximizes $\Pi(\mathbf{P},\varepsilon)$ for every possible value of ε. The proof of this is by contradiction. Suppose that there is a vector of CCPs $\mathbf{P}_0\neq\mathbf{P}^{\alpha^*}$ and a value ε_0 such that $\Pi(\mathbf{P}_0,\varepsilon_0)>\Pi(\mathbf{P}^{\alpha^*},\varepsilon_0)$. This implies that the optimal decision for ε_0 is the action a with the largest value of $\tilde{G}^{-1}(a,\mathbf{P}_0)+\varepsilon_0(a)$. But because $[\tilde{G}^{-1}(a,\mathbf{P}_0)-\tilde{G}^{-1}(j,\mathbf{P}_0)]\neq[\tilde{G}^{-1}(a,\mathbf{P}^{\alpha^*})-\tilde{G}^{-1}(j,\mathbf{P}^{\alpha^*})]=\pi(a)-\pi(j)$, the action that maximizes $\tilde{G}^{-1}(a,\mathbf{P}_0)+\varepsilon_0(a)$ is different to the action that maximizes $\pi(a)+\varepsilon(a)$. This contradicts that $\Pi(\mathbf{P}_0,\varepsilon_0)>\Pi(\mathbf{P}^{\alpha^*},\varepsilon_0)$.

Because $\mathbf{P}^{\alpha^*}$ maximizes $\Pi(\mathbf{P},\varepsilon)$ for every possible value of ε, it should be true that $\mathbf{P}^{\alpha^*}$ maximizes in $\mathbf{P}$ the "integrated" payoff function $\int\Pi(\mathbf{P},\varepsilon)dG(\varepsilon)$. It is straightforward to show that this integrated payoff function is the expected payoff function $\Pi^e(\mathbf{P})$. Therefore, $\mathbf{P}^{\alpha^*}$ maximizes the expected payoff function. By uniqueness of $\mathbf{P}^*$, this implies that $\mathbf{P}^{\alpha^*}=\mathbf{P}^*$.

Part (ii). The expected payoff function $\Pi^e(\mathbf{P})$ is continuously differentiable with respect to $\mathbf{P}$. Furthermore, $\Pi^e(\mathbf{P})$ goes to minus infinite as any of the choice probabilities in $\mathbf{P}$ goes to 0 or to 1, that is, when $\mathbf{P}$ goes to the frontier of the simplex $\mathcal{S}$. Therefore, the maximizer $\mathbf{P}^*$ should be in the interior of the simplex and it should satisfy the marginal conditions of optimality $\partial\Pi^e(\mathbf{P}^*)/\partial\mathbf{P}=0$. Finally, given the definition of the expected payoff function in Eq. (13), we have that

$$\frac{\partial\Pi^e(\mathbf{P})}{\partial P(a)}=\pi(a)-\pi(0)+e(a,\mathbf{P})-e(0,\mathbf{P})+\sum_{j=0}^{J}P(j)\frac{\partial e(j,\mathbf{P})}{\partial P(a)} \tag{A.2}$$

Proof of Proposition 2.

The proof of this proposition is a recursive application of Proposition 1. Let $W_t(\boldsymbol{x}_t, \varepsilon_t, \alpha_t, \mathbf{P}_{t'>t})$ be the ex-post valuation function associated with a current decision rule α_t and future CCPs $\mathbf{P}_{t'>t}$, such that

$$W_t(\boldsymbol{x}_t, \varepsilon_t, \alpha_t, \mathbf{P}_{t'>t}) = \sum_{a=0}^{J} 1\{\alpha_t(\boldsymbol{x}_t, \varepsilon_t) = a\}[v_t(a, \boldsymbol{x}_t, \mathbf{P}_{t'>t}) + \varepsilon_t(a)] \qquad \text{(A.3)}$$

and $v_t(a, \boldsymbol{x}_t, \mathbf{P}_{t'>t})$ is the conditional choice value $\pi_t(a, \boldsymbol{x}_t) + \beta \int W_{t+1}(\boldsymbol{x}_{t+1}, \mathbf{P}_{t+1}(\boldsymbol{x}_{t+1}), \mathbf{P}_{t'>t+1})\, f_t(\boldsymbol{x}_{t+1}|a, \boldsymbol{x}_t) d\boldsymbol{x}_{t+1}$. By Lemmas 1–2, there is a one-to-one relationship between $\mathbf{P}_t(\boldsymbol{x}_t)$ and α_t. Given this relationship, we can represent the ex-post valuation function associated with a decision rule α_t using the following function of $\mathbf{P}_t(\boldsymbol{x}_t)$:

$$\begin{aligned} W_t(\boldsymbol{x}_t, \varepsilon_t, \mathbf{P}_t(\boldsymbol{x}_t), \mathbf{P}_{t'>t}) \equiv \sum_{a=0}^{J} 1\{&\varepsilon_t(j) - \varepsilon_t(a) \leq \tilde{G}^{-1}(a, \mathbf{P}_t(\boldsymbol{x}_t)) \\ &- \tilde{G}^{-1}(j, \mathbf{P}_t(\boldsymbol{x}_t)) \text{ for any } j \neq a\}\ [v_t(a, \boldsymbol{x}_t, \mathbf{P}_{t'>t}) + \varepsilon_t(a)] \end{aligned} \qquad \text{(A.4)}$$

By definition of the optimal decision rule, given $\mathbf{P}^*_{t\prime>t}$ the decision rule α^*_t maximizes $W_t(\boldsymbol{x}_t, \varepsilon_t, \alpha_t, \mathbf{P}^*_{t\prime>t})$ for every possible value of ε_t. Then, as in Proposition 1, we have that by construction, $\mathbf{P}^{\alpha^*}_t(\boldsymbol{x}_t)$ maximizes $W_t(\boldsymbol{x}_t, \varepsilon_t, \mathbf{P}_t(\boldsymbol{x}_t), \mathbf{P}_{t'>t})$ for every possible value of ε_t. This implies that $\mathbf{P}^{\alpha^*}_t(\boldsymbol{x}_t)$ also maximizes the "integrated" valuation function $\int W_t(\boldsymbol{x}_t, \varepsilon_t, \mathbf{P}_t(\boldsymbol{x}_t), \mathbf{P}_{t'>t})\, dG(\varepsilon_t)$. But this integrated function is equal to the expected valuation function $W^e_t(\boldsymbol{x}_t, \mathbf{P}_t(\boldsymbol{x}_t), \mathbf{P}_{t'>t})$. Therefore, $\mathbf{P}^{\alpha^*}_t(x)$ maximizes $W^e_t(x, \mathbf{P}_t(x), \mathbf{P}_{t'>t})$. By uniqueness of $\mathbf{P}^*_t(x)$, this implies that $\mathbf{P}^{\alpha^*}_t(x) = \mathbf{P}^*_t(x)$.

The expected valuation function $W^e_t(x, \mathbf{P}_t(x), \mathbf{P}_{t'>t})$ is continuously differentiable with respect to $\mathbf{P}_t(x)$. The maximizer $W^e_t(x, \mathbf{P}_t(x), \mathbf{P}_{t'>t})$ with respect to $\mathbf{P}_t(x)$ should be in the interior of the simplex and it should satisfy the marginal conditions of optimality $\partial W^e_t(x, \mathbf{P}^*_t(x), \mathbf{P}^*_{t\prime>t}) / \partial \mathbf{P}^*_t(x) = 0$. Given the definition of the expected value function, we have that

$$\frac{\partial W^e_t}{\partial P_t(a|x)} = v_t(a, \boldsymbol{x}_t, \mathbf{P}_{t'>t}) - v_t(0, \boldsymbol{x}_t, \mathbf{P}_{t'>t}) + e_t(a, \mathbf{P}_t) - e_t(0, \mathbf{P}_t) + \sum_{j=0}^{J} P_t(j|x) \frac{\partial e_t(j, \mathbf{P}_t)}{\partial P_t(a|x)} \qquad \text{(A.5)}$$

Proof of Proposition 3.

For the derivation of the expressions below for the Lagrangian conditions, note that, by definition of $f_t^e(y_{t+1}|\mathbf{x}_t)$, we have that $\partial f_t^e(y_{t+1}|\mathbf{x}_t)/\partial P_t(a|\mathbf{x}_t) = \tilde{f}_t(y_{t+1}|a,\mathbf{x}_t) \equiv f_t(y_{t+1}|a,\mathbf{x}_t) - f_t(y_{t+1}|0,\mathbf{x}_t)$. For any $a>0$, the Lagrange condition $\partial \mathcal{L}_t/\partial P_t(a|\mathbf{x}_t) = 0$ implies that

$$\frac{\partial \Pi_t^e}{\partial P_t(a|\mathbf{x}_t)} + \beta \sum_{\mathbf{x}_{t+1}} \Pi_{t+1}^e(\mathbf{x}_{t+1})\ \tilde{f}_t(y_{t+1}|a,\mathbf{x}_t)\ f_z(z_{t+1}|z_t)$$
$$- \sum_{y_{t+2} \in \mathcal{Y}_{+2}(\mathbf{x}_t)} \lambda_t(y_{t+2},\mathbf{x}_t) \left[\sum_{x_{t+1}} f_{t+1}^e(y_{t+2}|x_{t+1})\ \tilde{f}_t(y_{t+1}|a,\mathbf{x}_t)\ f_z(z_{t+1}|z_t) \right] = 0 \tag{A.6}$$

We can also represent this expression as

$$\frac{\partial \Pi_t^e}{\partial P_t(a|\mathbf{x}_t)} + \beta \sum_{\mathbf{x}_{t+1}} \left[\Pi_{t+1}^e(x_{t+1}) - \mathbf{f}_{t+1}^e(x_{t+1})' \frac{\boldsymbol{\lambda}_t(\mathbf{x}_t)}{\beta} \right] \tilde{f}_t(y_{t+1}|a,\mathbf{x}_t)\ f_z(z_{t+1}|z_t) = 0 \tag{A.7}$$

where $\boldsymbol{\lambda}_t(\mathbf{x}_t)$ is the vector with dimension $|\mathcal{Y}_{+2}(\mathbf{x}_t)| \times 1$ with the Lagrange multipliers $\{\lambda_t(y_{t+2},\mathbf{x}_t) : y_{t+2} \in \mathcal{Y}_{+2}(\mathbf{x}_t)\}$, and $\mathbf{f}_{t+1}^e(.|\mathbf{x}_{t+1})$ is the vector of transition probabilities $\{f_{t+1}^e(y_{t+2}|\mathbf{x}_{t+1}) : y_{t+2} \in \mathcal{Y}_{+2}(\mathbf{x}_t)\}$. Similarly, for any $a>0$ and any $\mathbf{x}_{t+1} \in \mathcal{X}$, the Lagrange condition $\partial \mathcal{L}_t/\partial P_{t+1}(a|\mathbf{x}_{t+1}) = 0$ implies that

$$\beta \frac{\partial \Pi_{t+1}^e(\mathbf{x}_{t+1})}{\partial P_{t+1}(a|\mathbf{x}_{t+1})} - \sum_{y_{t+2} \in \mathcal{Y}_{+2}(\mathbf{x}_t)} \lambda_t(y_{t+2},\mathbf{x}_t)\ \tilde{f}_{t+1}(y_{t+2}|a,\mathbf{x}_{t+1}) = 0 \tag{A.8}$$

We can represent this system of equations in vector form as

$$\tilde{\mathbf{F}}_{t+1}(z_{t+1}) \frac{\boldsymbol{\lambda}_t(\mathbf{x}_t)}{\beta} = \frac{\partial \boldsymbol{\Pi}_{t+1}^e(z_{t+1})}{\partial \mathbf{P}_{t+1}(z_{t+1})} \tag{A.9}$$

$\boldsymbol{\lambda}_t(\mathbf{x}_t)$ is the vector of Lagrange multipliers defined above. $\partial \boldsymbol{\Pi}_{t+1}^e(z_{t+1})/\partial \mathbf{P}_{t+1}(z_{t+1})$ is a column vector with dimension $J|\mathcal{Y}_{+1}(\mathbf{x}_t)| \times 1$ that contains the partial derivatives $\{\partial \Pi_{t+1}^e(y_{t+1},z_{t+1})/\partial P_{t+1}(a|y_{t+1},z_{t+1})\}$ for every action $a>0$ and every value $y_{t+1} \in \mathcal{Y}_{+1}(\mathbf{x}_t)$ that can be reach from $\mathbf{x}_t$, and fixed value for z_{t+1}. And $\tilde{\mathbf{F}}_{t+1}(z_{t+1})$ is matrix with dimension $J|\mathcal{Y}_{+1}(\boldsymbol{x}_t)| \times |\mathcal{Y}_{+2}(\boldsymbol{x}_t)|$ that contains the probabilities $\tilde{f}_{t+1}(y_{t+2}|a,\boldsymbol{x}_{t+1})$ for every $y_{t+2} \in \mathcal{Y}_{+2}(\boldsymbol{x}_t)$, every $y_{t+1} \in \mathcal{Y}_{+1}(\boldsymbol{x}_t)$, and every action $a>0$, with fixed z_{t+1}. In general, the matrix $\tilde{\mathbf{F}}_{t+1}(z_{t+1})$ is full-column rank for any value of z_{t+1}. Therefore, for any value of z_{t+1}, the square matrix $\tilde{\mathbf{F}}_{t+1}(z_{t+1})'\ \tilde{\mathbf{F}}_{t+1}(z_{t+1})$ is non-singular and we can solve for the Lagrange multipliers as

$$\frac{\lambda_t(\boldsymbol{x}_t)}{\beta} = \left[\tilde{\mathbf{F}}_{t+1}(z_{t+1})'\tilde{\mathbf{F}}_{t+1}(z_{t+1})\right]^{-1}\left[\tilde{\mathbf{F}}_{t+1}(z_{t+1})'\frac{\partial \mathbf{\Pi}^e_{t+1}(z_{t+1})}{\partial \mathbf{P}_{t+1}(z_{t+1})}\right] \tag{A.10}$$

Solving this expression for the Lagrange multipliers into Eq. (A.7), we get the following Euler equation

$$\frac{\partial \Pi^e_t}{\partial P_t(a|\boldsymbol{x}_t)} + \beta \sum_{x_{t+1}} \left[\Pi^e_{t+1}(\boldsymbol{x}_{t+1}) - \mathbf{m}(\boldsymbol{x}_{t+1})'\frac{\partial \mathbf{\Pi}^e_{t+1}(z_{t+1})}{\partial \mathbf{P}_{t+1}(z_{t+1})}\right]\tilde{f}_t(y_{t+1}|a,\boldsymbol{x}_t)\, f_z(z_{t+1}|z_t) = 0 \tag{A.11}$$

where $\mathbf{m}(\boldsymbol{x}_{t+1})$ is a $J|\mathcal{Y}_{+1}(\boldsymbol{x}_t)| \times 1$ vector such that $\mathbf{m}(\boldsymbol{x}_{t+1})' = \mathbf{f}^e_{t+1}(\boldsymbol{x}_{t+1})'$ $[\tilde{\mathbf{F}}_{t+1}(z_{t+1})'\tilde{\mathbf{F}}_{t+1}(z_{t+1})]^{-1}, \tilde{\mathbf{F}}_{t+1}(z_{t+1})'$, and $\partial \mathbf{\Pi}^e_{t+1}(z_{t+1})/\partial \mathbf{P}_{t+1}(z_{t+1})$ is the vector of partial derivatives defined above.

APPROXIMATING HIGH-DIMENSIONAL DYNAMIC MODELS: SIEVE VALUE FUNCTION ITERATION

Peter Arcidiacono, Patrick Bayer,
Federico A. Bugni and Jonathan James

ABSTRACT

Many dynamic problems in economics are characterized by large state spaces which make both computing and estimating the model infeasible. We introduce a method for approximating the value function of high-dimensional dynamic models based on sieves and establish results for the (a) consistency, (b) rates of convergence, and (c) bounds on the error of approximation. We embed this method for approximating the solution to the dynamic problem within an estimation routine and prove that it provides consistent estimates of the modelik's parameters. We provide Monte Carlo evidence that our method can successfully be used to approximate models that would otherwise be infeasible to compute,

Structural Econometric Models
Advances in Econometrics, Volume 31, 45–95

ISSN: 0731-9053/doi:10.1108/S0731-9053(2013)0000032002

suggesting that these techniques may substantially broaden the class of models that can be solved and estimated.

Keywords: Large state space; dynamic decision problem; sieve approximation; value function; value function iteration

JEL classifications: C02; C44; C60; C63

1. INTRODUCTION

Dynamic problems in economics (and many other disciplines) are characterized by large state spaces that routinely make the model difficult or impossible to compute. Faced with these challenges, researchers proceed in a number of different ways including analyzing a static version of the problem, simplifying the dynamic problem to a setting where the state space is manageable, or employing a number of techniques for approximating the value and policy functions that characterize the solution to the problem. The problems analyzed in many broad literatures in economics ranging from models of market equilibrium (which are almost always treated in a static framework) to strategic or social interactions in networks (static or myopic dynamics) to dynamic games (typically characterized by a small number of players and states) to matching problems (almost always analyzed as static problems) remain limited by this large state space problem.

In recent years, techniques for approximating value functions in large state space problems have been developed using simulation and interpolation (Keane & Wolpin, 1994) or parametric policy iteration (PPI) (Béenitez-Silva, Hall, Hitsch, Pauletto, & Rust, 2000; Rust, 2000). The main idea behind these methods is to approximate the value function using flexible functions of the relevant state variables. Simulation and interpolation has been applied by Keane and Wolpin (1997) and Crawford and Shum (2005) among many others. PPI has been applied to a single agent setting in Hendel and Nevo (2006) and to a dynamic game in Sweeting (2011). While the potential application of these methods is great, the literature contains very few formal results regarding the quality of the approximation and, therefore, provides little formal or practical foundation for researchers to use as they apply these methods.

In this article, we consider an alternative, but related, method for approximating value functions that we refer to as sieve value function iteration

(SVFI).[1] We develop the method in the context of a generic single agent dynamic programming problem that can have either a finite or infinite horizon. The SVFI method involves approximating the integrated value function with a nonparametric sieve function. For any sieve function (i.e., for a particular choice of parameters), one can evaluate the Bellman equation and compute a notion of distance between the approximation and its contraction, and thus characterize how close the Bellman equation comes to holding. We approximate the value function by choosing the parameters of the sieve function that come as close as possible to making the Bellman equation hold exactly. Since the sieve space is a simple space, this minimization problem is relatively easy to solve. Moreover, as the sequence of sieve spaces becomes a better and better approximation of the original functional space $\mathcal{F}$, our approximation converges to the true value function.

In order to analyze the formal properties of the SVFI method, we assume that the complexity of the sieve space, n, increases to infinity. In this sense our SVFI approximation technique becomes nonparametric and we establish a number of results:

1. *Consistency:* We show that the sieve approximation converges to the true value function as the richness of the sieve space increases.
2. *Rates of convergence:* We provide the first results in the literature for the rate at which the approximating function converges to the true value function.
3. *Iteration of Bellman operator:* We characterize how rates of convergence are affected by iterating the Bellman operator, pointing out for the first time that this has the potential to improve performance in certain applications.
4. *Bound on the error of approximation:* Following arguments in Rust (2000), we provide an upper bound to the error of approximation to the unknown true value function that is feasible to compute.

While the consistency of the SVFI might be an expected result, establishing the rate of convergence of the SVFI approximation and understanding the effects of increasing the number of iterations on the quality of the approximation are two useful formal contributions to the literature. The fourth result can be related to results available in Rust (2000). The availability of bounds on the error of approximation is an incredibly valuable feature of SVFI because it ensures that one can bound the extent of approximation error relative to the true value function even when the true value function cannot be computed, that is, the case of relevance in very large state space problems. This also serves as a natural guide to researchers as they implement the SVFI, providing a clear sense of whether the approximation is reasonable for any given specification of the sieve function. Taken together, these results provide a formal foundation for the use of the SVFI for approximating large state space problems.

The SVFI approach is quite straightforward to understand and implement and, thus, has the potential to be widely applied in economics and other disciplines. The framework can also be flexibly implemented. It is possible, for example, to estimate the parameters of the sieve approximation function by minimizing the distance in the Bellman operator for only a large subset of the states in the state space. This is attractive for problems with large finite or infinite state spaces.

The method can be applied equally well to infinite and finite horizon problems. For finite horizon problems, we develop two strategies for approximating value function. First, we show how SVFI can be used to approximate the value functions at each time period using a traditional backwards recursion solution method. More interestingly, by including the time to the horizon as another state variable in the sieve function, we show how it is possible to approximate a single sieve function that provides an approximation of the value function at each point in time without solving the problem backwards. The particular features of the application in question will generally determine which of these approaches is computationally lighter or easier to implement.

Having developed this general method for approximating value functions, we then formally show how the SVFI can be used to estimate the structural parameters of large state space dynamic problems in empirical applications. Conceptually it is easy to see that for any particular guess of the model's structural parameters, the SVFI can be used to approximate the solution to the dynamic problem and thus compute the approximate value and policy functions as well as conditional choice probabilities (CCPs). By comparing these objects to their empirical counterparts in the data it is possible to compute a wide variety of objective functions that would be appropriate for estimating the structural parameters. We show that it is possible to consistently estimate the model's structural parameters by embedding the SVFI within the estimation algorithm.

We close the article by demonstrating the performance of SVFI in a particular Monte Carlo application, inspired by the famous bus-engine replacement problem of Rust (1987), in which a firm must dynamically manage its entire fleet of buses. We begin by analyzing an infinite horizon problem with a state space that is finite and relatively large but manageable, that is, for which it is still possible to compute the value function exactly at each state. We demonstrate that SVFI approximates value functions for this problem very closely in a tiny fraction of the time that it takes to compute the exact solution to the problem. We show that an accurate approximation can be obtained even when the Bellman operator is evaluated at a small, randomly, drawn subset of the full set of states and compare the speed and accuracy of alternative methods for minimizing this distance, including nonlinear least squares, an iterative least squares method, and methods that iterate the Bellman operator. We extend this problem to an infinite state space by adding a continuous state variable, again demonstrating that it is possible to approximate the solution exceptionally well in a reasonably short amount of computation time. We then analyze an analogous finite horizon problem, comparing the speed and accuracy of SVFI approximations using (a) the traditional backwards recursion solution method in which we compute a separate sieve approximation function at each point in time and (b) an approach that treats time to the horizon as a state variable, yielding a single time-interacted sieve approximation function.

We complete the Monte Carlo section of the article by evaluating the performance of SVFI approximation within the context of the estimation of the structural parameters of the model. Returning to the infinite horizon problem, we demonstrate that SVFI accurately estimates with only a minimal impact on the effective standard errors while being much faster to compute. In particular, we propose estimating the sieve parameters outside of the estimation of the structural parameters in a manner similar to Aguirregabiria and Mira (2002) swapping of the nested fixed point algorithm. Further, it is straightforward to examine how the estimated structural parameters are affected by the dimension of the sieve and, therefore, to ensure that the sieve is sufficiently rich such that its impact on the estimated structural parameters is minimal.

At this point, it is important to acknowledge that there is an existent operations research literature that develops approximation methods to dynamic programming problems like the ones addressed in this article. Extensive surveys of mayor developments can be found in Bertsekas and Tsitsiklis (1996), Powell (2011), and Bertsekas (2012). These references (and references therein) describe a variety of *approximation methods* or *architectures* based on polynomial functions. For example, Bertsekas and Tsitsiklis (1996, Section 6.10) consider parametric approximation based on "Bellman error methods" which is closely related to our SVFI approximation. Also, according to Bertsekas (2012, Chap. 6) our SVFI can be characterized as an "indirect approximation method" of the value function based on a "parametric architecture."

Just like in this article, the operations research literature derives bounds on the error of approximation and, with these, provide consistency type results (see, e.g., Bertsekas & Tsitsiklis, 1996, p. 332; Bertsekas, 2012, p. 500). The main difference between our methodological contribution and this literature lies on the nature of the asymptotic analysis. On the one hand, the operations research literature considers the behavior of the approximation using an iterative procedure *keeping the approximating parametric space constant*. On the other hand, our analysis does not involve iterative procedures[2] but it does require the sieve space to increase in complexity in order to derive formal results. Given that our interest is in deriving formal (asymptotic) results, the difference in the nature of the asymptotics implies that these two approaches are clearly distinct contributions. In addition to being theoretically interesting in its own right, the type of asymptotic analysis considered in this article becomes essential in order to establish the asymptotic properties of the estimation procedure that results from embedding the SVFI within the estimation algorithm.

The rest of the article proceeds as follows. In Section 2 we describe the optimization problem. Sections 3 and 4 develop formal results for infinite horizon problems and finite horizon problems, respectively. In particular, we establish properties of the approximation including consistency and rates of convergence. In Section 5, we show how to use SVFI in estimation as well as properties of the estimator. Section 6 investigates the small sample properties of our approximations, establishing both the speed and reliability of our methods. Section 7 concludes.

2. THE DYNAMIC DECISION PROBLEM

In this article, we are interested in approximating the value function of a single agent solving a dynamic decision problem. We begin by introducing the general problem. In every period $t \in \mathbb{N}$, the agent observes the current value of a state (x_t, ε_t) and chooses an action a_t in a finite choice set $A(x_t)$. The first component x_t is observed by the researcher whereas the second component $\varepsilon_t \equiv \{\varepsilon_t(a) : a \in A(x_t)\}$ is not. We assume that $x_t \in X$ and $\varepsilon_t \in E$. Conditional on this information, the agent solves the following optimization problem:

$$V_t(x_t, \varepsilon_t) = \sup_{\Pi_t} E\left\{ \sum_{j=t}^{T} \beta^{j-t}[u(x_j, a_j) + \varepsilon_j(a_j)] \mid x_t, \varepsilon_t \right\} \tag{2.1}$$

where $\Pi_t = \{\{a_j\}_{j=t}^{\infty} : a_t = A(x_t)\}$ and $u(x_t, a_t) + \varepsilon_t(a_t)$ denotes the period utility of making decision a_t in state (x_t, ε_t), $u(x_t, a_t)$ representing the structural part (possibly known up to a finite dimensional parameter) and $\varepsilon_t(a_t)$ representing the residual part, unobserved by the researcher.

The objective of this article is to provide a computationally feasible approximation to the value functions (i.e., $\{V_t(\cdot)\}_{t=1}^{T}$) and study its properties. In general, we might be interested in approximating these function because we want to do welfare analysis (i.e., which can be conducted directly using these functions) or because we are interested in any other feature of the problem that can be computed from these functions (i.e., optimal decision rules, CCPs, etc.).

The formulation in Eq. (2.1) encompasses both finite horizon problems (i.e., $T = \infty$) and infinite horizon problems (i.e., $T < \infty$). Following the dynamic programming literature, our strategy to approximate the value function in Eq. (2.1) is to show that it is the unique solution to a (functional) Bellman equation, and construct an approximation based on this representation. Given that the Bellman equation representation of the finite and infinite horizon problems are fundamentally different, it is convenient to divide the rest of the discussion into these two cases.

3. APPROXIMATION IN INFINITE HORIZON PROBLEMS

This section describes the application of nonparametric sieve methods to approximate the value functions in Eq. (2.1) when the dynamic problem has an infinite horizon (i.e., $T = \infty$). The distinctive feature of the infinite horizon problem is that the value function of the problem is stationary (i.e., $V_t(\cdot) = V(\cdot), \forall t \in \mathbb{N}$), provided that we impose mild additional assumptions to the problem. In particular, we follow Rust (1987, 1988) and assume that the joint stochastic process $\{x_t, \varepsilon_t, a_t\}$ is a controlled Markov process that satisfies the following conditional independence (CI) assumption:

$$\begin{aligned} dP(x_{t+1},\varepsilon_{t+1} | x_t,\varepsilon_t,a_t,x_{t-1},\varepsilon_{t-1},a_{t-1},\ldots) &= dP(x_{t+1},\varepsilon_{t+1} | x_t,\varepsilon_t,a_t)(\text{Markov}) \\ &= dP(\varepsilon_{t+1} | x_{t+1},x_t,\varepsilon_t,a_t) dP(x_{t+1} | x_t,\varepsilon_t,a_t) \\ &= dP(\varepsilon_{t+1} | x_{t+1}) dP(x_{t+1} | x_t,a_t)(\text{CI}) \end{aligned}$$

Under these assumptions, the literature provides several ways of formulating the value function in Eq. (2.1) as the recursive solution of a

Bellman equation. In particular, these include: (a) the *social surplus function* formulation discussed in Rust (1987, 1988), (b) the *conditional value function* formulation of Rust (1987), and (c) the *choice-specific value function* formulation of Rust (1988). Rather than describing each of these formulations in the main text, we now introduce a single *unified formulation* that encompasses all of these formulations.[3]

According to our unified formulation, the value functions in Eq. (2.1) are stationary and solve the following Bellman equation:

$$V(s) = \max_{a \in A(s)} \{u(s,a) + \beta E(F(V,s') \mid s,a)\}, \forall s \in S \tag{3.1}$$

where s is the current value of the state, s' is the future value of the state, S is the state space, a represents the action chosen by the agent, $A(s)$ is the set of actions available to the agent when the state is s, and F is a known functional of the value function $V(\cdot)$ and the future state s' that satisfies certain known properties.[4]

3.1. Approximating the Value Function

In order to discuss the approximation of V, we must first define the space to which this function belongs. In particular, assume that V belongs to a functional space, denoted $\mathcal{F}$. For example, we can take $\mathcal{F}$ to be the space of measurable, bounded, real-valued functions from S to $\mathbb{R}$. We define a metric d in this space, making $(\mathcal{F}, d)$ a normed vector space. If we do not indicate otherwise, the metric is the sup-norm metric, that is, for any $f_1, f_2 \in \mathcal{F}$:

$$d(f_1, f_2) = \sup_{s \in S} \mid f_1(s) - f_2(s) \mid \tag{3.2}$$

Furthermore, we assume that this metric space is complete, that is, it is a Banach space. Consider the following (functional) operator $\Gamma : \mathcal{F} \to \mathcal{F}$:

$$[\Gamma\theta]\ (s) \equiv \max_{a \in A(s)} \{u(s,a) + \beta E(F(\theta,s') \mid s,a)\}, \forall s \in S \tag{3.3}$$

According to the definition in Eq. (3.1), the value function is the fixed point of this operator. Furthermore, under Blackwell (1965) sufficient conditions (also see, e.g., Stokey & Lucas, 1989, Theorem 3.3), the operator Γ can be shown to be a contraction mapping. Thus, as a consequence of the contraction mapping theorem (see, e.g., Stokey & Lucas, 1989, Theorem

3.2), it follows that the value function is the *unique* fixed point of the contraction mapping, that is, the *unique* solution to:

$$\min_{\theta \in \mathcal{F}} d(\theta, \Gamma\theta) \tag{3.4}$$

As a consequence, if it is possible to solve the minimization problem in Eq. (3.4), then the solution has to be unique and equal to the value function. Unfortunately, there are several situations of practical relevance in which this minimization problem is computationally infeasible. In this article we focus on the difficulties that arise when the state space is too large, that is, the cardinality of the set S is either infinity or finite but too large to permit the use of traditional methods.

The approximation method we propose is inspired by the sieves nonparametric estimation method. Instead of solving the original minimization problem (i.e., Eq. (3.4)), we replace the original (possibly infinite dimensional) parameter space $\mathcal{F}$ with a sequence of simpler (often finite dimensional) parameter spaces, called sieves. Throughout this article, the sequence of sieve spaces will be denoted by $\{\Theta_n\}_{n\geq 1}$, where $n \in \mathbb{N}$ is an index that represents the complexity of the sieve space. In order for this replacement to produce an accurate approximation of the unknown value function, it will be required that the sieve space sequence $\{\Theta_n\}_{n\geq 1}$ to become increasingly more complex (i.e., for any $n \in \mathbb{N}$, $\Theta_n \subset \Theta_{n+1} \subseteq \mathcal{F}$) and dense in $\mathcal{F}$ as $n \to \infty$.

For a given sieve space Θ_n, our method produces an approximation, denoted $\hat{\theta}_n$. In essence, we replace the original parameter space $\mathcal{F}$ by the sieve parameter space Θ_n and, loosely speaking, our approximation will be given as:

$$\hat{\theta}_n \approx \arg\min_{\theta \in \Theta_n} d(\theta, \Gamma\theta)$$

That is, we will seek to choose the parameters of the sieve to get as close to a fixed point of the Bellman operator as possible. Naturally, the quality of the approximation will be determined by the sieve space Θ_n used to approximate the original parameter space $\mathcal{F}$.

We introduce a definition of consistency of the approximation and rate of convergence of the approximation.

Definition 3.1. (Consistency) $\hat{\theta}_n$ is a consistent approximation to V if and only if:

$$d(\hat{\theta}_n, V) = o_p(1), \text{ as } n \to \infty$$

To be precise, this is an approximation problem and not an estimation problem. In other words, there are no data and, hence, no random sampling error.[5]

Definition 3.2. (Rate of Convergence) $\hat{\theta}_n$ converges to V at a rate of γ_n^{-1} if and only if:

$$d(\hat{\theta}_n, V) \leq O_p(\gamma_n)$$

where $\gamma_n = o(1)$ as $n \to \infty$.

3.2. Assumptions

We now provide a list of the assumptions used in this section. As we show in Example 3.1, all of these assumptions are satisfied in dynamic decision problems that have a very large but finite state space.

Assumption A.1. $(\mathcal{F}, d)$ is a complete metric space of functions that map S into $\mathbb{R}$ and Γ defined in Eq. (3.3) is a contraction mapping with modulus $\beta \in (0, 1)$.

Assumption A.2. For any $n \in \mathbb{N}$, d_n is a pseudo-metric in $(\mathcal{F}, d)$ such that $\exists\, K_1, K_2 > 0$,

$$K_1\ d_n(f_1,f_2) - \eta_{1,n} \leq d(f_1,f_2) \leq K_2\ d_n(f_1,f_2) + \eta_{1,n}$$

where $\eta_{1,n} = O_p(\gamma_{1,n})$ and $\gamma_{1,n} = o(1)$, uniformly in $f_1, f_2 \in \mathcal{F}$.

Assumption A.3. For some $k \in \mathbb{N}$, we can find $\theta_n \in \Theta_n$ that satisfies:

$$d_n(\theta_n, \Gamma^k \theta_n) \leq \inf_{\theta \in \Theta_n} d_n(\theta, \Gamma^k \theta) + \eta_{2,n} \tag{3.5}$$

where Γ^k is the kth iteration of Γ, $\eta_{2,n} = O_p(\gamma_{2,n})$, and $\gamma_{2,n} = o(1)$.

Assumption A.4. For any $f \in \mathcal{F}$:

$$\inf_{\theta \in \Theta_n} d(\theta, f) = \eta_{3,n}(f)$$

where $\eta_{3,n}(f) = O_p(\gamma_{3,n}(f))$ and $\gamma_{3,n}(f) = o(1)$.

We now briefly comment on each of the assumptions. Even though Assumption A.1 might look innocuous, it is not. The definition of a contraction mapping is associated to a metric space $(\mathcal{F}, d)$ and, in particular, to the metric d. In other words, if $(\mathcal{F}, d)$ and $(\mathcal{F}, \breve{d})$ are two metric spaces, it is possible that a mapping Γ is a contraction mapping with respect to d but not with respect to $\breve{d}$. This is exactly what happens in the context of single agent dynamic decision problems. According to Blackwell (1965) sufficient conditions, Γ in Eq. (3.3) is a contraction mapping with respect to the sup-norm metric but it may not not be a contraction mapping with respect to more convenient metrics, such as the l_2-metric (see, e.g., the discussion in Bertsekas & Tsitsiklis, 1996, p. 369).

In cases in which the state space S is too large, it might not be computationally possible to work with the metric d, but we find convenient to replace this metric with an associated pseudo-metric d_n. In order for this replacement to produce interesting results, we need to assume that the difference between the metric d and the pseudo-metric d_n vanishes at a certain rate. This is what Assumption A.2 accomplishes.

If we had the computational capability to solve the minimization problem in Eq. (3.4), then the solution to this problem would be exactly object of interest. The motivation for this article, however, is to consider cases in which the size of the state space S makes solving the minimization problem in Eq. (3.4) impossible. Assumption A.3 describes the operation that is within our computational possibilities.

Instead of solving the problem in the original space $\mathcal{F}$, we replace the space with a simpler sieve space Θ_n that approximates $\mathcal{F}$. Assumption A.3 implies that, by the virtue of this simplification, we are now able to solve certain computational problems. In particular, we assume that we can: (i) compute the kth iteration of Γ for any function in the sieve space Θ_n and (ii) minimize an objective function within the sieve space Θ_n, possibly up to a small error denoted by $\eta_{2,n}$. In case the objective function can be exactly minimized, then $\eta_{2,n} = 0$. Even when restricted to the simpler sieve space Θ_n, the minimization problem in Assumption A.3 can appear to be computationally challenging. For this reason, Section 3.3 describes an algorithm than can be used to implement this step.

The strategy our our approximation is to replace the original parameter space $\mathcal{F}$ with a sequence of approximating sieve spaces $\{\Theta_n\}_{n \geq 1}$. In order to guarantee that this replacement does not affect the asymptotic properties, Assumption A.4 requires that any function $f \in \mathcal{F}$ can be approximated by an element in Θ_n, up to a small error denoted by $\eta_{3,n}(f)$. In order to guarantee a small error of approximation, it is convenient to choose the sieve space Θ_n that mimics the properties of the original parameter space $\mathcal{F}$.

In turn, in order to derive these properties, Stokey and Lucas (1989, Corollary 1, p. 52) can prove to be a very valuable tool.

In order to illustrate these assumptions, we consider the following example.

Example 3.1. (Large but finite state space) Suppose that the agent solves the value function in Eq. (3.1) where the state-space S is finite but large, that is, $\#S = N < \infty$. By Stokey and Lucas (1989, Corollary 1, p. 52) we can show that the value function belongs to $B(S)$, that is, the space of bounded functions that map S onto $[-B, B] \in \mathbb{R}$, for some $B < \infty$. This implies that we can take the relevant metric space to be $(\mathcal{F}, d)$, with $\mathcal{F} = B(S)$ and d equal to the sup-norm metric, that is,

$$d(f_1, f_2) = \sup_{s \in S} |f_1(s) - f_2(s)| = \max_{i \leq N} |f_1(s_i) - f_2(s_i)|, \ \forall f_1, f_2 \in \mathcal{F}$$

We now verify all of the assumptions. We begin with Assumption A.1. By arguments in Stokey and Lucas (1989, p. 47), $(\mathcal{F}, d)$ is a complete metric space of functions that map S onto $\mathbb{R}$. By the Blackwell (1965) sufficient conditions, it is easy to see that $\Gamma : \mathcal{F} \to \mathcal{F}$ is a contraction mapping with modulus $\beta \in (0, 1)$.

Given that $\#S = N$ is a large number, we might not be able to compute d exactly. Instead, for any $n \in \mathbb{N}$ with $n < N$, we might be able to compute:

$$d_n(f_1, f_2) = \max_{i \leq n} |f_1(s_i) - f_2(s_i)|, \ \forall f_1, f_2 \in \mathcal{F}$$

This is a pseudo-norm in $(\mathcal{F}, d)$, which we refer as the sup-norm pseudo-metric (this pseudo-norm becomes the sup-norm metric when $n = N$). Notice that:

$$|d_n(f_1, f_2) - d(f_1, f_2)| = \eta_{1,n}, \ \forall f_1, f_2 \in \mathcal{F}$$

with $\eta_{1,n} = \max_{i>n} |f_1(s_i) - f_2(s_i)| \leq \max\{N - n, 0\}B$, and so $\eta_{1,n} = O_p(\gamma_{1,n})$ and $\gamma_{1,n} = o(1)$. This verifies Assumption A.2 with $K_1 = K_2 = 1$.

As we have already pointed out, the sup norm (pseudo-)metric can complicated the associated optimization problem in Assumption A.3. For this reason, it is convenient to consider alternative pseudo-metrics. For example, one possibility is to use the l_2 pseudo-metric, given by:

$$d_n(f_1, f_2) = \sqrt{\sum_{i \leq n} |f_1(s_i) - f_2(s_i)|^2}, \ \forall f_1, f_2 \in \mathcal{F}$$

In order to verify Assumption A.2 we notice that:

$$d_n(f_1,f_2) \leq \max_{i \leq n} |f_1(s_i) - f_2(s_i)| \leq \sqrt{N}\, d_n(f_1,f_2)$$

and, therefore:

$$d_n(f_1,f_2) + \eta_{1,n} \leq d(f_1,f_2) \leq N^{1/2}\, d_n(f_1,f_2) + \eta_{1,n}$$

with $\eta_{1,n} = \max_{i>n} |f_1(s_i) - f_2(s_i)| \leq \max\{N-n, 0\}B$, and so it follows that $\eta_{1,n} = O_p(\gamma_{1,n})$ and $\gamma_{1,n} = o(1)$. This verifies Assumption A.2 with $K_1 = 1$ and $K_2 = \sqrt{N}$.

Assumption A.3 assumes that we have computational capabilities to (approximately) minimize a certain objective function. As we have already mentioned, the minimization problem can be approached by using the algorithm described in Section 3.3.

Finally, Assumption A.4 requires that the sieve space Θ_n can approximate the original space $\mathcal{F}$. The nonparametric sieve estimation literature describes many possible choices of sieve spaces that will produce this type of result. For example, for any $n \in \mathbb{N}$, we take Θ_n to be the set of polynomial functions defined in S of degree n. Then, the Weierstrass Theorem (see, e.g., Royden, 1988, p. 128) implies that:

$$\inf_{\theta \in \Theta_n} d(\theta, v) = o(1),\ \forall v \in \mathcal{F}$$

as required by Assumption A.4. Results on the rate of convergence of the $o(1)$ term are available from Chen (2007), and references therein (e.g., Lorentz, 1966; Powell, 1981, Chaps. 15–16).

3.3. An Iterative Procedure to Implement the Minimization

This article proposes an approximation method by replacing the original parameter space $\mathcal{F}$ in Eq. (3.4) with a simpler sieve space Θ_n in Eq. (3.5). Unfortunately, the single-step minimization problem in Eq. (3.5) can be computationally challenging to approach as is.

In order to deal with these challenges, we suggest the Algorithm 3.1. Relative to the original minimization problem, this algorithm replaces the single-step minimization problem with a iterative multistep procedure. We explain the relative advantages of this alternative procedure after introducing the algorithm.

Algorithm 3.1. Let $\{\varepsilon_n\}_{n\geq 1}$ be a tolerance sequence that satisfies $\varepsilon_n = o(1)$. For an arbitrary initial function $f \in \Theta_n$, consider the following iterative procedure:

1. Given f, choose a function $\theta_m \in \Theta_n$ such that:

$$\theta_m = \underset{\theta \in \Theta_n}{\arg\min}\ d_n(\theta, \Gamma^k f) \tag{3.6}$$

2. If $\max\{d_n(\theta_m, \Gamma^k f), d_n(\theta_m, f)\} \leq \varepsilon_n$, then stop the algorithm and define $\theta_n \equiv \theta_m$. Otherwise, set $f = \theta_m$ and return to step 1.
3. If the algorithm converges, then it can be shown that the resulting $\theta_n \in \Theta_n$ satisfies Eq. (3.5) with $\eta_{2,n} = O(\max\{\varepsilon_n, \eta_{1,n}\})$.[6]

The pseudo-norm d_n should be chosen so that it makes the minimization problem in Eq. (3.6) easy to solve. For example, if d_n is a weighted l_2 norm and if Θ_n is a finite dimensional linear sieve (i.e., a linear span of finitely many known basis functions[7]), then the minimization problem in Eq. (3.6) can be solved with a closed form by a least squares procedure.

Having defined the dynamic decision problem and laid out basic definitions and assumptions, we now introduce our method for approximating the value function and prove a series of results regarding the properties of this approximation. We begin by analyzing infinite horizon problems, taking up finite horizon problems in the following section of the article.

3.4. Definition of the Approximation

Under Assumption A.1, the contraction mapping theorem (see, e.g., Stokey & Lucas, 1989, Theorem 3.2, p. 50) indicates that the contraction mapping Γ defined by Eq. (3.3) has a unique fixed point. As we have explained, Eq. (3.1) implies this fixed point is the value function of interest, which we have denoted by $V \in \mathcal{F}$. As we have explained, this motivates us to consider the (unfeasible) optimization problem in Eq. (3.4) or, more generally, for some $k \in \mathbb{N}$, the following (equally unfeasible) optimization problem:

$$\inf_{\theta \in \mathcal{F}} d(\theta, \Gamma^k \theta)$$

Even though the objective function can be computed, the sample space of the problem under consideration makes the domain of the optimization,

$\mathcal{F}$, too complex to handle. In order to circumvent this issue, we consider replacing the space $\mathcal{F}$ with a sequence of approximating spaces or sieves. According to Assumption A.4, the sequence of spaces $\{\Theta_n\}_{n\geq 1}$ becomes a good approximation of $\mathcal{F}$ as our computational possibilities, n, diverge to infinity. In particular, this motives us to consider the following alternative optimization problem:

$$\inf_{\theta\in\Theta_n} d(\theta,\Gamma^k\theta)$$

In certain situations, minimizing with respect to the metric d might not be computationally easy or even possible. In those cases, it is convenient to consider replacing the metric d with a suitable pseudo-metric d_n according to Assumption A.2. This leads us to consider the following optimization problem:

$$\inf_{\theta\in\Theta_n} d_n(\theta,\Gamma^k\theta)$$

In certain settings, the above minimization problem might only be feasible up to a certain residual term that will vanish as n diverges to infinity. This is precisely the case described in Assumption A.3. This progression naturally leads to the definition of our SVFI approximation.

Definition 3.3. (Sieve Value Function Approximation) Assume Assumption A.3. Then the SVFI approximation of V is any $\hat{\theta}_n \in \Theta_n$ that satisfies:

$$d_n(\hat{\theta}_n,\Gamma^k\hat{\theta}_n) \leq \inf_{\theta\in\Theta_n} d_n(\theta,\Gamma^k\theta) + \eta_{2,n} \tag{3.7}$$

where $\eta_{2,n} = O_p(\gamma_{2,n})$ with $\gamma_{2,n} = o(1)$.

3.5. Properties of the Approximation

All of the findings of this section are corollaries of the following lemma.

Lemma 3.1. Assume Assumptions A.1–A.4. Then, the SVFI approximation satisfies:

$$d(\hat{\theta}_n, V) \leq \frac{(1+K_2K_1^{-1})\eta_{1,n} + K_2\eta_{2,n} + K_1^{-1}K_2(1+\beta^k)\eta_{3,n}(V)}{1-\beta^k} \tag{3.8}$$

where $V\in\mathcal{F}$ is the unique fixed point of Γ in $(\mathcal{F},d)$.

Lemma 3.1 is the key result to establish the consistency of the SVFI approximation, derive its rate of convergence, and investigate the finite sample properties of its approximation error. The following result establishes the consistency and the rate of convergence of the approximation.

Theorem 3.1. Assume Assumptions A.1–A.4. Then, the SVFI approximation satisfies:

$$d(\hat{\theta}_n, V) = O_p(\max\{\gamma_{1,n}, \gamma_{2,n}, \gamma_{3,n}(V)\})$$

where $\max\{\gamma_{1,n}, \gamma_{2,n}, \gamma_{3,n}(V)\} = o(1)$ as $n \to \infty$, and $V \in \mathcal{F}$ is the unique fixed point of Γ in $(\mathcal{F}, d)$. This implies that the SVFI approximation:

1. is consistent approximation of V, that is, $d(\hat{\theta}_n, V) = o_p(1)$, as $n \to \infty$.
2. converges to V at a rate of $\min\{\gamma_{1,n}^{-1}, \gamma_{2,n}^{-1}, \gamma_{3,n}^{-1}(V)\}$.

Theorem 3.1 implies that the rate of convergence of the approximation depends on the rate at which three errors converge to zero. These errors are:

1. The error of approximating the metric d with the approximate pseudo-metric d_n, denoted by $\eta_{1,n}$, which converges to zero at a rate of $\gamma_{1,n}^{-1}$.
2. The error of approximation when minimizing the objective function $d_n(\theta, \Gamma^k \theta)$, denoted by $\eta_{2,n}$, which converges to zero at a rate of $\gamma_{2,n}^{-1}$.
3. The error of approximating the value function $V \in \mathcal{F}$ with an element in the sieve space Θ_n, denoted by, which converges to zero at a rate of $\gamma_{3,n}^{-1}(V)$.

The slowest of these three rates determines the rate of convergence of the approximation. The motivation for introducing sieve approximations was the fact that working with the original space $\mathcal{F}$ was computationally infeasible, that is, the third source of error $\eta_{3,n}(V)$ cannot be avoided. However, it might be possible to avoid the other sources of error. In other words, it might be possible to use $d_n = d$, leading to $\gamma_{1,n} = 0$, or it might be possible to solve the minimization of $d_n(\theta, \Gamma^k \theta)$ exactly, leading to $\gamma_{2,n} = 0$. If so, then, the convergence rate of this source of error is infinity, effectively disappearing from the expression for the rate of convergence $\min\{\gamma_{1,n}^{-1}, \gamma_{2,n}^{-1}, \gamma_{3,n}^{-1}(V)\}$.

It is interesting to notice that the findings in Theorem 3.1 do not depend on the number of contraction mapping iterations k in Assumption A.3 (in particular, they hold even if $k = 1$). The choice of k affects several constants associated with the rates of convergence, which are "hidden" in the O_p notation. While these constants are not relevant for the asymptotic results, they can be very relevant for finite values of the computational power n.

Table 1. Value of Constants Associated to the Upper Bound on the Error of Approximation for Different Number of Iterations.[a]

	Number of Iterations: k						
	1	2	3	4	5	6	7
$1/(1-\beta^k)$	10	5.26	3.69	2.91	2.44	2.13	1.92
$(1+\beta^k)/(1-\beta^k)$	19	9.53	6.38	4.82	3.88	3.27	2.83

[a]The discount factor β is set to 0:9.

The right tool for this analysis is Eq. (3.8) in Lemma 3.1, which provides a concrete upper bound on the error of approximation that can be used to study the effect of changes in k that is valid for any value of n. This result reveals that the three sources of error are each associated with a constant that depend on k. In particular, the error terms $\eta_{1,n}$, $\eta_{2,n}$, and $\eta_{3,n}$ are associated to the constants $(1+K_2K_1^{-1})/(1-\beta^k)$, $K_2/(1-\beta^k)$, and $K_1^{-1}K_2(1+\beta^k)/(1-\beta^k)$, respectively. A corollary of this is that, ceteris paribus, an increase in the number of value function iterations k reduces the value of the upper bound of the error of approximation. In particular, Table 1 illustrates that there are significant gains in precision from raising the value of k when the discount factor is $\beta=0.9$. For example, changing the number of iterations from $k=1$ to $k=2$ reduces the (upper bound on the) error of approximation by approximately 50%.

We illustrate the tradeoffs associated with increasing the number of contraction mapping iterations k in the Monte Carlo analysis in Section 6.

4. APPROXIMATION IN FINITE HORIZON DYNAMIC PROBLEMS

This section describes the application of nonparametric sieve methods to approximate the value functions in Eq. (2.1) when the dynamic problem has a finite horizon (i.e., $T<\infty$). The distinctive feature of the finite horizon problem is that the value function of the problem is no longer stationary (i.e., $V_t(\cdot)$ depends on the time index). As time passes and the terminal period T approaches, the agent's value function changes.

Using backward induction, the value function in any given period can be expressed the optimized choice between instantaneous utility and the discounter value for the immediately proceeding period. By repeating the arguments used to develop the unified formulation used in the infinite horizon case, we use s to denote the current value of the state, s' to denote the future value of the state, S to denote the state space, a to denote the action chosen by the agent, $A(s)$ to denote the space of actions available to the agent when the state is s, and F to be a known functional of $V_{t+1}(\cdot)$ and s' that satisfies certain known properties. Based on this notation, in every period $t=1,\ldots,T$, the agent solves an optimization problem characterized by the following value function:

$$V_t(s) = \max_{a \in A(s)} \{u(s,a) + \beta E(F(V_{t+1}, s') \mid s, a)\}, \forall s \in S \tag{4.1}$$

where the variables and functions are defined as in Eq. (3.1) and:

$$V_{T+1}(s) = 0, \ \forall s \in S \tag{4.2}$$

Using the notation developed in Eq. (3.3), the sequence of value functions $\{V_t\}_{t=1}^{T}$ can be defined as follows: $V_T = \Gamma V_{T+1}$ with a zero terminal value, that is, $V_{T+1}(s)=0, \ \forall s \in S$.[8]

The approximation procedure developed for the infinite horizon problem must be modified to accommodate several distinct features of the finite horizon setup. First, the finite horizon problem requires an approximation for the value function at each point in time; the infinite horizon problem is stationary, that is, the agent solves the same problem every period, and thus only requires the approximation of a single value function V. Second, the approximation procedure developed for the infinite horizon problem required the value function V to be a fixed point in a contraction mapping. Clearly, this will not be true for the nonstationary finite horizon problem. As time progresses, the last period of the game approaches and this affects the value of participating in the game. Thus the value functions of the finite horizon problem are not fixed points to any mapping, but are instead a finite sequence of functions that are sequentially related.

With enough computational power, the set of functions $\{V_t\}_{t=1}^{T}$ could be computed exactly using backward induction. Nevertheless, for economic models with large state spaces, the exact implementation of backward induction might be too computationally challenging or even impossible. The objective of this section is to propose a sieve value function approximation for such settings. For a given computational power (i.e., for a given sieve space Θ_n), our approximation method produces a sequence of approximations: $\{\hat{\theta}_{n,t}\}_{t=1}^{T}$ where, for all $t=1, \ldots, T$, $\hat{\theta}_{n,t}$ is the sieve value function approximation for V_t.

We consider two approximation procedures. The first is, essentially, the sieve approximation version of a traditional backward induction. The value function is first approximated for the last period and this approximate function is used to solve for the (approximate) value function for the previous period. Continuing to work backwards yields an approximate value function for each period. Implementing this procedure requires using computational routines that are specifically tailored for the finite horizon setup.

The second procedure entails expanding the state space to include time as a state variable. To the best of our knowledge, this procedure is novel to our article. While this procedure is less intuitive than backward induction, it has the advantage of being implemented with the same computational routines developed above for the infinite horizon problem.

4.1. Approximation Using Backward Induction

The computation of the sequence of value functions $\{V_t\}_{t=1}^{T}$ by backward induction is well understood and requires no further discussion. This section proposes an approximation to these value functions using sieves. The approximation requires the following assumptions. By repeating previous arguments, it is easy to see that these assumptions are satisfied in dynamic decision problems that have a very large but finite state space.

Assumption B.1. $(\mathcal{F}, d)$ is a complete metric space of functions that map S onto $\mathbb{R}$, where d is the sup-norm metric, that is,

$$d(f_1, f_2) = \sup_{s \in S} \| f_1(s) - f_2(s) \|, \ \forall f_1, f_2 \in \mathcal{F}$$

Assumption B.2. For any $n \in \mathbb{N}$, d_n is a pseudo-metric in $(\mathcal{F}, d)$ such that $\exists\, K_1, K_2 > 0$,

$$K_1 \ d_n(f_1, f_2) - \lambda_{1,n} \leq d(f_1, f_2) \leq K_2 \ d_n(f_1, f_2) + \lambda_{1,n}$$

where $\lambda_{1,n} = O_p(\upsilon_{1,n})$ and $\upsilon_{1,n} = o(1)$, uniformly in $f_1, f_2 \in \mathcal{F}$.

Assumption B.3. For any $f \in \mathcal{F}$, we can find $\theta_n \in \Theta_n$ that satisfies:

$$d_n(\theta_n, f) \leq \inf_{\theta \in \Theta_n} d_n(\theta, f) + \lambda_{2,n}$$

where $\lambda_{2,n} = O_p(\upsilon_{2,n})$ and $\upsilon_{2,n} = o(1)$, uniformly in $f \in \mathcal{F}$.

Assumption B.4. For any $f \in \mathcal{F}$:

$$\inf_{\theta \in \Theta_n} d(\theta, f) = \lambda_{3,n}$$

where $\lambda_{3,n} = O_p(\upsilon_{3,n})$ and $\upsilon_{3,n} = o(1)$, uniformly in $f \in \mathcal{F}$.

Assumption B.5. For all $f_1, f_2 \in \mathcal{F}$, $a \in A(s)$, and $s \in S$:

$$E[F(f_1, s') - F(f_2, s') \mid s, a] \leq d(f_1, f_2)$$

We now briefly comment on each of the assumptions with focus on the differences with Assumptions A.1–A.4. With respect to Assumption A.1, Assumption B.1 eliminates the contraction mapping requirement with the requirement that d is the sup-norm metric. As we have already explained, these two assumptions are not that different, as the mapping Γ in Eq. (3.3) can be shown to be a contraction mapping with respect to the sup-norm metric but not with respect to other metrics. Assumption B.2 is identical to Assumption A.2. Assumption B.3 is very similar to Assumption A.3. The differences between the two are the following. First, Assumption A.3 assumed that one could (approximately) minimize a specific objective function within the sieve space Θ_n, whereas Assumption B.3 assumes that one can (approximately) find the best approximation within the sieve space Θ_n for any function in $\mathcal{F}$. Second, in accordance to the first point, Assumption B.3 requires that the error of minimization to converge to zero (in probability) uniformly in $f \in \mathcal{F}$. Assumption B.4 strengthens Assumption A.4 as it requires that $\inf_{\theta \in \Theta_n} d(\theta, f)$ converges to zero (in probability) uniformly in $f \in \mathcal{F}$. In other words, instead of requiring a vanishing error of approximation of any particular function, we require that the a vanishing error of approximation for the *worst* function in the class of functions $\mathcal{F}$. For references on these stronger results, see, for example, Lorentz (1966, Chap. 8). Finally, Assumption B.5 is a mild assumption about the properties of the mapping F. In particular, Lemma A.2 verifies that this assumption holds for all possible the formulations of the problem.

The approximation considered in this section is defined as follows:

Definition 4.1. (Sieve Value Function Approximation) Assume Assumption B.3. Then the approximation of $\{V_t\}_{t=1}^{T}$ is $\{\hat{\theta}_{n,t}\}_{t=1}^{T}$

constructed in the following iterative manner. For $z = 1, \ldots, T$, let $t = T + 1 - z$ and complete the following steps:

1. Define $\hat{\theta}^*_{t,n} : S \rightarrow \mathbb{R}$ as follows:

$$\hat{\theta}^*_{t,n}(s) \equiv [\Gamma\hat{\theta}_{t+1,n}](s) = \max_{a \in A(s)} \{u(s,a) + \beta E(F(\hat{\theta}_{t+1,n}, s') \mid s, a)\}, \forall s \in S$$

where either: $t = T$ and $\hat{\theta}_{t+1,n}(s) \equiv V_{T+1}(s) = 0$ $\forall s \in S$, or $t < T$ and $\hat{\theta}_{t+1,n}$ has been defined in a previous iteration of the algorithm.

2. Define $\hat{\theta}_{t,n} : S \rightarrow \mathbb{R}$ to be any $\hat{\theta}_{t,n} \in \Theta_n$ that satisfies:

$$d_n(\hat{\theta}_{t,n}, \hat{\theta}^*_{t,n}) \leq \inf_{\theta \in \Theta_n} d_n(\theta, \hat{\theta}^*_{t,n}) + \lambda_{2,n}$$

where $\lambda_{2,n} = O_p(\upsilon_{2,n})$ and $\upsilon_{2,n} = o(1)$.

It is evident from the description of the procedure that this method implements the traditional backward induction procedure using sieve approximations, that is, it performs an approximation of the value function of the terminal period and uses the approximation of the value function in a given period to conduct an approximation for the value function in the immediately preceding period. The following theorem establishes the asymptotic properties of the approximation.

Theorem 4.1 . Assume Assumptions B.1–B.5. Then, the approximation satisfies:

$$\max_{t=1,\ldots,T} d(\hat{\theta}_{t,n}, V_t) = O_p(\max\{\upsilon_{1,n}, \upsilon_{2,n}, \upsilon_{3,n}\})$$

where $\max\{\upsilon_{1,n}, \upsilon_{2,n}, \upsilon_{3,n}\} = o(1)$ as $n \rightarrow \infty$. This implies that for all $t = 1, \ldots, T$, the sieve value function approximation $\hat{\theta}_{t,n}$:

1. is a consistent approximation of V_t, that is, $d(\hat{\theta}_{t,n}, V_t) = o_p(1)$, as $n \rightarrow \infty$.
2. converges to V_t at a rate of $\min\{\upsilon_{1,n}^{-1}, \upsilon_{2,n}^{-1}, \upsilon_{3,n}^{-1}\}$.

As in Theorem 3.1, Theorem 4.1 indicates that the rate of convergence of the approximation depends on the rate at which three errors converge to zero. The slowest of these three rates determines the rate of convergence of the approximation.

4.2. Approximation Using Time as a State Variable

The approximation considered in this section entails considering the time dimension as part of the state of the problem. In some sense, it may seem counterintuitive to "increase" the state space for a problem in which the size of space was already deemed to large to compute directly. However, as we demonstrate in this section, the approximation is computationally feasible and can be implemented using the exact same computational tools as in the infinite horizon case.

Consider the state space that results from the cartesian product of the (time invariant) state space S with the time dimension 1,..., T + 1, that is, $\tilde{S} = S \times 1,\ldots,\mathrm{T}+1$. Throughout this section, we superscript with the symbol $\sim$ to denote objects in the new state space that includes the time dimension. For example, the new metric space is denoted by $(\tilde{\mathcal{F}}, \tilde{d})$, where $\tilde{\mathcal{F}}$ denotes a set functions from $\tilde{S}$ onto $\mathbb{R}$ and $\tilde{d}$ denotes the corresponding norm in this space. In this enlarged state space, the sequence of value functions $\{V_t\}_{t=1}^{T+1}$ defined by Eqs. (4.1) and (4.2) can be equivalently rewritten as follows:

$$V(s,t) \equiv V_t(s)$$

In the state space $\tilde{S}$ we can define an analogue to the function Γ, which we denote by $\tilde{\Gamma}$ and define as follows:

$$[\tilde{\Gamma}\theta](s,t) \equiv \sup_{a \in A(s)} \{u(s,a) + \beta E(F(\theta,(s',t+1) \mid (s,t),a)\} \times 1[t < T+1],\ \forall (s,t) \in \tilde{S} \tag{4.3}$$

In order to conduct the approximation in the state space $\tilde{S}$, we use a sequence of sieve spaces, denoted by $\{\tilde{\Theta}_n\}_{n \geq 1}$, where each $\tilde{\Theta}_n$ is a space of (simple) functions that map $\tilde{S}$ onto $\mathbb{R}$. We consider the following assumptions.

Assumption B.6. $(\tilde{\mathcal{F}}, \tilde{d})$ is a complete metric space of functions that map $\tilde{S}$ onto $\mathbb{R}$, where $\tilde{d}$ is the sup-norm metric, that is,

$$\tilde{d}(f_1,f_2) = \sup_{(s,t) \in \tilde{S}} \| f_1(s,t) - f_2(s,t) \|, \forall f_1, f_2 \in \tilde{\mathcal{F}}$$

Assumption B.7. For any $n \in \mathbb{N}$, $\tilde{d}_n$ is a pseudo-metric in $(\tilde{\mathcal{F}}, \tilde{d})$ such that $\exists K_1, K_2 > 0$,

$$K_1\tilde{d}_n(f_1,f_2) - \lambda_{1,n} \leq \tilde{d}(f_1,f_2) \leq K_2\tilde{d}_n(f_1,f_2) + \lambda_{1,n}$$

where $\lambda_{1,n} = O_p(\upsilon_{1,n})$ and $\upsilon_{1,n} = o(1)$, uniformly in $f_1,f_2 \in \tilde{\mathcal{F}}$.

Assumption B.8. For some $k \in \mathbb{N}$, we can find $\theta_n \in \Theta_n$ that satisfies:

$$\tilde{d}_n(\theta_n, \tilde{\Gamma}^k\theta_n) \leq \inf_{\theta \in \tilde{\Theta}_n} \tilde{d}_n(\theta, \tilde{\Gamma}^k\theta) + \lambda_{2,n}$$

where $\tilde{\Gamma}^k$ is the kth iteration of $\tilde{\Gamma}$, $\lambda_{2,n} = O_p(\upsilon_{2,n})$, and $\upsilon_{2,n} = o(1)$.

Assumption B.9. For any $f \in \tilde{\mathcal{F}}$:

$$\inf_{\theta \in \tilde{\Theta}_n} \tilde{d}(\theta,f) = \lambda_{3,n}(f)$$

where $\lambda_{3,n}(f) = O_p(\upsilon_{3,n}(f))$ and $\upsilon_{3,n}(f) = o(1)$.

Assumption B.10. For all $f_1,f_2 \in \tilde{\mathcal{F}}$, $a \in A(s)$, and $(s,t) \in \tilde{S}$:

$$E[F(f_1,(s',t+1)) - F(f_2,(s',t+1)) \mid (s,t),a] \leq d(f_1,f_2)$$

With the exception of the fact that the state space has been enriched with the time index, Assumptions B.6–B.10 are analogous to assumptions that have already been discussed in the article. On the one hand, Assumptions B.6, B.7, and B.10 are analogous to Assumptions B.1, B.2, and B.5 used to consider the sieve approximation to the backward induction solution in finite horizon problems. On the other hand, Assumptions B.8 and B.9 are analogous to Assumptions A.3 and A.4 used to consider the SVFI approximation in infinite horizon problems.

In the context of the SVFI approximation in infinite horizon problems, we provided an iterative algorithm to (approximately) minimizing the objective function. A similar iterative procedure can be developed in the present context.

Algorithm 4.1. *Let $\{\varepsilon_n\}_{n\geq 1}$ be a tolerance sequence that satisfies $\varepsilon_n = o(1)$. For an arbitrary initial function $f \in \tilde{\Theta}_n$, consider the following iterative procedure:*

1. *Given f, choose a function $\theta_m \in \tilde{\Theta}_n$ such that:*

$$\theta_m = \inf_{\theta \in \tilde{\Theta}_n} \tilde{d}_n(\theta, \tilde{\Gamma}^k f)$$

2. *If* $\max\{\tilde{d}_n(\theta_m, \tilde{\Gamma}^k f), \tilde{d}_n(\theta_m, f)\} \leq \varepsilon_n$, *then stop the algorithm and define* $\theta_n \equiv \theta_m$. *Otherwise, set* $f = \theta_m$ *and return to step 1.*

If the algorithm converges, then it can be shown that the resulting $\theta_n \in \tilde{\Theta}_n$ *satisfies Eq.* (3.5) *with* $\lambda_{2,n} = O(\max\{\varepsilon_n, \lambda_{1,n}\})$.[9]

The following result is the key to the asymptotic findings of this section.

Lemma 4.1. Assume Assumptions B.6 and B.10. Let $V \in \tilde{\mathcal{F}}$ be the function defined by: $V(t,s) \equiv V_t(s)$ for all $S \times 1, \ldots, \mathrm{T}+1$. Then:

1. $\tilde{\Gamma}$ is a contraction mapping with modulus β on $(\tilde{\mathcal{F}}, \tilde{d})$.
2. V is the unique fixed point of the contraction mapping $\tilde{\Gamma}$, that is, $\tilde{\Gamma}V = V$.

In the context of infinite horizon problems, Assumption A.1 indicated that the value function was the unique fixed point of a certain contraction mapping. This result was the key to proposing the SVFI approximation method. Lemma 4.1 indicates that an analogous result holds for in the context of finite horizon problem. In fact, if we combine this result with the remaining assumptions, the current setup satisfies all of the conditions required for the SVFI approximation. As a consequence, an analogous approximation to the the SVFI approximation will have the same asymptotic properties, that is, consistency and rates of convergence. This analogous approximation is defined next.

Definition 4.2. (Sieve Value Function Approximation) Assume Assumption B.8. Then the sieve approximation of $\{V_t\}_{t=1}^T$ is $\{\hat{\theta}_{t,n}\}_{t=1}^T$ where, for every $(s,t) \in S \times 1, \ldots, \mathrm{T}\}$, $\hat{\theta}_{t,n}(s) \equiv \hat{\theta}_n(s,t)$ and $\hat{\theta}_n \in \tilde{\Theta}_n$ is any function that satisfies:

$$\tilde{d}_n(\hat{\theta}_n, \tilde{\Gamma}^k \hat{\theta}_n) \leq \inf_{\theta \in \tilde{\Theta}_n} \tilde{d}_n(\theta, \tilde{\Gamma}^k \theta) + \lambda_{2,n}$$

where $\lambda_{2,n} = O_p(\upsilon_{2,n})$ and $\upsilon_{2,n} = o(1)$.

Based on the previous discussion, the following result is a simple corollary of Theorem 3.1 and Lemma 4.1.

Theorem 4.2. Assume Assumptions B.6–B.10. Then, the function $\hat{\theta}_n \in \tilde{\Theta}_n$ in Definition 4.2 satisfies:

$$\tilde{d}(\hat{\theta}_n, V) = O_p(\max\{\upsilon_{1,n}, \upsilon_{2,n}, \upsilon_{3,n}(V)\})$$

where $\max\{\upsilon_{1,n}, \upsilon_{2,n}, \upsilon_{3,n}(V)\} = o(1)$ as $n \to \infty$ and $V \in \tilde{\mathcal{F}}$ is the function defined by: $V(t,s) \equiv V_t(s)$ for all $S \times 1, \ldots, \mathrm{T}+1$. This implies that for all $t = 1, \ldots, T$, the sieve approximation $\hat{\theta}_{t,n}$:

1. is a consistent approximation of V_t, that is, $\sup_{s \in S} | \hat{\theta}_{t,n}(s) - V_t(s) | = o_p(1)$, as $n \to \infty$.
2. converges to V_t at a rate of $\min\{\upsilon_{1,n}^{-1}, \upsilon_{2,n}^{-1}, \upsilon_{3,n}^{-1}(V)\}$.

As in Theorems 3.1 and 4.1, Theorem 4.2 indicates that the rate of convergence of the approximation depends on the rate at which three errors converge to zero. Once again, the slowest of these three rates determines the rate of convergence of the approximation.

5. ESTIMATION

The results to this point in the article characterize the (approximate) computation of the value function (and associated object of interests) for a known vector parameters π that characterize the agent's dynamic decision problem. In this section, we now consider the problem of estimating π in a parameter space Π when the researcher has data on dynamic decisions and, again, the state space is too large to permit the direct computation of V for a given value of π.[10] As before, the associated value function V incorporates all the information that is relevant to the decision problem and depends on the parameter π, that is, $V(\cdot \mid \pi)$. In this setup, the approximation problem of previous sections entails the approximation of the value function V for a particular value of the parameter $\pi \in \Pi$. Let π^* denote the true parameter value, that is, $V(\cdot) \equiv V(\cdot \mid \pi^*)$.

For concreteness, consider an agent solving the value function in Eq. (3.1) with:

$$AS \equiv \{(a,s) : a \in A(s) \text{ and } \forall s \in S\}$$

instantaneous utility function given by:

$$u(s,a) = u(s,a \mid \pi_1), \ \forall (a,s) \in AS$$

transition probabilities given by:

$$dP(\varepsilon', x' \mid x, a) = dP(\varepsilon', x' \mid x, a, \pi_2), \ \forall (a,s) \in AS$$

and a discount factor $\beta = \pi_3$. Set $\pi \equiv (\pi_1, \pi_2, \pi_3) \in \Pi$. For each parameter value $\pi \in \Pi$, the corresponding value function is denoted $V(\cdot \mid \pi)$.

The SVFI approximation procedure described in Definition 3.3 provides a method for approximating the value function for any given set of primitives (i.e., choice set, utility function, discount factor, and transition probabilities). In this setting, these primitives are functions of the unknown parameter value π. To be consistent with this interpretation, we denote: $\theta_n \equiv \theta_n(\cdot \mid \pi)$.

If the value function (or some function derived from it) were observed for an arbitrary set of values, then the SVFI approximation procedure could be used to approximate it. Furthermore, the consistency result in Theorem 3.1 suggests that the parameter π could be estimated as follows:

$$\hat{\pi}_n = \underset{\pi \in \Pi}{\operatorname{argmin}} \; Q(\theta_n(\cdot \mid \pi)) \tag{5.1}$$

where $Q(\theta_n(\cdot \mid \pi))$ is an appropriately chosen function that measures the distance between $\theta_n(\cdot \mid \pi)$ and the value function V. For instance, Q could be the following function:

$$Q(\theta_n(\cdot \mid \pi)) = \int (V(s) - \theta_n(s \mid \pi))^2 \; d\mu(s)$$

where μ is any arbitrary positive measure over S. In practice, however, the estimator in Eq. (5.1) is unfeasible because the value function is not observed by the researcher and, consequently, Q is unknown.

In practice, the value function, or some feature derived from it (e.g., CCPs), can be estimated from the data. With some abuse of notation, let V_I denote the estimated value function using a sample of size I (observations are indexed $i = 1,\ldots,I$) and let Q_I denote the function that measures the distance between $\theta_n(\cdot \mid \pi)$ and V_I. Our previous discussion suggests that the parameter π could be estimated according to the following definition.

Definition 5.1. (Estimator based on the Sieve Value Function Approximation) Let $Q_I : \Pi \rightarrow \mathbb{R}_+$ be the function of the data that measures the distance between V_I and $\theta_n(\cdot \mid \pi)$ for any $\pi \in \Pi$ and let $n = n(I)$. The estimator of the true parameter value π^*, denoted $\hat{\pi}_I$, satisfies:

$$Q_I(\hat{\theta}_n(\cdot \mid \hat{\pi}_I)) \leq \inf_{\pi \in \Pi} \; Q_I(\hat{\theta}_n(\cdot \mid \pi)) + o_p(1), \text{ as } I \rightarrow \infty \tag{5.2}$$

In order to clarify the structure of the problem, we consider an illustrative example.

Example 5.1. In this case, we estimate the CCPs from a sample of I observed choices. In particular, if the set S is finite, then the following estimator:

$$\hat{P}_I = \{\hat{P}_I(a \mid s),\ \forall (a,s) \in AS\}$$

where:

$$\hat{P}_I(a \mid s) = \sum_{i=1}^{I} 1[a_i = a, s_i = s] / \sum_{i=1}^{I} 1[s_i = s]$$

is a $\sqrt{I}$-consistent estimator of the CCPs.

By definition, the CCPs can be derived from the value function. Let $J(\cdot \mid \pi) : \mathcal{F} \to [0,1]^{\#AS}$ be the mapping between the value function and the CCPs, that is,

$$J(V \mid \pi) = \{P(a \mid s),\ \forall (a,s) \in AS\}$$

where the conditioning on π indicates that the mapping itself could depend on the parameter value.[11] This discussion suggests the estimation of π with $\hat{\pi}_I$ as in Eq. (5.2), where the measure μ is set to be the empirical measure, that is,

$$Q_I(\theta_n(\cdot \mid \pi)) = \int (\hat{P}_I - J(\theta_n(\pi) \mid \pi))^2 \, d\hat{P}_I \tag{5.3}$$

$$= I^{-1} \sum_{i=1}^{I} 1[(a_i, s_i) = (a,s)](\hat{P}_I(a \mid s) - J_{(a,s)}(V \mid, \pi))^2 \tag{5.4}$$

In other words, we choose the parameter value that minimizes the integrated squared distance between the observed CCPs and the approximated CCPs, where the empirical measure is used as the measure of integration.

The objective of the rest of the section is to provide conditions under which $\hat{\pi}_I$ is consistent. To this end, we now provide a list of the assumptions that are exclusively used in this section.

Assumption C.1. $(\mathcal{F}_1, d_1)$ and $(\mathcal{F}_2, d_2)$ are metric spaces. The true value function $V = V(\cdot \mid \pi^*) \in \mathcal{F}_1$ and the true parameter value $\pi^* \in \Pi \subseteq \mathcal{F}_2$.

Assumption C.2. The SVFI approximation satisfies:

$$\sup_{\pi \in \Pi} d_1(\hat{\theta}_n(\cdot \mid \pi), V(\cdot \mid \pi)) = o_p(1), \text{ as } n \to \infty$$

Assumption C.3. There is a function $Q(\cdot) : \mathcal{F}_1 \to \mathbb{R}$ such that:

a. $\hat{c}(n,I) = o_p(\delta(n,I))$ where $\hat{c}(n,I) \equiv \sup_{f \in \Theta_n} | Q_I(f) - Q(f) |$.
b. Q is uniformly continuous in $\mathcal{F}_1$ under d_1, that is, for any $\delta > 0$, there exists $\varepsilon > 0$ such that $f_1, f_2 \in \mathcal{F}_1$ with $d_1(f_1, f_2) < \varepsilon$ implies $Q(f_1) - Q(f_2) \leq \delta$.
c. The function $Q(V(\cdot \mid \pi)) : \Pi \to \mathbb{R}$ is uniquely minimized at $\pi = \pi^*$.

Assumption C.4. $I \in \mathbb{N}$, $n = n(I)$ with $n(I) \to \infty$ and $\delta(n(I), I) \to 0$ as $I \to \infty$.

We now briefly comment on each of the assumptions. Assumption C.1 provides a label to relevant spaces, functions, and parameters. Assumption C.2 is a high level assumption which indicates that $\hat{\theta}_n(\cdot \mid \pi)$ is a consistent approximation of $V(\cdot \mid \pi)$, uniform over $\pi \in \Pi$. By repeating the arguments in Theorem 3.1, it is not hard to see that Assumption C.2 holds as a result of using the SVFI approximation procedure described in Definition 3.3 under Assumptions A.1-A.4, with the exception that Assumption A.4 is strengthened to hold uniformly in $f \in \mathcal{F}$ (i.e., as in Assumption B.4). Assumption C3 is similar to assumptions used in the literature on extremum estimators (see, e.g., Chen, 2007, Theorem 3.1) for conditions pertaining to sieve estimators, and Amemiya (1985, Theorem 4.1.1) or McFadden and Newey (1994, Theorem 2.1) for finite dimensional estimators). Finally, Assumption C.4 describes conditions that restrict the relationship between the data sample size and the complexity of the sieve.

Under these assumptions, it is possible to obtain consistent estimators of the parameters of large state space dynamic decision problems by embedding SVFI methods in the estimation algorithm.

Theorem 5.1. Assume Assumptions C.1–C.4. Then, the estimator in Eq. (5.1) is consistent, that is,

$$d_2(\hat{\pi}_I, \pi^*) = o_p(1), \text{ as } I \to \infty$$

6. MONTE CARLO SIMULATIONS

In this section we illustrate the small sample properties of sieve value function approximation in an infinite horizon single agent setting. We first demonstrate sieve approximation of the value function when the structural parameters are known. In the second part of this section, we show how sieves can be applied in the estimation of structural models. The Monte Carlo experiments are conducted in a framework similar to the bus engine replacement problem in Rust (1987). In our context though, the problem is modified so that rather than making the engine replacement decision of a single bus, the agent now endogenizes the purchasing and replacement decision over an entire fleet of buses, with the constraint that at most one bus can be replaced in any period. Allowing more buses increases the number of state variables, allowing us to study the approximation for both small and large scale problems. We consider a single bus setting where we can compare the sieve approximation to full solution methods and then study the performance of sieves in a more complex problem (10 buses) where full solution methods are infeasible.

Let J indicate the number of buses in the agent's fleet. The endogenous state vector x_t contains the current engine mileage for each bus j, $x_t(j)$. There are J endogenous state variables. In each period the agent has the option of reseting any (but only one) of the J engine mileages to zero. The choice set is defined as $a_t = \{0, 1, \ldots, J\}$, where $a_t = 0$ represents replacing no buses and $a_t = j$ corresponds replacing the engine in bus j. For these examples we assume that if a bus engine is not replaced the engine mileage transitions as an exponential random variable that is the same for all buses.

$$x_{t+1}(j) = \begin{cases} x_t(j) + \zeta_t(j), & \text{if } a_t \neq j \\ \zeta_t(j), & \text{if } a_t = j \end{cases}$$

where the probability density function of ζ is $P(\zeta \mid \lambda) = \lambda \exp(-\lambda\zeta)$.

Given the current mileage states x, the agent chooses to set at most one engine milage to zero in the current period. Contemporaneous utility is defined as $u(x, a_t) + \varepsilon_t(a_t)$, where ε is a random utility shock and mean flow utility is defined as

$$u(x_t, a_t) = \begin{cases} \alpha \sum_{j=1}^{J} x_t(j), & \text{if } a_t = 0 \\ \alpha \sum_{j=1}^{J} x_t(j) - \alpha x_t(a_t) + RC, & \text{if } a_t = \{1, \ldots, J\} \end{cases}$$

RC is the replacement cost of a bus engine.

The agent's problem is to make an optimal sequence of purchasing decisions to maximize the expected discounted flow of future per-period pay-offs. With discount factor β, we can formulate the value function using the recursive Bellman representation:

$$V(x_t, \varepsilon_t) = \max_{a_t \in \{0,1,\ldots,J\}} \{u(x_t, a_t) + \varepsilon_t(a_t) + \beta E[V(x_{t+1}, \varepsilon_{t+1}) \mid x_t, a_t]\}$$

where the expectation is taken with respect to all future milage shocks ζ and utility shocks ε.

The choice specific value functions (excluding the shocks) for choice $a \in \{0, 1, \ldots, J\}$ are

$$v(x_t, a) = u(x_t, a) + \beta E[V(x_{t+1}, \varepsilon_{t+1}) \mid x_t, a]$$

The agent's optimal decision in period t is then to choose a_t^* such that:

$$a_t^* = \arg \max_{a \in \{0,1,\ldots,J\}} \{v(x_t, a) + \varepsilon_t(a)\}$$

6.1. *Approximation*

Let θ_n denote the sieve approximation of the ex-ante value function, that is, $\theta_n(x_t) \approx E[\max_{a \in 0,1,\ldots,J\}}(v(x_t, a) + \varepsilon_t(a)) \mid x_t]$ where the expectation is over the random pay-off shock ε. Assuming the utility shocks are distributed type-I extreme value, we have a known closed form representation of the expectation:

$$E[V(x_t, \varepsilon_t) \mid x_t] = \ln\left(\sum\nolimits_{a \in 0,1,\ldots,J\}} \exp(v(x_t, a))\right) + \gamma \tag{6.1}$$

where γ is Euler's constant.

Therefore, for a chosen sieve space Θ_n, we seek an approximation of the expression in Eq. (6.1), $\theta_n \in \Theta_n$, such that:

$$\begin{aligned}\theta_n(x_t) &\approx \ln\left(\sum\nolimits_{a \in 0,1,\ldots,J\}} \exp(v(x_t, a))\right) + \gamma \\ &= \ln\left(\sum\nolimits_{a \in 0,1,\ldots,J\}} \exp(u(x_t, a) + \beta E[V(x_{t+1}, \varepsilon_{t+1}) \mid x_t, a])\right) + \gamma \\ &\approx \ln\left(\sum\nolimits_{a \in 0,1,\ldots,J\}} \exp(u(x_t, a) + \beta E[\theta_n(x_{t+1}) \mid x_t, a])\right) + \gamma\end{aligned} \tag{6.2}$$

The right hand side of Eq. (6.2) represents one contraction on the approximation, θ_n, defined as $\Gamma^1 \theta_n(x_{t+1} \mid x_t)$. Section 3.5 demonstrates that we can actually reduce the upper-bound of the approximation error by increasing the number of iterations of the contraction operator on the approximation. Rather than immediately plugging the approximation into the expected future value term, we could alternatively write this term using Eq. (6.1) as a function of next periods contemporaneous profit functions and a two-period away expected future value term. If we substitute the approximation into the two-period away expected future value function, this corresponds to two iterations of the contraction ($k=2$). We could continue in this way for $k>2$, though the computational burden increases exponentially with k.

In these example, we construct the sieve approximation using ordinary polynomials and piece-wise polynomials (splines). Given a value of the state vector, x and our chosen sieve space, the sieve approximation is defined as,

$$\theta_n(x) = \mathrm{W}_n(x)\rho$$

where ρ are the parameters that approximate the value function, and the elements of $\mathrm{W}_n(\cdot)$ are determined from our choice of polynomial function.

For any state variable x, the sieve approximation and its contraction will satisfy,

$$\mathrm{W}_n(x)\rho \approx \ln\left(\sum\nolimits_{a\in\{0,1,\ldots,J\}} \exp(u(x,a) + \beta E[\mathrm{W}_n(x')\rho \mid x, a])\right) + \gamma \tag{6.3}$$

A key convenience of constructing the approximation with a linear function is that the parameters ρ can be taken out of the expected value, with the expectation only applying to the state transitions, so we can replace $E[\mathrm{W}_n(x')\rho \mid x, a] = E[\mathrm{W}_n(x') \mid x, a]\rho$.

Given a sample of state vectors x_s for $s=1,\ldots,S$, the parameters ρ in (6.3) are found through the iterative Algorithm 3.1 using the sum of squared errors as the distance function. At iteration m, the parameters are updated for $m+1$ by solving:

$$\rho^{m+1} = \arg\max_{\rho} \sum_{s=1}^{S} \left[\mathrm{W}_n(x_s)\rho - \ln\left(\sum\nolimits_{a\in\{0,1,\ldots,J\}} \exp(u(x_s,a) + \beta E[\mathrm{W}_n(x'_s) \mid x_s, a]\rho^m)\right) + \gamma\right]^2 \tag{6.4}$$

Repeating until convergence.

Let X represent a matrix whose sth row contains $W_n(x_s)$. Similarly, $\overline{X}_a$ is a matrix who's sth row contains $E[W_n(x'_s) \mid x_s, a]$. The maximum of Eq. (6.4) has a closed form solution, so the iterative procedure finds a fixed point to the equation:

$$\rho^{m+1} = (X'X)^{-1}X'\left[\ln\left(\sum\nolimits_{a \in \{0,1,\ldots,J\}} \exp(u(X,a) + \beta\overline{X}_a\rho^m)\right) + \gamma\right] \tag{6.5}$$

The element inside the brackets on the right-hand side of Eq. (6.5) can be abbreviated as $\Gamma^1\theta(\rho^m)$ since it represents one contraction on the sieve function with parameters ρ^m.

Equation (6.5) has two important features. First, most of it's components, including $(X'X)^{-1}X'$ and $\overline{X}_a$ can be computed outside of the algorithm and do not need to be recomputed at each iteration. Second, since the sieve is a simple linear function, the elements of $\overline{X}_a$, the expectations of the sieve given the state transitions, are simply the raw moments of the random variables. In many cases, these moments have a closed form expression or can be approximated to any precision with simulation methods, which holds true for both continuous or discrete state variables.[12]

Before we move to the main analysis, the solid line in Fig. 1 plots the expected value function for the single bus replacement problem, which is the object we aim to approximate in these first set of exercises. The benefit of looking at the single state variable case first is that we can solve the value function exactly using full solution methods, providing a benchmark to compare our approximation. Fig. 1 also plots two different approximating functions using SVFI. These functions illustrate the basic insight of this article. The first function, represented by the dashed line, uses a spline with a single knot and a linear interaction. This choice of sieve space does a very poor job of approximating the true value function. The dotted line adds a quadratic term to the spline. The main result of this article shows that as we increase the complexity of the sieve space, we are guaranteed to get closer to the value function. In this example adding the quadratic reduced the maximum distance between the approximating function and true function from about 2.9 to 1.0.

Table 2 contains the details of the sieve approximation for the single bus case. The table is broken into three panels. For comparison, panel A shows the performance of traditional value function iteration where the state space is split into 250 grid points. Panel B shows the performance of SVFI using polynomials, where we consider up to a seventh order polynomial function. Finally, panel C shows the performance for SVFI using

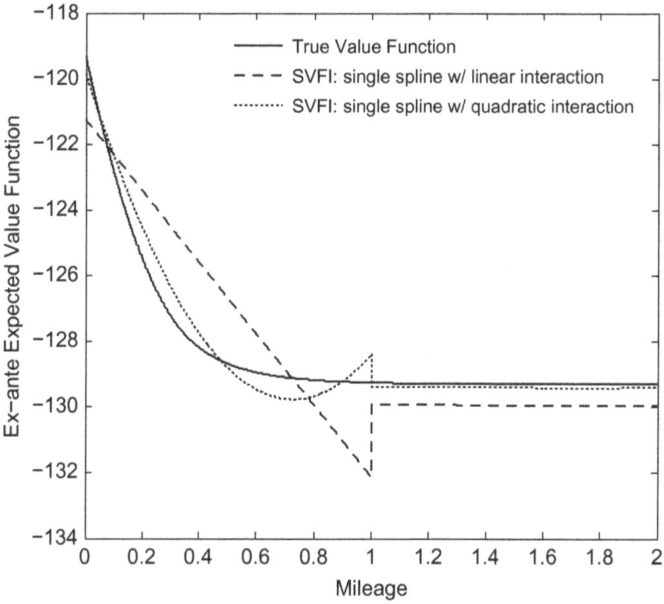

Fig. 1. Comparison of true value function to approximated value function.

piece-wise polynomials, where we hold fixed a fourth order polynomial for each spline and increase the number of knot points from one to seven. Since we know the true value function in this small problem, we can evaluate how close each method gets to the true function as we did in Fig. 1.

For each of the approximation methods, Table 2 includes the three measures of fit that can be computed within our approximation sample. These measures of fit will be very useful in practice as they indicate how well the contraction comes to holding. These include:

1. Mean squared errors: $||\theta - \Gamma^1\theta||_2/S$

$$\sum_{s=1}^{S} (\theta(x_s) - \Gamma^1\theta(x'_s \mid x_s))^2/S$$

2. Supremum norm: $||\theta - \Gamma^1\theta||_\infty$

$$\max\{|\theta(x_s) - \Gamma^1\theta(x'_s \mid x_s)|\}_{s=1}^{S}$$

Table 2. Sieve Approximation ($J = 1$).[a]

Method	Number of Parameters	Time (Sec.)	Within Approximation Sample Fit			Comparison to Truth	
			MSE(θ,$\Gamma\theta$)	$\|\|\theta - \Gamma\theta\|\|\infty$	R-squared[b]	$\|\|\theta - V^*\|\|\infty$	R-squared[c]
A: traditional value function iteration with fixed grid of 250 points							
	250	0.4803	–	–	–	0.3294	0.9790
B: SVFI with polynomials[d] *(order of highest polynomial)*							
2nd	3	0.003	0.04189	1.3506	0.7584	2.3327	0.4000
3rd	4	0.004	0.02043	0.7483	0.8649	1.2614	0.7232
4th	5	0.005	0.00816	0.3448	0.9411	0.4328	0.9061
5th	6	0.006	0.00220	0.0860	0.9836	0.1291	0.9759
6th	7	0.007	0.00170	0.0973	0.9873	0.1248	0.9793
7th	8	0.008	0.00142	0.0541	0.9894	0.0874	0.9844
C: SVFI with piece-wise polynomials (number of knots w/4th order poly)							
1	10	0.008	0.00120	0.0696	0.9910	0.0888	0.9859
2	15	0.010	0.00048	0.0439	0.9964	0.0700	0.9950
3	20	0.012	0.00006	0.0058	0.9996	0.0140	0.9994
4	25	0.015	0.00004	0.0027	0.9997	0.0049	0.9996
5	30	0.016	0.00002	0.0021	0.9999	0.0043	0.9997
6	35	0.017	0.00001	0.0009	0.9999	0.0029	0.9998
7	40	0.015	0.00001	0.0004	1.0000	0.0023	0.9998

[a]The "true" value function is solved through value function iteration with 25,000 grid points. It took 90 minutes. The parameters are set to $\alpha = -5$, $RC = -10$, $\lambda = 1/.05$ and $\beta = .99$.

[b]$1 - \frac{||\theta - \Gamma\theta||_2}{||\Gamma\theta - E(\Gamma\theta)||_2}$

[c]$1 - \frac{||\theta - V^*||_2}{||V^* - E(V^*)||_2}$

[d]Sieve approximation uses the same 250 points used in part A.

3. *R*-squared

$$1-\frac{||\theta-\Gamma^{1}\theta||_{2}}{||\Gamma^{1}\theta-E(\Gamma^{1}\theta)||_{2}}$$

Beginning with the polynomial approximation (panel B), the second order polynomial function does a very poor job approximating the value function. This is apparent in the with-in sample fit. In the second order case, the contraction is very far from holding, with the maximum distance between the function and its contraction being 1.35. Across the entire function, the *R*-squared in this case is 0.75. However, as suggested by the theoretical results, by increasing the sieve complexity we are able to achieve a better, in this csae when we reach the end of panel C, the piece-wise polynomial with seven knot points, we can get the approximation and its contraction to hold nearly exactly and an *R*-squared of 1.0.[13]

Table 3 displays the results of the sieve approximation method for a much larger problem containing 10 continuous state variables. Similar to the smaller problem, the measures of within approximation fit become successively better as the complexity of the sieve is increased. Although we have no method to compare the approximated value functions with the true value functions as we could with the smaller model, the fact that we can achieve similar measures of fit within the sample gives some indication that we are close to the true value function.

Table 3. Sieve Approximation ($J=10$).[a]

Method	Number of Parameters	Time (Sec.)	Within Approximation Sample Fit		
			$MSE(\theta,\Gamma\theta)$	$\|\|\theta-\Gamma\theta\|\|_\infty$	*R*-squared[b]
SVFI with polynomials (order of highest polynomial)					
1st	11	3	0.12952	70.6554	0:9192
2nd	66	27	0.00651	10.1523	0.9898
3rd	286	125	0.00441	6.8139	0.9921
4th	1001	268	0.00285	2.4845	0.9937
5th	3003	744	0.00214	1.4864	0.9954

[a]Sieve approximation uses 10,000 draws on the interval (0,2). The parameters are set to $\alpha=-5$, $RC=-10$, $\lambda=1/.05$ and $\beta=.99$

[b]$1-\frac{||\theta-\Gamma\theta||_{2}}{||\Gamma\theta-E(\Gamma\theta)||_{2}}$

6.2. Estimation

We now apply sieve value function approximation to estimate dynamic models, where we simultaneously solve for the structural parameters and the associated sieve value function approximation that maximizes the likelihood of observed choice data. We consider the single bus replacement case so that data can be generated from the true choice probabilities. In general, the data will contain fewer observations than are necessary to approximate the sieve function. This is not a problem because we are free to draw as many state vectors as we want from the state space to supplement the states that are actually observed. Since the observed sample contains the most relevant part of the state space, for example we will never observe buses with extraordinarily high mileages because they will have been replaced long before then, rather than randomly drawing from the state space for the approximation, we may be able to improve our approximation (and thus our structural parameter estimates) by focusing on the state space near the generated data. For these exercises we will draw 500 random points which will be perturbations around the observed data points.

Our model contains two unknown structural parameters, α and RC. Estimation is implemented by modifying the iterative algorithm used for approximation described in Section 3.3. The parameter of interest is denoted by $\pi \equiv (\alpha, RC)$. Let the observations be indexed by $i = 1,\ldots, I$, where I denotes the sample size, a_i denotes the observed choice for observation i, and x_i denotes the observed state for observation i.

The estimator of π is denoted by $\hat{\pi}_I$ and is computed according to the following procedure. First, we choose arbitrary initial values of $(\hat{\pi}_I^0, \hat{\theta}_n^0) \in \Pi \times \tilde{\Theta}_n$. Then, we set $m = 1$ and use the following iterative algorithm:

1. Choose $\hat{\pi}_I^m$ to maximize the (approximate) likelihood:

$$\hat{\pi}_I^m = \arg\max_{\pi \in \Pi} \sum_{i=1}^{I} \ln\left(\Pr(a_i \mid \pi, x_i, \hat{\theta}_n^{m-1}\right)$$

2. Choose $\hat{\theta}_n^m$ to solve the fixed point in Eq. (6.5) taking $\hat{\pi}_I^m$ as given.
3. If $\|\hat{\pi}_I^m - \hat{\pi}_I^{m-1}\| 10^{-6}$, then stop the algorithm and set $\hat{\pi}_I = \hat{\pi}_I^m$. Otherwise, set $m = m + 1$ and return to the first step.

This algorithm parallels Aguirregabiria and Mira (2002) in the sense that it swaps the calculation of the value function to outside of the maximization of the likelihood over the structural parameters. Results of the

Table 4. Sieve Estimation ($J=1$).[a]

	α	RC
Parameters	−5.000	−10.000
SVFI with polynomials (order of highest polynomial)		
2nd	−7.5762	−14.6496
	(1.5004)	(2.3318)
3rd	5.0129	−9.9637
	(0.5212)	(0.5374)
4th	−5:0159	−10.0036
	(0:2811)	(0.4897)

[a]Results from 2000 replications, each with 5,000 observations. Initial values of structural parameters and sieve approximation were set to zero.

estimation exercise for different values of sieve complexity are presented in Table 4. The results show that for the second order polynomial the parameter estimates are extremely biased, which is not surprising given that this function performed very poorly in approximating the value function in Table 2. However this bias completely disappears for the third order polynomial and above.

7. CONCLUSION

This article proposes a methodology to approximate the value function in single agent dynamic problems where a large state space makes value function iteration unfeasible. Our method is based on nonparametric sieve estimation, and we refer to it as SVFI. We provide a formal framework to analyze the approximation error. In particular, we show that the SVFI approximation converges to the value function as the complexity of the sieve increases, and we characterize the rate of this convergence. Furthermore, we provide a concrete upper bound on the error of approximation which can be used to analyze its contributing factors.

A Monte Carlo analysis reveals that the SVFI approximation is very successful in estimating the value function. These results suggest that our approximation can successfully be used to solve models that would otherwise be computationally infeasible, implying that these techniques may substantially broaden the class of models that can be solved and estimated.

Given the standard challenges with large state space problems, we expect SVFI to open up a wide variety of avenues of theoretical and empirical exploration of complex dynamic single agent and equilibrium problems. For example, in Arcidiacono, Bayer, Bugni, and James (2012), we consider sequential move dynamic games. Estimation of these games can be done via standard two-step procedures. Through the use of sieves, it is possible to calculate the CCPs of the finite horizon game which has a unique equilibrium, the limit of which is also an equilibrium in the infinite horizon game. It is then possible to compare the CCPs from the finite horizon equilibrium to those observed in the data, testing to see whether this equilibrium was played.

NOTES

1. For an excellent review of the method of sieves see Chen (2007).

2. As we explain later the minimization problem we propose can be computationally complex to implement. For this reason, we provide an iterative algorithm with the sole purpose of approximating a solution to this minimization problem. Nevertheless, if it were possible to solve the minimization problem directly (i.e., without using the iterative algorithm), then our methodology does not really require the use of iterations.

3. Appendix B describes each of these formulations and shows that all of them are special cases of our unified formulation.

4. Among other properties, $F : \mathcal{F} \times S$ satisfies: (a) monotonicity: for functions f_1, f_2 with $f_1(s) \leq f_2(s)$ for all $s \in S$, then $F(f_1, s') \leq F(f_2, s')$ and (b) discounting: for any function f and any $\alpha \in \mathbb{R}$, $\beta F(f + \alpha, s') = \beta F(f, s') + \beta \alpha$.

5. The reason to use $o_p(1)$ instead of $o(1)$ is that, in general, we allow for randomness in the approximation. The randomness can occur, for example, in the choice of the sieve space or the solution to the approximation problem.

6. See Lemma A.1 for the formal statement and its proof.

7. This is a widely used class of sieve spaces that includes polynomials, trigonometric functions, splines, and orthogonal wavelets (see, e.g., Chen, 2007, p. 5570).

8. It should be noted that each of the objects in Eq. (4.1), i.e., the set of possible actions $A(\cdot)$, the period utility function $u(\cdot)$, the expectation operator $E(\cdot)$, and the functional $F(\cdot)$, could be allowed to be time-specific without affecting any of the theoretical results to follow. We opted to keep these elements time invariant to simplify the exposition and to relate them easily to elements in Eq. (3.1).

9. This can be shown using a very similar argument to the one used for Algorithm 3.1 in Lemma A.1. The argument requires that $\tilde{\Gamma}$ is a contraction mapping with modulus β on $(\tilde{\mathcal{F}}, \tilde{d})$, which shown in Lemma 4.1.

10. Throughout this section, we pretend that the dynamic problem we refer to is the infinite horizon single agent decision problem. Nevertheless, by making slight notational changes, the results of this section can also be applied to a finite horizon problem.

11. The function J will depend on the specific formulation of the dynamic decision problem. See Appendix B for a description of each of the formulations and the definition of the function J in each case.

12. In our engine replacement problem, for example, if an element of the approximating function is the interaction of mileages between bus 1 and bus 2 (i.e., $x(1) \times x(2)$), and neither engine is replaced, then the expectation for the state transition next period is defined as:

$$E[(x(1)+\zeta(1))(x(2)+\zeta(2))] = x(1)x(2) + x(1)E[\zeta(2)] + x(2)E[\zeta(1)] + E[\zeta(1)\zeta(2)]$$

Given the assumption that ζ is an exponential random variable with parameter λ, $E[\zeta] = 1/\lambda$.

13. The computation time for the finite horizon problem for large T is essentially identical to the computation time for the infinite horizon case and is much less than the infinite horizon case when T is small. This is because the time to compute each update of the value function approximation in the infinite horizon case is equivalent to calculating the value function one period back in the backwards recursion problem. Eventually the value function from working backwards in the finite horizon case will converge to the infinite horizon solution as T goes to infinity.

ACKNOWLEDGMENT

Thanks to Pedro Mira, R. Vijay Krishna, and Peng Sun for useful comments and suggestions. Arcidiacono, Bayer, and Bugni thank the National Science Foundation for research support via grant SES-1124193.

REFERENCES

Aguirregabiria, V., & Mira, P. (2002). Swapping the nested fixed point algorithm: A class of estimators for discrete markov decision models. *Econometrica, 70*(2), 1519–1543.

Amemiya, T. (1985). *Advanced econometrics*. Cambridge, MA: Harvard University Press.

Arcidiacono, P., Bayer, P., Bugni, F. A., & James, J. (2012). *Sieve value function iteration for large state space dynamic games*. Duke University and Federal Reserve Bank of Cleveland, Mimeo.

Bénitez-Silva, H., Hall, G., Hitsch, G., Pauletto, G., & Rust, J. (2000). *A comparison of discrete and parametric approximation methods for continuous-state dynamic programming problems*. Yale University, S.U.N.Y. Stony Brook and University Geneva, Mimeo.

Bertsekas, D. P. (2012). *Dynamic programming and optimal control*. Approximate Dynamic Programming (4th ed., Vol. II). Nashua, NH: Athena Scientific.

Bertsekas, D. P., & Tsitsiklis, J. N. (1996). *Neuro-dynamic programming* (Vol. 2). Athena Scientific, Nashua, NH.

Blackwell, D. (1965). Discounted dynamic programming. *The Annals of Mathematical Statistics*, *36*(1), 226–235.

Chen, X. (2007). Large sample sieve estimation of semi-nonparametric models. *Handbook of Econometrics*, *6B*, 5550–5588.

Chiappori, P.-A., & Ekeland, I. (2009). The microeconomics of efficient group behavior: Identification. *Econometrica*, *77*(3), 763–799.

Crawford, G. S., & Shum, M. (2005). Uncertainty and learning in pharmaceutical demand. *Econometrica*, *73*(4), 1137–1173.

Del Boca, D., & Flinn, C. (2012). Endogenous household interaction. *Journal of Econometrics*, *166*(1), 49–65.

Hendel, I., & Nevo, A. (2006). Measuring the implications of sales and consumer inventory behavior. *Econometrica*, *74*(6), 1637–1673.

Keane, M. P., & Wolpin, K. I. (1994). The solution and estimation of discrete choice dynamic programming models by simulation and interpolation: Monte Carlo evidence. *The Review of Economics and Statistics*, *76*(4), 648–672.

Keane, M. P., & Wolpin, K. I. (1997). The career decisions of young men. *Journal of Political Economy*, *105*(3), 473–522.

Lorentz, G. (1966). *Approximation of functions*. New York, NY: Holt, Rinehart and Winston, Inc.

McFadden, D., & Newey, W. K. (1994). Large sample estimation and hypothesis testing. *Handbook of econometrics* (Vol. 4, pp. 2111–2245). North Holland, Amsterdam, The Netherlands: Elsevier Science B.V.

Powell, M. J. D. (1981). *Approximation theory and methods*. New York, NY: Cambridge University Press.

Powell, W. B. (2011). *Approximate dynamic programming: Solving the curses of dimensionality* (2nd ed.). Wiley Series in Probability and Statistic. Hoboken, NJ: Wiley.

Royden, H. L. (1988). *Real analysis*. Prentice Hall, Upper Saddle River, NJ.

Rust, J. (1987). Optimal replacement of GMC bus engines: An empirical model of harold zurcher. *Econometrica*, *55*, 999–1033.

Rust, J. (1988). Maximum likelihood estimation of discrete control processes. *SIAM Journal of Control and Optimization*, *26*, 1006–1024.

Rust, J. (2000). *Parametric policy iteration: An efficient algorithm for solving multidimensional dp problems*. University of Maryland, Mimeo.

Stokey, N. L., & Lucas, R. E. (1989). *Recursive methods in economic dynamics*. Cambridge, MA and London, England: Harvard University Press.

Sweeting, A. (2011). *Dynamic product positioning in differentiated product markets: The effect of fees for musical performance rights on the commercial radio industry*. Duke University, Mimeo.

APPENDIX A: TECHNICAL APPENDIX

Lemma A.1. Assume Assumptions A.1–A.2 and let $\theta_n \in \Theta_n$ be the result of a convergence in Algorithm 3.1. Then, θ_n satisfies Eq. (3.5) with $\eta_{2,n} = O(\max\{\varepsilon_n, \eta_{1,n}\})$.

Proof. By definition, the algorithm stops when: $d(f, \theta_n) \leq \varepsilon_n$ and $d_n(\theta_n, \Gamma^k f) \leq \varepsilon_n$ for some $\theta_n, f \in \Theta_n$. Based on this, consider the following argument:

$$\begin{aligned}
d_n(\theta_n, \Gamma^k \theta_n) &\leq d_n(\theta_n, \Gamma^k f) + d_n(\Gamma^k f, \Gamma^k \theta_n) \\
&\leq d_n(\theta_n, \Gamma^k f) + K_1^{-1} d(\Gamma^k f, \Gamma^k \theta_n) + K_1^{-1} \eta_{1,n} \\
&\leq d_n(\theta_n, \Gamma^k f) + K_1^{-1} \beta^k d(f, \theta_n) + K_1^{-1} \eta_{1,n} \\
&\leq d_n(\theta_n, \Gamma^k f) + K_1^{-1} \beta^k K_2 d_n(f, \theta_n) + K_1^{-1} \beta^k K_2 \eta_{1,n} + K_1^{-1} \eta_{1,n} \\
&\leq \varepsilon_n (1 + K_1^{-1} \beta^k K_2) + (K_1^{-1} \beta^k K_2 + K_1^{-1}) \eta_{1,n} \\
&\leq \inf_{\theta \in \Theta_n} d_n(\theta, \Gamma^k \theta) + \eta_{2,n}
\end{aligned}$$

where $\eta_{2,n} \equiv \varepsilon_n (1 + K_1^{-1} \beta^k K_2) + (K_1^{-1} \beta^k K_2 + K_1^{-1}) \eta_{1,n}$ and, thus, $\eta_{2,n} = O(\max\{\varepsilon_n, \eta_{1,n}\})$, as required. The first inequality follows from the triangular inequality (applied to the pseudo-metric d_n), the second and fourth inequalities follow from Assumption A.2, the third inequality follows from the fact that Γ is a contraction mapping with modulus β, the fifth inequality follows from the stopping rule in the algorithm, the final inequality follows from the definition of $\eta_{2,n}$ and the fact that the pseudo-metric d_n is positive. □

Proof of Lemma 3.1. We begin by showing that or any $\theta \in \mathcal{F}$ and $m \in \mathbb{N}$:

$$d(\theta, V) \leq d(\theta, \Gamma^m \theta)/(1 - \beta^m)$$

To see this, consider the following derivation:

$$\begin{aligned}
d(\theta, V) &\leq d(\theta, \Gamma^m \theta) + d(\Gamma^m \theta, \Gamma^m V) + d(\Gamma^m V, V) \\
&= d(\theta, \Gamma^m \theta) + d(\Gamma^m \theta, \Gamma^m V) \\
&\leq d(\theta, \Gamma^m \theta) + \beta^m \, d(\theta, V)
\end{aligned}$$

where the first inequality follows from the Triangle Inequality, the next equality follows from the fact that V is a fixed point, and the final inequality follows from the fact that Γ is a contraction mapping. Eq. (A) is a straightforward consequence of this result.

Let $\hat{\theta}_n \in \Theta_n \subseteq \mathcal{F}$ be the SVFI approximation in Definition 3.3. On the one hand, consider the following derivation:

$$\begin{aligned} d(\hat{\theta}_n, V)(1-\beta^k) &\leq d(\hat{\theta}_n, \Gamma^k \hat{\theta}_n) \\ &\leq K_2\, d_n(\hat{\theta}_n, \Gamma^k \hat{\theta}_n) + \eta_{1,n} \\ &\leq K_2 \inf_{\theta \in \Theta_n} d_n(\theta, \Gamma^k \theta) + \eta_{1,n} + K_2 \eta_{2,n} \\ &\leq K_1^{-1} K_2 \inf_{\theta \in \Theta_n} d(\theta, \Gamma^k \theta) + (1 + K_2 K_1^{-1}) \eta_{1,n} + K_2 \eta_{2,n} \end{aligned}$$

where the first inequality follows from Eq. (A), the second and fourth inequalities follow from Assumption A.2, and the third inequality follows from Eq. (3.7).

On the other hand, for any $\theta \in \mathcal{F}$, consider the following derivation:

$$\begin{aligned} d(\theta, \Gamma^k \theta) &\leq d(\theta, V) + d(V, \Gamma^k V) + d(\Gamma^k V, \Gamma^k \theta) \\ &= d(\theta, V) + d(\Gamma^k V, \Gamma^k \theta) \\ &\leq (1+\beta^k) d(\theta, V) \end{aligned}$$

where the first inequality follows from the triangle inequality, the next equality follows from the fact that V is a fixed point, and the final inequality follows from the fact that Γ is a contraction mapping in (d, Γ). If we take infimum of $\theta \in \Theta_n \subseteq \mathcal{F}$ on both sides:

$$\inf_{\theta \in \Theta_n} d(\theta, \Gamma^k \theta) \leq (1+\beta^k) \inf_{\theta \in \Theta_n} d(\theta, V) = (1+\beta^k) \eta_{3,n}(V)$$

The result follows directly from combining the previous results. □

Proof of Theorem 3.1. By combining Lemma 3.1 with Assumption A.4, it follows that:

$$\begin{aligned} d(\hat{\theta}_n, V) &\leq \{K_1^{-1} K_2 (1+\beta^k) \eta_{3,n}(V) + (1 + K_2 K_1^{-1}) \eta_{1,n} + K_2 \eta_{2,n}\} (1-\beta^k)^{-1} \\ &= O_p(\max\{\gamma_{1,n}, \gamma_{2,n}, \gamma_{3,n}(V)\}) \end{aligned}$$

where $\max\{\gamma_{1,n}, \gamma_{2,n}, \gamma_{3,n}(V)\} = o(1)$ as $n \to \infty$. Using elementary arguments, this result implies that: (1) $d(\hat{\theta}_n, V) = o_p(1)$ as $n \to \infty$ and (2) $d(\hat{\theta}_n, V)$ converges in probability to zero at a rate of $\max\{\gamma_{1,n}, \gamma_{2,n}, \gamma_{3,n}(V)\}^{-1} = \min\{\gamma_{1,n}^{-1}, \gamma_{2,n}^{-1}, \gamma_{3,n}(V)^{-1}\}$. □

Lemma A.2. Under Assumption B.1, Assumption B.5 is satisfied for all the formulations of the dynamic decision problem described in Appendix B.

Proof. We verify the result for each formulation described in Appendix B. We begin with the *conditional value function* formulation. In this case: $s=(x,\varepsilon)$ and $F(V,s')=V(s')$. Then:

$$E[F(f_1,s')-F(f_2,s') \mid s,a]=E(f_1(s')-f_2(s') \mid s,a)\leq d(f_1,f_2)$$

where the equality holds by definition of F and the inequality holds because d is the sup-norm metric.

We now consider the *social surplus function* formulation. In this case: $s=(x,a)$, $F(V,s')=G(V(x') \mid x')$, and $A(s)=\{a\}$. Then:

$$\begin{aligned}
E[F(f_1,s')-F(f_2,s') \mid s,a] &=E[G(f_1(s') \mid s')-G(f_2(s') \mid s') \mid s,a]\\
&=E[E[\max_{a'\in A(x')}(f_1(x',a')+\varepsilon(a'))-\max_{a'\in A(x')}(f_2(x',a')+\varepsilon(a')) \mid x'] \mid x,a]\\
&\leq E[\,|\,E[\max_{a'\in A(x')}(f_1(x',a')+\varepsilon(a'))-\max_{a'\in A(x')}(f_2(x',a')+\varepsilon(a')) \mid x']\,|\, \mid x,a]\\
&\leq E[\max_{a'\in A(x')}|f_1(x',a')-f_2(x',a')| \mid x,a]\leq d(f_1,f_2)
\end{aligned}$$

where the first equality holds by definition of F, the second equality holds by definition of G, the first and second inequalities hold by elementary arguments, and the final inequality holds because d is the sup-norm metric.

We conclude with the *choice-specific value function* formulation. In this case: $s=(x,a)$, $F(V,s')=G(\beta^{-1}u(x')+V(x') \mid x')$, and $A(s)=\{a\}$. Using the same arguments as in the social surplus function formulation, it is not hard to verify the result. □

Proof of Theorem 4.1. This proof proceeds by induction. Set $t=1$. By definition, $\hat{\theta}_{T+2-t,n}=V_{T+1}$ and, thus, $d(V_{T+2-t},\hat{\theta}_{T+2-t,n})=0$. We now prove the inductive step. Suppose that for some $t\geq 1$, $d(V_{T+2-t},\hat{\theta}_{T+2-t,n})=O_p(\max\{\upsilon_{1,n},\upsilon_{2,n},\upsilon_{3,n}\})$. We now show that: $d(V_{T+1-t},\hat{\theta}_{T+1-t,n})=o_p(1)$, as $n\to\infty$. By the triangular inequality:

$$d(V_{T+1-t},\hat{\theta}_{T+1-t,n})=d(V_{T+1-t},\hat{\theta}^*_{T+1-t,n})+d(\hat{\theta}^*_{T+1-t,n},\hat{\theta}_{T+1-t,n})$$

We now analyze each of the terms on the right hand side satisfies the desired property.

We begin with $d(V_{T+1-t}, \hat{\theta}^*_{T+1-t,n})$. Fix $s \in S$ arbitrarily. Let $a_{1,n}(s) \in A(s)$ be such that:

$$\hat{\theta}^*_{T+1-t,n}(s) = u(s, a_{1,n}(s)) + \beta E(F(\hat{\theta}_{T+2-t,n}, s') \mid s, a_{1,n}(s)) \tag{A}$$

that is, $a_{1,n}(s)$ is the maximizer, which exists due to the fact that $A(s)$ is a finite set. Then, consider the following derivation:

$$\begin{aligned}\hat{\theta}^*_{T+1-t,n}(s) &= u(s,a_{1,n}(s))+\beta E(F(\hat{\theta}_{T+2-t,n},s')\mid s,a_{1,n}(s)),\\ &\leq u(s,a_{1,n}(s))+\beta E(F(V_{T+2-t},s')\mid s,a_{1,n}(s))+\beta d(\hat{\theta}_{T+2-t,n},V_{T+2-t}),\\ &\leq V_{T+1-t}(s)+\beta d(\hat{\theta}_{T+2-t,n},V_{T+2-t}),\end{aligned}$$

where the first equality holds by Eq. (A), the next inequality holds by Assumption B.5, and the final inequality holds by Eq. (4.1). As a consequence, it follows that: $\sup_{s\in S}(\hat{\theta}^*_{T+1-t,n}(s) - V_{T+1-t}(s)) \leq \beta d(\hat{\theta}_{T+2-t,n}, V_{T+2-t})$. By a similar argument, one can show that $\sup_{s\in S}(V_{T+1-t}(s) - \hat{\theta}^*_{T+1-t,n}(s)) \leq \beta d(\hat{\theta}_{T+2-t,n}, V_{T+2-t})$. By combining both inequalities with Assumption B.1, it follows that:

$$d(\hat{\theta}^*_{T+1-t,n}, V_{T+1-t}) = \sup_{s\in S} \mid \hat{\theta}^*_{T+1-t,n}(s) - V_{T+1-t}(s) \mid \leq \beta d(\hat{\theta}_{T+2-t,n}, V_{T+2-t})$$

By the inductive assumption, it follows that: $d(\hat{\theta}^*_{T+1-t,n}, V_{T+1-t}) = O_p(\max\{\upsilon_{1,n}, \upsilon_{2,n}, \upsilon_{3,n}\})$.

We continue with $d(\hat{\theta}^*_{T+1-t,n}, \hat{\theta}_{T+1-t,n})$. Consider the following derivation:

$$\begin{aligned}d(\hat{\theta}^*_{T+1-t,n}, \hat{\theta}_{T+1-t,n}) &\leq K_2\ d_n(\hat{\theta}^*_{T+1-t,n}, \hat{\theta}_{T+1-t,n}) + \lambda_{1,n}\\ &\leq K_2 \inf_{\theta\in\Theta_n} d_n(\theta, \hat{\theta}^*_{T+1-t,n}) + \lambda_{1,n} + \lambda_{2,n}(\hat{\theta}^*_{T+1-t,n})\\ &\leq K_1^{-1}K_2 \inf_{\theta\in\Theta_n} d(\theta, \hat{\theta}^*_{T+1-t,n}) + \lambda_{1,n}(1+K_1^{-1}) + \lambda_{2,n}\\ &\leq K_1^{-1}K_2 \sup_{f\in\mathcal{F}} \lambda_{3,n}(f) + \lambda_{1,n}(1+K_1^{-1}) + \lambda_{2,n}\end{aligned}$$

where the first and third inequalities hold by Assumption B.2, the second inequality holds by Assumption B.3, and the final inequality holds by Assumption B.4. By the properties of $\lambda_{1,n}$, $\lambda_{2,n}$, and $\lambda_{3,n}$, it follows that $d(\hat{\theta}^*_{T+1-t,n}, \hat{\theta}_{T+1-t,n}) = O_p(\max\{\upsilon_{1,n}, \upsilon_{2,n}, \upsilon_{3,n}\})$. □

Proof of Lemma 4.1. **Part 1.** Consider a pair of functions $f_1, f_2 \in \tilde{\mathcal{F}}$. First, consider $t = T+1$. By definition, $\tilde{\Gamma} f_1(s,t) = \tilde{\Gamma} f_2(s,t) = 0\ \forall s \in S$, which implies that: $\sup_{s\in S} | \tilde{\Gamma} f_1(s,T+1) - \tilde{\Gamma} f_2(s,T+1) | = 0$. Next, consider $t = 1, \dots, T$. For any arbitrary $s \in S$:

$$
\begin{aligned}
|\tilde{\Gamma}f_1(s,t)-\tilde{\Gamma}f_2(s,t)| &= \left\{ \begin{array}{l} \sup\limits_{a\in A(s)} \{u(s,a)+\beta E(F(f_1,(s',t+1))|(s,t),a)\} \\ -\sup\limits_{a\in A(s)} \{u(s,a)+\beta E(F(f_2,(s',t+1))|(s,t),a)\} \end{array} \right\} \\
&\leq \beta \sup_{a\in A(s)} E(F(f_1,(s',t+1)) - F(f_2,(s',t+1))|(s,t),a) \\
&= \beta \sup_{a\in A(s)} E(F(f_{1,t+1},s') - F(f_{2,t+1},s')|s,a) \\
&\leq \beta \sup_{a\in A(s)} E(f_{1,t+1}(s') - f_{2,t+1}(s')|s,a) \\
&\leq \beta \sup_{s\in S} |f_{1,t+1}(s) - f_{2,t+1}(s)| = \beta \sup_{s\in S} |f_1(s,t+1) - f_2(s,t+1)|
\end{aligned}
$$

where for any $f \in \tilde{\mathcal{F}}$ and $(s,t) \in S \times \{1,\dots,T+1\}$, we use $f_t(s) \equiv f(s,t)$. Notice that we are also using the fact that conditional expectations are time invariant, but that is assumed for simplicity of notation, that is, the assumption can be eliminated by indexing expectations with a time index. By reversing the roles of f_1 and f_2, we deduce that: $\forall t = 1,\dots,T$:

$$\sup_{s\in S} | \tilde{\Gamma} f_1(s,t) - \tilde{\Gamma} f_2(s,t) | \leq \beta \sup_{s\in S} | f_1(s,t+1) - f_2(s,t+1) |$$

By combining information from all values of $t = 1,\dots,T+1$, it follows that:

$$
\begin{aligned}
\tilde{d}(\tilde{\Gamma}f_1, \tilde{\Gamma}f_2) = \max_{t=1,\dots,T+1} \sup_{s\in S} | \tilde{\Gamma} f_1(s,t) - \tilde{\Gamma} f_2(s,t) | \leq \beta \max_{t=1,\dots,T+1} \sup_{s\in S} \\
| f_1(s,t) - f_2(s,t) | = \beta \tilde{d}(f_1, f_2)
\end{aligned}
$$

Part 2. By the contraction mapping theorem (see, e.g., Stokey & Lucas, 1989, p. 50) the mapping $\tilde{\Gamma}$ has a unique fixed point in $\tilde{\mathcal{F}}$. It suffices to show that V is such fixed point, that is, $\tilde{d}(V, \tilde{\Gamma}V) = 0$. For $t = T+1$, the definition of $\tilde{\Gamma}V$ is: $(\tilde{\Gamma}V)(s,T+1) = 0 = V(T+1,s) \equiv V_{T+1}(s)$. For any other $t = 1,\dots,T$, it follows that:

$$
\begin{aligned}
(\tilde{\Gamma}V)(s,t) &= \sup_{a\in A(s)} \{u(s,a) + \beta E(F(V,(s',t+1)) | (s,t),a)\} \\
&= \sup_{a\in A(s)} \{u(s,a) + \beta E(F(V_{t+1},s')) | s,a)\} = V_t(s) = V(s,t)
\end{aligned}
$$

which completes the proof.

Proof of Theorem 4.2. By Lemma 4.1, the analogue of Assumptions A.2–A.4 hold for the state space $\tilde{S}$. Under these assumptions, the result is a corollary of Theorem 3.1.

Proof of Theorem 5.1. Fix $\varepsilon > 0$ arbitrarily. Then, $\exists \delta > 0$ such that $\forall \pi \in \Pi$: $d_2(\pi, \pi^*) > \varepsilon \Rightarrow Q(V(\cdot \mid \pi)) - Q(V(\cdot \mid \pi^*)) > \delta$. This implies that $\exists \delta > 0$ such that:

$$P(d_2(\hat{\pi}_I, \pi^*) \leq \varepsilon) \geq P(Q(V(\cdot \mid \hat{\pi}_I)) - Q(V(\cdot \mid \pi^*)) \leq \delta)$$

The strategy of the proof is to show that the RHS converges to one as $I \to \infty$. To this end, for a fixed $\delta > 0$, consider the following argument:

$$\begin{aligned}
&P(Q(V(\cdot \mid \hat{\pi}_I)) - Q(V(\cdot \mid \pi^*) \leq \delta) \\
&= P\begin{pmatrix} Q(V(\cdot \mid \hat{\pi}_I)) - Q(\hat{\theta}_n(\cdot \mid \hat{\pi}_I)) + Q(\hat{\theta}_n(\cdot \mid \hat{\pi}_I)) - Q_I(\hat{\theta}_n(\cdot \mid \hat{\pi}_I)) \\ + Q_I(\hat{\theta}_n(\cdot \mid \hat{\pi}_I)) - Q(V(\cdot \mid \pi^*)) \leq \delta \end{pmatrix} \\
&\geq P\begin{pmatrix} \{Q(V(\cdot \mid \hat{\pi}_I)) - Q(\hat{\theta}_n(\cdot \mid \hat{\pi}_I)) \leq \delta/3\} \cap \{Q(\hat{\theta}_n(\cdot \mid \hat{\pi}_I)) - Q_I(\hat{\theta}_n(\cdot \mid \hat{\pi}_I)) \leq \delta/3\} \\ \cap \{Q_I(\hat{\theta}_n(\cdot \mid \hat{\pi}_I)) - Q(V(\cdot \mid \pi^*)) \leq \delta/3 \end{pmatrix} \\
&\geq \begin{Bmatrix} P(Q(V(\cdot \mid \hat{\pi}_I)) - Q(\hat{\theta}_n(\cdot \mid \hat{\pi}_I)) \leq \delta/3) + P(Q(\hat{\theta}_n(\cdot \mid \hat{\pi}_I)) - Q_I(\hat{\theta}_n(\cdot \mid \hat{\pi}_I)) \leq \delta/3) \\ + P(Q_I(\hat{\theta}_n(\cdot \mid \hat{\pi}_I)) - Q(V(\cdot \mid \pi^*)) \leq \delta/3) - 2 \end{Bmatrix}
\end{aligned}$$

The last expression on the RHS includes three probability expressions. The proof is completed by showing that these expressions converge to one as $I \to \infty$.

Consider the first expression. By the uniform continuity of Q, there is $\eta > 0$ such that:

$$\sup_{\pi \in \Pi} d_1(\hat{\theta}_n(\cdot \mid \pi), V(\cdot \mid \pi)) < \eta \Rightarrow d_1(\hat{\theta}_n(\cdot \mid \hat{\pi}_I), V(\cdot \mid \hat{\pi}_I)) < \eta \Rightarrow Q(\hat{\theta}_n(\cdot \mid \hat{\pi}_I)) - Q(V(\cdot \mid \hat{\pi}_I)) \leq \delta/3$$

It follows then that:

$$P(Q(\hat{\theta}_n(\cdot \mid \hat{\pi}_I)) - Q(V(\cdot \mid \hat{\pi}_I)) \leq \delta/3) \to 1, \text{ as } n \to \infty$$

or, equivalently, as $I \to \infty$ because $n(I) \to \infty$ as $I \to \infty$.

Consider the second expression. Notice that:

$$Q(\hat{\theta}_n(\cdot \mid \hat{\pi}_I)) - Q_I(\hat{\theta}_n(\cdot \mid \hat{\pi}_I)) \leq \sup_{f \in \Theta_n} \mid Q_I(f) - Q(f) \mid = \hat{c}(n, I)$$

and since $\hat{c}(n, I) = o_p(\delta(n(I), I)) = o_p(1)$ as $I \to \infty$, it follows that:

$$P(Q(\hat{\theta}_n(\cdot \mid \hat{\pi}_I)) - Q_I(\hat{\theta}_n(\cdot \mid \hat{\pi}_I)) \leq \delta/3) \to 1, \text{ as } I \to \infty$$

Finally, consider the third expression. By definition of the estimation:

$$Q_I(\hat{\theta}_n(\cdot \mid \hat{\pi}_I)) \leq \inf_{\pi \in \Pi} Q_I(\theta_n(\cdot \mid \pi)) + o_p(1) \leq Q_I(\theta_n(\cdot \mid \pi^*)) + o_p(1)$$

as $I \to \infty$. This implies that:

$$\begin{aligned} Q_I(\hat{\theta}_n(\cdot \mid \hat{\pi}_I)) - Q(V(\cdot \mid \pi^*)) &\leq Q_I(\hat{\theta}_n(\cdot \mid \pi^*)) - Q(V(\cdot \mid \pi^*)) + o_p(1), \\ &= Q_I(\hat{\theta}_n(\cdot \mid \pi^*)) - Q(\hat{\theta}_n(\cdot \mid \pi^*)) + Q(\hat{\theta}_n(\cdot \mid \pi^*)) - Q(V(\cdot \mid \pi^*)) + o_p(1), \\ &\leq \sup_{f \in \Theta_n} \left| Q_I(f) - Q(f) \right| + Q(\hat{\theta}_n(\cdot \mid \pi^*)) - Q(V(\cdot \mid \pi^*)) + o_p(1). \end{aligned}$$

Repeating arguments used in previous expressions, it follows that:

$$P(Q_I(\hat{\theta}_n(\cdot \mid \hat{\pi}_I)) - Q(V(\cdot \mid \pi^*)) \leq \delta/3) \to 1, \text{ as } I \to \infty$$

completing the proof. □

APPENDIX B: ALTERNATIVE FORMULATIONS OF DECISION PROBLEM

As described in the main text of Section 2, there are three possible ways to formulate the dynamic decision problem of Eq. (2.1) as a recursive problem. The objective of this section is to describe each of these formulations and show that each of them is a special case of the unified formulation described in the main text.

B.1. Value Function Formulation

This formulation of the dynamic decision problem is the most obvious one but, as we will argue, the most computationally demanding in terms of the size of the state space. It is easy to verify that Eq. (2.1) can be represented as follows:

$$\begin{aligned} V(x,\varepsilon) &= \max_{a \in A(x)} \{u(x,a) + \varepsilon(a) + \beta \int V(x',\varepsilon') dP(x',\varepsilon' \mid x,\varepsilon,a)\} \\ &= \max_{a \in A(x)} \{u(x,a) + \varepsilon(a) + \beta E[V(x',\varepsilon') \mid x,\varepsilon,a]\} \end{aligned}$$

If we let $s \equiv (x,\varepsilon)$ and $S \equiv X \times E$, $V : S \rightarrow \mathbb{R}$ is the fixed point of the following mapping:

$$(\Gamma_1 m)(x,\varepsilon) = \max_{a \in A(x)} \{u(x,a) + \varepsilon(a) + \beta E[m(x',\varepsilon') \mid x,\varepsilon,a], \ \forall (x,\varepsilon) \in S$$

This corresponds to the conditional value function formulation of the problem (Rust, 1987, Eq. (4.4)). Notice that our derivations so far did not require the CI assumption. It is straightforward to verify that it is a contraction mapping (in the sup-norm) by using the Blackwell (1965) sufficient conditions for a contraction (see Stokey & Lucas, 1989, Theorem 3.3). This is an obvious object of interest, as it allows us to deduce optimal decision rules in the following way:

$$f(x,\varepsilon) = \arg \max_{a \in A(x)} \{u(x,a) + \varepsilon(a) + \beta E[V(x',\varepsilon') \mid x,\varepsilon,a]\}$$

with a related CCP:

$$P(a = \overline{a} \mid x) = \int_{\varepsilon} (\arg \max_{a \in A(x)} \{u(x,a) + \varepsilon(a) + \beta E[V(x',\varepsilon') \mid x,\varepsilon,a]\} = \overline{a}) \ dP(\varepsilon \mid x)$$

We now verify that this formulation is a particular case of the unified formulation. This is shown in Table 5, which explains how the objects in the unified notation are defined in terms of the primitive objects in Eq. (2.1). According to the table, F is defined as follows: $F(V, s') = V(s')$. It is straightforward to verify that this function satisfies all of the properties required for F.

Notice that the state space in this formulation is given by $s = (x, \varepsilon)$, which is relatively large as it includes $\varepsilon = \{\varepsilon(a) : a \in A(x)\}$ (i.e., has the cardinality of $A(x)$). By the nature of the type of problems under consideration it is reasonable to consider alternative formulations of the problem, where ε is not part of the state space.

B.2. Social Surplus Function Formulation

This formulation of the problem is developed in Rust (1988). In order to explain the formulation, it is necessary to define certain objects. Given a vector $v(x) = \{v(x, a) : a \in A(x)\}$, define the social surplus function as follows:

$$G(v(x) \mid x) \equiv \int_{\varepsilon} \max_{a \in A(x)} \{v(x, a) + \varepsilon(a) \, dP(\varepsilon \mid x) = E(\max_{a \in A(x)} \{v(x, a) + \varepsilon(a)\} \mid x)$$

If we let $s \equiv (x, a)$ and $S \equiv \{(x, a) : a \in A(x), x \in X\}$, Rust (1988, Theorem 3.2) indicates that:

$$V(x, \varepsilon) = \max_{a \in A(x)} [v(x, a) + \varepsilon(a)] \tag{B.2}$$

where $v : S \rightarrow \mathbb{R}$ is the unique fixed point of the following contraction mapping:

$$(\Gamma_2 m)(x, a) = u(x, a) + \beta E[G(m(x') \mid x') \mid x, a], \forall (x, a) \in S$$

Notice that, in the formula, $m(x')$ is shorthand for the vector $\{m(x', i') : i' \in A(x')\}$. Our assumptions imply that the mapping is a contraction mapping

Table 5. Representation of the Primitive Object of the Conditional Value Function Formulation in Terms of the Unified Formulation.

Primitive object	V	(x,ε)	$X \times E$	$A(x)$	a	$u(x,a)+\varepsilon$	$V(s')$
Unified formulation	V	s	S	$A(s)$	a	$u(s,a)$	$F(V,s')$

(in the sup-norm) by using the Blackwell (1965) sufficient conditions for a contraction (in this case, it is important to establish that G satisfies the properties in Rust (1988, Theorem 3.2)). Notice that the fixed point v is the object of interest because it allows us to recover the original value function V (using Eq. (B.2)) and, with it, we can then construct the rest of the objects of interest such as optimal decision rules and CCPs.

The advantage of working with this formulation of the dynamic decision problem is that the state space is (x, a), whose dimension is smaller than for the condition value function formulation. Another advantage is that the CCPs can be written simply as (see Rust, 1988, Theorem 3.4):

$$P(a=\overline{a} \mid x) = G_{\overline{a}}(v(x) \mid x)$$

where $G_{\overline{a}}$ denotes the derivative of the social surplus function (i.e., Eq. (B.2)) with respect to $v(x, \overline{a})$.

We now verify that this formulation is a particular case of the unified formulation. This is shown in Table 6, which explains how the objects in the unified notation are defined in terms of the primitive objects in Eq. (2.1). According to the table, F is defined as follows: $F(V, s') = G(V(x') \mid x')$, where G is the social surplus function (i.e., Eq. (B.2)) with its own choice set $A(x')$. Theorem 3.1 in Rust (1988) shows that the function G satisfies all of the desired properties.

B.3. Choice-Specific Value Function Formulation

This formulation is related to the social surplus function formulation and is explained in Rust (1988, p. 1014). As in the previous formulation, let $s \equiv (x, a)$ and $S \equiv \{(x, a) : a \in A(x), x \in X\}$. Under our assumptions, Rust (1988) indicates that:

$$v(x, a) = u(x, a) + \beta EV(x, a)$$

Table 6. Representation of the Primitive Object of the Social Surplus Function Formulation Formulation in Terms of the Unified Formulation.

Unified formulation	v	s	S	$A(s)$	a	$u(s,a)$	$F(V,s')$
Primitive object	V	(x,a)	$\{(x,a) : a \in A(x), x \in X\}$	$\{a\}$	a	$u(x,a)$	$G(V(x') \mid x')$

Table 7. Representation of the Primitive Object of the Choice-Specific Value Function Formulation Formulation in Terms of the Unified Formulation.

Unified formulation	V	s	S	$A(s)$	a	$u(s,i)$	$F(V,s')$
Primitive object	EV	(x,a)	$\{(x,a): i\in A(x), x\in X\}$	$\{a\}$	a	0	$G(\beta^{-1}u(x')+V(x')\mid x')$

where $v : S\rightarrow\mathbb{R}$ is the function in Eq. (B.2) and $EV : S\rightarrow\mathbb{R}$ is the fixed point in the following contraction mapping:

$$(\Gamma_3 m)(x,a) = E[G(u(x') + \beta m(x') \mid (x')) \mid x, a],\ \forall (x,a)\in S$$

This formulation is intimately related to the social surplus function formulation and shares all its advantages relative to the conditional value function formulation, that is, the state space is (x, a), which have a relatively smaller dimension, and the CCPs are relatively easy to compute using Eq. (B.2).

We now verify that this formulation is a particular case of the unified formulation. This is shown in Table 7, which explains how the objects in the unified notation are defined in terms of the primitive objects in Eq. (2.1). According to the table, F is defined as follows: $F(V,s') = G(\beta^{-1}u(x') + V(x') \mid x')$, where G is the social surplus function (i.e., Eq. (B.2)) with its own action set $A(x')$. Rust (1988, Theorem 3.1) shows that the function G satisfies all of the desired properties.

IDENTIFYING DYNAMIC GAMES WITH SERIALLY CORRELATED UNOBSERVABLES

Yingyao Hu and Matthew Shum

ABSTRACT

In this article, we consider the nonparametric identification of Markov dynamic games models in which each firm has its own unobserved state variable, which is persistent over time. This class of models includes most models in the Ericson and Pakes (1995) and Pakes and McGuire (1994) framework. We provide conditions under which the joint Markov equilibrium process of the firms' observed and unobserved variables can be nonparametrically identified from data. For stationary continuous action games, we show that only three observations of the observed component are required to identify the equilibrium Markov process of the dynamic game. When agents' choice variables are discrete, but the unobserved state variables are continuous, four observations are required.

Keywords: Dynamic games; identification; unobserved heterogeneity; serial correlation

JEL classifications: L13; C73; C14

Structural Econometric Models
Advances in Econometrics, Volume 31, 97–113

ISSN: 0731-9053/doi:10.1108/S0731-9053(2013)0000032003

INTRODUCTION

In this article, we consider nonparametric identification in Markovian dynamic games models where each agent may have its own serially correlated unobserved state variable. This class of models includes most models in the Ericson and Pakes (1995) and Pakes and McGuire (1994) framework.[1] These models have been the basis for much of the recent empirical applications of dynamic game models. Throughout, by "unobservable," we mean variables which are commonly observed by all agents, and condition their actions, but are unobserved by the researcher.

Consider a dynamic duopoly game in which two firms compete. It is straightforward to extend our assumptions and arguments to the case of N firms. A dynamic duopoly is described by the sequence of variables (W_{t+1},χ_{t+1}), $(W_t,\chi_t),\ldots,(W_1,\chi_1)$ where

$$W_t=(W_{1,t},W_{2,t})$$

$$\chi_t=(\chi_{1,t},\chi_{2,t})$$

$W_{i,t}$ stands for the observed information on firm i and $\chi_{i,t}$ denotes the unobserved heterogeneity of firm i at period t, which we allow to vary over time and be serially correlated.

In empirical dynamic games model, the observed variables $W_{i,t}$ consist of two variables:

$$W_{i,t}\equiv(Y_{i,t},M_{i,t})$$

where $Y_{i,t}$ denotes firm i's choice, or control variable in period t, and $M_{i,t}$ denotes the state variables of firm i which are observed by both the firms and the researcher. We assume that the serially correlated variables $\chi_{1,t}$ and $\chi_{2,t}$ are observed by both firms prior to making their choices of $Y_{1,t}, Y_{2,t}$ in period t, but the researcher never observes χ_t. For simplicity, we assume that each firm's variables $Y_{i,t}, M_{i,t}, \chi_{i,t}$ are scalar-valued.

Main Results: Our goal is to identify the density

$$f_{W_t,\chi_t|W_{t-1},\chi_{t-1}} \tag{1}$$

which corresponds to the equilibrium transition density of the choice and state variables along the Markov equilibrium path of the dynamic game.[2] The identification of this stochastic process plays a key role in the identification of dynamic games because it can be interpreted as the "reduced form" equations of the model and contains all the information that is needed to identify and estimate the structural parameters under standard exclusion restrictions.

In Markovian dynamic settings, the transition density can be factored into two components of interest:

$$f_{W_t,\chi_t|W_{t-1},\chi_{t-1}} = f_{Y_t,M_t,\chi_t|Y_{t-1},M_{t-1},\chi_{t-1}} = \underbrace{f_{Y_t|M_t,\chi_t}}_{\text{CCP}} \cdot \underbrace{f_{M_t,\chi_t|Y_{t-1},M_{t-1},\chi_{t-1}}}_{\text{state transition}} \tag{2}$$

The first term denotes the conditional choice probabilities (CCP) for the firms' actions in period t, conditional on the current state (M_t,χ_t). In the Markov equilibrium, firms' optimal strategies typically depends just on the current state variables (M_t,χ_t), but not past values. The second term denotes is the equilibrium Markovian transition probabilities for the state variables (M_t,χ_t). As shown in Hotz and Miller (1993) and Magnac and Thesmar (2002), once these two structural components are known, it is possible to recover the "deep" structural elements of the model, including the period utility functions.

In an earlier article (Hu & Shum (2013)), we focused on nonparametric identification of Markovian single-agent dynamic optimization models. There, we showed that in stationary models, four periods of data $W_{t+1},\ldots,W_{t-2}$ were enough to identify the Markov transition $W_t,\chi_t|W_{t-1},\chi_{t-1}$, while five observations $W_{t+1},\ldots,W_{t-3}$ were required for the nonstationary case. In this article, we focus on Markovian dynamic games. We show that, once additional features of the dynamic optimization framework are taken into account, only three observations $W_t,\ldots,W_{t-2}$ are required to identify $W_t,\chi_t|W_{t-1},\chi_{t-1}$ in the stationary case, when Y_t is a continuous choice variable. If Y_t is a discrete choice variable (while χ_t is continuous), then four observations are required for identification.

Related literature: Recently, there has been a growing literature related to identification and estimation of dynamic games. Papers include Aguirregabiria and Mira (2007), Pesendorfer and Schmidt-Dengler (2008), Bajari, Benkard, and Levin (2007), Pakes, Ostrovsky, and Berry (2007), and Bajari, Chernozhukov, Hong, and Nekipelov (2007). Our main contribution related to this literature is to provide nonparametric identification results for the case, where there are firm-specific unobserved state variables, which are serially correlated over time. Allowing for firm-specific and serially correlated unobservables is important, because the dynamic game models in Ericson and Pakes (1995) and Pakes and McGuire (1994) (see also Doraszelski & Pakes, 2007), which provide an important framework for much of the existing empirical work in dynamic games, explicitly contain firm-specific "product quality" variables which are typically unobserved by researchers.

A few recent papers have considered estimation methodologies for games with serially correlated unobservables.[3] Arcidiacono and Miller (2011) develop an EM-algorithm for estimating dynamic games where the unobservables are assumed to follow a discrete Markov process. Siebert and Zulehner (2008) extend the Bajari et al. (2007) approach to estimate a dynamic product choice game for the computer memory industry where each firm experiences a serially correlated productivity shock. Finally, Blevins (2008) develops simulation estimators for dynamic games with serially correlated unobservables, utilizing state-of-the-art recursive importance sampling ("particle filtering") techniques. However, all these papers focus on estimation of parametric models in which the parameters are assumed to be identified, whereas this article concerns nonparametric identification.

EXAMPLES OF DYNAMIC DUOPOLY GAMES

To make things concrete, we present two examples of a dynamic duopoly problem, both of which are in the "dynamic investment" framework of Ericson and Pakes (1995) and Pakes and McGuire (1994), but simplified without an entry decision.

Example 1 is a model of learning by doing in a durable goods market, similar to Benkard (2004). There are two heterogeneous firms $i=1,2$, with each firm described by two time-varying state variables $(M_{i,t},\chi_{i,t})$. $M_{i,t}$ denotes the "installed base" of firm i, which are the share of consumers who have previously bought firm i's product. $\chi_{i,t}$ is firm i's marginal cost, which is unobserved to the econometrician, and is an unobserved state variable. There is learning by doing, in the sense that increases in the installed base will lower future marginal costs. In each period, each firm's choice variable $Y_{i,t}$ is its period t price, which affects the demand for its product in period t and thereby the future installed base, which in turn affects future production costs.

In the following, let $Y_t \equiv (Y_{1,t}, Y_{2,t})$, and similarly for M_t and χ_t. Let $S_t \equiv (M_t, \chi_t)$ denote the common-knowledge state variables of the game in period t. $S_{i,t} \equiv (M_{i,t}, \chi_{i,t})$, for $i=1,2$, denotes firm i's state variables. Each period, firms earn profits by selling their products to consumers who have not yet bought the product. The demand curve for firm i's product is

$$q_i(Y_t, M_t, \eta_{i,t})$$

which depends on the price and installed base of both firms' products. Firm i's demand also depends on $\eta_{i,t}$, a firm-specific demand shock. As in Aguirregabiria and Mira (2007) and Pesendorfer and Schmidt-Dengler (2008), we assume that $\eta_{i,t}$ is privately observed by each firm; that is, only firm 1, but not firm 2, observes $\eta_{1,t}$, making this a game of incomplete information. Furthermore, we assume that the demand shocks $\eta_{i,t}$ are i.i.d. across firm and periods, and distributed according to a distribution K which is common knowledge to both firms. The main role of the variable $\eta_{i,t}$ is to generate randomness in $Y_{i,t}$, even after conditioning on (M_t, χ_t).

The period t profits of firm i can then be written:

$$\Pi_i(Y_t, S_t, \eta_{i,t}) = q_i(Y_t, M_t, \eta_{i,t}) * (Y_{i,t} - \chi_{i,t})$$

where $Y_{i,t} - \chi_{i,t}$ is firm i's margin from each unit that it sells.

Installed base evolves according to the conditional distribution:

$$M_{i,t+1} \sim G(\cdot | M_{i,t}, Y_{i,t}) \tag{3}$$

One example is to model the incremental change $M_{i,t+1} - M_{i,t}$ as a log-normal random variable:

$$\log(M_{i,t+1} - M_{i,t}) \sim q_i(Y_t, M_t, \eta_{i,t}) + \varepsilon_{i,t}, \quad \varepsilon_{i,t} \sim N(0, \sigma_\varepsilon^2), \quad \text{i.i.d.-}(i, t)$$

Marginal cost evolves according to the conditional distribution:

$$\chi_{i,t+1} \sim H(\cdot | \chi_{i,t}, M_{i,t+1}) \tag{4}$$

One example is

$$\chi_{i,t+1} = \chi_{i,t} - N(\gamma(M_{i,t+1} - M_{i,t}), \sigma_k^2)$$

where γ and σ_k are unknown parameters. This encompasses learning-by-doing because the incremental reduction in marginal cost $(\chi_{i,t+1} - \chi_{i,t})$ depends on the incremental increase in installed base $(M_{i,t+1} - M_{i,t})$.

In the dynamic Markov-perfect equilibrium, each firm's optimal pricing strategy will also be a function of the current S_t, and the current demand shock $\eta_{i,t}$:

$$Y_{i,t} = Y_i^*(S_t, \eta_{i,t}), \quad i = 1, 2 \tag{5}$$

where the strategy satisfies the equilibrium Bellman equation:

$$\begin{aligned} Y_i^*(S_t, \eta_{i,t}) = \operatorname{argmax}_y E_{\eta_{-i,t}} \{ &\Pi_i(S_t, y, Y_{-i,t} = Y_{-i}^*(S_t, \eta_{-i,t})) \\ &+ \beta E[V_i(S_{t+1}, \eta_{i,t+1}) | y, Y_{-i,t} = Y_{-i}^*(S_t, \eta_{-i,t})]\} \end{aligned} \tag{6}$$

subject to Eqs. (4) and (3). In the above equation, $V_i(S_t, \eta_{it})$ denotes the equilibrium value function for firm i, which is equal to the expected discounted future profits that firm i will make along the equilibrium path, starting at the current state (S_t, η_{it}). ■

Example 2 is a simplified version of the dynamic investment models estimated in the productivity literature. (See Ackerberg, Benkard, Berry, and Pakes (2007) for a detailed survey of this literature.) In this model, firms' state variables are $(M_{i,t}, \chi_{i,t})$, where $M_{i,t}$ denotes firm i's capital stock, and $\chi_{i,t}$ denotes its productivity shock in period t. $Y_{i,t}$, firm i's choice variable, denotes new capital investment in period t.

Capital stock $M_{i,t}$ evolves deterministically, as a function of $(Y_{i,t-1}, M_{i,t-1})$:

$$M_{i,t} = (1-\delta) \cdot M_{i,t-1} + Y_{i,t-1} \tag{7}$$

The productivity shock is serially correlated, and evolves according to the conditional distribution:

$$\chi_{i,t+1} \sim H(\cdot | \chi_{i,t}, M_{i,t}) \tag{8}$$

Each period, firms earn profits by selling their products. Let $q_i(p_{i,t}, p_{-i,t}, \eta_{i,t})$ denote the demand curve for firm i's product, which depends on the quality and prices of both firms' products. As in Example 1, $\eta_{i,t}$ denotes the privately observed demand shock for firm i in period t, which is distributed i.i.d. across firms and time periods.

The period t profits of firm i are

$$q_i(p_{i,t}, p_{-i,t}, \eta_{i,t}) * (p_{i,t} - c_i(S_{i,t})) - K(Y_{i,t})$$

where $c_i(\cdot)$ is the marginal cost function for firm i (we assume constant marginal costs) and $K(Y_{it})$ is the investment cost function.

Following the literature, we assume that each firm's price in period t are determined by a static equilibrium, given the current values of the state variables S_t, and the firm-specific demand shock $\eta_{i,t}$. Let $p_i^*(S_t, \eta_{i,t})$ denote the static equilibrium prices for each firm in period t. By substituting in the equilibrium prices in firm's profit function, we obtain each firm's "reduced-form" expected profits:

$$\Pi_i(S_t, Y_t, \eta_{i,t}) = E_{\eta_{-i,t}} q_i(p_1^*(S_t, \eta_{1,t}), p_2^*(S_t, \eta_{2,t}), \eta_{i,t}) \\ * [p_i^*(S_t, \eta_{i,t}) - c_i(S_{i,t})] - K(Y_{i,t}), \quad i = 1, 2$$

As in Example 1, the Markov equilibrium investment strategy for each firm just depends on the current state variables S_t, and the current shock $\eta_{i,t}$:

$$Y_t = Y_i^*(S_t, \eta_{it}), \quad i = 1, 2$$

subject to the Bellman equation (Eq. (6)) and the transitions (Eqs. (7) and (8)). ■

The substantial difference between Examples 1 and 2 is that in Example 2, the evolution of the observed state variable $M_{i,t}$ is deterministic, whereas in Example 1 there is randomness in $M_{i,t}$ conditional on $(M_{i,t-1}, Y_{i,t-1})$ (i.e., compare Eqs. (3) and (7)). As we will see below, this has important implications for nonparametric identification.

Moreover, as illustrated in these two examples, for the first part of the article, we focus on games with continuous actions, so that Y_t are continuous variables. Later, we will consider the important alternative case of discrete-action games, where Y_t is discrete-valued.

NONPARAMETRIC IDENTIFICATION

In this section, we present the assumptions for nonparametric identification in the dynamic game model. Our identification strategy requires a panel dataset with multiple markets and the asymptotics in the corresponding estimation is in the number of markets. The assumptions we make here are different than those in our earlier article (Hu & Shum, 2013), and are geared specifically for the dynamic games literature, and motivated directly by existing applied work utilizing dynamic games. We assume that for each market j, $\{(W_{t+1}, \chi_{t+1}), (W_t, \chi_t), \ldots, (W_1, \chi_1)\}_j$ is an independent random draw from the identical distribution $f_{W_{t+1},W_t,\ldots,W_1,\chi_{t+1},\chi_t,\ldots,\chi_1}$. This rules out across-market effects and spillovers. And the assumption of identical distribution across markets rules out the possibility of multiple equilibria. For each market j, $\{W_1,\ldots,W_T\}_j$ is observed, for $T\geq 4$.

After presenting each assumption, we relate it to the examples in the previous section. Define $\Omega_{<t}=\{W_{t-1},\ldots,W_1,\chi_{t-1},\ldots,\chi_1\}$. We assume the dynamic process satisfies:

Assumption 1. First-order Markov:

$$f_{W_t,\chi_t|W_{t-1},\chi_{t-1},\Omega_{<t-1}}=f_{W_t,\chi_t|W_{t-1},\chi_{t-1}} \tag{9}$$

Remark. The first-order Markov assumption is satisfied along the Markov-equilibrium path of both examples given in the previous section. ■

Without loss of generality, we assume that $W_t=(Y_t,M_t)\in\mathbb{R}^2$. We assume

Assumption 2.

(i) $f_{Y_t|M_t,\chi_t,Y_{t-1},M_{t-1},\chi_{t-1}}=f_{Y_t|M_t,\chi_t}$,

(ii) $f_{\chi_t|M_t,Y_{t-1},M_{t-1},\chi_{t-1}}=f_{\chi_t|M_t,M_{t-1},\chi_{t-1}}$.

Assumption 2(i) is motivated completely by the state-contingent aspect of the optimal policy function in dynamic optimization models. It turns out that this assumption is stronger than necessary for our identification, but it allows us to achieve identification only using three periods of data. Assumption 2(ii) implies that χ_t is independent of Y_{t-1} conditional on M_t, M_{t-1} and χ_{t-1}. This is consistent with the setup above.

Remarks. Assumption 2 is satisfied in both Examples 1 and 2. ■

The conditional independence Assumptions 1 and 2 imply that the Markov transition density (Eq. (1)) can be factored into

$$f_{W_t,\chi_t|W_{t-1},\chi_{t-1}}=f_{Y_t,M_t,\chi_t|Y_{t-1},M_{t-1},\chi_{t-1}}=f_{Y_t|M_t,\chi_t}\cdot f_{\chi_t|M_t,M_{t-1},\chi_{t-1}}\cdot f_{M_t|Y_{t-1},M_{t-1},\chi_{t-1}} \tag{10}$$

In the identification procedure, we will identify these three components of $f_{W_t,\chi_t|W_{t-1},\chi_{t-1}}$ in turn.

Next, we restrict attention to stationary equilibria in the dynamic game, which is natural given our focus on Markov equilibria. In stationary equilibria, the Markov transition density $f_{W_t,\chi_t|W_{t-1},\chi_{t-1}}$ is time-invariant.

Assumption 3. Stationarity of Markov kernel:

$$f_{W_t,\chi_t|W_{t-1},\chi_{t-1}}=f_{W_2,\chi_2|W_1,\chi_1}$$

For simplicity, we assume that $Y_{i,t}$, M_t, $\chi_{i,t} \in \{1, 2, ..., J\}$.[4] Consider the joint density of $\{Y_t, M_t, Y_{t-1}, M_{t-1}, Y_{t-2}\}$. We show in the appendix, that Assumptions 1 and 2 imply that

$$f_{Y_t,M_t,Y_{t-1}|M_{t-1},Y_{t-2}} = \sum_{\chi_{t-1}} f_{Y_t|M_t,M_{t-1},\chi_{t-1}} f_{M_t,Y_{t-1}|M_{t-1},\chi_{t-1}} f_{\chi_{t-1}|M_{t-1},Y_{t-2}} \tag{11}$$

where the final line follows from Assumptions 1 and 2. Note that the density $f_{Y_t,M_t,Y_{t-1}|M_{t-1},Y_{t-2}}$ on the left-hand side is nonparametrically identified everywhere under mild regularity conditions, and that Eq. (11) summarizes all the key restrictions that the model imposes on the densities on the righ-hand side.

In order to identify the unknown densities on the right-hand side, we use the identification strategy for the nonclassical measurement error models in Hu (2008). His results imply that two measurements and a dependent variable of a latent explanatory variable are enough to achieve identification. For fixed values of (M_t, M_{t-1}), we see that (Y_t, Y_{t-1}, Y_{t-2}) enter Eq. (11) separately in, respectively, the first, second, and third terms. This implies that we can use (Y_t, Y_{t-2}) as the two measurements and Y_{t-1} as the dependent variable of the latent variable χ_{t-1}.

We abuse the notation Y_t and define

$$Y_t = G(Y_{1,t}, Y_{2,t}) \equiv \begin{cases} 1 & \text{if} \quad (Y_{1,t}, Y_{2,t}) = (1,1) \\ 2 & \text{if} \quad (Y_{1,t}, Y_{2,t}) = (1,2) \\ \ldots & \qquad \ldots \\ J^2 & \text{if} \quad (Y_{1,t}, Y_{2,t}) = (J,J) \end{cases}$$

where the one-to-one function G maps a vector of discrete variables to a scalar discrete variable.[5] Similarly, we may also redefine $\chi_t = G(\chi_{1,t}, \chi_{2,t})$. Furthermore, we define the matrix $\mathbf{F}_{Y_t,m_t,y_{t-1}|m_{t-1},Y_{t-2}}$ for any given (m_t, y_{t-1}, m_{t-1}) in the support of (M_t, Y_{t-1}, M_{t-1}) and $i,j,k \in \mathcal{S} \equiv \{1, 2 \ldots, J^2\}$

$$\begin{aligned}
\mathbf{F}_{Y_t,m_t,y_{t-1}|m_{t-1},Y_{t-2}} &= [f_{Y_t,M_t,Y_{t-1}|M_{t-1},Y_{t-2}}(i, m_t, y_{t-1}|m_{t-1}, j)]_{i,j} \\
\mathbf{F}_{Y_t|m_t,m_{t-1},\chi_{t-1}} &= [f_{Y_t|M_t,M_{t-1},\chi_{t-1}}(i|m_t, m_{t-1}, k)]_{i,k} \\
\mathbf{D}_{y_{t-1}|m_t,m_{t-1},\chi_{t-1}} &= diag\{[f_{Y_{t-1}|M_t,M_{t-1},\chi_{t-1}}(y_{t-1}|m_t, m_{t-1}, k)]_k\} \\
\mathbf{D}_{m_t|m_{t-1},\chi_{t-1}} &= diag\{[f_{M_t|M_{t-1},\chi_{t-1}}(m_t|m_{t-1}, k)]_k\} \\
\mathbf{F}_{\chi_{t-1}|m_{t-1},Y_{t-2}} &= [f_{\chi_{t-1}|M_{t-1},Y_{t-2}}(k|m_{t-1}, j)]_{k,j}
\end{aligned}$$

where $diag\{V\}$ generates a diagonal matrix with diagonal entries equal to the corresponding ones in the vector V. As shown in the appendix, Eq. (11) can be written in matrix notation as (for fixed (m_t, y_{t-1}, m_{t-1})):

$$\mathbf{F}_{Y_t,m_t,y_{t-1}|m_{t-1},Y_{t-2}} = \mathbf{F}_{Y_t|m_t,m_{t-1},\chi_{t-1}} \mathbf{D}_{y_{t-1}|m_t,m_{t-1},\chi_{t-1}} \mathbf{D}_{m_t|m_{t-1},\chi_{t-1}} \mathbf{F}_{\chi_{t-1}|m_{t-1},Y_{t-2}} \tag{12}$$

Similarly, integrating our y_{t-1} in Eq. (11) leads to for any given (m_t, m_{t-1}):

$$\mathbf{F}_{Y_t,m_t|m_{t-1},Y_{t-2}} = \mathbf{F}_{Y_t|m_t,m_{t-1},\mathcal{X}_{t-1}} \mathbf{D}_{m_t|m_{t-1},\mathcal{X}_{t-1}} \mathbf{F}_{\mathcal{X}_{t-1}|m_{t-1},Y_{t-2}} \tag{13}$$

where

$$\mathbf{F}_{Y_t,m_t|m_{t-1},Y_{t-2}} = [f_{Y_t,M_t|M_{t-1},Y_{t-2}}(i, m_t|m_{t-1}, j)]_{i,j}$$

The identification of a matrix, for example, $\mathbf{F}_{Y_t|m_t,m_{t-1},\mathcal{X}_{t-1}}$, is equivalent to that of its corresponding density, for example, $f_{Y_t|M_t,M_{t-1},\mathcal{X}_{t-1}}$. Identification of $\mathbf{F}_{Y_t|m_t,m_{t-1},\mathcal{X}_{t-1}}$ from the observed $\mathbf{F}_{Y_t,m_t,y_{t-1}|m_{t-1},Y_{t-2}}$ requires

Assumption 4. For any (m_t, m_{t-1}), there exists a $y_{t-1} \in \mathcal{S}$ such that $\mathbf{F}_{Y_t,m_t|m_{t-1},Y_{t-2}}$ is invertible.

Assumption 4 rules out cases where the support of χ_{t-1} is larger than that of Y_t. Hence, in this section, we are restricting attention to the case where Y_t and χ_{t-1} have the same support.

Remark. This assumption implies that all the unknown matrices on the right-hand side are invertible. In particular, all the diagonal entries in $\mathbf{D}_{y_{t-1}|m_t,m_{t-1},\mathcal{X}_{t-1}}$ and $\mathbf{D}_{m_t|m_{t-1},\mathcal{X}_{t-1}}$ are nonzero. Furthermore, this assumption is imposed on the observed probabilities, and therefore, directly testable using the sample. ■

As in Hu (2008), if the latter matrix relation can be inverted (which is ensured by Assumption 4), we can combine Eqs. (12) and (13) to get

$$\mathbf{F}_{Y_t,m_t,y_{t-1}|m_{t-1},Y_{t-2}} \mathbf{F}^{-1}_{Y_t,m_t|m_{t-1},Y_{t-2}} = \mathbf{F}_{Y_t|m_t,m_{t-1},\mathcal{X}_{t-1}} \cdot \mathbf{D}_{y_{t-1}|m_t,m_{t-1},\mathcal{X}_{t-1}} \cdot \mathbf{F}^{-1}_{Y_t|m_t,m_{t-1},\mathcal{X}_{t-1}} \tag{14}$$

This representation shows that an eigenvalue-eigenfunction decomposition of the observed matrix $\mathbf{F}_{Y_t,m_t,y_{t-1}|m_{t-1},Y_{t-2}} \mathbf{F}^{-1}_{Y_t,m_t|m_{t-1},Y_{t-2}}$ yields the unknown density functions $f_{Y_t|m_t,m_{t-1},\mathcal{X}_{t-1}}$ as the eigenfunctions and $f_{y_{t-1}|m_t,m_{t-1},\mathcal{X}_{t-1}}$ as the eigenvalues.

The following assumption ensures the uniqueness of this decomposition, and restricts the choice of the $\omega(\cdot)$ function.

Assumption 5. For any (m_t, m_{t-1}), there exists a $y_{t-1} \in \mathcal{S}$ such that for $j \neq k \in \mathcal{S}$

$$f_{Y_{t-1}|M_t,M_{t-1},\mathcal{X}_{t-1}}(y_{t-1}|m_t, m_{t-1}, j) \neq f_{Y_{t-1}|M_t,M_{t-1},\mathcal{X}_{t-1}}(y_{t-1}|m_t, m_{t-1}, k)$$

Assumption 5 implies that the latent variable does change the distribution of Y_{t-1} given M_t in the two periods. Notice that Assumption 4 guarantees that $f_{y_{t-1}|m_t,m_{t-1},\chi_{t-1}} \neq 0$.

Remark. Assumption 5 requires that the conditional density $f_{Y_{t-1}|M_t,M_{t-1},\chi_{t-1}}(y_{t-1}|m_t,m_{t-1},\chi_{t-1})$ varies in χ_{t-1} given any fixed (m_t,m_{t-1}), so that the "eigenvalues" in the decomposition (Eq. (14)) are distinctive. Although this assumption is not imposed directly on observed probability, the probability $f_{Y_{t-1}|M_t,M_{t-1},\chi_{t-1}}$ for different values of χ_{t-1} is an eigenvalue of an matrix induced by observed probabilities. Therefore, Assumption 5 is also testable using the sample. For Example 1, given the preceding discussion, Assumption 5 should hold. For Example 2, the capital stock M_t evolves deterministically, so that $f_{Y_{t-1}|M_t,M_{t-1},\chi_{t-1}}(y_{t-1}|m_t,m_{t-1},\chi_{t-1}) = I(y_{t-1} = m_t - (1-\delta)m_{t-1})$. Since this does not change with χ_{t-1} for any fixed (m_t,m_{t-1}), Therefore, Assumption 5 fails. ■

Remark (complete information games). In some models, the choice variable Y_{it} is a deterministic function of the current state variables, that is,

$$Y_{i,t-1} = g_i(M_{t-1},\chi_{t-1}), \qquad i=1,2 \tag{15}$$

In Examples 1 and 2, this would be the case if we eliminated the privately observed demand shocks η_{1t} and η_{2t}. Assumption 5 becomes

$$f_{Y_{t-1}|M_{t-1},\chi_{t-1}}(y_{t-1}|m_{t-1},j) \neq f_{Y_{t-1}|M_{t-1},\chi_{t-1}}(y_{t-1}|m_{t-1},k)$$ ■

Remark. Notice that in the decomposition (Eq. (14)), y_{t-1} only appears in the eigenvalues. Therefore, if there are several values y_{t-1} which satisfy Assumption (5), the decompositions (Eq. (14)) using these different y_{t-1}'s should yield the same eigenfunctions. Hence, depending on the specific model, it may be possible to use this feature as a general specification check for Assumptions 1 and 2. We do not explore this possibility here. ■

Under the foregoing assumptions, the density $Y_t, m_t, y_{t-1}|m_{t-1}, Y_{t-2}$ can form a unique eigenvalue-eigenvector decomposition. In this decomposition, the eigenfunction corresponds to the density $f_{Y_t|m_t,m_{t-1},\chi_{t-1}} \times (\cdot|m_t,m_{t-1},\chi_{t-1})$ which can be written as

$$f_{Y_t|m_t,m_{t-1},\chi_{t-1}}(\cdot|m_t,m_{t-1},\chi_{t-1}) = f_{Y_{1,t},Y_{2,t}|m_t,m_{t-1},\chi_{1,t-1},\chi_{2,t-1}}(\cdot,\cdot|m_t,m_{t-1},\chi_{1,t-1},\chi_{2,t-1}) \tag{16}$$

The eigenvalue–eigenfunction decomposition only identifies this eigenfunction up to some arbitrary ordering of the $(\chi_{1,t-1},\chi_{2,t-1})$ argument. Hence, in order to pin down the right ordering of χ_{t-1}, an additional ordering assumption is required. In our earlier article (Hu & Shum, 2013), where χ_t was scalar-valued, a monotonicity assumption sufficed to pin down the ordering of χ_t. However, in dynamic games, χ_{t-1} is multivariate, so that monotonicity is no longer well-defined.

Consider the marginal density

$$f_{Y_{i,t}|m_t,m_{t-1},\chi_{1,t-1},\chi_{2,t-1}}(\cdot|m_t,m_{t-1},\chi_{1,t-1},\chi_{2,t-1})$$

which can be computed from Eq. (16) above. We make the following ordering assumption:

Assumption 6. For any given (m_t,m_{t-1}) and $j\neq k\in\mathcal{S}$

$$f_{Y_t|m_t,m_{t-1},\chi_{t-1}}(k|m_t,m_{t-1},k)>f_{Y_t|m_t,m_{t-1},\chi_{t-1}}(j|m_t,m_{t-1},k)$$

Remark. With this assumption, the mode of $f_{Y_{1,t},Y_{2,t}|m_t,m_{t-1},\chi_{1,t-1},\chi_{2,t-1}}(\cdot,\cdot|m_t,m_{t-1},j,k)$ is (j,k). Therefore, the value of the latent variable $\chi_{1,t-1},\chi_{2,t-1}$ can be identified from the eigenvectors. In other words, the "pattern" of the latent marginal cost is revealed at the mode of the price distribution of $(Y_{1,t},Y_{2,t})$. This assumption should be confirmed on a model-by-model basis. In example where the $Y_{i,t}$ is interpreted as a price and $\chi_{1,t}$ as a marginal cost variable, this assumption implies that a firm whose marginal cost is the k-th lowest would most likely has the k-th lowest price for given the installed base. ■

From the eigenvalue–eigenvector decomposition in Eq. (14), Hu (2008) implies that we can identify all the unknown matrices $\mathbf{F}_{Y_t|m_t,m_{t-1},\chi_{t-1}}$, $\mathbf{D}_{y_{t-1}|m_t,m_{t-1},\chi_{t-1}}$, $\mathbf{D}_{m_t|m_{t-1},\chi_{t-1}}$, and $\mathbf{F}_{\chi_{t-1}|m_{t-1},Y_{t-2}}$ for any (m_t,y_{t-1},m_{t-1}) and their corresponding densities $f_{Y_t|M_t,M_{t-1},\chi_{t-1}}$, $f_{Y_{t-1}|M_t,M_{t-1},\chi_{t-1}}$, $f_{M_t|M_{t-1},\chi_{t-1}}$, and $f_{\chi_{t-1}|M_{t-1},Y_{t-2}}$. That implies we can identify $f_{M_t,Y_{t-1}|M_{t-1},\chi_{t-1}}$ as

$$f_{M_t,Y_{t-1}|M_{t-1},\chi_{t-1}}=f_{Y_{t-1}|M_t,M_{t-1},\chi_{t-1}}f_{M_t|M_{t-1},\chi_{t-1}}$$

From the factorization:

$$f_{M_t,Y_{t-1}|M_{t-1},\chi_{t-1}}=f_{M_t|Y_{t-1},M_{t-1},\chi_{t-1}}\cdot f_{Y_{t-1}|M_{t-1},\chi_{t-1}}$$

we can recover $f_{M_t|Y_{t-1},M_{t-1},\chi_{t-1}}$ and $f_{Y_{t-1}|M_{t-1},\chi_{t-1}}$. Given stationarity, the latter density is identical to $f_{Y_t|M_t,\chi_t}$, so that from $f_{M_t,Y_{t-1}|M_{t-1},\chi_{t-1}}$ we have recovered the first two components of $f_{W_t,\chi_t|W_{t-1},\chi_{t-1}}$ in Eq. (10).

All that remains now is to identify the third component $f_{\chi_t|M_t,M_{t-1},\chi_{t-1}}$. To obtain this, note that the following matrix relation holds:

$$\mathbf{F}_{Y_t|m_t,m_{t-1},\chi_{t-1}} = \mathbf{F}_{Y_t|m_t,\chi_t}\mathbf{F}_{\chi_t|m_t,m_{t-1},\chi_{t-1}}$$

for given (m_t, m_{t-1}), and where for $i,l,k \in \mathcal{S}$

$$\mathbf{F}_{\chi_t|m_t,m_{t-1},\chi_{t-1}} = [f_{\chi_t|M_t,M_{t-1},\chi_{t-1}}(l|m_t, m_{t-1}, k)]_{l,k}$$
$$\mathbf{F}_{Y_t|m_t,\chi_t} = [f_{Y_t|M_t,\chi_t}(i|m_t, l)]_{i,l}$$

The invertibility of $\mathbf{F}_{Y_t|m_t,m_{t-1},\chi_{t-1}}$ implies that of $\mathbf{F}_{Y_t|m_t,\chi_t}$. Therefore, the final component in Eq. (10) can be recovered as

$$\mathbf{F}_{\chi_t|m_t,m_{t-1},\chi_{t-1}} = \mathbf{F}^{-1}_{Y_t|m_t,\chi_t}\mathbf{F}_{Y_t|m_t,m_{t-1},\chi_{t-1}} \tag{17}$$

where both terms on the right-hand side have already been identified in previous steps.

Finally, we summarize the identification results as follows:

Theorem 1. (Stationary case) Under the Assumptions 1, 2, 3, 4, 5, and 6, the density $f_{W_t,W_{t-1},W_{t-2}}$, for any $t \in \{3,\ldots T\}$, uniquely determines the time-invariant Markov equilibrium transition density $f_{W_2,\chi_2|W_1,\chi_1}$.

Proof. See the appendix. ■

This theorem implies that we may identify the Markov kernel density with three periods of data.

Without stationarity, the desired density $f_{Y_t|M_t,\chi_t}$ is not the same as $f_{Y_{t-1}|M_{t-1},\chi_{t-1}}$, which can be recovered from the three observations $f_{W_t,W_{t-1},W_{t-2}}$. However, in this case, we can repeat the whole foregoing argument for the three observations $f_{W_{t+1},W_t,W_{t-1}}$ to identify $f_{Y_t|M_t,\chi_t}$. Hence, the following corollary is immediate:

Corollary 1. (Nonstationary case) Under the Assumptions 1, 2, 4, 5, and 6, the density $f_{W_{t+1},W_t,W_{t-1},W_{t-2}}$ uniquely determines the time-varying Markov equilibrium transition density $f_{W_t,\chi_t|W_{t-1},\chi_{t-1}}$, for every period $t \in \{3,\ldots T-1\}$.

EXTENSIONS

Alternatives to Assumption 2(ii)

In this section, we consider alternative conditions of Assumption 2(ii). Assumption 2(ii) implies that χ_t is independent of Y_{t-1} conditional on M_t,

M_{t-1} and χ_{t-1}. There are other alternative "limited feedback" assumptions, which may be suitable for different empirical settings. Assumptions 1 and 2(i) imply

$$\begin{aligned} & f_{W_{t+1},W_t,W_{t-1},W_{t-2}} \\ & = f_{Y_{t+1},M_{t+1},Y_t,M_t,Y_{t-1},M_{t-1},Y_{t-2},M_{t-2}} \\ & = \int\int \left[f_{Y_{t+1},M_{t+1}|Y_t,M_t,\chi_t} f_{Y_t|M_t,\chi_t} f_{\chi_t,M_t|Y_{t-1},M_{t-1},\chi_{t-1}} \cdot f_{Y_{t-1}|M_{t-1},\chi_{t-1}} f_{\chi_{t-1},M_{t-1},Y_{t-2},M_{t-2}} \right] d\chi_t d\chi_{t-1} \end{aligned}$$

Assumption 2(ii) implies that the state transition density satisfies

$$f_{\chi_t,M_t|Y_{t-1},M_{t-1},\chi_{t-1}} = f_{\chi_t|M_t,M_{t-1},\chi_{t-1}} f_{M_t|Y_{t-1},M_{t-1},\chi_{t-1}}$$

Alternative "limited feedback" assumptions may be imposed on the density $f_{\chi_t,M_t|Y_{t-1},M_{t-1},\chi_{t-1}}$. One alternative to Assumption 2(ii) is

$$f_{\chi_t,M_t|Y_{t-1},M_{t-1},\chi_{t-1}} = f_{\chi_t|M_t,Y_{t-1},\chi_{t-1}} f_{M_t|Y_{t-1},M_{t-1},\chi_{t-1}} \quad (18)$$

which implies that M_{t-1} does not have a direct effect on χ_t conditional on M_t, Y_{t-1}, and χ_{t-1}. A second alternative is

$$f_{\chi_t,M_t|Y_{t-1},M_{t-1},\chi_{t-1}} = f_{M_t|\chi_t,Y_{t-1},M_{t-1}} f_{\chi_t|Y_{t-1},M_{t-1},\chi_{t-1}} \quad (19)$$

which is the "limited feedback" assumption used in our earlier study (Hu & Shum, 2013) of identification on single-agent dynamic optimization problems. Both alternatives (Eqs. (18) and (19)) can be handled using identification arguments similar to the one in Hu and Shum (2013).

A third alternative to Assumption 2(ii) is

$$f_{\chi_t,M_t|Y_{t-1},M_{t-1},\chi_{t-1}} = f_{\chi_t|M_t,Y_{t-1},M_{t-1},\chi_{t-1}} f_{M_t|M_{t-1},\chi_{t-1}} \quad (20)$$

This alternative can be handled in an identification framework similar to the one used in this article.

CONCLUSIONS

In this article, we show several results regarding nonparametric identification in a general class of Markov dynamic games, including many models in the Ericson and Pakes (1995) and Pakes and McGuire (1994) framework.

We show that only three observations $W_t, \ldots, W_{t-2}$ are required to identify $W_t, \chi_t | W_{t-1}, \chi_{t-1}$ in the stationary case, when Y_t is a continuous choice variable. If Y_t is a discrete choice variable (while χ_t is continuous), then four observations are required for identification.

In ongoing work, we are working on developing estimation procedures for dynamic games which utilize these identification results.

NOTES

1. Our framework is one of incomplete information but our results apply both to models of incomplete information and, as a particular case, to dynamic games of complete information.
2. Markov Perfect Equilibrium (MPE) is the equilibrium concept that has been used in this literature and this concept assumes that players' strategies depend only on payoff-relevant state variables.
3. Kasahara and Shimotsu (2009) consider a dynamic discrete choice model as a mixture model, where the unobserable is time-invariant. We use a general identification result for measurment error models (Hu, 2008) to identify a dynamic game with time-varying unobserved state variables. See also Hu, Kayaba, and Shum (2013) and An, Hu, and Shum (2010).
4. This restriction limits the support of the common knowledge unobservables to be discrete. An advantage of this restriction is that the identification procedure does not require high-level technical assumption, such as injectivity, and many assumptions are directly testable from the data. An obvious disadvantage is that it rules out continuous unobserved state variables.
5. The identification strategy for the continuous choice games is the same as that for the discrete choice games after discretization of the observed choice, as long as the latent unobservable is discrete. This can be seen in the transformation of $(Y_{1,t}, Y_{2,t})$ before introducing the matrices. For the continuous choice games, one may pick a function $\tilde{G}$ to map continuous $Y_{1,t}, Y_{2,t}$ to a discrete $Y_t = \tilde{G}(Y_{1,t}, Y_{2,t})$, then impose restrictions on Y_t.

REFERENCES

Ackerberg, D., Benkard, L., Berry, S., & Pakes, A. (2007). Econometric tools for analyzing market outcomes. In J. Heckman, & E. Leamer (Eds.), *Handbook of econometrics*, (Vol. 6A). North-Holland, Amsterdam.

Aguirregabiria, V., & Mira, P. (2007). Sequential estimation of dynamic discrete games. *Econometrica*, *75*, 1–53.

An, Y., Hu, Y., & Shum, M. (2010). Nonparametric estimation of first-price auctions when the number of bidders is unobserved: A misclassification approach. *Journal of Econometrics*, *157*, 328–341.

Arcidiacono, P., & Miller, R. (2011). Conditional choice probability estimation of dynamic discrete choice models with unobserved heterogeneity. *Econometrica*, *79*, 1823–1867.

Bajari, P., Benkard, L., & Levin, J. (2007). Estimating dynamic models of imperfect competition. *Econometrica*, *75*, 1331–1370.

Bajari, P., Chernozhukov, V., Hong, H., & Nekipelov, D. (2007). Nonparametric and semiparametric analysis of a dynamic game model," Manuscript, University of Minnesota.

Benkard, L. (2004). A dynamic analysis of the market for wide-bodied commercial aircraft. *Review of Economic Studies*, *71*, 581–611.

Blevins, J. (2008). *Sequential MC methods for estimating dynamic microeconomic models*, Duke University, working paper.

Doraszelski, U., & Pakes, A. (2007). A framework for dynamic analysis in IO. In M. Armstrong & R. Porter (Eds.), *Handbook of industrial organization* (Vol. 3). North-Holland, Amsterdam. Chap. 30.

Ericson, R., & Pakes, A. (1995). Markov-perfect industry dynamics: A framework for empirical work. *Review of Economic Studies*, *62*, 53–82.

Hotz, J., & Miller, R. (1993). Conditional choice probabilties and the estimation of dynamic models. *Review of Economic Studies*, *60*, 497–529.

Hu, Y. (2008). Identification and estimation of nonlinear models with misclassification error using instrumental variables: A general solution. *Journal of Econometrics*, *144*, 27–61.

Hu, Y., Kayaba, Y., & Shum, M. (2013). Nonparametric learning rules from bandit experiments: The eyes have it!. *Games and Economic Behavior*, *81*, 215–231.

Hu, Y., & Shum, M. (2013). Nonparametric identification of dynamic models with unobserved state variables. *Journal of Econometrics*, *171*, 32–44.

Kasahara, H., & Shimotsu, K. (2009). Nonparametric identification of finite mixture models of dynamic discrete choice. *Econometrica*, *77*, 135–175.

Magnac, T., & Thesmar, D. (2002). Identifying dynamic discrete decision processes. *Econometrica*, *70*, 801–816.

Pakes, A., & McGuire, P. (1994). Computing markov-perfect nash equilibria: Numerical implications of a dynamic dierentiated product model. *RAND Journal of Economics*, *25*, 555–589.

Pakes, A., Ostrovsky, M., & Berry, S. (2007). Simple estimators for the parameters of discrete dynamic games (with entry exit examples). *RAND Journal of Economics*, *38*, 373–399.

Pesendorfer, M., & Schmidt-Dengler, P. (2008). Asymptotic least squares estimators for dynamic games. *Review of Economic Studies*, *75*, 901–928.

Siebert, R., & Zulehner, C. (2008). *The impact of market demand and innovation on market Structure*. Working paper. Purdue University.

APPENDIX

Proof. (theorem 1) First, Assumptions 1 and 2 imply that the density of interest becomes

$$\begin{aligned} f_{W_t,\chi_t|W_{t-1},\chi_{t-1}} &= f_{Y_t,M_t,\chi_t|Y_{t-1},M_{t-1},\chi_{t-1}} \\ &= f_{Y_t|M_t,\chi_t,Y_{t-1},M_{t-1},\chi_{t-1}} f_{\chi_t|M_t,Y_{t-1},M_{t-1},\chi_{t-1}} f_{M_t|Y_{t-1},M_{t-1},\chi_{t-1}} \\ &= f_{Y_t|M_t,\chi_t} f_{\chi_t|M_t,M_{t-1},\chi_{t-1}} f_{M_t|Y_{t-1},M_{t-1},\chi_{t-1}} \end{aligned} \tag{21}$$

We consider the observed density $f_{W_t,W_{t-1},W_{t-2}}$. One can show that Assumptions 1 and 2(i) imply

$$\begin{aligned} & f_{W_t,W_{t-1},W_{t-2}} \\ &= \sum_{\chi_t} \sum_{\chi_{t-1}} f_{W_t,\chi_t|W_{t-1},W_{t-2},\chi_{t-1}} f_{W_{t-1},W_{t-2},\chi_{t-1}} \\ &= \sum_{\chi_t} \sum_{\chi_{t-1}} f_{Y_t|M_t,\chi_t} f_{\chi_t|M_t,Y_{t-1},M_{t-1},\chi_{t-1}} f_{M_t|Y_{t-1},M_{t-1},\chi_{t-1}} f_{Y_{t-1}|M_{t-1},\chi_{t-1}} f_{\chi_{t-1},M_{t-1},Y_{t-2},M_{t-2}} \\ &= \sum_{\chi_t} \sum_{\chi_{t-1}} f_{Y_t|M_t,\chi_t} f_{\chi_t|M_t,Y_{t-1},M_{t-1},\chi_{t-1}} f_{M_t,Y_{t-1}|M_{t-1},\chi_{t-1}} f_{\chi_{t-1},M_{t-1},Y_{t-2},M_{t-2}} \end{aligned}$$

After integrating out M_{t-2}, Assumption 2(ii) then implies

$$f_{Y_t,M_t,Y_{t-1},M_{t-1},Y_{t-2}} = \sum_{\chi_{t-1}} \left(\sum_{\chi_t} f_{Y_t|M_t,\chi_t} f_{\chi_t|M_t,M_{t-1},\chi_{t-1}} \right) f_{M_t,Y_{t-1}|M_{t-1},\chi_{t-1}} f_{\chi_{t-1},M_{t-1},Y_{t-2}}$$

The expression in the parenthesis can be simplified as $f_{Y_t|M_t,M_{t-1},\chi_{t-1}}$. We then have

$$f_{Y_t,M_t,Y_{t-1}|M_{t-1},Y_{t-2}} = \sum_{\chi_{t-1}} f_{Y_t|M_t,M_{t-1},\chi_{t-1}} f_{M_t,Y_{t-1}|M_{t-1},\chi_{t-1}} f_{\chi_{t-1}|M_{t-1},Y_{t-2}} \tag{22}$$

Straightforward algebra shows that this equation is equivalent to

$$\mathbf{F}_{Y_t,m_t,y_{t-1}|m_{t-1},Y_{t-2}} = \mathbf{F}_{Y_t|m_t,m_{t-1},\chi_{t-1}} \mathbf{D}_{y_{t-1}|m_t,m_{t-1},\chi_{t-1}} \mathbf{D}_{m_t|m_{t-1},\chi_{t-1}} \mathbf{F}_{\chi_{t-1}|m_{t-1},Y_{t-2}} \tag{23}$$

for any given (m_t, y_{t-1}, m_{t-1}). The identification results then follow from Theorem 1 in Hu (2008). ■

PART II
STRUCTURAL MODELS OF GAMES

PARTIAL IDENTIFICATION IN TWO-SIDED MATCHING MODELS

Federico Echenique, SangMok Lee and Matthew Shum

ABSTRACT

We propose a methodology for estimating preference parameters in matching models. Our estimator applies to repeated observations of matchings among a fixed group of individuals. Our estimator is based on the stability conditions in matching models; we consider both transferable (TU) and nontransferable utility (NTU) models. In both cases, the stability conditions yield moment inequalities which can be taken to the data. The preference parameters are partially identified. We consider simple illustrative examples, and also an empirical application to aggregate marriage markets.

Keywords: Two-sided matching; stability; partial identification

JEL classifications: C78; C51; D10

Structural Econometric Models
Advances in Econometrics, Volume 31, 117–139

ISSN: 0731-9053/doi:10.1108/S0731-9053(2013)0000032004

In this article, we propose a methodology for estimating preference parameters in matching models. Our estimator applies to repeated observations of matchings among a fixed group of individuals, which is a similar data structure as in Fox (2010). Our estimator is based on stability conditions in the matching models; we consider both transferable (TU) and nontransferable utility (NTU) models. In both cases, the stability conditions yield moment inequalities which can be taken to the data. The preference parameters are partially identified. We consider simple illustrative examples, and also an empirical application to aggregate marriage markets.

SETUP

Consider a setup where we observe repeated individual-level matchings among a group of N men and women. Index men (women) by $m=1,...,N(w=1,...,N)$. The set of men (women) is denoted $M(W)$. Each man $m\in M$ has a set of strict preferences $>_m$ over $W\cup\{m\}$; similarly, each woman $w\in W$ has a set of strict preferences $>_w$ over men $M\cup\{w\}$. We assume that matchings are one-to-one.

Moment conditions are defined for each potential pair of couples through the stability conditions. First, define the utility indicators, for $i,k\in M$ and $j,l\in W$

$$d_{ijl} := \mathbb{1}(j>_i l) \quad \text{and} \quad d_{jik} := \mathbb{1}(i>_j k)$$

For the *nontransferable utility (NTU) model*, the stability condition implies: for $i,k\in M$ and $j,l\in W$, with $i\neq k$ and $j\neq l$,

$$(i,j),(k,l)\text{ matched} \Rightarrow \begin{cases} d_{ilj}d_{lik}=0, \text{ and} \\ d_{jki}d_{kjl}=0 \end{cases} \tag{1}$$

This stability condition implies the moment inequality:

$$Pr((i,j),(k,l) \text{ matched}) \leq Pr(d_{ilj}d_{lik}=0, d_{jki}d_{kjl}=0)$$

For the *transferable utility (TU) model*, let $\mathcal{A}=(\alpha_{i,j})$ be a $|M|\times|W|$ matrix of non-negative real numbers. $\mathcal{A}$ is called a surplus matrix, in which $\alpha_{i,j}$ is the surplus jointly generated by man-i and woman-j.

A matching is called *optimal* if it achieves the maximum total surplus. It is well-known that optimality corresponds to the appropriate notion of stability for the TU model (Shapley & Shubik, 1971). The formal notion of stability requires a discussion of agents' payoffs; for reasons of space, we omit the definition of stability and focus instead on optimal matchings.

A *necessary condition* of the optimal matching is the *pairwise-stability* condition:

$$(i,j),(k,l)\text{ matched} \Rightarrow \alpha_{ij}+\alpha_{kl}\geq \alpha_{il}+\alpha_{kj}$$

This leads to the moment inequality:

$$Pr((i,j),(k,l)\ \text{ matched})\ \leq Pr(\alpha_{ij}+\alpha_{kl}\geq \alpha_{il}+\alpha_{kj};\beta)$$

For both NTU and TU models, the LHS of the moment inequalities can be obtained directly from the data, as sample frequencies when the number of repeated matchings grows large. The RHS of the moment inequalities will depend on the utility parameters, once we specify the utility functions. (A simple example will be presented in the next section.) The number of moment conditions then is the number of potential pairs of couples that can be observed; out of N men and women, there are N^2 potential couples that can be formed; hence, there are $N^{2*}(N-1)^2$ *pairs* of potential couples consisting of two distinct men and two distinct women.

Comparison with Other Estimation Approaches

Note that generally, parameters in both NTU and TU setting will be partially identified. For the NTU setting, this is due to the multiplicity of stable matchings, and echoes the partial identification results for game models with multiple equilibria (cf. Beresteanu, Molchanov, & Molinari, 2011; Ciliberto & Tamer, 2009). For the TU setting, even though the optimal matching is generally unique, we are using only *necessary conditions* for identification, and hence partial identification results. This contrasts with Fox (2010), who considers maximum score estimation of the TU model using the pairwise stability conditions, and obtains point identification of utility parameters.

EXAMPLE: NTU MODEL

Here we present a simple 2×2 example with two men (i,k) and two women (j,l). Utilities are

$$U_{m,w}=\beta_M|Age_m-Age_w|+\varepsilon_{m,w}$$
$$U_{w,m}=\beta_W|Age_m-Age_w|+\varepsilon_{w,m}$$

Utilities depend just on the age differences between the matched persons. The unobserved portion of utility, ε, is assumed to be distributed i.i.d. $N(0, \frac{1}{2})$ across all m, w, and identically for men and women.

With just two men and two women, there are only two pairs of distinct potential couples: $\{(i,j),(k,l)\}$ and $\{(i,l),(k,j)\}$. Hence there are two moment inequalities. Assume that, from the data, we have the following match frequencies:

$$Pr(\{(i,j),(k,l)\}) = 0.3$$
$$Pr(\{(i,l),(k,j)\}) = 1 - Pr(\{(i,j),(k,l)\}) = 0.7$$

We consider the NTU model here. Hence the first moment inequality says

$$Pr(\{(i,j),(k,l)\}) \leq Pr(d_{ilj}d_{lik} = 0, d_{jki}d_{kjl} = 0)$$

Given the utility specification above, this becomes (letting $\Delta_{ij} := |Age_i - Age_j|$):

$$\begin{aligned} Pr(\{(i,j),(k,l)\}) \leq & [1 - \Phi(\beta_M(\Delta_{il} - \Delta_{ij}))\Phi(\beta_W(\Delta_{il} - \Delta_{kl}))] \\ & \cdot [1 - \Phi(\beta_W(\Delta_{jk} - \Delta_{ji}))\Phi(\beta_M(\Delta_{kj} - \Delta_{kl}))] \end{aligned}$$

Analogously, for the second moment inequality, we have:

$$\begin{aligned} 1 - Pr(\{(i,j),(k,l)\}) \leq & [1 - \Phi(\beta_M(\Delta_{kl} - \Delta_{kj}))\Phi(\beta_W(\Delta_{kl} - \Delta_{il}))] \\ & \cdot [1 - \Phi(\beta_W(\Delta_{ij} - \Delta_{kj}))\Phi(\beta_M(\Delta_{ij} - \Delta_{il}))] \end{aligned}$$

For our example, we have that $\Delta_{kj} = \Delta_{il} = 0.5$, while $\Delta_{ij} = \Delta_{kl} = 0$.

The identified set for the NTU version of this simple example is shown in Fig. 1. To a certain degree, the admissible preferences of men and women have an "antipodal" feature. When $\beta_M \ll 0$, implying that men dislike a large age gap, then $\beta_W \gg 0$, implying that women prefer a larger age gap. When men prefer a larger age gap ($\beta_M > 0$), however, then women may be either indifferent or dislike a large age gap ($\beta_W \leq 0$).

Such antipodal preferences is consistent with a general logic of stability in NTU settings. In such a setting, an observed matching may not be indicative that each person is matched to a "most preferred" partner; rather, stability of the observed matching only implies that (say) each man is not able to find a more preferable partner who would also prefer to be matched with him rather than her current mate. It is this "no blocking pairs"

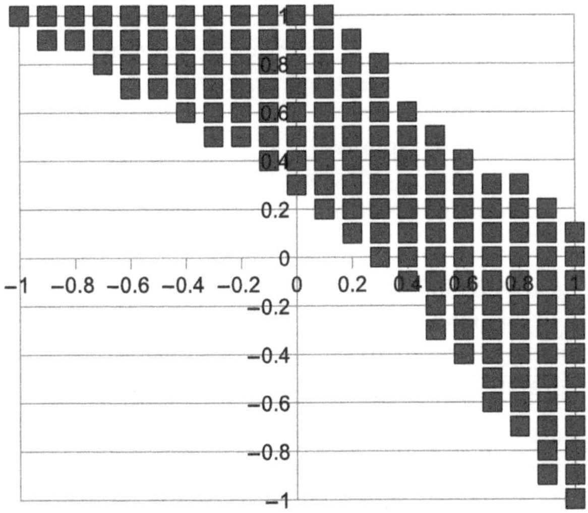

Fig. 1. Identified set for simple 2 × 2 example: NTU model *X*-axis: β_M; *Y*-axis: β_W.

requirement, which restricts the utility parameter values. In the example, we assumed that "unequal-aged matchings" (i.e., $\{(k,j),(i,l)\}$) occurred with probability 0.7, which is higher than the "equal-age matchings" (i.e., $\{(i,j),(k,l)\}$). The "no blocking pairs" conditions then implies that if men value an equal-aged partner (i.e., $\beta_M < 0$), then women must value an unequal-aged partner (i.e., $\beta_W > 0$), and vice versa. We see these implications in the identified set of admissible preference parameters.

AGGREGATE MATCHING MODEL

One problem with the present estimator is the need to observe repeated matchings from comparable populations. Also, the population should be relatively small, in order for the number of moment conditions to stay modest and manageable. Both of these requirements are difficult to fulfill in practice. Therefore, in this section we consider the robustness of our estimator when applied to *aggregate* data: that is, when the data available are tables of the match frequencies for different aggregate *types* of agents. We spell out the theory of such aggregate matchings in another article

(Echenique, Lee, Shum, & Yenmez, 2013). Here we introduce and define basic concepts, which will be used in the empirical application below.

An aggregate matching market is described by a triple $\langle M, W, > \rangle$, where

(1) M and W are disjoint, finite sets.
(2) $(> := ((>_m)_{m \in M}, (>_w)_{w \in W})$ is a profile of strict preferences: for each m and w, $>_m$ is a linear order over $W \cup \{m\}$ and $>_w$ is a linear order over $M \cup \{w\}$.

We call agents on one side men, and on the other side women, as is traditional in the matching literature. The elements of M are types of men, and the elements of W are *types of women.* Many applications are, of course, to environments different from the marriage matching market.

Note that preferences > above effectively rules out preference heterogeneity among agents of the same type. While this is restrictive relative to other aggregate matching models in the literature, such as Choo and Siow (2006), Galichon and Salanie (2010), both of these papers consider the TU model. For the NTU model (which is the focus of this section), stability conditions for a model with agent-specific preference heterogeneity has *no empirical implications* at the aggregate level (see Appendix A for further discussions). For this reason, we assume that all agents of the same type have identical preferences.

Consider an aggregate matching market $\langle M, W, > \rangle$, with $M = \{m_1, \ldots, m_K\}$ and $W = \{w_1, \ldots, w_L\}$. An *aggregate matching* is a $K \times L$ matrix $X = (X_{ij})$ with nonnegative integer entries. The interpretation of X is that X_{ij} is the number of type-i men and type-j women matched to each other. An aggregate matching X is canonical if $X_{ij} \in \{0, 1\}$. For any aggregate matching X, we can construct a canonical aggregate matching X^c by setting $X^c_{ij} = 0$ when $X_{ij} = 0$ and $X^c_{ij} = 1$ when $X_{ij} > 0$.

We consider, in turn, the nontransferable utility model and its empirical implementation, followed by the transferable utility model.

Nontransferable Utility Model

An aggregate matching X is *stable* if it is individually rational and there are no blocking pairs for X. Obviously, an aggregate matching X is stable if and only if the corresponding canonical matching X^c is stable. Therefore, our empirical results below pertain to canonical aggregate matchings.

Given a canonical matching X, we define an *anti-edge* as a pair of couples $\{(i,j),(k,l)\}$ with $i \neq k \in M$ and $j \neq l \in W$ such that $X_{ij} = X_{kl} = 1$. Then, stability of the canonical aggregate matching X is equivalent to

$$(i,j),(k,l) \text{ anti-edge} \Rightarrow \begin{cases} \mathbb{1}(w_l >_{m_i} w_j) \cdot \mathbb{1}(m_i >_{w_l} m_k) = 0, \text{ and} \\ \mathbb{1}(w_j >_{m_k} w_l) \cdot \mathbb{1}(m_k >_{w_j} m_i) = 0 \end{cases} \tag{2}$$

In our empirical work with the NTU model, Eq. (2) of the stability conditions forms the basis for the moment inequalities. The anti-edge condition (Eq. (2)) implies that

$$Pr((i,j),(k,l) \text{ anti-edge}) \leq Pr(d_{ilj} d_{lik} = 0, d_{jki} d_{kjl} = 0) \tag{3}$$

Given parameter values β, and our assumptions regarding the distribution of the ε's, these probabilities can be calculated. Hence, the moment inequality corresponding to Eq. (3) is

$$\mathbb{E}\underbrace{[1((i,j),(k,l)\text{anti-edge}) - Pr(d_{ilj} d_{lik} = 0, d_{jki} d_{kjl} = 0; \beta))]}_{g_{ijkl}(X;\beta)} \leq 0 \tag{4}$$

The identified set is defined as

$$\mathbb{B}_0 = \{\beta : \mathbb{E} g_{ijkl}(X;\beta) \leq 0, \ \forall i,j,k,l\}$$

These moment inequalities are quite distinct from the estimating equations considered in the existing empirical matching literature. For instance, Choo and Siow (2006), Dagsvik (2000), and Fox (2010) use equations similar to those in the multinomial choice literature, that each observed pair (i,j) represents, for both i and j, an "optimal choice" from some "choice set." The restrictions in Eq. (2) cannot be expressed in such a way.

Assume that we observe multiple aggregate matchings. Let T be the number of such observations, and X_t denote the t-th aggregate matching that we observe. Then the sample analog of the expectation in Eq. (4) is

$$\frac{1}{T}\sum_t \mathbb{1}((ij),(kl) \text{ is anti-edge in } X_t) - Pr(d_{ilj} d_{lik} = 0, d_{jki} d_{kjl} = 0; \beta) = \frac{1}{T}\sum_t g_{ijkl}(X_t;\beta) \tag{5}$$

If the number of types of men and woman were equal ($K = L$), then there would be $\frac{K^2 \times (K-1)^2}{2}$ such inequalities, corresponding to each couple of pairs.

Note that the expectation $\mathbb{E}$ above is over both the utility shocks ε's, as well as over the "equilibrium selection" process (which we are agnostic about).

There is by now a large methodological literature on estimating confidence sets for parameters in partially identified moment inequality models that cover the identified set $\mathbb{B}_0$ with some prescribed probability. (An incomplete list includes Andrews, Berry, & Jia, 2004; Beresteanu & Molinari, 2008; Chernozhukov, Hong, & Tamer, 2007; Pakes, Porter, Ho, & Ishii, 2007; Romano & Shaikh, 2010.) While there are a variety of objective functions one could use, we use here the simple sum of squares objective:

$$\mathbb{B}_n = \text{argmin}_\beta Q_n(\beta) = \sum_{i,j,k,l} \left[\frac{1}{T} \sum_{t=1}^{T} g_{ijkl}(X_t; \beta) \right]_+^2$$

where $[x]_+ := \max\{x, 0\}$.

Data and Empirical Implementation

In the empirical implementation, we use data on new marriages, as recorded by the US Bureau of Vital Statistics.[1] We consider new marriages in the year 1988, and treat data from each state as a separate, independent matching. We aggregate the matchings into age categories, and create canonical matchings. For this application, we only include the age variable in our definition of agent types, because it is the only variable which we observe for all the matchings.[2] Table 1 has examples of aggregate matchings, and the corresponding canonical matchings, for several states. In these matching matrices, rows denote age categories for the husbands, and the columns denote the age categories for the wives.

These aggregate canonical matchings have many 1's, and hence many anti-edges. Moreover, the matchings in Table 1 contain more nonzero entries below the diagonal, which means that in a preponderance of marriages, the husband is older than the wife.

In our empirical exercise, the specification of utility is very simple, and it only involves the ages of the two partners to a match. Suppose that man m of age Age_m is matched to woman w of age Age_w. The following utility functions capture preferences over age differences, and partner's age.

$$U_{m,w} = \beta_1 |Age_m - Age_w|^- + \beta_2 |Age_m - Age_w|^+ + \varepsilon_{m,w}$$

$$U_{w,m} = \beta_3 |Age_m - Age_w|^- + \beta_4 |Age_m - Age_w|^+ + \varepsilon_{w,m}$$

where $\varepsilon_{m,w}$ and $\varepsilon_{w,m}$ are assumed to follow a standard normal distributions.

Table 1. Aggregate Matchings and the Corresponding Canonical Matchings.

	Age	Aggregate Matchings							Canonical Matchings						
	♂↓,♀→	12–20	21–25	26–30	31–35	36–40	41–50	51–94	12–20	21–25	26–30	31–35	36–40	41–50	51–94
	12–20	231	47	8	0	0	1	0	1	1	1	0	0	1	0
	21–25	329	798	156	32	11	7	0	1	1	1	1	1	1	0
	26–30	71	477	443	136	27	8	0	1	1	1	1	1	1	0
MI	31–35	11	148	249	196	83	21	0	1	1	1	1	1	1	0
	36–40	2	41	105	144	114	51	1	1	1	1	1	1	1	1
	41–50	0	15	42	118	121	162	25	0	1	1	1	1	1	1
	51–94	0	2	11	11	35	137	158	0	1	1	1	1	1	1
	12–20	8	1	0	0	0	0	0	1	1	0	0	0	0	0
	21–25	17	31	4	0	0	0	0	1	1	1	0	0	0	0
	26–30	2	21	22	7	1	0	0	1	1	1	1	1	0	0
NV	31–35	0	4	10	5	3	0	0	0	1	1	1	1	0	0
	36–40	0	3	8	2	2	2	0	0	1	1	1	1	1	0
	41–50	0	1	1	2	6	3	3	0	1	1	1	1	1	1
	51–94	0	0	0	0	0	5	3	0	0	0	0	0	1	1
	12–20	307	83	12	6	0	0	0	1	1	1	1	0	0	0
	21–25	453	1165	214	64	10	6	1	1	1	1	1	1	1	1
	26–30	113	698	703	190	51	17	0	1	1	1	1	1	1	0
PA	31–35	17	184	393	277	78	26	2	1	1	1	1	1	1	1
	36–40	9	73	152	191	148	84	5	1	1	1	1	1	1	1
	41–50	3	27	83	146	187	273	28	1	1	1	1	1	1	1
	51–94	1	7	12	38	48	182	268	1	1	1	1	1	1	1

In this specification, we assume that utility is a piecewise linear function of age, with the "kink" occurring when the age gap between husband and wife is zero. To interpret the preference parameters, note that β_1 (β_3) is the coefficient in the husband's (wife's) utility, attached to the age gap when the wife is older than the husband. Thus, a finding that $\beta_1(\beta_3)>0$ means that, when the wife older, men (women) prefer a larger age gap: that is, men prefer older women, and women prefer younger men. Similarly, a finding that $\beta_2(\beta_4)>0$, implies that then when the husband is older than the wife, men (women) prefer a larger age gap: here, because the husband is older, a larger age gap means that men prefer younger women, and women prefer older men.

Relaxing the Stability Constraints

Stability (rationalizability) places very strong demands on the data that can be observed, since we often observe many 1's, and hence many anti-edges, in aggregate canonical matchings (see Eqs. (2) and (3)). Accordingly, we propose a relaxation of the stability constraint that is particularly useful in applied empirical work.

Namely, we assume that potential blocking pairs may not necessarily form. If preferences are such that the pair (m, w) would block X, the block actually occurs only with probability less than 1. The reason for not blocking could be simply the failure of m and w to meet or communicate (as in the literature on search and matching).

Specifically, we allow for the possibility that an observed edge between pairs (i,j) and (k,l) may imply nothing about the preferences of the affected types i,j,k,l, simply because the couples (i,j) and (k,l) fail to meet. In particular, define

$$\delta_{ijkl} = Pr(\text{types } (i,j), (k,l) \text{ communicate}).$$

We then modify the stability inequalities (Eq. (2)) as

$$\begin{pmatrix} (i,j),(k,l) \text{ is anti-edge} \\ (i,j),(k,l) \text{ meet} \end{pmatrix} \Rightarrow \begin{cases} d_{ilj}d_{lik} = 0 \\ d_{jki}d_{kjl} = 0 \end{cases} \tag{6}$$

This leads to the modified moment inequality:

$$Pr((i,j),(k,l)\,\text{anti-edge}) \leq \frac{Pr(d_{ilj}d_{lik} = 0, d_{jki}d_{kjl} = 0; \beta)}{\delta_{ijkl}} \tag{7}$$

As $\delta_{ijkl} \to 1$, the identified set $\mathbb{B}_0$ shrinks to the empty set. Thus the observed aggregate matchings cannot be rationalized without a positive probability that potential blocking pairs do not form. On the other hand, as $\delta_{ijkl} \to 0$, the identified set converges to the whole parameter space: the right-hand side of the moment inequality becomes larger than 1.

Here, the events $((i,j),(k,l)$ is anti-edge) and $((i,j),(k,l)$ meet) are independent. The first event depends on preferences and process that produces a stable matching in the first place. On the other hand, we allow δ_{ijkl} to depend on the relative number of matched (i,j) and (k,l) couples. So we are making the assumption that the probability of communication is independent of preferences and the matching.[3] Specifically, letting γ denote a scaling parameter, we set

$$\delta_{ijkl} = \min\left\{2 \cdot \gamma \cdot \frac{X_{ij}}{N} \cdot \frac{X_{kl}}{N}, 1\right\}$$

where N is the number of observed men (women).

To interpret this, consider a given pair of couples $(i,j),(k,l)$. If this couple constitutes an anti-edge, and the stability conditions fails, then two potential blocking pairs can be formed: (i,l) and (k,j). The specification for δ_{ijkl} represents one story for when a blocking pair which is present in the agents' preferences, actually blocks. With X_{ij}/N (resp. X_{kl}/N) being the relative populations of (i,j) (resp. (k,j)) couples, then δ_{ijkl} is set proportional to the frequency of potential blocking pairs $(j,l),(k,j)$ in the market; it is scaled by γ (and capped from above by 1). We scale by γ to allow the probability that a blocking pair forms to be smaller or larger than this frequency. A larger γ implies that blocking pairs form more frequently, so that there is less slackness in the stability restrictions.

More broadly, the δs weight the anti-edges in the sample moment inequalities. Intuitively, an anti-edge $\{(i,j),(l,k)\}$ should receive a higher weight when it involves many potential blocking pairs than when it only involves a few. Our specification achieves this idea, as it makes the probability of forming a blocking pair dependent on the number of agents involved.

Identified Sets

Table 2 summarizes the identified set for several levels of γ, and presents the highest and lowest values that each parameter attains in the identified set. The unrestricted interval in which we searched for each parameter was $[-2, 2]$. So we see that, for a value of $\gamma = 25$, the identified set contains the

Table 2. Unconditional Bounds of β.

	β_1		β_2		β_3		β_4	
γ	Min.	Max.	Min.	Max.	Min.	Max.	Min.	Max.
25	−2.00	2.00	−2.00	2.00	−2.00	2.00	−2.00	2.00
28	−2.00	1.60	−2.00	2.00	−2.00	1.60	−2.00	2.00
29	−2.00	0.40	−2.00	1.80	−2.00	0.40	−2.00	1.80
30	−2.00	−0.80	−2.00	0.60	−2.00	−0.85	−2.00	0.60

full parameter space, implying that the data impose no restrictions on parameters. At the other extreme, when $\gamma \geq 31$, the identified set becomes empty, implying that the observed matchings can no longer be rationalized.

For $\gamma = 30$, we see that β_1 and β_3 take negative values, while the values of β_2 and β_4 tend to take negative values but also contain small positive values. This suggests that husbands' utilities are decreasing in the wife's age when the wife is older, but when the wife is younger, his utility is less responsive to the wife's age. A similar picture emerges for wives' utilities, which are increasing in the husband's age when the husband is younger, but when the husband is older, the wife's utility is less responsive to her husband's age. All in all, our findings here support the conclusion that husbands' and wives' utilities are more responsive to the partner's age when the wife is older than the husband.

A richer picture emerges when we consider the joint values of parameters in the identified set. Fig. 2 illustrates the contour sets (at different values of γ) for the husband's preference parameters (β_1, β_2), holding the wife's preference parameters (β_3, β_4) fixed.

To simplify the interpretation of these findings in light of the stability restrictions, we recall two features of our aggregate matchings (as seen in Table 1): first, there are more anti-edges below the diagonal, where $Age_m > Age_w$. Second, there are more "downward-sloping" anti-edges than "upward-sloping" ones. That is, there are more anti-edges $\{(i,j), (k,l)\}$ with $k > i, l > j$ than with $i > k, l > j$, as illustrated here.

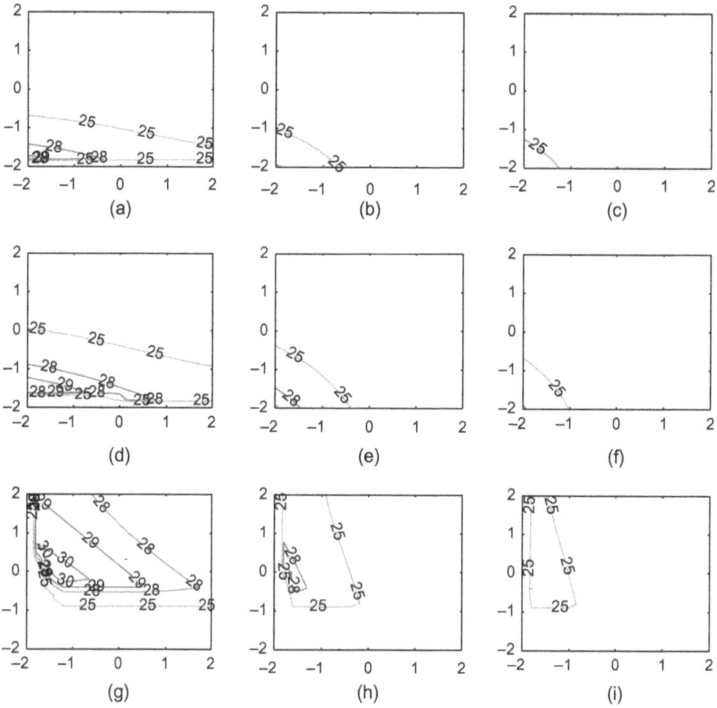

Fig. 2. Identified sets of (β_1,β_2) given (β_3,β_4) and γ. (a) $\beta_3=-2$ and $\beta_4=1$, (b) $\beta_3=0$ and $\beta_4=1$, (c) $\beta_3=1$ and $\beta_4=1$ (d) $\beta_3=-2$ and $\beta_4=0$, (e) $\beta_3=0$ and $\beta_4=0$, (f) $\beta_3=1$ and $\beta_4=0$ (g) $\beta_3=-2$ and $\beta_4=-2$, (h) $\beta_3=0$ and $\beta_4=-2$, (i) $\beta_3=1$ and $\beta_4=-2$.

Because of these features, we initially focus on the parameters (β_2,β_4), which describe preferences when the husband is older than the wife.

The graphs in the bottom row of Fig. 2 correspond to $\beta_4=-2$, corresponding to the case that the wife prefers a younger husband: with a downward-sloping anti-edge, this implies that it is likely that $d_{jik}=1$ and $d_{lki}=0$. In turn, using the stability restrictions (Eq. (2)), this implies that $d_{ilj}=0$ (that husbands prefer younger wives), but places no restrictions on the sign of d_{kjl}. For this reason, we find that in these graphs, β_2 tends to take positive values at the highest contour levels so that, when husbands are older than their wives, they prefer the age gap to be as large as possible.

By a similar reasoning, β_2 takes negative values when $\beta_4=1$. When wives prefer older husbands (which is the case when $\beta_4=1$), then with a downward-sloping anti-edge, this implies that $d_{jik}=0$ and $d_{lki}=1$. Consequently, stability considerations would restrict the husband's preferences so that $d_{kjl}=0$ (and husbands prefer older wives), leading to $\beta_2<0$.

On the other hand, because there are more downward-sloping anti-edges, when the wife is older than the husband, restriction (Eq. (2)) implies that one of two cases – either the husband prefers a younger wife, or the wife prefers an older husband – must be true. In Fig. 2, as β_3 increases from -2 to 1 (from the left to the right column), the wife's utilities becomes more favorable toward a younger husband. As a result, more restrictions are imposed to the husbands' utilities, which yields a tighter negative range for β_1 in the identified sets.

Overall, we see that $\beta_1<0$ and $\beta_3<0$, implying that as long as the wife is older than the husband, both prefer a smaller age gap. On the other hand, β_2 and β_4 are negatively correlated: as β_4 increases, β_2 decreases. This suggests that, when the husband is older than the wife, one side prefers a smaller gap but the other side is less responsive on the age gap.

Confidence Sets

Fig. 3 summarizes the 95% confidence sets with $\gamma=28$ (shaded lightly) and 30 (shaded darkly). In computing these confidence sets, we use the subsampling algorithm proposed by Chernozhukov et al. (2007). Comparing the confidence sets in Fig. 3 to their counterpart identified sets in Fig. 2, the confidence sets are slightly larger than the identified sets. This is not surprising, given the modest number of matchings (fifty-one: one for each state) which we used in the empirical exercise.

Nevertheless, the main findings from Fig. 1 are still apparent; $\beta_1<0$ across a range of values for (β_3,β_4), and $\beta_2<0$ (resp. > 0) when $\beta_4>0$ (resp. < 0). These somewhat "antipodal" preferences between a husband and wife are a distinctive consequence of the stability conditions of an NTU matching model.

Transferable Utility Model

For the TU model, we define the surplus obtained by matching of type-i man with type-j woman as

$$\alpha_{ij}=U_{ij}+U_{ji}=(\beta_1+\beta_3)|Age_m-Age_w|^- +(\beta_2+\beta_4)|Age_m-Age_w|^+ +\varepsilon_{ij}+\varepsilon_{ji}$$

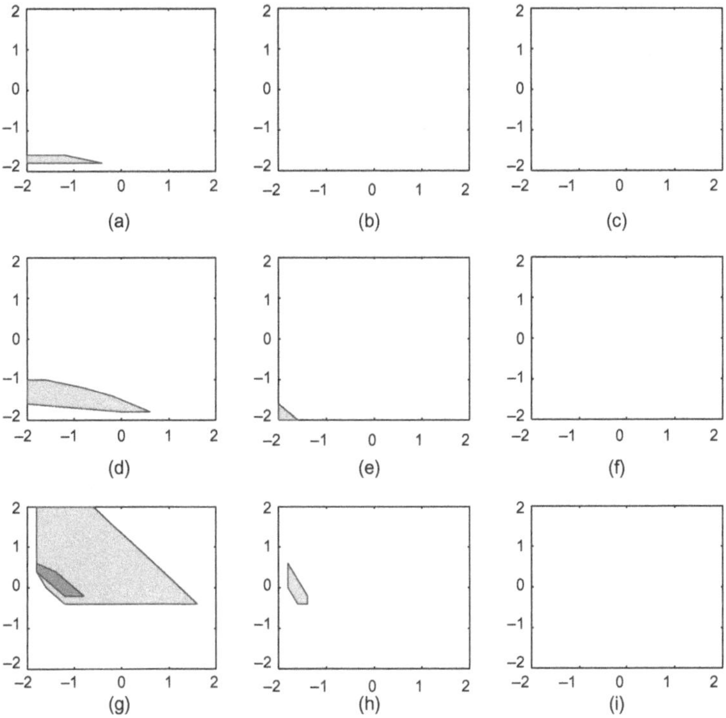

Fig. 3. 95% Confidence sets of (β_1, β_2) given (β_3, β_4) and $\gamma = 32$ (shaded lightly) and 35 (shaded darkly). (a) $\beta_3 = -2$ and $\beta_4 = 1$, (b) $\beta_3 = 0$ and $\beta_4 = 1$, (c) $\beta_3 = 1$ and $\beta_4 = 1$ (d) $\beta_3 = -2$ and $\beta_4 = 0$, (e) $\beta_3 = 0$ and $\beta_4 = 0$, (f) $\beta_3 = 1$ and $\beta_4 = 0$, (g) $\beta_3 = -2$ and $\beta_4 = -2$, (h) $\beta_3 = 0$ and $\beta_4 = -2$, (i) $\beta_3 = 1$ and $\beta_4 = -2$.

We work from the *pairwise stability* condition: for every anti-edge $\{(i,j),(k,l)\}$, we have

$$(i,j),(k,l)\ \text{anti-edge} \Rightarrow \alpha_{ij} + \alpha_{kl} \geq \alpha_{il} + \alpha_{kj}$$

This leads to the moment inequality:

$$Pr((i,j),(k,l)\ \text{ anti-edge}) \leq Pr(\alpha_{ij} + \alpha_{kl} \geq \alpha_{il} + \alpha_{kj}; \beta)$$

This condition derived via optimality. Given an aggregate matching X, suppose $\{(i,j),(k,l)\}$ is an anti-edge (i.e., $X_{ij} > 0$ and $X_{kl} > 0$). Consider an alternative aggregate matching X' where a pair of $\{(i,j),(k,l)\}$ couples are swapped:

$$X'_{ij} = X_{ij} - 1, \quad X'_{kl} = X_{kl} - 1$$
$$X'_{il} = X_{il} + 1, \quad X'_{kj} = X_{kj} + 1$$

By optimality of X, this swapping must lower surplus:

$$\begin{aligned}&\alpha_{ij}X_{ij} + \alpha_{il}X_{il} + \alpha_{kj}X_{kj} + \alpha_{kl}X_{kl} \geq \alpha_{ij}X'_{ij} + \alpha_{il}X'_{il} + \alpha_{kj}X'_{kj} + \alpha_{kl}X'_{kl}\\&= \alpha_{ij}(X_{ij} - 1) + \alpha_{il}(X_{il} + 1) + \alpha_{kj}(X_{kj} + 1) + \alpha_{kl}(X_{kl} - 1) \Rightarrow \alpha_{ij} + \alpha_{kl} \geq \alpha_{il} + \alpha_{kj}\end{aligned}$$

For the same reason as in the NTU model, we relax the stability constraints by introducing communication probabilities:

$$Pr((i,j),(k,l) \text{ anti-edge}) \leq \frac{Pr(\alpha_{ij} + \alpha_{kl} \geq \alpha_{il} + \alpha_{kj}; \beta)}{\delta_{ijkl}}$$

The identified set for the TU model takes the form $K_1 \leq \sum_{i=1}^{4} \beta_i \leq K_2$. First, if all (i,j), (i,l), (k,j), and (k,l) are "below the diagonal" (i.e., $Age_m > Age_w$):

$$\begin{aligned}\alpha_{ij} + \alpha_{kl} &= (\beta_2 + \beta_4)|Age_i - Age_j|^+ + (\beta_2 + \beta_4)|Age_k - Age_l|^+ + \Sigma_{ij,kl}\\&\quad (\text{since } Age_i > Age_j \text{ and } Age_k > Age_l) + \Sigma_{ij,kl}\\&= (\beta_2 + \beta_4)(Age_i - Age_j) + (\beta_2 + \beta_4)(Age_k - Age_l) + \Sigma_{ij,kl}\\&= (\beta_2 + \beta_4)(Age_i - Age_l) + (\beta_2 + \beta_4)(Age_k - Age_j) + \Sigma_{ij,kl}\\&= \alpha_{il} + \alpha_{kj} - \Sigma_{il,kj} + \Sigma_{ij,kl}\\&\quad (\text{since } Age_i > Age_l \text{ and } Age_k > Age_j)\end{aligned}$$

where we define the shorthand $\Sigma_{ij,kl} = \varepsilon_{ij} + \varepsilon_{ji} + \varepsilon_{kl} + \varepsilon_{lk}$. Since the event $\alpha_{ij} + \alpha_{kl} \geq \alpha_{il} + \alpha_{kj}$ is equivalent to $\Sigma_{ij,kl} \geq \Sigma_{il,kj}$, and involves no model parameters, stability (rationalizability) imposes no restriction on the data in the "below diagonal" case. Similarly, stability imposes no restriction on the observed matchings for (i,j), (k,l), (i,l), and (k,j) which are all above diagonal (i.e., $Age_m < Age_w$).

Therefore, identification is determined by moment conditions corresponding to men i and k, and women j and l, where we have a pair below diagonal, and a pair above diagonal. Suppose, for example, (i,j), (k,l), and

(k,j) are below diagonal, but (i,l) is above diagonal (i.e., $Age_k > Age_l > Age_i > Age_j$):

$$\begin{aligned}\alpha_{ij} + \alpha_{kl} &= (\beta_2 + \beta_4)|Age_i - Age_j|^+ + (\beta_2 + \beta_4)|Age_k - Age_l|^+ + \Sigma_{ij,kl} \\ &\quad \text{(since } Age_i > Age_j \text{ and } Age_k > Age_l\text{)} \\ &= (\beta_2 + \beta_4)(Age_i - Age_j) + (\beta_2 + \beta_4)(Age_k - Age_l) + \Sigma_{ij,kl}\end{aligned}$$

$$\begin{aligned}\alpha_{il} + \alpha_{kj} &= (\beta_1 + \beta_3)|Age_i - Age_l|^- + (\beta_2 + \beta_4)|Age_k - Age_j|^+ + \Sigma_{il,kj} \\ &\quad \text{(since } Age_i < Age_l \text{ and } Age_k > Age_j\text{)} \\ &= (\beta_1 + \beta_3)(Age_l - Age_i) + (\beta_2 + \beta_4)(Age_k - Age_j) + \Sigma_{il,kj}\end{aligned}$$

Therefore,

$$(\alpha_{ij} + \alpha_{kl}) - (\alpha_{il} + \alpha_{kj}) = (\beta_1 + \beta_2 + \beta_3 + \beta_4)(Age_i - Age_j) + \Sigma_{ij,kl} - \Sigma_{il,kj}$$

For all other cases, we have the same result: we can identify β up to $\sum_{i=1}^{4} \beta_i$.

The identified set is presented in Fig. 4, which is consistent with both antipodal and non-antipodal preferences.

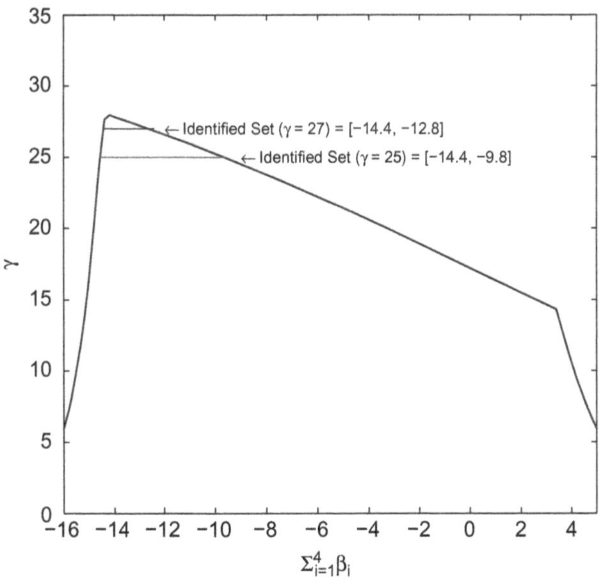

Fig. 4. Identified sets of $\sum_{i=1}^{4} \beta_i$ given γ.

CONCLUSIONS

In this article, we propose a methodology for estimating preference parameters in matching models. Our estimator applies to repeated observations of matchings among a fixed group of individuals. For both the transferable utility (TU) and nontransferable utility (NTU) models, we derive moment inequalities based on the restrictions which match stability places on the preferences of the agents.

NOTES

1. http://www.nber.org/data/marrdivo.html
2. Because stability is defined at the level of the matching, we did not want to exclude any marriage from the data due to missing variables.
3. We could relax this assumption by making δ dependent on the same covariates that enter into the agents preferences.
4. See, for instance, Choo and Siow (2006) and Galichon and Salanie (2010) for the TU model. For NTU model, Uetake and Watanabe (2012) take this utility specification with an assumption that the model generates unique stable matchings.
5. Galichon and Salanie (2010) also discuss this point (cf. p. 11).
6. These individual-level inequalities express the same notion of stability as the aggregate stability conditions (Eq. (2)), but can be written in this more succinct way here due to the summing-up requirements at the individual-level (i.e., that $\sum_j X_{ij} = 1$ for all i). These summing-up conditions do not hold for canonical aggregate matchings.

REFERENCES

Andrews, D., Berry, S., & Jia, P. (2004). *Confidence regions for parameters in discrete games with multiple equilibria, with an application to discount chain store location*. Mimeo, Yale University.

Beresteanu, A., Molchanov, I., & Molinari, F. (2011). Sharp identification regions in models with convex moment predictions. *Econometrica*, *79*(6), 1785–1821.

Beresteanu, A., & Molinari, F. (2008). Asymptotic properties for a class of partially identified models. *Econometrica*, *76*, 763–814.

Chernozhukov, V., Hong, H., & Tamer, E. (2007). Estimation and confidence regions for parameter sets in econometric models. *Econometrica*, *75*, 1234–1275.

Choo, E., & Siow, A. (2006). Who marries whom and why. *Journal of Political Economy*, *114*(1), 175–201.

Ciliberto, F., & Tamer, E. (2009). Market structure and multiple equilibria in airline markets. *Econometrica*, *77*, 1791–1828.

Dagsvik, J. K. (2000). Aggregation in matching markets. *International Economic Review*, *41*(1), 27–57.

Echenique, F., Lee, S., Shum, M., & Yenmez, M. (2013). The revealed preference theory of stable and extremal stable matchings. *Econometrica*, *81*, 153–171.

Fox, J. (2010). Identification in matching games. *Quantitative Economics*, *1*(2), 203–254.

Galichon, A., & Salanie, B. (2010). *Matching with trade-offs: Revealed preferences over competing characteristics*. Mimeo, Sciences Po.

Pakes, A., Porter, J., Ho, K., & Ishii, J. (2007). *Moment inequalities and their application*: Manuscript, Harvard University.

Romano, J., & Shaikh, A. (2010). Inference for the identified set in partially identified econometric models. *Econometrica*, *78*, 169–211.

Shapley, L., & Shubik, M. (1971). The assignment game I: The core. *International Journal of Game Theory*, *1*(1), 111–130.

Uetake, K., & Watanabe, Y. (2012). A note on estimation of two-sided matching models. *Economics Letters*.

APPENDIX A: INDIVIDUAL-LEVEL HETEROGENEITY

In our theoretical results, we have assumed that agents' preferences depend only on observables. This allowed us to obtain rather stark implications of stability for aggregate matchings. Maybe the implications are too stark, in the sense that most of the observed matchings in the data would not be rationalizable. If we add unobserved heterogeneity, then the theoretical implications become weaker and "probabilistic," but the main thrust of these implications are preserved.

So, in a matching model that captures how preferences depend on observables, but has additional noise, our conditions for rationalizability hold in a probabilistic sense. The econometric approach proposed here involves just such a probabilistic version of the model. Here we compare our approach to other papers in the literature.

One possible starting point is to assume that individuals of the same type have the same preferences up to individual-specific i.i.d. shocks, which is the assumption in most of the empirical literature.[4]

The i.i.d. shocks are a very limited form of unobserved heterogeneity: it allows two (say) type i men to differ in the utility they would obtain from a matching with a (say) type j woman. However, each of these men still remains indifferent between all type j women.[5] Thus two agents of the same type are still perceived as identical by the opposite side of the market.

The shocks ensure that each agent-type has a nonzero probability of being matched with any agent-type on the opposite side of the market; this reconciles the theory with the observed data. In this respect, the role of the preference shocks in these articles plays the same role as the "communication probability" δ_{ijkl} in our empirical analysis. The "communication probability" captures unobserved heterogeneity in the ability of agents to match, perhaps as a result of noisy search frictions. It serves the same purpose as i.i.d. preference shocks. The shocks, on the other hand, lead to trivial inequalities at the aggregate level. We state this result here, and prove it in the Appendix B.

Claim 1. In the NTU model, preference shocks at the individual-level lead to trivially-satisfied stability restrictions at the aggregate level.

Because of this result, then, i.i.d. individual-level preference shocks seem inappropriate in the aggregate NTU setting of our empirical work. Furthermore, the communication probability δ_{ijkl} plays a similar role in our empirical work as do preference shocks in others' work: namely, to better reconcile the theory to the data by enlarging the the sets of marriages which one could observe in a stable matching.

The sample moment inequality (Eq. (5)), with the modification in Eq. (6), becomes

$$\frac{1}{T}\sum_t g_{ijkl}(X_t;\beta)$$
$$=\left(\frac{1}{T}\sum_t \mathbb{1}((i,j),(k,l)\text{ anti-edge in }X_t)\right) * \delta_{ijkl} - Pr(d_{ilj}d_{lik}=0, d_{jki}d_{kjl}=0;\beta)$$

for all combinations of pairs (i,j) and (k,l).

APPENDIX B: DETAILS ON CLAIM 1

We consider a market where every woman (man) is acceptable to all men (women). The individual-level stability inequalities, for all pairs (i,j), are[6]

$$\sum_{k:k>ij} X_{ik} + \sum_{k:k>ji} X_{kj} + X_{ij} \geq 1.$$

Letting $d_{ikj} = \mathbb{1}\{k >_i j\}$, this can be written as

$$\sum_k X_{ik}d_{ikj} + \sum_k X_{kj}d_{jki} + X_{ij} \geq 1. \tag{8}$$

Here (i,j,k) all denote individual agents, not types. These inequalities cannot be taken directly to the data, because we do not observe the individual-level matching, but rather an aggregate-level matching.

One starting point is to treat both the X's and the d's as random variables, where the randomness derives from both the individual-level preference shocks, as well as from the procedure whereby the observed matching is selected among the set of stable matchings. We partition the men and women into types $t_1^M, \ldots t_L^M$ and $t_1^W, \ldots t_L^W$. Since individual-level preference shocks are i.i.d., we obtain that

$$Pr(d_{ijk}=1) = Pr(d_{i'j'k'}=1): \quad \forall (i,i') \in t_i^M,\ (j,j') \in t_j^M,\ (k,k') \in t_k^M. \tag{9}$$

That is, the distribution of d_{ijk} is identical for all individuals of the same type. Hence, below we will use the notation $Pr(d_{ijk}=1)$ and $Pr(t_j^W >_{t_i^M} t_k^W)$ interchangeably.

Given these assumptions, we can derive an aggregate version of Eq. (8). First, we take expectations:

$$\begin{aligned}&\textstyle\sum_k E[X_{ik}d_{ikj}] + \sum_k E[X_{kj}d_{jki}] + E[X_{ij}] \geq 1\\ &\quad\Leftrightarrow \textstyle\sum_k \overline{X}_{ikj} \cdot Pr(d_{ikj}=1) + \sum_k \overline{X}_{kji} \cdot Pr(d_{jki}=1) + E[X_{ij}] \geq 1\end{aligned}$$

with $\overline{X}_{ikj} \equiv E[X_{ik}d_{ikj} | d_{ikj}=1]$.

Next, we aggregate up to the type-level:

$$\textstyle\sum_l \left\{Pr\{t_l^W >_{t_i^M} t_j^W\}\overline{X}_{t_i^M t_l^W t_j^W}\right\} + \sum_l \left\{Pr\{t_l^M >_{t_j^W} t_i^M\}\overline{X}_{t_l^M t_j^W t_i^M}\right\} \geq \left|t_j^W\right|\left|t_i^M\right|(1-E[X_{ij}]). \tag{10}$$

Here $\overline{X}_{t_i^M t_l^W t_j^W} \equiv \sum_{k\in t_l^W}\sum_{i\in t_i^M}\sum_{j\in t_j^W}\overline{X}_{ikj}$ and $\overline{X}_{t_l^M t_j^W t_i^M} \equiv \sum_{j\in t_i^M}\sum_{j\in t_j^W}\sum_{i\in t_i^M}\overline{X}_{kji}$. In the above inequality, only the $\left|t_j^W\right|$ and $\left|t_i^M\right|$ are observed, but nothing else. This is of little use empirically.

On the other hand, because $d_{ijk} \geq 0$, for all (i,j,k), we also have

$$\begin{aligned}&E(X_{ik}d_{ikj}) = E(X_{ik}d_{ikj}|d_{ikj}=1)Pr(d_{ikj}=1) \leq E(X_{ik})\\ &\quad\Rightarrow \sum_{k\in t_l^W} E(X_{ik}d_{ikj}|d_{ikj}=1)Pr(d_{ikj}=1)\\ &\quad\leq \sum_{k\in t_l^W} E(X_{ik}) \Leftrightarrow Pr(t_l^W >_i j)\sum_{k\in t_l^W}\overline{X}_{ikj}\\ &\quad\leq \sum_{k\in t_l^W} E(X_{ik}) \Rightarrow \sum_{i\in t_i^M} Pr(t_l^W >_i j)\sum_{k\in t_l^W}\overline{X}_{ikj}\\ &\quad\leq \sum_{i\in t_i^M}\sum_{k\in t_l^W} E(X_{ik}) \Leftrightarrow Pr(t_l^W >_{t_i^M} j)\sum_{i\in t_i^M}\sum_{k\in t_l^W}\overline{X}_{ikj} \leq X_{t_i^M t_l^W}\\ &\quad\Rightarrow Pr(t_l^W >_{t_i^M} t_j^W)\sum_{j\in t_j^W}\sum_{i\in t_i^M}\sum_{k\in t_l^W}\tilde{X}_{ikj} \leq \left|t_j^W\right| X_{t_i^M t_l^W}\\ &\quad\Leftrightarrow Pr(t_l^W >_{t_i^M} t_j^W)\overline{X}_{t_i^M t_l^W t_j^M} \leq \left|t_j^W\right| X_{t_i^M t_l^W}\end{aligned} \tag{11}$$

Combining inequalities (Eqs. (10) and (11)), we get

$$\sum_l \left|t_j^W\right| X_{t_i^M t_l^W} + \sum_l \left|t_i^M\right| X_{t_l^M t_j^W} \geq \left|t_j^W\right| \left|t_i^M\right| (1 - E[X_{i,j}])$$

By the equalities $\sum_l X_{t_i^M t_l^W} = \left|t_i^M\right|$ and $\sum_l X_{t_l^M t_j^W} = \left|t_j^W\right|$, the above reduces to

$$2\left|t_i^M\right| \left|t_j^W\right| \geq \left|t_i^M\right| \left|t_j^W\right| (1 - E[X_{ij}]) \Rightarrow 2 \geq (1 - E[X_{ij}])$$

which is trivially satisfied.

IDENTIFICATION OF MATCHING COMPLEMENTARITIES: A GEOMETRIC VIEWPOINT

Alfred Galichon

ABSTRACT

We provide a geometric formulation of the problem of identification of the matching surplus function and we show how the estimation problem can be solved by the introduction of a generalized entropy function over the set of matchings.

Keywords: Matching; marriage; assignment

JEL classifications: C78; D61; C13

SETTING

We consider the Becker (1973) model of the marriage market as a bipartite matching game with transferable utility. Let $\mathcal{X}$ and $\mathcal{Y}$ be finite sets of "types" of men and women, where $|\mathcal{X}| = d_x$ and $|\mathcal{Y}| = d_y$. Assume that the number of men and women is equal, and that the number of men of type

Structural Econometric Models
Advances in Econometrics, Volume 31, 141–151

ISSN: 0731-9053/doi:10.1108/S0731-9053(2013)0000032005

x (resp. of women of type y) is p_x (resp. q_y). We normalize the total number of men and women to one, that is, we set $\sum_{x \in \mathcal{X}} p_x = 1$ and $\sum_{y \in \mathcal{Y}} q_y = 1$. Let $\Phi_{xy} \geq 0$ be the joint surplus (to be split endogenously across the pair) from matching a man of type x and a woman of type y. For the clarity of exposition we do not allow for unmatched individuals.

Recall that under transferable utility, in the Shapley and Shubik (1972) model, the stable matching also maximizes the total surplus

$$\sum_{x,y} \mu_{xy} \Phi_{xy}$$

over $\mu \in \mathcal{M}$ the set of *matchings*, defined by

$$\mathcal{M} = \left\{ \mu : \mu_{xy} \geq 0, \ \sum_y \mu_{xy} = p_x, \ \sum_x \mu_{xy} = q_y \right\}$$

where μ_{xy} is interpreted as the number of (x, y) pairs, which is allowed to be a fractional number.

Note that the equations defining $\mathcal{M}$ have $d_x + d_y - 1$ degrees of redundancy, hence the dimension of $\mathcal{M}$ is $d_x d_y - d_x - d_y + 1 = (d_x - 1)(d_y - 1)$.

Further, if μ and $\tilde{\mu}$ are in $\mathcal{M}$, then for $t \in [0, 1]$, $(t\mu + (1 - t)\tilde{\mu})$ is also in $\mathcal{M}$. Finally, $\mathcal{M}$ is obviously bounded in $\mathbb{R}^{d_x d_y}$. Hence:

Claim 1. The set of matchings $\mathcal{M}$ is a compact convex set of $\mathbb{R}^{d_x d_y}$.

IDENTIFICATION

One observes a matching $\hat{\mu} \in \mathcal{M}$ and one wonders whether $\hat{\mu}$ is rationalizable, that is, whether there exists some surplus function Φ such that $\hat{\mu}$ is the optimal matching in the problem with surplus Φ, that is

$$\hat{\mu} \in \arg\max_{\mu \in \mathcal{M}} \sum_{x,y} \mu_{xy} \Phi_{xy}$$

As it is classically the case in revealed preference analysis, some restrictions on Φ are needed in order to have a meaningful definition. Indeed, the null surplus function $\Phi_{xy} = 0$ always trivially rationalizes any matching; similarly, $\Phi_{xy} = f_x + g_y$ which also rationalizes any μ as the value of the total surplus evaluated at μ is $\sum_x p_x f_x + \sum_y q_y g_y$ irrespective of $\mu \in \mathcal{M}$. Hence in order to have some empirical bite, we need to impose

$$\arg\max_{\mu \in \mathcal{M}} \sum_{x,y} \mu_{xy} \hat{\Phi}_{xy} \neq \mathcal{M}$$

Let **S** be the set of Φ such that Φ_{xy} does not coincides with $f_x + g_y$ for some vectors (f_x) and (g_y). We shall thus seek Φ in **S**. The following assertion characterizes Φ in dimension two.

Claim 2. Assume $d_x = d_y = 2$. Then **S** is the set of (Φ_{xy}) such that $\Phi_{11} + \Phi_{22} \neq \Phi_{12} + \Phi_{21}$.

The previous considerations lead to the following definition:

Definition 1. $\hat{\mu} \in \mathcal{M}$ is rationalizable if there is $\hat{\Phi} \in \mathbf{S}$ such that

$$\hat{\mu} \in \arg\max_{\mu \in \mathcal{M}} \sum_{x,y} \mu_{xy} \hat{\Phi}_{xy} \tag{1}$$

Introducing $\mathcal{W}_0$ the *indirect surplus function*, defined as

$$\mathcal{W}_0(\Phi) = \max_{\mu \in \mathcal{M}} \langle \mu, \Phi \rangle \tag{2}$$

where the product $\langle \mu, \Phi \rangle$ is defined as

$$\langle \mu, \Phi \rangle = \sum_{xy} \mu_{xy} \Phi_{xy} \tag{3}$$

condition (Eq. (1)) is equivalent, by the Envelope theorem, to

$$\hat{\mu} \in \partial \mathcal{W}_0(\hat{\Phi})$$

where $\partial \mathcal{W}_0(\Phi)$ denotes the *subgradient* of $\mathcal{W}_0$ at Φ. See the appendix for some basic results on convex analysis. In the terminology of convex analysis, $\mathcal{W}_0$ is the *support function* of set $\mathcal{M}$, a geometric property that we shall develop in the next paragraph.

The following remark is obvious.

Claim 3. $\mathcal{W}_0$ is positive homogenous of degree one, hence for $t > 0$, one has

$$\mathcal{W}_0(t\Phi) = t\mathcal{W}_0(\Phi) \tag{4}$$

$$\partial \mathcal{W}_0(t\Phi) = \partial \mathcal{W}_0(\Phi) \tag{5}$$

GEOMETRY

The following result provides the geometric interpretation of rationalizability. Formula (1) means that for $\hat{\mu}$ to be rationalizable, it needs to maximize a linear functional over the compact convex set $\mathcal{M}$. As it is well known, a necessary and sufficient for this to hold is that $\hat{\mu}$ should belong to the boundary of $\mathcal{M}$.

Theorem 1. The following three conditions are equivalent:

(i) $\hat{\mu}$ is rationalizable,
(ii) $\hat{\mu}$ lies on $\overline{\mathcal{M}}\backslash\mathcal{M}^{int}$, the boundary of $\mathcal{M}$,
(iii) There is $\hat{\Phi} \in \mathbf{S}$ such that

$$\hat{\mu} \in \partial\mathcal{W}_0(\hat{\Phi}) \tag{6}$$

This theorem is illustrated in Fig. 1. While the equivalence between part (ii), of geometric kind and part (iii), of analytic nature follows from standard convex analysis, the insight of this result is to connect this to the economic notion of rationalizability (i), of revealed preference flavor. This result provides a geometric understanding of revealed preference analysis in matching models with transferable utility. See Echenique, Lee, Yenmez, and Shum (2012).

Geometrically, this means that the matchings that are rationalizable lie on the boundary of $\mathcal{M}$. We give a very simple example of a $\hat{\mu}$ which is rationalizable.

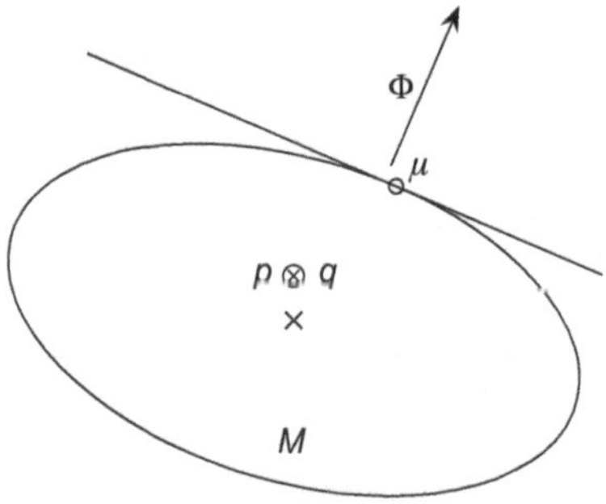

Fig. 1. Geometric view of rationalizability. In order for matching μ to be rationalized by surplus function Φ, μ need to lie on the geometric frontier of $\mathcal{M}$.

Example 1. Assume $d_x = d_y = 2$ and consider matrix

$$\hat{\mu} = \begin{pmatrix} 1 & 0 \\ 0 & 1 \end{pmatrix}$$

then any $\hat{\Phi}$ such that $\hat{\Phi}_{11} + \hat{\Phi}_{22} > \hat{\Phi}_{12} + \hat{\Phi}_{21}$ rationalizes $\hat{\mu}$.

We now give a very simple example of a $\hat{\mu}$ which *not* is rationalizable, that is, where $\hat{\mu}$ is in the strict interior of $\mathcal{M}$.

Example 2. *Assume $d_x = d_y = 2$ and consider matrix*

$$\hat{\mu} = \begin{pmatrix} 0.7 & 0.3 \\ 0.3 & 0.7 \end{pmatrix}$$

This matrix is equal to $0.7\begin{pmatrix} 1 & 0 \\ 0 & 1 \end{pmatrix} + 0.3\begin{pmatrix} 0 & 1 \\ 1 & 0 \end{pmatrix}$. *Hence for a production function Φ, we get*

$$\sum_{xy} \hat{\mu}_{xy} \Phi_{xy} = 0.7(\Phi_{11} + \Phi_{22}) + 0.3(\Phi_{12} + \Phi_{21})$$

Hence it cannot be rationalized by a production function Φ unless $\Phi_{11} + \Phi_{22} = \Phi_{12} + \Phi_{21}$. But in that case, set $a_1 = \Phi_{11}$, $b_1 = 0$, $a_2 = \Phi_{21}$, and $b_2 = \Phi_{12} - \Phi_{11}$, thus $\Phi_{ij} = a_i + b_j$ – which contradicts $\Phi \in \mathbf{S}$. Therefore $\hat{\mu}$ cannot be rationalized.

Example 3. *As another example, consider $p \otimes q$ defined by $(p \otimes q)_{xy} = p_x q_y$. Clearly, $p \otimes q \in \mathcal{M}$; intuitively this matching corresponds to matching randomly men and women, so that the characteristics of the partner are independent. This matching cannot be rationalized as it lies in the strict interior of $\mathcal{M}$. Indeed, $p \otimes q$ is the barycenter of the full set $\mathcal{M}$.*

ENTROPY

In practice, it is almost never the case that a matching $\hat{\mu}$ observed in the population is rationalizable. This is understandable using the geometric interpretation provided above: the locus of matchings that are rationalizable being the frontier of a convex set, it is "small" with respect to the set of matchings that are not rationalizable, which is the strict interior of this same convex set.

Mathematically speaking, we are looking for a solution $\Phi \in \mathbf{S}$ satisfying

$$\hat{\mu} \in \partial \mathcal{W}_0(\Phi) \tag{7}$$

If $\mathcal{W}_0$ was "well behaved," more precisely if $\mathcal{W}_0$ was strictly convex and continuously differentiable, then the gradient $\nabla\mathcal{W}_0$ would exist and be invertible with inverse $\nabla\mathcal{W}_0^*$, where $\mathcal{W}_0^*$ is the convex conjugate of $\mathcal{W}_0$. Then relation (Eq. (7)) would imply $\Phi = \nabla\mathcal{W}_0^*(\hat{\mu})$. But $\mathcal{W}_0$ is not strictly convex, so this approach does not work, and in fact relation (Eq. (7)) has no solution. Geometrically, it is quite clear why. As remarked above, the image of $\partial\mathcal{W}_0$ is included in the frontier of $\mathcal{M}$, hence if $\hat{\mu}$ does not lie on the geometric frontier of $\mathcal{M}$, then relation (Eq. (7)) cannot possibly have a solution.

In order to be able to estimate Φ based on the observation of $\hat{\mu}$, most of the literature following the seminal paper of Choo and Siow (2006) introduce heterogeneities in matching surpluses. Without trying to be exhaustive, let us mention Fox (2010, 2011), Galichon and Salanié (2010, 2012), Decker, Lieb, McCann, and Stephens (2012), and Chiappori, Salanié, and Weiss (2012). As argued in Galichon and Salanié (2012), this consists in essence in introducing a *generalized entropy function* $\mathcal{I}(\mu)$ which is strictly convex, and which is such that

$$\mathcal{I}(\mu) = +\infty \text{ if } \mu \notin \mathcal{M}$$

such that $\mathcal{I}$ is differentiable on $\mathcal{M}^{int}$ the interior of $\mathcal{M}$, with, for all $\mu \in \mathcal{M}^{int}$,

$$\nabla\mathcal{I}(\mu) \in \mathbf{S}$$

and such $\hat{\Phi}$ is identified by

$$\hat{\Phi} = \nabla\mathcal{I}(\hat{\mu}) \tag{8}$$

Noting that Eq. (8) is the first-order condition to the following optimization program

$$\mathcal{W}_{\mathcal{I}}(\Phi) = \max_{\mu \in \mathcal{M}} \langle \mu, \Phi \rangle - \mathcal{I}(\mu) \tag{9}$$

which, as argued in Galichon and Salanié (2010, 2012), can be interpreted in some cases as the social welfare of a matching model with unobserved heterogeneity.

Example 4. *Recall the definition $(p\otimes q)_{xy} = p_x p_y$, and remember that $p\otimes q$ is never on the frontier of $\mathcal{M}$, hence never rationalizable. When $\hat{\mu}$ is not rationalizable either, one may consider the smallest t such that $p\otimes q + t(\hat{\mu} - p\otimes q)$ is rationalizable. This number exists and is finite because the halfline which starts from $p\otimes q$ through $\hat{\mu}$ must cross the* *frontier of $\mathcal{M}$, which is a convex and compact set. Letting t^* be the corresponding value of t, and $\mu^* = p \otimes q + t^*(\hat{\mu} - p \otimes q)$, there exists by definition an element $\hat{\Phi} \in \mathbf{S} \backslash \{0\}$ such that $\mu^* \in \partial \mathcal{W}_0(\hat{\Phi})$, where $\mathcal{W}_0$ is as in (2). Note that if $\hat{\mu}$ is rationalizable, then $t^* = 1$ and $\mu^* = \mu$. See* Fig. 2.

This construction can be expressed in terms of $\mathcal{I}$. Letting

$$\mathcal{I}(\hat{\mu}) = -\max_{t \geq 1}\{t : p \otimes q + t(\hat{\mu} - p \otimes q) \in \mathcal{M}\} \text{ if } \hat{\mu} \in \mathcal{M} \tag{10}$$

$$= +\infty \text{ else} \tag{11}$$

so that $\mathcal{I}(\hat{\mu})$ can be formulated as a max-min problem, that is, for $\hat{\mu} \in \mathcal{M}$,

$$\mathcal{I}(\hat{\mu}) = -\max_{t \geq 1} \min_{\Phi \in S}\{t + \mathcal{W}_0(\Phi) - \langle \Phi, p \otimes q + t(\hat{\mu} - p \otimes q)\rangle\}$$

Because the objective function is convex in Φ and linear in t, this problem has a saddlepoint which will be denoted (Φ^*, t^*). Let $\mu^* = p \otimes q + t^*(\hat{\mu} - p \otimes q)$. By optimality with respect to Φ, $\mu^* \in \partial \mathcal{W}_0(\Phi^*)$, thus Φ^* rationalizes μ^*. By the envelope theorem

$$t^* \Phi^* = \nabla \mathcal{I}(\hat{\mu})$$

thus we take

$$\hat{\Phi} = t^* \Phi^*$$

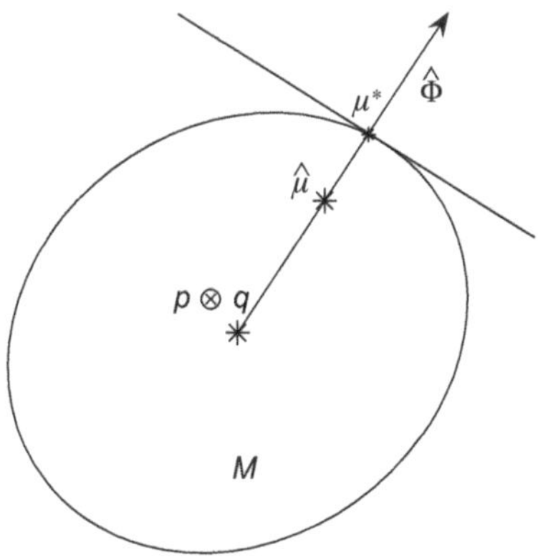

Fig. 2. Geometric illustration of example 4. $\hat{\mu}$ is not rationalizable, but it is associated to some proximate μ^* on the boundary of $\mathcal{M}$, which is itself rationalized by $\hat{\Phi}$.

and μ^* is the matching which is on the halfline which starts from $p \otimes q$ through $\hat{\mu}$ and which is rationalizable.

Example 5. *In the Choo and Siow (2006) model, the surplus function is* $\Phi_{ij} = \Phi(x, y) + \varepsilon_{iy} + \eta_{jx}$ *where* ε_{iy} *and* η_{jx} *are iid extreme value type I random variables. Choo and Siow use this model nonparametrically identifies* Φ. Galichon and Salanié (2010) *show that this model leads to the following specification of* $\mathcal{I}$:

$$\mathcal{I}(\mu) = \sum_{xy} \mu_{xy} \log \mu_{xy} \text{ if } \mu \in \mathcal{M} = +\infty \text{ else} \tag{12}$$

Example 6. Galichon and Salanié (2012) *argue that the model of Choo and Siow actually extends in the case where the matching surplus function in the presence of heterogeneities between man i of type x and woman j of type y is* $\Phi_{ij} = \Phi(x, y) + \varepsilon_{ixy} + \eta_{jxy}$, *and letting* $G_x(U) = \mathbb{E}[\max_y(U_{xy} + \varepsilon_{ixy})]$ *and* $H_y(V) = \mathcal{E}[\max_x(V_{xy} + \eta_{jxy})]$ *be the ex-ante indirect utilities of respectively the man of type x and the woman of type y, and letting* G^* *and* H^* *their respective convex conjugate transforms, that is*

$$G_x^*(\mu_{.|x}) = \sup_{U_{xy}} \left\{ \sum_y \mu_{y|x} U_{xy} - G_x(U) \right\} \text{ if } \sum_y \mu_{y|x} = 1 = +\infty \text{ else}$$

and

$$H_y^*(\mu_{.|y}) = \sup_{V_{xy}} \left\{ \sum_x \mu_{x|y} V_{xy} - H_y(V) \right\} \text{ if } \sum_x \mu_{x|y} = 1 = +\infty \text{ else}$$

Then $\mathcal{I}(\mu)$ *is given by*

$$\mathcal{I}(\mu) = \sum_x p_x G_x^*(\mu_{.|x}) + \sum_y q_y H_y^*(\mu_{.|y}) \tag{13}$$

which coincides with Eq. (12) in the case studied by Choo and Siow, hence the term "generalized entropy." As an important consequence, this paves the way to the continuous generalization of the Choo and Siow model. See Dupuy and Galichon (2012) and Bojilov and Galichon (2013).

Example 7. *Applying this setting,* Galichon and Salanié (2012, Example 3) *assume that* $\mathcal{X}$ *and* $\mathcal{Y}$ *are finite subsets of* $\mathbb{R}$, *and that* $\varepsilon_{ixy} = e_i y$ *while*

$\eta_{jxy} = f_j x$, where e_i and f_j are drawn from $\mathcal{U}([0,1])$ distributions. In this case the utility shocks are perfectly correlated across alternatives, in sharp contrast with Example 1, where they are independent. Then, letting $Q^{\mu}_{Y|X=x}$ be the conditional quantile of Y conditional on $X=x$ under distribution μ, one has

$$\mathcal{I}(\mu) = \sum_x p_x \int_0^1 Q^{\mu}_{Y|X=x}(t) t \, dt + \sum_y q_y \int_0^1 Q^{\mu}_{X|Y=y}(t) \; t \, dt$$

ACKNOWLEDGMENT

This research has received funding from the European Research Council under the European Union's Seventh Framework Programme (FP7/2007-2013)/ERC grant agreement No. 313699. Support from FiME, Laboratoire de Finance dés Marchés de l'Energie (www.fime-lab.org) is gratefully acknowledged. Gen Tang provided excellent research assistance. The author thanks a referee and the editors of this volume for comments that helped him improving this work.

REFERENCES

Becker, G. (1973). A theory of marriage, part I. *Journal of Political Economy*, *81*, 813–846.

Bojilov, R., & Galichon, A. (2013). *Closed-form formulas for multivariate matching*. Working paper.

Chiappori, P.-A., Oreffice, S., & Quintana-Domeque, C. (2012). Fatter attraction: Anthropometric and socioeconomic matching on the marriage market, to appear in the *Journal of Political Economy*.

Chiappori, P.-A., Salanié, B., & Weiss, Y. (2012). *Partner choice and the marital college premium*. Discussion Papers 1011-04, Columbia University.

Choo, E., & Siow, A. (2006). Who marries whom and why. *Journal of Political Economy*, *114*(1), 175–201.

Decker, C., Lieb, E., McCann, R., & Stephens, B. (2012). Unique equilibria and substitution effects in a stochastic model of the marriage market. To appear in the *Journal of Economic Theory*.

Dupuy, A., & Galichon, A. (2012). *Personality traits and the marriage market*. Working paper. Retrieve from SSRN: http://ssrn.com/abstract=2167565

Echenique, F., Lee, S., Yenmez, B., & Shum, M. (2012). The revealed preference theory of stable and extremal stable matchings. *Econometrica*, forthcoming.

Ekeland, I., & Temam, R. (1976). *Convex analysis and variational problems*. Amsterdam: North-Holland.

Fox, J. (2010). Identification in matching games. *Quantitative Economics*, *1*, 203–254.
Fox, J. (2011). *Estimating matching games with transfers*. Working paper. Mimeo, University of Michigan.
Galichon, A., & Salanié, B. (2010). *Matching with trade-offs: Revealed preferences over competing characteristics*. Technical report. Retrieved from SSRN: http://ssrn.com/abstract=1487307
Galichon, A., & Salanié, B. (2012). *Cupid's invisible hand: Social surplus and identification in matching models*. Working paper. Retrieved from SSRN: http://ssrn.com/abstract = 1804623
Shapley, L., & Shubik, M. (1972). The assignment game I: The core. *International Journal of Game Theory*, *1*, 111–130.

APPENDIX: FACTS FROM CONVEX ANALYSIS

The definitions below are included for completeness and the reader is referred to Ekeland and Temam (1976) for a thorough exposition of the topic.

Take any set $Y\,\mathbb{R}^d$; then the *convex hull* of Y is the set of points in $\mathbb{R}^d$ that are convex combinations of points in Y. We usually focus on its closure, the closed convex hull, denoted $cch(Y)$.

The *support function* S_Y of Y is defined as

$$S_Y(x) = \sup_{y \in Y} x \cdot y$$

for any x in Y, where $x \cdot y$ denotes the standard scalar product. It is a convex function, and it is homogeneous of degree one. Moreover, $S_Y = S_{\mathrm{cch}(Y)}$, where $\mathrm{cch}(Y)$ is the closed convex hull of Y, and $\partial S_Y(0) = \mathrm{cch}(Y)$.

A point in Y is an *boundary point* if it belongs in the closure of Y, but not in its interior.

Now let u be a convex, continuous function defined on $\mathbb{R}^d$. Then the gradient ∇u of u is well-defined almost everywhere and locally bounded. If u is differentiable at x, then

$$u(x') \geq u(x) + \nabla u(x) \cdot (x' - x)$$

for all $x' \in \mathbb{R}^d$. Moreover, if u is also differentiable at x', then

$$(\nabla u(x) - \nabla u(x')) \cdot (x - x') \geq 0.$$

When u is not differentiable in x, it is still *subdifferentiable* in the following sense. We define $\partial u(x)$ as

$$\partial u(x) = \{y \in \mathbb{R}^d : \forall x' \in \mathbb{R}^d, u(x') \geq u(x) + y \cdot (x' - x)\}.$$

Then $\partial u(x)$ is not empty, and it reduces to a single element if and only if u is differentiable at x; in that case $\partial u(x) = \{\nabla u(x)\}$.

Given a convex function u defined on a convex subset of $\mathbb{R}^d$, one defines its *convex conjugate* as

$$u^*(y) = \sup_{x \in \mathbb{R}^d} \{x \cdot y - u(x)\}.$$

One has $y \in \partial u(x)$ if and only if $x \in \partial u^*(y)$ if and only if $u(x) + u^*(y) = x \cdot y$.

COMPARATIVE STATIC AND COMPUTATIONAL METHODS FOR AN EMPIRICAL ONE-TO-ONE TRANSFERABLE UTILITY MATCHING MODEL

Bryan S. Graham

ABSTRACT

I show that the equilibrium distribution of matches associated with the empirical transferable utility one-to-one matching (TUM) model introduced by Choo and Siow (2006a, 2006b) corresponds to the fixed point of system of $K+L$ nonlinear equations; with K and L respectively equal to the number of discrete types of women and men. I use this representation to derive new comparative static results, showing how the match distribution varies with match surplus and the marginal distributions of agent types.

Keywords: Transferable Utility Matching (TUM); Choo–Siow Model; matching equilibrium; comparative statics

JEL classifications: C62; C68; C78

Structural Econometric Models
Advances in Econometrics, Volume 31, 153–181

ISSN: 0731-9053/doi:10.1108/S0731-9053(2013)0000032006

In the context of a single agent discrete choice problem, the assumption of utility maximization provides a tight link between the observed population distribution of choices and the unobserved population distribution of preferences (Manski, 1975; Matzkin, 2007; McFadden, 1974). In contrast the mapping from an observed distribution of matches between *two sets of heterogenous agents*, say men and women in a marriage market, and total match utility or surplus is less well-understood. In one-to-one matching problems two agents must agree to form a match. Rivalry is important, constraining choice: an individual's utility maximizing match partner may be unavailable, herself preferring to match with someone else. Rivalry, a consequence of the two-sided aspect of the problem, makes the problem of inferring the distribution of match surplus from information of who matches with whom difficult (Echenique, Lee, Shum, & Yenmez, 2013; Fox, 2010; Graham, 2011).

I study a variant of the structural matching model introduced by Choo and Siow (2006a, 2006b) (henceforth the "CS model").[1] Abstractly the CS model is a two-sided model of discrete choice subject to a market clearing, or adding-up, restriction (cf. Graham, 2011). The general equilibrium nature of the CS model makes a complete understanding of its economic properties difficult. In his Canadian Economics Association Presidential Address, Siow (2008) noted that (i) whether an equilibrium matching was globally unique was an open question and (ii) that the substitution patterns generated by the model were poorly understood. Decker (2010) and Decker, Lieb, McCann, and Stephens (2013) subsequently proved uniqueness of the CS matching and also derived some limited qualitative comparative static results. In independent work, Galichon and Salanie (2010, 2012) also showed uniqueness of the CS matching, but did not present comparative static results.

Let K and L denote the number of discrete types of men and women respectively (Table 1). A matching in the CS model consists of $K+L+KL$ terms. These terms correspond to the number of each type of woman and man who chooses to remain single in equilibrium ($K+L$), as well as the number of each type of feasible couple (KL). I show that an equilibrium CS matching corresponds to a fixed point of a certain system of $K+L$ nonlinear equations. The solution to these equations equals the number of "singles" of each type in equilibrium. The number of each type of couple is a closed form expression of the number singles and the model parameters (see Eq. (7) below).

I use the new equilibrium representation to derive comparative static results, showing how the equilibrium match distribution varies smoothly with model fundamentals. These results extend the qualitative ones derived

Table 1. Feasible Matchings.

W\M	Single(x_0)	x_1	$\cdots$	x_L	
Single(w_0)	–	$q_1 - \sum_{k=1}^{K} r_{k1}$	$\cdots$	$q_L - \sum_{k=1}^{K} r_{kL}$	–
w_1	$p_1 - \sum_{l=1}^{L} r_{1l}$	r_{11}	$\cdots$	r_{1L}	p_1
$\vdots$		$\vdots$	$\ddots$	$\vdots$	$\vdots$
w_K	$p_K - \sum_{l=1}^{L} r_{Kl}$	r_{K1}	$\cdots$	r_{KL}	p_K
	–	q_1	$\cdots$	q_L	

Note: Let $r_{kl} \geq 0$ denote the number of k-to-l matches. Feasibility of a matching imposes the $K+L$ adding up constraints $\sum_{l=1}^{L} r_{kl} \leq p_k$ for $k = 1, \ldots, K$ and $\sum_{k=1}^{K} r_{kl} \leq q_l$ for $l = 1, \ldots, L$.

by Decker et al. (2013). Specifically I derive inequalities on the magnitude of, and in some cases closed-form expressions for, various elasticities. These results provide insight into the substitution patterns implied by the CS model (i.e., how the distribution of matches changes in response to changes in the availability of different types of agents and other model parameters). These results speak to the testability of the model.

Identification of the parameters indexing the CS model from an equilibrium distribution of matches was first considered by Choo and Siow (2006a, 2006b). Additional results for their original model, as well as different extensions, can be found in Siow (2008), Galichon and Salanie (2010, 2012), Graham (2011), and Chiappori, Salanie, and Weiss (2012). Here I focus on characterizing the equilibrium and comparative static properties of the CS model, a topic, as noted above, also considered by Decker (2010) and Decker et al. (2013).

The first section outlines the version of the CS model I study. The second section shows that the equilibrium match distribution corresponds to the fixed point of a certain system of nonlinear equations. The third section presents comparative static results. The fourth section summarizes and discusses additional areas for research. Proofs and derivations are collected in the fifth section.

THE MATCHING MODEL

Preferences

Consider a single matching market composed of two large populations of, for concreteness, women and men. While I will often invoke language familiar from the marriage market application, there are numerous other empirically relevant examples of assignment games (cf. Fox, 2010; Koopmans & Beckmann, 1957; Shapley & Shubik, 1971). For each woman and man we respectively observe the discretely valued characteristics $W_i \in \mathbb{W} = \{w_1, \ldots, w_K\}$ and $X^j \in \mathbb{X} = \{x_1, \ldots, x_L\}$.[2] The K types of women and L types of men may encode, for example, different unique combinations of years-of-schooling and age. While K and L are assumed finite, they may be very large in practice.

Observationally identical women have heterogeneous preferences over different types of men, but are indifferent between men of the same type. Specifically female i's utility from matching with male j is given by

$$U(W_i, X^j, \varepsilon_i) = \alpha(W_i, X^j) + \tau(W_i, X^j) + \varepsilon_i(X^j)$$

where $\alpha(w_k, x_l)$ is the systematic utility a type $W_i = w_k$ women derives from matching with a type $X^j = x_l$ man, $\varepsilon_i(X^j) = \sum_{l=1}^{L} \mathbf{1}(X^j = x_l)\varepsilon_{il}$ captures unobserved heterogeneity in women's preferences over alternative *types* of men, and $\tau(w_k, x_l)$ is the *equilibrium* transfer that a type $X^j = x_l$ man must pay a type $W_i = w_k$ women in order to match. Transfers may be negative and their determination is discussed below. Here $\mathbf{1}(\bullet)$ denotes the indicator function. Since the stochastic component of female match utility, $\varepsilon_i(X^j)$, varies with male type alone (i.e., his specific identify does not matter), women are indifferent among observationally identical men. A similar restriction on male preferences ensures that the equilibrium transfer, $\tau(w_k, x_l)$, depends on agent types alone (as asserted) (cf. Galichon & Salanie, 2012).

A women may also choose to remained unmatched, or "single," in which case her utility is given by

$$\underline{U}(W_i, \varepsilon_i) = \underline{\alpha}(W_i) + \varepsilon_{i0}$$

Men also have heterogenous preferences. Man j's utility from matching with woman i is given by

$$V(W_i, X^j, \upsilon_i) = \beta(W_i, X^j) - \tau(W_i, X^j) + \upsilon^j(W_i)$$

where $\beta(w_k, x_l)$ is the systematic utility a type $X^j = x_l$ men derives from matching with a type $W_i = w_k$ woman and $\upsilon^j(W_i) = \sum_{k=1}^{K} \mathbf{1}(W_i = w_k)\upsilon_k^j$ is a heterogenous component of match utility. Here $\tau(w, x)$ enters with a negative sign as we conceptually imagine men "paying" women (recall that transfers may be negative). The utility from remaining unmatched is

$$\underline{V}(X^j, \upsilon^j) = \underline{\beta}(X^j) + \upsilon_0^j$$

Preference heterogeneity ensures that, for any given transfer function $\tau(w, x)$, observationally identical women will match with different types of men. If the support of the heterogeneity distribution is rich enough all types of matches will be observed in equilibrium.

Let $\underline{\varepsilon} = (\varepsilon_{i0}, \varepsilon_{i1}, \ldots, \varepsilon_{iL})'$ and $\underline{v} = (v_0^j, v_1^j, \ldots, v_K^j)'$. I assume that the components of these vectors are independently and identically distributed Type I extreme value random variables

$$F_{\underline{\varepsilon}|W}(\underline{e}|W = w_k) = \prod_{l=0}^{L} \exp\left(-\exp\left(-\frac{e_l}{\sigma_\varepsilon}\right)\right)$$

$$F_{\underline{v}|X}(\underline{v}|X = x_l) = \prod_{k=0}^{K} \exp\left(-\exp\left(-\frac{v_k}{\sigma_v}\right)\right) \tag{1}$$

Assumption (1) is slightly more general than that maintained by Choo and Siow (2006a, 2006b) who additionally impose the restriction $\sigma_\varepsilon = \sigma_v$. Chiappori et al. (2012) allow the scale parameters, σ_ε and σ_v, to vary with, respectively, k and l.[3]

Equilibrium

Let $\alpha_{kl} = \alpha(w_k, x_l)$, $\underline{\alpha}_{k0} = \underline{\alpha}(w_k)$, $\beta_{kl} = \beta(w_k, x_l)$, $\beta_{0l} = \underline{\beta}(x_l)$, and $\tau_{kl} = \tau(w_k, x_l)$. Let θ be a vector of model parameters – to be more precisely specified below – and $\underline{\tau}$ a $KL \times 1$ vector of transfers. The total number of type k women is given by p_k, that of type l men by q_l. Let $\mathbf{p} = (p_1, \ldots, p_K)'$ and $\mathbf{q} = (q_1, \ldots, q_L)'$. Denote the probability, given a hypothetical transfer vector $\underline{\tau}$, that a type k woman matches with a type l man by $e_{kl}^D(\theta; \underline{\tau})$. The probability of remaining unmatched is $e_{k0}^D(\theta, \underline{\tau}) = 1 - \sum_{l=1}^{L} e_{kl}^D(\theta, \underline{\tau})$. Under the Type I extreme value assumption we have for $k = 1, \ldots, K$ (McFadden, 1974):

$$e_{k0}^D(\theta, \underline{\tau}) = \frac{1}{1 + \sum_{n=1}^{L} \exp(\sigma_\varepsilon^{-1}[\alpha_{kn} - \underline{\alpha}_{k0} + \tau_{kn}])}$$

$$e_{kl}^D(\theta, \underline{\tau}) = \frac{\exp(\sigma_{\varepsilon k}^{-1}[\alpha_{kl} - \underline{\alpha}_{k0} + \tau_{kl}])}{1 + \sum_{n=1}^{L} \exp(\sigma_\varepsilon^{-1}[\alpha_{kn} - \underline{\alpha}_{k0} + \tau_{kn}])}, \quad l = 1, \ldots, L$$

Total "demand" for type l men by type k women is therefore

$$\begin{aligned} r_{k0}^{D}(\theta, \underline{\tau}, \mathbf{p}, \mathbf{q}) &\stackrel{def}{=} p_k e_{k0}^{D}(\theta, \underline{\tau}) \\ r_{kl}^{D}(\theta, \underline{\tau}, \mathbf{p}, \mathbf{q}) &\stackrel{def}{=} p_k e_{kl}^{D}(\theta, \underline{\tau}) \end{aligned} \tag{2}$$

which, after some manipulation, gives

$$\sigma_{\varepsilon} \ln\left(\frac{r_{kl}^{D}(\theta, \underline{\tau}, \mathbf{p}, \mathbf{q})}{r_{k0}^{D}(\theta, \underline{\tau}, \mathbf{p}, \mathbf{q})}\right) = \alpha_{kl} - \underline{\alpha}_{k0} + \tau_{kl} \tag{3}$$

For $l = 1, \ldots, L$ we get a conditional "supply" of type l men to each of the $k = 1, \ldots, K$ types of women equal to

$$\begin{aligned} r_{0l}^{S}(\theta, \underline{\tau}, \mathbf{p}, \mathbf{q}) &\stackrel{def}{=} q_l g_{0l}^{S}(\theta, \underline{\tau}) \\ r_{kl}^{S}(\theta, \underline{\tau}, \mathbf{p}, \mathbf{q}) &\stackrel{def}{=} q_l g_{kl}^{S}(\theta, \underline{\tau}) \end{aligned} \tag{4}$$

where

$$g_{0l}^{S}(\theta, \underline{\tau}) = \frac{1}{1 + \sum_{m=1}^{K} \exp(\sigma_{\upsilon}^{-1}[\beta_{ml} - \underline{\beta}_{0l} - \tau_{ml}])}$$

$$g_{kl}^{S}(\theta, \underline{\tau}) = \frac{\exp(\sigma_{\upsilon}^{-1}[\beta_{kl} - \underline{\beta}_{0l} - \tau_{kl}])}{1 + \sum_{m=1}^{K} \exp(\sigma_{\upsilon}^{-1}[\beta_{ml} - \underline{\beta}_{0l} - \tau_{ml}])}, \quad k = 1, \ldots, K$$

so that

$$\sigma_{\upsilon} \ln\left(\frac{r_{kl}^{S}(\theta, \underline{\tau}, \mathbf{p}, \mathbf{q})}{r_{0l}^{S}(\theta, \underline{\tau}, \mathbf{p}, \mathbf{q})}\right) = \beta_{kl} - \underline{\beta}_{0l} - \tau_{kl} \tag{5}$$

The transfer vector, $\underline{\tau}$, adjusts to equate the KL female "demands" with the KL male "supplies" so that in equilibrium

$$r_{kl}^{\text{eq}}(\theta, \underline{\tau}^{\text{eq}}, \mathbf{p}, \mathbf{q}) = r_{kl}^{D}(\theta, \underline{\tau}^{\text{eq}}, \mathbf{p}, \mathbf{q}) = r_{kl}^{S}(\theta, \underline{\tau}^{\text{eq}}, \mathbf{p}, \mathbf{q}), \quad k = 1, \ldots, K, \;\; l = 1, \ldots, L \tag{6}$$

with the "eq" superscript denoting an equilibrium quantity.

Let

$$\gamma_{kl} = \frac{\alpha_{kl} + \beta_{kl} - \underline{\alpha}_{k0} - \underline{\beta}_{0l}}{\sigma_\varepsilon + \sigma_\upsilon}, \quad \lambda = \frac{\sigma_\upsilon}{\sigma_\varepsilon + \sigma_\upsilon}$$

Imposing Eq. (6), adding Eqs. (3) and (5), exponentiating and rearranging yields

$$r_{kl}^{\text{eq}} = (r_{k0}^{\text{eq}})^{1-\lambda}(r_{0l}^{\text{eq}})^{\lambda}\exp(\gamma_{kl}) \tag{7}$$

where I let $r_{kl}^{\text{eq}} = r_{kl}^{\text{eq}}(\theta, \underline{\tau}^{\text{eq}}, \mathbf{p}, \mathbf{q})$ to economize on notation.

FIXED POINT REPRESENTATION OF THE EQUILIBRIUM MATCHING

This section develops a fixed point representation of the equilibrium match distribution or "matching." Taking the logarithm (7) and manipulating yields the following two equalities that hold in equilibrium for all (k, l) pairs:

$$\ln\left(\frac{r_{kl}^{\text{eq}}}{r_{k0}^{\text{eq}}}\right) = \gamma_{kl} + \lambda \ln\left(\frac{r_{0l}^{\text{eq}}}{r_{k0}^{\text{eq}}}\right) \tag{8}$$

$$\ln\left(\frac{r_{kl}^{\text{eq}}}{r_{0l}^{\text{eq}}}\right) = \gamma_{kl} - (1-\lambda) \ln\left(\frac{r_{0l}^{\text{eq}}}{r_{k0}^{\text{eq}}}\right) \tag{9}$$

Exponentiating both sides of Eqs. (8) and (9) and summing over, respectively, l and k yields

$$\left(\frac{\sum_{n=1}^{L} r_{kn}^{\text{eq}}}{r_{k0}^{\text{eq}}}\right) = \sum_{n=1}^{L} \exp\left[\gamma_{kn} + \lambda \ln\left(\frac{r_{0n}^{\text{eq}}}{r_{k0}^{\text{eq}}}\right)\right]$$

$$\left(\frac{\sum_{m=1}^{K} r_{ml}^{\text{eq}}}{r_{0l}^{\text{eq}}}\right) = \sum_{m=1}^{K} \exp\left[\gamma_{ml} - (1-\lambda) \ln\left(\frac{r_{0n}^{\text{eq}}}{r_{m0}^{\text{eq}}}\right)\right]$$

which, since $\sum_{n=1}^{L} r_{kn}^{eq} = p_k - r_{k0}^{eq}$ and $\sum_{m=1}^{K} r_{ml}^{eq} = q_l - r_{0l}^{eq}$, implies that the equilibrium number of *unmatched* agents of each type satisfies the $K+L$ implicit equations

$$r_{k0}^{eq} = \frac{p_k}{1+\sum_{n=1}^{L}\exp\left[\gamma_{kn}+\lambda\ln\left(\frac{r_{0n}^{eq}}{r_{k0}^{eq}}\right)\right]}, \quad k=1,\dots,K$$

$$r_{0l}^{eq} = \frac{q_l}{1+\sum_{m=1}^{K}\exp\left[\gamma_{ml}-(1-\lambda)\ln\left(\frac{r_{0l}^{eq}}{r_{m0}^{eq}}\right)\right]}, \quad l=1,\dots,L$$

for $\mathbf{r}_0 = (r_{10},\dots,r_{K0},r_{01},\dots,r_{0L})'$ and $\theta = (\gamma',\lambda)'$ with

$$\gamma = (\gamma_{11},\dots,\gamma_{1L},\dots,\gamma_{K1},\dots,\gamma_{KL})'$$

Let $B_{k0}(\mathbf{r}_0;\mathbf{p},\mathbf{q},\theta) \stackrel{def}{=} p_k\left[1+\sum_{n=1}^{L}\exp\left[\gamma_{kn}+\lambda\ln\left(\frac{r_{0n}}{r_{k0}}\right)\right]\right]^{-1}$ for $k=1,\dots,K$ and $B_{0l}(\mathbf{r}_0;\mathbf{p},\mathbf{q},\theta) \stackrel{def}{=} q_l\left[1+\sum_{m=1}^{K}\exp\left[\gamma_{ml}-(1-\lambda)\ln\left(\frac{r_{0l}^{eq}}{r_{m0}^{eq}}\right)\right]\right]^{-1}$ for $l=1,\dots,L$.

We have shown that $\mathbf{r}_0^{eq}$ – the $(K+L)\times 1$ vector giving the equilibrium number of agents of each type who choose not to match – is a solution to the $(K+L)\times 1$ vector of implicit functions

$$\mathbf{r}_0^{eq} - \mathbf{B}(\mathbf{r}_0^{eq};\mathbf{p},\mathbf{q},\theta) = 0 \tag{10}$$

with $\mathbf{B}(\mathbf{r}_0;\mathbf{p},\mathbf{q},\theta) = (B_{10}(\bullet),\dots,B_{K0}(\bullet),B_{01}(\bullet),\dots,B_{0L}(\bullet))'$. Given a solution to Eq. (10) we can solve for the number of each of the $K\times L$ types of matches in closed form using Eq. (7) above:

$$r_{kl}^{eq} = (r_{k0}^{eq})^{1-\lambda}(r_{0l}^{eq})^{\lambda}\exp(\gamma_{kl}) \tag{11}$$

for $k=1,\dots,K$ and $l=1,\dots,L$.

The representation of $\mathbf{r}_0^{eq}$ as a solution to Eq. (10) is, to my knowledge, a new result; one with, as I argue below, useful implications for estimation and inference.

From the prior work of Decker (2010), Decker et al. (2013), and Galichon and Salanie (2010, 2012) we know that the solution to Eq. (10) must be unique. Let $\mathbb{T}_\varepsilon = \{\mathbf{r}_0 : \varepsilon \le r_{k0} \le p_k - \varepsilon, \varepsilon \le r_{0l} \le q_l - \varepsilon, (k=1,\dots,K, l=1,\dots,L)\}$ be a closed rectangular region with ε some arbitrarily small positive constant and Γ be a closed and bounded subset of $\mathbb{R}^{KL}$.

Let $J(\mathbf{r}_0) = I_{K+L} - \nabla_{\mathbf{r}_0}\mathbf{B}(\mathbf{r}_0; \mathbf{p}, \mathbf{q}, \theta)$, with $\nabla_{\mathbf{r}_0}\mathbf{B}(\mathbf{r}_0; \mathbf{p}, \mathbf{q}, \theta) = \frac{\partial \mathbf{B}(\mathbf{r}_0; \mathbf{p}, \mathbf{q}, \theta)}{\partial \mathbf{r}_0'}$, be the $(K+L)\times(K+L)$ Jacobian matrix associated with Eq. (10). If $J(\mathbf{r}_0)$ is a P-matrix on $\mathbb{T}_\varepsilon$, meaning all its principal minors are positive, then Theorem 4 of Gale and Nikaido (1965) implies uniqueness of $\mathbf{r}_0^{\text{eq}}$ (on $\mathbb{T}_\varepsilon$) for all $(\gamma, \lambda) \in \Gamma \times (0, 1)$. Thus showing that $J(\mathbf{r}_0)$ is a P-matrix on $\mathbb{T}_\varepsilon$ would provide an alternative proof of equilibrium uniqueness in the CS model. Unfortunately verifying the P-matrix property can be computationally hard in practice, especially when the Jacobian is large, nonsymmetric, and otherwise complicated, as is the case here (cf. Coxson, 1994).[4] In results not reported here, I have shown that $J(\mathbf{r}_0^{\text{eq}})$ is a P-matrix (indeed a diagonally dominant matrix in the sense of McKenzie (1960)). However, I have been unable to show that the result holds for $\mathbf{r}_0 \neq \mathbf{r}_0^{\text{eq}}$ (although I conjecture that it does). It is also possible show that $\mathbf{B}(\mathbf{r}_0; \mathbf{p}, \mathbf{q}, \theta)$ is a contraction mapping in the neighborhood of $\mathbf{r}_0^{\text{eq}}$. This provides some justification for using fixed point iteration to find an equilibrium (as was done for the numerical examples reported below). However, proving that $\mathbf{B}(\mathbf{r}_0; \mathbf{p}, \mathbf{q}, \theta)$ is a contraction on all of $\mathbb{T}_\varepsilon$ remains a goal for future research.

Representation (10) suggests an interpretation of the CS model as an "as if" incomplete information game (e.g., Aradillas-Lopez, 2010; Bajari, Hong, Krainer, & Nekipelov, 2010).

Define the inclusive values

$$v_k^f(\mathbf{s}_0; \theta) = \ln\left(\sum_{n=1}^{L} \exp\left[\gamma_{kn} + \lambda \ln\left(\frac{q_n(1-s_{0n})}{p_k(1-s_{k0})}\right)\right]\right), \quad k = 1, \ldots, K$$
$$v_l^m(\mathbf{s}_0; \theta) = \ln\left(\sum_{m=1}^{K} \exp\left[\gamma_{ml} - (1-\lambda) \ln\left(\frac{q_l(1-s_{0l})}{p_m(1-s_{m0})}\right)\right]\right), \quad l = 1, \ldots, L \tag{12}$$

where $s_{k0} = (p_k - r_{k0})/p_k$ for $k = 1, \ldots, K$ and $s_{0l} = (q_l - r_{0l})/q_l$ for $l = 1, \ldots, L$. The $K + L$ vector of matching market entrance probabilities for each type of women and man is $\mathbf{s}_0 = (s_{10}, \ldots, s_{K0}, s_{01}, \ldots, s_{0L})'$. These probabilities are the unique solution to the $K + L$ system of nonlinear equations

$$s_{k0} = \frac{\exp(v_k^f(\mathbf{s}_0; \theta))}{1 + \exp(v_k^f(\mathbf{s}_0; \theta))}, \quad k = 1, \ldots, K$$
$$s_{0l} = \frac{\exp(v_l^m(\mathbf{s}_0; \theta))}{1 + \exp(v_l^m(\mathbf{s}_0; \theta))}, \quad l = 1, \ldots, L \tag{13}$$

Eq. (13) is identical in form to an incomplete information entry game with $K+L$ players. Multiplicity of equilibria in such games is frequent in practice (e.g., Bajari, Hahn, Hong, & Ridder, 2011). Here uniqueness evidently follows from the specific form of the inclusive values.

In an initial stage each agent decides whether to enter the matching market or remain unmatched. The probability of entry depends on the surplus associated with the different types of matches available to an agent (e.g., $\gamma_{k1}, \ldots, \gamma_{kL}$ for a type k female). It also depends on the participation rate of all other types of agents as well as their relative population sizes. The influence of these various factors is summarized by the inclusive value terms (12).

Once the "entry" decision has been made agents match with different types of partners according to the closed form rule (11).

COMPARATIVE STATICS

An attraction of the CS model, compared to reduced form models of the marriage market (e.g., Angrist, 2002; Schwartz, 2010) is that it allows the researcher to undertake counterfactual analysis. What would happen to the distribution of marriage if the number of college educated females increased? How would the marriage rate change in response to a decline in match surplus, induced by, for example, changes in tax policy or divorce laws? By comparing the observed matching with a counterfactual one computed under a different distribution of types or model parameters, these questions may be answered numerically. Representation (10) suggests that we may compute such counterfactuals by fixed point iteration, using the initial assignment for starting values.

Deriving analytic results on the substitution patterns implied by the CS model is more difficult. Such results are useful because they provide insight into the economic structure of the model. In a nonlinear system of equations comparative static analysis generally involves an application of the Implicit Function Theorem. To derive precise comparative static results requires a closed form expression for the inverse Jacobian matrix, $J(\mathbf{r}_0^{\text{eq}})^{-1}$. In the CS model explicit calculation of $J(\mathbf{r}_0^{\text{eq}})^{-1}$, as in other large nonlinear fixed point problems, appears difficult, however certain features of this matrix can be derived. Specifically I show that $J(\mathbf{r}_0^{\text{eq}})$ coincides with the similarity transform of a row stochastic matrix with certain diagonal dominance properties. These properties are sufficient to bound every element of $J(\mathbf{r}_0^{\text{eq}})^{-1}$.

Deriving these bounds involves linear algebra results on M-matrices and inverse M-matrices (e.g., Carlson & Markham, 1979; Fiedler & Ptak, 1962; Johnson, 1982).

My main result is:

Theorem 1. (*Comparative Statics*). Let $\mathbf{r_0} = \mathbf{B}(\mathbf{r}_0; \mathbf{p}, \mathbf{q}, \theta)$ be the equilibrium prevalence of single-hood, then

(i) *Type-specific elasticities of single-hood*: for $m = 1, \ldots, K$

$$\frac{\mathrm{d}r_{m0}}{\mathrm{d}p_k}\frac{p_k}{r_{m0}} \geq \begin{cases} \dfrac{1}{(1-\lambda)p_m + \lambda r_{m0}} \dfrac{p_k}{(1-\lambda)p_k + \lambda r_{k0}} \displaystyle\sum_{n=1}^{L} \dfrac{r_{mn}r_{kn}}{\lambda q_n + (1-\lambda)r_{0n}} > 0 & m \neq k \\ \dfrac{p_k}{(1-\lambda)p_k + \lambda r_{k0}} \left[1 + \dfrac{1}{(1-\lambda)p_k + \lambda r_{k0}} \displaystyle\sum_{n=1}^{L} \dfrac{r_{1n}r_{kn}}{\lambda q_n + (1-\lambda)r_{0n}} \right] > 1 & m = k \end{cases}$$

while for $l = 1, \ldots, L$

$$\frac{\mathrm{d}r_{0l}}{\mathrm{d}p_k}\frac{p_k}{r_{0l}} \leq -\frac{(1-\lambda)r_{kl}}{\lambda q_l + (1-\lambda)r_{0l}} \frac{p_k}{(1-\lambda)p_k + \lambda r_{k0}} < 0$$

and an analogous result holding for $\mathrm{d}\mathbf{r_0}/\mathrm{d}q_l$;

(ii) *Partial symmetry of semi-elasticities*:

$$\frac{\mathrm{d}r_{m0}}{\mathrm{d}p_k}\frac{1}{r_{m0}} = \frac{\mathrm{d}r_{k0}}{\mathrm{d}p_m}\frac{1}{r_{k0}}, \quad k, m = 1, \ldots, K$$

$$\frac{\mathrm{d}r_{0n}}{\mathrm{d}q_l}\frac{1}{r_{0n}} = \frac{\mathrm{d}r_{0l}}{\mathrm{d}q_n}\frac{1}{r_{0l}}, \quad l, n = 1, \ldots, L$$

$$\lambda\frac{\mathrm{d}r_{k0}}{\mathrm{d}q_l}\frac{1}{r_{k0}} = (1-\lambda)\frac{\mathrm{d}r_{0l}}{\mathrm{d}p_k}\frac{1}{r_{0k}}, \quad k = 1, \ldots, K, \ \ l = 1, \ldots, L$$

(iii) *Aggregate elasticity of single-hood*:

$$\frac{\mathrm{d}(\mathbf{r}_0{}'\iota_{K+L})}{\mathrm{d}p_k}\frac{p_k}{\mathbf{r}_0{}'\iota_{K+L}} = \frac{r_{k0}}{\sum_{k=1}^{K} r_{k0} + \sum_{l=1}^{L} r_{0l}}$$

for $k = 1, \ldots, K$ and an analogous result holding for $\mathrm{d}(\mathbf{r}_0{}'\iota_{K+L})/\mathrm{d}q_l$;

(iv) *Constant returns to scale*:

$$\sum_{k=1}^{K}\frac{\mathrm{d}r_{m0}}{\mathrm{d}p_k}\frac{p_k}{r_{m0}}+\sum_{l=1}^{L}\frac{\mathrm{d}r_{m0}}{\mathrm{d}q_l}\frac{q_l}{r_{m0}}=1,\quad m=1,\ldots,K$$

$$\sum_{k=1}^{K}\frac{\mathrm{d}r_{0n}}{\mathrm{d}p_k}\frac{p_k}{r_{0n}}+\sum_{l=1}^{L}\frac{\mathrm{d}r_{0n}}{\mathrm{d}q_l}\frac{q_l}{r_{0n}}=1,\quad n=1,\ldots,L$$

Proof. See section "Proof of Theorem 1 and Corollaries."

The first two implications of Theorem 1 generalize Theorem 2 of Decker et al. (2013). Implication (i) states that if the kth type of women becomes more abundant then (a) the prevalence of single-hood across all types of women increases (with the response being strongest among type k women) and (b) the prevalence of marriage increases across all types of men. These results are a consequence of more women "competing" for the same number of men. Implication (ii) extends the symmetry result of Decker et al. (2013) to the case where $\lambda \neq 1/2$.

Implication (iii), which is new, shows that the special structure of the CS model makes it possible to derive some equilibrium elasticities in closed form. Consider the probability that a random draw from the population, women *and* men, is single. How does this probability change in response to an increase in the size of a specific subgroup, say type k, women? Implication (i) of the Theorem suggests that single-hood rises across all women, and especially type k women, and declines across all men. Implication (iii) shows that the net effect is an overall increase in single-hood with the elasticity being equal to type k's share of all singles.

Implication (iv) confirms that the CS model exhibits constant results to scale. Holding the type distributions of men and women fixed, increasing market size has no effect on the probability of marriage.

It is well known that the independence of irrelevant alternatives (IIA) property of the conditional logit model structure places strong restrictions on substitution patterns in single agent discrete choice problems (McFadden, 1974). A concern is that similar problems arise here. Consider a model with three types of women: high school dropouts (type 1), high school graduates (type 2), and those with a 4-year degree (type 3). For simplicity assume there is only one type of man. Not all women secure a husband and vice versa. I assume that high school dropouts and high school graduates generate similar systematic match surpluses with $\gamma_{11}=\gamma_{21}=-1/2$. College graduates generate a systematic match surplus of $\gamma_{31}=0$.

Table 2 gives the equilibrium matching associated with this marriage market when $p_1 = 5/9$, $p_2 = 3/9$, and $p_3 = 1/9$. I set $q_1 = 1$ so that, initially, there are a sufficient number of men for all women. As expected, given the form of γ, high school dropouts and high school graduates are more likely than college graduates to remain unmarried.

Now consider a doubling of the population of high school dropout women. This influx of women increases the pools of unmarried among all types of women. We might also expect that the response is stronger for high school graduates than it is for college graduates. Since high school graduates are "similar" to dropouts in terms of the marriage surplus they generate, this group should be disproportionally affected. It turns out that this predicted elasticity ranking is incorrect. The number of unmarried high school graduate women increases by $100 \times (0.1724 - 0.1617)/0.1617 \approx 6.6$ percent, while the ranks of unmarried college graduates by $100 \times (0.0202 - 0.0176)/0.0176 \approx 15.8$ percent. As in the standard single agent discrete choice model, the source of these counter-intuitive substitution patterns is the assumed independence of υ_1^j and υ_2^j (Table 3).

Table 2. Substitution Patterns Implied by CS Model, Part 1.

W\M	Single(x_0)	x_1	
Single(w_0)	–	0.4951	–
w_1	0.3157	0.2398	$p_1 = 5/9$
w_2	0.1617	0.1716	$p_2 = 3/9$
w_3	0.0176	0.0935	$p_3 = 1/9$
	–	$q_1 = 1$	

Note: In the above simulated market $\gamma_{11} = \gamma_{21} = 0$ and $\gamma_{31} = 0.25$ with $\lambda = 1/2$.

Table 3. Substitution Patterns Implied by CS Model, Part 2.

W\M	Single(x_0)	x_1	
Single(w_0)	–	0.4080	–
w_1	0.7709	0.3402	$p_1 = 10/9$
w_2	0.1724	0.1609	$p_2 = 3/9$
w_3	0.0202	0.0909	$p_3 = 1/9$
	–	$q_1 = 1$	

Note: In the above simulated market $\gamma_{11} = \gamma_{21} = 0$ and $\gamma_{31} = 0.25$ with $\lambda = 1/2$.

Derived Results

It is possible to use Theorem 1 to derive some additional comparative static results.

First, consider the effect of a percent increase in the population size of women, holding is type composition fixed. We have, using (iii) of Theorem 1

$$\left.\frac{\mathrm{d}(\mathbf{r}_0'\iota_{K+L})}{d(\mathbf{p}'\iota_K)}\frac{(\mathbf{p}'\iota_K)}{(\mathbf{r}_0'\iota_{K+L})}\right|_{\frac{\mathrm{d}p_k}{p_k}\Big/\frac{\mathrm{d}(\mathbf{p}'\iota_K)}{(\mathbf{p}'\iota_K)}=1,\ k=1,\ldots,K} = \frac{\sum_{k=1}^{K} r_{k0}}{\sum_{k=1}^{K} r_{k0}+\sum_{l=1}^{L} r_{0l}} \tag{14}$$

Eq. (14) shows that CS model generates sharp implications for the effect of changes in the sex ratio on the marriage rate (cf. Angrist, 2002).

Second, the semi-elasticity of single-hood for type m females given an unit increase in the surplus parameter γ_{kl} is

$$\frac{\mathrm{d}r_{m0}}{\mathrm{d}\gamma_{kl}}\frac{1}{r_{m0}}=\frac{\mathrm{d}r_{m0}}{\mathrm{d}p_k}\frac{r_{kl}}{r_{m0}}+\frac{\mathrm{d}r_{m0}}{\mathrm{d}q_l}\frac{r_{kl}}{r_{m0}}$$

Since this is the sum of opposite-signed terms the sign of this effect is ambiguous (cf. Decker et al., 2013). However it turns out that we can get a sharper result if we consider the effect on *aggregate* single-hood of a unit increase in *all* γ_{kl} for $k=1,\ldots,K$ and $l=1,\ldots,L$. To motivate this counterfactual we can think of an economy-wide change in tax policy, divorce law, or contraceptive availability which changes the utility of marriage relative to single-hood. Calculations in the proof of Theorem 1 show that this semi-elasticity is a weighted average of type-specific population shares. Weights are greatest for types that are neither very likely, nor very unlikely, to be single under the status quo. Specifically we get the closed form expression

$$\left.\frac{\mathrm{d}(\mathbf{r}_0'\iota_{K+L})}{\mathrm{d}(\gamma'\iota_{KL})}\frac{(\gamma'\iota_{KL})}{(\mathbf{r}_0'\iota_{K+L})}\right|_{\frac{\mathrm{d}\gamma_{kl}}{\gamma_{kl}}\Big/\frac{\mathrm{d}(\gamma'\iota_{KL})}{(\gamma'\iota_{KL})}=1,\ k=1,\ldots,K,\ l=1,\ldots,L} = -\frac{\sum_{k=1}^{K} p_k e_{k0}(1-e_{k0})+\sum_{l=1}^{L} q_l e_{0l}(1-e_{0l})}{\sum_{k=1}^{K} p_k+\sum_{l=1}^{L} q_l} \tag{15}$$

This semi-elasticity measures the effect – on the unconditional probability of matching – of an economy-wide increase in the returns from doing so.

Third, observe that

$$\frac{\mathrm{d}\ln r_{kl}}{\mathrm{d}\ln p_o} = (1-\lambda)\frac{\mathrm{d}\ln r_{k0}}{\mathrm{d}\ln p_o} + \lambda\frac{\mathrm{d}\ln r_{0l}}{\mathrm{d}\ln p_o}$$

and hence that

$$\frac{\mathrm{d}\ln r_{mn}}{\mathrm{d}\ln p_o} - \frac{\mathrm{d}\ln r_{ml}}{\mathrm{d}\ln p_o} - \left[\frac{\mathrm{d}\ln r_{kn}}{\mathrm{d}\ln p_o} - \frac{\mathrm{d}\ln r_{kl}}{\mathrm{d}\ln p_o}\right] = 0$$

which implies the zero restriction

$$\frac{\mathrm{d}\ln\left(\frac{r_{mn}}{r_{ml}}\frac{r_{kl}}{r_{kn}}\right)}{\mathrm{d}\ln p_o} = 0$$

for $o = 1, \ldots, K$. The local assortativeness properties of the CS matching are unaffected by the type distribution of the population.

FURTHER AREAS FOR RESEARCH

This article has presented a systematic analysis of the equilibrium properties of the CS model, building on prior work by others. Theorem 1 indicates, perhaps unsurprisingly given its conditional logit foundation, that the CS model has strong comparative static implications. These implications could be used to test the empirical usefulness of the CS model, and also to guide the development of more general models. As in single agent discrete choice models, it seems fruitful to explore modeling frameworks that allow for correlation in the unobserved component of match utility associated with different types of partners.

Fixed point iteration could be useful for researchers interested in estimating models where K and/or L are large, but where $\gamma = \gamma(\eta)$ is parameterized in terms of a smaller dimensional η. In such a situation the researcher could use iteration to solve for the equilibrium matching associated with a particular choice of η and λ in order to evaluate a log likelihood function (Rust, 1987).[5] This method of computation would be especially attractive if it could be shown that $\mathbf{B}(\mathbf{r_0}; \mathbf{p}, \mathbf{q}, \theta)$ is a contraction on all of $\mathbb{T}_\varepsilon$.

PROOFS AND DERIVATIONS

In what follows we write, for example, $\mathbf{B}(\mathbf{r}_0; \mathbf{p}, \mathbf{q}, \theta) = \mathbf{B}(\mathbf{r}_0)$ when dependence on $\mathbf{p}$, $\mathbf{q}$, and θ is not germane.

Proof of Theorem 1 and Corollaries

The proof of Theorem 1 involves four steps. First the Jacobian matrix $J(\mathbf{r}_0)$ is calculated and evaluated at $\mathbf{r}_0 = \mathbf{r}_0^{\text{eq}}$. Second, $J(\mathbf{r}_0^{\text{eq}})$ is factored into the similarity transform of a row stochastic matrix $H(\mathbf{r}_0)$. Third, $H(\mathbf{r}_0)$ is partitioned and the Schur complements of its upper $K \times K$ and lower $L \times L$ diagonal blocks are shown to be row diagonal dominant Z-matrices (i.e., matrices with non-positive off diagonal elements). This is sufficient to show that the upper $K \times K$ and lower $L \times L$ diagonal blocks of $H(\mathbf{r}_0)^{-1}$ are positive matrices while the two off-diagonal blocks are non-positive. This identifies the sign structure of the inverse Jacobian. Fourth, the partitioned inverse formula is used to establish various bounds on the elements of the inverse Jacobian which in turn provide bounds for various elasticities. In what follows I drop the "eq" superscript from $\mathbf{r}_0$ to simplify the notation when doing so does not cause confusion.

Step 1: Calculation of Jacobian

The Jacobian, recalling that we set $\mathbf{r}_0 = \mathbf{r}_0^{\text{eq}}$ in what follows, is given by $J(\mathbf{r}_0) = I_{K+L} - \nabla_{\mathbf{r}_0}\mathbf{B}(\mathbf{r}_0; \mathbf{p}, \mathbf{q}, \theta)$ where

$$\nabla_{\mathbf{r}_0}\mathbf{B}(\mathbf{r}_0; \mathbf{p}, \mathbf{q}, \theta) = \nabla_{\mathbf{r}_0}\mathbf{B}(\mathbf{r}_0) = \begin{pmatrix} E_{11}(\mathbf{r}_0) & E_{12}(\mathbf{r}_0) \\ E_{21}(\mathbf{r}_0) & E_{22}(\mathbf{r}_0) \end{pmatrix}$$

with

$$E_{11}(\mathbf{r}_0) = \lambda \cdot \text{diag}\left\{ \sum_{n=1}^{L} e_{n|1}(\mathbf{r}_0), \ldots, \sum_{n=1}^{L} e_{n|K}(\mathbf{r}_0) \right\}$$

$$E_{12}(\mathbf{r}_0) = -\lambda \begin{pmatrix} \dfrac{r_{10}}{r_{01}} e_{1|1}(\mathbf{r}_0) & \cdots & \dfrac{r_{10}}{r_{0L}} e_{L|1}(\mathbf{r}_0) \\ \vdots & \ddots & \vdots \\ \dfrac{r_{K0}}{r_{01}} e_{1|K}(\mathbf{r}_0) & \cdots & \dfrac{r_{K0}}{r_{0L}} e_{L|K}(\mathbf{r}_0) \end{pmatrix}$$

$$E_{21}(\mathbf{r}_0) = -(1-\lambda)\begin{pmatrix} \frac{r_{0l}}{r_{10}} g_{1|1}(\mathbf{r}_0) & \cdots & \frac{r_{0l}}{r_{K0}} g_{K|1}(\mathbf{r}_0) \\ \vdots & \ddots & \vdots \\ \frac{r_{0L}}{r_{10}} g_{1|L}(\mathbf{r}_0) & \cdots & \frac{r_{0L}}{r_{K0}} g_{K|L}(\mathbf{r}_0) \end{pmatrix}$$

$$E_{22}(\mathbf{r}_0) = (1-\lambda)\cdot\mathrm{diag}\left\{\sum_{m=1}^{K} g_{m|1}(\mathbf{r}_0), \ldots, \sum_{m=1}^{K} g_{m|L}(\mathbf{r}_0)\right\}$$

where we define

$$e_{l|k}(\mathbf{r}_0) =^{\mathrm{def}} \frac{\exp\left[\gamma_{kl} + \lambda \ln\left(\frac{r_{0l}}{r_{k0}}\right)\right]}{1 + \sum_{n=1}^{L} \exp\left[\gamma_{kn} + \lambda \ln\left(\frac{r_{0n}}{r_{k0}}\right)\right]}$$

$$g_{k|l}(\mathbf{r}_0) =^{\mathrm{def}} \frac{\exp\left[\gamma_{kl} - (1-\lambda) \ln\left(\frac{r_{0l}}{r_{k0}}\right)\right]}{1 + \sum_{m=1}^{K} \exp\left[\gamma_{ml} - (1-\lambda) \ln\left(\frac{r_{0l}}{r_{m0}}\right)\right]}$$

Note that for all $\mathbf{r}_0 \in \mathbb{T}_\varepsilon$ and $k = 1, \ldots, K$ and $l = 1, \ldots, L$ we have $\sum_{l=1}^{L} e_{l|k}(\mathbf{r}_0) < 1$ and $\sum_{k=1}^{K} g_{k|l}(\mathbf{r}_0) < 1$. In what follows I will use the abbreviated notation $e_{l|k} = e_{l|k}(\mathbf{r}_0)$ and $g_{k|l} = g_{k|l}(\mathbf{r}_0)$.

Step 2: Factorization of Jacobian Matrix

By the Implicit Function Theorem we have

$$\frac{\mathrm{d}\mathbf{r}_0}{\mathrm{d}p_k} = J(\mathbf{r}_0)^{-1}\frac{\partial \mathbf{B}}{\partial p_k}$$
$$\frac{\mathrm{d}\mathbf{r}_0}{\mathrm{d}q_l} = J(\mathbf{r}_0)^{-1}\frac{\partial \mathbf{B}}{\partial q_l}$$
$$\frac{\mathrm{d}\mathbf{r}_0}{\mathrm{d}\gamma_{kl}} = J(\mathbf{r}_0)^{-1}\frac{\partial \mathbf{B}}{\partial \gamma_{kl}}$$

The $K+L\times 1$ vector of partial derivatives, $\partial\mathbf{B}/\partial p_k$, consists of a zero vector with the exception of the kth element which equals r_{k0}/p_k. The form of $\partial\mathbf{B}/\partial q_l$ is similar with $(K+l)$th element r_{0l}/q_l. The form of $\partial\mathbf{B}/\partial\gamma_{kl}$ consists of a zero vector with the exception of the kth and $(K+l)$th elements, which equal $-r_{k0}(1-r_{kl}/p_k)$ and $-r_{0l}(1-r_{kl}/q_l)$ respectively.

We begin by rewriting the Jacobian matrix in the form

$$J(\mathbf{r}_0)=C(\mathbf{r}_0)^{-1}(A(\mathbf{r}_0)+U(\mathbf{r}_0)B(\mathbf{r}_0)U(\mathbf{r}_0)^{-1}) \tag{16}$$

$$=U(\mathbf{r}_0)C(\mathbf{r}_0)^{-1}(A(\mathbf{r}_0)+B(\mathbf{r}_0))U(\mathbf{r}_0)^{-1} \tag{17}$$

where the second equality exploits the diagonality of $A(\mathbf{r}_0)$, $C(\mathbf{r}_0)$, and $U(\mathbf{r}_0)$, defined as

$$A(\mathbf{r}_0)=\begin{pmatrix}\mathrm{diag}\{\mathbf{p}-\lambda\mathbf{R}\iota_L\} & 0\\ 0 & \mathrm{diag}\{\mathbf{q}-(1-\lambda)\mathbf{R}'\iota_K\}\end{pmatrix}$$

$$B(\mathbf{r}_0)=\begin{pmatrix}0 & \lambda\mathbf{R}\\ (1-\lambda)\mathbf{R}' & 0\end{pmatrix}$$

$$C(\mathbf{r}_0)=\begin{pmatrix}\mathrm{diag}\{\mathbf{p}\} & 0\\ 0 & \mathrm{diag}\{\mathbf{q}\}\end{pmatrix}$$

$$U(\mathbf{r}_0)=\begin{pmatrix}\mathrm{diag}\{\mathbf{r}_{.0}\} & 0\\ 0 & \mathrm{diag}\{\mathbf{r}_{.0}\}\end{pmatrix}$$

Let $H(\mathbf{r}_0)=C(\mathbf{r}_0)^{-1}(A(\mathbf{r}_0)+B(\mathbf{r}_0))$. Writing out $H(\mathbf{r}_0)$ we get

$$\begin{pmatrix}
\frac{(1-\lambda)p_1+\lambda r_{10}}{p_1} & \cdots & 0 & \lambda\frac{r_{11}}{p_1} & \cdots & \lambda\frac{r_{1L}}{p_1}\\
\vdots & \ddots & \vdots & \vdots & \ddots & \vdots\\
0 & \cdots & \frac{(1-\lambda)p_K+\lambda r_{K0}}{p_K} & \lambda\frac{r_{K1}}{p_K} & \cdots & \lambda\frac{r_{KL}}{p_K}\\
\frac{(1-\lambda)r_{11}}{q_1} & \cdots & \frac{(1-\lambda)r_{K1}}{q_1} & \frac{\lambda q_1+(1-\lambda)r_{01}}{q_1} & \cdots & 0\\
\vdots & \ddots & \vdots & \vdots & \ddots & \vdots\\
\frac{(1-\lambda)r_{1L}}{q_L} & \cdots & \frac{(1-\lambda)r_{KL}}{q_L} & 0 & \cdots & \frac{\lambda q_L+(1-\lambda)r_{0L}}{q_L}
\end{pmatrix}$$

Observe that all the elements of $H(\mathbf{r}_0)$ are nonnegative and that its rows sum to one (i.e., $H(\mathbf{r}_0)\iota_{K+L}=\iota_{K+L}$). Therefore $H(\mathbf{r}_0)$ is a row stochastic matrix (cf. Horn & Johnson, 2013, p. 547) with an inverse whose rows also sum to one since

$$H(\mathbf{r}_0)^{-1}\iota_{K+L} = H(\mathbf{r}_0)^{-1}H(\mathbf{r}_0)\iota_{K+L} = I_{K+L}\iota_{K+L} = \iota_{K+L} \tag{18}$$

Step 3: Derivation of Z-Matrix Property

Let $D = \mathrm{diag}\{\lambda I_K, (1-\lambda)I_L\}$ and partition of $H^*(\mathbf{r}_0) = H(\mathbf{r}_0)D$ as

$$H^*(\mathbf{r}_0) = \begin{pmatrix} \lambda\mathrm{diag}(\mathbf{p})^{-1}\mathrm{diag}((1-\lambda)\mathbf{p}+\mathbf{l}\mathbf{r}_{.0}) & \lambda(1-\lambda)\mathrm{diag}(\mathbf{p})^{-1}\mathbf{R} \\ \lambda(1-\lambda)\mathrm{diag}(\mathbf{q})^{-1}\mathbf{R}' & (1-\lambda)\mathrm{diag}(\mathbf{q})^{-1}\mathrm{diag}(\lambda\mathbf{q}+(1-\lambda)\mathbf{r}_{0.}) \end{pmatrix}$$
$$= \begin{pmatrix} H_{11}^*(\mathbf{r}_0) & H_{12}^*(\mathbf{r}_0) \\ H_{21}^*(\mathbf{r}_0) & H_{22}^*(\mathbf{r}_0) \end{pmatrix}$$

Observe that $H^*(\mathbf{r}_0)$ is strictly diagonally dominant since, for $i = 1, \ldots, K$,

$$\sum_{j=1, j\neq i}^{K+L} \left|h_{ij}^*\right| = \lambda(1-\lambda)\sum_{n=1}^{L}\frac{r_{in}}{p_i} = \frac{\lambda(1-\lambda)(p_i - r_{i0})}{p_i} < \frac{\lambda r_{i0} + \lambda(1-\lambda)(p_i - r_{i0})}{p_i} = \left|h_{ii}^*\right|$$

and, for $i = K+1, \ldots, K+L$,

$$\sum_{j=1, j\neq i}^{K+L} \left|h_{ij}^*\right| = \lambda(1-\lambda)\sum_{m=1}^{K}\frac{r_{mi-K}}{q_{i-K}} = \frac{\lambda(1-\lambda)(q_{i-K} - r_{0i-K})}{q_{i-K}}$$
$$< \frac{(1-\lambda)r_{0i-K} + \lambda(1-\lambda)(q_{i-K} - r_{0i-K})}{q_{i-K}} = \left|h_{ii}^*\right|$$

The Schur complement of H_{11}^* in H^* equals $H_{22}^* - H_{21}^*(H_{11}^*)^{-1}H_{12}^*$ and that of H_{22}^* in H^* equals $H_{11}^* - H_{12}^*(H_{22}^*)^{-1}H_{21}^*$ (we suppress the dependence of these matrices on $\mathbf{r}_0$ in what immediately follows). Theorem 1 of Carlson and Markham (1979, p. 248) implies that both of these Schur complements are diagonally dominant (this also easily shown directly). Observe that

$$H_{22}^* - H_{21}^*(H_{11}^*)^{-1}H_{12}^* = (1-\lambda)H_{22} - \lambda H_{21}(\lambda H_{11})^{-1}(1-\lambda)H_{12}$$
$$= (1-\lambda)(H_{22} - H_{21}H_{11}^{-1}H_{12})$$

and also

$$H_{11}^* - H_{12}^*(H_{22}^*)^{-1}H_{21}^* = \lambda H_{11} - (1-\lambda)H_{12}((1-\lambda)H_{22})^{-1}\lambda H_{21}$$
$$= \lambda(H_{11} - H_{12}H_{22}^{-1}H_{21})$$

Partitioning $H(\mathbf{r}_0)$ conformably to the $H^*(\mathbf{r}_0)$ partition defined above we therefore have that the Schur complements of H_{11} and H_{22} in H are row diagonally dominant. Diagonality of H_{11} and H_{22}, positivity of the elements of $H_{21}H_{11}^{-1}H_{12}$ and $H_{12}H_{22}^{-1}H_{21}$, and diagonal dominance further imply that these matrices are Z-matrices (i.e., members of the class of real matrices with non-positive off-diagonal elements). By applying Theorem 4.3 of Fiedler and Ptak (1962) it follows that $H_{22}-H_{21}H_{11}^{-1}H_{12}$ and $H_{11}-H_{12}H_{22}^{-1}H_{21}$ are M-matrices and hence that $(H_{22}-H_{21}H_{11}^{-1}H_{12})^{-1}\geqq 0$ and $(H_{11}-H_{12}H_{22}^{-1}H_{21})^{-1}\geqq 0$. These results are sufficient to establish the sign structure of $H(\mathbf{r}_0)^{-1}$. Specifically we have, using the partitioned inverse formula

$$H(\mathbf{r}_0)^{-1}=\begin{pmatrix} W_{11} & W_{12} \\ W_{21} & W_{22}\end{pmatrix}=\begin{pmatrix} + & \vdots & - \\ \cdots & & \cdots \\ - & \vdots & + \end{pmatrix}$$

where

$$\begin{aligned}
W_{11} &= (H_{11}-H_{12}H_{22}^{-1}H_{21})^{-1} \\
&= H_{11}^{-1}+H_{11}^{-1}H_{12}(H_{22}-H_{21}H_{11}^{-1}H_{12})^{-1}H_{21}H_{11}^{-1} \\
W_{12} &= -(H_{11}-H_{12}H_{22}^{-1}H_{21})^{-1}H_{12}H_{22}^{-1} \\
&= -H_{11}^{-1}H_{12}(H_{22}-H_{21}H_{11}^{-1}H_{12})^{-1} \\
W_{21} &= -H_{22}^{-1}H_{21}(H_{11}-H_{12}H_{22}^{-1}H_{21})^{-1} \\
&= -(H_{22}-H_{21}H_{11}^{-1}H_{12})^{-1}H_{21}H_{11}^{-1} \\
W_{22} &= (H_{22}-H_{21}H_{11}^{-1}H_{12})^{-1} \\
&= H_{22}^{-1}+H_{22}^{-1}H_{21}(H_{11}-H_{12}H_{22}^{-1}H_{21})^{-1}H_{12}H_{22}^{-1}
\end{aligned}$$

Step 4: Derivation of the Structure of $H(\mathbf{r}_0)^{-1}$

The known sign structures of $(H_{22}-H_{21}H_{11}^{-1}H_{12})^{-1}$ and $(H_{11}-H_{12}\times H_{22}^{-1}H_{21})^{-1}$ and the partitioned inverse formula immediately yield the inequality relationships:

$$\begin{aligned}
W_{11} &\geq H_{11}^{-1} \\
W_{22} &\geq H_{22}^{-1}
\end{aligned}$$

and hence the refined inequalities

$$\begin{aligned}
W_{11} &= H_{11}^{-1}+H_{11}^{-1}H_{12}W_{22}H_{21}H_{11}^{-1}\geq H_{11}^{-1}+H_{11}^{-1}H_{12}H_{22}^{-1}H_{21}H_{11}^{-1} \\
W_{22} &= H_{22}^{-1}+H_{22}^{-1}H_{21}W_{11}H_{12}H_{22}^{-1}\geq H_{22}^{-1}+H_{22}^{-1}H_{21}H_{11}^{-1}H_{12}H_{22}^{-1}
\end{aligned}$$

where

$$
\begin{aligned}
W_{11} &\geq H_{11}^{-1} + H_{11}^{-1} H_{12} H_{22}^{-1} H_{21} H_{11}^{-1} \\
&= \operatorname{diag}\left\{ \frac{p_1}{(1-\lambda)p_1 + \lambda r_{10}}, \ldots, \frac{p_K}{(1-\lambda)p_K + \lambda r_{K0}} \right\} \\
&\quad + \lambda(1-\lambda) \begin{pmatrix}
\frac{1}{(1-\lambda)p_1 + \lambda r_{10}} \frac{p_1}{(1-\lambda)p_1 + \lambda r_{10}} \sum_{n=1}^{L} \frac{r_{1n} r_{1n}}{\lambda q_n + (1-\lambda) r_{0n}} & \cdots & \frac{1}{(1-\lambda)p_1 + \lambda r_{10}} \frac{p_K}{(1-\lambda)p_K + \lambda r_{K0}} \sum_{n=1}^{L} \frac{r_{1n} r_{Kn}}{\lambda q_n + (1-\lambda) r_{0n}} \\
\vdots & \ddots & \vdots \\
\frac{1}{(1-\lambda)p_K + \lambda r_{K0}} \frac{p_1}{(1-\lambda)p_1 + \lambda r_{10}} \sum_{n=1}^{L} \frac{r_{Kn} r_{1n}}{\lambda q_n + (1-\lambda) r_{0n}} & \cdots & \frac{1}{(1-\lambda)p_K + \lambda r_{K0}} \frac{p_K}{(1-\lambda)p_K + \lambda r_{K0}} \sum_{n=1}^{L} \frac{r_{Kn} r_{Kn}}{\lambda q_n + (1-\lambda) r_{0n}}
\end{pmatrix} > I_K
\end{aligned}
$$

$$
\begin{aligned}
W_{22} &\geq H_{22}^{-1} + H_{22}^{-1} H_{21} H_{11}^{-1} H_{12} H_{22}^{-1} \\
&= \operatorname{diag}\left\{ \frac{q_1}{\lambda q_1 + (1-\lambda) r_{01}}, \ldots, \frac{q_L}{\lambda q_L + (1-\lambda) r_{0L}} \right\} \\
&\quad + \lambda(1-\lambda) \begin{pmatrix}
\frac{1}{\lambda q_1 + (1-\lambda) r_{01}} \frac{q_1}{\lambda q_1 + (1-\lambda) r_{01}} \sum_{m=1}^{K} \frac{r_{m1} r_{m1}}{(1-\lambda)p_m + \lambda r_{m0}} & \cdots & \frac{1}{\lambda q_1 + (1-\lambda) r_{01}} \frac{q_L}{\lambda q_L + (1-\lambda) r_{0L}} \sum_{m=1}^{K} \frac{r_{m1} r_{mL}}{(1-\lambda)p_m + \lambda r_{m0}} \\
\vdots & \ddots & \vdots \\
\frac{1}{\lambda q_L + (1-\lambda) r_{0L}} \frac{q_1}{\lambda q_1 + (1-\lambda) r_{01}} \sum_{m=1}^{K} \frac{r_{mL} r_{m1}}{(1-\lambda)p_m + \lambda r_{m0}} & \cdots & \frac{1}{\lambda q_L + (1-\lambda) r_{0L}} \frac{q_L}{\lambda q_L + (1-\lambda) r_{0L}} \sum_{m=1}^{K} \frac{r_{mL} r_{mL}}{(1-\lambda)p_m + \lambda r_{m0}}
\end{pmatrix} > I_L
\end{aligned}
$$

This implies that the diagonal elements of $H(\mathbf{r}_0)^{-1}$ exceed one.

For the off-diagonal blocks of $H(\mathbf{r}_0)^{-1}$ we have

$$W_{12} \leq -H_{11}^{-1}H_{12}H_{22}^{-1}$$
$$W_{21} \leq -H_{22}^{-1}H_{21}H_{11}^{-1}.$$

Evaluating $-H_{11}^{-1}H_{12}H_{22}^{-1}$ and $-H_{22}^{-1}H_{21}H_{11}^{-1}$ yields

$$-H_{11}^{-1}H_{12}H_{22}^{-1}$$
$$= -\begin{pmatrix} \frac{\lambda r_{11}}{(1-\lambda)p_1 + \lambda r_{10}} \frac{q_1}{\lambda q_1 + (1-\lambda) r_{01}} & \cdots & \frac{\lambda r_{1L}}{(1-\lambda)p_1 + \lambda r_{10}} \frac{q_L}{\lambda q_L + (1-\lambda) r_{0L}} \\ \vdots & \ddots & \vdots \\ \frac{\lambda r_{K1}}{(1-\lambda)p_K + \lambda r_{K0}} \frac{q_1}{\lambda q_1 + (1-\lambda) r_{01}} & \cdots & \frac{\lambda r_{KL}}{(1-\lambda)p_K + \lambda r_{K0}} \frac{q_L}{\lambda q_L + (1-\lambda) r_{0L}} \end{pmatrix}$$

$$-H_{22}^{-1}H_{21}H_{11}^{-1}$$
$$= -\begin{pmatrix} \frac{(1-\lambda) r_{11}}{\lambda q_1 + (1-\lambda) r_{01}} \frac{p_1}{(1-\lambda)p_1 + \lambda r_{10}} & \cdots & \frac{(1-\lambda) r_{K1}}{\lambda q_1 + (1-\lambda) r_{01}} \frac{p_K}{(1-\lambda)p_K + \lambda r_{K0}} \\ \vdots & \ddots & \vdots \\ \frac{(1-\lambda) r_{1L}}{\lambda q_L + (1-\lambda) r_{0L}} \frac{p_1}{(1-\lambda)p_1 + \lambda r_{10}} & \cdots & \frac{(1-\lambda) r_{KL}}{\lambda q_L + (1-\lambda) r_{0L}} \frac{P_K}{(1-\lambda)p_K + \lambda r_{K0}} \end{pmatrix}$$

Theorem 2.5.12 of Horn and Johnson (1991, p. 125) further implies that the diagonal elements of $H^*(\mathbf{r}_0)^{-1}$ are larger in absolute value that any off diagonal element in the same column (i.e., $H^*(\mathbf{r}_0)^{-1}$ is strictly dominant in its column entries). Since $H^*(\mathbf{r}_0)^{-1} = D^{-1}H(\mathbf{r}_0)^{-1}$ with $D = \text{diag}\{\lambda I_K, (1-\lambda) I_L\}$ we have the upper-left $K \times K$ and lower-right $L \times L$ blocks of $H(\mathbf{r}_0)^{-1}$ strictly dominant in their column entries.

Step 5a: Type-Specific Elasticities of Single-Hood with Respect to Type Availability

Let $\mathbf{h}_k$ be a $K + L$ column vector of zeros with the exception of a one in the kth row. The $K + L$ elasticities of single-hood with respect to p_k are given by

$$\begin{aligned} U(\mathbf{r}_0)^{-1} \frac{\mathrm{d}\mathbf{r}_0}{\mathrm{d}p_k} p_k &= U(\mathbf{r}_0)^{-1} J(\mathbf{r}_0)^{-1} \frac{\partial \mathbf{B}}{\partial p_k} p_k \\ &= U(\mathbf{r}_0)^{-1} U(\mathbf{r}_0) H(\mathbf{r}_0)^{-1} U(\mathbf{r}_0)^{-1} \mathbf{h}_k \left(\frac{r_{k0}}{p_k}\right) p_k \\ &= H(\mathbf{r}_0)^{-1} \mathbf{h}_k \end{aligned}$$

The sign structure of $H(\mathbf{r}_0)^{-1}$ as well as strict dominance of its two diagonal blocks in their column entries gives part 1 of Theorem 1. Specifically, tedious calculation yields

$$\frac{\mathrm{d}r_{10}}{\mathrm{d}p_k}\frac{p_k}{r_{10}}=W_{11}[1,k]\geq\frac{1}{(1-\lambda)p_1+\lambda r_{10}}\frac{p_k}{(1-\lambda)p_k+\lambda r_{k0}}\sum_{n=1}^{L}\frac{r_{1n}r_{kn}}{\lambda q_n+(1-\lambda)r_{0n}}>0$$

$$\vdots$$

$$\frac{\mathrm{d}r_{k0}}{\mathrm{d}p_k}\frac{p_k}{r_{k0}}=W_{11}[k,k]\geq\frac{p_k}{(1-\lambda)p_k+\lambda r_{k0}}\left(1+\frac{1}{(1-\lambda)p_k+\lambda r_{k0}}\sum_{n=1}^{L}\frac{r_{kn}r_{kn}}{\lambda q_n+(1-\lambda)r_{0n}}\right)>1$$

$$\vdots$$

$$\frac{\mathrm{d}r_{K0}}{\mathrm{d}p_k}\frac{p_k}{r_{K0}}=W_{11}[K,k]\geq\frac{1}{(1-\lambda)p_K+\lambda r_{K0}}\frac{p_k}{(1-\lambda)p_k+\lambda r_{k0}}\sum_{n=1}^{L}\frac{r_{Kn}r_{kn}}{\lambda q_n+(1-\lambda)r_{0n}}>0$$

$$\frac{\mathrm{d}r_{01}}{\mathrm{d}p_k}\frac{p_k}{r_{01}}=W_{21}[1,k]\leq-\frac{(1-\lambda)r_{k1}}{\lambda q_1+(1-\lambda)r_{01}}\frac{p_k}{(1-\lambda)p_k+\lambda r_{k0}}<0$$

$$\vdots$$

$$\frac{\mathrm{d}r_{0L}}{\mathrm{d}p_k}\frac{p_k}{r_{0L}}=W_{21}[L,k]\leq-\frac{(1-\lambda)r_{kL}}{\lambda q_L+(1-\lambda)r_{0L}}\frac{p_k}{(1-\lambda)p_k+\lambda r_{k0}}<0$$

Step 5b: Limited Symmetry

The entire matrix of semi-elasticities can be written as

$$U(\mathbf{r}_0)^{-1}\frac{\mathrm{d}\mathbf{r}_0}{\mathrm{d}\begin{pmatrix}\mathbf{p}\\ \mathbf{q}\end{pmatrix}'}=U(\mathbf{r}_0)^{-1}U(\mathbf{r}_0)H(\mathbf{r}_0)^{-1}U(\mathbf{r}_0)^{-1}\mathrm{diag}\left\{\frac{r_{10}}{p_1},\ldots,\frac{r_{K0}}{p_K},\frac{r_{01}}{q_1},\ldots,\frac{r_{0L}}{q_L}\right\}$$

$$=H(\mathbf{r}_0)^{-1}\mathrm{diag}\{\mathbf{p}\prime,\mathbf{q}\prime\}^{-1}$$

Now observe that $\mathrm{diag}\left\{\frac{\mathbf{p}'}{\lambda},\frac{\mathbf{q}'}{1-\lambda}\right\}H(\mathbf{r}_0)$ is symmetric and hence, also using the calculation immediately above

$$U^{-1}\frac{\mathrm{d}\mathbf{r}_0}{\mathrm{d}\begin{pmatrix}\mathbf{p}\\ \mathbf{q}\end{pmatrix}'}=\left[\mathrm{diag}\left\{\frac{\mathbf{p}'}{\lambda},\frac{\mathbf{q}'}{1-\lambda}\right\}^{-1}\mathrm{diag}\left\{\frac{\mathbf{p}'}{\lambda},\frac{\mathbf{q}'}{1-\lambda}\right\}H(\mathbf{r}_0)\right]^{-1}\mathrm{diag}\{\mathbf{p}',\mathbf{q}'\}^{-1}$$

$$=\left[\mathrm{diag}\left\{\frac{\mathbf{p}'}{\lambda},\frac{\mathbf{q}'}{1-\lambda}\right\}H(\mathbf{r}_0)\right]^{-1}\mathrm{diag}\left\{\frac{\mathbf{p}'}{\lambda},\frac{\mathbf{q}'}{1-\lambda}\right\}\mathrm{diag}\{\mathbf{p}',\mathbf{q}'\}^{-1}$$

$$=\underbrace{\begin{pmatrix}+ & \vdots & -\\ \cdots & & \cdots\\ - & \vdots & +\end{pmatrix}}_{\text{symmetric}}\begin{pmatrix}\lambda^{-1}I_K & 0\\ 0 & (1-\lambda)^{-1}I_L\end{pmatrix}$$

from which the result follows.

Step 5c: Aggregate Elasticity of Single-Hood with Respect to Type Availability

The elasticity of single-hood with respect to p_k is given by

$$\begin{aligned}
&\left(\sum_{k=1}^{K} r_{k0} + \sum_{l=1}^{L} r_{0l}\right)^{-1}\left\{\sum_{m=1}^{K}\frac{\mathrm{d}r_{m0}}{\mathrm{d}p_k} + \sum_{n=1}^{L}\frac{\mathrm{d}r_{0l}}{\mathrm{d}p_k}\right\}p_k \\
&= \left(\sum_{k=1}^{K} r_{k0} + \sum_{l=1}^{L} r_{0l}\right)^{-1} \iota'_{K+L}\frac{\mathrm{d}\mathbf{r}_0}{\mathrm{d}p_k}p_k \\
&= \left(\sum_{k=1}^{K} r_{k0} + \sum_{l=1}^{L} r_{0l}\right)^{-1} \iota'_{K+L}U(\mathbf{r}_0)H(\mathbf{r}_0)^{-1}U(\mathbf{r}_0)^{-1}\times\frac{\partial\mathbf{B}}{\partial p_k}p_k \\
&= \left(\sum_{k=1}^{K} r_{k0} + \sum_{l=1}^{L} r_{0l}\right)^{-1} \iota'_{K+L}U(\mathbf{r}_0)H(\mathbf{r}_0)^{-1}U(\mathbf{r}_0)^{-1}\times\mathbf{h}_k\left(\frac{r_{k0}}{p_k}\right)p_k \\
&= \left(\sum_{k=1}^{K} r_{k0} + \sum_{l=1}^{L} r_{0l}\right)^{-1} \mathbf{h}'_kU(\mathbf{r}_0)H(\mathbf{r}_0)^{-1}\iota_{K+L} \\
&= \left(\sum_{k=1}^{K} r_{k0} + \sum_{l=1}^{L} r_{0l}\right)^{-1} \mathbf{h}'_kU(\mathbf{r}_0)\iota_{K+L} \\
&= \frac{r_{k0}}{\sum_{k=1}^{K} r_{k0} + \sum_{l=1}^{L} r_{0l}}
\end{aligned}$$

where I use the fact, shown above, that $H(\mathbf{r}_0)^{-1}\iota_{K+L} = \iota_{K+L}$.

Now consider the effect of an increase in the population size of women, holding its type distribution fixed (i.e., we increase $\mathrm{d}(\mathbf{p}'\iota_K)$ such that $\frac{\mathrm{d}p_k}{\mathrm{d}(\mathbf{p}'\iota_K)} = p_k/\mathbf{p}'\iota_K$ for $k=1,\ldots,K$). This yields

$$\begin{aligned}
\frac{\mathrm{d}(\mathbf{r}'_0\iota_{K+L})}{\mathrm{d}(\mathbf{p}'\iota_K)} &= \frac{1}{\mathbf{p}'\iota_K}\sum_{k=1}^{K}\left\{\sum_{m=1}^{K}\frac{\mathrm{d}r_{m0}}{\mathrm{d}p_k} + \sum_{n=1}^{L}\frac{\mathrm{d}r_{0l}}{\mathrm{d}p_k}\right\}p_k \\
&= \frac{1}{\mathbf{p}'\iota_K}\sum_{k=1}^{K}\iota'_{K+L}U(\mathbf{r}_0)H(\mathbf{r}_0)^{-1}U(\mathbf{r}_0)^{-1}\mathbf{h}_k\left(\frac{r_{k0}}{p_k}\right)p_k \\
&= \frac{1}{\mathbf{p}'\iota_K}\sum_{k=1}^{K}\mathbf{h}'_kU(\mathbf{r}_0)\iota_{K+L} = \frac{1}{\mathbf{p}'\iota_K}\sum_{k=1}^{K}r_{k0}
\end{aligned}$$

and hence

$$\left.\frac{\mathrm{d}(\mathbf{r}_0'\iota_{K+L})}{\mathrm{d}(\mathbf{p}'\iota_K)}\frac{(\mathbf{p}'\iota_K)}{(\mathbf{r}_0'\iota_{K+L})}\right|_{\frac{\mathrm{d}p_k/p_k}{\mathrm{d}(\mathbf{p}'\iota_K)/(\mathbf{p}'\iota_K)}=1,\ k=1,\dots,K} = \frac{\sum_{k=1}^{K} r_{k0}}{\sum_{k=1}^{K} r_{k0} + \sum_{l=1}^{L} r_{0l}}$$

This is reported in Eq. (14) of the main text.

Step 5d: Constant Returns to Scale

The demand functions for single-hood are homogenous of degree one since

$$\sum_{k=1}^{K} U(\mathbf{r}_0)^{-1}\frac{\mathrm{d}\mathbf{r_0}}{\mathrm{d}p_k}p_k + \sum_{l=1}^{L} U(\mathbf{r}_0)^{-1}\frac{\mathrm{d}\mathbf{r}_0}{\mathrm{d}q_l}q_l = U(\mathbf{r}_0)^{-1}U(\mathbf{r}_0)H(\mathbf{r}_0)^{-1}U(\mathbf{r}_0)^{-1}\mathbf{r}_0$$
$$= H(\mathbf{r}_0)^{-1}\iota_{K+L} = \iota_{K+L}$$

with the result following from Euler's Theorem

Step 5e: Semi-Elasticity of Single-Hood with Respect to γ_{kl}

The approximate percent increase in single-hood for each of the $K+L$ types of agents given a unit increase in γ_{kl} is given by

$$U(\mathbf{r}_0)^{-1}\frac{\mathrm{d}\mathbf{r_0}}{\mathrm{d}\gamma_{kl}} = U(\mathbf{r}_0)^{-1}J(\mathbf{r}_0)^{-1}\frac{\partial \mathbf{B}}{\partial \gamma_{kl}}$$
$$= -H(\mathbf{r}_0)^{-1}\mathrm{diag}\{\mathbf{p}\prime, \mathbf{q}\prime\}^{-1}(\mathbf{h}_k + \mathbf{h}_{K+l})r_{kl}$$
$$= -\begin{pmatrix} \frac{\mathrm{d}r_{10}}{\mathrm{d}p_k}\frac{1}{r_{10}} + \frac{\mathrm{d}r_{10}}{\mathrm{d}q_l}\frac{1}{r_{10}} \\ \vdots \\ \frac{\mathrm{d}r_{K0}}{\mathrm{d}p_k}\frac{1}{r_{K0}} + \frac{\mathrm{d}r_{K0}}{\mathrm{d}q_l}\frac{1}{r_{K0}} \\ \frac{\mathrm{d}r_{01}}{\mathrm{d}p_k}\frac{1}{r_{01}} + \frac{\mathrm{d}r_{01}}{\mathrm{d}q_l}\frac{1}{r_{01}} \\ \vdots \\ \frac{\mathrm{d}r_{0L}}{\mathrm{d}p_k}\frac{1}{r_{0L}} + \frac{\mathrm{d}r_{0L}}{\mathrm{d}q_l}\frac{1}{r_{0L}} \end{pmatrix} r_{kl}$$

where the final equality follows from the expression for $U(\mathbf{r}_0)^{-1}\frac{\mathrm{d}\mathbf{r}_0}{\mathrm{d}(p'\ q')}$ derived above.

To derive the effect of a unit increase in net marriage surplus – for all types of marriages – on the aggregate prevalence of single-hood we begin by noting that

$$\sum_{k=1}^{K}\sum_{l=1}^{L}\frac{\partial \mathbf{B}}{\partial \gamma_{kl}} = -\begin{pmatrix} r_{10}(1-r_{01}/p_1) \\ \vdots \\ r_{K0}(1-r_{K0}/p_K) \\ r_{01}(1-r_{01}/q_1) \\ \vdots \\ r_{0L}(1-r_{0L}/q_L) \end{pmatrix}$$

The required semi-elasticity is then, making use of the row stochastic structure of $H(\mathbf{r}_0)$,

$$\begin{aligned}
\iota'_{K+L}\frac{\mathrm{d}\mathbf{r}_0}{\mathrm{d}\bar{\gamma}} &= \iota'_{K+L}J(\mathbf{r}_0)^{-1}\sum_{k=1}^{K}\sum_{l=1}^{L}\frac{\partial \mathbf{B}}{\partial \gamma_{kl}} \\
&= -\iota'_{K+L}U(\mathbf{r}_0)H(\mathbf{r}_0)^{-1}U(\mathbf{r}_0)^{-1}\begin{pmatrix} r_{10}(1-r_{01}/p_1) \\ \vdots \\ r_{K0}(1-r_{K0}/p_K) \\ r_{01}(1-r_{01}/q_1) \\ \vdots \\ r_{0L}(1-r_{0L}/q_L) \end{pmatrix} \\
&= -\iota'_{K+L}U(\mathbf{r}_0)H(\mathbf{r}_0)^{-1}\begin{pmatrix} 1-r_{01}/p_1 \\ \vdots \\ 1-r_{K0}/p_K \\ 1-r_{01}/q_1 \\ \vdots \\ 1-r_{0L}/q_L \end{pmatrix} \\
&= -\begin{pmatrix} 1-r_{01}/p_1 \\ \vdots \\ 1-r_{K0}/p_K \\ 1-r_{01}/q_1 \\ \vdots \\ 1-r_{0L}/q_L \end{pmatrix}' U(\mathbf{r}_0)H(\mathbf{r}_0)^{-1}\iota_{K+L} \\
&= -\sum_{k=1}^{K} r_{k0}\left(1-\frac{r_{k0}}{p_k}\right) - \sum_{l=1}^{L} r_{0l}\left(1-\frac{r_{0l}}{q_l}\right)
\end{aligned}$$

Hence the change in the fraction of the population that is single equals

$$-\frac{\sum_{k=1}^{K} p_k e_{k0}(1-e_{k0}) + \sum_{l=1}^{L} q_l e_{0l}(1-e_{0l})}{\sum_{k=1}^{K} p_k + \sum_{l=1}^{L} q_l}$$

as reported in Eq. (15) of the main text.

NOTES

1. See Dagsvik (2000) for an earlier, and related, contribution.
2. The subscript "i" denotes a generic random draw from the population of women, while the superscript "j" one from men.
3. Galichon and Salanie (2012) consider other parametric families of distributions. Graham (2011) considers the case where $F_{\underline{\varepsilon}|W}$ and $F_{\underline{v}|X}$ are left nonparametric.
4. The difficulty of determining whether a Jacobian matrix is a P-matrix is one motivation for deriving alternative conditions which ensure invertibility (e.g., Berry, Gandhi, & Haile, 2012).
5. Alternatively other, more recent, approaches to parameter estimation in fixed point problems may be utilized (e.g., Aguirregabiria, 2004; Aguirregabiria & Mira, 2002, 2007, 2010; Su & Judd, 2012).

ACKNOWLEDGMENTS

I would like to thank Gary Chamberlain, Eugene Choo, Alfred Galichon, Michael Jansson, Konrad Menzel, Ariel Pakes, and numerous participants in the 2013 Advances in Econometrics Conference at Louisiana State University and a seminar at Harvard-MIT for helpful discussions. A special thanks to Gary Chamberlain, Eugene Choo, and Alfred Galichon for written feedback on an earlier draft. All the usual disclaimers apply.

REFERENCES

Aguirregabiria, V. (2004). Pseudo maximum likelihood estimation of structural models involving fixed-point problems. *Economics Letters*, *84*(3), 335–340.

Aguirregabiria, V., & Mira, P. (2002). Swapping the nested fixed point algorithm: A class of estimators for discrete Markov decision models. *Econometrica*, *70*(4), 1519–1543.

Aguirregabiria, V., & Mira, P. (2007). Sequential estimation of dynamic discrete games. *Econometrica*, *75*(1), 1–53.

Aguirregabiria, V., & Mira, P. (2010). Dynamic discrete choice structural models: A survey. *Journal of Econometrics*, *156*(1), 38–67.

Angrist, J. (2002). How do sex ratios affect the marriage and labor markets? Evidence from America's second generation. *Quarterly Journal of Economics*, *117*(3), 997–1038.

Aradillas-Lopez, A. (2010). Semiparametric estimation of a simultaneous game with incomplete information. *Journal of Econometrics*, *157*(2), 409–431.

Bajari, P., Hahn, J., Hong, H., & Ridder, G. (2011). A note on semiparametric estimation of finite mixtures of discrete choice models with application to game theoretic models. *International Economic Review*, *52*(3), 807–824.

Bajari, P., Hong, H., Krainer, J., & Nekipelov, D. (2010). Estimating static models of strategic interactions. *Journal of Business and Economic Statistics*, *28*(4), 469–482.

Berry, S., Gandhi, A., & Haile, P. (2012). *Connected substitutes and the invertibility of demand.* Mimeo.

Carlson, D., & Markham, T. L. (1979). Schur complements of diagonally dominant matrices. *Czechoslovak Mathematical Journal*, *29*(2), 246–251.

Chiappori, P.-A., Salanie, B., & Weiss, Y. (2012). *Partner choice and the marital college premium.* Mimeo.

Choo, E., & Siow, A. (2006a). Who marries whom and why? *Journal of Political Economy*, *114*(1), 175–201.

Choo, E., & Siow, A. (2006b). Estimating a marriage matching model with spillover effects. *Demography*, *43*(3), 464–490.

Coxson, G. E. (1994). The P-matrix problem is co-NP-complete. *Mathematical Programming*, *64*(1–3), 173–178.

Dagsvik, J. K. (2000). Aggregation in matching markets. *International Economic Review*, *41*(1), 27–57.

Decker, C. (2010). *When do systematic gains uniquely determine the number of marriages between different types in the Choo-Siow matching model? Sufficient conditions for a unique equilibrium.* Masters of Science thesis, University of Toronto.

Decker, C., Lieb, E. H., McCann, R. J., & Stephens, B. K. (2013). Unique equilibria and substitution effects in a stochastic model of the marriage market. *Journal of Economic Theory*, *148*(12), 778–792.

Echenique, F., Lee, S., Shum, M., & Yenmez, B. B. (2013). The reveal preference theory of stable and extremal stable matchings. *Econometrica*, *81*(1), 153–171.

Fiedler, M., & Ptak, V. (1962). On matrices with non-positive off-diagonal elements and positive principal minors. *Czechoslovak Mathematical Journal*, *12*(3), 382–400.

Fox, J. (2010). Identification in matching games. *Quantitative Economics*, *1*(2), 203–254.

Gale, D., & Nikaido, H. (1965). The Jacobian matrix and global univalence of mappings. *Mathematische Annalen*, *159*(2), 81–93.

Galichon, A., & Salanie, B. (2010). *Matching with trade-offs: Revealed preferences over competing characteristics.* Mimeo.

Galichon, A., & Salanie, B. (2012). *Cupid's invisible hand: Social surplus and identification in matching models.* Mimeo.

Graham, B. S. (2011). Econometric methods for the analysis of assignment problems in the presence of complementarity and social spillovers. In J. Benhabib, A. Bisin, & M. Jackson (Eds.), *Handbook of social economics* (Vol. 1B, pp. 965–1052). Amsterdam: North-Holland.

Horn, R. A., & Johnson, C. R. (1991). *Topics in matrix analysis*. Cambridge: Cambridge University Press.

Horn, R. A., & Johnson., C. R. (2013). *Matrix analysis* (2nd ed.). Cambridge: Cambridge University Press.

Johnson, C. R. (1982). Inverse M-matrices. *Linear Algebra and its Applications*, *47*, 195–216.

Koopmans, T. C., & Beckmann, M. (1957). Assignment problems and the location of economic activities. *Econometrica*, *25*(1), 53–76.

Manski, C. F. (1975). Maximum score estimation of the stochastic utility model of choice. *Journal of Econometrics*, *3*(3), 205–228.

Matzkin, R. (2007). Heterogeneous choice. In R. Blundell, W. Newey, & T. Persson (Eds.), *Advances in economics and econometrics: Theory and applications* (Vol. 3, pp. 75–110). Cambridge: Cambridge University Press.

McFadden, D. (1974). Conditional logit analysis of qualitative choice behavior. In P. Zarembka (Ed.), *Frontiers in econometrics* (pp. 105–142). New York, NY: Academic Press.

McKenzie, L. (1960). Matrices with dominant diagonals and economic theory. In K. J. Arrow, S. Karlin, & P. Suppes (Eds.), *Mathematical methods in the social sciences, 1959* (pp. 47–62). Stanford: Stanford University Press.

Rust, J. (1987). Optimal replacement of GMC bus engines: An empirical model of Harold Zurcher. *Econometrica*, *55*(5), 999–1033.

Schwartz, C. (2010). Earnings inequality and the changing association between spouse's earnings. *American Journal of Sociology*, *115*(5), 1524–1557.

Shapley, L. S., & Shubik., M. (1971). The assignment game I: The core. *International Journal of Game Theory*, *1*(1), 111–130.

Siow, A. (2008). How does the marriage market clear? An empirical framework. *Canadian Journal of Economics/Revue Canadienne D'économique*, *41*(4), 1121–1155.

Su, C.-L., & Judd., K. L. (2012). Constrained optimization approaches to estimation of structural models. *Econometrica*, *80*(5), 2213–2230.

A TEST FOR MONOTONE COMPARATIVE STATICS

Federico Echenique and Ivana Komunjer

ABSTRACT

In this article we design an econometric test for monotone comparative statics (MCS) often found in models with multiple equilibria. Our test exploits the observable implications of the MCS prediction: that the extreme (high and low) conditiona l quantiles of the dependent variable increase monotonically with the explanatory variable. The main contribution of the article is to derive a likelihood-ratio test, which to the best of our knowledge is the first econometric test of MCS proposed in the literature. The test is an asymptotic "chi-bar squared" test for order restrictions on intermediate conditional quantiles. The key features of our approach are: (1) we do not need to estimate the underlying non-parametric model relating the dependent and explanatory variables to the latent disturbances; (2) we make few assumptions on the cardinality, location, or probabilities over equilibria. In particular, one can implement our test without assuming an equilibrium selection rule.

Keywords: Multiple equilibria; comparative statics; quantiles; chi-bar squared

JEL classifications: C12; C51

Structural Econometric Models
Advances in Econometrics, Volume 31, 183–232

ISSN: 0731-9053/doi:10.1108/S0731-9053(2013)0000032007

INTRODUCTION

Comparative statics predictions – or how exogenous variables affect endogenous variables – are important to establish in economic models.[1] Often, the models possess multiple equilibria, and a *monotone comparative statics* (MCS) prediction holds: There is a smallest and a largest equilibrium, and these change monotonically with explanatory variables (see, e.g., Milgrom & Roberts, 1990b; Milgrom & Shannon, 1994; Villas-Boas, 1997). MCS is a feature found in many well-known economic models. Examples are single-person decision models such as models of optimal growth (see, e.g., Barro & Sala-I-Martin, 2003; Ljungqvist & Sargent, 2004) and firms' investment decisions (see, e.g., Hayashi, 1982; Hayashi & Inoue, 1991), oligopoly models à la Berry, Levinsohn, and Pakes (1995), games with network externalities (see, e.g., Ackerberg & Gowrisankaran, 2006), as well as many other models in industrial organization (IO) (see Vives, 1999, for survey).

Recent work in econometrics has shown that MCS is a useful property that can aid with model identification. Molinari and Rosen (2008) study the identification power of MCS in an oligopoly pricing game. Lazzati (2012) uses MCS to derive identification results for treatment response models with endogenous social interactions.[2] In both works, the identification analysis is made complicated because of the presence of multiple equilibria (see, e.g., de Paula, 2013, for a survey on multiple equilibria in econometrics of games). Though recognizing the usefulness of MCS in dealing with equilibrium multiplicity, current econometric literature has largely remained silent on the issue of formal tests for MCS.[3] The goal of this article is to fill this gap.

There are two challenges in testing the MCS hypothesis. The first is to obtain testable implications; the second is to construct a formal statistical test and study its properties. In the context of structural models, Echenique and Komunjer (2009) solve the first, but not the second challenge. They obtain testable implications of the MCS property in the form of restrictions on the conditional quantiles of the dependent variable given the explanatory variable.

In this article, we derive similar restrictions on conditional quantiles in the context of reduced form models with multiple equilibria. Our main contribution is to show how to test those restrictions in a way that is not affected by equilibrium selections. In general, the latter are unknown and have to be treated as nuisance parameters of the problem. Our approach is to first estimate the conditional quantiles nonparametrically, then use those to construct an asymptotic likelihood-ratio (LR) test of the order restrictions implied by the MCS. The test relies only on the asymptotic distribution results; it is an extension of the "chi-bar squared" test by Gourieroux, Holly, and Monfort (1982) and Kodde and Palm (1986) to restrictions on conditional quantiles.

It is worth pointing out that we work under quite weak assumptions on the equilibrium selection procedure. All we need to assume is that the latter places nonzero probabilities on the extremal equilibria, and that the equilibrium probabilities do not depend on the unobservables in the model. These assumptions are considerably weaker than assuming the probabilities of various equilibrium realizations known (see, e.g., Bjorn & Vuong, 1984; Jia, 2008) or finitely parameterized (see, e.g., Ackerberg & Gowrisankaran, 2006; Bajari, Hong, & Ryan, 2010; Bjorn & Vuong, 1985; McKelvey & Palfrey, 1995; Sweeting, 2009). They are also weaker than an assumption that only one equilibrium is played in the data (see, e.g., Aguirregabiria & Mira, 2007).

Example. Here is an example that illustrates how to use our results. Say that one is interested in testing whether an exogenous change in a policy causes the prices in the market for cars to increase. When there are complementarities between the policy and the agents' choice variables, the effect on prices takes the form of MCS. In the case of car prices, policy changes which increase marginal cost would cause the smallest and largest equilibria to increase. Examples of these policies are environmental regulations (Pakes, Berry, & Levinsohn, 1993) and voluntary export restraints (VERs) (Berry, Levinsohn, & Pakes, 1999).

Concretely, let Y denote the price and X the policy dummy; further, suppose that an economic theory posits a reduced form model for Y that has the form $Y=g(X)U$, where one observes an "intended equilibrium" $g(X)$, subject to a multiplicative shock U. Here, g is generally unknown. A multiplicative error model is chosen so as to preserve the positivity of the price variable Y. Note, however, that by taking logarithms our entire analysis applies to models with additive errors.

We now explain how this setup would arise in a simplified version of the Berry et al. (1999) model. For this, assume there are only two firms in the market (American and Japanese), each producing only one car. The Japanese firm is subject to a VER that is implemented as an implicit tax on firms' production. On the demand side, the consumers choose among the two cars based on a random utility specification. For simplicity, assume that all the observed product characteristics entering the random utilities, except the price, as well as all the observed marginal cost shifters have been taken out of the model (or, alternatively, think of the analysis as being conditional on those variables). In this setup, Y would be the American and Japanese car prices, X the dummy indicating whether a particular car is subject to the VER, and U would capture any unobservables in the model (such as unobserved product characteristics and unobserved productivity terms).

Many models which yield predictions for price competition – such as Berry et al. (1995, 1999) – are also likely to have multiple equilibria. We capture this by letting g be a correspondence (a set valued map) instead of a function (single valued map), so there is generally a set ε_{XU} of equilibrium predictions for Y. We assume further that there is an unknown equilibrium selection procedure which results in a distribution P_X over ε_{XU}. This multiple equilibrium model gives rise to a mixture conditional distribution for Y given X.

For example, in the Berry et al. (1999) model, the realizations of U could vary from one period to the next, thus inducing the variation in prices across periods (one can also think of each time period as being a different market in which prices are observed). This results in a distribution of car prices given the VER dummy that due to the presence of multiple equilibria in each period takes a mixture form.

Fig. 1 illustrates the effect on the price Y that may result from a change in the policy X. Before the change in the policy, we have three elements in the mixture, and after we have five. The probabilities under each element are result of some equilibrium selection procedure. The case in Fig. 1 presents a challenge as the conditional expectation of Y given X decreases. This means that, in expectation, the car prices *decrease* following the increase in marginal costs. And one can construct examples where following a change in X, the conditional mean of Y increases. Thus – as a result of equilibrium

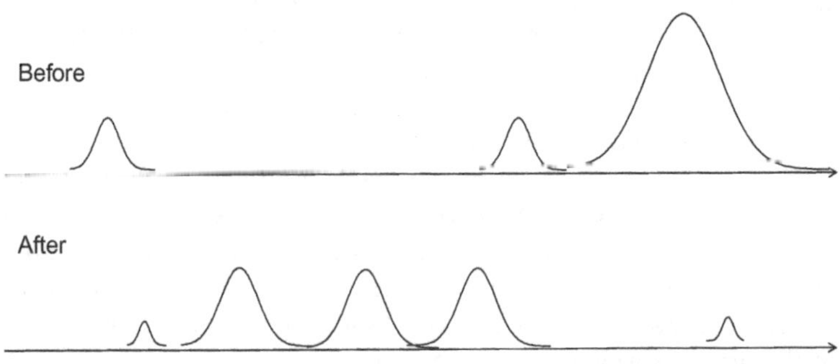

Fig. 1. Price distribution before the change in policy, and after.

multiplicity – standard practices such as an OLS regression of prices on the policy dummy can be very misleading: the testable implications of the MCS property are not on the conditional mean of prices.

Our solution is to work with restrictions that MCS implies irrespective of the way equilibria are selected. As already said, those restrictions are on the conditional quantiles of Y given X, and we derive them following a reasoning similar to that in Echenique and Komunjer (2009). It is important to stress that we make few assumptions on the true equilibrium distribution. We only assume that P_X puts a positive probability on the extremal equilibria. Similarly, our assumptions on the distribution of the equilibrium deviations U are weak; we need them to belong to a well-known class of distributions in extreme-value theory. This class includes most distributions commonly used in empirical work, such as Gaussian, lognormal, and exponential distributions.

Once the appropriate implications of the MCS hypothesis derived, we proceed with a construction of an LR test. In particular, our test is a test for order restrictions on the conditional quantiles of Y given X. We use a two-step approach: first, we construct nonparametric estimators for the conditional quantiles of Y given X. The key difficulty here is that the MCS prediction holds only for quantiles that are extreme; hence, we need to use a nonstandard framework to derive their asymptotic distribution (Chernozhukov, 2005; Chernozhukov & Fernandez-Val, 2011; Dekkers & de Haan, 1989).

In the second step, we construct an LR test for order restrictions based on the asymptotic distributions of our conditional quantile estimators. This step presents important challenges as the existing results (Gourieroux et al., 1982; Kodde & Palm, 1986) apply only to the conditional means; hence, we need to extend them to our extreme conditional quantile framework. Perhaps an even greater difficulty comes from the presence of numerous nuisance parameters – unknown equilibrium selection probabilities – that we need to eliminate from our test statistic. Unfortunately, the standard approaches of dealing with nuisance parameters fail to work once we exit the usual asymptotic framework. Our solution is to first consider the problem in the exact case (as, e.g., in Bartholomew, 1959a, 1959b), then extend the obtained solution to our asymptotic framework.

The remainder of the article is organized as follows: we introduce the model in the second secion, and present the intuition behind our main results in the third section. In the fourth section we present the basic statistical framework, and develop an approach to estimation in the fifth section. Finally, in the sixth section we present our test. Last section concludes.

The technical details including the proofs of the results stated in the main text as well as some additional useful results are relegated to Appendices A and B, respectively.

SETUP

Multiple Equilibrium Model

Consider a familiar nonlinear regression model with a multiplicative error:

$$Y = g(X)U \tag{1}$$

that relates a dependent variable $Y \in \mathbb{R}_{++}$, an explanatory variable $X \in \mathcal{X}$ with $\mathcal{X}$ finite in $\mathbb{R}$, and a latent disturbance $U \in \mathbb{R}_{++}$.[4] The map $g: \mathcal{X} \to \mathbb{R}_{++}$ in Eq. (1) is unknown; we assume however that g is positive valued, so that the positivity of the dependent variable is preserved. When the map g is known up to some finite dimensional parameter θ, one can write $g(X, \theta)$ in Eq. (1). While the explanatory and dependent variables X and Y are observable, the disturbance U is not; U can be thought of as unaccounted heterogeneity in the model. Finally, note that the random variables Y and U are assumed to be continuous, whereas X is restricted to be discrete.[5] Hereafter, we shall use the lowercase letters y, x and u to denote the realizations of the random variables Y, X and U, respectively.

Underlying the model in Eq. (1) is the assumption that, given the explanatory variable X, a unique value of the dependent variable Y can be assigned to each value of the disturbance U. In other words, conditional on X, the mapping from the unobservables to the observables is single valued, and g in Eq. (1) is a function. In models that possess multiple equilibria, this letter property is generally violated as more than one value of Y can be associated with each value of U.

In order to adapt our model to multiple equilibria for Y, we shall assume that the map g in Eq. (1) is a correspondence $g : \mathbb{R} \rightrightarrows \mathbb{R}_{++}$, which, to each $x \in \mathcal{X}$, assigns the set $\Gamma_x \equiv \{g_i(x), \ldots, g_{N_x}(x) : g_1(x) < \ldots \leq g_{N_x}(x)\}$. The maps g_i which define the image set Γ_x are single valued so every $g_i : \mathbb{R} \to \mathbb{R}_{++}$ is a function. We do not make any assumptions regarding continuity or differentiability of g_i's except that they are Borel-measurable. As a result, there are multiple equilibria for the dependent variable Y in Eq. (1) given by $Y_i = g_i(X)U$ with $i = 1, \ldots, N_X$. We then let $\varepsilon_{XU} \equiv \{Y_1, \ldots, Y_{N_X}\}$ denote the equilibrium set.[6] Note that all equilibria for Y are ordered in ε_{XU}, i.e. $Y_1 \leq \ldots \leq Y_{N_X}$. We shall work with the following definition.

Definition 1. A multiple equilibrium model is a collection $(\varepsilon_{XU}, P_X, F_{U|X})$ such that for every $(x, x', u) \in \mathcal{X}^2 \times \mathbb{R}_{++}$ we have:

(i) $\varepsilon_{xu} \subseteq \mathbb{R}_{++}$ is finite and nonempty;
(ii) $x < x'$ implies that $\min \varepsilon_{xu} < \min \varepsilon_{x'u}$ and $\max \varepsilon_{xu} < \max \varepsilon_{x'u}$;
(iii) P_x is a probability distribution over ε_{xu}, $P_x(\min \varepsilon_{xu}) > 0$ and $P_x(\max \varepsilon_{xu}) > 0$;
(iv) $F_{U|X=x}$ is a twice-differentiable distribution function with positive density on $\mathbb{R}_{++}$.

We assume that $\varepsilon_{XU} \subseteq \mathbb{R}_{++}$ is finite, so we accommodate multiple, but finitely many, equilibria. The assumption is common, and often justified by standard genericity arguments: in parameterized families of economic models, one obtains finitely many equilibria except on sets of measure zero (see, e.g., Mas-Colell, Whinston, & Green, 1995). Our results shall build on the MCS property in item (ii) of Definition 1: an increase in X causes the smallest and largest equilibria in ε_{XU} to increase.

The probability distribution P_X in item (iii) of Definition 1 reflects some equilibrium selection procedure. It is important to note that while the elements of the equilibrium set ε_{XU} vary with U, the probabilities assigned to them by P_X can only depend on X. In other words, the probability π_{Xi} of choosing the ith equilibrium Y_i under P_X $(i = 1, \ldots, N_X)$ must not depend on U. In particular, this means that in our setup, the equilibrium selection mechanism can depend on X, as well as on other possibly unobserved variables, provided the latter are independent of U conditional on X.

Our multiple equilibrium model implies the following: given the explanatory variable X, the dependent variable Y is distributed as $F_{Y|X}$, where $F_{Y|X}$ is a discrete mixture of continuous distributions:

$$F_{Y|X}(y) = \sum_{i=1}^{N_X} \pi_{Xi} F_{U|X}\left(\frac{y}{g_i(X)}\right) \tag{2}$$

for any $y \in \mathbb{R}_{++}$, where π_{Xi} $(i = 1, \ldots, N_X)$ is the probability of choosing the ith equilibrium Y_i under P_X. The assumptions on $F_{U|X}$ imply that $F_{Y|X}$ is twice differentiable on $\mathbb{R}_{++}$ with density $f_{Y|X}$ that is positive on $\mathbb{R}_{++}$.

Given $\alpha \in (0,1)$, we let $q_{Y|X}(\alpha)$ denote the α-quantile under $F_{Y|X}$: $q_{Y|X}(\alpha) \equiv \inf\{y \in \mathbb{R}_{++} : F_{Y|X}(y) > \alpha\}$, which under our assumptions also equals $q_{Y|X}(\alpha) = F_{Y|X}^{-1}(\alpha)$. In what follows, we devote particular attention to the distribution tails of the dependent variable: $\overline{F}_{Y|X} \equiv 1 - F_{Y|X}$. Similarly, we let $\overline{F}_{U|X} \equiv 1 - F_{U|X}$. Note that given $\alpha \in (0,1)$, we have the following simple relation:

$$q_{Y|X}(\alpha) = \overline{F}^{-1}_{Y|X}(1-\alpha) \tag{3}$$

On the Model Assumptions

We now comment on the restrictions we have made in our multiple equilibrium model.

Multiplicative Error Model

We have defined the equilibrium set ε_{XU} using the multiplicative error model specification in Eq. (1), with g being a correspondence. Alternatively, one can take the mixture in Eq. (2) to be one of the primitive assumptions of our multiple equilibrium model. As we shall show in subsequent sections, the mixture property in Eq. (2) is instrumental in deriving our results. In particular, the latter do not explicitly use the multiplicative error specification in Eq. (1).

This raises the question of the plausibility of the mixture assumption for $F_{Y|X}$. In Echenique and Komunjer (2009) we provide a general result on how such mixtures arise in structural econometric models of the form $r(Y,X)=U$ under fairly weak assumptions on the structural function r.

Assumptions on P_X

We have assumed that the largest and smallest equilibria in ε_{XU} have positive probability under P_X – this is our only deviation from being agnostic regarding P_X. We actually need something somewhat weaker, and it will be clear that, without our weaker assumption, no testable implications are possible. We argue here that our assumption is reasonable.

To fix ideas, let $\mathcal{X}=\{\underline{x},\overline{x}\subseteq\}\mathbb{R}$ with $\underline{x}<\overline{x}$. We need that for every $u \in \mathbb{R}_{++}$, the largest equilibrium in $\varepsilon_{\underline{x}u}$, *of those with positive $P_{\underline{x}}$ probability*, be smaller than the largest equilibrium in $\varepsilon_{\overline{x}u}$ with positive $P_{\overline{x}}$ probability. This is a weaker requirement than the one we have imposed above. It says that the equilibrium selection mechanism implicit in P_X should have the right correlation with respect to changes in X.

We claim that this correlation can be expected to hold: suppose agents are playing an equilibrium in $\varepsilon_{\underline{x}u}$ when the explanatory variable changes to $\overline{x}$. Then a broad class of learning dynamics must lead them to play a larger equilibrium; Echenique (2002) presents a formal statement and proof.

Assumptions on $F_{U|X}$

Our multiple equilibrium model assumes that $F_{U|X}$ is a continuous distribution with support $\mathbb{R}_{++}$. It is worth pointing out that we let $F_{U|X}$ be unknown. In some cases, it might be preferable to assume $F_{U|X}$ known, at least up to some finite-dimensional parameter; in such cases, the conditional distribution of Y in Eq. (2) could in principle be estimated via maximum likelihood methods, provided the equilibrium selection probabilities P_X are either known or finitely parameterized. However, the presence of unknown equilibrium probabilities P_X in $F_{Y|X}$ causes almost all the practical problems of implementation and model estimation with maximum likelihood methods.[7]

NATURE OF THE PROBLEM AND RESULTS

We first explain our results informally. Consider again our example in which $\mathcal{X} = \{\underline{x}, \bar{x}\} \subseteq \mathbb{R}$, $\underline{x} < \bar{x}$ where $\underline{x}$ and $\bar{x}$ denote low- and high-level of the explanatory variable. In addition, letting $\underline{y}_i$ and $\bar{y}_j$ denote the equilibrium levels when $(X = \underline{x}, U = u)$ and $(X = \bar{x}, U = u)$, respectively, assume that $\varepsilon_{\underline{x}u} = \{\underline{y}_1, \underline{y}_2, \underline{y}_3\}$ and $\varepsilon_{\bar{x}u} = \bar{y}_1, \bar{y}_2, \bar{y}_3, \bar{y}_4, \bar{y}_5$, where $\underline{y}_i = g_i(\underline{x})u$ and $\bar{y}_i = g_i(\bar{x})u$. The situation is represented in Fig. 2.

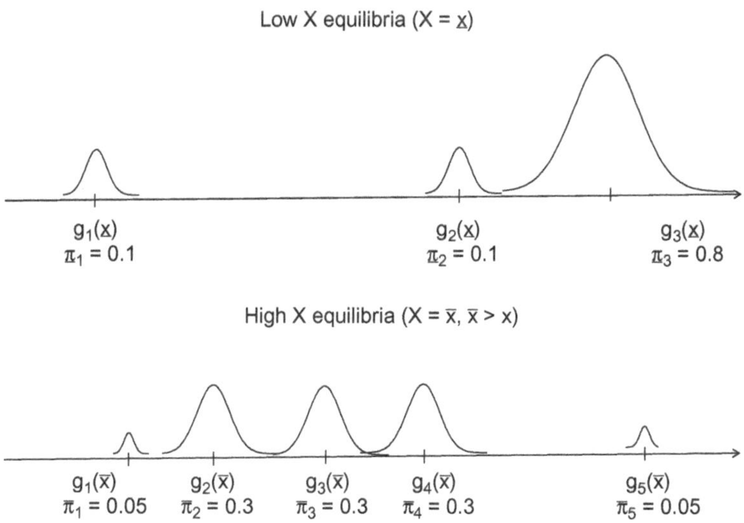

Fig. 2. Equilibrium distributions.

The problem of obtaining testable implications is to say how the distributions $F_{Y|X=\underline{x}}$ and $F_{Y|X=\bar{x}}$ must differ ($F_{Y|X}$ was defined in Eq. (2)). All we have to work with is that $\underline{y}_3 < \bar{y}_5$ (and $\underline{y}_1 < \bar{y}_1$), but the probability of the $\bar{y}_5$ equilibrium is very low, that of $\underline{y}_3$ is very high, and there are three equally likely equilibria with high sum of probabilities, $\bar{y}_2, \bar{y}_3$ and $\bar{y}_4$, that are smaller than $\underline{y}_3$.

Note that the mean (and median) of the dependent variable under $F_{Y|X=\bar{x}}$ is smaller than that under $F_{Y|X=\underline{x}}$. Thus the conditional mean (and median) of Y does not change monotonically in X. One can change the example so the conditional mean increases instead of decreasing; thus the MCS property in item (ii) of Definition 1 produces no testable implications for the conditional mean of the dependent variable. One is also more likely to observe a realization under $F_{Y|X=\underline{x}}$ that is larger than under $F_{Y|X=\bar{x}}$ than vice versa.

Our solution to finding testable implications is to assume the right structure on the distribution tails, so the effect of $\underline{y}_3 < \bar{y}_5$ is felt for large enough values of the dependent variable, irrespective of the values of the corresponding probabilities $P_{\underline{x}}$ and $P_{\bar{x}}$. We show how, for large enough realizations y of Y, the distribution tails $\overline{F}_{Y|X=\underline{x}} \equiv 1 - F_{Y|X=\underline{x}}$ and $\overline{F}_{Y|X=\bar{x}} \equiv 1 - F_{Y|X=\bar{x}}$ must satisfy $\overline{F}_{Y|X=\underline{x}}(y) < \overline{F}_{Y|X=\bar{x}}(y)$.

To further simplify the notation, let $\underline{\pi}_i$ (resp. $\bar{\pi}_j$) denote the probabilities assigned to the elements of $\varepsilon_{\underline{x}u}$(resp. $\varepsilon_{\bar{x}u}$) under $P_{\underline{x}}$(resp. $P_{\bar{x}}$). Note that the tail $\overline{F}_{Y|X}$ is related to $\overline{F}_{U|X} \equiv 1 - F_{U|X}$ via:

$$\overline{F}_{Y|X=\underline{x}}(y) = \underline{\pi}_3 \overline{F}_{U|X=\underline{x}}(y/g_3(\underline{x})) + \underline{\pi}_2 \overline{F}_{U|X=\underline{x}}(y/g_2(\underline{x})) + \underline{\pi}_1 \overline{F}_{U|X=\underline{x}}(y/g_1(\underline{x})) \quad (4)$$

Assume that the tails of $F_{U|X=\underline{x}}$ satisfy the following property:

$$\lim_{u \to \infty} \frac{\overline{F}_{U|X=\underline{x}}(\lambda u)}{\overline{F}_{U|X=\underline{x}}(u)} = 0 \quad (5)$$

whenever $\lambda > 1$. Property (5) requires that the tail of the distribution $F_{U|X}$ is not too heavy. As we explain below, it is a well-known condition in the statistics of extreme values, and it is satisfied by most distributions familiar to practitioners.

Now,

$$\frac{\overline{F}_{U|X=\underline{x}}(y/g_2(\underline{x}))}{\overline{F}_{U|X=\underline{x}}(y/g_3(\underline{x}))} = \frac{\overline{F}_{U|X=\underline{x}}(\lambda z)}{\overline{F}_{U|X=\underline{x}}(z)}$$

where we have let $z \equiv y/g_3(\underline{x})$ and $\lambda \equiv g_3(\underline{x})/g_2(\underline{x}) > 1$, and similarly with g_1 in place of g_2. So, dividing by $\overline{F}_{U|X=\underline{x}}(y/g_3(\underline{x}))$ throughout Eq. (4), and using Property (5), we obtain that:

$$\overline{F}_{Y|X=\underline{x}}(y) \sim \underline{\pi}_3 \overline{F}_{U|X=\underline{x}}(y/g_3(\underline{x})) \text{ as } y \text{ goes to } \infty$$

In other words, the behavior of $\overline{F}_{Y|X=\underline{x}}(y)$ for large y is driven solely by the largest equilibrium $\underline{y}_3$. Under analogous assumptions on the tails of $F_{U|X=\overline{x}}$, it is easy to show that $\overline{F}_{Y|X=\overline{x}}(y)$ behaves like $\overline{\pi}_5 \overline{F}_{U|X=\overline{x}}(y/g_5(\overline{x}))$. Thus:

$$\frac{\overline{F}_{Y|X=\underline{x}}(y)}{\overline{F}_{Y|X=\overline{x}}(y)} \sim \underbrace{\left[\frac{\underline{\pi}_3}{\overline{\pi}_5}\right]}_{A} \underbrace{\left[\frac{\overline{F}_{U|X=\underline{x}}(y/g_3(\underline{x}))}{\overline{F}_{U|X=\underline{x}}(y/g_5(\overline{x}))}\right]}_{B} \underbrace{\left[\frac{\overline{F}_{U|X=\underline{x}}(y/g_5(\overline{x}))}{\overline{F}_{U|X=\overline{x}}(y/g_5(\overline{x}))}\right]}_{C} \tag{6}$$

From item (iii) in Definition 1, we know that the term A is bounded. Since $\underline{y}_3 < \overline{y}_5$, our assumption on $F_{U|X=\underline{x}}$ in Eq. (5) implies that the B term goes to 0 as y grows. If, in addition, we assume that:

$$\frac{\overline{F}_{U|X=\underline{x}}(y)}{\overline{F}_{U|X=\overline{x}}(y)} \text{ is bounded as } y \text{ goes to } \infty \tag{7}$$

then the C term is bounded. So $\overline{F}_{Y|X=\underline{x}}(y)/\overline{F}_{Y|X=\overline{x}}(y)$ converges to 0 irrespective of the probabilities under $P_{\underline{x}}$ and $P_{\overline{x}}$. Hence, for large enough y, the tail of $F_{Y|X=\overline{x}}(y)$ is thicker than that of $F_{Y|X=\underline{x}}(y)$; this is the essence of our testable implication.

To summarize, Statements (5) and (7) together ensure that the ratio of $\overline{F}_{Y|X=\underline{x}}$ to $\overline{F}_{Y|X=\overline{x}}$ goes to zero. This is our testable implication: $\overline{F}_{Y|X=\underline{x}}(y)/\overline{F}_{Y|X=\overline{x}}(y)$ for y large enough. As a result, large enough population quantiles must be larger under $F_{Y|X=\overline{x}}$ than under $F_{Y|X=\underline{x}}$. In the next section we show how this result generalizes.

ECONOMETRIC FRAMEWORK

A useful statistical framework to formalize the basic ideas in the third section is that of regularly varying functions. We first give some preliminary definitions, and results on regularly varying functions. We then exploit this theory to develop statistical tests for the models inthe second section.

Regular Variation Theory

In this section, H denotes a distribution function with positive density h on $\mathbb{R}_{++}$ and distribution tail $\overline{H} \equiv 1 - H$. We shall focus on the behavior of $\overline{H}$ in $+\infty$, knowing that analogous results can be obtained at zero.

Definition 2. A distribution tail $\overline{H} : \mathbb{R}_{++} \to (0, 1)$ is regularly varying at c, $0 \leq c \leq \infty$, with index ρ, $-\infty \leq \rho < \infty$, denoted $\overline{H} \in \mathcal{R}_\rho$ at c, if for $\lambda > 0$:

$$\lim_{x \to c} \frac{\overline{H}(\lambda x)}{\overline{H}(x)} = \lambda^\rho \tag{8}$$

The notion of regular variation was first introduced by Karamata (1930) (see Resnick, 1987, for an exposition). When c is understood we shall often abuse notation and write $\overline{H} \in \mathcal{R}_\rho$.

We focus on regular variation at $c = \infty$ with index $\rho = -\infty$, denoted by $\mathcal{R}_{-\infty}$ at ∞. Most of the distributions employed in economics, such as the Gaussian, exponential and lognormal distributions, are in $\mathcal{R}_{-\infty}$ at ∞. The distributions in $\mathcal{R}_{-\infty}$ at ∞ are also called "$(-\infty)$-varying" or "rapidly varying." They are moderately heavy-tailed, or light-tailed, meaning that their tails decrease to zero faster than any power law $x^{-\alpha}$.[8]

Note that the special case of $\overline{H}(\cdot)$ being in $\mathcal{R}_{-\infty}$ at ∞ is defined by

$$\lim_{x \to \infty} \frac{\overline{H}(\lambda x)}{\overline{H}(x)} = \begin{cases} 0 & \text{if} \quad \lambda > 1 \\ \infty & \text{if} \quad \lambda < 1 \end{cases} \tag{9}$$

The discussion in the third section should suggest that Statement (9) is a useful property. Now, the property in Statement (9) does not control the rate at which $\overline{H}(\lambda x)/\overline{H}(x)$ converges. By using a subclass of $(-\infty)$-varying distribution tails, called Γ (see, e.g., de Haan, 1970), we can exercise this control.

Definition 3. A distribution tail $\overline{H}$ belongs to the *class* Γ, $\overline{H} \in \Gamma$, if there exists a function $a : \mathbb{R}_{++} \to \mathbb{R}_{++}$ such that for $\lambda > 0$:

$$\lim_{x \to \infty} \frac{\overline{H}(x + \lambda a(x))}{\overline{H}(x)} = \exp(-\lambda) \tag{10}$$

a is called the auxiliary function of $\overline{H}$.

When $\overline{H} \in \Gamma$, one can show that a can be chosen as $a \equiv \overline{H}/h$ (we shall often make this choice).

That $\Gamma \subseteq \mathcal{R}_{-\infty}$ is a direct consequence of Theorem 1.5.1 in de Haan (1970). Examples of distributions whose tails in Γ are: exponential, two-parameter Gamma, Gaussian, lognormal, and Weibull (see, e.g., Embrechts, Kluppelberg, & Mikosch, 1997).

The tail properties in Eqs. (8) and (10) translate into similar properties for the inverse function $\overline{H}^{-1}: (0,1) \to \mathbb{R}_{++}$ (see Lemma 5) and the class of regularly varying functions is closed under inversion. The inverses of functions in Γ, however, do not belong to Γ but form a class called Π (see, e.g., de Haan, 1970, 1974).

Definition 4. A function $\overline{H}^{-1}: (0,1) \to \mathbb{R}_{++}$ belongs to the *class* Π, $\overline{H}^{-1} \in \Pi$, if there exist functions $b: \mathbb{R}_{++} \to \mathbb{R}_{++}$ and $a: \mathbb{R}_{++} \to \mathbb{R}_{++}$ such that, for $\mu \in (0,1)$:

$$\lim_{y \downarrow 0} \frac{\overline{H}^{-1}(\mu y) - b(y)}{a(y)} = -\ln\mu \tag{11}$$

When $\overline{H}$ belongs to Γ with auxiliary function $\tilde{a}$, Eq. (11) holds with $b(y) \equiv \overline{H}^{-1}(y)$ and $a(y) \equiv \tilde{a}(\overline{H}^{-1}(y))$.

Testable Implications: General Result

We now return to our multiple equilibrium model $(\varepsilon_{XU}, P_X, F_{U|X})$ and impose structure on the distribution tails $\overline{F}_{U|X}$ of the disturbances.

Assumption 1. Say that a multiple equilibrium model $(\varepsilon_{XU}, P_X, F_{U|X})$ satisfies Assumption 1 if, for every $x \in \mathcal{X}$, $\overline{F}_{U|X=x}$ is in $\mathcal{R}_{-\infty}$ at ∞.

We now show how the properties of the tails $\overline{F}_{U|X}$ translate into properties of the tail of the conditional distribution of the dependent variable $\overline{F}_{Y|X}$ in Eq. (2). Recall that π_{XN_X} denotes the probability of choosing the largest equilibrium $Y_{N_X} = g_{N_X}(X)U$ under P_X.

Lemma 1. If $(\varepsilon_{XU}, P_X, F_{U|X})$ satisfies Assumption 1, then for every $x \in \mathcal{X}$:

(i) $\overline{F}_{Y|X=x}$ is in $\mathcal{R}_{-\infty}$ at ∞, and $\overline{F}_{Y|X=x}(y) \sim \pi_{xN_x} \overline{F}_{U|X=x}(y/g_{N_x}(x))$ as $y \to \infty$;

(ii) $\overline{F}^{-1}_{U|X=x}$ and $\overline{F}^{-1}_{Y|X=x}$ are in $\mathcal{R}_0$ at 0, and $\overline{F}^{-1}_{Y|X=x}(v) \sim g_{N_x}(x) \overline{F}^{-1}_{U|X=x}(v)$ as $v \downarrow 0$.

Thus, the limit behavior of the distribution tail $\overline{F}_{Y|X}$ is determined by the largest equilibrium in ε_{XU} and its probability. In the limit, the conditional quantiles of Y are proportional to the quantiles under $F_{U|X}$, and the constant of proportionality equals $g_{N_X}(X)$.

In order to generalize the argument in the third section we need to strengthen our assumption:

Assumption 2. Say that a multiple equilibrium model $(\varepsilon_{XU}, P_X, F_{U|X})$ satisfies Assumption 2 if it satisfies Assumption 1 and, in addition, for every $(x, x') \in \mathcal{X}^2$ such that $x < x'$, we have:

$$\frac{\overline{F}_{U|X=x}(u)}{\overline{F}_{U|X=x'}(u)} \text{ is bounded as } u \text{ goes to } \infty \tag{12}$$

Using the above assumptions together with Lemma 1 allows us to derive our first main result:

Theorem 1. If $(\varepsilon_{XU}, P_X, F_{U|X})$ satisfies Assumption 2, then for any $(x, x') \in \mathcal{X}^2$ there is $\overline{y} \in \mathbb{R}_{++}$ such that $x < x'$ implies $\overline{F}_{Y|X=x}(y) < \overline{F}_{Y|X=x'}(y)$ for all $y \geq \overline{y}$. Equivalently, there is $\overline{\alpha} \in (0,1)$ such that $x < x'$ implies $q_{Y|X=x}(\alpha) < q_{Y|X=x'}(\alpha)$ for all $\alpha \in [\overline{\alpha}, 1)$.

The idea of Theorem 1 is that, if the distribution $F_{U|X}$ is not too heavy-tailed, the effect of X on the largest equilibrium in ε_{XU} will eventually be noticed in the tail of $F_{Y|X}$. In a sense, there is a race between the potentially damaging effect of other equilibria in ε_{XU}, and the effect of the largest equilibrium Y_{N_X}. Since P_X is arbitrary, P_X can work in favor of the other equilibria in ε_{XU}, as in Fig. 2. But the $(-\infty)$-varying condition on $\overline{F}_{U|X}$ and Property (12) together guarantee that the largest equilibrium wins the race. Hence, for large values of y, the conditional distributions $F_{Y|X=x}(y)$ of the dependent variable have tails that increase monotonically with x, a property akin to monotonicity in first-order stochastic dominance. Equivalently, Theorem 1 has consequences for the quantiles of Y conditional on X. In the limit, the conditional quantiles of the dependent variable given X are monotone increasing in X.

Further Model Implications

Theorem 1 suggests one can use estimates of conditional quantiles under $F_{Y|X}$ for testing, but there are several difficulties. First, the theorem does not determine $\overline{y}$ or $\overline{\alpha}$; it does not identify the quantiles for which we have testable implications. Second, we need to know the (asymptotic) distribution of the conditional quantile estimates – the key is to derive the latter by imposing structure on the distributions while maintaining our agnosticism about the P_X distributions. Third, given the asymptotic distributions of estimates for quantiles under $F_{Y|X}$, we need to derive a test that is not influenced by the P_X distributions nor the non-extremal values in ε_{XU}, for which our model makes no predictions.

In order to deal with the asymptotics, we need to impose further structure on the distribution tail $\overline{F}_{U|X}$: in addition to being $(-\infty)$-varying, $\overline{F}_{U|X}$ is now assumed to belong to the class Γ.

Assumption 3. Say that a multiple equilibrium model $(\varepsilon_{XU}, P_X, F_{U|X})$ satisfies Assumption 3 if it satisfies Assumption 1 and, in addition, for every $x \in \mathcal{X}$ we have $\overline{F}_{U|X=x} \in \Gamma$ with auxiliary function a_x^U.

This allows us to show the following results on the tails of conditional distributions $F_{Y|X}$ of the dependent variable.

Lemma 2 . If $(\varepsilon_{XU}, P_X, F_{U|X})$ satisfies Assumption 3, then for every $x \in \mathcal{X}$:

(i) $\overline{F}_{Y|X=x} \in \Gamma$ with auxiliary function $a_x^Y(y) = g_{N_x}(x) a_x^U(y/g_{N_x}(x))$ for all $y > 0$;
(ii) $\overline{F}^{-1}_{U|X=x}$ and $\overline{F}^{-1}_{Y|X=x}$ are in Π with auxiliary functions $a_x^U \circ \overline{F}^{-1}_{U|X=x}$ and $a_x^Y \circ \overline{F}^{-1}_{Y|X=x}$ in $\mathcal{R}_0$ at 0, and $a_x^Y(\overline{F}^{-1}_{Y|X=x}(v)) \sim g_{N_x}(x) a_x^U(\overline{F}^{-1}_{U|X=x}(v))$ as $v \downarrow 0$.

Lemma 2 presents two results: First, that the Γ (resp. Π) properties of $\overline{F}_{U|X}$(resp. $\overline{F}^{-1}_{U|X}$) continue to hold for $\overline{F}_{Y|X}$(resp. $\overline{F}^{-1}_{Y|X}$). Hence, we will only need to make assumptions on the behavior of $\overline{F}_{U|X}$ in Eq. (2) in order to fully characterize the behavior of $\overline{F}_{Y|X}(y)$ as y gets large. Note that this result is particularly important if we want to preserve our agnosticism about the probabilities P_X over equilibria in ε_{XU}.

The second result of Lemma 2 is to show how $a_X^Y \circ \overline{F}^{-1}_{Y|X}$ relates to $a_X^U \circ \overline{F}^{-1}_{U|X}$. We shall prove that these expressions are involved in the formulation of the central limit theorem for empirical conditional quantiles under $F_{Y|X}$. In other words, the results of Lemma 2 are essential for understanding the asymptotic properties of the estimators for conditional quantiles of Y given X, and hence for constructing an econometric test of the implication derived in Theorem 1.

ESTIMATION

Notation and Setup

Fix $x \in \mathcal{X}$ and assume that the econometrician observes some large number T_x of realizations of the dependent variable Y obtained when the explanatory variable X takes the value x. More formally, let $(Y_{x,1}, \ldots, Y_{x,T_x})$ be a random sample of size T_x from a distribution function $F_{Y|X=x}$. Let $(y_{x,1}, \ldots, y_{x,T_x})$ denote the realizations of $(Y_{x,1}, \ldots, Y_{x,T_x})$ and write $\hat{F}_{Y|X=x}$ to be the empirical distribution function, $\hat{F}_{Y|X=x}(y) \equiv T_x^{-1} \sum_{t=1}^{T_x} \mathbb{1}(y_{x,t} \leq y)$ for $y > 0$. For a given α, $0 < \alpha < 1$, the empirical quantile under $F_{Y|X=x}$ is then given by:

$$\hat{q}_{Y|X=x}(\alpha) \equiv \inf\{y \in \mathbb{R}_{++} : \hat{F}_{Y|X=x}(y) > \alpha\} \tag{13}$$

Under standard regularity conditions, the estimator in Eq. (13) is consistent for the true α-quantile under $F_{Y|X=x}$. Consistency of $\hat{q}_{Y|X=x}(\alpha)$ can be extended to cases where $(Y_{x,1}, \ldots, Y_{x,T_x})$ is a weakly dependent time-series, provided additional assumptions hold (Chernozhukov, 2005; Chernozhukov & Fernandez-Val, 2011; Koenker & Zhao, 1996; Komunjer, 2005; Pollard, 1991; Portnoy, 1991); for the sake of simplicity, we focus on the independent case.

To alleviate the notation, we drop the reference to x when doing so introduces no ambiguities. Hence we use the notation $(Y_1, \ldots, Y_T)$, T, $\hat{F}$ and $\hat{q}(\alpha)$ to denote the random sample under $F_{Y|X=x}$, its size, the corresponding empirical distribution function, and the α-quantile estimator in Eq. (13).

As pointed out previously, the main object of interest are α-quantiles with probabilities α close to unity. How close α is to 1 is determined by the sample size T; hence we let this probability be a function of the sample size, and we denote it by α_T. Knowing how α varies with T will then enable us to answer the question: for a given sample size T how large α needs to be for the ordering in Theorem 1 to hold.

Central Limit Theory for Intermediate Empirical Quantiles

We now derive the asymptotic distribution of $\hat{q}(\alpha_T)$ in Eq. (13) when $\lim_{T\to\infty} \alpha_T = 1$ and when $(1-\alpha_T)T$ has a positive limit as T goes to infinity. In particular, we consider the case where $\lim_{T\to\infty}(1-\alpha_T)T = \infty$. This last condition describes how fast α has to go to unity relative to the sample size

T; knowing $T^{-1} = o(1-\alpha_T)$ we can use an appropriate limit theory result to derive an asymptotic distribution of the α-quantile estimator $\hat{q}(\alpha_T)$ in Eq. (13).

We shall need the following lemma.

Lemma 3 . Consider a random sample $(Y_1, ..., Y_T)$ of size T from F and let $\hat{q}(\alpha_T)$ be the corresponding empirical α_T-quantile. If the distribution tail $\overline{F} \in \Gamma$ with auxiliary function a and with density f which is eventually non-increasing, then, provided $\lim_{T \to \infty} \alpha_T = 1$ and $\lim_{T \to \infty}(1-\alpha_T)T = \infty$ we have:

$$\sqrt{T(1-\alpha_T)}\ \frac{\hat{q}(\alpha_T) - q(\alpha_T)}{a(q(\alpha_T))} \xrightarrow{d} \mathcal{N} \quad \text{and} \quad \frac{\hat{q}(\beta_T) - \hat{q}(\alpha_T)}{a(q(\alpha_T))} \xrightarrow{p} \ln \rho$$

where $\mathcal{N}$ is a standard normal random variable and β_T is such that $\alpha_T < \beta_T < 1$ and $(1-\alpha_T)/(1-\beta_T) \to \rho$ with $\rho > 1$.

Lemma 3 presents two limit results. The first was proved by Falk (1989). The second is new. The first result in the lemma shows the asymptotic behavior of intermediate empirical quantiles when α_T depends on the sample size T. It is an extension of the well-known result for central α-quantiles with $\alpha \in (0,1)$ fixed (see, e.g., Bahadur, 1966; Bassett & Koenker, 1978; Mosteller, 1946; Powell, 1984, 1986; Siddiqui, 1960; Smirnov, 1952) to the case where α increases with the sample size T. Dekkers and de Haan (1989), Chernozhukov (2005), and Chernozhukov and Fernandez-Val (2011) prove this extension under an additional assumption on the tail behavior of F. While it is not new, we include a proof of the first result to make the article self-contained, and because it requires little beyond what we need to prove the second result.

The second limit result of Lemma 3 is important because it gives us a consistent estimator of the variance of the empirical quantile. Recall that Theorem 1 says that the conditional quantiles of Y given X must be increasing in X. With consistent estimators of quantiles in hand, a test seems easy to derive. The problem, though, is that we do not know how the asymptotic variances of the quantile estimators change with X. Our second result in Lemma 3 allows us to solve the problem.

The second limit result of Lemma 3 extends a result on the asymptotic distribution of the quantile spacings derived by Dekkers and de Haan (1989) for the case $\rho = 2$ (see also Chernozhukov, 2005; Chernozhukov & Fernandez-Val, 2011). The result by Dekkers and de Haan (1989) requires that $d\overline{F}^{-1}(v)/dv$ be in $\mathcal{R}_{-1}$ at 0, an assumption that we need to avoid because it implies a restriction on the equilibrium selection P_X. By focusing on consistency, and not on the asymptotic distribution of quantile spacings, we obtain a result only assuming that $\overline{F}$ in Γ and that f if eventually non-increasing. Consistency, in turn, is sufficient for our testing procedure.

We should note that the assumption that f be eventually non-increasing imposes no restriction on the equilibrium selection probabilities π_{Xi} in Eq. (2), and follows from requiring the density of $F_{U|X}$ to be eventually non-increasing.

Estimates for Conditional Quantiles Under $(\varepsilon_{XU}, P_X, F_{U|X})$.

We now assume a collection of random samples for different values $x \in \mathcal{X}$ of the explanatory variable X. Concretely, consider a multiple equilibrium model $(\varepsilon_{XU}, P_X, F_{U|X})$, and assume we observe realizations from $k \geq 2$ random samples $(Y_{x_1,1}, \ldots, Y_{x_1,T_{x_1}})$ to $(Y_{x_k,1}, \ldots, Y_{x_k,T_{x_k}})$ of sizes T_{x_1} to T_{x_k}, respectively. To ease the notation, for any $j = 1,\ldots,k$, we let $(Y_{j,1}, \ldots, Y_{j,T_j})$ denote $(Y_{x_j,1}, \ldots, Y_{x_j,T_{x_j}})$; in other words, we replace the subscript x_j with j whenever doing so does not introduce any ambiguity. The k samples are assumed independent and drawn from the distributions $F_{Y|X=x_1}$ to $F_{Y|X=x_k}$, respectively, with $(x_1, \ldots, x_k) \in \mathcal{X}^k$.

In order to use the results of Lemma 3 we need to impose the following assumption on the tails of $F_{U|X}$:

Assumption 4. Say that a multiple equilibrium model $(\varepsilon_{XU}, P_X, F_{U|X})$ satisfies Assumption 4 if it satisfies Assumption 3 and, in addition, the densities $h_{U|X}$ are eventually non-increasing.

The limit results of Lemma 3 then yield the following result:

Theorem 2. Assume $(\varepsilon_{XU}, P_X, F_{U|X})$ satisfies Assumption 4, and consider k independent random samples $(Y_{j,1}, \ldots, Y_{j,T_j})$, $j = 1, \ldots, k$, each of size $T_j \geq 1$ and drawn from $F_{Y|X=x_j}$ with $x_j \in \mathcal{X}$. If for every j we have: $0 < \alpha_{T_j} < \beta_{T_j} < 1$, $\lim_{T_j \to \infty} \alpha_{T_j} = 1$, $\lim_{T_j \to \infty}(1 - \alpha_{T_j})T_j = \infty$ and $\lim_{T_j \to \infty}(1 - \alpha_{T_j})/(1 - \beta_{T_j}) = \rho_j$ with $\rho_j > 1$, then as $T \to \infty$:

$$\frac{\hat{q}_{Y|X=x_j}(\alpha_{T_j}) - \mu_j}{\sigma_j} \xrightarrow{d} \mathcal{N}_j \quad \text{with } \mu_j \equiv q_{Y|X=x_j}(\alpha_{T_j}) \text{ and } \sigma_j \equiv \frac{a^Y_{x_j}(\mu_j)}{\sqrt{(1 - \alpha_{T_j})T_j}}$$

where $a^Y_{x_j}$ is the auxiliary function of $F_{Y|X=x_j}$, $a^Y_{x_j} = \overline{F}_{Y|X=x_j}/f_{Y|X=x_j}$, and $\mathcal{N}_1, \ldots, \mathcal{N}_k$ are k independent standard normal random variables. Moreover, the scaling constants σ_j can be consistently estimated via:

$$\frac{\hat{\sigma}_j}{\sigma_j} \equiv \sigma_j^{-1} \frac{\hat{q}_{Y|X=x_j}(\alpha_{T_j}) - \hat{q}_{Y|X=x_j}(\beta_{T_j})}{\ln \rho_j \sqrt{(1-\alpha_{T_j})T_j}} \xrightarrow{p} 1$$

For any given $k \geq 2$, the results of Theorem 2 allow us to determine the asymptotic behavior of estimates for conditional quantiles under $F_{Y|X}$. With conditional quantile estimators in hand, we can then test the implications in Theorem 1.

For the purpose of testing, we make an assumption on the rate of growth of the different samples. The assumption ensures that the $(1-\alpha_{T_j})T_j$ grow at the same speed, and that we consider the same α_T-quantile, for all k samples. We can then formulate our results in the standard asymptotic framework, i.e. as $T \to \infty$. Concretely, assume that the sample sizes $(T_1, \ldots, T_k)$ and the corresponding probabilities $(\alpha_{T_1}, \ldots, \alpha_{T_k})$ are such that for every j there exist α_T and c_j that satisfy:

$$\alpha_{T_j} = \alpha_T \text{ and } T_j = c_j T, \quad \text{with } 0 < \alpha_T < 1, \lim_{T \to \infty} (1-\alpha_T)T = \infty, \quad \text{and } c_j > 0 \quad (14)$$

TESTING

Test Hypotheses

From Theorem 1, the observable restriction of our multiple equilibrium model $(\varepsilon_{XU}, P_X, F_{U|X})$ is that $x_1 < \ldots < x_k$ implies $q_{Y|X=x_1}(\alpha_T) < \ldots < q_{Y|X=x_k}(\alpha_T)$ as $\alpha_T \to 1$. Hence, we are interested in testing weather an increase in the explanatory variable results in an increase in the conditional quantiles of the dependent variable. The opposite case of interest is the one in which an increase in X produces no effect on the conditional quantiles of Y given X, so that we have $x_1 < \ldots < x_k$ and $q_{Y|X=x_1}(\alpha_T) = \ldots = q_{Y|X=x_k}(\alpha_T)$. Those two cases define our alternative and null hypotheses, respectively.

More formally, for given values $x_1 < \ldots < x_k$ in $\mathcal{X}^k$ we test the null hypothesis $H_0 : q_{Y|X=x_1}(\alpha_T) = \ldots = q_{Y|X=x_k}(\alpha_T)$, as $\alpha_T \to 1$, against an ordered alternative $H_1 : q_{Y|X=x_1}(\alpha_T) \leq \ldots \leq q_{Y|X=x_k}(\alpha_T)$, as $\alpha_T \to 1$, with strict inequality for at least one value of j, $1 \leq j \leq k$.

Our test statistic is a function of estimates for conditional quantiles under $F_{Y|X}$; from Theorems 1 and 2 we know that the latter satisfies the following property:

Corollary 1. Assume $(\varepsilon_{XU}, P_X, F_{U|X})$ satisfies Assumptions 2 and 4, and let $(Y_{j,1}, \ldots, Y_{j,c_jT})$, $j=1,\ldots,k$, be k independent random samples of size c_jT (with $T \geq 1$) drawn from $F_{Y|X=x_j}$, $x_j \in \mathcal{X}$. If $0<\alpha_T<\beta_T<1$, $\lim_{T\to\infty}\alpha_T=1$, $\lim_{T\to\infty}(1-\alpha_T)T=\infty$ and $\lim_{T\to\infty}(1-\alpha_T)/(1-\beta_T)=\rho$, with $\rho>1$, then as $T\to\infty$:

$$x_1 < \ldots < x_k \text{ implies } \mu_1 < \ldots < \mu_k$$

where $\mu_j \equiv q_{Y|X=x_j}(\alpha_T)$, and

$$\frac{\hat{q}_{Y|X=x_j}(\alpha_T)-\mu_j}{\hat{\sigma}_j} \xrightarrow{d} \mathcal{N}_j \text{ with } \hat{\sigma}_j \equiv \frac{\hat{q}_{Y|X=x_j}(\alpha_T)-\hat{q}_{Y|X=x_j}(\beta_T)}{\ln\rho\sqrt{c_j(1-\alpha_T)T}}$$

where $\mathcal{N}_1, \ldots, \mathcal{N}_k$ are k independent standard normal random variables.

Note that the asymptotic distribution result in Corollary 1 exploits the sample size growth assumptions made in Eq. (14). It follows by applying Slutsky's theorem to the results derived in Theorem 2.

Exact Test for Order Restrictions

Assume for the moment that all the distribution results from Corollary 1 are exact rather than being asymptotic, i.e. assume that for some probability α_T close to 1 and for large enough T, $(\hat{q}_{Y|X=x_1}(\alpha_T), \ldots, \hat{q}_{Y|X=x_k}(\alpha_T))$ is a sample from k independent and normally distributed random variables with means $(\mu_1, \ldots, \mu_k)$ and variances $(\hat{\sigma}_1^2, \ldots, \hat{\sigma}_k^2)$. Our null and alternative hypotheses are then equivalent to $H_0 : \mu_1 = \ldots = \mu_k$ and $H_1 : \mu_1 \leq \ldots \leq \mu_k$ with at least one strict inequality. Note that having observed $\hat{q}_{Y|X=x_j}(\alpha_T)$ and $\hat{q}_{Y|X=x_j}(\beta_T)$, the variances $\hat{\sigma}_j^2$ are known. So the implications of our multiple equilibrium model $(\varepsilon_{XU}, P_X, F_{U|X})$ can be restated in terms of the means $(\mu_1, \ldots, \mu_k)$ of k independent Gaussian random variables with known variances.

An LR test of H_0 against H_1 is now available from the existing literature (see, e.g., Barlow, Bartholomew, Bremner, & Brunk, 1972; Bartholomew, 1959a, 1959b; Robertson & Wegman, 1978). We shall review Bartholomew's results, as the results are instrumental in showing how the extension of exact results works in the asymptotic case.

We introduce the following notation: $\hat{q} \equiv (\hat{q}_{Y|X=x_1}(\alpha_T), \ldots, \hat{q}_{Y|X=x_k}(\alpha_T))'$, $\mu \equiv (\mu_1, \ldots, \mu_k)'$ and $\hat{\Sigma} \equiv diag(\hat{\sigma}_1^2, \ldots, \hat{\sigma}_k^2)$. Hence, for a given value of T, the k-vector $\hat{q}$ is multivariate normal with mean μ and diagonal covariance matrix $\hat{\Sigma}$. Letting A be a $(k-1) \times k$-matrix defined as:

$$A \equiv \begin{bmatrix} 1 & -1 & & (0) \\ & \ddots & \ddots & \\ (0) & & 1 & -1 \end{bmatrix}$$

we can write the null and the alternative hypotheses as:

$$H_0 : \{A\mu = 0\} \text{ against } H_1 : \left\{A\mu \preccurlyeq 0 \text{ and } A\mu \neq 0\right\} \tag{15}$$

where the inequalities $\preccurlyeq$ is understood as component wise.

The test in Eq. (15) is based on the LR statistic:

$$\hat{\xi}_{LR} \equiv -2 \ln \frac{\max\limits_{A\mu=0} L(\hat{q}|\mu, \hat{\Sigma})}{\max\limits_{A\mu \preccurlyeq 0} L(\hat{q}|\mu, \hat{\Sigma})} \tag{16}$$

where $L(\hat{q}|\mu, \hat{\Sigma})$ is the likelihood function:

$$L(\hat{q}|\mu, \hat{\Sigma}) = \frac{1}{(2\pi)^{k/2}(\det\hat{\Sigma})^{1/2}} \exp\left[-(\hat{q}-\mu)'\hat{\Sigma}^{-1}(\hat{q}-\mu)\right] \tag{17}$$

Combining Eqs. (16) and (17) then yields:

$$\hat{\xi}_{LR} = \min_{A\mu=0}(\hat{q}-\mu)'\hat{\Sigma}^{-1}(\hat{q}-\mu) - \min_{A\mu \preccurlyeq 0}(\hat{q}-\mu)'\hat{\Sigma}^{-1}(\hat{q}-\mu) \tag{18}$$

Barlow et al. (1972) show that the test statistic in Eq. (18) – similar to the χ^2 statistic used to test H_0 against the most general form of alternative $H_2 : \mu_1 \neq \ldots \neq \mu_k$ – is a weighted average of χ^2 distributions with d degrees of freedom (χ_d^2) with $0 \leq d \leq k-1$, and is denoted $\overline{\chi}_k^2$ (χ_0^2 denotes a point mass at 0).

The $\overline{\chi}_k^2$ distribution of the LR test statistic $\hat{\xi}_{LR}$ depends on the number of quantiles being compared k, as well as their variances $\hat{\sigma}_j^2$ through the probability weights attached to each distribution χ_d^2. For example, when $k=2$ and 3, the distribution of $\hat{\xi}_{LR}$ is given by:

$$\hat{\xi}_{LR} \stackrel{d}{=} \frac{1}{2}\chi_0^2 + \frac{1}{2}\chi_1^2, \quad \text{for } k=2 \tag{19}$$

$$\hat{\xi}_{LR} \overset{d}{=} \frac{\hat{\alpha}}{2\pi}\chi_0^2 + \frac{1}{2}\chi_1^2 + \left[\frac{1}{2} - \frac{\hat{\alpha}}{2\pi}\right]\chi_2^2, \text{ for } k=3 \tag{20}$$

and $\hat{\alpha} \equiv \arccos\left[\hat{\sigma}_2^2/\sqrt{(\hat{\sigma}_1^2+\hat{\sigma}_2^2)(\hat{\sigma}_2^2+\hat{\sigma}_3^2)}\right]$ is a constant, $-\pi < \hat{\alpha} < \pi$.

In the special case where the variances $\hat{\sigma}_j^2$ are equal, Bartholomew (1959b) computes the $\overline{\chi}_k^2$ critical values for a number of values for k $(2 \leq k \leq 12)$. When the variances are different, exact critical values for $\overline{\chi}_k^2$ are hard to compute analytically if $k \geq 5$, though there is no difficulty in obtaining their numerical values for any k (see, e.g., Barlow et al. 1972). Stochastic upper and lower bounds for the distribution of $\hat{\xi}_{LR}$ have been obtained by Robertson and Wright (1982) and Dardanoni and Forcina (1998).

Asymptotic Test

We shall now derive a test for the implication obtained in Corollary 1, where normality is only asymptotic. Using the notation of section Exact Test for Order Restrictions, the k-vector $\hat{\Sigma}^{-1/2}(\hat{q}-\mu)$ is asymptotically multivariate normal with mean vector 0_k and identity covariance matrix Id_k.

Note that the standard way of dealing with asymptotically valid order restriction tests (see, e.g., Gourieroux et al. 1982; Kodde & Palm, 1986) does not apply here, as the components of the scaling matrix $\hat{\Sigma}$ are not all proportional to $T^{-1/2}$. In order to make sure that $\hat{\Sigma}$ does not become ill-scaled as T gets large – that some of the variance terms $\hat{\sigma}_j$ become infinitely large compared to others – we assume the following:

Assumption 5. Say that a multiple equilibrium model $(\varepsilon_{XU}, P_X, F_{U|X})$ satisfies Assumption 5 if it satisfies Assumption 4 and, in addition, U is independent of X.

When the distribution $F_{U|X}$ does not depend on X, the same is true for the quantities involved in the previously derived limit results. In particular, under Assumption 5 we have that $a_x^U \circ \overline{F}_{U|X=x}^{-1} = a^U \circ \overline{F}_U^{-1}$ for all $x \in \mathcal{X}$, so:

$$\frac{\sigma_j}{\sigma_i} = \frac{a_{x_j}^Y(q_{Y|X=x_j}(\alpha_T))/\sqrt{c_j(1-\alpha_T)T}}{a_{x_i}^Y(q_{Y|X=x_i}(\alpha_T))/\sqrt{c_i(1-\alpha_T)T}} = \sqrt{\frac{c_i}{c_j}\frac{a_{x_j}^Y \circ \overline{F}_{Y|X=x_j}^{-1}(\alpha_T)}{a_{x_i}^Y \circ \overline{F}_{Y|X=x_i}^{-1}(\alpha_T)}} \sim \sqrt{\frac{c_i}{c_j}\frac{g_{N_{x_i}}(x_i)}{g_{N_{x_j}}(x_j)}} \text{ as } \alpha_T \to 1 \tag{21}$$

where the last equality uses the asymptotic proportionality of $a_X^Y \circ \overline{F}_{Y|X}$ and $a^U \circ \overline{F}_U$ that was established in Lemma 2(ii).

Now, consider again the limit results derived in Corollary 1. The asymptotic equivalence result established in Eq. (21) guarantees that the scaling constants σ_j that control how fast the empirical quantiles $\hat{q}_{Y|X=x_j}(\alpha_T)$ converge to the true quantiles $q_{Y|X=x_j}(\alpha_T)$ are all of the same size. In that case, we have have the following result.

Theorem 3. Assume $(\varepsilon_{XU}, P_X, F_{U|X})$ satisfies Assumption 5. If for $T \geq 1$, $(Y_{j,1}, \ldots, Y_{j,c_jT})$, $j = 1, \ldots, k$, are k independent random samples of size c_jT drawn from $F_{Y|X=x_j}$, $x_j \in \mathcal{X}$, then as $T \to \infty$, the likelihood-ratio statistic $\hat{\xi}_{LR}$ is asymptotically distributed as $\overline{\chi}^2_k$, with weights that are consistently estimated by weights obtained in the exact Gaussian case.

For example, when $k = 2$ and 3, the asymptotic distribution of $\hat{\xi}_{LR}$ is that derived in Eqs. (19) and (20).

It is worth pointing out that the conclusion of Theorem 3 remains valid if, instead of being independent of X, the distribution $F_{U|X}$ is such that for any $(x, x') \in \mathcal{X}^2$ we have:

$$\lim_{v \downarrow 0} \frac{f_{U|X=x}(\overline{F}^{-1}_{U|X=x}(v))}{f_{U|X=x'}(\overline{F}^{-1}_{U|X=x'}(v))} \text{ exists, is strictly positive and independent of } (x, x'). \tag{22}$$

The requirement in Eq. (22) is weaker than that of independence, since it only restricts the behavior of the auxiliary function a_X^U evaluated at the tail quantiles $\overline{F}^{-1}_{U|X}$. In particular, if the auxiliary function a_X^U is constant, as in the case of exponentially distributed random variables, the requirement in Eq. (22) holds without imposing independence of U and X.

Limitations

Finally, we briefly discuss some important limitations of our approach. First, note that since we only use the MCS prediction to derive our test, the latter is based solely on the extremal conditional quantiles of Y given X. Our approach is not equilibria other than the largest and the smallest one, thus our test is not based on the observations that would correspond to those equilibria. While this allows us to cover a variety of models in which MCS holds, it comes at a cost in terms of the power of our test. Indeed, if one knows that the MCS prediction needs to hold at equilibria other than the largest and the smallest one (e.g. all the stable equilibria), then incorporating this additional information in the testing procedure will likely result in improved power properties since the test will now be based on a larger set of observations.

Second, the implementation of our test requires a choice for the probability α_T that satisfies the conditions in Eq. (14). Since there are a number of possible choices for α_T, a data-dependent rule for determination of an "optimal" α_T would be useful in practice. This, however, is likely to be quite a difficult problem, akin to developing rigorous rules for bandwidth selection in nonparametric methods. We therefore leave this issue for future research.

CONCLUSION

In this article we design an econometric test for MCS predictions suited for testing models with multiple equilibria. Our approach may be characterized as nonparametric as we do not make assumptions on the cardinality, location or probabilities over equilibria. In particular, one can implement our test without assuming an equilibrium selection rule.

First, we show how MCS predictions translate into observable implications on the distribution of the dependent variable. In particular, we show that high enough conditional quantiles of the dependent variable increase when the explanatory variable increases.

Second, we construct an LR test for equality of high conditional quantiles against an ordered alternative, as predicted by the MCS arguments. The test is an asymptotic extension of the "chi-bar squared" test. Even though the focus of this article is on quantiles with probabilities close to one, all of our results – when properly transposed – continue to hold for probabilities close to zero.

Finally, we point out some extensions: our LR test can be accommodated to test other hypotheses of interest, such as the unrestricted order among conditional quantiles. Provided that quantile probabilities increase toward one at the same speed as the sample size – which would satisfy the requirement of "large enough" quantile in our paper – this would give rise to other limit distributions. It would be interesting to compare our existing test with one based on such extreme conditional quantiles. In order to carry out our LR test, we needed to eliminate the nuisance parameters – quantile variances – by replacing them with their probability limits. An alternative approach is to use the asymptotic distribution results of the quantile spacings and derive a better approximation to standardized quantiles in the small sample. Finally, a regression-based approach – in which the conditional quantile is modeled as a function of the explanatory variable – would offer an interesting alternative way of testing the monotonicity prediction.

NOTES

1. According to Samuelson (1947): "The usefulness of our theory emerges from the fact that by our analysis we are often able to determine the nature of the changes in our unknown variables resulting from a designated change in one or more parameters."
2. See also Fox and Lazzati (2012) for additional examples.
3. We note that Athey and Stern (1998) discuss tests for monotone comparative statics, however, only in the context of firms' choice of organizational form. Complementarities play an important role in organizational design, as discussed, for example, Brynjolfsson and Milgrom (2012), and Milgrom and Roberts (1990a). Our results can potentially be of interest to this literature.
4. All of our results are easily transposable to additive error models of the form $Y = g(X) + U$ with $Y \in \mathbb{R}$, $U \in \mathbb{R}$, $X \in \mathcal{X}$ and $g : \mathcal{X} \to \mathbb{R}$, by taking logarithms.
5. Recall that X is a policy variable, which in the applications described in the Introduction took the form of a dummy variable. In the general setup, we allow X to be discrete. However, extending our analysis to continuous $X's$ is nontrivial and thus outside the scope of this article.
6. Note that while we explicitly allow the cardinality of the equilibrium set N_x to vary with x, we can also accommodate the case in which the latter varies with u provided $Card(\varepsilon_{xu})$ remains bounded by some M_x for every $u \in \mathbb{R}_{++}$.
7. For example, if the estimation is carried out by using the EM-algorithm, both the location of different equilibria and the probabilities attached to them need to be estimated (see, e.g., Carroll, Ruppert, & Stefanski, 1995).
8. This implies that all the moments of a random variable with a $(-\infty)$-varying distribution tail are finite. Examples of distributions with ρ-varying tails, $\rho > -\infty$, which *do not* have finite moments are: (1) a stable law with index α, $0 < \alpha < 2$, for which $\rho = -\alpha$; (2) a Cauchy distribution, for which $\rho = -1$. Hence the use of those distributions is not permitted in our framework.

ACKNOWLEDGMENTS

We would like to thank the editors and an anonymous referee for valuable comments. All errors are our own. The second author gratefully acknowledges financial support from the National Science Foundation SES-0962473.

REFERENCES

Ackerberg, D. A., & Gowrisankaran, G. (2006). Quantifying equilibrium network externalities in the ACH banking industry. *The RAND Journal of Economics*, *37*(3), 738–761.

Aguirregabiria, V., & Mira, P. (2007). Sequential estimation of dynamic discrete games. *Econometrica*, *75*(1), 1–53.

Athey, S., & Stern, S. (1998). *An empirical framework for testing theories about complementarity in organizational design*. NBER Working Paper 6600.

Bahadur, R. R. (1966). A note on quantiles in large samples. *The Annals of Mathematical Statistics*, *37*, 577–580.

Bajari, P., Hong, H., & Ryan, S. P. (2010). Identification and estimation of a discrete game of complete information. *Econometrica*, *78*(5), 1529–1568.

Barlow, R., Bartholomew, D., Bremner, J., & Brunk, H. (1972). *Statistical inference under order restrictions*. New York, NY: Wiley.

Barro, R. J., & Sala-I-Martin, X. (2003). *Economic growth*. Cambridge, MA: MIT Press.

Bartholomew, D. J. (1959a). A test of homogeneity for ordered alternatives. *Biometrika*, *46*, 36–48.

Bartholomew, D. J. (1959b). A test of homogeneity for ordered alternatives II. *Biometrika*, *46*, 328–335.

Bassett, Jr, G., & Koenker, R. (1978). Asymptotic theory of least absolute error regression. *Journal of the American Statistical Association*, *73*(363), 618–622.

Berry, S. T., Levinsohn, J., & Pakes, A. (1995). Automobile prices in market equilibrium. *Econometrica*, *63*(4), 841–890.

Berry, S. T., Levinsohn, J., & Pakes, A. (1999). Voluntary export restraints on automobiles: Evaluating a trade policy. *American Economic Review*, *89*(3), 400–430.

Bjorn, P. A., & Vuong, Q. H. (1984). *Simultaenous equations models for dummy endogenous variables: A game theoretic formulation with an application to labor force participation*. Caltech Social Science Working Paper 577.

Bjorn, P. A., & Vuong, Q. H. (1985). *Econometric modeling of a stackelberg game with an application to labor force participation*. Caltech Working Paper 537.

Brynjolfsson, E., & Milgrom, P. (2012). Complementarity in organizations. In R. Gibbons & J. Roberts. (Eds.), *The handbook of organizational economics*. Princeton: Princeton University Press.

Carroll, R. J., Ruppert, D., & Stefanski, L. A. (1995). *Measurement error in nonlinear models*. Chapmann & Hall.

Chernozhukov, V. (2005). Extremal quantile regression. *Annals of Statistics*, *33*, 806–839.

Chernozhukov, V., & Fernandez-Val, I. (2011). Inference for extremal conditional quantile models, with an application to market and birthweight risks. *The Review of Economic Studies*, *78*(2), 559–589.

Dardanoni, V., & Forcina, A. (1998). A unified approach to likelihood inference on stochastic orderings in a nonparametric context. *Journal of the American Statistical Association*, *93*, 1112–1123.

de Haan, L. (1970). *On regular variation and its application to the weak convergence of sample extremes*. University of Amsterdam, Mathematical Centre Tract 32.

de Haan, L. (1974). Equivalence classes of regularly varying functions. *Stochastic Processes and their Applications*, *2*, 243–259.

de Paula, A. (2013). Econometric analysis of games with multiple equilibria. *Annual Review of Economics*, *5*(1), 107–131.

Dekkers, A. L., & de Haan, L. (1989). On the estimation of the extreme-value index and large quantile estimation. *Annals of Statistics*, *17*, 1795–1832.

Echenique, F. (2002). Comparative statics by adaptive dynamics and the correspondence principle. *Econometrica*, *70*(2), 833–844.

Echenique, F., & Komunjer, I. (2009). Testing models with multiple equilibria by quantile methods. *Econometrica*, *77*, 1281–1297.

Embrechts, P., Kluppelberg, C., & Mikosch, T. (1997). *Modelling extremal events for insurance and finance*. Berlin Heidelberg: Springer-Verlag.

Falk, M. (1989). A note on uniform asymptotic normality of intermediate order statistics. *Annals of the Institute of Statistical Mathematics*, *41*, 19–29.

Fox, J. T., & Lazzati, N. (2012). *Identification of potential games and demand models for bundles*. Unpublished manuscript, University of Michigan.

Gourieroux, C., Holly, A., & Monfort, A. (1982). Likelihood ratio test, Wald test, and Kuhn-Tucker test in linear models with inequality constraints on the regression parameters. *Econometrica*, *50*, 63–80.

Hayashi, F. (1982). Tobin's marginal q and average q: A neoclassical interpretation. *Econometrica*, *50*(1), 213–224.

Hayashi, F., & Inoue, T. (1991). The relation between firm growth and q with multiple capital goods: Theory and evidence from panel data on Japanese firms. *Econometrica*, *59*(3), 731–753.

Jia, P. (2008). What happens when Wal-Mart comes to town: An empirical analysis of the discount retailing industry. *Econometrica*, *76*(6), 1263–1316.

Karamata, J. (1930). Sur un mode de croissance régulière des fonctions. *Mathematica*, *5*, 38–53.

Kodde, D. A., & Palm, F. C. (1986). Wald criteria for jointly testing equality and inequality restrictions. *Econometrica*, *54*, 1243–1248.

Koenker, R., & Zhao, Q. (1996). Conditional quantile estimation and inference for ARCH models. *Econometric Theory*, *12*, 793–813.

Komunjer, I. (2005). Quasi-Maximum likelihood estimation for conditional quantiles. *Journal of Econometrics*, *128*, 137–164.

Lazzati, N. (2012). *Treatment response with social interactions: Partial identification via monotone comparative statics*. Working Paper. University of Michigan.

Ljungqvist, L., & Sargent, T. J. (2004). *Recursive macroeconomic theory* (2nd ed.). Cambridge, MA: MIT Press.

Mas-Colell, A., Whinston, M. D., & Green, J.R. (1995). *Microeconomic theory*. New York: Oxford University Press.

McKelvey, R. D., & Palfrey, T. R. (1995). Quantal response equilibria for normal form games. *Games and Economic Behavior*, *10*(1), 6–38.

Milgrom, P., & Roberts, J. (1990a). The economics of modern manufacturing: Technology, strategy, and organization. *The American Economic Review*, *80*(3), 511–528.

Milgrom, P., & Roberts, J. (1990b). Rationalizability, learning and equilibrium in games with strategic complementarities. *Econometrica*, *58*(6), 1255–1277.

Milgrom, P., & Shannon, C. (1994). Monotone comparative statics. *Econometrica, 62*(1), 157–180.

Molinari, F., & Rosen, A. M. (2008). The identification power of equilibrium in games: The supermodular case. *Journal of Business & Economic Statistics, 26*(3), 297–302.

Mosteller, F. (1946). On some useful Inefficient statistics. *Annals of Mathematical Statistics, 17*, 377–408.

Pakes, A., Berry, S., & Levinsohn, J. A. (1993). Applications and limitations of some recent advances in empirical industrial organization: Price indexes and the analysis of environmental change. *American Economic Review, 83*(2), 240–246.

Pollard, D. (1991). Asymptotics for least aboslute deviation regression estimators. *Econometric Theory, 7*, 186–199.

Portnoy, S. (1991). Behavior of regression quantiles in non-stationary, dependent cases. *Journal of Multivariate Analysis, 38*, 100–113.

Powell, J. L. (1984). Least absolute deviations estimation for the censored regression model. *Journal of Econometrics, 25*, 303–325.

Powell, J. L. (1986). Censored regression quantiles. *Journal of Econometrics, 32*, 143–155.

Renyi, A. (1953). On the theory of order statistics. *Acta Mathematica Hungarica, 4*, 191–231.

Resnick, S.I. (1987). *Extreme values, regular variation, and point processes.* New York: Springer-Verlag.

Robertson, T., & Wegman, E. J. (1978). Likelihood ratio tests for order restrictions in exponential families. *Annals of Statistics, 6*, 485–505.

Robertson, T., & Wright, F. T. (1982). Bounds on mixtures of distributions arising in order restricted inference. *Annals of Statistics, 10*, 302–306.

Samuelson, P.A. (1947). *Foundations of economic analysis.* Cambridge, MA: Harvard University Press.

Siddiqui, M. (1960). Distribution of quantiles in samples form a bivariate population. *Journal of Research of the National Bureau of Standards – B. Mathematics and Mathematical Physics, 64B*, 145–150.

Smirnov, N. (1952). Limit distributions for the terms of a variational series. *American Mathematical Society Translations, 67*, 82–143.

Sweeting, A. (2009). The strategic timing incentives of commercial radio stations: An empirical analysis using multiple equilibria. *RAND Journal of Economics, 40*(4), 710–742.

Villas-Boas, J. M. (1997). Comparative statics of fixed points. *Journal of Economic Theory, 73*(1), 183–198.

Vives, X. (1999). *Oligopoly pricing.* Cambridge, MA: MIT Press.

Watts, V. (1980). The almost sure representation of intermediate order statistics. *Zeitschrift Fur Wahrscheinlichkeitstheorie und Verwandte Gebiete, 54*, 281–285.

APPENDIX A: PROOFS OF RESULTS STATED IN THE TEXT

Proof of Lemma 1. Fix $x \in \mathcal{X}$ and assume $\overline{F}_{U|X=x} \in \mathcal{R}_{-\infty}$ at ∞. Let $R_x : \mathbb{R}_{++} \to \mathbb{R}_{++}$ be given by:

$$R_x(y) \equiv \pi_{xN_x} \frac{\overline{F}_{U|X=x}(y/g_{N_x}(x))}{\overline{F}_{Y|X=x}(y)} \tag{A.1}$$

Note that R_x is well defined, as from item (iv) in Definition 1 and Eq. (2) we know $\overline{F}_{Y|X=x}(y) > 0$, for all $y > 0$. Moreover:

$$R_x(y) = \frac{\pi_{xN_x}\overline{F}_{U|X=x}(y/g_{N_x}(x))}{\pi_{xN_x}\overline{F}_{U|X=x}(y/g_{N_x}(x))\left[1 + \sum_{1 \leqslant i < N_x} \frac{\pi_{xi}\overline{F}_{U|X=x}(y/g_i(x))}{\pi_{xN_x}\overline{F}_{U|X=x}(y/g_{N_x}(x))}\right]} \tag{A.2}$$

Given that $\overline{F}_{U|X=x}$ is $(-\infty)$-varying at ∞, we have:

$$\lim_{y \to \infty} \frac{\overline{F}_{U|X=x}(y/g_i(x))}{\overline{F}_{U|X=x}(y/g_{N_x}(x))} = \lim_{z \to \infty} \frac{\overline{F}_{U|X=x}(zg_{N_x}(x)/g_i(x))}{\overline{F}_{U|X=x}(z)} = 0 \tag{A.3}$$

with $z = y/g_{N_x}(x)$. Moreover, from item (iii) in Definition 1 we know that π_{xi}/π_{xN_x} is bounded, so:

$$\lim_{y \to \infty} R_x(y) = 1 \tag{A.4}$$

and

$$\overline{F}_{Y|X=x}(y) \sim \pi_{xN_x}\overline{F}_{U|X=x}(y/g_{N_x}(x)) \text{ as } y \to \infty \tag{A.5}$$

From Eq. (A.5), we have:

$$\lim_{y \to \infty} \frac{\overline{F}_{Y|X=x}(\lambda y)}{\overline{F}_{Y|X=x}(y)} = \lim_{y \to \infty} \frac{\overline{F}_{U|X=x}(\lambda y/g_{N_x}(x))}{\overline{F}_{U|X=x}(y/g_{N_x}(x))} = \lim_{z \to \infty} \frac{\overline{F}_{U|X=x}(\lambda z)}{\overline{F}_{U|X=x}(z)}$$

so $\overline{F}_{Y|X=x} \in \mathcal{R}_{-\infty}$ at ∞, which together with Eq. (A.5) shows that item (i) holds.

We shall now prove item (ii). Using Lemma 5, $\overline{F}^{-1}_{U|X=x}$ is 0-varying at 0: for $\lambda > 0$:

$$\lim_{v \downarrow 0} \frac{\overline{F}^{-1}_{U|X=x}(\lambda v)}{\overline{F}^{-1}_{U|X=x}(v)} = 1 \tag{A.6}$$

On the other hand, $\lim_{y\to\infty}\overline{F}_{Y|X=x}(y)=0$ and Eq. (A.4) together imply that $\lim_{y\to\infty}\overline{F}_{Y|X=x}(y)R_x(y)/\pi_{xN_x}=0$, and

$$\lim_{y\to\infty}\frac{\overline{F}_{Y|X=x}(y)R_x(y)/\pi_{xN_x}}{\overline{F}_{Y|X=x}(y)}=\frac{1}{\pi_{xN_x}}$$

That $\overline{F}^{-1}_{U|X=x}$ is 0-varying at 0 then implies, by Lemma 6:

$$\lim_{y\to\infty}\frac{\overline{F}^{-1}_{U|X=x}(\overline{F}_{Y|X=x}(y)R_x(y)/\pi_{xN_x})}{\overline{F}^{-1}_{U|X=x}(\overline{F}_{Y|X=x}(y))}=[\pi_{xN_x}]^0=1 \tag{A.7}$$

Now, using the definition of $R_x(y)$ in Eq. (A.1), we have:

$$\frac{\overline{F}^{-1}_{U|X=x}(\overline{F}_{Y|X=x}(y)R_x(y)/\pi_{xN_x})}{\overline{F}^{-1}_{U|X=x}(\overline{F}_{Y|X=x}(y))}=\frac{y/g_{xN_x}(x)}{\overline{F}^{-1}_{U|X=x}(\overline{F}_{Y|X=x}(y))} \tag{A.8}$$

so Eq. (A.7) implies that $y/g_{xN_x}(x)\sim\overline{F}^{-1}_{U|X=x}(\overline{F}_{Y|X=x}(y))$ as y goes to ∞. Letting $v=\overline{F}_{Y|X=x}(y)$ we then have:

$$\overline{F}^{-1}_{Y|X=x}(v)\sim g_{xN_x}(x)\overline{F}^{-1}_{U|X=x}(v) \quad as \quad v\downarrow 0 \tag{A.9}$$

Eqs. (A.6) and (A.9) give:

$$\lim_{v\downarrow 0}\frac{\overline{F}^{-1}_{Y|X=x}(\lambda v)}{\overline{F}^{-1}_{Y|X=x}(v)}=1 \quad for \quad \lambda>0$$

so $\overline{F}^{-1}_{Y|X=x}$ is 0-varying at 0 which together with Equations (A.6) and (A.9) shows (ii), and thus completes the proof of Lemma 1.

Proof of Theorem 1. The proof of Theorem 1 follows from Lemma 1 easily by the argument used in the third section. We include it here for completeness. Consider $(x_1,x_2)\in\mathcal{X}^2$ such that $x_1<x_2$. From Lemma 1(i):

$$\frac{\overline{F}_{Y|X=x_1}(y)}{\overline{F}_{Y|X=x_2}(y)}\sim\frac{\pi_{x_1N_{x_1}}\overline{F}_{U|X=x_1}(y/g_{N_{x_1}}(x_1))}{\pi_{x_2N_{x_2}}\overline{F}_{U|X=x_2}(y/g_{N_{x_2}}(x_2))},\quad \text{as}\quad y\to\infty$$

Now note that:

$$\frac{\overline{F}_{U|X=x_1}(y/g_{N_{x_1}}(x_1))}{\overline{F}_{U|X=x_2}(y/g_{N_{x_2}}(x_2))}=\frac{\overline{F}_{U|X=x_1}(y/g_{N_{x_1}}(x_1))}{\overline{F}_{U|X=x_1}(y/g_{N_{x_2}}(x_2))}\frac{\overline{F}_{U|X=x_1}(y/g_{N_{x_2}}(x_2))}{\overline{F}_{U|X=x_2}(y/g_{N_{x_2}}(x_2))} \tag{A.10}$$

From item (ii) in Definition 1 we have $g_{N_{x_2}}(x_2) > g_{N_{x_1}}(x_1)$, and by Assumption 1 $\overline{F}_{U|X=x_1} \in \mathcal{R}_{-\infty}$ at ∞, so:

$$\lim_{y\to\infty} \frac{\overline{F}_{U|X=x_1}(y/g_{N_{x_1}}(x_1))}{\overline{F}_{U|X=x_1}(y/g_{N_{x_2}}(x_2))} = \lim_{z\to\infty} \frac{\overline{F}_{U|X=x_1}(zg_{N_{x_2}}(x_2)/g_{N_{x_1}}(x_1))}{\overline{F}_{U|X=x_1}(z)} = 0$$

where $z \equiv y/g_{N_{x_2}}(x_2)$. So the first term on the right-hand side of Eq. (A.10) goes to 0 as y gets large. From Property (12) in Assumption 2 and given $x_1 < x_2$, we know that the second term of the right-hand side of Eq. (A.10) is bounded as y increases. Finally, we know that $\pi_{x_1 N_{x1}}/\pi_{x_2 N_{x_2}} < \infty$ since from item (iii) in Definition 1 $\pi_{x_2 N_{x_2}} > 0$. Combining the facts above:

$$\lim_{y\to\infty} \frac{\overline{F}_{Y|X=x_1}(y)}{\overline{F}_{Y|X=x_2}(y)} = 0$$

so there is $\overline{y}_1 > 0$ such that, if $y \geq \overline{y}_1$ then $\overline{F}_{Y|X=x_1}(y) < \overline{F}_{Y|X=x_2}(y)$. Since $\mathcal{X}$ is finite, there is $\overline{y}$ such that if $y \geq \overline{y}$ then $\overline{F}_{Y|X=x}(y) < \overline{F}_{Y|X=x'}(y)$ for all $(x, x') \in \mathcal{X}^2$ with $x < x'$. Note that for any $x \in \mathcal{X}$ and $v \in (0,1)$, $\overline{F}^{-1}_{Y|X=x}(v) = q_{Y|X=x}(1-v)$. From the above we know that, for any $(x_1, x_2) \in \mathcal{X}^2$ such that $x_1 < x_2$, there is $\underline{v}1 \in (0,1)$ such that if $v \leq \underline{v}1$ then $q_{Y|X=x_1}(1-v) < q_{Y|X=x_2}(1-v)$. Equivalently, letting $\overline{\alpha}_1 \equiv 1 - \underline{v}1$, for $\alpha \in [\overline{\alpha}_1, 1)$ we have $q_{Y|X=x_1}(\alpha) < q_{Y|X=x_2}(\alpha)$. $\mathcal{X}$ being finite guarantees that the result holds for any $(x, x') \in \mathcal{X}^2$ by the same reasoning as above.

Proof of Lemma 2. Fix $x \in \mathcal{X}$ and assume $\overline{F}_{U|X=x}$ is in Γ with auxiliary function a^U_x; for R_x defined in Eq. (A.1) we have:

$$\frac{R_x(g_{N_x}(x)y + g_{N_x}(x)\lambda a^U_x(y))}{R_x(g_{N_x}(x)y)} = \left[\frac{\pi_{xN_x}\overline{F}_{U|X=x}(y+\lambda a^U_x(y))}{F_{Y|X=x}(g_{N_x}(x)y + g_{N_x}(x)\lambda a^U_x(y))}\right]\left[\frac{F_{Y|X=x}(g_{N_x}(x)y)}{\pi_{xN_x}\overline{F}_{U|X=x}(y)}\right] \tag{A.11}$$

From Eq. (A.4), the left-hand side in Eq. (A.11) converges to 1 as $y \to \infty$. On the other hand:

$$\lim_{y\to\infty} \frac{\pi_{xN_x}\overline{F}_{U|X=x}(y + \lambda a^U_x(y))}{\pi_{xN_x}\overline{F}_{U|X=x}(y)} = \exp(-\lambda)$$

since a_x^U is the auxiliary function of $\overline{F}_{U|X=x}$. Then we have:

$$\begin{aligned}\exp(\lambda) &= \lim_{y\to\infty} \frac{\overline{F}_{Y|X=x}(g_{N_x}(x)y)}{\overline{F}_{Y|X=x}(g_{N_x}(x)y + g_{N_x}(x)\lambda a_x^U(y))} \\ &= \lim_{z\to\infty} \frac{\overline{F}_{Y|X=x}(z)}{\overline{F}_{Y|X=x}(z + g_{N_x}(x)\lambda a_x^U(z/g_{N_x}(x)))}\end{aligned}$$

using the change of variable $z \equiv g_{N_x}(x)y$. Hence $\overline{F}_{Y|X=x} \in \Gamma$:

$$\lim_{y\to\infty} \frac{\overline{F}_{Y|X=x}(y + \lambda a_x^Y(y))}{\overline{F}_{Y|X=x}(y)} = \exp(-\lambda) \tag{A.12}$$

with auxiliary function a_x^Y defined as $a_x^Y(y) \equiv g_{N_x}(x) a_x^U(y/g_{N_x}(x))$ for all $y>0$, which shows item (i).

In order to show item (ii) we exploit the fact that for any sequence $\{\varphi_s\}_{s>0}$ of monotone increasing functions $\varphi_s : \mathbb{R}^+ \to (0,1)$, $\lim_{s\to\infty} \varphi_s(x) = \varphi(x)$ for all continuity points $x>0$ of φ, implies $\lim_{s\to\infty} \varphi_s^{-1}(z) = \varphi^{-1}(z)$ for all continuity points $z \in (0,1)$ of φ^{-1} (see, e.g., Lemma 1.9 in de Haan, 1974). Let then:

$$\varphi_s(y) \equiv 1 - \frac{\overline{F}_{U|X=x}(s + y a_x^U(s))}{\overline{F}_{U|X=x}(s)} \text{ for all } y>0$$

That $\overline{F}_{U|X=x} \in \Gamma$ implies $\lim_{s\to\infty} \varphi_s(y) = 1 - \exp(-y)$ for all $y>0$. Letting $\varphi(y) \equiv 1 - \exp(-y)$, we then have for $t \in (0,1)$:

$$\lim_{s\to\infty} \frac{\overline{F}^{-1}_{U|X=x}((1-t)\overline{F}_{U|X=x}(s)) - s}{a_x^U(s)} = \lim_{s\to\infty} \varphi_s^{-1}(t) = \varphi^{-1}(t) = -\ln(1-t)$$

Letting $\nu \equiv \overline{F}_{U|X=x}(s)$ and $\mu \equiv 1-t$ gives:

$$\lim_{\nu\downarrow 0} \frac{\overline{F}^{-1}_{U|X=x}(\nu\mu) - \overline{F}^{-1}_{U|X=x}(\nu)}{a_x^U(\overline{F}^{-1}_{U|X=x}(\nu))} = -\ln\mu \;\text{ for } \mu \in (0,1) \tag{A.13}$$

Thus $\overline{F}^{-1}_{U|X=x} \in \Pi$ as in Definition 4 with auxiliary function $a_x^U \circ \overline{F}^{-1}_{U|X=x}$. Moreover, for any $\lambda>0$, letting $\mu \equiv \lambda$ and $\nu \equiv \lambda^{-1}$ we have:

$$\frac{a_x^U(F^{-1}_{U|X=x}(\lambda\nu))}{a_x^U(F^{-1}_{U|X=x}(\nu))} = -\left[\frac{F^{-1}_{U|X=x}(\mu\nu) - F^{-1}_{U|X=x}(\nu)}{a_x^U(F^{-1}_{U|X=x}(\nu))}\right]\left[\frac{a_x^U(F^{-1}_{U|X=x}(\lambda\nu))}{F^{-1}_{U|X=x}(\lambda\nu\nu) - F^{-1}_{U|X=x}(\lambda\nu)}\right] \tag{A.14}$$

Eqs. (A.13) and (A.14) together imply:

$$\lim_{v\downarrow 0}\frac{a_x^U\circ\overline{F}_{U|X=x}^{-1}(\lambda v)}{a_x^U\circ\overline{F}_{U|X=x}^{-1}(v)}=\frac{\ln\mu}{-\ln\nu}=1 \tag{A.15}$$

so $a_x^U\circ\overline{F}_{U|X=x}^{-1}\in\mathcal{R}_0$ at 0. We now study $\overline{F}_{Y|X=x}$: if for any $x\in\mathcal{X}$, we let $\varphi_{x,s}(y)\equiv 1-\overline{F}_{Y|X=x}(s+ya_x^Y(s))/\overline{F}_{Y|X=x}(s)$ for all $y>0$, we have $\lim_{s\to\infty}\varphi_{x,s}(y)=\varphi(y)$. Same reasoning as previously then implies:

$$\lim_{v\downarrow 0}\frac{\overline{F}_{Y|X=x}^{-1}(v\mu)-\overline{F}_{Y|X=x}^{-1}(v)}{a_x^Y(\overline{F}_{Y|X=x}^{-1}(v))}=-\ln\mu \ \text{ for } \mu\in(0,1) \tag{A.16}$$

So $\overline{F}_{Y|X=x}^{-1}\in\Pi$ as in Definition 4 with auxiliary function $a_x^Y\circ\overline{F}_{Y|X=x}^{-1}$. Eq. (A.16) and the fact that:

$$\frac{a_x^Y(\overline{F}_{Y|X=x}^{-1}(\lambda v))}{a_x^Y(\overline{F}_{Y|X=x}^{-1}(v))}=-\left[\frac{\overline{F}_{Y|X=x}^{-1}(\mu v)-\overline{F}_{Y|X=x}^{-1}(v)}{a_x^Y(\overline{F}_{Y|X=x}^{-1}(v))}\right]\left[\frac{a_x^Y(\overline{F}_{Y|X=x}^{-1}(\lambda v))}{\overline{F}_{Y|X=x}^{-1}(\lambda\nu v)-\overline{F}_{Y|X=x}^{-1}(\lambda v)}\right]$$

with $\lambda>0$, $\mu\equiv\lambda$ and $\nu\equiv\lambda^{-1}$, then imply that $a_x^Y\circ\overline{F}_{Y|X=x}^{-1}\in\mathcal{R}_0$ at 0.

Given Eq. (A.9) and the definition of a_x^Y it is not surprising to see that $a_x^Y(\overline{F}_{Y|X=x}^{-1}(v))\sim g_{N_x}(x)a_x^U(\overline{F}_{U|X=x}^{-1}(v))$ as $v\downarrow 0$; however we need a formal proof of that statement. We start by showing that:

$$\lim_{s\to\infty}F_{Y|X=x}^{s}(A_s\lambda+b_s)=\exp[-\exp(-\lambda)] \tag{A.17}$$

with $A_s\equiv a_x^Y(b_s)$ and $b_s\equiv\overline{F}_{Y|X=x}^{-1}(1/s)$. In Eq. (A.12) let $y\equiv\overline{F}_{Y|X=x}^{-1}(1/s)$ so $y\to\infty$ as $s\to\infty$; then:

$$\begin{aligned}&\lim_{s\to\infty}\frac{F_{Y|X=x}(F_{Y|X=x}^{-1}(1/s)+\lambda a_x^Y(F_{Y|X=x}^{-1}(1/s)))}{F_{Y|X=x}(F_{Y|X=x}^{-1}(1/s))}\\&=\lim_{s\to\infty}s\overline{F}_{Y|X=x}(a_x^Y(\overline{F}_{Y|X=x}^{-1}(1/s))\lambda+\overline{F}_{Y|X=x}^{-1}(1/s))\\&=\exp(-\lambda).\end{aligned} \tag{A.18}$$

Let $b_s\equiv\overline{F}_{Y|X=x}^{-1}(1/s)$ and $A_s\equiv a_x^Y(b_s)$; the last equality in Eq. (A.18) together with Lemma 2.2.2 in de Haan (1970) then imply Eq. (A.17). We now derive a similar equality involving $F_{U|X=x}$: the last equality in Eq. (A.18) and the tail equivalence property in Eq. (A.5) together imply:

$$\lim_{s\to\infty} s\overline{F}_{U|X=x}((A_s/g_{N_x}(x))\lambda+(b_s/g_{N_x}(x)))=\exp(-\lambda-\ln\pi_{xN_x})$$

Using again Lemma 2.2.2 in de Haan (1970) then gives:

$$\lim_{s\to\infty} F^s_{U|X=x}((A_s/g_{N_x}(x))\lambda+(b_s/g_{N_x}(x)))=\exp(-\exp(-\lambda-\ln\pi_{xN_x})) \quad \text{(A.19)}$$

On the other hand, $\overline{F}_{U|X=x}\in\Gamma$ as in Definition 3 with auxiliary function a_x^U, together with Lemma 2.2.2 in de Haan (1970) imply:

$$\lim_{s\to\infty} F^s_{U|X=x}(\tilde{A}_s\lambda+\tilde{b}_s)=\exp(-\exp(-\lambda)) \quad \text{(A.20)}$$

with $\tilde{A}_s\equiv a_x^U(\tilde{b}_s)$ and $\tilde{b}_s\equiv\overline{F}^{-1}_{U|X=x}(1/s)$. Combining Eqs. (A.19) and (A.20) and applying the results of Lemma 2.4.1 in de Haan (1970) on the change of norming constants (with $A=1$ and $B=\ln\pi_{xN_x}$), then gives:

$$\frac{(A_s/g_{N_x}(x))}{\tilde{A}_s}\to 1 \text{ and } \frac{(b_s/g_{N_x}(x))-\tilde{b}_s}{\tilde{A}_s}\to \ln\pi_{xN_x} \text{as } s\to\infty$$

So from the first of the above limit results, we get:

$$a_x^Y(\overline{F}^{-1}_{Y|X=x}(v))\sim g_{N_x}(x)a_x^U(\overline{F}^{-1}_{U|X=x}(v)) \text{ as } v\downarrow 0,$$

which completes the proof of item (ii).

Proof of Lemma 3. Given a random sample $(Y_1,\ldots,Y_T)$ let $\{Y^{(T)}_{(k)}\}_{k=1}^T$ be the ascending order statistics: $Y^{(T)}_{(1)}\leq\ldots\leq Y^{(T)}_{(T)}$. Then for any, α_T, $0<\alpha_T<1$, we have:

$$\hat{q}(\alpha_T)=Y^{(T)}_{(m)} \text{ with } m\equiv\lfloor\alpha_T T\rfloor+1 \quad \text{(A.21)}$$

where $\lfloor\cdot\rfloor$ denotes the greatest integer function, $\lfloor x\rfloor\equiv\max\{n\in\mathbb{N}:n\leq x\}$ for $x>0$. Note that m depends on T. Similarly, for $\beta_T:\hat{q}(\beta_T)=Y^{(T)}_{(k)}$, where $k\equiv\lfloor\beta_T T\rfloor+1$.

First we record the following facts, which follow trivially from the definition of m and the hypotheses on α_T in the theorem:

$$\lim_{T\to\infty} T-m=\infty \quad \text{(A.22)}$$

$$\lim_{T\to\infty}\frac{T-m}{T}=0 \quad \text{(A.23)}$$

$$\lim_{T\to\infty} \frac{T-m}{(1-\alpha_T)T} = \lim_{T\to\infty} \frac{T-m+1}{(1-\alpha_T)T} = 1 \tag{A.24}$$

The hypotheses on β_T imply properties (A.22)–(A.24) for k, and, in addition, that

$$\lim_{T\to\infty} \frac{T-m}{T-k} = \rho \tag{A.25}$$

Second, we have:

$$\begin{aligned}
&\sqrt{T(1-\alpha_T)}\left[\frac{\hat{q}(\alpha_T)-q(\alpha_T)}{a(q(\alpha_T))}\right] = \sqrt{T(1-\alpha_T)}\left[\frac{Y^{(T)}_{(\lfloor\alpha_T T\rfloor+1)} - F^{-1}(1-\alpha_T)}{a(F^{-1}(1-\alpha_T))}\right]\\
&= \sqrt{T-m+1}\left[\frac{Y^{(T)}_{(m)} - F^{-1}((T-m)/T)}{a(F^{-1}((T-m)/T))} + \frac{F^{-1}((T-m)/T) - F^{-1}(1-\alpha_T)}{a(F^{-1}((T-m)/T))}\right]\\
&\cdot \frac{a(F^{-1}((T-m)/T))}{a(F^{-1}(1-\alpha_T))}\sqrt{\frac{T(1-\alpha_T)}{T-m+1}}
\end{aligned} \tag{A.26}$$

and

$$\begin{aligned}
\frac{\hat{q}(\beta_T)-\hat{q}(\alpha_T)}{a(q(\alpha_T))} - \ln\rho = \Bigg\{ &\left[\frac{Y^{(T)}_{(k)} - Y^{(T)}_{(m)}}{a(Y^{(T)}_{(m)})} - \ln\rho\right]\frac{a(Y^{(T)}_{(m)})}{a(F^{-1}((T-m)/T))}\\
&+ \ln\rho\left[\frac{a(Y^{(T)}_{(m)})}{a(F^{-1}((T-m)/T))} - 1\right]\Bigg\}\frac{a(F^{-1}((T-m)/T))}{a(F^{-1}(1-\alpha_T))}.
\end{aligned} \tag{A.27}$$

The proof of the theorem is done in three steps. We first show (Step 1) that:

$$\sqrt{T-m+1}\left[\frac{Y^{(T)}_{(m)} - \overline{F}^{-1}((T-m)/T)}{a(\overline{F}^{-1}((T-m)/T))}\right] \xrightarrow{d} \mathcal{N} \tag{A.28}$$

$$\frac{Y^{(T)}_{(k)} - Y^{(T)}_{(m)}}{a(Y^{(T)}_{(m)})} \xrightarrow{P} \ln\rho \tag{A.29}$$

where $\mathcal{N}$ is a standard Gaussian random variable. We then show (Step 2):

$$\lim_{T\to\infty}\sqrt{T-m+1}\left[\frac{\overline{F}^{-1}((T-m)/T)-\overline{F}^{-1}(1-\alpha_T)}{a(\overline{F}^{-1}((T-m)/T))}\right]=0 \tag{A.30}$$

$$\lim_{T\to\infty}\frac{a(\overline{F}^{-1}((T-m)/T))}{a(\overline{F}^{-1}((1-\alpha_T))}=1 \tag{A.31}$$

Finally, we show (Step 3):

$$\frac{a(Y_{(m)}^{(T)})}{a(\overline{F}^{-1}((T-m)/T))}\xrightarrow{p}1 \tag{A.32}$$

The first limit result of Lemma 3 then follows from (A.26) by (A.28), (A.30) and (A.31) using (A.24) and Lemma 2.4.1 in de Haan (1970). The second limit result in Lemma 3 follows from (A.27) by (A.29) and (A.32) using (A.31), (A.24), and Slutsky's theorem.

Step 1: This step takes a key idea from the proof of Theorem 3.1 in Dekkers and de Haan (1989). Let $A_1,\ldots,A_T$ be independent and identically distributed standard exponential random variables. Let $A_{(1)}^{(T)}\leq\ldots\leq A_{(T)}^{(T)}$ be the ascending order statistics of $(A_1,\ldots,A_T)$. Then, by using the probability integral transform, we have $\left\{Y_{(m)}^{(T)}\right\}_{m=1}^{T}=^d\left\{\overline{F}^{-1}\left(\exp\left(-A_{(m)}^{(T)}\right)\right)\right\}_{m=1}^{T}$.

Now, let $W(x)\equiv\overline{F}^{-1}(\exp(-x))$ for $x>0$; we have $Y_{(m)}^{(T)}=^d W(A_{(m)}^{(T)})$ and $W(\ln(T/(T-m)))=\overline{F}^{-1}((T-m)/T)$. Moreover:

$$a(W(x))=\frac{\exp(-x)}{f(W(x))}=W'(x)$$

Let $\eta_T\equiv\ln(T/(T-m))$, then $a(\overline{F}^{-1}((T-m)/T))=W'(\eta_T)$. So the expression in Statement (A.28) can be written as:

$$\begin{aligned}\sqrt{T-m+1}\left[\frac{Y_{(m)}^{(T)}-F^{-1}((T-m)/T)}{a(F^{-1}((T-m)/T))}\right]&\stackrel{d}{=}\sqrt{T-m+1}\left[\frac{W(A_{(m)}^{(T)})-W(\eta_T)}{W'(\eta_T)}\right]\\&\stackrel{d}{=}\sqrt{T-m+1}\int_0^{Z_T/\sqrt{T-m+1}}\frac{W'(\eta_T+s)}{W'(\eta_T)}ds\end{aligned} \tag{A.33}$$

where $Z_T\equiv\sqrt{T-m+1}\,[A_{(m)}^{(T)}-\ln(T/(T-m))]$.

Then, by Lemma 10, $Z_T\to^d\mathcal{N}_1$ as $T\to\infty$. But Lemma 7(i) and Statement (A.19) imply that the integrand on the right-hand side of Eq. (A.33) converges uniformly to 1 on compact intervals, as $T\to\infty$. So Lemma 8 implies Statement (A.28).

The proof of Statement (A.29) is similar. We have:

$$\frac{Y_{(k)}^{(T)}-Y_{(m)}^{(T)}}{a(Y_{(m)}^{(T)})}-\ln\rho \overset{d}{=} \frac{W(A_{(k)}^{(T)})-W(A_{(m)}^{(T)})}{W'(A_{(m)}^{(T)})}-\ln\rho$$

$$\overset{d}{=}\left[\sqrt{\frac{T-m}{\rho-1}}\int_0^{V_T/\sqrt{\frac{T-m}{\rho-1}}}\frac{W'(A_{(m)}^{(T)}+\ln\rho+s)}{W'(A_{(m)}^{(T)})}ds\right]\sqrt{\frac{\rho-1}{T-m}}$$

$$+\int_0^{\ln\rho}\left[\frac{W'(A_{(m)}^{(T)}+s)}{W'(A_{(m)}^{(T)})}-1\right]ds \tag{A.34}$$

where $V_T\equiv\sqrt{(T-m)/(\rho-1)}[A_{(k)}^{(T)}-A_{(m)}^{(T)}-\ln\rho]$. Note that $\{V_T\}$ and $\{A_{(m)}^{(T)}\}$ are independent (Renyi, 1953) and that $A_{(m)}^{(T)}\to^{as}\infty$ (see, e.g., Theorem 4 in Watts, 1980). By Lemma 10, we have $V_T\to^{d}\mathcal{N}_2$ as $T\to\infty$, and the integrand in the first term of Eq. (A.34) converges uniformly to 1 on compact intervals. Hence, using Lemma 8 and Statement (A.17) the first term in brackets in Eq. (A.34) converges in distribution. It is multiplied by $[(\rho-1)/(T-m)]^{-1/2}$, which goes to zero. So the first summand of expression (A.34) converges in probability to 0 (it converges in distribution to the constant 0, so it converges in probability). On the other hand, the second summand in expression (56) converges to 0 a.s.: Note that $A_{(m)}^{(T)}\to^{as}\infty$ a.s. (by, e.g., Theorem 4 in Watts, 1980) and the integrand converges to 0 uniformly on compact intervals (Lemma 7(i)), so the integral converges to 0 for a full measure of realizations of $\{A_{(m)}^{(T)}\}$. This establishes Statement (A.29).

Step 2: We now prove Eqs. (A.30) and (A.31). Using the notation in Step 1:

$$\sqrt{T-m+1}\left[\frac{F^{-1}((T-m)/T)-F^{-1}(1-\alpha_T)}{a(F^{-1}((T-m)/T))}\right]$$

$$=\sqrt{T-m+1}\left[\frac{W(\eta_T)-W(\ln(1/(1-\alpha_T)))}{W'(\eta_T)}\right]$$

$$=\sqrt{T-m+1}\int_{-\ln(1-\alpha_T)-\eta_T}^{0}\frac{W'(\eta_T+s)}{W'(\eta_T)}ds$$

$$\sim\sqrt{T-m+1}\left[0-\ln\frac{T-m}{(1-\alpha_T)T}\right]\ as\ T\to\infty \tag{A.35}$$

The equivalence in Statement (A.35) follows by exchanging the limit and the integral, using the uniform convergence established in Lemma 7(i), and the fact that Statement (A.24) implies:

Using $\left|\ln\{(T-m)/[(1-\alpha_T)T]\}\right| \leq \left|(T-m)/[(1-\alpha_T)T]-1\right|$, we then get:

$$\begin{aligned}\sqrt{T-m+1}\left|\ln\frac{T-m}{(1-\alpha_T)T}\right| &\leq \sqrt{T-m+1}\left|\frac{T-m}{(1-\alpha_T)T}-1\right| \\ &= \sqrt{T-m+1}\left|\frac{\alpha_T T-\lfloor\alpha_T T\rfloor-1}{(1-\alpha_T)T}\right| \\ &\leq 2\frac{\sqrt{T-m+1}}{(1-\alpha_T)T}\to 0,\ as\ T\to\infty\end{aligned}$$

where the convergence to 0 follows from Statement (A.24). By Statement (A.35), then, this proves (A.30). To prove (A.31), note that Lemma 2(ii) implies that $a\circ\overline{F}^{-1}\in\mathcal{R}_0$ at 0. So Statements (A.23) and (A.24), and Lemma 6 give (A.31).

Step 3: The proof of (A.32), in turn is similar to that of (A.28) in Step 1. We have:

$$\begin{aligned}\frac{a(Y_{(m)}^{(T)})}{a(F^{-1}((T-m)/T))}-1 &\stackrel{d}{=} \frac{W'(A_{(m)}^{(T)})-W'(\eta_T)}{W'(\eta_T)} \\ &\stackrel{d}{=} \left[\sqrt{T-m}\int_0^{Z_T/\sqrt{T-m+1}}\frac{W''(\eta_T+s)}{W'(\eta_T)}ds\right]\frac{1}{\sqrt{T-m}}\end{aligned} \tag{A.36}$$

where as previously $Z_T=\sqrt{T-m+1}\,[A_{(m)}^{(T)}-\ln(T/(T-m))]$. Then, by Lemma 10, $Z_T\stackrel{d}{\to}\mathcal{N}_1$ as $T\to\infty$. But Lemma 7(ii) implies that the integrand on the right-hand side of Eq. (A.36) converges uniformly to 0 on compact intervals. So Lemma 9 and Statement (A.17) imply Statement (A.32).

Proof of Theorem 2. If $(\varepsilon_{XU}, P_X, F_{U|X})$ satisfies Assumption 4 then it satisfies Assumption 3; hence we can use Lemma 2(i) to show that for any

$x_j \in \mathcal{X}$, $1 \le j \le k$, the conditional distribution tails $\overline{F}_{Y|X=x_j} \in \Gamma$. Moreover, from Eq. (2) we know that for any $1 \le j \le k$:

$$f_{Y|X=x_j}(y) = \sum_{i=1}^{N_{x_j}} \frac{\pi_{x_j i}}{g_i(x_j)} f_{U|X=x_j}\left(\frac{y}{g_i(x_j)}\right) \text{for any } y > 0$$

Under Assumption 4 the densities $f_{U|X=x_j}$ are all eventually non-decreasing; hence the same holds for $f_{Y|X=x_j}$. If for each $1 \le j \le k$, we have $0 < \alpha_{T_j} < \beta_{T_j} < 1$, $\lim_{T_j \to \infty} \alpha_{T_j} = 1$, $\lim_{T_j \to \infty}(1-\alpha_{T_j})T_j = \infty$ and $\lim_{T_j \to \infty}(1-\alpha_{T_j})/(1-\beta_{T_j}) = \rho_j$ with $\rho_j > 1$, then the results of Lemma 3 apply for all $1 \le j \le k$, i.e.

$$\sqrt{T_j(1-\alpha_{T_j})} \frac{\hat{q}_{Y|X=x_j}(\alpha_{T_j}) - q_{Y|X=x_j}(\alpha_{T_j})}{a^Y_{x_j}(q_{Y|X=x_j}(\alpha_{T_j}))} \xrightarrow{d} \mathcal{N}_j$$

and

$$\frac{\hat{q}_{Y|X=x_j}(\beta_{T_j}) - \hat{q}_{Y|X=x_j}(\alpha_{T_j})}{a^Y_{x_j}(q_{Y|X=x_j}(\alpha_{T_j}))} \xrightarrow{p} \ln \rho_j$$

where $a^Y_X \equiv \overline{F}_{Y|X}/f_{Y|X}$ is the auxiliary function of $F_{Y|X}$ and $\mathcal{N}_j$, $1 \le j \le k$, are k independent standard normal random variables. The conclusion Theorem 2 follows by letting $\mu_j \equiv q_{Y|X=x_j}(\alpha_{T_j})$ and $\sigma_j \equiv a^Y_{x_j}(\mu_j)/\sqrt{T_j(1-\alpha_{T_j})}$, and using the independence of different samples $(Y_{j,1}, \ldots, Y_{j,T_j})$.

Proof of Theorem 3. The proof is done in five steps:

Step 1: We work with the first minimization problem in Eq. (18):

$$\min_{\mu} (\mu - \hat{q})' \hat{\Sigma}^{-1} (\mu - \hat{q}) \tag{A.37}$$

$$\text{subject to } A\mu = 0$$

Let $\mathcal{L} : \mathbb{R}^{2k-1} \to \mathbb{R}$ be the corresponding Lagrangian $\mathcal{L}(\mu, \lambda) = (\mu - \hat{q})' \hat{\Sigma}^{-1} (\mu - \hat{q}) + \lambda' A\mu$, where λ denotes the $(k-1)$-vector of Lagrange multipliers (dual variables) associated with the constraint $A\mu = 0$. A is full rank and the (Lagrange) dual function $g:\mathbb{R}^{k-1}\to\mathbb{R}\cup-\infty$ is $g(\lambda)\equiv \inf_{\mu}\mathcal{L}(\mu,\lambda)=-\frac{1}{4}\lambda' A\hat{\Sigma}A'\lambda+\lambda' A\hat{q}$. The dual problem is then:

$$\max_{\lambda} -\frac{1}{4}\lambda' A\hat{\Sigma}A'\lambda+\lambda' A\hat{q} \tag{A.38}$$

with λ unconstrained. The solutions to the dual and primal problems (A.38) and (A.37) are:

$$\lambda_0=2(A\hat{\Sigma}A')^{-1}A\hat{q} \tag{A.39}$$

$$\mu_0=\hat{q}-\frac{1}{2}\hat{\Sigma}A'\lambda_0=\hat{q}-\hat{\Sigma}A'(A\hat{\Sigma}A')^{-1}A\hat{q} \tag{A.40}$$

and we have:

$$(\mu_0-\hat{q})'\hat{\Sigma}^{-1}(\mu_0-\hat{q})=\hat{q}'A'(A\hat{\Sigma}A')^{-1}A\hat{q}=-\frac{1}{4}\lambda_0' A\hat{\Sigma}A'\lambda_0+\lambda_0' A\hat{q} \tag{A.41}$$

Similarly, we consider the dual of the second minimization problem in Eq. (18):

$$\min_{\mu}(\mu-\hat{q})'\hat{\Sigma}^{-1}(\mu-\hat{q}) \tag{A.42}$$

$$\text{subject to } A\mu\leqslant 0$$

The dual is:

$$\max_{\lambda} -\frac{1}{4}\lambda' A\hat{\Sigma}A'\lambda+\lambda' A\hat{q} \tag{A.43}$$

$$\text{subject to } \lambda\geqslant 0$$

Letting λ_1 and μ_1 denote the solutions to the dual and primal problems (A.43) and (A.42) we again have:

$$(\mu_1-\hat{q})'\hat{\Sigma}^{-1}(\mu_1-\hat{q})=-\frac{1}{4}\lambda_1' A\hat{\Sigma}A'\lambda_1+\lambda_1' A\hat{q} \tag{66}$$

Step 2: Using Eqs. (A.41) and (A.44) the LR statistic in Eq. (18) then equals:

$$\begin{aligned}\hat{\xi}_{LR} &= \max_{\lambda}\left(-\frac{1}{4}\lambda' A\hat{\Sigma}A'\lambda + \lambda' A\hat{q}\right) - \max_{\lambda:\lambda\geqslant 0}\left(-\frac{1}{4}\lambda' A\hat{\Sigma}A'\lambda + \lambda' A\hat{q}\right)\\
&= \max_{\lambda}\left[\hat{q}'\hat{\Sigma}^{-1}\hat{q} - \left(\frac{1}{2}\hat{\Sigma}A'\lambda - \hat{q}\right)'\hat{\Sigma}^{-1}\left(\frac{1}{2}\hat{\Sigma}A'\lambda - \hat{q}\right)\right]\\
&\quad - \max_{\lambda:\lambda\geqslant 0}\left[\hat{q}'\hat{\Sigma}^{-1}\hat{q} - \left(\frac{1}{2}\hat{\Sigma}A'\lambda - \hat{q}\right)'\hat{\Sigma}^{-1}\left(\frac{1}{2}\hat{\Sigma}A'\lambda - \hat{q}\right)\right]\\
&= \min_{\lambda:\lambda\geqslant 0}\left[\left(\frac{1}{2}\hat{\Sigma}A'\lambda - \hat{q}\right)'\hat{\Sigma}^{-1}\left(\frac{1}{2}\hat{\Sigma}A'\lambda - \hat{q}\right)\right]\\
&\quad - \min_{\lambda}\left[\left(\frac{1}{2}\hat{\Sigma}A'\lambda - \hat{q}\right)'\hat{\Sigma}^{-1}\left(\frac{1}{2}\hat{\Sigma}A'\lambda - \hat{q}\right)\right]\\
&= \min_{\lambda:\lambda\geqslant 0}\left[\left(\frac{1}{2}\hat{\Sigma}A'\lambda_0 - \frac{1}{2}\hat{\Sigma}A'\lambda\right)'\hat{\Sigma}^{-1}\left(\frac{1}{2}\hat{\Sigma}A'\lambda_0 - \frac{1}{2}\hat{\Sigma}A'\lambda\right)\right]\end{aligned}$$

where the last equality follows by a simple geometric argument. Combining the above with Eqs. (A.39) and (A.40) then gives:

$$\hat{\xi}_{LR} = \min_{\lambda:\lambda\geqslant 0} \|\hat{\Sigma}^{-1/2}(\hat{q} - \mu_0) - \frac{1}{2}\hat{\Sigma}^{1/2}A'\lambda\|^2$$

where $\|X\|^2 \equiv X'X$ for any $X \in \mathbb{R}^k$. Letting $\hat{R} \equiv (A\hat{\Sigma}A')^{-1}A\hat{\Sigma}^{1/2}$ and $\nu \equiv \frac{1}{2}\hat{\Sigma}^{1/2}A'\lambda$ (so that $\lambda = 2\hat{R}\nu$) we then have:

$$\hat{\xi}_{LR} = \min_{\nu:\hat{R}\nu\geqslant 0} \|\hat{\Sigma}^{-1/2}(\hat{q} - \mu_0) - \nu\|^2 \tag{A.45}$$

Step 3: We consider the dual of the minimization problem in Eq. (A.45):

$$\max_{\beta:\beta\geqslant 0}\left[-\frac{1}{4}\beta'\hat{R}\hat{R}'\beta - \beta'\hat{R}\hat{\Sigma}^{-1/2}(\hat{q} - \mu_0)\right] \tag{A.46}$$

where β is a $(k-1)$-vector of Lagrange multipliers. Note that

$$\begin{aligned}-\frac{1}{4}\beta'\hat{R}\hat{R}'\beta - \beta'\hat{R}\hat{\Sigma}^{-1/2}(\hat{q} - \mu_0) &= \|(A\hat{\Sigma}A')^{-1/2}A(\hat{q} - \mu_0)\|^2\\
&\quad - \|\tfrac{1}{2}(A\hat{\Sigma}A')^{-1/2}\beta + (A\hat{\Sigma}A')^{-1/2}A(\hat{q} - \mu_0)\|^2\end{aligned}$$

so the quantity in Eq. (A.46) is equivalent to:

$$\|(A\hat{\Sigma}A')^{-1/2}A(\hat{q}-\mu_0)\|^2 - \min_{\beta:\beta\geqslant 0}\|\frac{1}{2}(A\hat{\Sigma}A')^{-1/2}\beta + (A\hat{\Sigma}A')^{-1/2}A(\hat{q}-\mu_0)\|^2 \tag{A.47}$$

Now, let:

$$\hat{Z} \equiv -(A\hat{\Sigma}A')^{-1/2}A(\hat{q}-\mu_0) \text{ and } \gamma \equiv \frac{1}{2}(A\hat{\Sigma}A')^{-1/2}\beta \tag{A.48}$$

(so $\beta = 2(A\hat{\Sigma}A')^{1/2}\gamma$); combining Eqs. (A.45)–(A.47) then yields:

$$\hat{\xi}_{LR} = \|\hat{Z}\|^2 - \min_{\gamma:(A\hat{\Sigma}A')^{1/2}\gamma\geqslant 0}\|\hat{Z}-\gamma\|^2 \tag{A.49}$$

Let $P_{\hat{C}}\hat{Z}$ denote the orthogonal projection of $\hat{Z}$ on the cone $\hat{C}$, defined as: $\hat{C} \equiv \{\gamma \in \mathbb{R}^{k-1} : (A\hat{\Sigma}A')^{1/2}\gamma \geqslant 0$. The LR statistic in Eq. (A.49) then equals:

$$\hat{\xi}_{LR} = \|P_{\hat{C}}\hat{Z}\|^2 \tag{A.50}$$

Step 4: Under the null hypothesis H_0 we have $A\mu = 0$ (in addition to $A\mu_0 = 0$) so that the quantity in Eq. (A.48) can be written as $\hat{Z} = BV$, with $B \equiv -(A\hat{\Sigma}A')^{-1/2}A\hat{\Sigma}^{1/2}$ and $V \equiv \hat{\Sigma}^{-1/2}(\hat{q}-\mu)$. Under conditions of Corollary 1, the k-vector V converges in distribution to $V \to^d \mathcal{N}(0_k, Id_k)$ as $T \to \infty$, and the $(k-1)\times k$-matrix B is such that $BB' = Id_{k-1}$; hence as $T \to \infty$, we have $\hat{Z} \to^d Z \equiv \mathcal{N}(0_{k-1}, Id_{k-1})$, under the null hypothesis H_0. Now, for every j, $1 \leq j \leq k$, let:

$$\sigma_j \equiv \frac{a^Y_{x_j}(q_{Y|X=x_j}(\alpha_T))}{\sqrt{c_j T(1-\alpha_T)}}$$

and consider the matrix $\sigma_1^{-2}(A\hat{\Sigma}A')$; its entries are:

$$\sigma_1^{-2}(A\hat{\Sigma}A') = \begin{bmatrix} \frac{\hat{\sigma}_1^2}{\sigma_1^2} + \frac{\sigma_2^2}{\sigma_1^2}\frac{\hat{\sigma}_2^2}{\sigma_2^2} & -\frac{\sigma_2^2}{\sigma_1^2}\frac{\hat{\sigma}_2^2}{\sigma_2^2} & & (0) \\ -\frac{\sigma_2^2}{\sigma_1^2}\frac{\hat{\sigma}_2^2}{\sigma_2^2} & \frac{\sigma_2^2}{\sigma_1^2}\frac{\hat{\sigma}_2^2}{\sigma_2^2} + \frac{\sigma_3^2}{\sigma_1^2}\frac{\hat{\sigma}_3^2}{\sigma_3^2} & -\frac{\sigma_3^2}{\sigma_1^2}\frac{\hat{\sigma}_3^2}{\sigma_3^2} & \\ & & \ddots & \\ (0) & & -\frac{\sigma_{k-1}^2}{\sigma_1^2}\frac{\hat{\sigma}_{k-1}^2}{\sigma_{k-1}^2} & \frac{\sigma_{k-1}^2}{\sigma_1^2}\frac{\hat{\sigma}_{k-1}^2}{\sigma_{k-1}^2} + \frac{\sigma_k^2}{\sigma_1^2}\frac{\hat{\sigma}_k^2}{\sigma_k^2} \end{bmatrix}$$

From Lemma 3 and Theorem 2 we know that for every j, $1 \leq j \leq k$, $\sigma_j^{-2}\hat{\sigma}_j^2 \rightarrow^p 1$. Moreover, using Lemma 2(ii), and the fact that $F_{U|X}$ does not depend on X so we can write it as $F_{U|X} = F_U$ with auxiliary function a^U, we have:

$$\frac{\sigma_j}{\sigma_1} \sim \sqrt{\frac{c_1}{c_j}\frac{g_{N_{x_j}}(x_j)}{g_{N_{x_1}}(x_1)}\frac{a^U(\overline{F}_U^{-1}(\alpha_T))}{a^U(\overline{F}_U^{-1}(\alpha_T))}} = \sqrt{\frac{c_1}{c_j}\frac{g_{N_{x_j}}(x_j)}{g_{N_{x_1}}(x_1)}}$$

so as $T \rightarrow \infty$ we have $\sigma_1^{-2}(A\hat{\Sigma}A') \rightarrow^p \Omega$ with a symmetric $(k-1)\times(k-1)$-matrix Ω given by:

$$\Omega \equiv \begin{bmatrix} 1+\frac{c_1 g_{N_{x_2}}(x_2)^2}{c_2 g_{N_{x_1}}(x_1)^2} & -\frac{c_1 g_{N_{x_2}}(x_2)^2}{c_2 g_{N_{x_1}}(x_1)^2} & & (0) \\ -\frac{c_1 g_{N_{x_2}}(x_2)^2}{c_2 g_{N_{x_1}}(x_1)^2} & \frac{c_1 g_{N_{x_2}}(x_2)^2}{c_2 g_{N_{x_1}}(x_1)^2}+\frac{c_{t1} g_{N_{x_3}}(x_3)^2}{c_3 g_{N_{x_1}}(x_1)^2} & -\frac{c_{t1} g_{N_{x_3}}(x_3)^2}{c_3 g_{N_{x_1}}(x_1)^2} & \\ \ddots & & \ddots & \\ (0) & -\frac{c_1 g_{N_{x_{k-1}}}(x_{k-1})^2}{c_{k-1} g_{N_{x_1}}(x_1)^2} & & \frac{c_1 g_{N_{x_{k-1}}}(x_{k-1})^2}{c_{k-1} g_{N_{x_1}}(x_1)^2}+\frac{c_1 g_{N_{x_k}}(x_k)^2}{c_k g_{N_{x_1}}(x_1)^2} \end{bmatrix} \tag{A.51}$$

Hence, using the fact that $\hat{C}$ equals $\hat{C} = \{\gamma \in \mathbb{R}^{k-1} : \sigma_1^{-2}(A\hat{\Sigma}A')^{1/2}\gamma \geqslant 0$, we have that the minimand in Eq. (A.49) converges in probability to a well defined limit:

$$\hat{\xi}_{LR} \xrightarrow{p} \xi_{LR} \equiv \|Z\|^2 - \min_{\gamma:\Omega^{1/2}\gamma \geqslant 0} \|Z-\gamma\|^2 = \|P_C Z\|^2 \tag{A.52}$$

where $Z =^d \mathcal{N}(0_{k-1}, \mathrm{Id}_{k-1})$, and $P_C Z$ denotes the orthogonal projection of Z on the cone $C \equiv \{\gamma \in \mathbb{R}^{k-1} : \Omega^{1/2}\gamma \geqslant 0$ with Ω as defined in Eq. (A.51).

Step 5: In order to determine the distribution of ξ_{LR} in Eq. (A.52) we use the following lemma:

Lemma 4. (Gourieroux et al., 1982). Let Z be a standard normal random vector of dimension $k-1 \geq 1$, i.e. $Z =^d \mathcal{N}(0_{k-1}, \mathrm{Id}_{k-1})$ and let C be a nonsingular symmetric $(k-1)\times(k-1)$-matrix whose columns are denoted $C_j, j=1,\ldots,k-1$. To each vector $C_j, j=1,\ldots,k-1$, we associate a vector $C_j^{\perp} \in \mathbb{R}^{k-1}$ such that $C_j^{\perp}$ is orthogonal to any $C_i, i \neq j$, and $C_J' C_j^{\perp} < 0$. For each subset S of the set $\{1, \ldots, k-1$ we define the cone:

$$\mathcal{C}_S \equiv \{y \in \mathbb{R}^{k-1} : y = \sum_{i=1}^{k-1} \alpha_i A_i, \text{ with } \alpha_i \leqslant 0,\ i = 1, \ldots, k-1, \text{ and} \\ A_i = C_i \text{ when } i \notin S \text{ and } A_i = C_i^{\perp} \text{ when } i \in S$$

Consider the orthogonal projection of Z on the cone $\mathcal{C}_{(1,\ldots,k-1)}$ denoted $P_{\mathcal{C}_{(1,\ldots,k-1)}} Z$. Then the distribution of $\|P_{\mathcal{C}_{(1,\ldots,k-1)}} Z\|^2$ is a mixture of chi-square distributions:

$$\|P_{\mathcal{C}_{(1,\ldots,k-1)}} Z\|^2 \stackrel{d}{=} \sum_{d=0}^{k-1} \omega(d) \chi^2(d) \textit{ with } \omega(d) = \sum_{S:\dim S = d} \Pr\{P_{\mathcal{C}_{(1,\ldots,k-1)}} Z \in \mathcal{C}_S$$

where the sequence of weights $\omega(d), d = 0, \ldots, k-1$ satisfies $\omega(d) \geq 0$ and $\sum_{d=0}^{k-1} \omega(d) = 1$ and $\chi^2(0)$ denotes the point mass distribution at zero.

Apply Lemma 4 to the $(k-1) \times (k-1)$-matrix $\Omega^{1/2}$ by letting $C \equiv \Omega^{1/2}$. Using the notation from Lemma 4, we then have that $\mathcal{C} = \mathcal{C}_{\{1,\ldots,k-1\}}$. Combining Lemma 4 with Eq. (A.52) then yields the result of Theorem 3. Note that the entries of Ω can be consistently estimated using $\hat{\sigma}_1^{-2}(A\hat{\Sigma}A')$; hence the probability weights $\omega(d)$ can be consistently estimated by $\hat{\omega}(d)$, where $\hat{\omega}(d)$ are the weights obtained in the exact Gaussian case.

APPENDIX B: AUXILIARY LEMMAS

Lemmas 5–7 are simple translations of results in de Haan (1970) to our problem. Lemmas 8–10 present more substantial preliminary results we shall need in the proof of Lemma 3. In the sequel, $\overline{H}$ is a distribution tail $\overline{H}:\mathbb{R}_{++}\rightarrow(0,1)$ and $\overline{H}^{-1}$ the corresponding quantile function $\overline{H}^{-1}:(0,1)\rightarrow\mathbb{R}_{++}$.

Lemma 5. If $\overline{H}\in\mathcal{R}_{-\infty}$ at ∞, then $\overline{H}^{-1}\in\mathcal{R}_0$ at 0.

Proof of Lemma 5. Let $U(x)\equiv\overline{H}(x)$ for all $x>0$; U is non-increasing. If U is $-\infty$-varying at ∞, then by Corollary 1.2.1 (5) in de Haan (1970), the function $x\mapsto\inf\{y|U(y)\leq 1/x\}$ is 0-varying at ∞. It is easy to verify that this function is $x\mapsto\overline{H}^{-1}(1/x)$. Then for $\lambda>0$, $\lim_{y\downarrow 0}\overline{H}^{-1}(\lambda y)/\overline{H}^{-1}(y)=\lim_{s\rightarrow\infty}\overline{H}^{-1}(\lambda/s)/\overline{H}^{-1}(1/s)=1$ where $s\equiv 1/y$. Thus $\overline{H}^{-1}$ is 0-varying at 0.

Lemma 6 . If $\overline{H}^{-1}\in\mathcal{R}_0$ at 0, then for all sequences $\{a_N\}$ and $\{a'_N\}$ of positive numbers with $\lim_{N\rightarrow\infty}a_N=\lim_{N\rightarrow\infty}a'_N=0$ and $\lim_{N\rightarrow\infty}a_N/a'_N=c$ (with $0<c<\infty$), we have:

$$\lim_{N\rightarrow\infty}\frac{\overline{H}^{-1}(a_N)}{\overline{H}^{-1}(a'_N)}=1$$

Proof of Lemma 6. Let $U(x)\equiv\overline{H}^{-1}(1/x)$ for all $x>1$ so $U\in\mathcal{R}_0$ at ∞. Let $\{\alpha_N\}$ and $\{\alpha'_N\}$ be sequences of positive numbers with $\alpha_N\equiv 1/a_N$ and $\alpha'_N\equiv 1/a'_N$ so that $\lim_{N\rightarrow\infty}\alpha_N=\lim_{N\rightarrow\infty}\alpha'_N=\infty$ and $\lim_{N\rightarrow\infty}\alpha_N/\alpha'_N=1/c$ $(0<1/c<\infty)$. By applying Corollary 1.2.1 (2) in de Haan (1970) we then have $\lim_{N\rightarrow\infty}\overline{H}^{-1}(a_N)/\overline{H}^{-1}(a'_N)=\lim_{N\rightarrow\infty}U(\alpha_N)/U(\alpha'_N)=(1/c)^0=1$.

Lemma 7. Consider a distribution tail $\overline{H}\in\Gamma$ with auxiliary function a. Let H be twice differentiable on $\mathbb{R}_{++}$ with a density h that is eventually non-increasing. Let $W(x)\equiv\overline{H}^{-1}(\exp(-x))$, for $x>0$. Then W is twice continuously differentiable on $\mathbb{R}_{++}$ with $W'(x)=a[\overline{H}^{-1}(\exp(-x))]$, for $x>0$, and for any real interval a,b we have:

(i) $\lim_{x\rightarrow\infty}W'(x+s)/W'(x)=1$, uniformly for s in a,b;
(ii) $\lim_{x\rightarrow\infty}W''(x+s)/W'(x)=0$, uniformly for s in a,b.

Proof of Lemma 7. First we prove (i). Note that $a(W(x)) = \exp(-x)/h(W(x)) = W'(x)$. From Lemma 2 we know that $a \circ \overline{H}^{-1} \in \mathcal{R}_0$ at 0, so:

$$\lim_{x \to \infty} \frac{W'(x+s)}{W'(x)} = \lim_{x \to \infty} \frac{a(\overline{H}^{-1}(\exp(-x-s)))}{a(\overline{H}^{-1}(\exp(-x)))} = 1, \quad \text{for } s > 0 \qquad \text{(B.1)}$$

By Corollary 1.2.1 in de Haan (1970), the convergence is uniform on intervals $[a, b]$ with $a > 0$. This implies that the convergence is uniform on arbitrary intervals $[a, b]$ by the change of variables $y = x - |a| - \eta$, for some $\eta > 0$ (and for $x > |a| + \eta$) by the resulting uniform convergence on $[\eta, b + |a| + \eta]$.

We now prove (ii). First note that $a(W(x)) = W'(x)$ implies that

$$\frac{W''(x+s)}{W'(x)} = \frac{W'(x+s)}{W'(x)} a'(W(x+s)) \qquad \text{(B.2)}$$

The bracketed term on the right-hand side of Eq. (B.2) converges to 1 uniformly on $[a, b]$ by item (i) of the lemma. We shall prove that $a'(W(x+s)) \to 0$ as $x \to \infty$ uniformly on $[a, b]$; combined, these two properties establish (ii).

Now $a(x) = \overline{H}(x)/h(x)$, so $a'(x) = -1 - \overline{H}(x)h'(x)/[h(x)]^2$. Then, $\overline{H} \in \Gamma$ implies, by Theorem 2.7.4 in de Haan (1970) (or Proposition 1.18 in Resnick (1987)), that

$$\lim_{x \to \infty} \frac{\overline{H}(x)h'(x)}{[h(x)]^2} = -1, \quad \text{i.e.} \quad \lim_{x \to \infty} a'(x) = 0 \qquad \text{(B.3)}$$

Fix $x > 0$ large enough so that $x + a > 0$. The range of $a'(W(x+s))$ when $s \in [a, b]$ is the same as the range of $a'(y)$ when $y \in [W(x+a), W(x+b)]$, as W is monotone increasing. Since a' is continuous, we can let $y(x)$ be such that:

$$a'(y(x)) = \sup_{y \in [W(x+a), W(x+b)]} a'(y) \qquad \text{(B.4)}$$

Now, $y(x) \to \infty$ as $x \to \infty$ because W is monotone increasing. Then the right-hand-side of Eq. (B.4) converges to 0 as $x \to \infty$, because a' converges to 0 (B.3). This proves the needed uniform convergence of $a'(W(x+s))$ in Eq. (B.2).

Lemma 8. Let c_T be a sequence of strictly positive real numbers such that $\lim_{T\to\infty} c_T = \infty$, and consider $f : \mathbb{R} \to \mathbb{R}$. Let X_T and Y_T be two independent stochastic processes. If:

(1). $X_T \to^d X$, as $T \to \infty$, for some X with continuous distribution F;
(2). $Y_T \to^{as} \infty$, as $T \to \infty$;
(3). for each $K > 0$, $\lim_{y\to\infty} f(x+y) = 1$ uniformly in $x \in [-K, K]$.

Then:

$$c_T \int_0^{X_T/c_T} f(x+Y_T)dx \overset{d}{\to} X, \text{ as } T \to \infty$$

Proof of Lemma 8. Fix a realization $\{y_T\}$ of $\{Y_T\}$ such that $\lim_{T\to\infty} y_T = \infty$; the almost sure convergence in item 2 ensures that $\{y_T\}$ with $\lim_{T\to\infty} y_T = \infty$ have full measure. Let $z \in \mathbb{R}_+$ and denote by B_T the event:

$$\left\{ c_T \int_0^{X_T/c_T} f(x+y_T)dx \leq z \right\}$$

Let $\varepsilon > 0$. We shall prove that there is a T such that $T \geq T$ implies that $|P(B_T) - F(z)| < \varepsilon$; here P denotes the probability measure on the space on which $\{X_T\}$ is defined.

Fix $\delta > 0$ such that $F(z/(1-\delta)) - F(z/(1+\delta)) < \varepsilon/4$. Let $K \in \mathbb{R}$ be large enough that $K > z/(1-\delta)$, $F(-K) < \varepsilon/4$ and $1 - F(K) < \varepsilon/4$. Since $X_T \to^d X$, there is T_1 such that $n \geq T_1$ implies:

$$P\{|X_T| > K\} < \varepsilon/2 \tag{B.5}$$

$$F(z/(1+\delta)) - \varepsilon/4 < P\{X_T \leq z/(1+\delta) \tag{B.6}$$

$$P\{X_T \leq z/(1-\delta)\} < F(z/(1-\delta)) + \varepsilon/4 \tag{B.7}$$

Let $B_T^K = B_T \cap X_T \leq K$. Then, by Statement (B.5), $T \geq T_1$ implies that $P(B_T) - P(B_T^K) \leq P\{X_T > K\} < \varepsilon/2$.

The convergence in item 3 is uniform on $[-K,K]$, so there is T such that $T \geq T_1$ and such that $T \geq T$ implies that for all $\tilde{x} \in [-K,K]$, $(1-\delta) < f(\tilde{x}+y_T) < (1+\delta)$. Then, $T \geq T$ implies:

$$\tilde{x}(1-\delta) < c_T \int_0^{\tilde{x}/c_T} f(x+y_T)dx < \tilde{x}(1+\delta)$$

if $\tilde{x} \geq 0$, and:

$$\tilde{x}(1+\delta) < c_T \int_0^{\tilde{x}/c_T} f(x+y_T)dx < \tilde{x}(1-\delta)$$

if $\tilde{x}<0$. Then $P\{X_T(1+\delta) \leq z, X_T \geq 0\} \leq P(B_T^K) \cap \{X_T \geq 0\} \leq P\{X_T(1-\delta) \leq z, X_T \geq 0\}$. And since $z \geq 0$, $P\{X_T(1-\delta) \leq z, X_T < 0\} = P(B_T^K) \cap \{X_T < 0\} = P\{X_T(1+\delta) \leq z, X_T < 0\}$. Hence, $P\{X_T(1+\delta) \leq z\} \leq P(B_T^K) \leq P\{X_T(1-\delta) \leq z\}$.

Now, $|F(z) - P\{X_T(1+\delta) \leq z\}| \leq |F(z) - F(z/(1+\delta))| + |F(z/(1+\delta)) - P\{X_T(1+\delta) \leq z\}| \leq \varepsilon/4 + \varepsilon/4$, by the definition of δ and Statement (B.6). And similarly for $P\{X_T(1-\delta) \leq z\}$. So $|F(z) - P(B_T^K)| < \varepsilon/2$. Finally, then, $T \geq T$ implies that:

$$\left|F(x) - P(B_T)\right| \leq \left|F(z) - P(B_T^K)\right| + \left|P(B_T) - P(B_T^K)\right| < \varepsilon/2 + \varepsilon/2$$

The argument for $z<0$ is analogous. The proof follows because X_T and Y_T are independent.

Lemma 9. Let $\{c_T\}$ be a sequence of strictly positive real numbers such that $\lim_{T\to\infty} c_T = \infty$, and consider $f: \mathbb{R} \to \mathbb{R}$. Let $\{X_T\}$ be a stochastic process and $\{y_T\}$ a sequence of strictly positive real numbers. If:

(1) $X_T \to^d X$, as $T \to \infty$, for some X with continuous distribution F;
(2) $\lim_{T\to\infty} y_T = \infty$;
(3) for each $K>0$, $\lim_{y\to\infty} f(x+y) = 0$ uniformly in $x \in [-K,K]$.

Then:

$$c_T \int_0^{X_T/c_T} f(x+y_T)dx \xrightarrow{p} 0, \text{ as } T \to \infty$$

Proof of Lemma 9. Let $\eta>0$ and denote by B_T the event:

$$\left\{\left|c_T \int_0^{X_T/c_T} f(x+y_T)dx\right| \leq \eta\right\}$$

We shall prove that $P(B_T) \to 1$.

Let $\varepsilon > 0$. Let $K > 0$ be large enough that $F(-K) < \varepsilon/2$ and $1 - F(K) < \varepsilon/2$. By the uniform convergence of f on $[-K, K]$, there is T such that $T \geq T$ implies that, for all $\tilde{x} \in [-K, K]$, $|f(\tilde{x} + y_T)| < \eta/K$. Then, for all $T \geq T$ and $\tilde{x} \in [-K, K]$:

$$\left| c_T \int_0^{\tilde{x}/c_T} f(x + y_T) dx \right| \leq \tilde{x}\eta/K \leq \eta$$

as $\tilde{x} \leq K$. So $T \geq T$ implies that $P(B_T) \geq P\{X_T \leq K\} > 1 - \varepsilon$, by the definition of K.

Lemma 10. Let $A_1, \ldots, A_T$ be a random sample from $F_A(x) = 1 - \exp(-x)$ with $x > 0$, and let $A_{(1)}^{(T)} \leq \ldots \leq A_{(T)}^{(T)}$ be the ascending order statistics of $(A_1, \ldots, A_T)$. Consider orders $(m, k) \in \mathbb{T}^2$ such that $m < k \leq T$. If $m \to \infty$, $k \to \infty$ and $T \to \infty$ in a way that $(T - m) \to \infty$, $(T - m)/T \to 0$, $(T - k) \to \infty$, $(T - k)/T \to 0$ and $(T - m)/(T - k) \to \rho$ where $\rho > 1$, then:

$$\sqrt{T - m + 1}\left[A_{(m)}^{(T)} - \ln\frac{T}{T - m}\right] \overset{d}{\to} \mathcal{N}_1 \text{ and } \sqrt{T - m}\left[\frac{A_{(k)}^{(T)} - A_{(m)}^{(T)} - \ln\rho}{\sqrt{\rho - 1}}\right] \overset{d}{\to} \mathcal{N}_2$$

where $\mathcal{N}_1$ and $\mathcal{N}_2$ are two independent standard normal random variables.

Proof of Lemma 10. Using Renyi's (1953) representation, we know that $\{A_{(T-k+1)}^{(T)} - A_{(T-k)}^{(T)}\}_{k=1}^T =^d \{Z_k/k\}_{k=1}^T$ where $A_{(0)}^{(T)} \equiv 0$ and where $Z_1, \ldots, Z_T$ are independent and identically distributed standard exponential random variables. Then for any m, $1 \leq m \leq T$, and any k, $m < k \leq T$, we have:

$$A_{(m)}^{(T)} \overset{d}{=} \sum_{j=T-m+1}^{T} \frac{Z_j}{j} \text{ and } A_{(k)}^{(T)} - A_{(m)}^{(T)} \overset{d}{=} \sum_{l=T-k+1}^{T-m} \frac{Z_l}{l} \tag{B.8}$$

which are independent. When $m \to \infty$, $k \to \infty$ and $T \to \infty$ in a manner that $(T - m) \to \infty$, $(T - m)/T \to 0$, $(T - k) \to \infty$, $(T - k)/T \to 0$ and $(T - m)/(T - k) \to \rho$ with $\rho > 1$, we can apply the central limit theorem in Liapunov's form to the sums of random variables in Eq. (B.8) (see, e.g., Theorem 4 in Renyi (1953)) to get:

$$\frac{A_{(m)}^{(T)} - M_1}{S_1} \overset{d}{\to} \mathcal{N}_1 \text{ and } \frac{A_{(k)}^{(T)} - A_{(m)}^{(T)} - M_2}{S_2} \overset{d}{\to} \mathcal{N}_2 \tag{B.9}$$

with $\mathcal{N}_1$ and $\mathcal{N}_2$ two independent standard normal random variables where:

$$\begin{aligned} M_1 &\equiv \sum_{j=T-m+1}^{T} \frac{1}{j} = \sum_{l=1}^{T} \frac{1}{l} - \sum_{n=1}^{T-m} \frac{1}{n} \\ &= \ln T + \gamma + O(T^{-1}) - \ln(T-m) - \gamma + O((T-m)^{-1}) \\ &= \ln \frac{T}{T-m} + O((T-m)^{-1}) \end{aligned} \tag{B.10}$$

and

$$\begin{aligned} S_1^2 &\equiv \sum_{j=T-m+1}^{T} \frac{1}{j^2} = \frac{1}{T-m+1} - \frac{1}{T} + \frac{\theta}{(T-m)(T-m+1)} \\ &= \frac{1}{T-m+1} + o((T-m)^{-1}) \end{aligned} \tag{B.11}$$

where γ is the Euler-Mascheroni constant and $0<\theta<1$; similarly:

$$\begin{aligned} M_2 &\equiv \sum_{j=T-k+1}^{T-m} \frac{1}{j} = \sum_{l=1}^{T-m} \frac{1}{l} - \sum_{n=1}^{T-k} \frac{1}{n} = \ln \frac{T-m}{T-k} + O((T-m)^{-1}) \\ &= \ln \rho + O((T-m)^{-1}) \end{aligned} \tag{B.12}$$

and

$$\begin{aligned} S_2^2 &\equiv \sum_{j=T-k+1}^{T-m} \frac{1}{j^2} \\ &= \frac{1}{T-k+1} - \frac{1}{T-m} + \frac{\phi}{(T-k)(T-k+1)} \\ &= \frac{\rho-1}{T-m} + o((T-m)^{-1}) \end{aligned} \tag{B.13}$$

where $0<\phi<1$ and $\rho>1$. Combining Equations (B.9)–(B.13) then yields the result.

ESTIMATING SUPERMODULAR GAMES USING RATIONALIZABLE STRATEGIES

Kosuke Uetake and Yasutora Watanabe

ABSTRACT

We propose a set-estimation approach to supermodular games using the restrictons of rationalizable strategies, which is a weaker solution concept than Nash equilibrium. The set of rationalizable strategies of a supermodular game forms a complete lattice, and are bounded above and below by two extremal Nash equilibria. We use a well-known alogrithm to compute the two extremal equilibria, and then construct moment inequalities for set estimation of the supermodular game. Finally, we conduct Monte Carlo experiments to illustrate how the estimated confidence sets vary in response to changes in the data generating process.

Keywords: Supermodular games; rationalizability; moment inequalities

JEL classifications: C13; C81

Structural Econometric Models
Advances in Econometrics, Volume 31, 233–247

ISSN: 0731-9053/doi:10.1108/S0731-9053(2013)0000032008

INTRODUCTION

Recently, a number of studies have estimated supermodular games (e.g., Ackerberg & Gowrisankaran, 2006; Jia, 2008; Matvos & Ostrovsky, 2010; Nishida, 2012). One of the main issues on estimating a supermodular game is how to address (potential) multiplicity of equilibria. Supermodular games may have multiple equilibria, and identifying which equilibrium is played in the data is not straightforward in general. In such a case, some sort of equilibrium selection rule is imposed a priori in most cases.

In this note, we propose a way to estimate supermodular games without imposing any equilibrium selection rule. In particular, we relax the Nash equilibrium assumption that researchers typically impose in order to estimate game-theoretic models, and use rationalizability as a solution concept in our estimation.[1] More precisely, we exploit the lattice property of the set of rationalizable strategies of supermodular games, and then apply a moment inequality estimator. The set of rationalizable strategies in supermodular games has a lattice structure, which implies that the set of rationalizable strategies is bounded above and below by the strategies of the two extremal Nash equilibria, say $\overline{s}$ and $\underline{s}$. These two extremal Nash equilibrium strategies bound any rationalizable strategies s^* for each player, that is, $s_i^* \geq \underline{s}_i$ and $\overline{s}_i \geq s_i^*$ for all i, where $\geq$ denotes appropriately specified partial order over the set of strategies.

Furthermore, we utilize the well-known result by Milgrom and Roberts (1990): The two extremal Nash equilibrium strategies $\overline{s}_i$ and $\underline{s}_i$ can be found by applying the best response correspondences iteratively starting from the largest and the smallest elements in the set of strategies (which monotonically converges to $\overline{s}$ and $\underline{s}$, respectively). Thus, we can easily compute $\overline{s}$ and $\underline{s}$, which allows us to construct moment inequalities based on $s_i^* \geq \underline{s}_i$ and $\overline{s}_i \geq s_i^*$.[2]

After proposing our estimation strategy, we present the results of Monte Carlo experiments to show how our estimation strategy works using a simple investment game with complementarity. We find that the obtained confidence set includes the true parameter value. Also, we illustrate how confidence sets vary with changes in the data generating process.

This note relates to a few strands of the literature on estimation of games. First, this note adds to the literature on estimation of games without equilibrium assumptions such as Nash equilibrium. In particular, it is related to Aradillas-Lopez and Tamer (2008), which considers the identification power of rationalizability as well as level-k rationality in comparison with Nash equilibrium. This note differs from theirs by considering supermodular games specifically. Because we focus on supermodular games, we can exploit the theoretical properties of rationalizable strategies in our estimation. In their comment to Aradillas-Lopez and Tamer (2008), Molinari and Rosen (2008) propose a similar approach to ours for level-k rationality for differentiated product pricing game, which is a specific examples of supermodular games. This note differs from theirs as our focus is on rationalizability instead of level-k rationality. Also, we add to their approah by using monotone comparative statics results in constructing moment inequalities based on utilitities.

The second related literature is the literature that studies identification and estimation of models using monotone comparative statics. Echenique and Komunjer (2009) proposes a test on complementarities using monotone comparative statics property when the model may have multiple equilibria. Lazzati (2012) also uses monotone comparative statics to study partial identification of treatment response models with endogenous social interactions. Third, the note more broadly relates to studies addressing the issue of multiple equilibria in games using a moment inequality estimator (e.g., Ciliberto & Tamer, 2009; Ho, 2009; Kawai & Watanabe, 2013).

We define supermodular games and summarize several important results of supermodular games in the next section. In the third section, we discuss our strategy to estimate supermodular games. We present our Monte Carlo experiments in the fourth section, and the conclusion follows in the fifth section.

SUPERMODULAR GAMES

Consider a n-player normal form game $G=(I,\{S_i, \succcurlyeq_i\}_{i\in I},\{u_i\}_{i\in I})$. We denote the set of players by I, that is, $i\in I=\{1,2,\ldots,n\}$. Each player i's strategy space $(S_i, \succcurlyeq_i)$ is a complete lattice. Let $S=\prod_{i=1}^{n} S_i$. Each player i's utility function $u_i : S\rightarrow \mathbb{R}$ is order upper-semicontinuous (see Milgrom & Roberts, 1990, for definition). Now, we define a supermodular game.

Definition 1. A normal form game $G=(I,\{S_i, \succcurlyeq_i\}_{i\in I},\{u_i\}_{i\in I})$ is a supermodular game if

1. u_i is supermodular in S_i, that is, for all $s_i, s_i'\in S_i$, and for all $s_{-i}\in S_{-i}$

$$u_i(s_i\wedge s_i', s_{-i})+u_i(s_i\vee s_i', s_{-i})\geq u_i(s_i, s_{-i})+u_i(s_i', s_{-i})$$

and

2. u_i has increasing difference in S_i and S_{-i}, that is, for all $s_i, s_i' \in S_i$ and $s_{-i}, s_{-i}' \in S_{-i}$ such that $s_i \succeq_i s_i'$ and $s_{-i} \succeq_{-i} s_{-i}'$,

$$u_i(s_i, s_{-i}) - u_i(s_i', s_{-i}) \geq u_i(s_i, s_{-i}') - u_i(s_i', s_{-i}')$$

The following example is a complete information chain-store entry game studied by Jia (2008).

Example 1. (Jia, 2008) Consider an entry game by two chain stores, Walmart and Kmart, that is, $I = \{\text{Walmart, Kmart}\}$. Each chain store's entry decision in market m is denoted by $s_{im} \in \{0, 1\}$, where 0 means stay out and 1 entry. Then, player i's strategy space is $S_i = \{0, 1\}^M$ and $s_i \succeq_i s_i'$ if and only if $s_{im} \geq s_{im}'$ for all $m = 1, 2, \ldots, M$, where M is the number of markets. The (simplified) utility function Jia uses is as follows:

$$u_i(s_i, s_j) = \sum_{m=1}^{M} \left[s_{im} \times \left(\delta_{ii} \sum_{l \neq m} \left(\frac{s_{il}}{Z_{ml}} \right) + \delta_{ij} s_{jm} + \varepsilon_{im} \right) \right]$$

where Z_{ml} is the distance between market m and l, δ_{ii} is the positive spillover effect of firm i's entry in market l on firm i's profit of market m, δ_{ij} is the business stealing effect by the existence of firm j, and ε_{im} is shock on profits, which is not observed by an econometrician. She shows that the chain-store game with two players is a supermodular game if $\delta_{ii} > 0$.

Other empirical applications of supermodular games include a technology adoption game with network effects in the banking industries studied by Ackerberg and Gowrisankaran (2006) and mutual funds' proxy voting decisions with peer effects as in Matvos and Ostrovsky (2010). Also, Nishida (2012) extends Jia's analysis by incorporating multiple branching decisions in the Japanese convenience store industry.

In supermodular games, the existence of Nash equilibrium and its characterization are given by Tarski's fixed point theorem (Tarski, 1955) and Topkis's monotonicity theorem (Topkis, 1968, 1998).[3] To apply Tarski's fixed point theorem to supermodular game G, we first note that $s* \in S$ is a Nash equilibrium if and only if the best-response correspondence, $BR_i(s) = \arg\max_{s_i \in S_i} u_i(s_i, s_{-i})$, satisfies $s_i^* \in BR_i(s^*)$ for all $i \in I$. In other words, the set of Nash equilibria is the set of fixed points of best response correspondences $BR : S \rightrightarrows S$, where $BR = \{BR_i\}_{i \in I}$. Moreover, for supermodular games, it is known that the best-response correspondence is non-decreasing.[4]

Now, we summarize important results by Milgrom and Roberts (1990), which we will use for estimation. Applying Tarski's fixed point theorem and Topkis's monotonicity theorem, Milgrom and Roberts (1990) give useful characterizations of the set of Nash equilibria and rationalizable strategies of supermodular games. The first two results concern characterizations of the set of Nash equilibria, while the third result discusses characterization of rationalizable strategies, on which our estimation strategy is relied.

Theorem 1. (Milgrom & Roberts, 1990) The set of Nash equilibria of a supermodular game is a complete lattice. Hence, it has a largest and smallest element.

Moreover, we can compute the greatest and smallest element of the set of Nash equilibria using the following iterative best response algorithm.

Corollary 1. (Milgrom & Roberts, 1990) There exist the largest and smallest element in the set of Nash equilibria, $\bar{s}^*$ and $\underline{s}^*$. Moreover, these extremal equilibria are achieved by applying $BR : S \rightrightarrows S$ recursively starting from $\underline{s} = \inf S$ and $\bar{s} = \sup S$, respectively.

Furthermore, it is known that the two extremal Nash equilibria, $\bar{s}^*$ and $\underline{s}^*$, in fact provide lower and upper bounds for the set of rationalizable strategies.[5]

Theorem 2. (Milgrom & Roberts, 1990) The set of rationalizable strategies of a supermodular game has largest and smallest elements. Moreover, those extremal strategy profiles correspond to extremal Nash equilibrium strategy profiles $\bar{s}^*$ and $\underline{s}^*$.

In the estimation section below, we use these results to construct moment inequalities.

ESTIMATION

In this section, we propose an estimation strategy for supermodular games based on moment inequalities. Our estimation strategy exploits the lattice structure of the set of rationalizable strategies which allows partial ordering over the set of strategies. We use this property to construct inequalities and apply a moment inequalities estimator.

We provide two ways to construct moment inequalities in this section. The first approach is to construct moment inequalities in the strategy space,

S, and the second approach is to do so in the utility space, $\mathbb{R}$. In both of the cases, we use the property that strategies or utilities corresponding to the two extremal equilibria bound (above and below) all rationalizable strategies or corresponding utilities.

Moment Inequalities Based on Strategy

Consider a supermodular game $G=(I,\{S_i,\succcurlyeq_i\}_{i\in I},\{u_i\}_{i\in I})$. We specify the player i's utility function as $u_i(s)=f(s,\mathbf{x}_i,\mathbf{z};\theta)+\varepsilon_{is_i}$, where $f(\cdot)$ is the deterministic part of the utility, $\mathbf{x}_i$ is the vector of each player i's characteristics and $\mathbf{z}$ is the vector of exogenous market-level characteristics. The error term ε_{is} captures random payoff shock drawn from distribution g, which is observed by the players but unobserved by the econometrician. We parameterize the utility function and the distribution of the taste shock g by parameter $\theta\in\Theta$. The data environment we consider is the case in which the econometrician observes the game to be played independently across M markets, indexed by $m\in\{1,\ldots,M\}$, where M is large. Note also that we consider that observations $(I_m, s_m^{DATA}, \mathbf{x}_m, \mathbf{z}_m)$, $m=1,2\ldots,M$, are realized as one of the rationalizable strategies conditional on $\mathbf{x}_m$ and $\mathbf{z}_m$, that is, we do not assume that the data is a realization of a Nash equilibrium.

Let S^* be the set of all Nash equilibria, that is, $S^*=\{s\in S: s^*\in BR(s^*)\}$, and denote the two extremal Nash equilibria as $\bar{s}^*=\sup S^*$ and $s^*=\inf S^*$. Note that the extremal equilibrium is a function of all players' characteristics, $\mathbf{x}=\{\mathbf{x}_i\}_{i\in I}$, market characteristics, $\mathbf{z}$, and the parameter θ. The researcher cannot identify which rationalizable strategy corresponds to the observed data. However, the observed data s^{DATA}, which correspond to one of the rationalizable outcomes, is ordered between $\bar{s}^*$ and $\underline{s}^*$ as evident from the fact that the set of rationalizable strategies of supermodular games has the lattice structure, and bounded by $\bar{s}^*$ and $\underline{s}^*$ as in Theorem 2. Hence, we obtain the following relationships given a set of shocks: for all $i\in I$,

$$\bar{s}_i^* \succcurlyeq_i s_i^{DATA} \tag{1}$$

$$s_i^{DATA} \succcurlyeq_i \underline{s}_i^* \tag{2}$$

This is the basis of our estimation strategy using moment inequalities.

The relationship above cannot be directly used in the estimation, because the inequality relationships, $\succcurlyeq_i$, is not defined in terms of real values, but in terms of the partial order on S_i. In most applications, however, we can find a way to transform the space of S_i such that we can define some distance between s_i and $s'_i \in S_i$ without losing the partial ordering $\succcurlyeq_i$. For notational simplicity, we consider the case that S_i is simply $\mathbb{R}$ in the following. Then, we can construct the moment inequalities as

$$E\left[\sum_{i \in I} (\bar{s}_i^*(\theta, \mathbf{x}, \mathbf{z}) - s_i^{DATA}) \middle| \mathbf{x}, \mathbf{z}\right] \geq 0 \tag{3}$$

$$E\left[\sum_{i \in I} (s_i^{DATA} - \underline{s}_i^*(\theta, \mathbf{x}, \mathbf{z})) \middle| \mathbf{x}, \mathbf{z}\right] \geq 0 \tag{4}$$

and the corresponding sample analogues are written as

$$\frac{1}{M} \sum_{m \in M} \sum_{i \in I_m} (\bar{s}_{i,m}^*(\theta, \mathbf{x}_m, \mathbf{z}_m) - s_{i,m}^{DATA}) \times g(\mathbf{x}_m, \mathbf{z}_m) \geq 0$$

$$\frac{1}{M} \sum_{m \in M} \sum_{i \in I_m} (s_{i,m}^{DATA} - \underline{s}_{i,m}^*(\theta, \mathbf{x}_m, \mathbf{z}_m)) \times g(\mathbf{x}_m, \mathbf{z}_m) \geq 0$$

where $g(\cdot)$ is any nonnegative valued function of firm and market characteristics.

Moment Inequalities Based on Utility

In some cases, constructing moment inequalities based on utility (instead of strategy) can be easier because the mapping between strategy and utility may not be very straightforward. In such a case, one can also construct moment inequalities in terms of utility associated with rationalizable strategies. First, we describe the cases in which such construction is possible. To do so, we first define *positive spillover* property as follows.

Definition 2. Utility function $u_i(s)$ satisfies positive spillover property if $u_i(s_i, s_{-i}) \geq u_i(s_i, s'_{-i})$ for all i whenever s_{-i} S_i, $\succcurlyeq_{-i} s'_{-i}$.

This property means that the degree of complementarity increases as "greater" strategy is chosen by other players. Milgrom and Roberts (1990) show monotone comparative statistics results for supermodular games with positive spillover.

Theorem 3. (Milgrom & Roberts, 1990) Suppose $G_\theta = ((I, \{S_i, \succcurlyeq_i\}_{i\in I}, \{u_i\}_{i\in I}), \theta)$ is a supermodular game with positive spillovers. Then the rationalizable strategies are ordered in accordance with Pareto preference, that is, for any rationalizable strategies $s*$,

$$u_i(\bar{s}^*(\theta)) \geq u_i(s^*;\theta) \geq u_i(\underline{s}^*(\theta)), \forall i \in I \tag{5}$$

Theorem 4 does not necessarily imply the largest Nash equilibrium $\bar{s}^*$ is Pareto optimal. This theorem shows that the largest Nash equilibrium $\bar{s}^*$ is most preferred to any rationalizable strategies for any player, and the smallest Nash equilibrium $\underline{s}^*$ is least preferred to any other rationalizable strategies for any player. As in Eqs. (3) and (4), observed strategies provide utilities between the largest and smallest Nash equilibria, and we can construct moment inequalities as follows:

$$E\left[\sum_{i\in I} u_i(\bar{s}*(\theta, \mathbf{x}, \mathbf{z})) - u_i(s^{DATA};\theta)|\mathbf{x}, \mathbf{z}\right] \geq 0 \tag{6}$$

$$E\left[\sum_{i\in I} u_i(s^{DATA};\theta) - u_i(\underline{s}^*(\theta, \mathbf{x}, \mathbf{z}))|\mathbf{x}, \mathbf{z}\right] \geq 0 \tag{7}$$

The corresponding sample analogues of moment inequalities are written as

$$\frac{1}{M}\sum_{m\in M}\sum_{i\in I_m}(u_{i,m}(\bar{s}*(\theta, \mathbf{x}_m, \mathbf{z}_m)) - u_{i,m}(s^{DATA};\theta)) \times g(\mathbf{x}_m, \mathbf{z}_m) \geq 0,$$

$$\frac{1}{M}\sum_{m\in M}\sum_{i\in I_m}(u_{i,m}(s^{DATA};\theta) - u_{i,m}(\underline{s}*(\theta, \mathbf{x}_m, \mathbf{z}_m))) \times g(\mathbf{x}_m, \mathbf{z}_m) \geq 0.$$

Comments on Estimation

A few comments are in order. First, our estimation strategy is computationally simple and do not assume any equilibrium selection mechanism.

In fact we use rationalizability as a solution concept, which is a much weaker concept than Nash equilibrium, and do not assume which rationalizable strategy is realized in the data a priori. Since any rationalizable strategy, including one observed in the data, is bounded by $\overline{s}^*$ and $\underline{s}^*$, we do not need any assumption about selection mechanism. Another approach, for example, would be to use an equilibrium assumption and apply the estimation strategy by Bajari, Hong, and Ryan (2010), in which one can use Echenique (2007) that provides an efficient algorithm to compute all Nash equilibria of a supermodular game.

Second, the identified set defined by these moment inequalities is not sharp in general. Berry and Tamer (2006) define the sharp identified set as the set of parameters θ that are consistent with the data and the model. Heuristically, we say θ is in the identified set if and only if there exists a (proper) equilibrium selection mechanism such that the induced probability distribution of outcome of the game matches the choice probabilities observed in the data almost everywhere. If Nash equilibrium were used as our solution concept, our identified set would not be sharp, because it might include infeasible parameters θ for which it is not possible to find any equilibrium selection mechanism. The identified set is sharp in case if there are only two players or in case if we use correlated rationalizability as a solution concept. This is due to the fact that the set of serially undominated strategies coincides with the set of rationalizable strategies in these two cases. Since we use rationalizability as our solution concept, however, the identified set is not necessarily sharp.

Estimation Algorithm

Let us denote the moment inequalities by $E[h(\mathbf{x},\mathbf{z};\theta)] \geq 0$. Our inference is based on observations from many markets indexed by $m = 1, 2, \ldots, M$. The estimation procedure is as follows:

1. Fix parameter θ. For each market $m = 1, \ldots, M$, draw large number of $\varepsilon^{ms} = \{\varepsilon_{is_i}^{ms}\}_{i=1}^{I}$ from g, where the number of simulation draws is S, and s denotes s-th simulation draw.
2. For each draw ε^{ms} in each market m, compute $\overline{s}^*(\theta, \mathbf{x}, \mathbf{z}, \varepsilon^{ms})$ and $\underline{s}^*(\theta, \mathbf{x}, \mathbf{z}, \varepsilon^{ms})$ by iteratively applying the best response correspondence for each player.
3. Construct sample analogue of moment inequalities using $\overline{s}^*(\theta, \mathbf{x}, \mathbf{z}, \varepsilon^{ms})$ and $\underline{s}^*(\theta, \mathbf{x}, \mathbf{z}, \varepsilon^{ms})$ (or $u_{i,m}(\overline{s}^*(\theta, \mathbf{x}, \mathbf{z}, \varepsilon^{ms}))$ and $u_{i,m}(\underline{s}^*(\theta, \mathbf{x}, \mathbf{z}, \varepsilon^{ms})))$ as well as the observation on s^{DATA} (or $u_{i,m}(s^{DATA})$):

$$\frac{1}{MS}\sum_{m=1}^{M}\sum_{s=1}^{S}\sum_{i\in I_m} h(\mathbf{x}_m, \mathbf{z}_m, \varepsilon^{ls}; \theta) \geq 0$$

4. Use moment inequalities estimator, such as Chernozhukov, Hong, and Tamer (2007), Andrews and Soares (2010), and Pakes, Porter, Ho, and Ishii (2011).

MONTE CARLO EXPERIMENT

In this section, we present the results of Monte Carlo experiments. For these experiments, we consider a simple supermodular game; two-player investment game with complementarity. Player $i \in \{1,2\}$ chooses whether to make an investment ($s_i = 1$) or not ($s_i = 0$).[6] The utility function of Player i is written as

$$u_i(s_i, s_{-i}) = \begin{cases} \theta_1 \sum_{i\in\{1,2\}} s_i - x_i^{\theta_2} + \varepsilon_i & \text{if } s_i = 1 \\ 0 & \text{if } s_i = 0 \end{cases}$$

where (θ_1, θ_2) are parameters to be estimated, x_i is Player i's characteristics that affects i's cost of investment, and ε_i is an idiosyncratic shock.[7] We can interpret θ_1 as a parameter measuring complementarity of investments, and θ_2 as a parameter capturing convexity of the investment cost (we assume $\theta_1 > 0$ and $\theta_2 > 1$). As is clear from the specification of the utility function, each player's investment has complementarity and the game is a supermodular game.

The best response function of Player i given the strategy of the other player is written as

$$BR_i(s_j = 0) = \begin{cases} 1 & \text{if } \theta_1 - x_i^{\theta_2} > -\varepsilon_i \\ 0 & \text{otherwise} \end{cases}$$

$$BR_i(s_j = 1) = \begin{cases} 1 & \text{if } 2\theta_1 - x_i^{\theta_2} > -\varepsilon_i \\ 0 & \text{otherwise} \end{cases}$$

Thus, given θ_1, θ_2, and x_i, we can draw the Nash equilibrium outcomes corresponding to the realizations of $(\varepsilon_1, \varepsilon_2)$ as in Fig. 1. Points A and B in the Figure corresponds to $(2\theta_1 - x_1^{\theta_2}, 2\theta_1 - x_2^{\theta_2})$ and $(\theta_1 - x_1^{\theta_2}, \theta_1 - x_2^{\theta_2})$,

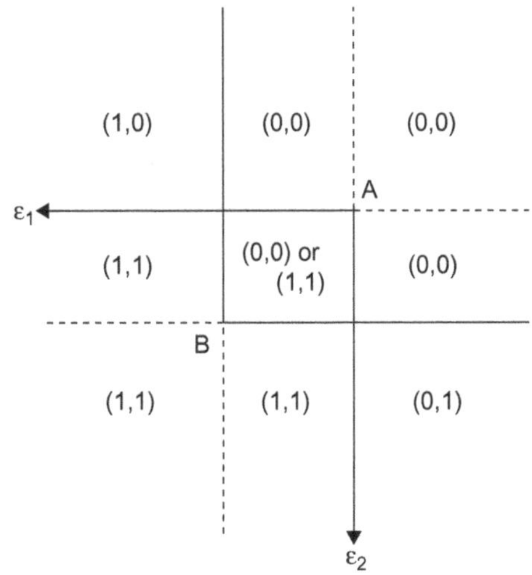

Fig. 1. Numbers in each parenthesis corresponds to (s_1^*, s_2^*). Points A and B correspond to $(2\theta_1 - x_1^{\theta_2}, 2\theta_1 - x_2^{\theta_2})$ and $(\theta_1 - x_1^{\theta_2}, \theta_1 - x_2^{\theta_2})$, respectively. The area in the middle corresponds to the region with multiple equilibria.

respectively. The region in the middle of the figure corresponds to the case that there are multiple equilibrium outcomes, while the rest of the regions have a unique equilibrium outcome. For example, very large values of ε_1 and ε_2 result in both players to invest (corresponding to the south-west corner of the figure), while a large value of ε_1 and a small value of ε_2 result in Player 1 to invest and Player 2 not to invest (corresponding to the north-west corner of the figure).

For the Monte Carlo experiments, we use the parameter values of $\theta_1 = 2$ and $\theta_2 = 2$. The number of markets is set at $M = 2000$. The value (x_1, x_2) of players' characteristics are uniformly distributed over the discrete values in the sets X_1 and X_2, respectively, where $X_1 = \{1.1,\ 1.2,\ 1.3,\ 1.4,\ 1.5\}$ and $X_2 = \{1.9,\ 2.8,\ 3.7,\ 4.6,\ 5.5\}$ in $m \in \{1, \ldots, 1000\}$, and $X_1 = \{1.9,\ 2.8,\ 3.7,\ 4.6,\ 5.5\}$ and $X_2 = \{1.1,\ 1.2,\ 1.3,\ 1.4,\ 1.5\}$ in $m \in \{1001, \ldots, 2000\}$. Finally, we specify that the error term ε_i follows a normal distribution with mean 0 and standard error of 0.05.

In our experiment, we have three different data generating processes. In case if multiple equilibrium outcome is possible, we let the outcomes $(0,0)$ and $(1,1)$ to occur with probabilities p and $1-p$, and we vary the value of p. Specifically, we use three values $p = 0.1,\ 0.5$, and 0.9 in the experiment. Fig. 2 is the plot of the confidence set in each case. In our implementation, we construct 95% confidence sets using Andrews and Soares' (2010) generalized moment selection.

Fig. 2 presents the 95% confidence set for all three cases, and Table 1 presents the minimum and the maximum of the parameter values for each dimension of the confidence set. In all cases, the true parameter value of (θ_1, θ_2) is included in the confidence set regardless of the data generating process. Thus, the approach we propose works fine in our Monte Carlo experiments regardless of which equilibrium is actually used in the data generating process.

Another observation is that the confidence set for the case of $p=0.1$ is included in the confidence set for the case of $p=0.5$, while the confidence sets for $p=0.5$ and for $p=0.9$ are very close to each other. Given that the

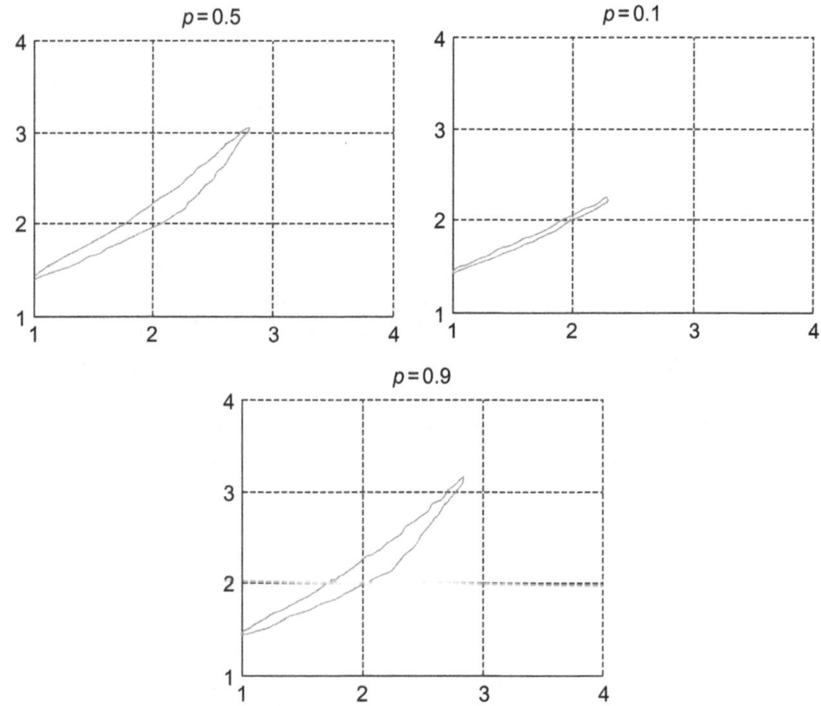

Fig. 2. 95% confidence set for $p=0.5$, 0.1, and 0.9. The horizontal axis in θ_1 and the vertical axis is θ_2. True parameter value is $(2, 2)$.

Table 1. Minimum and Maximum of the 95% Confidence Set for Each Parameter for Different Data Generating Processes.

DGP	Parameter	Confidence Set
$p=0.5$		
	θ_1	[1.00, 2.80]
	θ_2	[1.42, 3.08]
$p=0.1$		
	θ_1	[1.02, 2.28]
	θ_2	[1.42, 2.20]
$p=0.9$		
	θ_1	[1.02, 2.84]
	θ_2	[1.44, 3.14]

data generating process for the case of multiple equilibrium outcomes is different (while the realizations of (X_1, X_2) are the same), it is natural to think that the confidence set for the three cases differ from one another. However, we could not analytically show how these are related with each other in this case.

CONCLUSION

This note proposes an approach to estimate supermodular games using moment inequalities. Our approach differs from the approaches taken by the existing studies by addressing the issue of multiplicity of equilibria by adopting a set inference. We also differ form existing studies by using rationalizability as a solution concept, which in general is a weaker restriction than Nash equilibrium. Finally, we conduct Monte Carlo experiments to show that the method works, and presented how the confidence set varies as the data generating process changes.

NOTES

1. Rationalizability (Bernheim, 1984; Pearce, 1984) is a weaker concept than Nash equilibrium. Hence, all Nash equilibria are rationalizable, while rationalizability does not imply that the strategy profile constitutes a Nash equilibrium.
2. The approach we propose is similar to Uetake and Watanabe (2012b), which estimate a two-sided matching model to study banks' entry and merger decisions.

They use the property that the set of stable matchings in two-sided matching models can be characterized by Tarski's fixed point theorem in the similar way as the set of equilibria of supermodular games. Uetake and Watanabe (2012a) propose another way to exploit the lattice property of the stable matching to estimate two-sided matching models with non-transferable utilities.

3. Formally, Tarski's fixed point theorem is as follows: If a set T is a complete lattice and $f: T \rightarrow T$ is a non-decreasing function, then f has a fixed point. Moreover, the set of fixed points has its largest ad smallest element in T. Moreover, Topkis's monotonicity theorem is as follows: Let X be a complete lattice and T a partially ordered set. Suppose $F: X \times T \rightarrow R$ has increasing differences in $(x, t) \in X \times T$ and is supermodular in $x \in X$. Then $\text{argmax}_{x \in X} F(x, t)$ is monotone non-decreasing in (x, t).

4. Formally, we can use a Topkis's (1968) result in order to prove that the best response correspondence is non-decreasing.

5. For the formal definition of rationalibale strategy, see, e.g., Bernheim (1984) or Pearce (1984).

6. We focus on pure strategies in our analysis.

7. We assume that the probability distribution of ε_i is continuous. Hence, the probability that two choices give exactly the same payoff is zero.

ACKNOWLEDGEMENT

We thank the editors, Eugene Choo and Matt Shum, and an anonymous referee for providing us with useful comments, which significantly improved the article.

REFERENCES

Ackerberg, D. A., & Gowrisankaran, G. (2006). Quantifying equilibrium network externalities in the ACH banking industry. *RAND Journal of Economics*, *37*(3), 738–761.

Andrews, D. W. K., & Soares, G. (2010). Inference for parameters defined by moment inequalities using generalized moment selection. *Econometrica*, *78*, 119–157.

Aradillas-Lopez, A., & Tamer, E. (2008). The identification power of equilibrium in simple games. *Journal of Business and Economic Statistics*, *26*(3), 261–283.

Bajari, P., Hong, H., & Ryan, S. (2010). Identification and estimation of discrete games of complete information. *Econometrica*, *78*(5), 1529–1568.

Bernheim, B. D. (1984). Rationalizable strategic behavior. *Econometrica*, *52*, 1007–1028.

Berry, S., & E. Tamer (2006). Identification in models of oligopoly entry. In R. Blundell, W. Newey, & T. Persson (Eds.), *Advances in economics and econometrics. Theory and applications, ninth world congress* (Vol. 2, pp. 46–85). Econometric Society Monographs: Cambridge University Press.

Chernozhukov, V., Hong, H., & Tamer, E. (2007). Estimation and confidence regions for parameter sets in econometric models. *Econometrica*, *75*, 1243–1284.
Ciliberto, F., & Tamer, E. (2009). Market structure and multiple equilibria in airline markets. *Econometrica*, *77*, 1791–1828.
Echenique, F. (2007). Finding all equilibria in games with strategic complements. *Journal of Economic Theory*, *135*(1), 514–532.
Echenique, F., & Komunjer, I. (2009). Testing models with multiple equilibria by quantile methods. *Econometrica*, *77*(4), 1281–1298.
Ho, K. E. (2009). Insurer-provider networks in the medical care market. *American Economic Review*, *99*(1), 393–430.
Jia, P. (2008). What happens when Wal-Mart comes to town: An empirical analysis of the discount retailing industry. *Econometrica*, *76*(6), 1263–1316.
Kawai, K., & Watanabe, Y. (2013). Inferring strategic voting. *American Economic Review*, *103*(2), 624–662.
Lazzati, N. (2012). *Treatment response with social interactions: Partial identification via monotone comparative statics*: mimeo.
Matvos, G., & Ostrovsky, M. (2010). Heterogeneity and peer effects in mutual fund proxy voting. *Journal of Financial Economics*, *98*(1), 90–112.
Milgrom, P., & Roberts, J. (1990). Rationalizability, learning, and equilibrium in games with strategic complementarities. *Econometrica*, *58*(6), 1255–1277.
Molinari, F., & Rosen, A. (2008). The identification power of equilibrium in games: The supermodular case. *Journal of Business and Economic Statistics*, *26*(3), 297–302.
Nishida, M. (2012). Estimating a model of strategic network choice: The convenience-store industry in Okinawa, Mimeo.
Pakes, A., Porter, J., Ho, K., & Ishii, J. (2011). *Moment inequalities and their applications*. Mimeo.
Pearce, D. (1984). Rationalizable strategic behavior and the problem of perfection. *Econometrica*, *52*, 1029–1050.
Tarski, A. (1955). A lattice-theoretical fixpoint theorem and its applications. *Pacific Journal of Mathematics*, *5*, 285–309.
Topkis, D. (1968). *Ordered Optimal Solution*. Doctoral Dissertation, Stanford University, 1968.
Topkis, D. (1998). *Supermodularity and complementarity*. NJ: Princeton University Press.
Uetake, K., & Watanabe, Y. (2012a). A note on estimation of two-sided matching models. *Economics Letters*, *116*(3), 535–537.
Uetake, K., & Watanabe, Y. (2012b). *Entry by merger: Estimates from a two-sided matching model with externalities*. Mimeo.

PART III
APPLICATIONS OF STRUCTURAL ECONOMIC MODELS

ESTIMATION OF THE LOAN SPREAD EQUATION WITH ENDOGENOUS BANK-FIRM MATCHING

Jiawei Chen

ABSTRACT

This article estimates the loan spread equation taking into account the endogenous matching between banks and firms in the loan market. To overcome the endogeneity problem, I supplement the loan spread equation with a two-sided matching model and estimate them jointly. Bayesian inference is feasible using a Gibbs sampling algorithm that performs Markov chain Monte Carlo (MCMC) simulations. I find that medium-sized banks and firms tend to be the most attractive partners, and that liquidity is also a consideration in choosing partners. Furthermore, banks with higher monitoring ability charge higher spreads, and firms that are more leveraged or less liquid are charged higher spreads.

Keywords: Loan spread equation; two-sided matching; Bayesian inference; Gibbs sampling

JEL classifications: G21; C78; C11

Structural Econometric Models
Advances in Econometrics, Volume 31, 251–289

ISSN: 0731-9053/doi:10.1108/S0731-9053(2013)0000032009

INTRODUCTION

Bank loans are an important source of credit to firms. For instance, in 2010 the U.S. marketplace for bank loans is roughly $1.5 trillion in size, representing 17% of the overall corporate debt issuance and making bank loans a significant component of the capital markets (Stoeckle, 2011). Moreover, bank loans constitute the critical "lending" channel of monetary policy transmission and have substantial impact on investment and aggregate economic activity (Kashyap & Stein, 1994).

Not surprisingly, empirical researchers have long been interested in the pricing of bank loans. In particular, loan spreads (markups of loan interest rates over a benchmark rate) are regressed on the characteristics of banks, firms, and loans to examine the relationship between collateral and risk in financial contracting (Berger & Udell, 1990), and to provide evidence of the bank lending channel of monetary transmission (Hubbard, Kuttner, & Palia, 2002). However, the nonrandomness of the bank-firm pairs in the loan samples is typically ignored.

In this article, we argue that banks and firms prefer to match with partners that have higher quality, so banks choose firms, firms choose banks, and the matching outcome is endogenously determined. We show that, as a result, the regressors in the loan spread equation are correlated with the error term. In order to overcome this endogeneity problem, we develop a two-sided matching model to supplement the loan spread equation. We find that medium-sized banks and firms tend to be the most attractive partners, and that liquidity is also a consideration in choosing partners. Furthermore, banks with higher monitoring ability charge higher spreads, and firms that are more leveraged or less liquid are charged higher spreads.

Both firms and banks have strong economic incentives to select their partners. When a bank lends to a firm, the bank not only supplies credit to the firm but also provides monitoring, expert advice, and endorsement based on reputation (e.g., Diamond, 1984, 1991). Empirical evidence suggests that those " by-products" are important for firms. For instance, Billet, Flannery, and Garfinkel (1995) and Johnson (1997) show that banks' monitoring ability and reputation have significant positive effects on borrowers' performance in the stock market.

The size of a bank – the amount of its total assets – also plays an important role in firms' choices. First, a larger bank is likely to have better diversified assets and a lower risk, making it more attractive to firms. Second, the small size of a bank may place a constraint on its lending, which is undesirable for a borrowing firm, since its subsequent loan requests could be denied and it might have to find a new lender and pay a switching cost. Third, large banks usually have more organizational layers and face more severe information distortion problems than small banks, so they are generally less effective in processing and communicating borrower information, making them less able to provide valuable client-specific monitoring and expert advice. Fourth, Brickley, Linck, and Smith (2003) observe that employees in small to medium-sized banks own higher percentages of their banks' stocks than employees in large banks. As a result the loan officers in small to medium-sized banks have stronger incentives and will devote more effort to collecting and processing borrower information, which helps the banks better serve their clients. Thus the size of a bank has multiple effects on its quality perceived by firms and those effects operate in opposite directions. Which bank size is most attractive is determined by the net effect.

Banks' characteristics affect how much benefit borrowing firms will receive, so firms prefer banks that are better in those characteristics, for example, banks with higher monitoring ability, better reputation, suitable size, and so on. Banks are ranked by firms according to a composite quality index that combines those characteristics.

Now consider banks' choices. In making their lending decisions, loan officers in a bank screen the applicants (firms) and provide loans only to those who are considered creditworthy. Firms with lower leverage ratios (total debt/total assets) or higher current ratios (current assets/current liabilities) are usually considered less risky and more creditworthy. Larger firms also have an advantage here, because they generally have higher repaying ability and better diversified assets, and are more likely to have well-documented track records and lower degrees of information opacity.

However, the large size of a firm also has negative effects on its attractiveness. Because larger firms have stronger financial needs, the loan made to a larger firm usually has a larger amount and accounts for a higher percentage of the bank's assets, thus reducing the bank's diversification. Since banks prefer well diversified portfolios, the large size of a borrowing firm may be considered unattractive. In addition, lending to a large firm means that the bank's control over the firm's investment decisions will be relatively small, which is undesirable.[1] Therefore, the size of a firm also has multiple effects on its quality perceived by banks, and which firm size is most attractive depends on the relative magnitudes of those effects. Firms are ranked by banks according to a composite quality index that combines firms' characteristics, such as their risk and their sizes.

The above analysis shows that there is endogenous two-sided matching in the loan market: banks choose firms, firms choose banks, and they all prefer partners that have higher quality. Thus we need to address the endogeneity issue when we estimate the loan spread equation, as discussed below.

In our model banks' and firms' quality are multidimensional, but to illustrate the consequence of the endogenous matching, we assume for a moment that a bank's quality is solely determined by its liquidity risk, and that a firm's quality is solely determined by its information opacity. Further assume that banks' liquidity risk, firms' information opacity, and non-price loan characteristics such as maturity and loan size are determinants of loan spreads. The spread equation is

$$r_{ij} = \alpha_0 + \kappa L_i + \lambda I_j + N'_{ij}\alpha_3 + \nu_{ij}, \nu_{ij} \sim N(0, \sigma_\nu^2) \tag{1}$$

where r_{ij} is the loan spread if bank i lends to firm j, L_i is bank i's liquidity risk, I_j is firm j's information opacity, and N_{ij} is the non-price loan characteristics.

Liquidity risk and information opacity are not perfectly observed, and the bank's ratio of cash to total assets and the firm's ratio of property, plant, and equipment (PP&E) to total assets are used as their proxies, respectively. Assume

$$L_i = \rho C_i + \eta_i, \eta_i \sim N(0, \sigma_\eta^2)$$

and

$$I_j = \sigma P_j + \delta_j, \delta_j \sim N(0, \sigma_\delta^2)$$

where C_i is bank i's ratio of cash to total assets, and P_j is firm j's ratio of PP&E to total assets. Now Eq. (1) becomes

$$\begin{aligned} r_{ij} &= \alpha_0 + \kappa(\rho C_i + \eta_i) + \lambda(\sigma P_j + \delta_j) + N'_{ij}\alpha_3 + \nu_{ij} \\ &= \alpha_0 + \kappa\rho C_i + \lambda\sigma P_j + N'_{ij}\alpha_3 + \kappa\eta_i + \lambda\delta_j + \nu_{ij} \end{aligned} \tag{2}$$

Note that the error term contains η_i and δ_j, the unobserved quality. Because of the endogenous matching, the unobserved quality of a bank or a firm affects its matching outcome, and therefore correlates with its partner's characteristics. As a result, the regressors in the spread equation are correlated with the error term, giving rise to an endogeneity problem. Such endogeneity problem introduced by the use of proxies in the matching setting is pointed out by Ackerberg and Botticini (2002) in their analysis of contract choices.

The current study takes a full information approach to address the endogeneity problem. We develop a many-to-one two-sided matching model in the loan market that supplements the spread equation to permit nonrandom matching of banks and firms.[2] In the matching model, the set of participants are different in different markets, which provides exogenous variation in agents' matching outcome and solves the endogeneity problem for the same intuitive reason as the traditional instrumental variable method. In addition to addressing the endogeneity problem in estimation of the loan spread equation, the matching model also allows us to investigate the factors that determine banks' and firms' quality, enabling us to better understand how banks and firms choose each other in the loan market.

Our matching model is a special case of the College Admissions Model, for which an equilibrium matching always exists (Gale & Shapley, 1962; Roth & Sotomayor, 1990). Two-sided matching models are applied to markets in which agents are divided into two sides and each participant chooses a partner or partners from the other side. Examples include the labor market, the marriage market, the education market, and so on. There are a few studies on two-sided matching in financial markets. Fernando, Gatchev, and Spindt (2005) study the matching between firms and their underwriters, and Sorensen (2007) studies the matching between venture capitalists and the companies in which they invest. Park (2008) introduces the use of matching models into the merger setting and studies the incentives of acquirers and targets in the mutual fund industry.

We obtain Bayesian inference using a Gibbs sampling algorithm (Gelfand & Smith, 1990; Geman & Geman, 1984; Geweke, 1999) with data augmentation (Albert & Chib, 1993; Tanner & Wong, 1987). The method iteratively simulates each block of the parameters and the latent variables conditional on all the others to recover the joint posterior distribution. It transforms an integration problem into a simulation problem and overcomes the difficulty of integrating a highly nonlinear function over thousands of dimensions, most of which correspond to the latent variables. As a result, computational burden is substantially reduced. Related Markov chain Monte Carlo (MCMC) algorithms have been applied to the estimation of the optimal job search model (Lancaster, 1997) and the selection model of hospital admissions (Geweke, Gowrisankaran, & Town, 2003), among others. Sorensen's (2007) paper on venture capital is the first study that uses the method to estimate a two-sided matching model.

Our empirical analysis uses a sample of 1,369 U.S. loan facilities between 455 banks and 1,369 firms from 1996 to 2003. We find that positive assortative matching of sizes is prevalent in the loan market, that is, large banks tend to match with large firms, and vice versa. We show that for agents on both sides of the market there are similar relationships between quality and size, which lead to similar size rankings for both sides and explain the positive assortative matching of sizes. Medium-sized banks and firms are the most preferred partners, and liquidity is also a consideration in choosing partners. Furthermore, banks with higher monitoring ability charge higher spreads, and firms that are more leveraged or less liquid are charged higher spreads.

The remainder of the article is organized as follows: the second section provides the specification of the model, the third section presents the empirical method, the fourth section describes the data, the fifth section presents and interprets the empirical results, and the sixth section concludes.

MODEL

The first component of our model is a spread equation, in which the loan spread is a function of the bank's characteristics, the firm's characteristics, and the non-price characteristics of the loan. A two-sided matching model in the loan market supplements the spread equation to permit nonrandom matching of banks and firms.

Spread Equation

We are interested in estimating the following spread equation:

$$r_{ij} = \alpha_0 + \boldsymbol{B}_i'\alpha_1 + \boldsymbol{F}_j'\alpha_2 + \boldsymbol{N}_{ij}'\alpha_3 + \varepsilon_{ij} \equiv \boldsymbol{U}_{ij}'\alpha + \varepsilon_{ij}, \varepsilon_{ij} \sim N(0, \sigma_\varepsilon^2) \tag{3}$$

where r_{ij} is the loan spread if bank i lends to firm j, $\boldsymbol{B}_i$ is a vector of bank i's characteristics, $\boldsymbol{F}_j$ is a vector of firm j's characteristics, and $\boldsymbol{N}_{ij}$ is the non-price loan characteristics.

Prior studies, such as Hubbard et al. (2002) and Coleman, Esho, and Sharpe (2006), suggest that the bank's monitoring ability and risk, as well as the firm's risk and information opacity are important determinants of the loan spread. Those characteristics are not perfectly observed, so we follow the literature and use proxies for them in the spread equation. Because estimation of our model is numerically intensive, we choose a parsimonious specification to keep estimation feasible, focusing on a set of key variables.

Bank's Monitoring Ability

According to the hold-up theory in Rajan (1992) and Diamond and Rajan (2000), a bank that has superior monitoring ability can use its skills to extract higher rents. Moreover, Leland and Pyle (1977), Diamond (1984, 1991), and Allen (1990) show that banks' monitoring plays an important role in firms' operation and provides value to them. Therefore, we expect a bank that has higher monitoring ability to charge a higher spread.

A bank's salaries-expenses ratio, defined as the ratio of salaries and benefits to total operating expenses, is a proxy for its monitoring ability. Coleman et al. (2006) show that monitoring activities are relatively labor intensive, and that salaries can reflect the staff's ability and performance in these activities.

Bank's Risk

A bank's risk comes from two sources, inadequate capital and low liquidity. Both of them affect the bank's cost of funds and may have an impact on the spread (see, e.g., Hubbard et al. 2002).

A bank's capital-assets ratio is a proxy for its capital adequacy, and its ratio of cash to total assets is a proxy for its liquidity risk. The size of a bank (its total assets) is also a proxy for its risk, since a larger bank is likely to have better diversified assets and lower risk.

Firm's Risk

Proxies for a firm's risk include the leverage ratio (total debt/total assets), the current ratio (current assets/current liabilities), and the size of the firm.

Risk is positively related to the leverage ratio, so a firm that has a higher leverage ratio is charged a higher spread, all else being equal. On the other hand, a firm with a higher current ratio is more liquid and less risky, so it is typically charged a lower spread. Due to the diversification effects of increasing firm size, firm risk is negatively associated with firm assets, and a larger firm can usually get a loan with a lower spread.

Firm's Information Opacity

In general smaller firms pose larger information asymmetries because they typically lack well-documented track records, so the size of a firm is also a proxy for information opacity.

Another proxy for a firm's information opacity is the ratio of PP&E to total assets, which indicates the relative significance of tangible assets in the firm. A firm with relatively more tangible assets poses smaller information asymmetries. Consequently it can borrow at a lower spread, all else being equal.

Non-Price Loan Characteristics

Non-price loan characteristics are included on the right-hand side of the spread equation as control variables. They are maturity (in months), natural log of the loan facility size, purpose dummies such as "acquisition" and "recapitalization," type dummies such as "a revolver credit line with duration shorter than one year," and a secured dummy. The definitions of these variables are presented in the fourth section. In this article we follow the approach in the literature (e.g., Berger & Udell, 1990; Hubbard et al., 2002; John, Lynch, & Puri, 2003) and take the non-price loan characteristics as exogenous.

Two-Sided Matching Model

A two-sided matching model is developed to supplement the spread equation and address the endogeneity problem resulting from the nonrandom matching between banks and firms:

$$r_{ij} = \alpha_0 + \boldsymbol{B}_i'\alpha_1 + \boldsymbol{F}_j'\alpha_2 + \boldsymbol{N}_{ij}'\alpha_3 + \varepsilon_{ij} \equiv \boldsymbol{U}_{ij}'\alpha + \varepsilon_{ij}, \varepsilon_{ij} \sim N(0, \sigma_\varepsilon^2) \tag{4}$$

$$Q_i^b = \boldsymbol{B}_i'\beta + \eta_i, \eta_i \sim N(0, \sigma_\eta^2) \tag{5}$$

$$Q_j^f = \boldsymbol{F}_j'\gamma + \delta_j, \delta_j \sim N(0, \sigma_\delta^2) \tag{6}$$

$$m_{ij} = \mathrm{I}(\text{bank}\, i \text{ lends to firm}\, j) \tag{7}$$

where Q_i^b is the quality index of bank i, Q_j^f is the quality index of firm j, and $\mathrm{I}(\cdot)$ is the indicator function. r_{ij}, $\boldsymbol{N}_{ij}$ are observed iff the match indicator $m_{ij} = 1$. η_i and δ_j are allowed to be correlated with ε_{ij}.

In the two-sided matching model, whether m_{ij} equals one or zero is determined by both banks' choices and firms' choices, and the outcome corresponds to the unique equilibrium matching (defined later), which depends on the Q_i^b's and the Q_j^f's.

We assume that in the matching process, each agent has complete information on the quality indexes of the agents on the other side of the market. We consider this assumption a reasonable approximation of the portion of the loan market that we analyze, since we focus on the upper portion of the market, which consists of large banks and large, publicly traded firms. As a result, a two-sided matching model is more suitable here than a job-search model.

Miller and Bavaria (2003) and Yago and McCarthy (2004) document that during the 1990s, "market-flex language" became common in the loan market, which lets the pricing of a loan be determined after the loan agreement is made. This practice is consistent with the fact that banks commonly employ loan pricing formulas and strive to keep the weights assigned to different risk factors constant for a given period of time across all borrowers, leaving not much room for negotiation on loan spreads (Bhattacharya, 1997, pp. 688–689). These institutional features suggest that loan spreads are determined by a combination of pre-specified loan pricing formulas and bargaining between banks and firms. Consequently, the matching process in the loan market falls between two matching frameworks: (1) the transferable utility framework, in which the transfers between banks and firms (including the loan spreads) are endogenously determined by their bargaining, and (2) the nontransferable utility framework, in which the transfers follow prespecified formulas and are exogenous to the matching process.

In this article we approximate the loan matching process using the nontransferable utility framework. We model the loan spreads as determined by the characteristics of banks, firms, and loans, and do not consider endogenous transfers between partners. Note that the loan spread equation, which is a major motivation for this study, is compatible with the nontransferable utility framework but not the transferable utility framework, as the loan spread equation assumes that loan spreads are determined by the characteristics of banks, firms, and loans, and not by the bargaining between banks and firms.

In a related paper, Chen and Song (2013) take a different route and approximate the loan matching process using a transferable utility matching model, in which the price and non-price characteristics of loans are endogenously determined at the time of the matching, and an agent is willing to trade away match quality in order to obtain better terms in the loan. They investigate the two-sided matching in the loan market but not the loan spread equation (incompatible with the transferable utility framework).

Agents, Quotas, and Matches

Let I_t and J_t denote, respectively, the sets of banks and firms in market t, where $t = 1, 2, \ldots, T$. I_t and J_t are finite and disjoint. The market subscript t is sometimes dropped to simplify the notation.

In the empirical implementation of our model, a market is specified to contain all the firms that borrow during a half-year and all the banks that lend to them. In the data the vast majority of firms borrow only once during a half-year, whereas a bank often lends to multiple firms. We therefore model the loan market using a many-to-one two-sided matching model, also known as the College Admissions Model (Gale & Shapley, 1962; Roth & Sotomayor, 1990). In market t, bank i lends to q_{it} firms and firm j borrows from only one bank. q_{it} is known as the *quota* of bank i in the matching literature, and every firm has a quota of one. We assume that each agent uses up its quota in equilibrium.

The set of all potential loans, or *matches*, is given by $M_t = I_t \times J_t$. A *matching*, μ_t, is a set of matches such that $(i, j) \in \mu_t$ if and only if bank i and firm j are matched in market t.

Let $\mu_t(i)$ denote the set of firms that borrow from bank i in market t, and let $\mu_t(j)$ denote the set of banks that lend to firm j in market t, which is a singleton. We then have

$$m_{ij} = 1 \Leftrightarrow (i,j) \in \mu_t \Leftrightarrow j \in \mu_t(i) \Leftrightarrow i \in \mu_t(j) \Leftrightarrow \{i\} = \mu_t(j)$$

Equilibrium Matching

The matching of banks and firms is determined by the equilibrium outcome of a two-sided matching process. The payoff firm j receives if it borrows from bank i is Q_i^b, and the payoff bank i receives if it lends to the firms in the set $\mu_t(i)$ is $\sum_{j \in \mu_t(i)} Q_j^f$. Consequently, each bank prefers firm j to firm j' iff $Q_j^f > Q_{j'}^f$, and each firm prefers bank i to bank i' iff $Q_i^b > Q_{i'}^b$. The quality indexes are assumed to be distinct so there are no "ties."

A matching is an equilibrium if it is stable, that is, if there is no blocking coalition of agents. A coalition of agents is blocking if they prefer to deviate from the current matching and form new matches among them. Formally, μ_t is an equilibrium matching in market t iff there does not exist $\tilde{I} \subset I_t$, $\tilde{J} \subset J_t$ and $\tilde{\mu}_t \neq u_t$ such that $\tilde{\mu}_t(i) \subset \tilde{J} \cup \mu_t(i)$ and $\sum_{j \in \tilde{\mu}_t(i)} Q_j^f > \sum_{j \in \mu_t(i)} Q_j^f$ for all $i \in \tilde{I}$, and $\tilde{\mu}_t(j) \in \tilde{I}$ and $Q_{\tilde{\mu}_t(j)}^b > Q_{\mu_t(j)}^b$ for all $j \in \tilde{J}$.

The above stability concept is group stability. A related stability concept is pair-wise stability. A matching is pair-wise stable if there is no blocking pair. In the College Admissions Model, Roth and Sotomayor (1990) prove that pair-wise stability is equivalent to group stability and that an equilibrium always exists. Appendix A shows that there exists a unique equilibrium matching in our model, which is a special case of the College Admissions Model.

The unique equilibrium matching is characterized by a set of inequalities, based on the fact that there is no blocking bank-firm pair. For each bank, stability requires that its worst borrower be better than any other firm whose lender is worse than this bank. Similarly, for each firm, stability requires that its lender be better than any other bank whose worst borrower is worse than this firm. Appendix B derives the lower and upper bounds on the agents' quality indexes, $\underline{Q}_i^b$, $\underline{Q}_j^f$, $\overline{Q}_i^b$, and $\overline{Q}_j^f$, such that

$$\mu_t = \mu_t^e \Leftrightarrow Q_i^b \in (\underline{Q}_i^b, \overline{Q}_i^b), \forall i \in I_t \text{ and } Q_j^f \in (\underline{Q}_j^f, \overline{Q}_j^f), \forall j \in J_t \quad (8)$$

where μ_t^e denotes the unique equilibrium matching in market t. This characterization of the equilibrium matching is used in the estimation method in the next section.

ESTIMATION

Two-sided matching in the loan market presents numerical challenges when it comes to estimation. Maximum likelihood estimation requires integrating a highly nonlinear function over thousands of dimensions, most of which correspond to the latent quality indexes. Instead we use a Gibbs sampling algorithm that performs MCMC simulations to obtain Bayesian inference, and augment the observed data with simulated values of the latent data on quality indexes so that the augmented data are straightforward to analyze. The method iteratively simulates each block of the parameters and the latent variables conditional on all the others to recover the joint posterior distribution. It transforms a high-dimensional integration problem into a simulation problem and substantially reduces the computational burden.

In our model, variation in the set of participants across different markets provides exogenous variation in agents' matching outcome, which solves the endogeneity problem for the same intuitive reason as the traditional instrumental variable method.

Error Terms and Prior Distributions

Estimation of the quality index equations is subject to the usual identification constraints in discrete choice models, so σ_η and σ_δ are set to one to fix the scales, and the constant and market characteristics are excluded to fix the levels.

To allow for correlation among the error terms, we assume $\varepsilon_{ij} = \kappa\eta_i + \lambda\delta_j + \nu_{ij}$, $\nu_{ij} \sim N(0, \sigma_\nu^2)$, with

$$\begin{pmatrix} \varepsilon_{ij} \\ \eta_i \\ \delta_j \end{pmatrix} \sim N\left(0, \begin{bmatrix} \kappa^2 + \lambda^2 + \sigma_\nu^2 & \kappa & \lambda \\ \kappa & 1 & 0 \\ \lambda & 0 & 1 \end{bmatrix}\right)$$

The signs in the two-sided matching model are identified by requiring λ to be non-positive, as theory predicts that firms with higher unobserved quality (lower unobserved risk or lower degrees of unobserved information opacity) are charged lower loan spreads, everything else being equal.[3]

The prior distributions are multivariate normal for α, β, γ, normal for κ, and truncated normal for λ (truncated on the right at zero). The means of these prior distributions are zeros, and the variance-covariance matrices are $10I$, where I is an identity matrix. The prior distribution of $1/\sigma_\nu^2$ is gamma, $1/\sigma_\nu^2 \sim G(2, 1)$. We try larger variances and other changes in the priors and the estimates are largely unchanged.

Conditional Posterior Distributions

In the model, the exogenous variables are $\boldsymbol{B}_i$, $\boldsymbol{F}_j$, and $\boldsymbol{N}_{ij}$, which are abbreviated as $\boldsymbol{X}$. The observed endogenous variables are r_{ij} (the loan spread) and m_{ij} (the match indicator). The unobserved quality indexes are Q_i^b and Q_j^f. The parameters are α, β, γ, κ, λ, and $1/\sigma_\nu^2$, which are abbreviated as θ. In market t, let $\boldsymbol{X}_t$, r_t, μ_t and Q_t^* represent the above variables, where μ_t embodies all the m_{ij}'s and Q_t^* denotes all the quality indexes.

The joint density of the endogenous variables and the quality indexes conditional on the exogenous variables and the parameters is as follows:

$$\begin{aligned} p(r_t, \mu_t, Q_t^* \mid \boldsymbol{X}_t, \theta) = {} & \mathrm{I}(Q_i^b \in (\underline{Q}i^b, \overline{Q}_i^b), \forall i \in I_t \text{ and } Q_j^f \in (\underline{Q}j^f, \overline{Q}_j^f), \forall j \in J_t) \\ & \times \textstyle\prod_{(i,j)\in\mu_t} \phi(r_{ij} - \boldsymbol{U}_{ij}'\alpha - \kappa(Q_i^b - \boldsymbol{B}_i'\beta) - \lambda(Q_j^f - \boldsymbol{F}_j'\gamma); 0, \sigma_\nu^2) \\ & \times \textstyle\prod_{i\in I_t} \phi(Q_i^b - \boldsymbol{B}_i'\beta; 0, 1) \times \prod_{j\in J_t} \phi(Q_j^f - \boldsymbol{F}_j'\gamma; 0, 1) \end{aligned} \quad (9)$$

where $\mathrm{I}(\cdot)$ is the indicator function and $\phi(\cdot; \mu, \sigma^2)$ is the $N(\mu, \sigma^2)$ pdf. To obtain the likelihood function for market t $L_t(\theta) = p(r_t, \mu_t \mid \boldsymbol{X}_t, \theta)$, we need to integrate $p(r_t, \mu_t, Q_t^* \mid \boldsymbol{X}_t, \theta)$ over all possible values of the quality indexes.

Due to endogenous matching in the market, the bounds on each agent's quality index depend on other agents' quality indexes, so the integral can not be factored into a product of lower-dimensional integrals. The Gibbs sampling algorithm with data augmentation transforms this high-dimensional integration problem into a simulation problem and makes estimation feasible.

To keep our study tractable, we model the markets as independent, so the product of $p(r_t, \mu_t, Q_t^* \mid X_t, \theta)$ for $t = 1, 2, \ldots, T$ gives the joint density $p(r, \mu, Q^* \mid X, \theta)$ for all the markets. From Bayes' rule, the density of the posterior distribution of Q^* and θ conditional on the data is

$$p(Q^*, \theta \mid X, r, \mu) = p(\theta) \times p(r, \mu, Q^* \mid X, \theta)/p(r, \mu \mid X) \propto p(\theta) \times p(r, \mu, Q^* \mid X, \theta) \tag{10}$$

where $p(\theta)$ is the prior densities of the parameters. The conditional posterior distributions are described in Appendix C. They are truncated normal for Q_i^b, Q_j^f, and λ, multivariate normal for α, β, and γ, normal for κ, and gamma for $1/\sigma_\nu^2$.

Simulation

In the algorithm, the parameters and the quality indexes are partitioned into blocks. Each of the parameter vectors (α, β, γ, κ, λ, and $1/\sigma_\nu^2$) and the quality indexes is a block. In market t the number of quality indexes is equal to the number of agents, $|I_t| + |J_t|$, so altogether we have $\sum_{t=1}^{T}(|I_t| + |J_t|) + 6$ blocks. In each iteration of the algorithm, each block is simulated conditional on all the others according to the conditional posterior distributions, and the sequence of draws converge in distribution to the joint distribution.[4]

Estimation results reported in the fifth section are based on 20,000 draws from which the initial 2,000 are discarded to allow for burn-in. Visual inspection of the draws shows that convergence to the stationary posterior distribution occurs within the burn-in period. To formally examine whether the posterior simulator is correct and whether convergence has been achieved, three sets of tests are conducted. First, joint distribution tests of the posterior simulator (Geweke, 2004) using 1,224 test functions (the 48 first moments and 1,176 second moments of the 48 parameters in the model) yield one rejection in tests of size 0.05 and none in tests of size 0.01, showing that the posterior simulator is correct. Second, the

Raftery–Lewis (1992) test using all the draws shows that a small amount of burn-in (6 draws) and a total of 8,700 draws are needed for the estimated 95% highest posterior density intervals (HPDIs) to have actual posterior probabilities between 0.94 and 0.96 with probability 0.95, indicating that satisfactory accuracy can be achieved using the draws we have. Finally, based on draws 2,001–3,800 (the first 10% after burn-in) and draws 11,001–20,000 (the last 50% after burn-in), Geweke's (1992) convergence diagnostic is less than 1.96 in absolute value for all parameters, showing that convergence of the MCMC algorithm has been achieved.

DATA

We obtain information on loans from the DealScan database produced by the Loan Pricing Corporation. We obtain information on bank characteristics by matching the banks in DealScan to those in the Reports of Condition and Income (known as the Call reports, from the Federal Reserve Board). And we obtain information on firm characteristics by matching the firms in DealScan to those in the Compustat database (a product of Standard & Poor's).

Sample

The DealScan database contains detailed information on lending to large businesses in the U.S. dating back to 1988. For each loan facility, DealScan reports the identities of the borrower and the lender, the pricing information (spread and fees), and the information on non-price loan characteristics, such as maturity, secured status, purpose of the loan, and type of the loan.

We focus on loan facilities between U.S. banks and U.S. firms from 1996 to 2003, and divide them into 16 markets, each containing the lenders and the borrowers in a same half-year: January to June or July to December.[5] We use data on banks' and firms' characteristics from the quarter that precedes the market. Our sample consists of 1,369 loan facilities between 455 banks and 1,369 firms.

Variables

Information on loan spreads comes from the all-in spread drawn (AIS) reported in the DealScan database. The AIS is expressed as a markup over the London interbank offering rate (LIBOR). It equals the sum of the coupon spread, the annual fee, and any one-time fee divided by the loan maturity. In DealScan, the AIS is given in basis points (1 basis point = 0.01%). We divide the AIS by 100 to obtain r_{ij}, expressed in percentage points.

The matching of banks and firms (μ) is given by the names of the matched agents recorded in our loan facilities data.

The right-hand side of the spread equation includes a constant, year dummies, and three groups of exogenous variables. The first group includes the following bank characteristics: salaries-expenses ratio (salaries and benefits/total operating expenses), capital-assets ratio (total equity capital/total assets), ratio of cash to total assets (cash/total assets), and four size dummies. Each size dummy corresponds to one-fifth of the banks with the cutoffs being approximately \$5 billion, \$13 billion, \$32 billion, and \$76 billion in assets. The size dummy for the smallest one-fifth is dropped. The size dummies enable us to detect nonlinear relationships between sizes and loan spreads.

The second group includes the following firm characteristics: leverage ratio (total debt/total assets), current ratio (current assets/current liabilities), ratio of PP&E to total assets (PP&E/total assets), and four size dummies. Each size dummy corresponds to one-fifth of the firms with the cutoffs being approximately \$65 million, \$200 million, \$500 million, and \$1,500 million in assets. The size dummy for the smallest one-fifth is dropped.

The third group includes the following non-price loan characteristics: maturity (in months), natural log of facility size, purpose dummies, type dummies, and a secured dummy. The loan purposes reported in DealScan are combined into five categories: acquisition (acquisition lines and takeover), general (corporate purposes and working capital), miscellaneous (capital expenditure, equipment purchase, IPO related finance, mortgage warehouse, project finance, purchase hardware, real estate, securities purchase, spinoff, stock buyback, telecom build-out, and trade finance), recapitalization (debt repayment/debt consolidation/refinancing and recapitalization), and other. The purpose dummy for "other" is dropped. There are three categories of loan types: revolver/line <1 year (a revolving credit line whose duration is less than one year), revolver/line ≥ 1 year, and other. The type dummy for "other" is dropped. A secured dummy is also included, which equals one if the borrower is required to pledge collateral for the loan, and equals zero otherwise.

The right-hand side variables in the quality index equations are bank characteristics and firm characteristics, respectively. Bank assets, firm assets, and facility size are deflated using the GDP (chained) price index

Table 1. Variable Definitions and Sources.

Variable	Definition	Source
Dependent variable		
Loan spread	All-in spread drawn above LIBOR/100; in percentage points	DealScan
Independent variables		
Bank characteristics		
Salaries-expenses ratio	Salaries and benefits/total operating expenses	Call reports
Capital-assets ratio	Total equity capital/total assets	Call reports
Ratio of cash to total assets	Cash/Total assets	Call reports
Bank_Size2	Dummy = 1 if the bank has \$5–13 billion assets	Call reports
Bank_Size3	Dummy = 1 if the bank has \$13–32 billion assets	Call reports
Bank_Size4	Dummy = 1 if the bank has \$32–76 billion assets	Call reports
Bank_Size5	Dummy = 1 if the bank has more than \$76 billion assets	Call reports
Firm characteristics		
Leverage ratio	Total debt/total assets	Compustat
Current ratio	Current assets/current liabilities	Compustat
Ratio of property, plant, and equipment to total assets	PP&E/Total assets	Compustat
Firm_Size2	Dummy = 1 if the firm has \$65–200 million assets	Compustat
Firm_Size3	Dummy = 1 if the firm has \$200–500 million assets	Compustat
Firm_Size4	Dummy = 1 if the firm has \$500–1,500 million assets	Compustat
Firm_Size5	Dummy = 1 if the firm has more than \$1,500 million assets	Compustat
Non-price loan characteristics		
Maturity	Loan facility length in months	DealScan
Natural log of facility size	Log(tranche amount)	DealScan
Acquisition	Dummy = 1 if specific purpose is acquisition	DealScan
General	Dummy = 1 if specific purpose is general	DealScan
Miscellaneous	Dummy = 1 if specific purpose is miscellaneous	DealScan
Recapitalization	Dummy = 1 if specific purpose is recapitalization	DealScan
Revolver/Line < 1 Year	Dummy = 1 if the loan is a revolving credit line with duration < 1 year	DealScan
Revolver/Line ≥ 1 Year	Dummy = 1 if the loan is a revolving credit line with duration ≥ 1 year	DealScan
Secured	Dummy = 1 if the loan is secured	DealScan

Table 2. Summary Statistics.

Variable	Number of Observations	Mean	Standard Deviation	Minimum	Maximum
Loan spread	1,369	1.89	1.20	0.15	10.80
Salaries-expenses ratio	455	0.25	0.09	0.03	0.59
Capital-assets ratio	455	0.09	0.03	0.05	0.32
Ratio of cash to total assets	455	0.07	0.04	3.35E-05	0.44
Bank assets ($ million)	455	72311.19	124219.52	15.98	625255.55
Leverage ratio	1,369	0.26	0.23	0	1.95
Current ratio	1,369	2.26	2.29	0.08	31.68
Ratio of PP&E to total assets	1,369	0.31	0.25	0	0.96
Firm assets ($ million)	1,369	1807.32	6327.17	1.06	172827.99
Maturity	1,369	32.91	22.97	2	280
Facility size ($ million)	1,369	192.54	491.94	0.20	10202
Acquisition	1,369	0.10	0.30	0	1
General	1,369	0.46	0.50	0	1
Miscellaneous	1,369	0.04	0.21	0	1
Recapitalization	1,369	0.29	0.45	0	1
Revolver/Line < 1 year	1,369	0.06	0.24	0	1
Revolver/Line ≥ 1 year	1,369	0.67	0.47	0	1
Secured status	1,369	0.66	0.48	0	1

reported in the Historical Tables in the Budget of the U.S. Government for Fiscal Year 2005, with the year 2000 being the base year. Table 1 provides the definitions and sources of the variables, and Table 2 presents summary statistics.

FINDINGS

In this section, we first present evidence that positive assortative matching of sizes is prevalent in the loan market, that is, large banks tend to match with large firms, and vice versa. We then show that for agents on both sides of the market there are similar relationships between quality and size: after controlling for other factors, the medium-sized agents are regarded as having the highest quality, followed by the largest agents, and the smallest agents are at the bottom of the list. Consequently there are similar size rankings on both sides, which explain the positive assortative matching of sizes. Liquidity is also a consideration in choosing partners. Finally, the effects of bank characteristics, firm characteristics, and non-price loan characteristics on loan spreads are examined.

Positive Assortative Matching of Sizes

It is recognized in the literature that large banks tend to lend to large firms and vice versa. See, for example, Hubbard et al. (2002) and Berger, Miller, Peterson, Rajan, and Stein (2005). To verify this positive assortative matching of sizes, two OLS regressions using the matched pairs are run: the bank's size (natural log of total assets) on the firm's characteristics and the firm's size (natural log of total assets) on the bank's characteristics. The results (not reported) show that in matched pairs the bank's size and the firm's size are strongly positively correlated. The coefficients on partner's size are both positive and have t statistics around 20, indicating that there is indeed positive assortative matching of sizes.

Quality Indexes

Table 3 reports the posterior means and standard deviations of the coefficients in the quality index Eqs. (5) and (6).

Sizes of the Agents

All the size dummies have positive coefficients and for most of them the 90% HPDIs do not include zero, indicating that on both sides of the market, the group of the smallest agents – the omitted group – is considered the worst in terms of quality.[6] On the lenders' side, the smallest banks suffer from severe lending constraints and low reputation associated with their small sizes. On the borrowers' side, the smallest firms are considered the least creditworthy because they have low repaying ability and less diversified assets, and lack well-documented track records.

A closer look at the coefficients reveals that on both sides of the market, it is the medium-sized agents who have the highest quality. Banks with assets between the 40th and the 80th percentiles (group 3 and group 4) and firms with assets between the 40th and the 60th percentiles (group 3) are

Table 3. Estimates of Quality Index Equations.

	Mean	Standard Deviation
Bank quality index		
Salaries-expenses ratio	0.17	0.58
Capital-assets ratio	0.31	1.89
Ratio of cash to total assets	2.58	1.17**
Bank_Size2	0.41	0.15***
Bank_Size3	0.53	0.15***
Bank_Size4	0.54	0.15***
Bank_Size5	0.30	0.15**
Firm quality index		
Leverage ratio	−0.05	0.13
Current ratio	0.03	0.01**
Ratio of PP&E to total assets	0.02	0.12
Firm_Size2	0.11	0.08
Firm_Size3	0.29	0.09***
Firm_Size4	0.17	0.09*
Firm_Size5	0.11	0.09
κ	0.17	0.09**
λ	−0.10	0.08
$1/\sigma_v^2$	1.51	0.06***

The dependent variables are the quality indexes.
Posterior means and standard deviations are based on 20,000 draws from the conditional posterior distributions, discarding the first 2,000 as burn-in draws.
*, **, and *** indicate that zero is not contained in the 90%, 95%, and 99% highest posterior density intervals, respectively.

the most attractive. The largest agents are less attractive than the medium-sized ones, but are better than the smallest ones.

As the size of a bank increases, it has lower risk and greater lending capacity, making it more attractive. On the other hand, larger banks typically have more severe information distortion problems, and their loan officers have weaker incentives in collecting and processing borrower information. For the group of the largest banks, these negative effects outweigh the banks' advantages over the medium-sized banks in terms of risk and lending capacity.

Similarly, as the size of a firm increases, its repaying ability grows, its assets are more diversified, and it poses smaller information asymmetries. However, the group of the largest firms are less attractive than the medium-sized firms because lending to the largest firms means that the bank's assets will be less diversified and that its control over the firms' investment decisions will be weaker, and these disadvantages of the largest firms outweigh their advantages over the medium-sized firms.

Note that the negative effect of a firm's large size on its quality is likely understated, since in our model the limit on the number of loans a bank can make is binding and the limit on the total amount of loans is nonbinding. If we take into account that sometimes the binding limit is on the total amount of loans, then lending to a large firm should be less attractive: the size of the loan will typically be large, which means that the bank may have to sacrifice more than one lending opportunity elsewhere in order to lend to this large firm, impairing the bank's assets diversification.

The size rankings for both sides of the loan market are similar. From the highest quality to the lowest quality, the size ranking is 4-3-2-5-1 for the banks and 3-4-2-5-1 for the firms, where the numbers represent the size groups. All else being equal, the medium-sized agents have higher quality than the largest ones, which in turn have higher quality than the smallest ones. That explains the positive assortative matching of sizes. Medium-sized banks lend to medium-sized firms because both groups are the top candidates on their respective sides. Among the remaining agents, who face restricted choice sets, the largest banks and the largest firms are the top candidates, so they are matched. Finally, the smallest banks and the smallest firms have the lowest quality, and they have no choice but to match with each other.

Other Factors

On the banks' side, the coefficient on the ratio of cash to total assets is positive with a 95% HPDI that does not include zero, reflecting the negative impact of banks' liquidity risk on their quality. The coefficients on the salaries-expenses ratio and the capital-assets ratio are both positive, consistent with the hypothesis that banks with higher monitoring ability and/or higher capital adequacy are more attractive. Zero is included in the 90% HPDIs for these two coefficients, though, suggesting that in our sample the influence of these two ratios on the banks' quality is weak.

On the firms' side, the current ratio has a positive coefficient whose 95% HPDI does not include zero, supporting the view that a firm's quality is negatively related to its risk, especially the liquidity risk, for which the current ratio is a proxy. The other two variables both have the expected signs. The coefficient on the leverage ratio is negative, indicating that firms with higher leverage ratios are less attractive because they are riskier. The coefficient on the ratio of PP&E to total assets has a positive sign, suggesting that firms with relatively more tangible assets have higher quality because they pose smaller information asymmetries. The fact that the 90% HPDIs for these two coefficients include zero indicates that in our sample these two ratios are not important concerns of the banks when they rank the borrowers.

Effects on Matching Preference

To assess the importance of a variable in the matching process, we calculate an agent's probability advantage in being preferred to another agent due to a difference in that variable, everything else being equal. In order to obtain assessment that is independent of our choice of the ratio variables' units, we examine certain percentiles of these variables in the data. Table 4 reports the 10th, 30th, 50th, 70th, and 90th percentiles of each of the ratio variables.

Table 5 uses such percentiles and reports the variables' effects on matching preferences. Specifically, for each variable, the agents (banks or firms) are divided into five percentile groups: 0th–20th, 20th–40th, 40th–60th, 60th–80th, and 80th–100th. For the size variables, these groups simply correspond to the size groups in Table 3. For the ratio variables, the median of each group is used to represent that group. Each cell in Table 5 then reports one of the last four group's probability advantage in being preferred to the default group (the lowest 20%), everything else being equal.

The probability advantage that bank i has relative to bank i' is

$$\begin{aligned}
\Pr(\boldsymbol{B}_i'\beta + \eta_i > \boldsymbol{B}_{i'}'\beta + \eta_{i'}) - \Pr(\boldsymbol{B}_{i'}'\beta + \eta_{i'} > \boldsymbol{B}_i'\beta + \eta_i) \\
= 2 \times \Pr(\boldsymbol{B}_i'\beta + \eta_i > \boldsymbol{B}_{i'}'\beta + \eta_{i'}) - 1 \\
= 2 \times \Pr(\eta_{i'} - \eta_i < \boldsymbol{B}_i'\beta - \boldsymbol{B}_{i'}'\beta) - 1 \\
= 2 \times \Phi\left(\frac{\boldsymbol{B}_i'\beta - \boldsymbol{B}_{i'}'\beta}{\sqrt{2}}\right) - 1
\end{aligned}$$

Table 4. 10th, 30th, 50th, 70th, and 90th Percentiles of Ratio Variables.

	Percentiles				
	10th	30th	50th	70th	90th
Bank ratio variables					
Salaries-expenses ratio	0.13	0.20	0.24	0.28	0.35
Capital-assets ratio	0.06	0.07	0.08	0.09	0.11
Ratio of cash to total assets	0.03	0.05	0.06	0.08	0.12
Firm ratio variables					
Leverage ratio	0.00	0.10	0.23	0.36	0.53
Current ratio	0.76	1.28	1.72	2.39	3.95
Ratio of PP&E to total assets	0.05	0.13	0.22	0.40	0.73

Table 5. Effects of Bank and Firm Characteristics on Matching Preference.

	Percentile Groups			
	20th–40th	40th–60th	60th–80th	80th–100th
Bank characteristics				
Salaries-expenses ratio	0.66%	1.03%	1.41%	2.01%
Capital-assets ratio	0.18%	0.33%	0.49%	0.88%
Ratio of cash to total assets	2.80%	5.26%	7.96%	13.80%
Bank size	22.53%	28.94%	29.48%	16.76%
Firm characteristics				
Leverage ratio	−0.26%	−0.59%	−0.94%	−1.39%
Current ratio	0.86%	1.60%	2.71%	5.29%
Ratio of PP&E to total assets	0.09%	0.20%	0.40%	0.78%
Firm size	6.41%	16.23%	9.29%	6.38%

Each cell reports the group's probability advantage in being preferred to the default group (the lowest 20%), everything else being equal. For a ratio variable, the median of each group is used to represent that group.

where $\Phi(\cdot)$ is the standard normal cdf.[7] The probability advantage that firm j has relative to firm j' is obtained analogously. Consider a borrower's choice between two banks. If the two banks have no difference in their observed characteristics, then the choice is completely determined by the unobserved quality, and the probability of each bank being preferred to the other is 50%. Now suppose one bank is in the smallest size group and the other is in the middle size group, then the probability that the middle-sized bank is preferred to the small bank is 64.47%, representing a probability advantage that equals $64.47 - 35.53\% = 28.94\%$ and giving the middle-sized bank a nearly 2-to-1 advantage if both hope to match with the same borrower. Table 5 shows that most of the size dummies have positive and noticeable effects, indicating that size plays an important role in agents' quality. In particular, medium-sized agents are the most preferred partners on both sides of the market. Furthermore, the two proxies for liquidity (the ratio of cash to total assets for banks and the current ratio for firms) have the largest effects among the ratio variables, suggesting that liquidity is also a consideration in choosing partners. For example, a bank with a ratio of cash to total assets in the highest 20% enjoys a probability advantage of 13.80% relative to a bank with a ratio in the lowest 20%. These effects, however, are not so substantial as those of the size dummies, and we therefore conclude that size appears to be the most important factor in the matching.

Loan Spread Determinants

The covariance between the error terms in the loan spread equation and the bank quality index equation, κ, is found to have a 95% HPDI that does not include zero (Table 3). That is evidence that the matching process is correlated with the loan spread determination and cannot be ignored. To see that the m_{ij}'s (i.e., the match indicators) are correlated with the ε_{ij}'s, rewrite the spread equation as follows, noting that each firm borrows once in a market:

$$r_j = \alpha_0 + m_j'\boldsymbol{B}\alpha_1 + \boldsymbol{F}_j'\alpha_2 + \boldsymbol{N}_j'\alpha_3 + \varepsilon_j \tag{11}$$

$$= \alpha_0 + m_j'\boldsymbol{B}\alpha_1 + \boldsymbol{F}_j'\alpha_2 + \boldsymbol{N}_j'\alpha_3 + \kappa m'_j\eta + \lambda\delta_j + \nu_j, \nu_j \sim N(0, \sigma_\nu^2) \tag{12}$$

where r_j is the spread that firm j pays, $m_j = (m_{1j}, m_{2j}, \ldots, m_{Ij})'$ is the vector of match indicators, $\boldsymbol{B} = (\boldsymbol{B}_1, \boldsymbol{B}_2, \ldots, \boldsymbol{B}_I)'$ is the matrix of bank characteristics, $\boldsymbol{N}_j$ is the non-price loan characteristics of the loan firm j borrows, and $\eta = (\eta_1, \eta_2, \ldots, \eta_I)'$ is the vector of error terms in the bank quality index equation. If m_j were in fact independent of ε_j – as it would be if firms were randomly matched to banks – then m_j would be exogenous in Eq. (11). However, the evidence above against $\kappa = 0$ implies that m_j is correlated with ε_j. Thus the regressors are correlated with the error term, giving rise to an endogeneity problem. In this article, the inclusion of a two-sided matching model to supplement the spread equation overcomes this endogeneity problem. Estimates of the spread equation are presented in Table 6.

Bank Characteristics

The coefficients on the bank size dummies are all negative and most of them have 90% HPDIs that do not include zero, supporting the view that larger banks are likely to have better diversified assets and hence lower risk, so that they charge lower loan spreads. As expected, these coefficients exhibit a downward trend. Compared to banks with assets below the 20th percentile, banks with assets between the 20th and the 60th percentiles charge loan spreads that are around 15 basis points lower, whereas banks with assets above the 60th percentile charge loan spreads that are nearly 30 basis points lower.

The salaries-expenses ratio has a positive coefficient whose 99% HPDI does not include zero, showing that banks with superior monitoring ability indeed charge higher loan spreads. The coefficients on the capital-assets ratio and the ratio of cash to total assets have 90% HPDIs that include

Table 6. Estimates of Loan Spread Equation, Controlling for Endogenous Matching.

	Mean	Standard Deviation
Constant	1.60	0.21***
Salaries-expenses ratio	1.83	0.33***
Capital-assets ratio	1.51	1.19
Ratio of cash to total assets	0.15	0.68
Bank_Size2	−0.18	0.10*
Bank_Size3	−0.14	0.11
Bank_Size4	−0.27	0.10***
Bank_Size5	−0.28	0.08***
Leverage ratio	0.91	0.11***
Current ratio	−0.04	0.01***
Ratio of PP&E to total assets	−0.07	0.10
Firm_Size2	−0.22	0.08***
Firm_Size3	−0.32	0.10***
Firm_Size4	−0.27	0.11**
Firm_Size5	−0.46	0.13***
Maturity	0.00	0.00
Natural log of facility size	−0.20	0.02***
Acquisition	0.04	0.11
General	0.02	0.09
Miscellaneous	0.20	0.13
Recapitalization	0.06	0.09
Revolver/Line < 1 year	0.16	0.11
Revolver/Line ≥1 year	−0.11	0.06*
Secured	0.88	0.06***

The dependent variable is the loan spread.
Posterior means and standard deviations are based on 20,000 draws from the conditional posterior distributions, discarding the first 2,000 as burn-in draws.
*, **, and *** indicate that zero is not contained in the 90%, 95%, and 99% highest posterior density intervals, respectively.
Dummies for years 1997–2003 are included on the RHS of the spread equation.

zero, suggesting that in our sample, banks' capital adequacy risk and liquidity risk do not have significant impact on loan spreads.

To ensure that our assessment of the ratio variables' impact on loan spread is independent of our choice of these variables' units, we again use the percentiles reported in Table 4 to calculate the differences in the spreads charged by banks in different percentile groups. The results are reported in Table 7. For example, the table shows that a bank with a salaries-expenses

Table 7. Effects of Bank and Firm Characteristics on Loan Spread.

	Percentile Groups			
	20th–40th	40th–60th	60th–80th	80th–100th
Bank characteristics				
Salaries-expenses ratio	0.13	0.20	0.27	0.39
Capital-assets ratio	0.02	0.03	0.04	0.08
Ratio of cash to total assets	0.00	0.01	0.01	0.01
Bank size	−0.18	−0.14	−0.27	−0.28
Firm characteristics				
Leverage ratio	0.09	0.20	0.32	0.48
Current ratio	−0.02	−0.04	−0.06	−0.13
Ratio of PP&E to total assets	−0.01	−0.01	−0.02	−0.05
Firm size	−0.22	−0.32	−0.27	−0.46

Each cell reports the difference in loan spread (in percentage points) between the group and the default group (the lowest 20%), everything else being equal. For a ratio variable, the median of each group is used to represent that group.

ratio in the highest 20% charges a premium of 39 basis points relative to a bank with a ratio in the lowest 20%. In our sample, the average loan spread is 1.89%, or 189 basis points, so a 39 basis point premium represents an increase of more than 20%, clear evidence that banks charge a premium for superior monitoring ability.

Firm Characteristics

In Table 6, all the firm size dummies have negative coefficients whose 95% HPDIs do not include zero, consistent with the hypothesis that larger firms are charged lower loan spreads because they are less risky and have lower degrees of information opacity. The coefficients on the firm size dummies also exhibit a downward trend. For example, compared to firms with assets below the 20th percentile, firms with assets between the 20th and the 40th percentiles are charged loan spreads that are 22 basis points lower, whereas firms with assets above the 80th percentile are charged loan spreads that are 46 basis points lower.

Two firm ratios have 99% HPDIs that do not include zero: the leverage ratio (positive) and the current ratio (negative). A higher leverage ratio or a lower current ratio (indicating a lower liquidity) represents a higher borrower risk, so the signs of the coefficients confirm that firms with higher risk are charged higher loan spreads. The coefficient on the ratio of PP&E

to total assets has a 90% HPDI that includes zero, suggesting that the ratio does not significantly affect borrowers' costs of funds.

Table 7 shows the characteristics' impact on loan spread. For example, we see that a firm with a leverage ratio in the highest 20% is charged a premium of 48 basis points relative to a firm with a ratio in the lowest 20%. On the other hand, a firm with a current ratio in the highest 20% is given a discount of 13 basis points relative to a firm with a ratio in the lowest 20%. These numbers attest to the substantial impact of firms' leverage and liquidity on loan spreads charged.

Non-Price Loan Characteristics

In Table 6, three non-price loan characteristics have coefficients whose 90% HPDIs do not include zero: the natural log of facility size, the revolver/line > =1 year dummy, and the secured dummy.

The negative coefficient on the natural log of facility size is likely due to economies of scale in bank lending. The processes of loan approval, monitoring, and review are relatively labor intensive, and the labor costs in these processes increase less than proportionally when the size of the loan increases. As a result, a larger loan has a lower average labor costs and is therefore charged a lower loan spread.

The dummy for revolving credit lines whose durations are greater than or equal to one year has a negative coefficient. Since that type of loans are by far the most common, accounting for 67% of all loans, the negative coefficient may reflect that other types of loans are nonstandard or even custom-made, and are charged higher loan spreads to compensate for the banks' extra administrative costs resulting from the loans' nonstandard nature.

Related to the interpretation of the secured dummy, there are two major theories on the relationship between collateral and risk. In the first theory (referred to as the "sorting-by-observed-risk paradigm" by Berger & Udell, 1990), observably risky borrowers are *required* to pledge collateral, while observably safe borrowers are not. In the second theory (referred to as the "sorting-by-private-information paradigm" by Berger & Udell), because of informational asymmetry, borrower risk is unobservable to the banks and certain borrowers *choose* to pledge collateral to signal their quality and/or to lower borrowing costs. While it is likely that both theories apply to some cases, Berger and Udell (1990) find that empirically the sorting-by-observed-risk paradigm clearly dominates the sorting-by-private-information paradigm (also see the references and anecdotal evidence cited in their paper, e.g., on p. 23). Furthermore, given the nature of the loans included in our sample – large bank loans made to large and publicly traded companies, informational asymmetry is not a first-order concern. Therefore, the sorting-by-observed-risk paradigm is most relevant here and we thus take the secured status of a loan as a requirement of the bank due to the borrower being judged as risky, rather than a choice of the borrower (empirically testing between the two theories is beyond the scope of this article).

The sorting-by-observed-risk interpretation is also consistent with the common definition of an unsecured loan. According to Fitch (2006), an unsecured loan is also called a character loan or a good faith loan, and is granted by the lender on the strength of the borrower's creditworthiness, rather than a pledge of assets as collateral. The coefficient on the secured dummy reported in Table 6 shows that a sizeable 88 basis point premium is charged if the borrower is below the threshold for an unsecured loan, consistent with the finding in prior empirical studies (e.g., Berger & Udell, 1990; Focarelli, Pozzolo, & Casolaro, 2008; John et al., 2003) that the value of the recourse against collateral does not fully offset the higher risk of secured borrowers.

Loan Spread Determinants: Effects of Controlling for Endogenous Matching

In this subsection, we consider the reduced-form results from estimating the loan spread equation ignoring the matching process. Comparing these results to the ones we report earlier allows us to examine the effects of controlling for the endogenous matching.

Comparison of Estimates

Here we compare the estimates of the loan spread equation presented in Table 6 (controlling for the endogenous matching; call them $\hat{\theta}$) and Table 8 (OLS estimates ignoring the endogenous matching; call them $\tilde{\theta}$). The average absolute percentage difference, defined as the average of $|(\tilde{\theta}-\hat{\theta})/\hat{\theta}|$ across all the variables, is 23%. Eight variables (the bank's ratio of cash to total assets, the firm's current ratio, and six size dummies) are significant in the endogenous matching process, in the sense that they have 90% HPDIs that do not include zero in the quality index equations. As expected, it is on those eight variables that the two sets of estimates differ the most – the average absolute percentage difference for those variables is 39% (Table 9). These differences suggest that it is important to control for the endogenous

Table 8. OLS Estimates of Loan Spread Equation, Ignoring Endogenous Matching.

	Coefficient	Standard Error
Constant	1.67	0.20***
Salaries-expenses ratio	1.83	0.31***
Capital-assets ratio	1.53	1.13
Ratio of cash to total assets	−0.11	0.61
Bank_Size2	−0.21	0.09**
Bank_Size3	−0.21	0.09**
Bank_Size4	−0.34	0.08***
Bank_Size5	−0.32	0.08***
Leverage ratio	0.89	0.11***
Current ratio	−0.04	0.01***
Ratio of PP&E to total assets	−0.07	0.10
Firm_Size2	−0.21	0.08***
Firm_Size3	−0.28	0.09***
Firm_Size4	−0.25	0.11**
Firm_Size5	−0.44	0.13***
Maturity	0.00	0.00
Natural log of facility size	−0.19	0.03***
Acquisition	0.03	0.11
General	0.03	0.09
Miscellaneous	0.20	0.13
Recapitalization	0.05	0.10
Revolver/Line < 1 year	0.16	0.11
Revolver/Line ≥1 year	−0.11	0.06*
Secured	0.90	0.06***

The dependent variable is the loan spread.
*, **, and *** indicate significance at the 10%, 5%, and 1% levels, respectively.
Dummies for years 1997–2003 are included on the RHS of the spread equation.

matching. For instance, the spread differential between a bank in the smallest size group and a bank in the middle size group is overstated by 46% when the endogenous matching is ignored.

Directions of the Differences

The unobserved quality of banks has two components that affect the loan spreads in opposite directions: unobserved monitoring ability and unobserved risk. If the first component dominates, then the unobserved bank quality will be positively correlated with the loan spreads, because banks with higher unobserved monitoring ability have higher unobserved quality

Table 9. Comparison: Estimates of Loan Spread Equation.

	OLS	Controlling for Endogenous Matching	$\lvert\Delta\%\rvert$
Bank's ratio of cash to total assets	−0.11	0.15	175%
Bank_Size2	−0.21	−0.18	18%
Bank_Size3	−0.21	−0.14	46%
Bank_Size4	−0.34	−0.27	26%
Bank_Size5	−0.32	−0.28	14%
Firm's current ratio	−0.04	−0.04	7%
Firm_Size3	−0.28	−0.32	13%
Firm_Size4	−0.25	−0.27	9%
			Average: 39%

The dependent variable is the loan spread.
The variables in the quality index equations for which the 90% HPDIs do not include zero are reported.
$\lvert\Delta\%\rvert$ is the absolute percentage difference.

and will charge higher loan spreads, all else being equal. On the other hand, if the second component dominates, then the unobserved bank quality will be negatively correlated with the loan spreads, because banks with lower unobserved risk have higher unobserved quality and will charge lower loan spreads, all else being equal. The positive sign of κ (reported in Table 3) shows that the unobserved monitoring ability dominates the unobserved risk to be the main component in banks' unobserved quality. The result is an indication that the proxies for banks' risk do a better job than the proxy for banks' monitoring ability.

The unobserved quality of firms has two components that affect the loan spreads in the same direction: unobserved risk and unobserved information opacity. Firms with either higher unobserved risk or higher degrees of unobserved information opacity have lower unobserved quality and are charged higher loan spreads, all else being equal. The negative sign of λ (reported in Table 3) is consistent with this relationship.

Given the signs of κ and λ, the directions of the differences between the two sets of estimates (OLS vs. controlling for the endogenous matching) of the loan spread equation are intuitively explained. Five coefficients in the bank quality index equation have 90% HPDIs that do not include zero: the ratio of cash to total assets and the four size dummies. All these variables positively affect banks' quality. Now take the ratio of cash to total assets for example. Suppose all firms are identical except that they have different unobserved quality, and consider two banks that differ only in their ratios of cash to total assets. The bank with a higher ratio has a higher quality, so it matches with a firm that has a higher unobserved quality. Since λ is negative, the higher unobserved quality of the firm means that the spread charged by this bank has a smaller unobserved component. In an OLS regression of the loan spread equation, the effect of that smaller unobserved component on the loan spread is attributed to the difference in the ratio, resulting in underestimation (downward bias) of the ratio's coefficient. Similarly, the coefficients on the four bank size dummies are all underestimated in the OLS regression.

In the firm quality index equation, three coefficients have 90% HPDIs that do not include zero: the current ratio and two size dummies. All these variables positively affect firms' quality. Since κ is positive, by an analogous argument, the OLS regression of the loan spread equation should result in overestimation (upward bias) of the coefficients on all these variables. The results reported in Tables 6 and 8 confirm this prediction.

CONCLUSION

We have the potential to learn a lot about financial markets and the effects of monetary policy by investigating the pricing of bank loans. For example, empirical evidence on determinants of loan spreads can provide insights into risk premiums in financial contracting and transmission mechanisms of monetary policy. This article shows that there is endogenous matching in the bank loan market, and that we face an endogeneity problem in estimation of the loan spread equation when some characteristics of banks or firms are not perfectly observed and proxies are used. To control for the endogenous matching, we develop a two-sided matching model to supplement the loan spread equation. Because estimation of the model is numerically intensive, we choose a parsimonious specification to keep estimation feasible, focusing on a set of key variables. We obtain Bayesian inference using a Gibbs sampling algorithm with data augmentation, which transforms a high-dimensional integration problem into a simulation problem and overcomes the computational difficulty.

Using a sample of 1,369 U.S. loan facilities between 455 banks and 1,369 firms from 1996 to 2003, we find evidence of positive assortative matching of sizes in the market, that is, large banks tend to match with large firms, and vice versa. We then show that for agents on both sides of the market there are similar relationships between quality and size, which lead to similar size rankings for both sides and explain the positive assortative matching of sizes. Medium-sized banks and firms are the most preferred partners. Liquidity is also a consideration in choosing partners. Furthermore, banks with higher monitoring ability charge higher spreads, whereas larger banks charge lower spreads. On the other side of the market, firms that are more leveraged or less liquid are charged higher spreads, whereas larger firms are charged lower spreads.

The two-sided matching model not only addresses the endogeneity problem in estimation of the loan spread equation, but also provides a way to assess agents' quality and to understand how agents choose each other. The latter is an important issue in various two-sided markets. For instance, in an empirical study of academic achievements or job outcomes of college students, a two-sided matching model can be used to estimate the colleges' quality and the students' ability. Other examples include the matchings between teams and athletes (in NBA, for instance), corporations and CEOs, firms and underwriters, and so on. Furthermore, the two-sided matching model enables us to identify the factors that contribute to agents' quality, which can point the way for agents who try to improve their standing, such as colleges that want to attract better students. This suggests that understanding the quality indexes can play an important role in such markets. We view those issues as interesting avenues for future research.

NOTES

1. See Rajan (1992) for a discussion on banks' control over borrowers' investment decisions.

2. A similar full information approach is used by Ackerberg and Botticini (2002) to overcome the endogeneity problem, in which they include an ordered probit matching equation to supplement the contract choice equation.

3. For the model to be identified, the sign of one of the parameters in β, γ, κ and λ must be specified, because both $(\beta, \gamma, \kappa, \lambda)$ and $(-\beta, -\gamma, -\kappa, -\lambda)$ would be admissible given the same observed (endogenous and exogenous) variables. Here we follow theory prediction and assume λ to be non-positive. If the truth is $\lambda>0$, we would obtain a set of estimates of the quality index equations in which all the good factors have negative coefficients and all the bad factors have positive coefficients. Theory allows us to determine which of the two opposite scenarios is reasonable.

4. The sufficient condition for convergence set forth in Roberts and Smith (1994) is satisfied.

5. Changing the market definition from a half-year to a year leaves our main findings unaffected.

6. HPDIs are used for model comparison in an ad hoc fashion. With two models $M_1 : \beta_j = 0$ and $M_2 : \beta_j \neq 0$, a finding that the HPDI under M_2 does not include zero is evidence against M_1. On the other hand, using posterior odds ratios for model comparison that involves equality restrictions typically requires the elicitation of informative priors (see Koop, 2003, pp. 38–45).

7. Point estimate of the probability advantage is obtained as $2 \times E_{\beta|\mathbf{X},r,\mu} \times \Phi((\boldsymbol{B}_i'\beta - \boldsymbol{B}_{i'}'\beta)/\sqrt{2}) - 1$.

ACKNOWLEDGMENT

I thank Jan Brueckner, Linda Cohen, Joseph Harrington, Ivan Jeliazkov, Ali Khan, Robert Moffitt, Dale Poirier, Matt Shum, Tiemen Woutersen, and seminar participants at Brown, Iowa, Johns Hopkins, St. Louis Fed, UC Irvine, USC, Williams College, and the 13th Advances in Econometrics Conference for their helpful comments.

REFERENCES

Ackerberg, D. A., & Botticini, M. (2002). Endogenous matching and the empirical determinants of contract form. *Journal of Political Economy*, *110*(3), 564–91.

Albert, J., & Chib, S. (1993). Bayesian analysis of binary and polychotomous response data. *Journal of the American Statistical Association*, *88*, 669–79.

Allen, F. (1990). The market for information and the origin of financial intermediation. *Journal of Financial Intermediation*, *1*, 3–30.

Berger, A. N., Miller, N. H., Peterson, M. A., Rajan, R. G., & Stein, J. C. (2005). Does function follow organizational form? Evidence from the lending practices of large and small banks. *Journal of Financial Economics*, *6* (2), 237–69.

Berger, A. N., & Udell, G. F. (1990). Collateral, loan quality, and bank risk. *Journal of Monetary Economics*, *25*, 21–42.

Bhattacharya, H. (1997). *Banking strategy, credit appraisal and lending decisions: A risk-return framework*. Oxford University Press.

Billet, M., Flannery, M., & Garfinkel, J. (1995). The effect of lender identity on a borrowing firm's equity return. *Journal of Finance*, *50*(2), 699–718.

Brickley, J. A., Linck, J. S., & Smith, C. W. (2003). Boundaries of the firm: Evidence from the banking industry. *Journal of Financial Economics*, *70*, 351–83.

Chen, J., & Song, K. (2013). Two-sided matching in the loan market. *International Journal of Industrial Organization*, *31*, 145–52.

Coleman, A. D. F., Esho, N., & Sharpe, I. G. (2006). Does bank monitoring influence loan contract terms? *Journal of Financial Services Research*, *30*, 177–98.

Diamond, D. (1984). Financial intermediation and delegated monitoring. *Review of Economic Studies*, *51*, 393–414.

Diamond, D. (1991). Monitoring and reputation: The choice between bank loans and directly placed debt. *Journal of Political Economy*, *99*, 689–721.

Diamond, D., & Rajan, R. (2000). A theory of bank capital. *Journal of Finance*, *55*(6), 2431–65.

Fernando, C. S., Gatchev, V. A., & Spindt, P. A. (2005). Wanna dance? How firms and underwriters choose each other. *Journal of Finance*, *60*(5), 2437–69.

Fitch, T. (2006). *Dictionary of banking terms* (p. 496). Barron's Educational Series, Inc.

Focarelli, D., Pozzolo, A. F., & Casolaro, L. (2008). The pricing effect of certification on syndicated loans. *Journal of Monetary Economics*, *55*, 335–49.

Gale, D., & Shapley, L. (1962). College admissions and the stability of marriage. *American Mathematical Monthly*, *69*, 9–15.

Gelfand, A., & Smith, A. (1990). Sampling-based approaches to calculating marginal densities. *Journal of the American Statistical Association*, *85*, 398–409.

Geman, S., & Geman, D. (1984). Stochastic relaxation, Gibbs distributions and the Bayesian restoration of images. *IEEE Transactions on Pattern Analysis and Machine Intelligence*, *6*, 721–41.

Geweke, J. (1992). Evaluating the accuracy of sampling-based approaches to the calculation of posterior moments (with discussion). In J. M. Bernardo, J. O. Berger, A. P. Dawid, & A. F. M. Smith (Eds.), *Bayesian statistics* (Vol. 4, pp. 169–93). Oxford University Press.

Geweke, J. (1999). Using simulation methods for bayesian econometric models: Inference, development and communication (with discussion and rejoinder). *Econometric Reviews*, *18*, 1–126.

Geweke, J. (2004). Getting it right: Joint distribution tests of posterior simulators. *Journal of the American Statistical Association*, *99*, 799–804.

Geweke, J., Gowrisankaran, G., & Town, R. (2003). Bayesian inference for hospital quality in a selection model. *Econometrica*, *71*(4), 1215–39.

Hubbard, R. G., Kuttner, K. N., & Palia, D. N. (2002). Are there bank effects in borrowers' costs of funds? Evidence from a matched sample of borrowers and banks. *Journal of Business*, *75*, 559–81.

John, K., Lynch, A., & Puri, M. (2003). Credit ratings, collateral, and loan characteristics: Implications for yield. *Journal of Business*, *76*, 371–409.

Johnson, S. (1997). The effects of bank reputation on the value of bank loan agreements. *Journal of Accounting, Auditing and Finance*, *24*, 83–100.

Kashyap, A.K., & Stein, J.C. (1994). Monetary Policy and Bank Lending. In N. G. Mankiw (Ed.), *Monetary policy* (pp. 221–56). University of Chicago Press.

Koop, G. (2003). *Bayesian econometrics*. Wiley.

Lancaster, T. (1997). Exact structural inference in optimal job-search models. *Journal of Business and Economic Statistics*, *15*(2), 165–79.

Leland, H., & Pyle, D. (1977). Informational asymmetries, financial structure and financial intermediation. *Journal of Finance*, *32*(2), 371–87.

Miller, S., & Bavaria, S. (2003, October). *A guide to the U.S. loan market*. Standard & Poor's. Retrieve from https://www.lcdcomps.com/d/pdf/LoanMarketguide.pdf

Park, M. (2008). *An empirical two-sided matching model of acquisitions: Understanding merger incentives and outcomes in the mutual fund industry*. Unpublished.

Raftery, A. E., & Lewis, S. (1992). How Many Iterations in the Gibbs Sampler? In J. M. Bernardo, J. O. Berger, A. P. Dawid, & A. F. M. Smith (Eds.), *Bayesian statistics* (Vol. 4, pp. 763–73). Oxford University Press.

Rajan, R. (1992). Insiders and outsiders: The choice between informed and arms-length debt. *Journal of Finance*, *47*, 1367–406.

Roberts, G. O., & Smith, A. F. M. (1994). Simple conditions for the convergence of the Gibbs sampler and metropolis-hastings algorithms. *Stochastic Processes and Their Applications*, *49*, 207–16.

Roth, A., & M. Sotomayor (1990). *Two-sided matching: A study in game-theoretic modeling and analysis*. Econometric Society Monograph Series. Cambridge: Cambridge University Press.

Sorensen, M. (2007). How smart is smart money? A two-sided matching model of venture capital. *Journal of Finance*, *62*, 2725–62.

Stoeckle, G. (2011, March). *Investment insights: Bank loans within the broader market*. Invesco. Retrieve from http://www.institutional.invesco.com/portal/file/invescoinst/pdf/II-BL2011-IVP-4-E.pdf

Tanner, T., & Wong, W. (1987). The calculation of posterior distributions by data augmentation. *Journal of the American Statistical Association*, *82*, 528–49.

Yago, G., & D. McCarthy (2004, October), *The U.S. leveraged loan market: A primer*. Milken Institute Research Report. Retrieve from http://www.milkeninstitute.org/pdf/loan_primer_1004.pdf

APPENDIX A: UNIQUENESS OF EQUILIBRIUM MATCHING

The existence of an equilibrium matching in the College Admissions Model is proved in Roth and Sotomayor (1990). Below we show that there exists a unique equilibrium matching in our model, which is a special case of the College Admissions Model.

Re-index the banks and the firms according to the preference orderings, so that $i \succ_j i'$, $\forall i > i'$, $\forall j$, and $j \succ_i j'$, $\forall j > j'$, $\forall i$, where $i \succ_j i'$ denotes that firm j prefers bank i to bank i' and $j \succ_i j'$ denotes that bank i prefers firm j to firm j'. Let q_{it} be the quota of bank i. The following J-step algorithm produces the unique equilibrium matching, in which there is perfect sorting. In step 1, firm J matches with bank I. In step 2, firm $J-1$ matches with bank I if $q_{It} \geq 2$, otherwise it matches with bank $I-1$. In step 3, firm $J-2$ matches with bank I if $q_{It} \geq 3$, otherwise it matches with bank $I-1$ if $q_{It} + q_{I-1,t} \geq 3$, otherwise it matches with bank $I-2$. And so on.

First, μ is an equilibrium matching. Suppose not, then there exists at least one blocking pair (i', j') such that $i' > \mu(j')$ and $j' > \min\{j : j \in \mu(i')\}$. That is a contradiction, since by construction if $i' > \mu(j')$ then $j'' > j'$, $\forall j'' \in \mu(i')$, so $j' > \min\{j : j \in \mu(i')\}$ can not be true.

Second, the equilibrium matching is unique. Suppose not, then there exists $\tilde{\mu} \neq \mu$ such that $\tilde{\mu}$ is also an equilibrium matching. There is at least one match that is in μ but not in $\tilde{\mu}$. Now consider the first step in the algorithm that forms a match that is not in $\tilde{\mu}$. Call that match (i', j'). It follows that $\min\{j : j \in \tilde{\mu}(i')\} < j'$ and that $\tilde{\mu}(j') < i'$, since all the matches formed in the earlier steps are in both μ and $\tilde{\mu}$. Therefore, (i', j') is a blocking pair for $\tilde{\mu}$, a contradiction.

APPENDIX B: INEQUALITIES CHARACTERIZING THE UNIQUE EQUILIBRIUM MATCHING

The unique equilibrium matching is characterized by a set of inequalities, based on the fact that there is no blocking bank-firm pair. For each bank, stability requires that its worst current borrower be better than any other firm whose current lender is worse than this bank. Similarly, for each firm, stability requires that its current lender be better than any other bank whose worst current borrower is worse than this firm.

Consider a matching in market t, μ_t. Suppose bank i and firm j are not matched in μ_t. (i,j) is a blocking pair iff $Q_j^f > \min_{j' \in \mu_t(i)} Q_{j'}^f$ and $Q_i^b > Q_{\mu_t(j)}^b$. So (i, j) is not a blocking pair iff $Q_j^f < \min_{j' \in \mu_t(i)} Q_{j'}^f$ or $Q_i^b < Q_{\mu_t(j)}^b$. Equivalently, (i, j) is not a blocking pair iff $Q_j^f < \overline{Q}_{ji}^f$ and $Q_i^b < \overline{Q}_{ij}^b$, where

$$\overline{Q}_{ji}^f = \begin{cases} \min\limits_{j' \in \mu_t(i)} Q_{j'}^f & \textit{if } Q_i^b > Q_{\mu_t(j)}^b \\ \infty & \text{otherwise} \end{cases}$$

and

$$\overline{Q}_{ij}^b = \begin{cases} Q_{\mu_t(j)}^b & \textit{if } Q_j^f > \min\limits_{j' \in \mu_t(i)} Q_{j'}^f \\ \infty & \text{otherwise} \end{cases}$$

Now suppose bank i and firm j are matched in μ_t. Bank i or firm j is part of a blocking pair iff $Q_j^f < \max_{j' \in f(i)} Q_{j'}^f$ or $Q_i^b < \max_{i' \in f(j)} Q_{i'}^b$, where $f(i)$ is the set of firms that do not currently borrow from bank i but would prefer to do so, and $f(j)$ is the set of banks that do not currently lend to firm j but would prefer to do so. These two sets contain the feasible deviations of the agents and are given by

$$f(i) = \{j \in J_t \backslash \mu_t(i) : Q_i^b > Q_{\mu_t(j)}^b\}$$

and

$$f(j) = \{i \in I_t \backslash \mu_t(j) : Q_j^f > \min_{j' \subset \mu_t(i)} Q_{j'}^f\}$$

Therefore, neither bank i nor firm j is part of a blocking pair iff $Q_j^f > \underline{Q}_{ji}^f$ and $Q_i^b > \underline{Q}_{ij}^b$, where $\underline{Q}_{ji}^f = \max_{j' \in f(i)} Q_{j'}^f$ and $\underline{Q}_{ij}^b = \max_{i' \in f(j)} Q_{i'}^b$.

Let μ_t^e denote the unique equilibrium matching in market t. The above analysis leads to the following characterization of the equilibrium matching:

$$\mu_t = \mu_t^e \Leftrightarrow Q_i^b \in (\underline{Q}_i^b, \overline{Q}_i^b), \forall i \in I_t \text{ and } Q_j^f \in (\underline{Q}_j^f, \overline{Q}_j^f), \forall j \in J_t$$

where

$$\underline{Q}_i^b = \max_{j \in \mu_t(i)} \underline{Q}_{ij}^b \quad \overline{Q}_i^b = \min_{j \notin \mu_t(i)} \overline{Q}_{ij}^b \quad \underline{Q}_j^f = \underline{Q}_{j,\mu_t(j)}^f \quad \overline{Q}_j^f = \min_{i \notin \mu_t(j)} \overline{Q}_{ji}^f$$

APPENDIX C: CONDITIONAL POSTERIOR DISTRIBUTIONS

We obtain the conditional posterior distributions by examining the kernels of the conditional posterior densities. The conditional posterior distribution of Q_i^b is $N(\hat{Q}_i^b, \hat{\sigma}^2_{Q_i^b})$ truncated to the interval $(\underline{Q}_i^b, \overline{Q}_i^b)$, where

$$\hat{Q}_i^b = \boldsymbol{B}_i'\beta + \frac{\kappa \sum_{j \in \mu_t(i)} [r_{ij} - \boldsymbol{U}_{ij}'\alpha - \lambda(Q_j^f - \boldsymbol{F}_j'\gamma)]}{\sigma_\nu^2 + \kappa^2 q_{it}}$$

and

$$\hat{\sigma}^2_{Q_i^b} = \frac{\sigma_\nu^2}{\sigma_\nu^2 + \kappa^2 q_{it}}$$

The conditional posterior distribution of Q_j^f is $N(\hat{Q}_j^f, \hat{\sigma}^2_{Q_j^f})$ truncated to the interval $(\underline{Q}_j^f, \overline{Q}_j^f)$, where

$$\hat{Q}_j^f = \boldsymbol{F}_j'\gamma + \frac{\lambda[r_{\mu_t(j),j} - \boldsymbol{U}_{\mu_t(j),j}'\alpha - \kappa(Q_{\mu_t(j)}^b - \boldsymbol{B}_{\mu_t(j)}'\beta)]}{\sigma_\nu^2 + \lambda^2}$$

and

$$\hat{\sigma}^2_{Q_j^f} = \frac{\sigma_\nu^2}{\sigma_\nu^2 + \lambda^2}$$

The prior distributions of α, β, γ, and κ are $N(\overline{\alpha}, \overline{\Sigma}_\alpha)$, $N(\overline{\beta}, \overline{\Sigma}_\beta)$, $N(\overline{\gamma}, \overline{\Sigma}_\gamma)$, and $N(\overline{\kappa}, \overline{\sigma}_\kappa^2)$, respectively. The prior distribution of λ is $N(\overline{\lambda}\ \overline{\boldsymbol{\sigma}}_\lambda^2)$, truncated on the right at 0. The prior distribution of $1/\sigma_\nu^2$ is gamma, $1/\sigma_\nu^2 \sim G(a, b)$, $a, b > 0$.

The conditional posterior distribution of α is $N(\hat{\alpha}, \hat{\Sigma}_\alpha)$, where

$$\hat{\Sigma}_\alpha = \left\{ \overline{\Sigma}_\alpha^{-1} + \sum_{t=1}^{T} \sum_{(i,j) \in \mu_t} \frac{1}{\sigma_\nu^2} \boldsymbol{U}_{ij}\boldsymbol{U}_{ij}' \right\}^{-1}$$

and

$$\hat{\alpha} = -\hat{\Sigma}_\alpha \left\{ -\overline{\Sigma}_\alpha^{-1}\overline{\alpha} - \sum_{t=1}^{T} \sum_{(i,j)\in\mu_t} \frac{1}{\sigma_\nu^2} \boldsymbol{U}_{ij}(r_{ij} - \kappa(Q_i^b - \boldsymbol{B}_i'\beta) - \lambda(Q_j^f - \boldsymbol{F}_j'\gamma)) \right\}$$

The conditional posterior distribution of β is $N(\hat{\beta}, \hat{\Sigma}_\beta)$, where

$$\hat{\Sigma}_\beta = \left\{ \overline{\Sigma}_\beta^{-1} + \sum_{t=1}^{T} \sum_{i\in I_t} \frac{\sigma_\nu^2 + \kappa^2 q_{it}}{\sigma_\nu^2} \boldsymbol{B}_i \boldsymbol{B}_i' \right\}^{-1}$$

and

$$\hat{\beta} = -\hat{\Sigma}_\beta \left\{ -\overline{\Sigma}_\beta^{-1}\overline{\beta} + \sum_{t=1}^{T} \left[\sum_{(i,j)\in\mu_t} \frac{\kappa}{\sigma_\nu^2} \boldsymbol{B}_i(r_{ij} - \boldsymbol{U}_{ij}'\alpha - \kappa Q_i^b - \lambda(Q_j^f - \boldsymbol{F}_j'\gamma)) - \sum_{i\in I_t} Q_i^b \boldsymbol{B}_i \right] \right\}$$

The conditional posterior distribution of γ is $N(\hat{\gamma}, \hat{\Sigma}_\gamma)$, where

$$\hat{\Sigma}_\gamma = \left\{ \overline{\Sigma}_\gamma^{-1} + \sum_{t=1}^{T} \sum_{j\in J_t} \frac{\sigma_\nu^2 + \lambda^2}{\sigma_\nu^2} \boldsymbol{F}_j \boldsymbol{F}_j' \right\}^{-1}$$

and

$$\hat{\gamma} = -\hat{\Sigma}_\gamma \left\{ -\overline{\Sigma}_\gamma^{-1}\overline{\gamma} + \sum_{t=1}^{T} \left[\sum_{(i,j)\in\mu_t} \frac{\lambda}{\sigma_\nu^2} \boldsymbol{F}_j(r_{ij} - \boldsymbol{U}_{ij}'\alpha - \kappa(Q_i^b - \boldsymbol{B}_i'\beta) - \lambda Q_j^f) - \sum_{j\in J_t} Q_j^f \boldsymbol{F}_j \right] \right\}$$

The conditional posterior distribution of κ is $N(\hat{\kappa}, \hat{\sigma}_\kappa^2)$, where

$$\hat{\sigma}_\kappa^2 = \left\{ \frac{1}{\overline{\sigma}_\kappa^2} + \sum_{t=1}^{T} \sum_{i\in I_t} \frac{q_{it}(Q_i^b - \boldsymbol{B}_i'\beta)^2}{\sigma_\nu^2} \right\}^{-1}$$

and

$$\hat{\kappa} = -\hat{\sigma}_\kappa^2 \left\{ -\frac{\overline{\kappa}}{\overline{\sigma}_\kappa^2} - \sum_{t=1}^{T} \sum_{(i,j)\in\mu_t} \frac{(r_{ij} - \boldsymbol{U}_{ij}'\alpha - \lambda(Q_j^f - \boldsymbol{F}_j'\gamma))(Q_i^b - \boldsymbol{B}_i'\beta)}{\sigma_\nu^2} \right\}$$

The conditional posterior distribution of λ is $N(\hat{\lambda}, \hat{\sigma}_\lambda^2)$ truncated on the right at 0, where

$$\hat{\sigma}_\lambda^2 = \left\{ \frac{1}{\overline{\sigma}_\lambda^2} + \sum_{t=1}^{T} \sum_{j\in J_t} \frac{(Q_j^f - \boldsymbol{F}_j'\gamma)^2}{\sigma_\nu^2} \right\}^{-1}$$

and

$$\hat{\lambda} = -\hat{\sigma}_{\lambda}^{2}\left\{-\frac{\bar{\lambda}}{\bar{\sigma}_{\lambda}^{2}} - \sum_{t=1}^{T}\sum_{(i,j)\in\mu_t}\frac{(r_{ij} - \boldsymbol{U}_{ij}'\alpha - \kappa(Q_i^b - \boldsymbol{B}_i'\beta))(Q_j^f - \boldsymbol{F}_j'\gamma)}{\sigma_{\nu}^{2}}\right\}$$

Let $n = \sum_{t=1}^{T} |J_t|$ denote the total number of loans in all the markets. The conditional posterior distribution of $1/\sigma_{\nu}^2$ is $G(\hat{a}, \hat{b})$, where

$$\hat{a} = a + \frac{n}{2}$$

and

$$\hat{b} = \left[\frac{1}{b} + \frac{1}{2}\sum_{t=1}^{T}\sum_{(i,j)\in\mu_t}(r_{ij} - \boldsymbol{U}_{ij}'\alpha - \kappa(Q_i^b - \boldsymbol{B}_i'\beta) - \lambda(Q_j^f - \boldsymbol{F}_j'\gamma))^2\right]^{-1}$$

THE COLLECTIVE MARRIAGE MATCHING MODEL: IDENTIFICATION, ESTIMATION, AND TESTING

Eugene Choo and Shannon Seitz

ABSTRACT

We develop and estimate an empirical collective model with endogenous marriage formation, participation, and family labor supply. Intra-household transfers arise endogenously as the transfers that clear the marriage market. The intra-household allocation can be recovered from observations on marriage decisions. Introducing the marriage market in the collective model allows us to independently estimate transfers from labor supplies and from marriage decisions. We estimate a semiparametric version of our model using 1980, 1990, and 2000 US Census data. Estimates of the model using marriage data are much more consistent with the theoretical predictions than estimates derived from labor supply.

Keywords: Marriage matching; intra-household allocation; collective model; labor supply

JEL classifications: D10; D13; J12; J22

Structural Econometric Models
Advances in Econometrics, Volume 31, 291–336

ISSN: 0731-9053/doi:10.1108/S0731-9053(2013)0000032010

INTRODUCTION

An influential empirical model of intra-household allocations is the collective model of Chiappori (1988, 1992). There are several reasons for its popularity. The collective model is appealing from a theoretical standpoint because it assumes individuals, as opposed to households, have distinct preferences. Under a minimal set of assumptions, it is possible to separately identify the preferences and relative bargaining power of each member of a married couple from observations on labor supply in the collective framework.[1] This is an extremely useful result for empirical work and policy analysis: many policy changes can be expected to cause redistribution *between* and *within* the households and the collective model is able to quantify both effects. A large body of empirical evidence (e.g., Chiappori, Fortin, & Lacroix, 2002 (CFL hereafter); Duflo, 2003; Fortin & Lacroix, 1997; Lundberg, 1988; Thomas, 1990) finds the restrictions implied by the unitary model, where the spousal preferences coincide, are rejected while those implied by the collective model are not.[2] The existing theoretical work highlights, and the empirical work confirms, that substantial redistribution may occur within households. To measure the welfare implications of changes in policy, it is important to take intra-household redistribution into account. The collective model makes such measurement possible.

While the collective model has been a useful tool for opening the "black box" of household decision making, it is silent on other questions that also have welfare implications: Why do some marriages form and not others? How is bargaining power determined? Lundberg and Pollak (1996), and many others, recognize that "marriage is an important determinant of distribution between men and women." Furthermore, many studies (e.g., Amuedo-Dorantes & Grossbard-Schectman, 2007; Chiappori et al., 2002; among others) find that features of the marriage market, including sex ratios and divorce laws, are determinants of household labor supply behavior. Such studies suggest there may be strong connections between the marriage market and redistribution within marriage. These studies provide motivation to empirically investigate the joint determination of marriage matching and intra-household allocations. In Choo, Seitz, and Siow (2008; CSS hereafter), we develop the collective marriage matching model, a model that integrates the collective model of Chiappori and the marriage matching model of Choo and Siow (2006a; hereafter CS). The collective marriage matching model allows us to analyze both marriage matching and the intra-household allocation of resources.

The general form of the collective marriage matching model presented in CSS includes risk sharing and public goods in marriage. The goal of the current article is to present identification, testing, and estimation results for a more modest version of the collective marriage matching model that is amenable to empirical work. The particular collective model we employ here is based on CFL. As in CFL, our attention is limited to households in which all consumption and leisure is private. In such a setting, the household's Pareto problem can be decentralized and the resource allocation in the household can be summarized by a lump sum transfer of income, the *sharing rule*.

The decentralization of the household's problem generates indirect utilities for each spouse which are functions of own wages and the sharing rule. In the marriage market, individual marriage decisions are made by comparing the indirect utilities that can be obtained from different marriage choices, including the option to remain unmarried. Changes in shares of nonlabor incomes via changes in the sharing rule will affect the level of spousal utility obtained in a particular marriage. Our collective model extends CFL by producing a sharing rule that is the equilibrium outcome of marriage matching. This article shows that partial derivatives of the equilibrium sharing rules are identified from marriage data. Our debt to Chiappori (1988, 1992) and CFL is clear: we exploit the indirect utilities generated by the pure private goods collective model to estimate marital choice models.

In deciding whether to enter into a marriage, both potential spouses have to consider the marital gains relative to alternative choices. We focus on the nonlabor incomes and gains in utility that a potential couple could obtain if they match. The inclusion of such "alternative" nonlabor incomes fundamentally changes the interpretation of how nonlabor income affect bargaining within the marriage. In our framework, where own alternative nonlabor are included in estimation, an increase in nonlabor income *within the current match* makes the current match more desirable *relative to available alternatives*, decreasing one's bargaining power in the current match. On the other hand, increases in nonlabor incomes when in alternative living arrangements, holding all else constant, increase one's bargaining power within the current marriage. The inclusion of alternative nonlabor incomes in the sharing rule and their interpretation are new to the collective marriage matching model.

We establish two new identification results. First, by incorporating the marriage decision in the collective model, we are able to generate two independent sets of estimates of the sharing rule: one from labor supplies and one from marriage decisions. As a result, our framework generates overidentifying restrictions that allow us to test whether the sharing rule which clears the marriage market is consistent with the sharing rule that determines labor supplies in households where both spouses work. Since the two different ways of estimating the determinants of the sharing rule are based on different identifying assumptions and data, depending on circumstances, one way may be more advantageous than the other.

Second, in the case where one spouse does not work, the sharing rule cannot be identified in the CFL framework as is well known.[3] If the spouses who do not work are ex-ante identical to individuals who chose to remain unmarried and have positive labor supply, then we can identify the sharing rule using marriage data on couples in which one spouse does not work and on unmarried men and women.[4]

Our new results are due to the integration of the collective model with a marriage matching model. The standard collective model does not imply any a priori restriction on the sharing rule. The restrictions on the sharing rule in this article are due to an *additional* assumption that the sharing rule clears the marriage market. If our marriage matching assumption is incorrect, then the sharing rule restrictions in this article will be invalid.

We estimate the collective matching model for nonspecialized couples using a sample of young adults from the 1980, 1990, and 2000 United States Census. As pointed out by Blundell, Browning, and Crawford (2003) in a related context, a rejection of the collective framework using parametric tests could arise due to a failure of the collective model itself or to a misspecified functional form for preferences. To this end, we estimate a semiparametric version of the model. In general, the marriage market estimates are much more consistent with the theory than are the labor supply estimates. As expected, individuals are more likely to marry when economic opportunities are better for married couples. We find that increases in male's wage and nonlabor income of singles lower the odds ratio of marriage while increases in nonlabor income of married couples increase the odds ratio of marriage.

From the reduced form estimates, we compute two independent estimates of the partial derivatives of the sharing rule, one from the odds ratio marriage estimates and one from household labor supplies. In general, it is the case that the sharing rule derivatives computed from the marriage estimates are more consistent with the theoretical predictions of the model: all 6 of the derivatives from the marriage estimates have the correct sign while only 2 out of 6 derivatives from the labor supply estimates are consistent with the theory. The sharing rule estimates derived from the marriage equations, in particular, predict that increases in marital nonlabor income are shared by the husband and the wife: of an increase in marital nonlabor income of one dollar, approximately 50 cents goes to the wife. Increases in the husband's (wife's) wage serves to decrease (increase) transfers to wives as higher male's (female's) wages increase their bargaining power within marriage. By the same reasoning increases in the nonlabor income of single men (women) makes marriage less attractive to men. Intra-household transfers to wives has to decrease (increase) so as to make marriage as attractive to men (women) as before.

After estimating the model, we test the restrictions on labor supplies and marriage decisions implied by the collective marriage matching model. We formulate a semiparametric test of our collective matching model which involves comparing the partial derivatives of the sharing rule from labor supplies to those from marriage decisions.[5] We reject the null of equality of the sharing rule derivatives from the marriage and labor supply estimates for all determinants with the exception of single nonlabor incomes for men and women.

The remainder of the article is organized as follows. We survey the related literature in the second section. In the third section, we describe our benchmark version of the collective model and the marriage market. In the fourth section, we establish conditions under which the structural parameters of the model (preference parameters and the sharing rule) are identified. In the fifth section, we show how the restrictions of our model can be tested. We estimate our model using data from the 1980, 1990 and 2000 US Census and present the estimation results in the seventh section. The eighth section concludes.

RELATED LITERATURE

We are indebted to several literatures. The study of intra-household allocations began with, among others, Becker (1973, 1974; summarized in 1991), the bargaining models of Manser and Brown (1980) and McElroy and Horney (1981), McElroy (1990) and the collective model of Chiappori (1988, 1992). A related literature, encompassing a diverse set of models, has studied the link between marriage market conditions and marriage rates. Becker (1973) was the first to consider the relationship between sex ratios and marriage rates. Brien (1997) tests the ability of several measures of marriage market conditions to explain racial differences in marriage rates.

The link between sex ratios and household outcomes was also extended to the labor supply decision. Grossbard-Schectman (1984) constructs a model where more favorable conditions in the marriage market improve the bargaining position of individuals within marriage. One implication of Grossbard-Schectman and related models that has been tested extensively in the literature is that, for example, an improvement in marriage market conditions for women translates into a greater allocation of household resources towards women, which has a direct income effect on labor supply. Tests of this hypothesis have received support in the literature (see among others, Amuedo-Dorantes & Grossbard-Schectman, 2007; Becker, 1991; Chiappori et al., 2002; Grossbard-Schectman, 1984, 1993; Grossbard-Schectman & Granger, 1998; Seitz, 2009).[6] Our empirical work considers the link between the sex ratio and both marriage and labor supply decisions in a general version of the collective model with matching.

Several important predecessors of our work integrate the collective model and the marriage market (Becker & Murphy, 2000; Browning, Chiappori, & Weiss, 2003) and extend the integrated model to consider premarital investments (Chiappori, Iyigun, & Weiss, 2009; Iyigun & Walsh, 2007). In these integrated collective models and in our work the sharing rule arises endogenously in the marriage market. Our article differs from this recent work in focus. Our goal is to develop an empirical framework that minimizes a priori restrictions on marriage matching and labor supply patterns. In this respect, our empirical framework can be used to test some of the qualitative predictions of the existing integrated models.

Our treatment of discrete labor supply choices within the collective model, while different in formulation, was influenced by the work of Blundell et al. (2007). Blundell, et al. (2007) establish identification of the collective model in the case where the labor supply decision of one spouse is discrete and of the other spouse is continuous. In contrast to Blundell et al. (2007), information on marriage behavior can be used to identify the sharing rule in our framework, even in the case where both household members are not working.

Our work is complementary to the recent literature that estimates search and matching models of marriage. The vast majority of articles in this literature are parametric and dynamic (e.g., Brien, Lillard, & Stern, 2006; Del Boca & Flinn, 2006, 2012; Seitz, 2004). Del Boca and Flinn (2006, 2012), Jacquement and Robin (2011), and Seitz (2009) incorporate both time allocation within the household and marriage decisions.

We assume spouses have access to binding marital agreements and there is no divorce. There is an active empirical literature studying dynamic intra-household allocations and marital behavior. Mazzocco and Yamaguchi (2006) study savings, marriage, and labor supply decisions in a collective framework in which an individual's weight in the household's allocation process depends on the outside options of each spouse, in this case, divorce. As pointed out by Lundberg and Pollak (2003), bargaining within marriage may not lead to efficient outcomes in the absence of binding commitments. Del Boca and Flinn (2006, 2012) estimate models of household labor supply where the household members can choose to interact in either a cooperative or a noncooperative fashion. Seitz (2009) estimates a dynamic model of marriage and employment decisions, where intra-household allocations are inefficient. Our focus here is on developing and estimating an empirical model of intrahousehold allocations and matching that imposes a minimal set of assumptions. To this end, Pareto efficiency is a maintained assumption.

Choo and Siow (2006a) developed the basic the frictionless marriage matching CS framework. Using Canadian data, Choo and Siow (2006b) applied the CS framework to analyze how the baby boom and differential mortality affected the marriage and cohabitation distributions. Choo (2012) extends the CS model to allow for dynamics. CSS and the article here develop and apply the collective marriage matching model.

THE COLLECTIVE MARRIAGE MATCHING MODEL

Consider a society that is composed of many segmented marriage markets. For expositional ease, assume there is one type of man and one type of woman within each society. We extend our analysis to multiple types in the empirical analysis described in the fifth section. All men and women within the same market have the same ex-ante opportunities and preferences. Let m be the number of men and f be the number of women within a market.

Although this is a simultaneous model of intrahousehold allocations and marriage matching, it is pedagogically convenient to discuss the model as if decisions are made in two stages. In the first stage, individuals choose whether to marry and whether the wife works within the marriage. Wages and assets are known prior to marriage, and the distribution of spousal bargaining power is determined in equilibrium as described in detail below. In the second stage, labor supply decisions for working spouses and consumption allocations are chosen to realize the indirect utilities which were anticipated by their first stage choices.

We refer to marriages in which the wife does not work in the labor market as specialized marriages (s) and marriages in which both spouses work as nonspecialized marriages (n). The index k, $k \in \{n, s\}$ describes whether a married couple is nonspecialized or specialized. For simplicity, all men and all unmarried women are assumed to have positive hours of work.[7]

Preferences

Let C and c be the private consumption of women and men, respectively, and H and h denote their respective labor supplies. Preferences are described by

$$U_k(C, 1-H) + \Gamma_k + \varepsilon_k$$

for married women and

$$u_k(c, 1-h) + \gamma_k + \epsilon_k$$

for married men. For both spouses, the first term is defined over consumption and leisure and affects the intrahousehold allocation. The last two terms, as in CS, affect marriage behavior but do not directly influence the intrahousehold allocation.

The parameters Γ_k and γ_k capture invariant gains to a marriage of type k for wives and husbands, respectively and are assumed to be separable from consumption and leisure. For each man and woman, idiosyncratic, additively separable, and independent and identically distributed preference shocks (ε_k and ϵ_k) are realized before marriage decisions are made. It is assumed that the preference shocks do not depend on the specific identity of the spouse, but are specific to the individual and the type of match. As will be shown later, since different individuals of the same gender receive different preference shocks, they will make different marital choices.

Intrahousehold Allocations

We begin by considering the second stage intrahousehold decision process. This is the familiar setting of the collective model, first developed by Chiappori (1988, 1992). We first describe the second stage problem for unmarried individuals. Next, we consider the intrahousehold allocation problem for nonspecialized and specialized couples.

Singles

The problem facing a single woman is

$$\max_{\{C,H\}} U_0(C, 1-H) + \Gamma_0 + \varepsilon_0$$

subject to the budget constraint

$$C \leq WH + A_0$$

and likewise for a single man:

$$\max_{\{c,h\}} u_0(c, 1-h) + \gamma_0 + \epsilon_0$$

subject to the budget constraint

$$c \leq wh + a_0$$

Nonspecialized Couples

Consider a husband and wife in a couple where both partners work. Total nonlabor family income, denoted by A_n, and wages for the husband and wife are realized before marriage decisions are made. The social planner's problem for the household is

$$\max_{\{c,C,h,H\}} U_n(C, 1-H) + \Gamma_n + \varepsilon_n + \omega_n[u_n(c, 1-h) + \gamma_n + \epsilon_n] \qquad \text{(PN)}$$

subject to the family budget constraint:

$$c + C \leq A_n + WH + wh$$

where the Pareto weight on the husband's utility in nonspecialized marriages is ω_n and the Pareto weight on the wife's utility is normalized to one.

A major insight of Chiappori (1988) is that, if household decisions are Pareto efficient, the above program can be decentralized into each spouse solving an individual maximization problem with their own private budget constraint. The wife's budget constraint is characterized by her earnings and a lump sum transfer or sharing rule, denoted $\tau_n(\cdot)$. The husband's budget constraint is characterized by his earnings and household nonlabor income A_n net of the sharing rule $\tau_n(\cdot)$. The sharing rule is a known function: given W, w, A_n, and ω_n, the planner constructs $\tau_n(\cdot)$. Then, the spouses solve separate individual optimization problems in the second stage.

The decentralized problem for the wife in the second stage is

$$\max_{\{C,L\}} U_n(C, 1-H) + \Gamma_n + \varepsilon_n$$
$$\text{subject to} \quad C \leq WH + \boldsymbol{\tau}_n(W, w, A_n, \omega_n)$$

and the problem facing husbands in the second stage is

$$\max_{\{c,l\}} u_n(c, 1-h) + \gamma_n + \epsilon_n$$
$$\text{subject to} \quad c \leq wh + A_n - \boldsymbol{\tau}_n(W, w, A_n, \omega_n)$$

The sharing rule in the decentralized problem and the Pareto weights in the social planner's problem are treated as predetermined at the point consumption and leisure allocations are chosen. The large literature on collective models is, with few exceptions, agnostic regarding the origins of the sharing rule. A central focus of our article is to derive a sharing rule from marriage market clearing.

Specialized Couples

For households in which the wife does not work, the social planner's problem is

$$\max_{\{c,C,h\}} U_s(C, 1) + \Gamma_s + \varepsilon_s + \omega_s[u_s(c, 1-h) + \gamma_s + \epsilon_s] \tag{PS}$$

subject to the family budget constraint:

$$c + C \leq A_s + wh$$

where the Pareto weight on the husband's utility in specialized marriages is ω_s and the wife's Pareto weight is again normalized to one. The decentralized problem for the husband is

$$\max_{\{c,l\}} u_s(c, 1-h) + \gamma_s + \epsilon_s$$
$$\text{subject to} \quad c \leq wh + A_s - \boldsymbol{\tau}_s(w, A_s, \omega_s)$$

and the wife simply receives

$$\mathbf{Q}_s(\boldsymbol{\tau}_s) = U_s(C, 1) + \Gamma_s + \varepsilon_s$$

where

$$C = \boldsymbol{\tau}_s(w, A_s, \omega_s)$$

Since the wife is not working, the husband's Pareto weight in specialized marriages only depends on the husband's wage, nonlabor income, and the distribution factors.[8]

The Marriage Decision

In the first period, agents decide whether to marry and whether to specialize. Once the idiosyncratic gains from marriage, ε_k and ϵ_k, are realized, individuals choose the household structure that maximizes utility. Individuals have three alternatives: remain single, enter a specialized marriage, or enter a nonspecialized marriage. For women, the indirect utility from remaining single is

$$\mathbf{V}_0(\varepsilon_0) = \mathbf{Q}_0[W, A_0] + \Gamma_0 + \varepsilon_0$$

from entering a specialized marriage is

$$\mathbf{V}_s(\varepsilon_s) = \mathbf{Q}_s[\boldsymbol{\tau}_s] + \Gamma_s + \varepsilon_s$$

and from entering a nonspecialized marriage is

$$\mathbf{V}_n(\varepsilon_n) = \mathbf{Q}_n[W, \boldsymbol{\tau}_n] + \Gamma_n + \varepsilon_n$$

The functions $\mathbf{Q}_0[W, A_0]$, $\mathbf{Q}_s[\boldsymbol{\tau}_s(\cdot)]$, and $\mathbf{Q}_n[W, \boldsymbol{\tau}_n(\cdot)]$ are the indirect utilities resulting from the second stage consumption and labor supply decisions. Given the realizations of ε_0, ε_n, and ε_s, she will choose the marital status which maximizes her utility. The utility from her optimal choice will satisfy

$$\mathbf{V}^*(\varepsilon_0, \varepsilon_s, \varepsilon_n) = \max[\mathbf{V}_0(\varepsilon_0),\ \mathbf{V}_s(\varepsilon_s),\ \mathbf{V}_n(\varepsilon_n)] \quad (1)$$

The problem facing men in the first stage is analogous to that of women. The indirect utility from remaining single is

$$\mathbf{v}_0(\epsilon_0) = \mathbf{q}_0[w, a_0] + \gamma_0 + \epsilon_0$$

from entering a specialized marriage is

$$\mathbf{v}_s(\epsilon_s) = \mathbf{q}_s[w, A_s - \boldsymbol{\tau}_s] + \gamma_s + \epsilon_s$$

and from entering a nonspecialized marriage is

$$\mathbf{v}_n(\epsilon_n) = \mathbf{q}_n[w, A_n - \boldsymbol{\tau}_n] + \gamma_n + \epsilon_n$$

where $\mathbf{q}_0[w, a_0]$, $\mathbf{q}_s[w, A_s - \tau_s(\cdot)]$, and $\mathbf{q}_n[w, A_n - \tau_n(\cdot)]$ are the husband's second stage indirect utilities for remaining single, entering a specialized marriage, and entering a nonspecialized marriage, respectively. The utility from his optimal choice satisfies

$$v^*(\epsilon_0, \epsilon_s, \epsilon_n) = \max[v_0(\epsilon_0), v_s(\epsilon_s), v_n(\epsilon_n)] \tag{2}$$

The Marriage Market

In this section, we construct supply and demand conditions in the marriage market and define an equilibrium for this market. Our model of the marriage market closely follows CS. Assume that there are many women and men in the marriage market, each woman is solving (Eq. (1)) and each man is solving (Eq. (2)). Let ρ_k be the probability of woman that enters a relationship of type k, $k \in \{s, n\}$:

$$\rho_j = \mathbb{P}\,[j = \arg\max\{\mathbf{Q}_0[\cdot] + \Gamma_0, \mathbf{Q}_s[\cdot] + \Gamma_s, \mathbf{Q}_n[\cdot] + \Gamma_n\}]$$

and define ϱ_j similarly for men

$$\varrho_j = \mathbb{P}\,[j = \text{argmax}\{\mathbf{q}_0[\cdot] + \gamma_0,\ \mathbf{q}_s[\cdot] + \gamma_s,\ \mathbf{q}_n[\cdot] + \gamma_n\}]$$

Under the assumption ε_k and ϵ_k are i.i.d. Type I Extreme Value random variables, McFadden (1974) shows that, within a market, the number of marriages relative to the number of females can be expressed as the probability women prefer entering a type k marriage relative to all other alternatives, including remaining single:

$$\rho_k = \frac{\exp(\Gamma_k + \mathbf{Q}_k[\cdot])}{\sum_{l \in \{0,s,n\}} \exp(\Gamma_l + \mathbf{Q}_l[\cdot])} \tag{3}$$

Similarly, for every man

$$\varrho_k = \frac{\exp(\gamma_k + \mathbf{q}_k[\cdot])}{\sum_{l \in \{0,s,n\}} \exp(\gamma_l + \mathbf{q}_l[\cdot])} \tag{4}$$

The maximum likelihood estimators for the choice probabilities of females are $\hat{\rho}_k = \Pi_k / f$, where Π_k is the supply of wives into type k marriages. Similarly for men $\hat{\varrho}_k = \pi_k / m$, where π_k is the demand of wives into type k marriages. Marriage market clearing requires the supply of wives to be equal to the demand for wives for each type of marriage:

$$\Pi_k = \pi_k = \Pi_k^* \ \forall\, k \tag{5}$$

The following feasibility constraints ensure that the stocks of married and single agents of each gender and type do not exceed the aggregate stocks of agents of each gender in the market:

$$f = \Pi_0 + \sum_k \Pi_k^* \tag{6}$$

$$m = \pi_0 + \sum_k \Pi_k^* \tag{7}$$

where Π_0 is the number of females who choose to remain unmarried, and π_0 is the number of males who choose to remain unmarried.

We can now define a rational expectations equilibrium for our version of the collective marriage matching model. An equilibrium is defined and a proof of existence for a more general version of the collective matching model is provided in CSS. There are two parts to the equilibrium, corresponding to the two stages at which decisions are made by the agents. The first corresponds to decisions made in the marriage market; the second to the intra-household allocation. In equilibrium, agents make marital status decisions optimally, the sharing rules clear each marriage market, and conditional on the sharing rules, agents choose consumption and labor supply optimally. Formally:

Definition 1. A rational expectations equilibrium consists of a distribution of males and females across marital status and type of marriage $\{\Pi_0, \pi_0, \Pi_k^*\}$, a set of decision rules for marriage $\{\mathbf{V}^*(\varepsilon_{0G}, \varepsilon_{sG}, \varepsilon_{nG}), \mathbf{v}^*(\epsilon_{0g}, \epsilon_{sg}, \epsilon_{ng})\}$, a set of decision rules for spousal consumption and leisure $\{C_0, C_k, c_0, c_k, L_0, L_n, l_0, l_k\}$, exogenous marriage and labor market conditions $W, w, A_k, A_0, a_0, m, f,$ the sharing rules $\{\boldsymbol{\tau}_k(\cdot)\}$, and a set of Pareto weights $\{\omega_k\}, k \in \{n, s\}$, such that:

1. *The decision rules* $\{\mathbf{V}^*(\cdot), \mathbf{v}^*(\cdot)\}$, *solve Eqs. (1) and (2);*
2. *All marriage markets clear implying Eqs. (5), (6), (7) hold;*
3. *For a type n marriage, the decision rules* $\{C_n, c_n, L_n, l_n\}$ *solve (PN);*
4. *For a type s marriage, the decision rules* $\{c_s, l_s\}$ *solve (PS).*

Theorem 2. A rational expectations equilibrium exists.

Proof: The proof of this theorem is presented in CSS.

In general, the equilibrium Pareto weights will depend on all the exogenous variables in society. The equilibrium stocks of marriages of each type, as well as the stocks of singles of each type, will depend on wages and non-labor incomes, as well as labor and marriage market conditions across all alternatives, summarized by $\mathbf{R}=\{W,\ w,\ A_k,\ A_0,\ a_0,\ m,\ f\}$ and are denoted

$$\Pi_k^*(\mathbf{R}),\ \Pi_0^*(\mathbf{R}),\ \text{and}\ \pi_0^*(\mathbf{R})$$

Let $\mathbf{R}_n=\{w,\ W,\ A_k,\ A_0,\ a_0,\ m,\ f\}$ and $\mathbf{R}_s=\{w,\ W,\ A_k,\ A_0,\ a_0,\ m,\ f\}$. In the collective literature, $\mathbf{R}_k$ is known as a set of distribution factors, factors that only influence the allocation through the Pareto weight for marriages of type $k,\ k\in\{n,s\}$. Equilibrium transfers will therefore be

$$\boldsymbol{\tau}_n(W,w,A_n,\mathbf{R}_n)=\boldsymbol{\tau}_n(W,w,A_n,\omega_n(\mathbf{R}))$$
$$\boldsymbol{\tau}_s(w,A_s,\mathbf{R}_s)=\boldsymbol{\tau}_s(w,A_s,\omega_s(\mathbf{R}))$$

IDENTIFICATION

In this section, we demonstrate how information on spousal labor supplies and on marriage decisions can be used to identify the preferences of individual household members as well as the sharing rule.

Nonspecialized Couples

Marriage Matching Restrictions

Eqs. (3) and (4) imply that the odds ratio of a nonspecialized marriage relative to remaining single for men and women respectively takes the form:

$$\frac{\rho_n}{\rho_0}=\exp(\Gamma_n-\Gamma_0+\mathbf{Q}_n[W,\ \boldsymbol{\tau}_n]-\mathbf{Q}_0[W,A_0]) \tag{8}$$

$$\frac{\varrho_n}{\varrho_0}=\exp(\gamma_n-\gamma_0+\mathbf{q}_n[w,A_n-\boldsymbol{\tau}_n]-\mathbf{q}_0[w,a_0]) \tag{9}$$

Eqs. (8) and (9) represent a system of supply and demand equations for spouses. Let the odds ratio be denoted by $\mathbf{P}_k=\rho_k/\rho_0$ and $\mathbf{p}_k=\varrho_k/\varrho_0$. Then for women in a nonspecialized marriage, $\mathbf{P}_n$ is a function of the mean utilities $\mathbf{Q}_n(W,\ \boldsymbol{\tau}_n)+\Gamma_n$ and $\mathbf{Q}_0(W,A_0)+\Gamma_0$, that is

$$\mathbf{P}_n=\mathbf{P}_n[\mathbf{Q}_n(W,\ \boldsymbol{\tau}_n)+\Gamma_n,\ \mathbf{Q}_0(W,A_0)+\Gamma_0]$$

For men, $\mathbf{p}_n$ is a function of $\mathbf{q}_n(w, A_n - \boldsymbol{\tau}_n) + \gamma_n$ and $\mathbf{q}_0(w, a_0) + \gamma_0$, that is

$$\mathbf{p}_n = \mathbf{p}_n[\mathbf{q}_n(w, A_n - \boldsymbol{\tau}_n) + \gamma_n, \mathbf{q}_0(w, a_0) + \gamma_0]$$

A natural estimator for the odds ratio would be $\hat{\mathbf{P}}_n = \Pi_n^*/\Pi_0$ and $\hat{\mathbf{p}}_n = \Pi_n^*/\pi_0$.

The following proposition shows that the structure of the marriage choice probabilities imposes testable restrictions on marriage behavior that allow us to uncover the partial derivatives of the sharing rule without using information on labor supplies:

Proposition 3. *Take any point such that* $\mathbf{P}_{nA} \cdot \mathbf{p}_{nA} \neq 0$. *Then, the following results hold: (i) If there exists exactly one distribution factor such that* $\mathbf{p}_{nR_1}\mathbf{P}_{nA} \neq \mathbf{P}_{nR_1}\mathbf{p}_{nA}$, *the following conditions are necessary for any pair* $(\mathbf{P}_n, \mathbf{p}_n)$ *to be consistent with marriage market clearing for some sharing rule* $\boldsymbol{\tau}_n(W, w, A_n, \mathbf{R}_n)$:

$$\frac{\partial}{\partial j}\boldsymbol{\tau}_{ni} = \frac{\partial}{\partial i}\boldsymbol{\tau}_{nj}, \quad i, j, \in \{W, w, A_n, \mathbf{R_n}\}$$

$$\text{and} \quad \frac{\mathbf{P}_{nR_l}}{\mathbf{p}_{nR_l}} = \frac{\mathbf{P}_{nR_1}}{\mathbf{p}_{nR_1}}, \quad l \in \{A_s, A_0, a_0, m, f\}$$

(ii) Under the assumption that the conditions in (i) hold, the sharing rule is defined up to an additive constant η. *The partial derivatives of the sharing rule are given by*

$$\boldsymbol{\tau}_{nA_n} = \frac{\mathbf{p}_{nR_1}\mathbf{P}_{nA}}{\mathbf{p}_{nR_1}\mathbf{P}_{nA} - \mathbf{P}_{nR_1}\mathbf{p}_{nA}}$$

$$\boldsymbol{\tau}_{nR_l} = \frac{\mathbf{P}_{nR_1}\mathbf{p}_{nR_l}}{\mathbf{p}_{nR_1}\mathbf{P}_{nA} - \mathbf{P}_{nR_1}\mathbf{p}_{nA}} \qquad R_l \in \{A_s, m, f\}$$

$$\boldsymbol{\tau}_{ni} = \frac{\mathbf{P}_{nR_1}\mathbf{P}_{ni}}{\mathbf{p}_{nR_1}\mathbf{P}_{nA} - \mathbf{P}_{nR_1}\mathbf{p}_{nA}} \qquad i \in \{W, A_0\}$$

$$\boldsymbol{\tau}_{nj} = \frac{\mathbf{P}_{nj}\mathbf{p}_{nR_l}}{\mathbf{p}_{nR_1}\mathbf{P}_{nA} - \mathbf{P}_{nR_1}\mathbf{p}_{nA}} \qquad j \in \{w, a_0\}$$

Proof: See Appendix A1. Thus, information on marriage decisions allows us to identify the partial derivatives of the sharing rule independently of the partial derivatives identified from labor supplies.

Labor Supply Restrictions

Consider couples in which both partners work strictly positive hours. Assume that the unrestricted labor supplies for husbands and wives are continuously differentiable. The Marshallian labor supply functions associated with the collective framework are related to the reduced form according to

$$\mathbf{H}_n(W, w, A_n, \mathbf{R}_n) = \mathbf{H}_n[W, \tau_n(W, w, A_n, \mathbf{R}_n)] \tag{10}$$

$$\mathbf{h}_n(W, w, A_n, \mathbf{R}_n) = \mathbf{h}_n[w, A_n - \tau_n(W, w, A_n, \mathbf{R}_n)] \tag{11}$$

This is exactly the setting of CFL. As in CFL, it is straightforward to show that the partial derivatives of the sharing rule can be recovered from labor supplies. For completeness, we reproduce the identification results of CFL here. Let R_1 be the 1st element of $\mathbf{R}_n$. The following proposition outlines the necessary and sufficient conditions for identification of the sharing rule.

Proposition 4. *Take any point such that* $\mathbf{H}_{nA} \cdot \mathbf{h}_{nA} \neq 0$. *If* R_1 *is such that* $\mathbf{h}_{nR_1}\mathbf{H}_{nA} \neq \mathbf{H}_{nR_1}\mathbf{h}_{nA}$, *the sharing rule is defined up to an additive constant* κ. *The partial derivatives of the sharing rule are given by*

$$\tau_{nA} = \frac{\mathbf{h}_{nR_1}\mathbf{H}_{nA}}{\mathbf{h}_{nR_1}\mathbf{H}_{nA} - \mathbf{H}_{nR_1}\mathbf{h}_{nA}}$$

$$\tau_{nj} = \frac{\mathbf{h}_{nR_1}\mathbf{H}_{nj}}{\mathbf{h}_{nR_1}\mathbf{H}_{nA} - \mathbf{H}_{nR_1}\mathbf{h}_{nA}}, \quad \text{where } j \in \{A_s, A_0, a_0, m, f\},$$

$$\tau_{nW} = \frac{\mathbf{h}_{nW}\,\mathbf{H}_{nR_1}}{\mathbf{h}_{nR_1}\mathbf{H}_{nA} - \mathbf{H}_{nR_1}\mathbf{h}_{nA}}$$

$$\text{and} \quad \tau_{nw} = \frac{\mathbf{h}_{nR_1}\mathbf{H}_{nw}}{\mathbf{h}_{nR_1}\mathbf{H}_{nA} - \mathbf{H}_{nR_1}\mathbf{h}_{nA}}$$

Proof: See Proposition 3 and the appendix in CFL. Identification from labor supplies is identical to that in CFL in the case where both partners work.

Propositions 3 and 4 provide us with a set of overidentifying restrictions. In particular, the partial derivatives of the sharing rule from the household labor supplies are equal to the partial derivatives of the sharing rule derived from the marriage odds ratio equations if the collective model is to be consistent with market clearing.

Specialized Couples

Marriage

Denote the probability of choosing to be in a specialized marriage as ρ_s for women and ρ_s for men. The odds ratio of choosing a specialized marriage relative to remaining single for women is

$$\mathbf{P}_s = \frac{\rho_s}{\rho_0} = \exp(\Gamma_s - \Gamma_0 + \mathbf{Q}_s[\boldsymbol{\tau}_s] - \mathbf{Q}_0[W, A_0])$$

and for men

$$\mathbf{p}_s = \frac{\rho_s}{\rho_0} = \exp(\gamma_s - \gamma_0 + \mathbf{q}_s[w, A_s - \boldsymbol{\tau}_s] - \mathbf{q}_0[w_0, a_0])$$

As is the case for nonspecialized marriages, the following proposition shows that it is straightforward to derive the partial derivatives of the sharing rule from marriage decisions. Then

Proposition 5. *Take any point such that $\mathbf{P}_{nA} \cdot \mathbf{p}_{nA} \neq 0$. Then, the following results hold: (i) If $\mathbf{p}_{sR_1}\mathbf{P}_{sA} \neq \mathbf{P}_{sR_1}\mathbf{p}_{sA}$, the following conditions are necessary for any pair $(\mathbf{P}_s, \mathbf{p}_s)$ to be consistent with marriage market clearing for some sharing rule $\boldsymbol{\tau}_s(w_s, A_s, \mathbf{R_s})$:*

$$\boldsymbol{\tau}_{sA} = \frac{\mathbf{p}_{sR_1}\mathbf{P}_{sA}}{\mathbf{p}_{sR_1}\mathbf{P}_{sA} - \mathbf{P}_{sR_1}\mathbf{p}_{sA}}$$

$$\boldsymbol{\tau}_{sR_l} = \frac{\mathbf{p}_{sR_1}\mathbf{P}_{sR_l}}{\mathbf{p}_{sR_1}\mathbf{P}_{sA} - \mathbf{P}_{sR_1}\mathbf{p}_{sA}} \qquad R_l \in \{A_n, m, f\}$$

$$\boldsymbol{\tau}_{si} = \frac{\mathbf{p}_{sR_l}\mathbf{P}_{si}}{\mathbf{p}_{sR_1}\mathbf{P}_{sA} - \mathbf{P}_{sR_1}\mathbf{p}_{sA}} \qquad i \in \{w, a_0\}$$

and

$$\boldsymbol{\tau}_{sj} = \frac{\mathbf{P}_{sR_l}\mathbf{p}_{sj}}{\mathbf{p}_{sR_1}\mathbf{P}_{sA} - \mathbf{P}_{sR_1}\mathbf{p}_{sA}} \qquad j \in \{W, A_0\}$$

Proof: See Appendix A2. Thus, it is possible to identify the sharing rule, up to an additive constant, for specialized couples if we observe changes in marriage behavior in response to changes in wages, nonlabor incomes, or population supplies.[9] A conclusion that immediately follows from the above is that it is always possible to identify the sharing rule from marriage decisions in the absence of data on labor supply.

Labor Supply
Consider couples in which only the husband works in the labor market. The Marshallian labor supply function for husbands in specialized marriages is

$$\mathbf{h}_s(w, A_s, \mathbf{R_s}) = \mathbf{h}_s(w, A_s - \boldsymbol{\tau}_s(w, A_s, \mathbf{R_s}))$$

The partial derivatives of the labor supply function are

$$\mathbf{h}_{sw} = \mathbf{h}_{sw} - \mathbf{h}_{sy}\boldsymbol{\tau}_{sw}, \qquad \mathbf{h}_{sA} = \mathbf{h}_{sy}(1 - \boldsymbol{\tau}_{sA})$$
$$\text{and} \qquad \mathbf{h}_{sj} = -\mathbf{h}_{sy}\boldsymbol{\tau}_{sj}, \qquad j \in \{W, A_0, a_0, A_n, m, f\}$$

The above system has 11 equations and 13 unknowns. It is clear that if we only observe variation in the husband's labor supply it is not possible to uncover preferences and the sharing rule.

ECONOMETRIC SPECIFICATION AND MODEL TESTS

In this section, we outline our strategy for estimating and testing the collective matching model. We start by describing the data used to estimate our model. We next describe our estimation strategy and outline how we test whether the restrictions in Propositions 4 and 3 hold for nonspecialized couples.

Data

We use data from the 1980, 1990, and 2000 US Census to estimate our model. For the purposes of our empirical analysis, we allow for the presence of many segregated marriage markets and many discrete types of men and women, where i denotes the male's type and j the female's types. The type of each individual is defined by the combination of race, education, and age. There are four race categories (black, white, Hispanic, other) and three education types (less than high school, high school graduate, and/or some college, college graduate). To ensure that labor supply decisions are closely linked to marriage decisions, we focus primarily on young couples aged 21–30, grouped into two 5-year age categories. There are thus 24 potential types of women and men in the marriage market. As in

CFL, we further assume that each state at each census year constitutes a separate marriage market r in year t. Our unit of observation is $(ijrt)$ and there are a total of 86,400 possible cells or categories.

Our goal is to test the overidentifying restrictions implied by the collective matching model for nonspecialized couples. To this end, we limit our sample to couples in which both spouses work strictly positive hours and unmarried individuals who work strictly positive hours.

The marital choice for women (men) is defined as the ratio of the number ijr marriages at t to the number of jr single women (ir single men) at year t. Table 1 presents summary statistics on marriage for the age groups in our sample. In the pooled sample, the proportion of women between 21 and 25 years of age that are married is around 40% and for the 26- to 30-year-old group is 60%. Women are working in the majority of marriages for this age range and time period; only one-third of marriages are specialized. The proportion of men between 21 and 25 years of age that are married is around 30% and is roughly twice as high for the 26- to 30-year-old group. While the proportion of male marriages where the spouse does not work is smaller than that of women, roughly a third of male marriages are specialized. Men tend to be within the same age range or slightly older than their wives; the proportion of women marrying men above the age of 30 is 43% for 26- to 30-year-old women, while the proportion of 21- to 25-year-old women marrying men below the age of 21 is only 2%.

Matches across ethnic or education categories are relatively uncommon. Statistics on the ethnic and education composition of marriages are presented in Tables 2 and 3, respectively. More detailed tabulations by Census Year are presented in Tables 11 and 12. As is well known from previous studies, the vast majority of marriages (98%) are between men and women of the same race, with marriages between white men and white women comprising 95% of all marriages. With respect to education, individuals

Table 1. Summary Statistics on Marriages in Pooled Sample.

	Women Aged		Men Aged	
	21–25	26–30	21–25	26–30
Proportion that are married	39.5	60.06	29.13	59.67
Proportion of marriages:				
that are specialized	30.02	36.21	28.45	32.99
where spouse is younger than 21	1.78	00.16	17.03	1.55
where spouse is older than 30	10.08	43.14	2.38	12.17

Table 2. Ethnic Distribution of Marriages for the Pooled Sample.

		Nonspecialized Couples				
		Husbands				
		White	Black	Hispanic	Other	Total
	White	94.83	0.03	0.51	0.04	95.41
	Black	0.00	2.66	0.00	0.00	2.66
Wives	Hispanic	0.62	0.00	1.13	0.01	1.76
	Other	0.05	0.00	0.00	0.11	0.17
	Total	95.50	2.70	1.64	0.16	100.00
Number of couples				4,075,704		

Table 3. Education Distribution of Marriages in the Pooled Sample.

		Nonspecialized Couples			
		Husbands			
		<High school	High school	College	Total
	<High school	0.32	0.84	0.01	1.17
Wives	High school	2.97	53.46	10.68	67.10
	College	0.02	10.36	21.36	31.74
	Total	3.30	64.66	32.04	100.00
Number of couples			4,075,704		

are also very likely to match within own-education categories (75% of marriages) but not to the same extent as for race.

Our measure of labor supply is annual hours of work. Wages are measured by average hourly earnings, constructed by dividing total labor income by annual hours. Nonlabor income is measured as the sum of several income sources including social security income, welfare, interest, dividend and rental income, and other income. Wages, hours of work, and nonlabor income are subsequently aggregated up to the cell level using the household sampling weights and converted to 1990 prices.[10] Table 4 contains descriptive statistics for our nonspecialized sample. On average, men work more hours per year and have higher wages than women, as expected. While nonlabor incomes are similar across single men and women, married couples tend to have higher nonlabor income than singles.

Table 4. Household Characteristics for the Pooled Sample.

	Nonspecialized Couples	
	Mean	Standard deviation
Nonlabor income	728.74	(426.63)
Sex ratio by race:		
white	0.92	(0.26)
black	0.82	(0.22)
mix race	2.19	(6.17)
Sex ratio by education:		
high school	0.88	(0.18)
college	0.83	(0.33)
mix education group	1.89	(2.05
Sex Ratio across all types	1.17	(0.97)
# of types *ijrt*	2124	
# weighted married couples	3,910,235	
	Single males	Single females
Annual hours	2106.70	1780.28
	(137.53)	(140.11)
Average hourly wage	11.21	8.94
	(2.03)	(1.98)
Nonlabor income	518.92	547.94
	(222.92)	(213.39)

The sex ratio *ijrt* in each sample is defined as the total number of men of type *i* divided by the total number of women of type *j* in state or market *r* at time *t*. Our final sample has a 2,124 types. When we restrict the sample same race pairing, ignoring education and age, the weighted mean sex ratio is slightly higher for whites than blacks and close to 0.9. When we allow for mix race matching as in our final sample, the mean sex ratio more than doubles. Similarly when we restrict the sample to just education pairing that are the same level, the mean sex ratio is close to 0.9 with the mean sex ratio for high school couples slightly higher than college couple. When we allow for education pairing that are not the same, the mean sex ratio again more than doubles. When we allow for age, race and education pairing as in the final sample, the mean sex ratio is 1.17 with a standard deviation close to 1.

We impose the following additional restrictions on the sample used in estimation. We eliminate cells with less than five observations and observations for which nonlabor income is negative. We restrict our sample to couples without children. The final sample used in estimation includes husband–wife race pairing that are {*white-white, black-black, white-hispanic, hispanic-white*}. For husband–wife education pairing, we include the following types of matches, {*Less than hs-hs, hs-hs, hs-college, college-hs, college-college*}. To eliminate outliers in the nonspecialized sample, we trim the top and bottom 3% of the distribution of wages and nonlabor income. We also eliminate observations with sex ratio less than 0.1 and greater than 5.

Econometric Specification

Our tests of the collective matching model do not rely upon any particular functional form for preferences, thus it is desirable to impose as few parametric assumptions on preferences as possible in our empirical analysis. The goal of this section is to outline a strategy for obtaining semiparametric estimates of the collective matching model.

The reduced form marriage odds-ratio and labor supply equations are

$$\mathbf{P}_{ij}^{rt}(W_j^{rt}, w_i^{rt}, A_{ij}^{rt}, A_{0j}^{rt}, a_{i0}^{rt}, R_{ij}^{rt}) = \mathbf{P}_{ij}[W_j^{rt}, \boldsymbol{\tau}_{ij}(W_j^{rt}, w_i^{rt}, A_{ij}^{rt}, A_{0j}^{rt}, a_{i0}^{rt}, R_{ij}^{rt}), A_{0j}^{rt}]$$

$$\mathbf{p}_{ij}^{rt}(W_j^{rt}, w_i^{rt}, A_{ij}^{rt}, A_{0j}^{rt}, a_{i0}^{rt}, R_{ij}^{rt}) = \mathbf{p}_{ij}[w_i^{rt}, A_{ij}^{rt} - \boldsymbol{\tau}_{ij}(W_j^{rt}, w_i^{rt}, A_{ij}^{rt}, A_{0j}^{rt}, a_{i0}^{rt}, R_{ij}^{rt}), A_{i0}^{rt}]$$

and

$$\mathbf{H}_{ij}^{rt}(W_j^{rt}, w_i^{rt}, A_{ij}^{rt}, A_{0j}^{rt}, a_{i0}^{rt}, R_{ij}^{rt}) = \mathbf{H}_{ij}[W_j^{rt}, \boldsymbol{\tau}_{ij}(W_j^{rt}, w_i^{rt}, A_{ij}^{rt}, A_{0j}^{rt}, a_{i0}^{rt}, R_{ij}^{rt})]$$

$$\mathbf{h}_{ij}^{rt}(W_j^{rt}, w_i^{rt}, A_{ij}^{rt}, A_{0j}^{rt}, a_{i0}^{rt}, R_{ij}^{rt}) = \mathbf{h}_{ij}[w_i^{rt}, A_{ij}^{rt} - \boldsymbol{\tau}_{ij}(W_j^{rt}, w_i^{rt}, A_{ij}^{rt}, A_{0j}^{rt}, a_{i0}^{rt}, R_{ij}^{rt})]$$

respectively. In theory, the full set of distribution factors includes all wages, nonlabor incomes, and population supplies for men and women of every potential type and marital status. It is not feasible to estimate a model with so many distribution factors. Furthermore, it would be difficult to precisely estimate the effect of each factor due to multicollinearity. Therefore, we assume the vector of distribution factors is summarized by the match-specific sex ratio R_{ij}^{rt}, the ratio of men of type i to women of type j in state r at t, as this is a measure of marriage market conditions commonly adopted in the literature.

We introduce subscripts for the match type (ij) and the state of residence r and time t to highlight two points. The first is that our framework (and our empirical analysis) is general enough to accommodate heterogeneity in preferences and sharing rules by match type. The second point we wish to highlight is that we are imposing the identifying assumption that preferences can vary across different types of matches, but not across locations or time t. Thus, the partial derivatives of the marriage odds ratio ratios and the labor supplies (and therefore the sharing rules) will be identified off cross-state-time variation in marriage rates and hours worked within match type. Estimation entails two stages:

Stage 1: Estimate a semiparametric partially linear version of the model:

$$\mathbf{P}_{ij}^{rt}(W_j^{rt}, w_i^{rt}, A_{ij}^{rt}, A_{0j}^{rt}, a_{i0}^{rt}, R_{ij}^{rt}) = \mathbf{P}[W_j^{rt}, \boldsymbol{\tau}_{ij}, A_{0j}^{rt}] + \alpha_{ij}^{P} + \beta_t^{P} + e_{ij}^{Prt}$$
$$\mathbf{p}_{ij}^{rt}(W_j^{rt}, w_i^{rt}, A_{ij}^{rt}, A_{0j}^{rt}, a_{i0}^{rt}, R_{ij}^{rt}) = \mathbf{p}[w_i^{rt}, A_{ij}^{rt} - \boldsymbol{\tau}_{ij}, A_{i0}^{rt}] + \alpha_{ij}^{p} + \beta_t^{p} + e_{ij}^{prt}$$

and

$$\mathbf{H}_{ij}^{rt}(W_j^{rt}, w_i^{rt}, A_{ij}^{rt}, A_{0j}^{rt}, a_{i0}^{rt}, R_{ij}^{rt}) = \mathbf{H}[W_j^{rt}, \boldsymbol{\tau}_{ij}] + \alpha_{ij}^{H} + \beta_t^{H} + e_{ij}^{Hrt}$$
$$\mathbf{h}_{ij}^{rt}(W_j^{rt}, w_i^{rt}, A_{ij}^{rt}, A_{0j}^{rt}, a_{i0}^{rt}, R_{ij}^{rt}) = \mathbf{h}[w_i^{rt}, A_{ij}^{rt} - \boldsymbol{\tau}_{ij}] + \alpha_{ij}^{h} + \beta_t^{h} + e_{ij}^{hrt}$$

The function $\boldsymbol{\tau}_{ij} = \boldsymbol{\tau}_{ij}(W_j^{rt}, w_i^{rt}, A_{ij}^{rt}, A_{0j}^{rt}, a_{i0}^{rt}, R_{ij}^{rt})$. Our econometric specification differs from the most general version of our model in two respects. First, we restrict the match type ij so that it only affects the marriage odds ratio ratios and the labor supplies through an intercept. This allows differences in match-specific characteristics to affect individual marriage market decisions and labor supply, albeit in a limited way. Second, we introduce i.i.d. cell-specific error terms $(e_{ij}^{Prt}, e_{ij}^{prt}, e_{ij}^{Hrt}, e_{ij}^{hrt})$ that are independent of wages, other incomes, and the sex ratio.

We estimate the above specification model using a combination of Robinson (1988) and Speckman (1988) estimators and local linear estimation (Ruppert & Wand, 1994).[11] Details are presented in Appendix B.

Stage 2: Construct semiparametric estimates of the partial derivatives of the sharing rule from the first stage estimates and test the equality of the model restrictions.

Recall, we are interested in a test of whether the sharing rule that is consistent with market clearing is also consistent with household labor supplies. The set of restrictions associated with this test are

$$\tau_{nA} = \frac{\mathbf{h}_{nR}\mathbf{H}_{nA}}{\mathbf{h}_{nR}\mathbf{H}_{nA} - \mathbf{H}_{nR}\mathbf{h}_{nA}} = \frac{\mathbf{p}_{nR}\mathbf{P}_{nA}}{\mathbf{p}_{nR}\mathbf{P}_{nA} - \mathbf{P}_{nR}\mathbf{p}_{nA}}$$
$$\tau_{nR} = \frac{\mathbf{h}_{nR}\mathbf{H}_{nR}}{\mathbf{h}_{nR}\mathbf{H}_{nA} - \mathbf{H}_{nR}\mathbf{h}_{nA}} = \frac{\mathbf{p}_{nR}\mathbf{P}_{nR}}{\mathbf{p}_{nR}\mathbf{P}_{nA} - \mathbf{P}_{nR}\mathbf{p}_{nA}}$$
$$\tau_{nW} = \frac{\mathbf{h}_{nW}\mathbf{H}_{nR}}{\mathbf{h}_{nR}\mathbf{H}_{nA} - \mathbf{H}_{nR}\mathbf{h}_{nA}} = \frac{\mathbf{p}_{nW}\mathbf{P}_{nR}}{\mathbf{p}_{nR}\mathbf{P}_{nA} - \mathbf{P}_{nR}\mathbf{p}_{nA}}$$
$$\tau_{nw} = \frac{\mathbf{h}_{nR}\mathbf{H}_{nw}}{\mathbf{h}_{nR}\mathbf{H}_{nA} - \mathbf{H}_{nR}\mathbf{h}_{nA}} = \frac{\mathbf{p}_{nR}\mathbf{P}_{nw}}{\mathbf{p}_{nR}\mathbf{P}_{nA} - \mathbf{P}_{nR}\mathbf{p}_{nA}}$$
$$\tau_{nA_0} = \frac{\mathbf{h}_{nR}\mathbf{H}_{nA_0}}{\mathbf{h}_{nR}\mathbf{H}_{nA} - \mathbf{H}_{nR}\mathbf{h}_{nA}} = \frac{\mathbf{p}_{nA_0}\mathbf{P}_{nR}}{\mathbf{p}_{nR}\mathbf{P}_{nA} - \mathbf{P}_{nR}\mathbf{p}_{nA}}$$
and
$$\tau_{na_0} = \frac{\mathbf{h}_{nR}\mathbf{H}_{na_0}}{\mathbf{h}_{nR}\mathbf{H}_{nA} - \mathbf{H}_{nR}\mathbf{h}_{nA}} = \frac{\mathbf{p}_{nR}\mathbf{P}_{na_0}}{\mathbf{p}_{nR}\mathbf{P}_{nA} - \mathbf{P}_{nR}\mathbf{p}_{nA}}$$

Our semiparametric procedure computes an estimate of the partial derivatives of the marriage and labor supply equations for each observation in the sample. We then compute the sharing rule estimates at each point. The point estimates of the sharing rule and the partial derivatives presented below represent the weighted average of the point estimates, where the weights are the household sampling weights from the Census.

The standard errors for all the estimates and test statistics are generated using bootstrap methods. Details of the bootstrap procedure are given in Appendix C.

COMPARATIVE STATICS FOR A SPECIAL CASE

To provide intuition for the interpretation of the empirical results, consider a society where there is one type of man and one type of woman, and only one type of marriage, nonspecialized marriages. Then each individual simply chooses whether to enter a nonspecialized marriage or not. Let m and f denote the number of single men and women respectively and $\Pi()$ denote the equilibrium number of marriages. In this case, the net gains equations become

$$\begin{aligned}\mathbf{N}(W,w,A,A_0,a_0,R) &= \mathbf{\Pi}(W,w,A,A_0,a_0,R)/[f - \mathbf{\Pi}(W,w,A,A_0,a_0,R)]\\ &= \exp[\Gamma_k - \Gamma_0 + \mathbf{Q}[W, \boldsymbol{\tau}(W,w,A,A_0,a_0,R)] - \mathbf{Q}_0[W,A_0]]\end{aligned}$$

for women and

$$\mathbf{n}(W, w, A, A_0, a_0, R) = \mathbf{\Pi}(W, w, A, A_0, a_0, R)/[m - \mathbf{\Pi}(W, w, A, A_0, a_0, R)]$$
$$= \exp[\gamma_k - \gamma_0 + \mathbf{q}[w, A - \boldsymbol{\tau}(W, w, A, A_0, a_0, R)] - \mathbf{q}_0[w, a_0]]$$

for men.

These are two equations that can be solved for the two unknowns, $\Pi(\cdot)$ and $\tau(\cdot)$ and it is straightforward to derive a set of comparative statics for the net marital gains equations. The sign predictions for the comparative statics have implications for the signs of the reduced form odds ratio marriage equations, the reduced form labor supplies, and the sharing rules. A summary of the sign predictions is presented in Table 5. Columns 1 and 2 contain the sign predictions for the partial derivatives of the reduced form odds-ratio of marriage regressions for women and men, respectively. Columns 3 and 4 contain the sign predictions for the corresponding labor supply regressions. Finally, Column 5 of Table 5 contains the predicted signs of the sharing rule derivatives.

It is worth emphasizing that our restrictions on the sharing rule are due to the *additional* assumption that the sharing rule must clear the marriage market. These restrictions are not present in the standard collective model such as CFL.

The comparative statics for the net gains equations above are as follows:

$$\mathbf{\Pi}_W \gtrless 0,\ \theta_W = \text{sign}(\mathbf{\Pi}_W) \text{ where } \theta = \{n, N\}, \psi_W = -\text{sign}(\mathbf{\Pi}_W) \text{ where } \psi = \{\boldsymbol{\tau}, h\},$$
$$\mathbf{\Pi}_w \gtrless 0,\ \delta_w = \text{sign}(\mathbf{\Pi}_w) \text{ where } \delta = \{\boldsymbol{\tau}, n, N\}, \text{ and } \mathbf{H}_w = -\text{sign}(\mathbf{\Pi}_w).$$

The effect of an increase in female wages on marriage depends on the difference in the marginal utility from wages within marriage relative to that from being single, $\partial\mathbf{Q}/\partial W - \partial\mathbf{Q}_0/\partial W$. A higher marginal utility from female wages within marriage makes marriage more attractive relative to

Table 5. Theoretical Sign Predictions of the Marriage Choices, Labor Supplies, and Sharing Rule Partial Derivatives for Nonspecialized Couples.

	Marriage		Labor Supply		Sharing
	Women (N)	Men (n)	Wives (H)	Husbands (h)	Rule (τ)
Other income (A)	+	+	−	−	(0,1)
Husband's wage (w)	sign(τ_w)	sign(τ_w)	−sign(τ_w)	?	±
Wife's wage (W)	−sign(τ_W)	−sign(τ_W)	?	sign(τ_W)	±
Sex ratio (R)	+	−	−	+	+
Single male income (a_0)	−	−	+	−	−
Single female income (A_0)	−	−	−	+	+

remaining single. To attract more men into marriage, $\boldsymbol{\tau}$ falls and $\mathbf{\Pi}$ increases. Since the spouse's wage affects the husbands labor supply only through the sharing rule, the husband's labor supply falls as $\boldsymbol{\tau}$ falls. An increase in female wages W can also make marriage less attractive to women if the within marriage marginal utility from female wages is less than the marginal utility from being single. The model predicts that $\boldsymbol{\tau}_W$ and $\mathbf{\Pi}_W$ to have opposite signs and $\boldsymbol{\tau}_W$ and $\mathbf{h}_W$ to have the signs as $\mathbf{\Pi}_W$.

A similar arguments applies to an increase in men's wage w. It will make marriage more attractive to men if the within marriage marginal utility exceed the marginal utility from being single, that is $\partial \mathbf{q}/\partial w > \partial \mathbf{q}_0/\partial w$. To attract more women into marriage, $\boldsymbol{\tau}$ increases and $\mathbf{\Pi}$ increases. An increase in transfer will affect the wife's labor supply only through an income effect, wive's labor supply falls. If the marginal utility from being single exceed that from marriage, the effects will go in the opposite direction. The model predicts that $\boldsymbol{\tau}_w$ and $\mathbf{\Pi}_w$ to have the same signs and $\boldsymbol{\tau}_w$ and $\mathbf{H}_w$ to have opposite signs. The own wage effect in the labor supply equation is ambiguous due to the standard income and substitution effects found in the unitary model.

Comparing our results to the collective model without marriage matching (i.e., CFL), they expect and found $\boldsymbol{\tau}_W > 0$.

$$\mathbf{\Pi}_A > 0 \quad 1 > \boldsymbol{\tau}_A > 0 \quad \mathbf{N}_A > 0 \quad \mathbf{n}_A > 0 \quad \mathbf{H}_A < 0 \quad \mathbf{h}_A < 0$$

When A increases, the payoff to marriage increases, thus more individuals marry. Both husbands and wives can benefit from increases in marital nonlabor income; thus it is expected that gains will be shared by both spouses, consistent with a sharing rule derivative between 0 and 1. Since $0 < \boldsymbol{\tau}_A < 1$, both spousal labor supplies must decrease as A increases, a standard income effect.

$$\begin{array}{llllll} \mathbf{\Pi}_{A_0} < 0 & \boldsymbol{\tau}_{A_0} > 0 & \mathbf{N}_{A_0} < 0 & \boldsymbol{n}_{A_0} < 0 & \mathbf{H}_{A_0} < 0 & \boldsymbol{h}_{A_0} > 0 \\ \mathbf{\Pi}_{a_0} < 0 & \boldsymbol{\tau}_{a_0} < 0 & \mathbf{N}_{a_0} < 0 & \boldsymbol{n}_{a_0} < 0 & \mathbf{H}_{a_0} > 0 & \boldsymbol{h}_{a_0} < 0 \end{array}$$

As nonlabor income of single women, A_0 increase, women find it less attractive to enter marriage. To reduce the number of marriages, $\boldsymbol{\tau}$ falls and $\mathbf{\Pi}$ also falls. A similar argument applies to increases in a_0. Transfers to women within marriage are therefore predicted to rise if the wages and nonlabor incomes they face when single increase and are expected to fall with the nonlabor incomes and wages of single men increase, consistent with a bargaining interpretation.

$$1 > \mathbf{\Pi}_f > 0 \quad \tau_f < 0 \quad \mathbf{N}_f < 0 \quad n_f > 0 \quad \mathbf{H}_f > 0 \quad h_f < 0$$
$$1 > \mathbf{\Pi}_m > 0 \quad \tau_m > 0 \quad \mathbf{N}_m > 0 \quad n_m < 0 \quad \mathbf{H}_m < 0 \quad h_m > 0$$

As f increases, more women want to marry. To attract more men into marriage, τ falls and $\mathbf{\Pi}$ increases but by less than the increase in f. This implies $\mathbf{N}_f < 0$ and $\mathbf{n}_f > 0$. A similar argument holds for the increase in m. As is standard in the literature, an increase in the sex ratio is expected to increase transfers to women within marriage as men face greater competition for spouses, resulting in a rise in labor supply for married men and a fall for married women.

RESULTS

In this section, we present semiparametric estimates of the collective matching model. We start by presenting estimates of the reduced form odds ratio marriage and labor supplies regressions. We use these reduced form estimates to construct two independent sets of estimates of the sharing rule derivatives, presented in the section "Econometric Specification," and test the model restrictions discussed above. Finally, we consider the sensitivity of our estimates to several alternative model specifications.

Reduced form Marriage and Labor Supply Estimates

The estimates of the marriage and labor supply regressions for our benchmark specification are presented in Table 6. In all of the following tables, instances where the estimated signs are consistent with the theoretical predictions from Table 5 are denoted by †. The first two columns contain semiparametric estimates of the reduced form odds ratio marriage regressions for men and women. The third and fourth columns contain semiparametric estimates of the reduced form labor supply equations for husbands and wives in nonspecialized marriages, respectively.

The results for the odds ratio marriage regressions are very consistent with the theoretical sign predictions. Column 1 of Table 6 contains the estimation results for men, while Column 2 contains the corresponding estimates for women. As expected, an increase in the number of type i men relative to type j women reduces the odds ratio of an ij marriage for men and increases the odds ratio of an ij marriage for women (relative to remaining single). The estimated effects of an increase in the sex ratio is statistically

Table 6. Semiparametric Marriage and Labor Supply Estimates for Nonspecialized Couples.

	Marriage		Labor Supply	
	Men (n)	Women (N)	Husbands (h)	Wives (H)
Other income (A)	0.0002†	0.0002†	−0.0017†	−0.0029†
	(4.4340)	(4.5370)	(0.1303)	(0.2215)
Sex ratio (R)	−0.6336†	0.7403†	68.6957†	−9.3121†
	(4.7540)	(4.8169)	(2.2996)	(0.2661)
Male's wage (w)	−0.0517†	−0.0329†	7.5317	1.4910†
	(2.4502)	(1.5354)	(1.3210)	(0.2662)
Female's wage (W)	−0.0097†	−0.0194†	8.1042†	23.4986
	(0.3808)	(0.7479)	(1.2294)	(3.4747)
Single male income (a_0)	−1.0E-6†	−0.0002†	−0.0623†	−0.0007
	(0.0075)	(1.1642)	(1.8615)	(0.0195)
Single female income (A_0)	−0.0004†	−0.0003†	−0.0733	−0.0542†
	(3.9189)	(2.9375)	(2.3658)	(1.7808)
Observations		2,124		

Notes: Absolute value of t-statistic in parentheses. † denotes an estimated sign that is consistent with the theory.

significant for both regressions. An increase in the nonlabor income of singles has the expected negative effect on the marriage odds ratio for men and women. These effects are statistically significant only for an increase in the nonlabor income of single women. An increase in the nonlabor income of married couples has a positive and statistically significant effect on the marriage odds ratio of men and women. In general, increases in wages tend to decrease the odds ratio of marriage. In particular, increases in the men's wages has a statistically significant and negative effect on the odds ratio of marriage for men. The effect on female odds ratio of marriage is insignificant as are the estimates from an increase in female's wages.

Turning to the labor supply estimates, an increase in nonlabor income has the expected negative (though not statistically significant) effect on labor supply for both married men and married women. The effect of an increase in the sex ratio on the husband's labor supply is also consistent with the theory: a 10% increase in the sex ratio is predicted to result in a very modest 7 hour increase in annual labor supply for married men. In contrast to the marriage estimates, however, the labor supply estimates often have different signs than those predicted by the theory. There is no clear pattern, for example, in the effect of male and female wages on household labor supply: it is often the case that increases in wages or non-labor incomes have the same effect on the husband's and wife's labor supply when the theory predicts the effects should be opposite in sign.

Estimates of the Sharing Rule from Marriage and Labor Supply Decisions

Previous work on the collective model (e.g., CFL) generated estimates of the sharing rule from labor supplies or from consumption demands. We make two original contributions to the empirical literature on the collective model. First, we produce new and independent estimates of the sharing rule from marriage decisions. Second, since we can also produce estimates of the sharing rule from household labor supply as done in previous studies, we assess the extent to which our estimates of the sharing rule from labor supplies are consistent with our sharing rule estimates derived from marriage decisions.

The marriage estimates and the labor supply estimates presented in Table 6 are subsequently used to generate two independent sets of estimates of the sharing rule. These estimates are presented in Columns 1 and 2 of Table 7, respectively. Column 1 contains estimates of the partial derivatives

Table 7. Sharing Rule Estimates for Nonspecialized Couples.

	Marriage	Labor Supply	*t*-Statistic
Other income (A)	0.4990[†]	0.7946[†]	−1.9342
	(5.1454)	(6.4727)	
Sex ratio (R)	842.8942[†]	−179.4041	3.5424
	(5.4677)	(0.7664)	
Male's wage (w)	−52.1237[†]	67.3220[†]	−2.0410
	(1.7136)	(1.3654)	
Female's wage (W)	102.2030[†]	−28.0693	1.9059
	(2.0037)	(0.6099)	
Single male income (a_0)	−0.2001[†]	−0.6159	0.7580
	(1.0431)	(1.2241)	
Single female income (A_0)	0.9706[†]	0.4112	1.4684
	(3.4914)	(1.9570)	
Observations	2,124		

Notes: Absolute value of *t*-statistics in parentheses. [†] denotes an estimated sign that is consistent with the theory.

of the sharing rule with respect to each argument from the odds ratio of nonspecialized marriages versus remaining single for men and women. Column 2 contains corresponding estimates from the labor supply estimates for nonspecialized couples. The former sharing rule can be interpreted as the sharing rule that is consistent with marriage market clearing; the latter can be interpreted as the intra-household allocation that is consistent with family labor supply.

The sharing rule estimates in Table 7 derived from the odds ratio marriage regressions are very consistent with the theoretical sign predictions. The estimates also highlight many similarities across the marriage and labor supply sharing rules. The sharing rule determinant of nonlabor income for married couples is precisely estimated in both specifications, and the parameter estimates are both positive and less than one, consistent with our theoretical predictions. A dollar increase in other income for married couples is predicted to increase transfers to wives by 80 cents based on the labor supply estimates and 50 cents based on the marriage estimates.

The effect of increases in the sex ratio on the sharing rule from the marriage odds ratio regression is positive and significant, consistent with our theoretical predictions. A 10% increase in the sex ratio is predicted to result in a modest \$84 (measured in 1990 prices) increase in annual transfers. The estimate of increases in sex ratio from the labor supply regression is insignificant. The sharing rule is decreasing in male's wages and increasing in the female's wages. The model predicts that increases in male's wage to have the same sign on the sharing rule as the marriage odds ratio regression for men and women. As for increases in female's wage, the model predicts that the effect on the sharing rule to have opposite sign compared to the marriage odds ratio regression for men and women. Both of these theoretical predictions hold in the marriage market specification of the sharing rule.

The t-statistic for a test of equality of the sharing rule estimates from the labor supply and marriage regressions is presented in Column 3. With the exception of single male and female nonlabor income, we generally reject the the equality of the sharing rule derivatives from the marriage and labor regressions for the remaining determinants.

Figs. 1, 2, and 3 present the partial derivatives of the sharing rule from the marriage and labor supply regressions with respect to female's wage, sex ratio, and single female's nonlabor income, respectively. With the exception of single female's nonlabor income, the figures demonstrate the substantial nonlinearity in the sharing rule derivatives. Figs. 1 and 2 also highlights considerable differences in the estimates of the derivatives

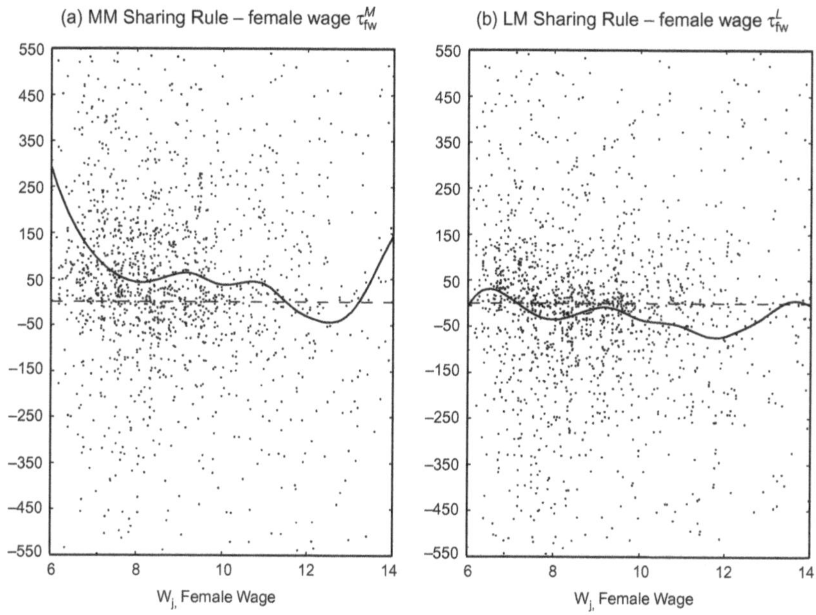

Fig. 1. Partial derivatives of the sharing rule from marriage and LS data – female wage.

derived from the two sets of regression. It is not surprising that we reject the equality of the derivatives for the case of female's wage and sex ratio.

The estimation results presented here suggest that estimation of the collective model from marriage decisions as opposed to labor supply might be a promising direction for future research. It is perhaps not surprising that marriage decisions appear to be more consistent with the predictions of the model: it is likely that bargaining power is most responsive to changes in wages and nonlabor incomes at the point the marriage decision is made. After forming a match, the presence of divorce costs and marriage-specific investments likely reduce the effects of outside conditions in the marriage market on intra-household allocations.

Selection and Alternative Specifications

In this section, we consider two alternative specifications to assess the robustness of the estimation results from the benchmark specification.

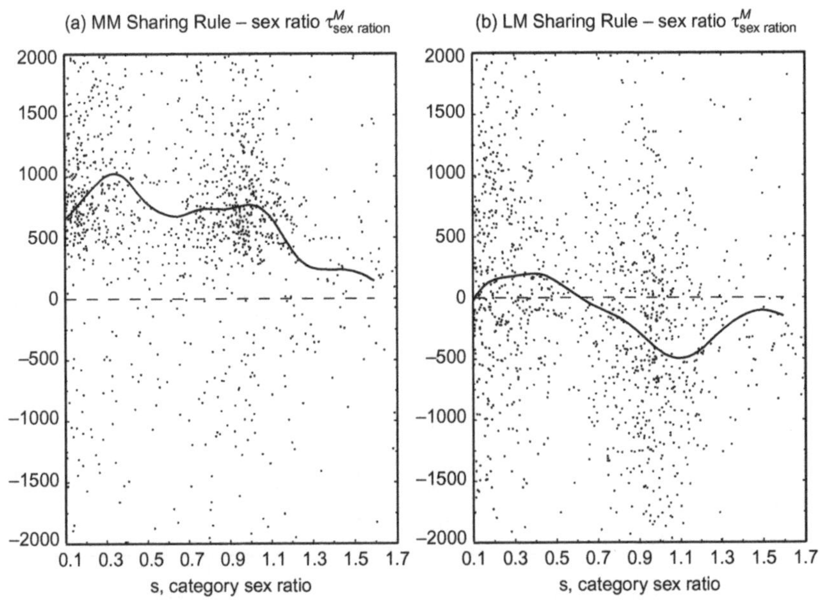

Fig. 2. Partial derivatives of the sharing rule from marriage and LS data – sex ratio.

First, we impose a more parametric structure on our model in the spirit of CFL. We estimated a much simpler linear model to assess the importance of nonlinearities in the data. In a second alternative specification, we restrict our sample to only white couples. Given that most marriages are between white men and white women, this restriction will eliminate marriage types with thinner number of observations. Omitting matches involving blacks and Hispanic couples would help investigate the much our results depend on these observations.

The results for the odds ratio marriage regressions are presented in Table 8. Columns 1 and 4 contain the estimation results for the benchmark specification for comparison purposes. Columns 2 and 5 contain the results from the linear model for wives and husbands, respectively. Columns 2 and 5 contain the results for the odds ratio regression using the restricted only whites sample for wives and husbands, respectively. Comparing the results from the restricted whites only sample with that of the benchmark model, the results of the partial derivatives of the odds ratio marriage regression

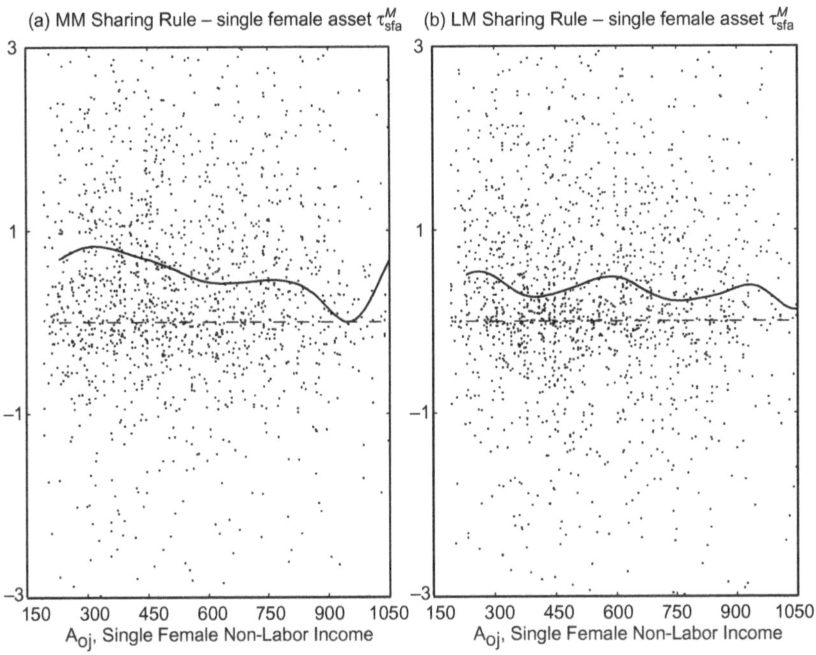

Fig. 3. Partial derivatives of the sharing rule from marriage and LS data – single female asset.

appears very robust across these two samples. With the exception of the derivative of the husband's marriage odds ratio with respect to single male's nonlabor income, the estimates from the two samples are very similar of in terms of both sign and magnitude.

In the specification where we impose parametric linearity in the model, the estimates in general differ considerably compared to the estimates from the benchmark model. The coefficient on the sex ratio for husbands changes sign and is insignificant in the linear specification. The estimates on wages in both the husbands and wives regressions are no longer consistent with theoretical predictions once we take into account the results of the sharing rule estimates in Table 10. The corresponding results for the labor supply regressions are presented in Table 9. We observe a similar trend in the results from the labor supply regressions from the two specifications. The estimates using the restricted whites only sample appears very

Table 8. Alternative Marriage Odds-Ratio Estimates.

	Women(N)			Men(n)		
	Benchmark	Linear model	White only sample	Benchmark	Linear model	White only sample
Other income (A)	0.0002†	−2.9E-5	0.0002†	0.0002†	3.6E-6†	0.0002†
	(4.5370)	(0.5980)	(4.1379)	(4.4340)	(0.0795)	(3.9821)
Sex ratio (R)	0.7403†	0.1364†	0.6848†	−0.6336†	−0.2813†	−0.6488†
	(4.8169)	(3.2124)	(5.1918)	(4.7540)	(5.7357)	(5.1045)
Male wage (w)	−0.0329†	−0.0123	−0.0313†	−0.0517†	−0.0474	−0.0523†
	(1.5354)	(0.6734)	(1.2340)	(2.4502)	(2.4156)	(2.0910)
Female wage (W)	−0.0194†	−0.0543	−0.0109†	−0.0097†	−0.0198	0.0037
	(0.7479)	(2.3376)	(0.3879)	(0.3808)	(0.8078)	(0.1350)
Single male income (a_0)	−0.0002†	−0.0001†	−0.0003†	−1.0E-6†	−0.0002†	−0.0001†
	(1.1642)	(1.0389)	(1.7547)	(0.0075)	(1.2728)	(0.7727)
Single female income (A_0)	−0.0003†	2.4E-5	−0.0003†	−0.0004†	−0.0001†	−0.0004†
	(2.9375)	(0.2078)	(2.5746)	(3.9189)	(1.1039)	(3.1923)
Observations	2124		1879	2124		1879

Notes: Absolute value of t-statistic in parentheses. † denotes an estimated sign that is consistent with the theory.

similar in signs and magnitude to the estimates from the benchmark specifications. Again there is considerable difference once we impose parametric linearity. The results in Tables 8 and 9 highlight the importance of nonlinearities in both the odds ratio and labor supply regressions. Imposing misspecified functional form leads to results that are inconsistent with theoretical predictions.

A comparison of the estimates of the sharing rule for all three specifications is presented in Table 10. The estimate of the sharing rule from the whites only sample is roughly consistent with estimates from the benchmark specification. The estimates using the linear specification tends to vary widely when compared to the benchmark specifications. In general, more of the derivatives of the sharing rule from the marriage regressions are significant. Very few of the estimates from the labor supply regressions are precisely estimated. Taking advantage of data on marriage decisions may be a more attractive in general than using data on household labor supply or consumption for married couples in general. Since all individuals in the data make marriage decisions, data on both singles and married couples can

Table 9. Alternative Labor Supply Estimates.

	Wives (H)			Husbands (h)		
	Benchmark	Linear model	White only sample	Benchmark	Linear model	White only sample
Other income (A)	−0.0029†	−0.0092†	0.0078	−0.0017†	−0.0180†	−0.0008†
	(0.2215)	(0.6581)	(0.5531)	(0.1303)	(1.5521)	(0.0546)
Sex ratio (R)	−9.3121†	−34.4818†	−4.1155†	68.6957†	−3.0316	79.0736†
	(0.2661)	(2.5097)	(0.1224)	(2.2996)	(0.2441)	(2.5838)
Male wage (w)	1.4910†	2.4291	3.4530†	7.5317	4.2365	7.2436
	(0.2662)	(0.4760)	(0.5586)	(1.3210)	(0.8077)	(1.1297)
Female wage (W)	23.4986	28.4060	24.1977	8.1042†	7.0876	10.3450†
	(3.4747)	(4.5229)	(3.2722)	(1.2294)	(1.2205)	(1.4075)
Single male income (a_0)	−0.0007	−0.0693	−0.0050	−0.0623†	0.0015	−0.0411†
	(0.0195)	(1.6396)	(0.1402)	(1.8615)	(0.0446)	(1.1101)
Single female income (A_0)	−0.0542†	−0.0696†	−0.0401†	−0.0733	−0.0578	−0.0696
	(1.7808)	(1.8679)	(1.2452)	(2.3658)	(1.7826)	(2.1118)
Observations	2,124		1,879	2,124		1,879

Notes: Absolute value of t-statistic in parentheses. †denotes an estimated sign that is consistent with the theory.

Table 10. Alternative Sharing Rule Estimates.

	Marriage			Labor Supply		
	Benchmark	Linear model	White only sample	Benchmark	Linear model	White only sample
Other income (A)	0.4990*†	1.0636*†	0.5488*†	0.7946*†	−0.0471	0.7338*†
	(5.1454)	(2.9796)	(5.8604)	(6.4727)	(0.0983)	(5.5913)
Sex ratio (R)	842.8942*†	−4961.0741	781.9008*†	−179.4041	−175.9491	76.2699†
	(5.4677)	(1.0551)	(4.3205)	(0.7664)	(0.1611)	(0.2951)
Male wage (w)	−52.1237*†	446.4904	−18.7437†	67.3220†	12.3948	58.1074†
	(1.7136)	(0.7215)	(0.5027)	(1.3654)	(0.0776)	(1.0373)
Female wage (W)	102.2030*†	−348.4918	44.4384†	−28.0693	411.3458	−9.0441
	(2.0037)	(0.7945)	(0.7641)	(0.6099)	(0.6502)	(0.2108)
Single male income (a_0)	−0.2001†	4.6309	−0.2693†	−0.6159	−0.3534	−0.5299
	(1.0431)	(0.8500)	(1.0955)	(1.2241)	(0.1449)	(0.8655)
Single female income (A_0)	0.9706*†	−2.3819	0.9204*†	0.4112	−3.3533	0.2710
	(3.4914)	(0.9034)	(2.6860)	(1.9570)*	(0.6149)	(1.1183)
Observations	2124		1879	2124		1879

Notes: Absolute values of t-statistics in parentheses. Value of t-statistics of equality denoted by * for 10% significance. †denotes an estimated sign that is consistent with the theory.

Table 11. Ethnic Distribution of Marriages by Census Year.

		Nonspecialized couples 1980				
		White	Black	Hispanic	Other	Total
				Husbands		
	White	95.09	0.02	0.43	0.02	95.56
	Black	0.00	2.94	0.00	0.00	2.94
Wives	Hispanic	0.49	0.00	0.90	0.00	1.39
	Other	0.01	0.00	0.00	0.10	0.11
	Total	95.60	2.95	1.33	0.12	100.00
Number of couples				1,942,480		
		Nonspecialized couples 1990				
				Husbands		
		White	Black	Hispanic	Other	Total
	White	95.10	0.03	0.54	0.02	95.69
	Black	0.00	2.35	0.00	0.00	2.35
Wives	Hispanic	0.67	0.01	1.10	0.00	1.78
	Other	0.01	0.00	0.01	0.16	0.18
	Total	95.78	2.40	1.64	0.18	100.00
Number of couples				1,296,379		
		Nonspecialized couples 2000				
				Husbands		
		White	Black	Hispanic	Other	Total
	White	93.79	0.06	0.63	0.12	94.60
	Black	0.00	2.50	0.00	0.00	2.50
Wives	Hispanic	0.84	0.00	1.74	0.03	2.61
	Other	0.22	0.00	0.00	0.07	0.29
	Total	94.85	2.57	2.37	0.22	100.00
Number of couples				836,845		

be used to estimate the sharing rule which has two advantages: (i) it allows the researcher to utilize a larger sample, and (ii) it reduces the potential for sample selection bias as it is no longer necessary to restrict the analysis to observations on married couples.

Table 12. Education Distribution of Marriages by Census Year.

		Husbands			
		<High school	High school	College	Total
		Nonspecialized couples in 1980			
		Husbands			
	High school	0.61	1.45	0.03	2.08
Wives	High school	4.35	52.27	13.10	69.72
	College	0.02	8.32	19.85	28.20
	Total	4.98	62.04	32.98	100.00
Number of couples			1,942,480		
		Nonspecialized couples in 1990			
		Husbands			
		<High school	High school	College	Total
	<High school	0.08	0.37	0.00	0.46
Wives	High school	2.17	56.11	9.51	67.80
	College	0.01	10.69	21.05	31.74
	Total	2.26	67.18	30.56	100.00
Number of couples			1,296,379		
		Nonspecialized couples in 2000			
		Husbands			
		<High school	High school	College	Total
	<High school	0.00	0.13	0.00	0.13
Wives	High school	0.99	52.08	6.86	59.93
	College	0.01	14.61	25.32	39.94
	Total	1.00	66.82	32.18	100.00
Number of couples			836,845		

CONCLUSION

In this article, we develop an empirical collective matching model that embeds the collective model of Chiappori et al. (2002) in the nonparametric matching model of Choo and Siow (2006). We show that the matching model generates an equilibrium sharing rule used to allocate resources in the intra-household problem of married couples. Further, we show that this sharing rule can be independently identified from commonly available labor supply and marital sorting data.

We estimate semiparametric sharing rules from 2000 US data and test the restrictions on labor supplies and marriage decisions implied by our collective matching model. For a sample of young adults, we find that the sharing rule consistent with household labor supplies is also consistent with marriage market clearing. The estimates provide evidence in favor of integrating the collective model and our non-transferable utility model of marriage, although the results should be interpreted with caution, as many of the estimates are imprecisely estimated. In general, the estimates of the collective model from marriage data are more robust and more consistent with the theory, suggesting a fruitful avenue for future research.

Our framework abstracts from two additional important issues which are beyond the scope of the current article. The first is dynamics. As we mention in the second section, Choo (2012), Seitz (2009), Mazzocco and Yamaguchi (2006) and others make important first steps in this direction. The second is unobserved heterogeneity and how this heterogeneity might influence marriage and labor supply decisions. How to resolve the latter issue is an open question in the literature. In this article, we provide a framework that allows for rich observed individuals heterogeneity and show how observed heterogeneity might influence matching and labor supply decisions.

NOTES

1. The standard identifying assumptions in this version of the collective model are that household allocations are Pareto efficient and preferences are egotistic or caring. For further details, see Browning and Chiappori (1998) and Chiappori and Ekeland (2009).

2. There are exceptions: for example, Dauphin, El-Lahga, Fortin and Lacroix (2011) reject the collective model in several specifications.

3. Blundell, Chiappori, Magnac, and Meghir (2007) establish identification of the collective model from labor supply data in the case where the labor supply decision of one spouse is discrete and of the other spouse is continuous.

4. Our result can be generalized to any discrete choice of hours, including zero hours, part-time and full-time work.

5. It should be emphasized that our identification results are still parametric in the sense that some assumptions on the functional form of preferences are imposed, namely that preferences are egotistic. Chiappori (1988) develops nonparametric

identification results for the collective model. In recent work, Cherchye, De Rock, and Vermeulen (2007) extend the results of Chiappori to a collective framework with externalities and public goods.

6. A number of studies have shown that the negative correlation between female labor supply and the sex ratio may not hold outside the United States, for example the recent studies by Fukuda (2006) and Emery and Ferrer (2009).

7. It is straightforward to extend our model to allow for zero hours of work for all single and married men and women.

8. Although individual types have been suppressed here for convenience, the sharing rule will in general depend on characteristics of both spouses and also on the society in which the couple resides.

9. As is the case for non-specialized couples, the indirect utilities and the sharing rules can both be identified up to an additive constant. Once the partial derivatives of the sharing rule are known, it is straightforward to recover the partial derivatives of the Marshallian labor supply function for husbands $\mathbf{h}_y$ and $\mathbf{h}_w$.

10. Note that measurement error in earnings and hours at the individual level is reduced when the data are aggregated up to the cell level.

11. See Li and Racine (2007) for a nice exposition of both methods.

ACKNOWLEDGEMENT

We would like to thank Karim Chalak, Don Cox, Anyck Dauphin, Ryan Davies, Peter Gottschalk, Arthur Lewbel, and seminar participants at many seminars and conferences for helpful comments. Choo and Seitz gratefully acknowledges the support of the Social Sciences and Humanities Research Council of Canada.

REFERENCES

Amuedo-Dorantes, C., & Grossbard-Schectman, S. (2007). Cohort level sex ratio effects on women's labor force participation. *Review of Economics of the Household*, *5*(3), 249–278.

Becker, G. (1973). A theory of marriage: Part I. *Journal of Political Economy*, *81*(4), 813–846.

Becker, G. (1974). A theory of marriage: Part II. *Journal of Political Economy*, *82*(2), S11–S26.

Becker, G. (1991). *A treatise on the family* (2nd ed.). Harvard University Press.

Becker, G., & Murphy, K. (2000). *Social economics*. Cambridge, MA: Harvard University Press.

Blundell, R., Browning, M., & Crawford, I. (2003). Nonparametric engel curves and revealed preference. *Econometrica*, *71*(1), 205–240.

Blundell, R., Chiappori, P.-A., Magnac, T., & Meghir, C. (2007). Collective labour supply: Heterogeneity and non-participation. *Review of Economic Studies*, *74*(2), 417–445.

Brien, M. (1997). Racial differences in marriage and the role of marriage markets. *Journal of Human Resources*, *32*(4), 741–778.

Brien, M., Lillard, L., & Stern, S. (2006). Cohabitation, marriage, and divorce in a model of match quality. *International Economic Review*, *47*(2), 451–494.

Browning, M., & Chiappori, P.-A. (1998). Efficient intra-household allocations: A general characterization and empirical tests. *Econometrica*, *66*(6), 1241–1278.

Browning, M., Chiappori, P.-A., & Weiss, Y. (2003). *A simple matching model of the marriage market*. University of Chicago, unpublished manuscript.

Cherchye, L., De Rock, B., & Vermeulen, F. (2007). The collective model of household consumption: A nonparametric characterization. *Econometrica*, *75*(2), 553–574.

Chiappori, P.-A. (1988). Rational household labor supply. *Econometrica*, *56*(1), 63–90.

Chiappori, P.-A. (1992). Collective labor supply and welfare. *Journal of Political Economy*, *100*(3), 437–467.

Chiappori, P.-A., Fortin, B., & Lacroix, G. (2002). Household labor supply, sharing rule, and the marriage market. *Journal of Political Economy*, *110*(1), 37–72.

Chiappori, P.-A., & Ekeland, I. (2009). The microeconomics of efficient group behavior: Identification. *Econometrica*, *77*(3), 763–799.

Chiappori, P.-A., Iyigun, M., & Weiss, Y. (2009). Investment in schooling and the marriage market. *American Economic Review*, *99*(5), 1689–1713.

Choo, E. (2012). *Dynamic marriage matching: An empirical framework*. Working Paper, Department of Economics, University of Calgary.

Choo, E., Seitz, S., & Siow, A. (2008). *Marriage matching, risk sharing and spousal labor supplies*. Working Paper No. tecipa-332. Department of Economics, University of Toronto.

Choo, E., & Siow, A. (2006a). Who marries whom and why. *Journal of Political Economy*, *114*(1), 175–201.

Choo, E., & Siow, A. (2006b). Estimating a marriage matching model with spillover effects. *Demography*, *43*(3), 463–488.

Dauphin, A., El-Lahga, A.-R., Fortin, B., & Lacroix, G. (2011). Are children decision makers within the household. *Economic Journal*, *121*(553), 871–903.

Del Boca, D., & Flinn, C. (2006). *Household time allocation and modes of behavior: A theory of sorts*. NYU Working Paper No. 8, Department of Economics, Collegio Carlo Alberto.

Del Boca, D., & Flinn, C. (2012). Endogenous household interaction. *Journal of Econometrics*, *166*(1), 49–65.

Duflo, E. (2003). Grandmothers and granddaughters: Old age pension and intra-household allocation in South Africa. *World Bank Economic Review*, *17*(1), 1–25.

Emery, H., & Ferrer, A. (2009). Marriage market imbalances and labor force participation of Canadian women. *Review of Economics of the Household*, *7*(1), 43–57.

Fortin, B., & Lacroix, G. (1997). A test of the unitary and collective models of household labour supply. *Economic Journal*, *107*(443), 933–955.

Fukuda, K. (2006). A cohort analysis of female labor participation rates in the U.S. and Japan. *Review of Economics of the Household*, *4*(4), 379–393.

Grossbard-Schectman, S. (1984). A theory of allocation of time in markets for labour and marriage. *The Economic Journal*, *94*(376), 863–882.

Grossbard-Schectman, S. (1993). *On the economics of marriage: A theory of marriage, labor, and divorce, boulder*. Colorado: Westview Press.

Grossbard-Schectman, S., & Granger, C. (1998). Women's jobs and marriage, baby-boom versus baby-bust. *Population*, *53*, 731–752, September 1998.

Iyigun, M., & Walsh, R. (2007). Building the family nest: Premarital investments, marriage markets, and spousal allocations. *Review of Economic Studies*, *74*(2), 507–535.

Jacquement, N., & Robin, J.-M. (2011). *Assortative matching and search with labor supply and home production*, CES Working Paper #2011–50.

Li, Q., & Racine, J. (2007). *Nonparametric econometrics*. Princeton University Press.

Lundberg, S. (1988). Labor supply of husbands and wives: A simulataneous equations approach. *The Review of Economics and Statistics*, *70*(2), 224–235.

Lundberg, S., & Pollak, R. (1996). Bargaining and distribution in marriage. *Journal of Economic Perspectives*, *10*(4), 139–158.

Lundberg, S., & Pollak, R. (2003). Efficiency in marriage. *Review of Economics of the Household*, *1*, 153–167.

Manser, M., & Brown, M. (1980). Marriage and household decision-making: A bargaining analysis. *International Economic Review*, *21*(1), 31–44.

Mazzocco, M., & Yamaguchi, S. (2006). *Labor supply, wealth dynamics, and marriage decisions*. University of Wisconsin-Madison, unpublished manuscript.

McElroy, M. (1990). The empirical content of nash-bargained household behavior. *The Journal of Human Resources*, *25*(4), 559–583.

McElroy, M., & Horney, M.-J. (1981). Nash-bargained household decisions: Toward a generalization of the theory of demand. *International Economic Review*, *22*(2), 333–349.

McFadden, D. (1974). Conditional logit analysis of qualitative choice behavior. In P. Zarembka (Ed.), *Frontiers in econometrics*. New York, NY: Academic Press.

Robinson, P. (1988). Root N-consistent semiparametric regression. *Econometrica*, *56*, 931–954.

Ruppert, D., & Wand, M. (1994). Multivariate locally weighted least squares regression. *The Annals of Statistics*, *22*(3), 1346–1370.

Seitz, S. (2009). Accounting for racial differences in marriage and employment. *Journal of Labor Economics*, *27*(3), July.

Speckman, P. (1988). Kernel smoothing in partial linear models. *Journal of the Royal Statistical Society, Series B*, *50*, 413–446.

Thomas, D. (1990). Intra-household resource allocation: An inferential approach. *The Journal of Human Resources*, *25*(4), 635–664.

APPENDIX A: IDENTIFICATION

A1 Marriage, Nonspecialized Couples

Denote the probability of choosing to be in a nonspecialized marriage ρ_n and the probability of being single ρ_0, respectively, for women and ϱ_n and ϱ_0 for men. Under the extreme value assumption for we can express the ratio of the choice probabilities for nonspecialized marriage relative to remaining single as

$$\frac{\rho_n}{\rho_0} = \frac{\exp(\boldsymbol{Q}_n[W, \tau_n(W, w, A_n, A_0, a_0, \mathbf{R}_n)] + \Gamma_n)}{\exp(\boldsymbol{Q}_0[W, A_0] + \Gamma_0)}$$

for women and

$$\frac{\varrho_n}{\varrho_0} = \frac{\exp(\boldsymbol{q}_n[w, A_n - \tau_n(W, w, A_n, A_0, a_0, \mathbf{R}_n)] + \gamma_n)}{\exp(\boldsymbol{q}_0[w, a_0] + \gamma_0)}$$

Denote $\boldsymbol{P}_n = \frac{\rho_n}{\rho_0}$ and $\boldsymbol{p}_n = \frac{\varrho_n}{\varrho_0}$. Differentiating with respect to each argument yields

$$\begin{aligned}
\boldsymbol{P}_{nA} &= \boldsymbol{Q}_{nY}\boldsymbol{\tau}_{nA}\\
\boldsymbol{P}_{nR_i} &= \boldsymbol{Q}_{nY}\boldsymbol{\tau}_{nR_i}, \quad R_i \in \mathbf{R}_n\\
\boldsymbol{P}_{nW} &= \boldsymbol{Q}_{nW} + \boldsymbol{Q}_{nY}\boldsymbol{\tau}_{nW}\\
\boldsymbol{P}_{nw} &= \boldsymbol{Q}_{nY}\boldsymbol{\tau}_{nw}\\
\boldsymbol{P}_{nA_0} &= \boldsymbol{Q}_{nY}\boldsymbol{\tau}_{A_0} - \boldsymbol{Q}_{0A_0}\\
\boldsymbol{P}_{na_0} &= \boldsymbol{Q}_{nY}\boldsymbol{\tau}_{a_0}
\end{aligned}$$

for women and

$$\begin{aligned}
\boldsymbol{p}_{nA} &= \boldsymbol{q}_{ny}(1 - \boldsymbol{\tau}_{nA})\\
\boldsymbol{p}_{nR_i} &= -\boldsymbol{q}_{ny}\boldsymbol{\tau}_{nR_i}, \quad R_i \in \mathbf{R}_n\\
\boldsymbol{p}_{nw} &= \boldsymbol{q}_{nw} - \boldsymbol{q}_{ny}\boldsymbol{\tau}_{nw}\\
\boldsymbol{p}_{nW} &= -\boldsymbol{q}_{ny}\boldsymbol{\tau}_{nW}\\
\boldsymbol{p}_{nA_0} &= -\boldsymbol{q}_{ny}\boldsymbol{\tau}_{A_0}\\
\boldsymbol{p}_{na_0} &= -\boldsymbol{q}_{ny}\boldsymbol{\tau}_{a_0} - \boldsymbol{q}_{0a_0}
\end{aligned}$$

A2 Marriage, Specialized Couples

Denote the probability of choosing to be in a specialized marriage ρ_s and the probability of being single ρ_0, respectively, for women and ϱ_s and ϱ_0 for men. Under the extreme value assumption for we can express the ratio of the choice probabilities for specialized marriage relative to remaining single as

$$\frac{\rho_s}{\rho_0} = \frac{\exp(\boldsymbol{Q}_s[\boldsymbol{\tau}_s(w, A_s, A_0, a_0, \mathbf{R}_s)] + \Gamma_s)}{\exp(\boldsymbol{Q}_0[W, A_0] + \Gamma_0)}$$

for women and

$$\frac{\varrho_s}{\varrho_0} = \frac{\exp(\boldsymbol{q}_s[w_s, A_s - \boldsymbol{\tau}_s(w_s, A_s, W_0, w_0, A_0, a_0, \mathbf{R}_s)] + \gamma_s)}{\exp(\boldsymbol{q}_0[w_0, a_0] + \gamma_0)}$$

for men. Denote $\boldsymbol{P}_s = \frac{\rho_s}{\rho_0}$ and $\boldsymbol{p}_s = \frac{\varrho_s}{\varrho_0}$. Differentiating with respect to each argument yields

$$\begin{aligned}
&\boldsymbol{P}_{sA} = \boldsymbol{Q}_{sY}\boldsymbol{\tau}_{sA} \\
&\boldsymbol{P}_{sR_i} = \boldsymbol{Q}_{sY}\boldsymbol{\tau}_{sR_i}, \quad R_i \in \mathbf{R}_s \\
&\boldsymbol{P}_{sw} = \boldsymbol{Q}_{sY}\boldsymbol{\tau}_{sw} \\
&\boldsymbol{P}_{sA_0} = \boldsymbol{Q}_{sY}\boldsymbol{\tau}_{A_0} - \boldsymbol{Q}_{0A_0} \\
&\boldsymbol{P}_{sa_0} = \boldsymbol{Q}_{sY}\boldsymbol{\tau}_{a_0}
\end{aligned}$$

for women and

$$\begin{aligned}
&\boldsymbol{p}_{sA} = \boldsymbol{q}_{sy}(1 - \boldsymbol{\tau}_{sA}) \\
&\boldsymbol{p}_{sR_i} = -\boldsymbol{q}_{sy}\boldsymbol{\tau}_{sR_i}, \quad R_i \in \mathbf{R}_s \\
&\boldsymbol{p}_{sw} = \boldsymbol{q}_{sw} - \boldsymbol{q}_{sy}\boldsymbol{\tau}_{sw} \\
&\boldsymbol{p}_{sA_0} = -\boldsymbol{q}_{sy}\boldsymbol{\tau}_{A_0} \\
&\boldsymbol{p}_{sa_0} = -\boldsymbol{q}_{sy}\boldsymbol{\tau}_{a_0} - \boldsymbol{q}_{0a_0}
\end{aligned}$$

APPENDIX B: FIRST STAGE ESTIMATION

The first stage estimation entails the following four steps:

Step 1: Take the conditional expectation of $\boldsymbol{H}_n$ with respect to the non-parametric part of the model. Let **s** denote a vector containing $W, w, A, \mathbf{R}$, where subscripts are eliminated for expositional convenience. Then

$$E[\boldsymbol{H}_n|s] = E[X|s]'\beta_H + \boldsymbol{H}_n(s) \tag{12}$$

and we difference from the labor supply equation to obtain:

$$\boldsymbol{H}_n - E[\boldsymbol{H}_n|\mathbf{s}] = [\mathbf{X} - E[\mathbf{X}|\mathbf{s}]]'\beta_H + \nu_H \tag{13}$$

Step 2: Estimate $E[\boldsymbol{H}_n|\mathbf{s}]$ and $E[\mathbf{X}|\mathbf{s}]$ by local linear regression. The local linear estimator of the conditional mean function at $\mathbf{s} = (W, w, A, \mathbf{R})$ is $\hat{\alpha}$ and the derivative at this point is $\hat{\rho}$. The local linear estimator for $E[\boldsymbol{H}_n|\mathbf{s}]$ is

$$\min_{\alpha,\rho} \sum_i \{\boldsymbol{H}_{ni} - \alpha - \rho'(S_i - s)\}^2 \prod_{h=1}^{4} K\left(\frac{S_{ih} - s_h}{b_h}\right) \tag{14}$$

where $K(\cdot)$ is a one-dimensional kernel function, the bandwidth for the ith covariate is b_i and the kernel weight function is a product kernel. From standard weighted least squares theory, the local linear estimator for the conditional mean is

$$\hat{H}_n(\mathbf{s}) = e_1(\mathbf{S}'_s\mathbf{W}_s\mathbf{S}_s)^{-1}\mathbf{S}'_s\mathbf{W}_s\boldsymbol{H}_\mathbf{n} \tag{15}$$

where e_1 is a $5+1$ vector with 1 for the first element and 0 everywhere else, $\boldsymbol{H}_\mathbf{n} = (\boldsymbol{H}_{n1}, \boldsymbol{H}_{n2}, \ldots \boldsymbol{H}_{nN})'$ where N is the number of observations,

$$\mathbf{W}_s = diag\left\{\prod_{i=1}^{4} K\left(\frac{S_{i1} - s_{i1}}{b_i}\right) \ldots \prod_{i=1}^{4} K\left(\frac{S_{iN} - s_{iN}}{b_i}\right)\right\} \tag{16}$$

and

$$S_s = \begin{pmatrix} 1 & (\mathbf{S}_1 - \mathbf{s})' \\ \vdots & \vdots \\ 1 & (\mathbf{S}_N - \mathbf{s})' \end{pmatrix} \tag{17}$$

To get an estimate of the derivative of $\boldsymbol{H}_n(\mathbf{S})$ with respect to to the kth derivative,

$$\frac{\partial \hat{\boldsymbol{H}}_n(\mathbf{s})}{\partial s_k} = e_{k+1}(\mathbf{S}'_s \mathbf{W}_s \mathbf{S}_s)^{-1} \mathbf{X}'_s \mathbf{W}_s \mathbf{H}_n \tag{18}$$

Currently the ith covariate bandwidth is set according to a rule of thumb of $c\sigma_i/n^{d+4}$, where σ_i is the standard deviation of the ith covariate and n is the sample size. Refer to Ruppert and Wand (1994) for expressions of the bias and variance on the derivative estimate.

Step 3: Estimate

$$\boldsymbol{H}_n - \hat{E}[\boldsymbol{H}_n|\mathbf{s}] = [\mathbf{X} - \hat{E}[\mathbf{X}|\mathbf{s}]]'\beta_H + \nu_H$$

using OLS to obtain $\hat{\beta}_H$.

Step 4: We can obtain an estimate of $\boldsymbol{H}_n(W, w, A, \mathbf{R})$ as

$$\boldsymbol{H}_n(W, w, A, \mathbf{R}) = \hat{E}[\boldsymbol{H}_n|\mathbf{s}] - \hat{E}[\mathbf{X}|\mathbf{s}]'\beta_H \tag{19}$$

APPENDIX C: BOOTSTRAPPED STANDARD ERROR

For example, consider the derivative estimates with respect to R from the male labor supply in the nonspecialized case, $\hat{h}_{nR}$.Let the sample size be N and let B denote the number of bootstrap replications, each of which is of size N. For all the reported standard errors, B is set to 1499. For each replication, we compute the weighted average point estimate $\hat{\boldsymbol{h}}^*_{nR1}, \ldots, \hat{\boldsymbol{h}}^*_{nRB}$ and the bootstrap variance estimate for $\hat{\boldsymbol{h}}_{nR}$ using the standard formula:

$$s^2_{\hat{h}_{nR}B} = \frac{1}{B-1}\sum_{b=1}^{B}(\hat{\boldsymbol{h}}^*_{nRb} - \hat{\boldsymbol{h}}^*_{nR}), \quad \text{where} \quad \hat{\boldsymbol{h}}^*_{nR} = B^{-1}\sum_{b=1}^{B}\hat{\boldsymbol{h}}^*_{nRb}$$

Let $\hat{\boldsymbol{\tau}}^L_{nR}$ and $\hat{\boldsymbol{\tau}}^M_{nR}$ be the weighted point estimates of the sharing rule derivatives with respect to R from the labor and marriage market, respectively, for nonspecialized couples. To test the hypothesis that $\boldsymbol{H}_0 : \boldsymbol{\tau}^L_{nR} = \boldsymbol{\tau}^M_{nR}$, we use the test statistic:

$$t = \frac{\hat{\boldsymbol{\tau}}^L_{nR} - \hat{\boldsymbol{\tau}}^M_{nR}}{s_{\hat{d}_{nR}B}} = \frac{\hat{d}_{nR}}{s_{\hat{d}_{nR}B}}$$

To compute the bootstrap standard error, $s_{\hat{d}_{nR}B}$, we compute the weighted point estimate for each bootstrap replication $\hat{d}^*_{nR1}, \ldots, \hat{d}^*_{nRB}$. The variance of the difference in the sharing rule estimates is calculated according to

$$s^2_{\hat{d}_{nR}B} = \frac{1}{B-1}\sum_{b=1}^{B}(\hat{\boldsymbol{d}}^*_{nRb} - \overline{\hat{d}}^*_{nR}), \quad \text{where} \quad \overline{\hat{d}}^*_{nR} = B^{-1}\sum_{b=1}^{B}(\hat{\boldsymbol{\tau}}^{*L}_{nRb} - \hat{\boldsymbol{\tau}}^{*M}_{nRb}) \qquad (37)$$

DEFLATION IN DURABLE GOODS MARKETS: AN EMPIRICAL MODEL OF THE TOKYO CONDOMINIUM MARKET

Migiwa Tanaka

ABSTRACT

Throughout the 1990s, the supply of new condominiums in Tokyo significantly increased while prices persistently fell. This article investigates whether the market power of condominium developers is a factor in explaining the outcome in this market and whether there is a relationship between production cost trend and the degree of market power that the developers were able to exercise. In order to respond to these questions, we construct and structurally estimate a dynamic durable goods oligopoly model of the condominium market – one incorporating time-variant costs and a secondary market – using a nested GMM procedure. We find that the data provide no evidence that firms in the primary market have substantial market power in this industry. Moreover, the counterfactual experiment provides evidence that inflationary and deflationary expectations on production cost trends have asymmetric effects to the market power of condominium producers. The increase in their markup

Structural Econometric Models
Advances in Econometrics, Volume 31, 337–386

ISSN: 0731-9053/doi:10.1108/S0731-9053(2013)0000032011

when cost inflation is anticipated is significantly higher than the decrease in the markup when the same magnitude of cost deflation is anticipated.

Keywords: Durable goods; dynamic oligopoly; housing market

JEL classifications: L11; L13; R31

INTRODUCTION

Throughout the 1990s, the supply of new condominiums in Tokyo increased significantly while prices of condominiums fell persistently. In 1994, the annual supply of condominium units surged from 8,000 units to 20,200 units and has maintained an increasing trend till 2005. Meanwhile, the average rate of decrease in condominium prices is 5.2 percent. It has been believed that a major cause of this deflationary price trend is land price depreciation – that has taken place since the burst of the asset price bubble in the Japanese economy, inasmuch as land is the most expensive factor of condominium production. At the same time, the top 15 developers have maintained control of about one-half of the market, despite the entrance of new developers. This fact may suggest that those top firms exercise market power, and, therefore, the price fall of condominiums may not only be due to the cost reduction but also to the change in their markup. This article addresses the following two questions about this market. First, how much market power do the large developers exercised in the Tokyo condominium market? Second, how does the deflationary cost trend affect the market power of durable goods producers?

In the durable goods market, with focus on a secondary market such as the condominium market, the degree of market power possessed by producers is worth investigating further because theoretical predictions are ambiguous. When there is no secondary market, it has been well known since Coase (1972) that rational expectations of consumers can erode the market power of a durable good producer by generating competition with one's past self as well as one's future self, unless one can commit to a future price path; buyers will not purchase a product at their valuation of the product since they correctly anticipate the producer's incentive to cut its price in the future.[1] When there is a secondary market, however, theoretical predictions are inconclusive regarding the degree of market power because of the several competing effects of the secondary market on the primary market. On one hand, the secondary market provides more varieties of imperfect substitutes to newly produced goods within and across time, and thus it reduces the market power of producers. On the other hand, the secondary market provides an opportunity for owners of durable goods to replace current holdings more easily, and, thus, it increases the demand for new goods and market power. Furthermore, given future resale possibilities, consumers may prefer the goods that yield higher resale values rather than simply inexpensive goods. Hence, the degree of market power of producers depends on which of those effects dominates in a market and it has to be examined empirically.

In order to measure the degree of market power in the Tokyo condominium market and investigate the relationship between the market power and cost deflation, we construct a dynamic Cournot oligopoly model based on Esteban (2003) that explicitly incorporates the secondary market. In our model, the products are differentiated by vintage, and producers face a cost function that varies across time. Using building-level supply data, the proposed model is structurally estimated via a nested GMM procedure, in which, following Rust (1987), Markov perfect Nash equilibrium of the model is solved for at each iteration. Using estimated parameter values, we performed several counterfactual experiments.

The results are summarized as follows: First, there is no evidence that firms in the primary market have substantial market power in this industry. Thus, the imperfect competition does not contribute to the observed deflation of prices and increased output. Second, the counterfactual experiment provides evidence that inflationary and deflationary expectations on production cost trends have asymmetric effects to the market power of condominium producers. The inflation in the production costs strengthens the market power of the condominium producers. On the other hand, deflation of the production costs exacerbates the erosion of the market power derived from the durability of condominiums. Moreover, increase in markup when cost inflation is anticipated is significantly higher than decrease in markup when the same magnitude of cost deflation is anticipated.

In the rest of this section, we relate this study to the received literature. There are few empirical studies on supply dynamics of durable goods. Notable exceptions are Ramey (1989) and Esteban and Shum (2007) on the US automobile market, Zhao (2008) on the digital camera market, Goettler and Gordon (2011) on the CPU market, and Nair (2007) on the video game console market. However, none of these article takes into account resale possibility. Esteban and Shum extend Esteban's model into a vertically differentiated product framework. They find that secondary markets allow firms to exploit their asymmetries. A producer of goods at the high end of the quality spectrum tends to produce more, as this can hurt the profits of producer of low-quality products without seriously hurting his or her own profit; this is because his or her product will act more as a substitute for newly produced low-quality goods once it reaches the secondary market.[2] In contrast to Esteban and Shum, our model is not restricted to vertical differentiation; thus, the problem is not formulated as a linear quadratic but as a more general dynamic problem.

Relative to literature on durable goods supply, there is a growing empirical literature on demand dynamics of consumer durables where the supply dynamics are a given, beginning with Melnikov (2000). He models the consumer's purchase behavior as an optimal stopping problem and develops an estimation procedure by extending the framework of Berry, Levinsohn, and Pakes (1995). Subsequent works on this framework include Nair (2007), Gowrisankaran and Rysman (2012), Gordon (2009), Carranza (2007), Schiraldi (2011), and Ishihara and Ching (2012); all except for Schiraldi (2011) and Ishihara and Ching (2012), give no explicit consideration of the presence of the secondary market.

The relationship between the production cost and market power of a durable goods producer is investigated by Kahn (1986). He suggests that increasing marginal costs of production mitigates the Coase problem inasmuch as buyers believe correctly that the producer benefits from spreading production over time, and, thus, will not cut prices in the near future.[3] Based on Kahn's intuition, it is expected that, faced with rising costs, producers will have incentives to produce now rather than in the future. Correspondingly, consumers will correctly believe that producers will not cut prices in the future. On the contrary, deflationary costs provide firms with incentives to postpone production in order to cut costs. Our model incorporates time varying component in the cost function of durable good producer. With structural estimation of our model and counterfactual experiments, we confirm that this is indeed the case in the Tokyo condominium market.

Durability is also considered an important characteristic in the literature on housing supply. Within that literature, the closest approach to the one used in our article is the investment approach, whereby consumers consider a residential building as an investment good, the price of which is determined by the present discount value of the rental price (i.e., the price of the service derived from the structure).[4] The rental price is a function of the level of the existing housing stock. Consumers, therefore, do not explicitly make distinctions between vintages. Homebuilders maximize the present discount value of the profit by taking the price as given. Poterba (1984) and Topel and Rosen (1988) are the examples in this strand. They all assume a competitive market, something rationalized by the fact that new construction is a small part of the existing stock; consequently, builders do not have any control over it. In our application, inasmuch as there seems to exist a distinction between newly constructed units and old units in the minds of consumers, we allow for strategic interactions between builders. To our knowledge, this is the first attempt at considering the housing market in an oligopolistic framework using an investment-based approach. One of a few micro level empirical studies on housing supply is Rosenthal (1999), who tests the efficiency market hypothesis that implies perfect competition. He finds that the deviation between new building prices and construction costs disappears faster than the time required for construction, indicating that the builders of single-family housing in Vancouver do not have excess profit opportunities. This article approaches the housing market in a more structural manner, both on the demand and supply sides.

This article proceeds in the following manner. The next section gives a description of the Tokyo condominium market. The third section introduces a dynamic oligopoly model of condominium suppliers. The fourth section explains the estimation method for the model. The fifth section reports the estimation results followed by the simulation results. The last section concludes.

THE TOKYO CONDOMINIUM MARKET

Definition of the Market and the Product

This article studies the market for newly constructed condominiums in the Tokyo metropolitan area. A condominium is defined as multiunit housing that consists of five or more units, with three stories or more, and with a steel-reinforced concrete structure. In this article, we only consider those units that are developed by private companies.[5] We define the market as encompassing 23 central districts in Tokyo. It is 621.45 square kilometers in size, and, in 1995, consisted of about 3.5 million households.[6] Throughout the 1990s, population growth was moderate within this area, while the number of households grew at an annual rate of 1 percent. This growth is mostly accounted for by an increase in single-person households. Condominiums have become an increasingly common form of housing in the area – as of 1998, multiunit housing owned by individuals accounted for 20 percent of all housing in the Tokyo metropolitan area. As of 2001, more than half of all households purchasing new housing chose a condominium unit rather than a single detached house. This ratio was about 45 percent on average throughout the 1990s.[7]

Based on the national tax law as of 1999, the statutory useful life of a condominium unit is 47 years. In reality, most existing condominiums are said to require either large scale repair or rebuilding after about 30 years. However, the physical and quality depreciation of a condominium depends on the maintenance quality over the years. Thus, the vintage may not be the best proxy for quality. This fact motivates us to incorporate other characteristics in the demand specification at the estimation stage, which is described in the fourth section.[8]

The Market Environment

Fig. D1 summarizes the various price indices relating to the housing market between 1986 and 2009, taking 1995 as the base year. The expansion of the economy started in 1986. During the subsequent four years, the annual real GDP growth rate in Japan was about 5 percent. The burst of the asset price bubble started at the stock market during 1990 and the real GDP growth rate in the following decade was about 1 percent, on average. The burst of the land market bubble gradually prevailed in 1991, a year later than the stock market crash. By that time, the residential land prices in Tokyo had risen by 154 percent from their 1986 level. Since the burst, land prices have been consistently decreasing. In the face of the devastated economy and declining asset prices, quite a few business entities had to sell their unused lots, some of which were suitable for condominium construction: for all condominiums built between 1995 and 2000 in central areas of Tokyo, about 60 percent of sites were formerly owned by the corporate sector. The prices of new condominiums in Tokyo showed almost identical movement with land prices before 1995, presumably because land was the most expensive factor in condominium production.[9] Meanwhile, construction work price deflators reflecting the material and labor costs in the construction industry displayed a gradual increase, but the movement was very modest compared with the fluctuation in land-related prices. The rental index (not shown in Fig. D1) exhibited a slight decrease over time, but again, the change has been mild compared with that for land prices, and might reflect the fact that land prices have not been fully adjusted for non-bubble prices.[10] After 1995, land price series and new condominium price series started to show a divergence. Land prices depreciated, on average, 2.6 percent more rapidly than condominium prices between 1995 and 2003. It might suggest the presence of market power. In other words, the decline in factor price may not be fully reflected in sales prices. Alternative explanations can be that the construction costs become more expensive relative to land prices, and, thus, the total cost falls slower than the land prices.[11] Furthermore, technological innovation made it possible to build taller condominiums, and, thus, the average size of land and the average cost of land for each unit decreased. In this article, we focus on the possibility that the market outcome is dictated by the market power and capture the transition of cost structure and technological progress by introducing cost components that evolves exogenously over time.

The Industry

Condominium production involves at least two types of firms: developers and construction companies. Developers acquire land, plan condominium development projects and contract with the construction companies for construction. Developers sell the units to consumers either through through dealer companies or directly. In this study, developers are assumed to produce and sell condominium units directly to consumers and the role of construction companies is abstracted away.

One of the contributors to the surge in the supply in 1994 was new entrants to the market. The transition in market participants is summarized in Table D1. The number of active firms was 111 in 1993, which increased to 205 in 1994, and has stayed around 230 since then. For each year, about 13–27 percent of firms appeared in the data set only once over the sample period of seven years. Those firms or individuals seemed to take advantage of the market expansion to sell their unused land. At the same time, the top 15 firms maintained a market share of more than 50 percent during the period of analysis, despite the large number of entries. Yet, one might consider that this aggregate statistics is relatively low concentration however one should note that there are regional variations in the market concentration within Tokyo: the Herfindahl Hirshiman index in the east area of Tokyo has been around 1,000 over years.[12] In addition, in the part of the central district, Chiyoda ward, the HHI has been between 1,000 and 5,020 during the period of analysis. These facts indicate the possibility that the developers' market power could play large role in Tokyo.

On average, condominium construction takes 15 months.[13] The average time lag in the sample between construction and sales is about 198 days and about 10 percent of the properties are sold before the completion of construction. It is common to divide the units from one project into groups and sell them at different phases. Our dataset is organized by the sales phases. While the actual production decisions tend to be made well ahead of sales time, we assume that transaction and production choices occur at the same time.

The Secondary Markets

It is said that the resale housing market in Japan is less developed than its counterpart in North America. The trade volume in the secondary market has been estimated at 50,000 units annually in the Tokyo metropolitan area alone. This accounts for 3 percent of the condominium stock in the area.[14]

Three factors are commonly recognized as sources of the low volume of transactions in the secondary market. First, there is a strong preference toward newly constructed housing in Japan. According to the survey of housing demand conducted by the Ministry of Land, Infrastructure and Transport, more than 50 percent of households preferred newly built housing in 2003. Second, there are substantial information asymmetry problems in the Japanese real estate market. Real estate brokers tend to be small scale and specialize in specific areas; they are thus inclined to monopolize local information. This leads to higher search costs for potential buyers and higher opportunity costs derived from vacancies for owners or potential sellers. Shimizu, Nishimura, and Asami (2004) focus on this point and find that there would be substantial cost savings if there were an information agency that provided relevant information to all (potential) market participants on all properties for resale, for almost zero cost. Note that in the market of newly constructed condominiums, most properties are sold by dealers, who are contracted with developers and real estate agents rarely involves in those transactions. Although above study suggests that information asymmetry may be important in this market, this article maintains the assumption of a perfectly competitive secondary market. Third, the transactions cost is rather high. There are various fees in housing markets including real estate acquisition tax, the national registration tax, stamp duty, capital gains tax if the sales are for replacement, brokerage fees, as well as the opportunity costs for sellers mentioned above. Additionally, Kanemoto (1997) points out that the favorable loan treatment for home-buyers of newly constructed houses by the Japan Housing Loan Corporation increases the relative cost of purchasing aged housing.[15] Nevertheless we maintain the assumption that the secondary market is perfect as above issues are beyond the scope of this article.

MODEL OF THE CONDOMINIUM MARKET

This section gives a description of the dynamic oligopoly model for the primary market for condominiums. The model is constructed based on the discrete-time semidurable goods oligopoly model of Esteban (2003), wherein both firms and consumers are forward looking. The behavior of consumers is modeled using a multinomial logit framework but the model incorporates the dynamics arising from durability.[16] Firms are quantity-setting oligopolists facing a macro cost shock and stochastically evolving fringe competitors.

The Environment and the Transition of the States

Condominiums are durable and are assumed to last for D periods. Newly constructed condominiums are traded in the oligopoly market, whereas older condominiums are traded in competitive secondary markets. Thus, the producers do not have direct control over the outcome in secondary markets. The condominium units are differentiated by vintage, implying that they are homogeneous within the same vintage. There are three types of state variables in this model: the stock of condominiums, $\vec{s}_t$, the macro cost shock, $\tilde{c}_t$, and the supply of fringe competitors, x_t.

In the market, there exist J firms producing and selling durable condominiums. Firms are indexed by j and are assumed to be homogenous. A typical firm j produces q_{jt} units of condominiums at time t. Besides J firms, there are fringe competitors who take the price as a given. They collectively produce x_t units at time t. It is assumed that x_t evolves due to an AR(1) process (i.e., $x_t = \bar{x} + \vartheta x_{t-1} + \xi_t$, where ξ_t is distributed mean 0 and is finite variance σ_ξ^2).[17] Therefore, x_t eventually converges to the steady-state level, x^{ss}. If current x_t is below x^{ss}, it would be in a growth phase. The condominium market for each vintage clears for each period.

Thus, all existing units are transacted in the secondary market of each vintage until they reach age D. A condominium unit depreciates at an annual rate of $1-\delta$ before age D. Note that units above age D stay in the market, but as part of an outside alternative. In other words, after age D, the specific links of used units with new or younger units are lost. Stock of age d is expressed as:

$$s_t^d = \delta\left(\sum_{j=1}^{J} q_{j,t-d} + x_{t-d}\right), d = 1\ldots D$$

Firm j incurs cost to produce $q_{j,t}$ according to the quadratic cost function:

$$C(q_{j,t}^0, \tilde{c}_t) = (\overline{c}_1 + \tilde{c}_t)q_{j,t} + \overline{c}_2 q_{j,t}^2 \tag{1}$$

where $\overline{c}_1$ and $\overline{c}_2$ are constants, while $\tilde{c}_t$ is stochastic, following an AR(1) process to capture macro shocks to the market. Formally, it is expressed as $\tilde{c}_{t+1} = \rho\tilde{c}_t + \eta_{t+1}$, where $\rho \in (0,1)$ is the persistence parameter and η_{t+1} is white noise (i.e., independently and identically distributed over time with mean zero and a finite variance, σ_η^2). The cost function is common among the J firms, which observe $\tilde{c}_t$ when making production decisions.

Let $\vec{\boldsymbol{q}}_t$ be a vector consisting of the production of the J firms. The above specifications on stock, exogenous production and cost determine the law of motion, as follows:

$$\begin{bmatrix} s_{t+1}^1 \\ s_{t+1}^2 \\ \vdots \\ s_{t+1}^D \\ x_{t+1} \\ \tilde{c}_{t+1} \end{bmatrix} = \begin{bmatrix} \mathbf{0}_0 \\ \overline{x} \\ 0 \end{bmatrix} + \begin{bmatrix} \mathbf{B}_1 & \mathbf{0}_1 \\ \mathbf{0}_2 & \mathbf{B}_2 \end{bmatrix} \begin{bmatrix} s_t^1 \\ s_t^2 \\ \vdots \\ s_t^D \\ x_t \\ \tilde{c}_t \end{bmatrix} + \begin{bmatrix} \delta & \ldots & \delta \\ \vdots & \vdots & \vdots \\ 0 & \ldots & 0 \\ 0 & \ldots & 0 \end{bmatrix} \vec{\boldsymbol{q}}_t + \begin{bmatrix} 0 \\ \vdots \\ 0 \\ 1 \end{bmatrix} \eta_{t+1} + \begin{bmatrix} 0 \\ \vdots \\ 1 \\ 0 \end{bmatrix} \xi_{t+1} \tag{2}$$

Note $\mathbf{B}_1(i,k) = \begin{cases} 0 & \text{if } k = i+1, \\ \delta & \text{otherwise,} \end{cases}$ and $\mathbf{B}_2 = \begin{bmatrix} \vartheta & 0 \\ 0 & \rho \end{bmatrix}$. $\mathbf{0}_0$ is a $D \times 1$ vector of zeros, $\mathbf{0}_1$ is a $D \times 2$ matrix of zeros and $\mathbf{0}_2$ is a $2 \times D$ matrix of zeros. For notational convenience, we denote the vector of the state variables as $\vec{S}_t = [\vec{s}_t' \; x_t \; \tilde{c}_t]'$, where $\vec{s}_t$ is defined by $[s_t^1, s_t^2, \ldots s_t^D]'$.

Consumers

The decision of consumers about condominium purchases are modeled using a discrete-choice logit framework. There are M consumers in the market and they are indexed by i. For each period, a typical consumer i purchases, at most, one unit from a set of condominiums, of age $0, 1, \ldots D$. The age 0 product is traded in the primary market while older units are traded in a competitive secondary market. The owner of a new condominium unit can sell it in the secondary market after holding it for at least a year. The owner of a condominium unit of age D receives a terminal value $\bar{p}$ at the end of the year. The product is indexed by its age, denoted by d. The outside alternative is denoted by $d=n$, and it includes the choice of purchasing single-unit housing, condominiums older than D, or not buying any type of housing (i.e., renting).

The flow utility of consumer i from purchasing a good of vintage d at time t is given by the following quasi-linear form:

$$u_{it}(d) = \begin{cases} g(d) - \alpha p_t^d + e_{it}^d & \text{if } d = 0, 1, \ldots D \\ e_{it}^d & \text{if } d = n \end{cases} \tag{3}$$

where $g(.)$ is a function of the age of the product (d) and measures the quality of the product, p_t^d is the price of the product, and e_{it}^d captures the heterogeneity of consumers that is unobservable by the econometrician.[18] These follow some zero mean finite-variance distributions independently across time and age. Let $\mathbf{J} = [1, \ldots, J]$ be a set of active firms in the market and $\mathbf{D} = [0, 1, \ldots D]$ a set of available vintages for those products. Consumer i maximizes the sum of his or her present discounted utility flow by making choice (d) from set $\mathbf{D}+\mathbf{1}$. Given the consumer's time discount factor, β, the problem for the consumer i is given by:

$$\max_{\{d_\tau\}_{\tau=t}^{\infty}} \sum_{\tau=t}^{\infty} \beta^{\tau-t} u_{i\tau}(d) \tag{4}$$

This problem involves cumbersome dynamic programming. However, it is known that the problem can be simplified to a static one by assuming that there are no transaction costs. Berkovec (1985) and Esteban and Shum (2007) show that problem (4) can be replaced by:

$$\max_{d \in \mathbf{D}+\mathbf{1}} \mathrm{UG}_{it}(d)$$

where the utility gain $\mathrm{UG}_{it}(d)$ is defined by:

$$\mathrm{UG}_{it}(d) = \begin{cases} g(d) - \alpha \mathrm{ECC}_t^d + e_{it}^d & \text{if } d \leq D \\ e_{it}^d & \text{if } d = n \end{cases}$$

The expected capital cost ECC_t^d is defined by:

$$\mathrm{ECC}_t^d = \begin{cases} p_t^d - \beta p_{t+1}^{d+1} & \text{if } d < D \\ p_t^d - \beta \overline{p} & \text{if } d = D \end{cases}$$

where $\overline{p}$ is the terminal or scrap value of the condominium when it reaches age D in period $t+1$. It implies that a consumer's dynamic decision is equivalent to a comparison of the utility gains from the choices available in the period. The utility gain consists of terms $g(d)$, the benefit from the consumption of the goods for the given period, and $p_t^d - \beta p_{t+1}^{d+1}$, the implicit rental price under the assumption of no transaction costs. Here, consumers have perfect foresight, such that $E_t(p_{t+k}^{d+k}) = p_{t+k}^{d+k}$ for all t and $k = 0, 1, D+1$. This assumption is relaxed at the estimation stage.[19]

The unobserved heterogeneity of consumers, e_{it}^d, is assumed to be identically and independently distributed with respect to the type I extreme value distribution across consumers (i), vintage (d) and time (t). Integrating ε_{it}^d then yields a market share equation for each vintage as follows:

$$\mu_t^d(p_t, p_{t+1}) = \begin{cases} \dfrac{\exp(g(d) - \alpha \mathrm{ECC}_t^d)}{1 + \sum_{d'=0}^{D} \exp(g(d) - \alpha \mathrm{ECC}_t^{d'})} & \text{for } d \leq D \\ \dfrac{1}{1 + \sum_{d'=0}^{D} \exp(g(d) - \alpha \mathrm{ECC}_t^{d'})} & \text{for } d = n \end{cases} \tag{5}$$

Applying the transformation method of Berry:1994, the logarithms of μ_t^d and μ_t^n are taken and their differences are given by the following expression:

$$\ln \mu_t^d(p_t, p_{t+1}) - \ln \mu_t^n(p_t, p_{t+1}) = g(d) - \alpha ECC_t^d \tag{6}$$

$$= g(d) - \alpha p_t^d + \alpha \beta p_{t+1}^{d+1} \tag{7}$$

for $t=1,\ldots T$, $d=0,1,\ldots D$. Note that the market share of each type is defined by:

$$\mu_t^d = \begin{cases} \dfrac{x_t + \sum_j q_{jt}}{M} & \text{if } d=0 \\ \dfrac{s_t^d}{M} & \text{if } d=1,2,\ldots D \\ 1 - \dfrac{\left(\sum_j q_{jt} + \sum_d s_t^d + x_t\right)}{M} & \text{if } d=n \end{cases} \tag{8}$$

Iterating over the future expected capital cost ECC, together with some manipulations, yields the following expression for the price of each new unit produced by firm j:

$$p_t^0 = \frac{1}{\alpha}\left[\sum_{d=0}^{D} \beta^d (\ln \mu_{t+d}^n - \ln \mu_{t+d}^d + g(d)\right] + \beta^{D+1}\overline{p}_{t+D+1} \tag{9}$$

$$= P^0(\vec{s}_t, x_t, x_{t+1}, \ldots, x_{t+D}, \vec{q}_t, \vec{q}_{t+1}, \ldots \vec{q}_{t+D}) \tag{10}$$

It shows that the price of each new product depends not only on today's production $(\vec{q}_t, x_t)$, but also on that of the future $(\vec{q}_{t+k}, x_{t+k}, k=1,\ldots D)$ and of the past $(\vec{s}_t)$, through the outside market share μ_{t+d}^n.

Given this inverse demand function, the description of a firm's problem is given in the next section.

Firms

Firms are competing in a Cournot quantity setting game. Condominium development requires a long period of planning and it is difficult to make quick adjustments in terms of the number of units being supplied once a development plan is approved by the authorities. Thus, it is reasonable to consider the production level as a strategic variable of a firm. Given the inverse demand function of a new product (9) and the cost function (1), firm j chooses the level of production to maximize its present discounted profit stream:

$$\sum_{\tau=t}^{\infty} \beta^{\tau-t} E_t \left[p_\tau^0 q_{j\tau} - C(q_{j\tau}, \tilde{c}_\tau) \right] \tag{11}$$

Because of the dependence of new condominium prices on the current, future and past production of the entire condominium stock (i.e., of all firms), any given firm's production strategy may depend on the entire history of its production. The convenient assumption is to allow the production plans of all firms at time t to depend only on the all available stock of condominiums at any given time. This assumption corresponds to the concept of a Markov perfect Nash equilibrium, which is a subgame perfect equilibrium where actions are only functions of payoff-relevant state variables, as defined in Maskin and Tirole (1988a,b). In the current problem, the payoff-relevant variables are the state variables ($\vec{S}_t$), as defined in section "The Environment and the Transition of the States."

Formally a firm's problem is given by:

$$\max_{q_{jt}^0} \sum_{\tau=t}^{\infty} \beta^{\tau-t} E_t \left[p_\tau^0 q_{j\tau} - C(q_{j\tau}, \tilde{c}_\tau) \right] \tag{12}$$

subject to Eq. (2) and

$$q_{jt} = h_j(\vec{S}_t) \tag{13}$$

and

$$q_{jt} \leq M - \sum_{d'=1}^{D} s_t^{d'} - x_t - \sum_{j' \neq j} q_{j't} \tag{14}$$

given

$$q_{j't} = h_{j'}(\vec{S}_t),\ j' = 1, 2, \ldots j-1, j+1, \ldots. J \tag{15}$$

where $h_l(\cdot)$ is the stationary policy function for firm l. The constraints (13) and (15) ensure that the solution is a Markov perfect Nash equilibrium. The expectation operator in the infinite sum in problem (12) is over the

η_s and ξ_s, $s=t,t+1,\ldots$. The constraint (14) restricts the choice of production so there is no oversupply. At equilibrium, the policy functions that rational firms use to forecast future production, both their own and that of competitors, coincides with the optimal policy for each. Note that, in this case, the equilibrium strategy is time consistent.

The problem stated by Eqs. (12)–(15) gives the following Bellman equation:

$$V_j(\vec{S}_t)=\max_{q_{jt}}[\mathrm{E}\pi_{jt}(\vec{S}_t,q_{jt},\vec{q}_{-jt},\{\vec{q}_\tau\}_{\tau=t+1}^{D})+\beta EV_j(\vec{S}_{t+1}|\vec{q}_t)] \tag{16}$$

subject to (2), and (13) for $j=1,\ldots,J$. $\vec{q}_{-jt}$ denotes a vector of production at time t, for all firms but j. It can be further simplified as follows:

$$V_j(\vec{S}_t)=\max_{q_{jt}}[\mathrm{E}\pi_{jt}(\vec{S}_t,q_{jt},\vec{q}_{-jt},\{H(\vec{S}_\tau)\}_{\tau=t+1}^{D})+\beta EV_j(\vec{S}_{t+1})] \tag{17}$$

where the vector $H(\vec{S}_\tau)=[h_1(\vec{S}_\tau),\ldots,h_J(\vec{S}_\tau)]'$ stands for the vector of (expected) future production given the state $\vec{S}_\tau$. To obtain tractability and overcome the computational burden, we focus only on symmetric equilibria, so that $h_j(\vec{S}_\tau)=h(\vec{S}_\tau)$ for all j. Note that the uniqueness of the equilibrium is not guaranteed in this model. Nevertheless, by the solution algorithm described in Appendix A, the solutions starting from various initial value always converged to the same one.

Discussions about Some Assumptions

In this section, we discuss four assumptions that, while important in implementing the estimation, are certainly not innocuous in other respects. First, products are differentiated only by vintage. Thus, condominiums are homogeneous within the same vintage and the quality of the product in a given vintage is constant for each given time. Although the data suggests that each year there exists great variation in the characteristics of new condominiums, and that those characteristics change over time, this assumption is nonetheless maintained, as the focus of the current article is on the durability of condominiums.[20] This simplification implies that firms take the quality of each rival's product as a given; likewise, that they consider a stated quality as being the same as their own.

Second, firms are homogeneous. This restriction, together with the first assumption, greatly reduces the dimensionality of the problem by allowing a structure wherein the policy function only depends on common variables (i.e., total stock, exogenous production, and macro cost shock), rather than also on firm-specific variables. It also enables us to impose a symmetric equilibrium when solving the model. If firm-specific variables are included in the set of state variables, the dimension of the problem grows with the number of the firms, and the problem becomes intractable. The gain from these assumptions is that we are only required to solve the problem as if it is a single agent problem. A drawback from this restriction is that the model does not explain the variation in the production level across firms, something which is observed in the data. Instead, this is dealt with using idiosyncratic production errors, as described in the fourth section.

Third, the terminal value of the condominium unit is fixed. This assumption permits us to obtain an analytical expression for the inverse demand function in a very simple manner. There are two shortcomings, however. First, we get a high price elasticity of demand and a low sensitivity of price to output, in as much as the terminal value does not depend on the stock or production. Second, it is likely that $\tilde{c}$ is correlated with $\overline{p}$, because of the certainty that the value of the physical building depreciates over time; thus, the price gets much closer to the land price as it ages. Nevertheless, it is difficult to infer the relationship between these variables unless we impose further structure on them, as we do not directly observe $\tilde{c}$.

Fourth, $\tilde{c}$ is treated as being exogenous. Hence, the cost, mainly as reflecting the land price, is not allowed to be endogenous; if the project involves the development of a large community, large-scale condominium construction could raise the value of the land.

ESTIMATION

The set of structural parameters in the model described above is $\Theta = [x, \vartheta, \sigma_\xi^2, \alpha, \beta, \delta, \overline{p}, \{g(d)|d = 0, 1, \ldots D\}, \overline{c}_1, \overline{c}_2, \rho, \sigma_\eta^2]$. This section describes the estimation strategy of those parameters in three steps. The third step involves the dynamic programming algorithm in the standard GMM procedure following Rust (1987). Note that various estimation approaches for dynamic games have been recently developed; among others, Hotz, Miller, Sanders, and Smith (1994), Aguirregabiria and Mira (2002), Bajari, Benkard, and Levin (2007), and Imai, Jain, and Ching (2009) are computationally less expensive compared with the nested fixed point approach. However, two features of our model – a continuous choice variable and a state variable that is serially correlated and common to all agents but unobservable to econometrician – do not easily allow the direct application of those methods.[21]

Data

The data for this study are obtained from two sources: primary market data for the years from 1990 to 2000 are taken from the yearly publication "Condominium Apartment Market Trends," as constructed by the Real Estate Economic Institute; and secondary market data are taken from periodical advertisements entitled "Weekly Housing Information," for the years 1992–2002, as published by Recruit Co. Ltd.

The unit of observation in the first dataset corresponds to a group of units in one development project that are sold at the same sales timing, called a phase. While 26 units on average are sold in a phase from one project, one phase could contain as many as 319 units. The data include the names of buildings, their addresses, the closest train stations, distances to stations, the names of developers, the names of builders, as well as other characteristics. Some of those variables are summarized in Table D2. The fifth column reports the mean of the variables weighted by the number of units to grasp the distribution of the variables in terms of units. This table displays the large variety of characteristics in the sample, as is common in any real estate data at the micro level. As described in the previous section, the model imposes that all products within the same vintage are homogeneous. However, we took advantage of the richness of the micro level data.

The second set of data is organized by unit. Two datasets are merged using common information such as the names of buildings and addresses. However, for each given time, the majority of condominiums are not traded; furthermore, the "Weekly Housing Information" advertisements do not cover all the properties on the market; 27 percent of the observations have corresponding secondary market data. For these reasons, prices for unobserved units are imputed using a linear regression of prices for each age on variables for various characteristics using data on observed units. Appendix B describes the method in detail.

The last two sections in Table D2 report the summary statistics for imputed prices. Prices are adjusted for inflation using a GDP deflator. The base year is 1995. In order to obtain numerical stability in the nested algorithm, prices are rescaled by one millionth, and the units are rescaled by one thousandth.

Our model classifies firms into two types: oligopolistic firms and fringe firms. The firms are selected by the ranking of the cumulative production during the sample period. The estimation is performed for the models of the a five-firm oligopoly (model I) and a 10-firm oligopoly (model II).[22]

Fixed Parameters

Some parameters that are fixed in the estimation procedure are summarized in Table D3; these are fixed in order to implement the estimation.

Two parameters that dictate durability in the model – the lifespan of a condominium unit, D, and the depreciation factor, δ – are fixed for computational reasons. The value of D is fixed at one calendar year; thus, a condominium unit lasts in the market for two years, in order to reduce the dimensionality. Note that as D increases, the number of vintages included in the state vector increases accordingly. To see the consequence of this treatment, the production paths of monopolists over a period of 25 years for $D=1$ and $D=2$ are simulated using the same parameter values. The results are shown in Fig. D2. The diagram indicates that there are no substantial differences in the nature of the two series. Although the same parameter values are used, additions to the vintage increase the value of a steady state; thus, we see the difference in the levels of production. Since what is important for the estimation and for the purpose of this study is the property of the series, this treatment does not cause any substantial differences in the results.[23] It is unlikely that a condominium unit physically depreciates over the first two years of its life. However, we set its annual depreciation rate, $1-\delta$, at 0.01 for two reasons. First, since the precise data of the stock of condominiums are unavailable, the parameter value cannot be estimated. Second, the numerical stability of the nested dynamic programming algorithm requires $1-\delta$ to be strictly greater than zero.[24]

The common discount factor for firms and consumers is fixed at $\beta=0.975$, which reflects the interest rate during this period and follows the convention found in the IO literature. It is known, in general, that the discount factor tends to be collinear to other parameters in a dynamic model, and, thus, it is difficult to identify.

As discussed in the previous section, to obtain an analytical expression of the inverse demand function, the price of a two-year-old unit, $\overline{p}$, is considered constant. In the estimation, it is fixed at 42.3 million yen, which corresponds to the weighted average (imputed) price of a two-year-old unit between 1994 and 2002.[25]

The cost parameter $\overline{c}_1$ is set at 24.71 million yen, which is equivalent to 61 percent of the projected cost for 2002.[26] This parameter is thought of as constituting the steady state of the level of the constant portion of the marginal cost. For numerical optimization, we restrict the sum of $\overline{c}_1$ and the macro shock, $\tilde{c}_t$, so that it is bounded below by zero. If this parameter is to be estimated, the range of $\tilde{c}_t$ must be adjusted for each iteration, something that increases the computation time. The variance of the macro cost shock, σ_η^2, is normalized at unity, as the policy function is very insensitive to this parameter. The market size, M, is fixed at 3,514,000, which is equal to the number of households in the area in 1995, a figure obtained from the census data. Thus, outside alternatives include not only condominiums older than two years but also all types of housing, inclusive of single-unit ownership and rental housing.

Given these fixed parameters, the set of structural parameters to be estimated is reduced to $\Theta = [\overline{x}, \vartheta, \sigma_\xi^2, \alpha, g(0), g(1), \overline{c}_2, \rho]$. In the next subsection, structural errors are introduced. Subsequently, the three-step estimation procedure is described.

Econometric Model

To carry out a statistical inference of the model, unobservable stochastic terms must be introduced so that variations observed in the data are generated by the model.

The key equations for the estimation are the market share equations (6) and the equilibrium production rule (13). For the demand-side relationship, the assumption about a consumer's expectation (i.e., perfect foresight) is relaxed, and a rational expectation is assumed instead. Specifically, the price of product aged $d+1$ at time $t+1$ can be written as follows[27]:

$$p_{t+1}^{d+1} = E_t(p_{t+1}^{d+1} | \Omega_t) + \nu_{t,t+1}^{d+1} \tag{18}$$

where Ω_t is the information available at time t and $\nu_{t,t+1}^{d+1}$ is the forecast error for vintage d.

For the supply side, an error λ_{jt} for firm j at time t is introduced; thus, the relation between the observed data and the optimal production rule can be written as:

$$q_{jt} = h(\vec{\mathbf{S}}_t) + \lambda_{jt}, j = 1, \ldots, J \tag{19}$$

where it is assumed that λ_{jt} is unobserved by any firm when making a decision, and that it is independently and identically distributed as $N(0, \sigma_\lambda^2)$ across firms and time. This implies that a producer integrates out not only its own production errors, but also those of its rivals when solving the problem (17) although they are not state variables. Note that λ_{jt}s do not affect the equilibrium policy function but still allow for the heterogeneity in the realized production. This change in the assumption adds one more parameter to estimate, σ_λ^2.[28] The assumption that there may be unexpected adjustments in production at the time of planning may sound restrictive. However, it is observed that, in some cases, condominium developers purchase condominium buildings from other developers. Hence λ_{jt} can be thought of as constituting such adjustments.

Additionally, the forecast error $\nu_{t,t+1}^{d+1}$ and λ_{jt} are assumed to be independent across time, firms and vintages. With this assumption, the introduction of $\nu_{t,t+1}^{d+1}$ does not change the problem for the producer.[29]

Using forecast errors as the basis for an estimation is not a common approach in the empirical discrete choice literature, which assumes the existence of unobserved heterogeneity. In this model, the time-invariant heterogeneity is captured by the term $g(d)$, while time-variant heterogeneity cannot be introduced, as it will not be consistent with the dynamic problem solved by the producers unless $\nu_{t,t+1}^{d+1}$ is treated as another state variable. This is not feasible because of computational difficulties. An alternative structure is the introduction of measurement errors. However, as the equilibrium production rule (19) is not linear for state variables measured using past errors, the construction of the GMM objective function requires an integration of all past errors. This is not available, however, given the current computational ability.

The First Step – Estimation of x_t Process $(\bar{x}, \vartheta, \sigma_\xi^2)$

The evolution of x_t, the production level of fringe competitors, is estimated using data from 1992 to 2000, by regressing it on its lagged variable (i.e., x_{t-1}). From the residuals, we obtain an estimate for σ_ξ^2. The variable x_t is constructed for each model by subtracting the aggregated production of oligopolistic firms from the total production in each year.

The Second Step – Estimation of the Demand Parameters $(\alpha, g(0), g(1))$
Since the model treats all condominiums of the same vintage as homogeneous, the corresponding data are aggregated by year. Inasmuch as the aggregation makes the number of observations too few for reasonable estimation, we employ sales phase data (i.e., the lowest level of aggregation) to estimate the parameters α, $g(0)$ and $g(1)$. Thus, the available variables at this stage are the averages of the characteristics and prices for the group of units that are sold by a particular firm at a particular location in a given sales phase. We index the unit of observation by k and let K denote the total number of groups of newly produced units. To capture quality variations across products as produced by different firms, a characteristic vector, $\vec{\boldsymbol{X}}^{d}_{k,t}$, is introduced.

Introducing forecast errors $\nu^{d+1}_{k,t,t+1}$ and using phase-level data modify Eq. (6) as follows:

$$\begin{aligned}\ln \mu^{d}_{k,t} - \ln \mu^{n}_{t} &= \vec{\boldsymbol{X}}^{d}_{k,t}\boldsymbol{\Gamma} - \alpha(p^{d}_{k,t} - \beta E p^{d+1}_{k,t+1}) = \vec{\boldsymbol{X}}^{d}_{k,t}\boldsymbol{\Gamma} - \alpha(p^{d}_{k,t} - \beta p^{d+1}_{k,t+1} - \beta \nu^{d+1}_{k,t,t+1}) \\ &= \vec{\boldsymbol{X}}^{d}_{k,t}\boldsymbol{\Gamma} - \alpha CC^{d}_{k,t} + \omega^{d+1}_{k,t+1}, k = 1, \ldots K, \ \ d = 0, 1, t = 1, \ldots T \end{aligned} \quad (20)$$

where $CC^{d}_{k,t}(= p^{d}_{k,t} - \beta p^{d+1}_{k,t+1})$ denotes the realized capital cost of a unit in group k of age d at time t.

As the disturbance $(\omega^{d+1}_{k,t+1} = \alpha\beta\nu^{d+1}_{k,t+1})$ is due to a forecast error, its definition gives the orthogonality condition as below (i.e., given the information set at time t, the expected error on the forecast is zero). Note that the number of observations increases proportionally to D because each new condominium will be one-year-old stock in the next period. Between ages, only prices and the amount of stock vary, since other observed characteristics do not change over time:

$$\begin{aligned} E(\omega^{d+1}_{k,t+1} | \Omega_t) &= 0 \\ E(y_{k,t} \cdot \omega^{d+1}_{k,t+1}) &= 0 \end{aligned} \quad (21)$$

where $y_{k,t}$ consists of variables that are known at time t. Note that Ω_t cannot include $q_{k,t}$, as it is not known when consumers make their choices. The vector $y_{k,t}$ includes a constant and some characteristic variables. Consistent estimation of the demand parameters, $(\alpha, \boldsymbol{\Gamma})$, can be obtained using a GMM estimator. The parameters for the next estimation step, $g(0)$, and $g(1)$, are obtained by calculating the mean characteristic vector for each vintage across k and t $(\vec{\boldsymbol{X}}^{d} = \sum\sum_{kt}\vec{\boldsymbol{X}}^{d}_{k,t})$, and by evaluating $\hat{g}(d) = \vec{\boldsymbol{X}}^{d}\hat{\boldsymbol{\Gamma}}$ for

$d=0,1$. By doing this, $g(d)$ becomes fixed to the mean of the quality for vintage d across time.

The Third Step – Estimation of the Supply Parameters

Given the estimates from the previous steps, we estimate the cost-related parameters, $(\rho, \sigma_\lambda^2, \overline{c}_2)$, by estimating Eq. (19), using the nested GMM procedure. In this model, where the parametric form of the policy function is unknown, our data-matching procedure utilizes a function approximation technique. Note that the alternative method such as utilizing equilibrium conditions cannot avoid obtaining a solution of the dynamic programming problem because current price is a function of future productions. Given the variables $\vec{z}_{jt}$, which are orthogonal to λ_{jt}, we are able to obtain the moment condition:

$$E(\vec{z}_{jt}' \cdot \lambda_{jt}) = 0 \tag{22}$$

Under the assumptions for λ_{jt}, the instruments are the constant, lagged production for two periods with the exception of its own, and exogenous production (i.e., $\vec{z}_{jt} = [1, q_{-j,t-1}, q_{-j,t-2}, x_t]$). The distribution assumptions for λ_{jt} give another moment restriction, based on the second moment for λ_{jt}, namely:

$$E[\vec{z}_{jt}'[\lambda_{jt}^2 - \sigma_\lambda^2]] = 0 \tag{23}$$

The stacking conditions (22) and (23), together yield $E(Z_{jt} {}^* \Lambda_{jt}) = 0$, where Z_{jt} is the block diagonal matrix. Its sample analogue is given by:

$$\Upsilon_s = \frac{1}{TJ} \sum_{t=1}^{T} \sum_{j=1}^{J} Z_{jt} {}^* \Lambda_{jt} \tag{24}$$

For each evaluation of the set of parameter values, the firms' dynamic programming problem has to be solved, as the function $h(\,)$ is a function of parameters $(\rho, \sigma_\lambda^2, \overline{c}_2)$.

The GMM criterion function (24) is, however, not available due to an initial condition problem – one of the state variables, $\tilde{c}$, is unobservable and serially correlated. The feasible objective function is obtained by integrating out the sequence of $\tilde{c}$ from Eq. (24) using the density of $\tilde{c}$. Nevertheless, as none of $\tilde{c}$ are observable, the serial dependence of $\tilde{c}$

requires a further assumption on its initial value (or terminal value). In this application, the terminal value $\tilde{c}_T$ is assumed to be nonstochastic and fixed to the value based on informal information on the cost of condominium production in the late 1990s. See Appendix C for how we calibrated this value. The feasible moment condition is thus given by:

$$\Upsilon_{si} = \frac{1}{J}\sum_{j=1}^{J} \int \cdots \int Z_{jt} * \Lambda_{jt}(\vec{c}) f(\vec{c}\,|c_T) d\vec{c} \tag{25}$$

Given a positive definite weighting matrix $\hat{\Xi}_s$, the GMM estimator minimizes $\Upsilon'_{si}\hat{\Xi}_s\Upsilon_{si}$. In the first-stage estimation, we used the inverse of the squared instrument matrix as $\hat{\Xi}_s$. The results reported in this article involve the optimal GMM estimator, which uses a consistent estimator for $E(\Upsilon_{si} * \Upsilon'_{si})$ as a weighting matrix.

Identification

As explained in the first and the second estimation steps, identifications of parameters for the process of production by fringe competitors and the demand system are obtained using cross-sectional and time-series variations of observables: market shares, observed capital costs, and aggregate production by fringe competitors. However, the identification in the third step is not trivial.[30] Although the model in this article fully specifies the parametric form of the return function, those assumptions alone do not guarantee identification. Stated more formally, the objective function for the estimation (i.e., the optimally weighted quadratic form of the GMM conditions) must be reasonably sensitive to changes in the parameter values.

In order to gain some ideas about its sensitivity to the parameter values in which we are interested, we present simulated production paths of a monopolist for different values of $\bar{c}_2$ and ρ in Fig. D3. The initial value of each simulation is set at the observed value for 1991, and each run consists of 10,000 simulations over nine periods. The panel on the left shows that the increase in $\bar{c}_2$, the coefficient of the quadratic term in the cost function, decreases the production at each period but does not greatly change the shape of the path. Thus, it determines the level of the optimal production. The panel on the right indicates that a low value of ρ, which implies a smaller persistence of the macro cost shock, $\tilde{c}$, generates a hump-shaped path by making $\tilde{c}$ reach its steady-state level faster. Hence, the peak of the production occurs later, as ρ increases. At a higher level of ρ, the peak is not realized within nine periods. Therefore, observed variations of the level of production can identify $\tilde{c}$, and observed shapes of the production paths can identify ρ. The variance of idiosyncratic production shock, σ_{λ}^{2}, can be identified by cross-sectional variations in production because all heterogeneity among the firms are summarized in λ_{jt} in the model.

RESULTS

The Parameter Estimates

The empirical results are reported in Tables D4, D5, and D6 respectively, for each estimation step.

The process for x_t is estimated for model I (a five-firm oligopoly) and model II (a 10-firm oligopoly) using the aggregated data from 1992 to 2000. For both models, the AR(1) coefficient, ϑ, is significantly positive, and less than one, as seen in Table D4. However, the Dicky–Fuller test does not reject the unit root for both models. The constant term, however, is positive, although not significant. These parameter estimates imply that the process of x_t gradually converges toward a positive steady-state value, x^{ss}, which is estimated to be 32,200 units with model I; and 31,160 units with model II.

The demand system is estimated using demand data for the period 1994–1999. This period includes the year during which the consumption tax rate changed and a new tax preferential system for homebuyers was implemented; both are likely to have had a large impact on housing purchase behavior. Nevertheless, we assume that all consumers and firms anticipated these events at the beginning of the period.[31] All observations appear twice in the estimation in the dataset, as any given year's new condominiums become one-year-old units the following year, with the amount depreciating by $1-\delta$. Overall, the dataset consists of 10,113 observations.

Columns (i) and (ii) in Table D5 report the estimates for the demand parameters, by OLS and GMM, respectively. Since imputed prices are used as the values of the condominium stock, standard errors must be adjusted for the noise caused by imputation. The correction is performed using the bootstrap method. Possible endogeneity for expected capital cost is dealt with using the log of its height and the log of the distance from the nearest train station. Both are known at the time of purchase by potential buyers, and correlate with the value of the property; the distance from the nearest train station is negatively correlated with the land prices, while the height of the building is positively correlated with the production costs. The coefficient for expected capital cost, $-\alpha$, is estimated to be negative and significant for both model specifications, although the magnitude's absolute value is larger when instruments are used, indicating that the forecast error, ω_{jt}, causes a bias toward zero. The negative value of $-\alpha$ suggests that consumers prefer a good with a lower capital cost, as expected. The tests for relevance of instruments (the canonical correlations likelihood-ratio test), endogeneity, and the overidentification restriction show that the adopted instruments are acceptable. Dummy variables for age, which measure the quality of each vintage after controlling for other characteristic variables, are negative and significant for all ages and for all specifications, implying that, relative to the outside alternative, consumers value condominium units less. Among condominiums, new condominiums are valued more than older condominiums, as is shown by the larger estimated coefficient of the age-0 dummy relative to the age-1 dummy. Having obtained estimated parameters for the age dummies and the other characteristic variables, the vintage quality parameters $g(d), d=0,1$ are calculated using the mean values for all characteristic variables. These are reported in Table D5, and represent the average valuations of consumers for condominium units for each vintage relative to outside goods. For the two specifications, the rankings of these two parameters by age are the same as that for the age dummies.

The cost parameters estimated in the third step are reported in Table D6 Firm-level data for 5- and 10-oligopolistic firms over seven periods (from 1994 to 2000) are used. The estimates for ρ indicate that the macro cost shock is a stationary process for both specifications. These estimates from models I and II, imply that the linear coefficient of the cost function, $\overline{c}_1 + \tilde{c}_t$, is deflating on average, at 2.4 percent and 1.5 percent, respectively. The estimated value of $\overline{c}_2$ is positive and significant, confirming that this industry's technology has decreasing returns to scale. This result reflects the fact that, relative to small firms, large developers are more apt to construct costly units such as large-scale buildings and high-rise complexes. This implies that large condominium developers have an incentive to spread production across time, as predicted by Kahn (1986); thus, they have some ability to commit to a future production plan.

The Numerical Solution of the Model

In this section, the solution of the producers' problem with the estimated parameters is presented. The solution for the model is obtained using a policy function iteration algorithm, that utilizes a function approximation technique, known as the collocation method, which is described in Appendix A. The nature of the solution is the same for all values of J (the number of oligopolistic firms). Consequently, the result reported in this section is based on model II ($J = 10$).

The panels in Fig. D4 display the contour maps of the resulting policy function corresponding to Eq. (19), the value function, and the price of a new condominium as a function of the macro cost shock, $\tilde{c}_t$, and the production of fringe competitors, x_t, at the steady-state stock level, ($s_t = s^{ss} = 31.16$).

Both the policy and value functions decreases for all of the state variables for the age-1 stock, s_t, the fringe competitors, x_t, and the macro cost shock, $\tilde{c}_t$. To understand the nature of the optimal production policy, it is useful to break down the states based on the values of the exogenous state variables, $\tilde{c}_t$ and x_t, relative to their steady states. For instance, if $\tilde{c}_t$ is above zero, the process shows a decreasing trend; thus, the state describes a deflationary period for $\tilde{c}_t$. If x_t is below the steady-state value, the process shows an increasing trend and the state describes a growth period. Table D7 reports the elasticities of the policy function with respect to the state variables for the different exogenous state phases. For example, when the macro cost shock is deflationary and the exogenous competitor is growing, an one-percent change in the one-year-old stock results in a 0.02 percent change in production. From this analysis, three more properties of the policy function are derived.

First, as measured by elasticities, the policy is more responsive to the production of the fringe competitors, x_t, than to the one-year-old stock, s_t; This is true for all states. For example, a 1 percent increase in x_t leads to a decrease of between a 0.07 percent and 0.33 percent in production, while a 1 percent increase in s_t leads to roughly a 0.02 percent decrease in production. The intuition behind this result is that, inasmuch as it is a part of current production, x_t influences the market longer through future stock than through one-year-old stock.

Second, production is more responsive to exogenous state variables when the cost is in a deflationary period ($\tilde{c} > 0$) and exogenous production is contracting ($x > 31.16$). Conversely, production is less responsive when the macro cost shock is appreciating and exogenous production is growing.

This reflects the effect of consumers' expectations; since the policy function is a decreasing function of both $\tilde{c}$ and x, cost inflation and growth in exogenous production imply lower production in the future. As a result, consumers are convinced that there will not be a drastic price cut in the future. Consequently, producers do not have to respond to changes in the market environment so much. As a result, adjustment toward the steady state is slower. With the opposite scenario, where cost depreciates and the production of fringe competitors contracts, producers have to respond relatively more, as consumers expect greater production and lower prices. Therefore, the convergence to the steady state occurs more rapidly than with the inflationary phase. This property corresponds to the result in Kahn (1986), wherein a decreasing return-to-scale cost function helps firms to credibly implement a low production plan, although in this case, the cost varies over time. Furthermore, in the deflationary phase of the macro cost shock, consumers correctly expect a future price cut, on account of which, producers quickly lose their market power. This point is investigated further in the next section.

Third, the response to the one-year-old stock does not vary a great deal with respect to the exogenous variables. This is partly due to the fact that, in the next period, the stock will move from the market to the outside alternative; consequently, the stock does not have a direct impact on the future market.

Simulations

In this section, several simulation results are presented to show the dynamics in the market. Unless otherwise noted, all simulations consist of over 10,000 independent seven-period simulations of the dynamic model. For the initial condition of s_t and x_t, the actual observations for 1994 are used. For $\tilde{c}_t$, which cannot be observed directly, we set $\tilde{c}_{2000}$ as the calibrated value of $\tilde{c}$, based on industry information and the estimated parameter value.

The predictive power of the Model

Table D8 compares the simulated statistics and the observations for total production, new condominium prices and the production of fringe competitors for models I and II. Performance is especially good for the prices. The second last row in the table reports the percentages of time within which the predictions fall within the 15 percent intervals from the observations. In both cases, the percentages for prices are close to 100 percent. For production, however, in models I and II, they are 24.4 percent and 37.7 percent, respectively. The performances with respect to production may indicate the limitations in the assumption that all oligopolistic firms are homogeneous. For the rest of the simulation exercises, the set of parameter estimates for model II is adopted because that model yields higher predictive power. Furthermore, it is statistically more reliable because it is based on more observations than is the case for model I. Additionally, alternative assumptions on the number of oligopolistic firms(J) are explored. These indicate that the predictive power increases with J, suggesting that the market is closer to being competitive.

Market power and profits

The mean prediction of markup, evaluated at the marginal cost, is reported in the last raw of Table D8. The average markup is between 0.48 percent and 0.56 percent; these are small values, and they indicate that firms may not possess substantial market power.[32]

Given our quadratic production costs specification, however, markups evaluated at the marginal costs for firms are not indicative of profits. The average profit margin measured using the average costs in simulated data is 8.4 percent and 12.4 percent for models I and II, respectively. These levels of profit margin are comparable to the profit margins reported in the financial statements of developers during the late 1990s, which suggests that the condominium business yields a profit margin of about 10 percent.[33]

The Role of Cost variations

For the purpose of examining the relationship between production cost trends and the market power of durable goods producers, we compare the markups in a cost increasing phase and a cost decreasing phase. To make a valid comparison, the following two paths are compared. The path of the decreasing phase is generated using the estimated parameter value, and then setting the initial value of the macro cost shock at $\tilde{c}_t = C$, where C has a positive value. To see the effect only of the cost variation trend, the path being compared should initiate from the same marginal cost function at the beginning. Thus, $\bar{c}_1 + \tilde{c}_t$ should be at the same level and $\tilde{c}_t$ should have the same absolute value but with a negative sign; consequently, $\tilde{c}_t = -C$. Producers in both cases then face the same speed of convergence in terms of $\tilde{c}_t$. To align the value of the marginal cost, the solution of the producer's problem, where $\bar{c}_1$ equals the sum of the previously set value (24.71 million yen) and twice the value, is set as the point of comparison ($2 \times C$). This solution is used to simulate the path in the cost increasing phase. For the initial value of exogenous production and one-year-old stock, the observed values for 2,000 are used in both paths. For the value of C, the terminal value of the macro cost shock obtained in the estimation, $\tilde{c}_{2000}$, is used.

Fig. D5 compares the simulated markups over 11 periods; the dotted line indicates the markup for the cost increasing phase and the solid line indicates that for the cost decreasing phase. At the initial point, the markup under the increasing phase is 31 percent higher than that under the decreasing phase. As the time passes, the difference in markups increases. By the 11th period, the markup in the increasing phase is 2.9 times more than that of the decreasing phase. This comparison indicates that the firms have significantly more market power during the cost increasing phase than during the cost decreasing phase.

Underlying these results is the change in the incentive of producers compared with that under a time-invariant cost structure. When cost is increasing, a firm has an incentive to produce more now rather than later, since it will be more costly to produce in the future. On the other hand, when cost is decreasing, a firm has an incentive to postpone production, as it can save on the cost by accruing a lower marginal cost in the future. Forward-looking consumers are aware of these incentives to firms. Therefore, cost increases lead consumers to believe that firms will not flood the market in the future; hence, their willingness to pay does not decrease. Conversely, cost decreases lead to a reduction in a willingness to pay. Hence, the Coase problem of firms becoming less serious during the cost increasing phase, but the problem is worse during the cost decreasing phase. Given that, on average, factor prices in the Tokyo market were on a decreasing trend throughout the 1990s up through the mid 2000s, this result suggests that condominium developers had more difficulty in making profits during the 1990s than during preceding decades.

Factors of Price Deflation between 1994 and 2000

In this section, the contributors to the price deflation between 1994 and 2000 are decomposed using the parameter estimates from model II. The result here, however, should be interpreted with caution given the way oligopolistic firms are selected in the estimation.

For this purpose, we obtain the following simulated price paths: (i) the benchmark price path reported at the beginning of this section; (ii) the price path where $\tilde{c}$, and x_t are fixed at the initial levels for all simulation periods;

and (iii) the price path using the actual values of x_t and with a fixed $\tilde{c}$. By comparing these series, we are able to obtain how much of the variation in price is accounted for by increased exogenous competition. Table D9 presents the results of the simulation. Column (iv) reports the percentage of the price deflation since 1994 that is accounted for by the increased competition caused by exogenous fringe competitors.

Note that the contribution of fringe competitors dropped from 45 percent to 13 percent in 1997 and revived to 25 percent in 1998. For those two years, the overall output dropped compared with that for 1996. This shift is likely due to the effects of the consumption tax hike introduced in 1997 and the change in the tax preferential system, which was expected to go into effect in 1999. With the anticipation of the first event that was announced in 1994, forward-looking consumers were apt to engage in last-minute purchases in the period leading up to 1997 and to reduce purchases following the change in the tax rate.[34] In anticipation of the second event, potential buyers had a strong incentive to postpone their purchases so as to benefit from the new system. Thus, prices after 1996 up through 1999 decreased due to the components not accommodated for in the model. In this simulation, all the remaining change is the contribution of $\tilde{c}_t$. Excluding those two years, the contribution of x_t is about 50 percent. One thing to note is the possibility that x_t is correlated with cost factors. It is likely that, generally speaking, competition intensifies as costs decline. Nevertheless, this is beyond the scope of this article, and is left for future research.

Column (v) reports the price path if oligopolistic firms act as price takers. By comparing this path with the benchmark path (i), the effect of imperfect competition on the market price can be measured. Column (vi) reports these measures in percentage terms; they are very close to zero. On average, the benchmark price is 0.09 percent or 36,000 yen higher than the competitive price, suggesting that the market power was not a key factor in explaining the divergence of the condominium prices and land prices that is observed in Fig. D1.

CONCLUSION

This article examines the market phenomenon of the primary market for condominiums in Tokyo between 1994 and 2000. During this period, increased output and persistent falls in the prices of condominiums, land,

and other factors of production were observed. The main question posed here is whether market power played any role in explaining this outcome.

We focus on the durability of the condominiums and the presence of a secondary market, and developed a dynamic oligopoly model that is based on Esteban (2003). The model incorporates an important feature found in this industry: the persistent factor price variations that affect the dynamics of the market on account of the expectations of all agents. This framework allows for an investigation of the relationship between the trend in production costs and the degree of market power possessed by the durable goods producers.

The structural parameters of the proposed model are estimated using a three-step estimation procedure, one which includes a nested GMM method, in which the algorithm solves the dynamic programming problem of producers for each evaluation of the GMM objective function.

For each estimated set of parameter values, the model yields an optimal policy for oligopolists as a decreasing function for all state variables (i.e., condominium stock, exogenous production and macro cost shock). The optimal policy is the most responsive to the macro cost shock, followed by exogenous competitors as measured by elasticities. Furthermore, the model shows that firms respond to changes in the market environment more drastically during the deflationary phase than during the inflationary phase.

In the estimation and simulation experiments, we find two major results. First, the data provides no evidence that the firms in the primary market had substantial market power in this industry. Contrary to our conjecture, therefore, imperfect competition did not play a role during this period. Second, increasing and decreasing expectations on production cost trends have asymmetric effects to the market power of condominium producers: an increase in their markup when cost increases are anticipated is significantly higher than a decrease in markup when the same magnitude of cost decreases are anticipated. Therefore, Coase problem is more severe when the cost is in deflationary phase.

Those results may call for caution on the part of policymakers when considering the effects of policy instruments in durable goods markets. For instance, for policies such as modifications in the tax codes, quality improvement in stock of durable goods, and the evaluation of merger cases, one should carefully assess how the prices of factors of production are expected to evolve over time when they are implemented. It is particularly relevant in recent years because the prices of raw materials are in increasing trend in many durable good industries.

NOTES

1. This stark conjecture by Coase – that monopoly results in a perfectly competitive outcome – was later formally shown by several researchers, among them Stokey (1981), Bulow (1982), and Gul, Sonnenschein, and Wilson (1986).

2. Porter and Sattler (1999) point out that there exists similar benefits of a second-hand market for durable goods producers as in the differentiated product market. The number of units sold is increased by giving low-valuation consumers a chance to obtain durable goods, and by reducing the incentive of producers to cut prices in order to sell to those low-valuation consumers. Chen, Esteban, and Shum (2013) further studied the effect of having secondary market to profitability of durable goods producer by calibration.

3. Bulow (1982) points out that the capacity constraint might work similarly to increasing costs in an infinite horizon framework. Karp and Perloff (1996) endogenize the technology choice made by a monopolist, thus showing that he or she is able to benefit from an inferior technology as it allows him or her to credibly commit to low production. Kutsoati and Zabojnik (2005) also find that there exists an incentive for a durable goods monopolist seller to adopt an inferior technology using a model of technology selection where "learning-by-doing" is present.

4. The alternative is the urban spatial approach, which considers an equilibrium wherein the stock of housing always equals the size of the urban population. Under such conditions, the supply of housing is equal to the inflow of new persons (i.e., the increase in the population). Land is defined here as a distinct input and its price is endogenously determined by the housing stock.

5. The public entity known as the Japan Public Housing Corporation (JPHC) has been the alternative seller of condominiums and has provided both rental housing and housing for sale since 1955. Its average annual national supply of housing units for sale of all types was approximately 13,000 units. Those units are excluded from our analysis, as the influence of this entity on the Tokyo market is likely to be insignificant. Additionally, given the growing trend toward privatization and the abundance of housing in urban areas, it retreated from the sales business in 1999.

6. The corresponding statistics for New York City in 2004 are as follows: an area of 785 square kilometers (approximately 303 square miles), encompassing 3 million households and 8.1 million people.

7. These data are from the Tokyo Metropolitan Government Bureau of Housing (2004) and the Mizuho Corporate Bank Industry Survey Division (2003).

8. In 2002, units that were older than 30 years constituted 6 percent of the total condominiums in Tokyo. The increasing proportion of aged stock for condominiums is becoming a regulatory concern for safety reasons. In particular, condominiums built before 1981 were designed under a weaker regulation code, and, thus, do not satisfy current building standards. In many cases, the rebuilding of condominiums has proven difficult, as the law requires an approval of rebuilding plans by four-fifths of the owners of units in the building.

9. The greater part of condominium ownership included sectional ownership of land.

10. Under an efficient market assumption, the theoretical price of an asset is the present discount value of the expected flow of income gain from the asset. Thus, the

value of a house has to be equal to the present discount value of a future rental stream. For example, if the expected rent is fixed to today's level, the land price is proportional to the rent. This means that the land price and rental price indices must be identical.

11. It may not be applicable, however, to condominium construction costs since there were news reports that the large contractors took orders at very low prices facing decreasing profitable orders from the public sector during the 1990s.

12. These areas include Adachi, Arakawa, Edogawa, Sumida, and Katsushika.

13. This data is according to Maeda (2005).

14. The percentage of aged home transactions in all home transactions in Japan was 11.8 percent in 2001. It is exceptionally small compared with the corresponding figures in the United States (76.1 percent), the United Kingdom (88.2 percent), and France (71.4 percent).

15. Japan Housing Loan Corporation was a government affiliated and the largest single mortgage lender in Japan. The corporation is privatized in 2006.

16. This modeling approach is employed by Berkovec (1985) with respect to car consumption.

17. This treatment of exogenous competitors is similar to that of exporters in the US automaker model used by Esteban and Shum (2007). However, they assumed the stochastic process to be a random walk without drift.

18. Therefore, consumers are risk neutral in this model.

19. Berkovec (1985) considers stochastic breakdown and the possibility of scrap for automobiles. Correspondingly, the expected capital cost takes these possible events into consideration. In the case of condominiums, because a complete breakdown is seldom observed, we disregard this possibility.

20. Treating the products of oligopolistic firms and the product of fringe firms is unlikely to be problematic. The estimation of the probability that a unit is provided by a fringe firm, controlling for characteristics and year effects, using the probit indicates that there are no substantial differences between the products of two types of firms.

21. The issue of serially correlated unobservable state variable in estimating dynamic game is addressed by some papers. For example, Gallant, Hong, and Khwaja (2010) propose to apply Bayesian MCMC methods for estimating such a model. Arcidiacono and Miller (2011) propose to incorporate Expectation-Maximization algorithm in conditional choice probability estimator of Hotz et al. (1994) to deal with unobserved heterogeneity.

22. Top 10 firms are Daikyo, Mitsui, Recruit Cosmos, Sumitomo, Towa, Cesar, Marubeni, Asahi Construction, Dia Construction, and Nomura Real Estate. These are ordered by the value of the cumulative production. The top five firms were within the top 15 for nine consecutive years between 1992 and 2000.

23. For the initial value of this simulation, we used the value corresponding to the 1991 observations for stock and exogenous production, and the calibrated value for the macro cost shock. The method of calculation for the initial value of the macro cost shock is described in Appendix C.

24. Note that the optimal policy does not substantially change at each set of state variables when δ is reduced further.

25. The simple average of the imputed unit price for the same period was 45.52 million yen, with a standard deviation of 29.18 million yen.

26. Based on an estimate by the industry analyst, non-land costs (i.e., construction cost and sales service cost) accounts for 61 percent of total cost per unit. For the determination of this parameter, the total cost for 2002 is projected by setting the average margin to 10 percent for 2000 and applying the growth rate of each cost index.

27. Note that the product that was aged d at time t becomes age $d+1$ at $t+1$.

28. One of the advantages of the GMM procedure over other methods, such as the maximum likelihood estimation, is that it does not require a parametric assumption of the error term. However, in this model, a parametric assumption is required, as the current price and profit depends on ω_{jt}, and each firm solves its own profit maximization problem with regard to expectation.

29. It is because the forecast errors are entered additively to the expected price function that the expected current period profit function is identical to the one without $\nu_{t,t+1}^{d+1}$, so long as it is independent of q or λ.

30. For a more precise discussion of nonparametrical identification of the dynamic Markov decision problem, see Rust (1994).

31. The consumption tax was raised from 3 to 5 percent in April 1997, in order to compensate for the fiscal loss from the income tax cut of 1994. Note that the consumption tax is imposed on any consumption expenditure, inclusive of residential buildings while the value of the land is not subject to it. As a part of its economic stimulus package, in 1999, the government extended the existing tax preferential system to include mortgage payments on housing loans. The change, which went into effect in 1999 as planned, increased the maximum tax benefit from 1.7 million yen to 5.9 million yen, a 245 percent increase.

32. In general, the model with the estimated parameter values yields a low level of markup across all ranges of states where the problem is solved. Using simulations, we assess to what extent an assumption that firms produce differentiated products can lead to higher markups.

33. For example, the average operating margin of the firms in the sample were 8–12 percent in 1994–2000. The profit breakdown estimate for the unit price around 2,000, performed by an industry analyst indicates that the margin was about 10 percent.

34. For a description of these events, see footnote 26.

35. We thank Koichi Hiraga for providing this information.

ACKNOWLEDGMENT

I wish to thank Matthew Shum and Joseph Harrington for their helpful comments and encouragement. I would also like to thank Susanna Esteban, Hiroshi Fujiki, Tanjim Hossain, Toshiaki Iizuka, Christopher Mayer, John Rust, and Katsumi Shimotsu for their valuable comments. Comments from the seminar audience at Aoyama Gakuin University, the Bank of Canada, the Bank of Japan, GRIPS, HKUST, Japan Economic Association 2008 Spring Meeting, Johns Hopkins University, La Pietra-Mondragone

Workshop (2007), NBER 2008 Japan Project Meeting, Nihon University, and ISER at Osaka University, Advances in Econometrics Research Conference (2013) are likewise gratefully acknowledged. All remaining errors are mine.

REFERENCES

Aguirregabiria, V., & Mira, P. (2002). Swapping the nested fixed point algorithm: A Class of estimators for discrete markov decision models. *Econometrica, 70*(4), 1519–1543.

Arcidiacono, P., & Miller, R. A. (2011). Conditional choice probability estimation of dynamic discrete choice models with unobserved heterogeneity. *Econometrica, 7*(6), 1823–1868.

Bajari, P., Benkard, C. L., & Levin, J. (2007). Estimating dynamic models of imperfect competition. *Econometrica, 75*, 1331–1370.

Berkovec, J. (1985). New car sales and used car stocks: A model of the automobile market. *RAND Journal of Economics, 16*(2), 195–214.

Berry, S. T. (1994). Estimating discrete-choice model of product differentiation. *RAND Journal of Economics, 25*(2), 242–262.

Berry, S., Levinsohn, J., & Pakes, A. (1995). Automobile prices in market equilibrium. *Econometrica, 63*(4), 841–890.

Bulow, J. (1982). Durable goods monopolists. *Journal of Political Economy, 90*, 314–332.

Carranza, J. E. (2007). *Estimation of demand for differentiated durable goods*. Mimeo, University of Wisconsin-Madison, WI.

Chen, J., Esteban, S., & Shum, M. (2013). When do secondary markets harm firms? *American Economic Review*. Forthcoming.

Coase, R. (1972). Durability and monopoly. *Journal of Law and Economics, 15*, 143–149.

Esteban, S. (2003). *Equilibrium dynamics in semi-durable goods markets*. Mimeo, Penn State University, PA.

Esteban, S., & Shum, M. (2007). Durable-goods oligopoly with secondary markets: The case of automobiles. *RAND Journal of Economics, 38*(2), 332–354.

Gallant, R., Hong, H., & Khwaja, A. (2010). *Bayesian estimation of a dynamic game with endogenous, partially observed, serially correlated state*. Working Paper. Economic Research Initiatives at Duke (ERID) Working Paper No. 118.

Goettler, R., & Gordon, B. R. (2011). Does AMD spur intel to innovate more. *Journal of Political Economy, 119*(6), 1141–1200.

Gordon, B. R. (2009). A dynamic model of consumer replacement cycles in the PC processor industry. *Marketing Science, 28*(5), 846–867.

Gowrisankaran, G., & Rysman, M. (2012). Dynamics of consumer demand for new durable goods. *Journal of Political Economy, 120*, 1173–1219.

Gul, F., Sonnenschein, H., & Wilson, R. (1986). Foundation of dynamic monopoly and the coase conjecture. *Journal of Economic Theory, 39*, 155–190.

Hotz, V. J., Miller, R. A., Sanders, S., & Smith, J. (1994). A simulation estimator for dynamic models of discrete choice. *Review of Economic Studies, 61*(2), 265–289.

Imai, S., Jain, N., & Ching, A. (2009). Bayesian estimation of dynamic discrete choice models. *Econometrica, 77*(6), 1865–1899.

Ishihara, M., & Ching, A. (2012). *Dynamic demand for new and used durable goods without physical depreciation: The case of japanese video games*. Rotman School of Management Working Paper No. 2189871. University of Toronto, Canada.

Kahn, C. (1986). The durable goods monopolist and consistency with increasing costs. *Econometrica, 54*(2), 275–294.

Kanemoto, Y. (1997). The housing question in Japan. *Regional Science and Urban Economics, 27*, 613–641.

Karp, L. S., & Perloff, J. M. (1996). The optimal suppression of a low-cost technology by a durable-good monopoly. *RAND Journal of Economics, 27*(2), 346–364.

Kutsoati, E., & Zabojnik, J. (2005). The effects of learning-by-doing on product innovation by a durable good monopolist. *International Journal of Industrial Organization, 23*(1–2), 83–108.

Maeda, S. (2005). *The outlook for the market for houses built for sale – Inventory of condominiums*. The Japanese Economy Insight. Mizuho Research Institute.

Maskin, E., & Tirole, J. (1988a). A theory of dynamic oligopoly, I: Overview and quantity competition with large fixed costs. *Econometrica, 56*(3), 546–569.

Maskin, E., & Tirole, J. (1988b). A theory of dynamic oligopoly, II: Price competition, kinked demand curves, and edgeworth cycles. *Econometrica, 56*(3), 571–599.

Melnikov, O. (2000). *Demand for differentiated durable products: The case of the U.S. computer printer market*. Mimeo, Yale University, CT.

Miranda, M. J., & Fackler, P. L. (2002). *Applied computational economics and finance*. Cambridge, MA: MIT Press.

Mizuho Corporate Bank Industry Survey Division. (2003). *Mizuho industry survey: An overview of the condominium market in the Tokyo metropolitan area*. (In Japanese).

Nair, H. (2007). Intertemporal price discrimination with forward-looking consumers: Application to the US market for console video-games. *Quantitative Marketing and Economics, 5*(3), 239–292.

Ono, H., Takatsuji, H., & Shimizu, C. (2002). *Development of hedonic housing price index for secondhand condominium market in tokyo metropolitan area*. Working Paper No. 3. Reitaku Instutute of Political Economics and Social Studies. In Japanese.

Porter, R. H., & Sattler, P. (1999). *Patterns of trade in the market for used durables: Theory and evidence*. NBER Working Paper No. 7149. MA: National Bureau of Economic Research.

Poterba, J. M. (1984). Tax subsidies to owner occupied housing: An asset market approach. *Quarterly Journal of Economics, 99*(4), 729–752.

Ramey, V. A (1989). *Durable goods monopoly behavior in the automobile industry*. Working Paper, Department of Economics, D-008, University of California, San Diego, CA.

Rosenthal, S. S. (1999). Residential buildings and the cost of construction: New evidence on the efficiency of the housing market. *The Review of Economics and Statistics, 81*, 288–302.

Rust, J. (1987). Optimal replacement of GMC bus engines: An empirical model of Harold Zurcher. *Econometrica, 55*, 999–1033.

Rust, J. (1994). Structural estimation of markov decision process. In R. Engle & D. McFadden (Eds.), *Handbook of econometrics* (Vol. 4, pp. 3081–3143). Amsterdam, Netherland and Oxford, UK: Elsevier Sicence Publisher B.V. Chap. 51. Retrieved from http://books.google.ca/books?id = no5DetlGbMoC&pg = PR11&lpg = PR11&dq = Chapter + 51 + Structural + estimation + of + markov + decision + processes&source = bl&ots = Ugihx5LUx5&sig = p13MvNoP6qk5bshh1mxHAQU6HJc&hl = en&sa = X&ei = eLV6Uu_YJMG_sQS20IEo&ved = 0CEsQ6AEwBA#v = onepage&q = Chapter%2051%20Structural%20estimation%20of%20markov%20decision%20processes&f = false

Schiraldi, P. (2011). Automobile replacement: A dynamic structural approach. *RAND Journal of Economics*, *42*(2), 266–291.

Shimizu, C., Nishimura, K. G., & Asami, Y. (2004). Search and vacancy costs in the Tokyo housing market: Attempt to measure social costs of imperfect information. *Regional Science and Urban Economics*, *16*(3), 210–230.

Stokey, N. (1981). Rational expectations and durable goods pricing. *Bell Journal of Economics*, *12*, 112–128.

Tokyo Metropolitan Government Bureau of Housing. (2004). *Tokyo Housing White Paper – Fiscal Year 2003*. In Japanese.

Topel, R., & Rosen, S. (1988). Housing investment in the United States. *Journal of Political Economy*, *96*(4), 718–740.

Zhao, Y. (2008). *Why are prices falling fast? An empirical study of the US digital camera market*. Mimeo, City University of New York, NY.

APPENDIX A: SOLUTION ALGORITHM – THE COLLOCATION METHOD

With few exceptions, the Markov decision problems have no analytical solutions. In such cases, one needs to rely on the numerical solution – which is an approximation of the true solution – in order to understand the dynamics of the model. We describe here in this note one of the solution methods for a discrete-time continuous Markov decision problem, the collocation method. Among the difficulties in solving such problems is the fact that the unknown of the dynamic programming is not a particular variable, but rather consists of two functions, usually known as the value function and the optimal policy function. In collocation methods, this difficulty is overcome by approximating the value function by using a linear combination of prespecified functions, called a basis function, and evaluating it at predetermined state nodes. For details, see Miranda and Fackler (2002).

The collocation method suggests an approximation of the value function, $V(\cdot)$, as in Eq. (16) with a linear combination of n prespecified functions; these functions are evaluated only at the prespecified n state nodes. More specifically, the function V can be expressed as follows:

$$V(s) \approx \sum_{l=1}^{n} c_l \phi_l(\mathbf{s}) \tag{A.1}$$

where $\mathbf{s}$ denotes a vector of state variables, $\mathbf{q}$ denotes the vector of choice variables by all firms, c_l is a scalar, and $\phi_l(\mathbf{s})$ is a nonlinear function. The numerical analysis theory offers several choices of functional form for $\phi_l(s)$ and the associated state nodes, such as the Chebyshev polynomial basis and node, and the piecewise polynomial splines and nodes. Based on this approximation, I can rewrite the problem as follows:

$$\sum_{l=1}^{n} c_l \phi_l(\mathbf{s}) = \max_{x} \pi(\mathbf{s}, \mathbf{q}, h(g(\mathbf{s}, \mathbf{q}))\ldots) + \beta \sum_{l=1}^{n} c_l \phi_l(g(\mathbf{s}, \mathbf{q}))$$

where he function $g(s, q)$ describes the transition of a state vector, given the choice of firms in the previous period.

The task then is to obtain the optimal policy function, $h(\cdot)$, and coefficient, $c_l, l = 1, 2, \ldots, n$. Note that since my problem impose the symmetric equilibrium, I need to solve for common policy function for all firms. Once $\phi_l(\cdot)$s and s are selected, the optimal policy and value function can be obtained using the algorithm below. Before describing the algorithm, several notations need to be introduced. Let $\boldsymbol{s}$ be the vector (or matrix if s is a vector) of interpolation nodes $[s_1, s_2, \ldots s_n]$. Using $\phi_l(\cdot)$s and s, we can construct a matrix, Φ, in which the ilth element is $\phi_l(s_k)$, where s_k is the kth interpolation node. Note that this matrix will not change over the solution algorithm. Let $\boldsymbol{c} = [c_1, c_2, \ldots, c_n]'$ be the vector of the approximation coefficients. Let $\boldsymbol{v}$ be the column vector $[v(s_1), v(s_2), \ldots, v(s_n)]'$, where s_k denotes each interpolation node. We can then write (A.1) in vector notation:

$$\boldsymbol{v} = \Phi \boldsymbol{c}$$

The outer loop solves for the value function approximation (obtaining coefficient value, c_l^*, $l = 1, 2, \ldots n$), while the inner loop solves for the optimal policy and the associated value function. Note that the superscripts for c and h indicate for the number of iteration steps involved/found in the outer loop in the description below.

Step 1: At the beginning of the program, both the initial guess for the coefficient vector, $\boldsymbol{c}^0$ (which approximates the value function), and the initial guess for the optimal policy, $h^0(\cdot)$, are determined.

Step 2: Given $\boldsymbol{c}^i$ and $h^i(\cdot)$ as own future policy and competitors' current and future policy, the inner loop solves the Bellman equation and the return policy function and the value at the interpolation nodes, s. More specifically, for each interpolation node, s, we obtain scalar q_j, thus satisfying the Karush–Kuhn–Tucker condition: $\frac{\partial \pi_j}{\partial q_j} + \beta \sum_{l=1}^{n} c_l^i \phi_l'(g(s,q)) \frac{\partial g}{\partial q_j} = 0$, where ϕ_l' is the first derivative of ϕ_l. To evaluate this condition, h_i has to be approximated with $\Phi \boldsymbol{c}^*$. This allows us to gain the expected future production. Note that Φ is the same matrix for the approximation of $\boldsymbol{v}$. This step yields $q = h^{i+1}(s)$ and the optimal value, $v^{i+1}(s)$.

Step 3: Given $\boldsymbol{v}^{i+1}$, $\boldsymbol{c}^i$ can be updated by the following rule: $\boldsymbol{c}^{i+1} = \Phi^{-1}\boldsymbol{v}^{i+1}$. Alternatively, it can be updated using Newton's method, which uses the iteration rule,

$\boldsymbol{c}^{i+1} = \boldsymbol{c}^i + [\Phi - \boldsymbol{v}^{i+1'}]^{-1}[\Phi \boldsymbol{c}^i - \boldsymbol{v}^{i+1}]$, where $\boldsymbol{v}^{i+1'}$ is the Jacobian of $\boldsymbol{v}^{i+1}$. It goes back to step 2 until $\|\boldsymbol{c}^{i+1} - \boldsymbol{c}^i\|$ reaches a particular level of tolerance.

Note that Miranda and Fackler (2002) provides the MATLAB toolkit, which constructs a vector from the basis function and the corresponding interpolations nodes with the user's type of choice.

APPENDIX B: IMPUTING FUTURE PRICES IN THE SECONDARY MARKET

As mentioned in section "Data," not all condominium units are traded every year, and not all of the data for those that were traded are available. Thus, future prices (p^*_{jt+n}) must be imputed from the observed data. We followed two steps, as described in this sequel.

First, the secondary market data from the classified magazines documented in section 4.1. are matched with the primary market data by name and address. Of the entire primary market sample, about 27 percent of the entries correspond to at least one secondary market entry between 1992 and 2002.

Second, we estimate an imputation equation in the following specification. Note that we use prices per square meter instead of unit prices so as to control for size differences:

$$\log(p^*_{jt+n}) = a_0 + a_1 \log(p^*_{jt}) + a_3' \boldsymbol{x} + u_{jt} \tag{B.1}$$

where p^*_{jt} is the price of the property when it was sold as new, $\boldsymbol{x}$ is a vector of the characteristics of the condominiums, inclusive of cohort dummies and transaction year dummies, and u_{jt} is an error term. Note that the OLS estimation of (B.1) is inclined to be biased, as the error term u_{jt}, is likely to be correlated with regressors due to selection bias. There are at least two potential sources of selection bias. First, prices in the secondary market are only observed if properties are on the market (i.e., if there is incidental truncation). Second, as the sample is drawn from weekly classified magazines, only the subgroup for secondary market transactions is included. To correct these biases, Heckman's two-step method is applied. Table D10 reports the estimation of Eq. (B.1) for selected variables from the OLS and selection model. For vector $\boldsymbol{x}$, we include the log of total units sold initially in the same phase, the log of the distance from the nearest train station, the log of the total area that was sold in the same phase, birth cohort dummies, transaction year dummies, vintage dummies, ward dummies, building height dummies, floor plan dummies, and railroad dummies. The selection of variables is based on Ono,Takatsuji, and Shimizu (2002), who study the hedonic price index using data from the same source as this article. As our data do not include some information, such as the detailed characteristics of each unit, an initial price p^*_{jt} is included in the regression to control for unobserved quality variation. In both models, the higher the price in the secondary market, the higher the initial price in the primary market. The negative and significant coefficient estimates for the distance from the nearest train station suggests that the future value of the unit is higher if it is closer to a train station. This is because, generally speaking, most people commute to work or school by train and stores tend to be concentrated around train stations. Thus, the distance to a train station measures the degree of convenience. As expected, the estimates of the vintage dummies are all negative and significant, and the magnitude increases monotonically with the vintage, suggesting that older units are less expensive. The transaction year dummies are negative and monotonically decrease with the year. This implies that properties have become less expensive in recent years, something which reflects the overall housing market trend. The birth cohort dummies are positive and increase with the year, until 1996. There is no distinct incident that seems to drive this result. A comparison of models (a) and (b) shows the direction of the bias due to selection. The variables whose coefficients are the most biased are the vintage and year dummies; the coefficients for the birth cohort dummies are underestimated in terms of magnitude. The coefficients for the vintage dummies are underestimated, while those for the transaction year dummies are overestimated.

APPENDIX C: CALCULATION OF THE TERMINAL CONDITION FOR $\tilde{c}$

The terminal condition for $\tilde{c}$, both for estimations and simulations, is calibrated based on the costs and profit breakdown estimate for the unit price around 2,000 performed by an industry analyst.[35]

First, from this information, we know that the average profit per unit was approximately 10 percent around 2000. Since the weighted average price of new condominiums (age zero) in the data for the year 2000 was 4.78 million yen, the average cost of production is set at 4.32 million yen (=4.78*.9). Second, since the average cost corresponds to the expression in the text, $\tilde{c} + \overline{c}_1 + \overline{c}_2{}^*q$, and $\overline{c}_1$ is fixed to 24.71, the value of $\tilde{c}^{2000}$ is obtained using average production of five firms for q.

APPENDIX D: TABLES AND FIGURES

Table D1. Number of Firms and Concentration Measures.

Year	(A) Number of Active Firms	(B) Number of Single Appearance[a]	= (B)/(A)	(C) 5-Firm[b]	10-Firm[b]	15-Firm[b]
1992	89	35	0.393	0.383	0.523	0.614
1993	111	26	0.234	0.402	0.538	0.618
1994	205	56	0.273	0.309	0.442	0.540
1995	228	48	0.211	0.293	0.416	0.498
1996	227	29	0.128	0.297	0.412	0.501
1997	231	35	0.152	0.306	0.443	0.511
1998	221	32	0.145	0.259	0.385	0.480
1999	230	33	0.143	0.312	0.417	0.495
2000	231	44	0.190	0.317	0.433	0.516
Total	1,773	338	0.191	0.310	0.433	0.518

[a]The number of firms that appeared in the dataset only once during the sample period.
[b]x-firm concentration ratio is the sum of the market share of the top x firms.

Table D2. Summary Statistics[a].

Variable	Notation	Obs	Mean	Weighted Mean[b]	Standard Deviation	Min	Max
Distance from NTS[c]	dist	5,522	701.31	734.44	913.61	0	13,880
Height of the building	height	5,522	8.72	9.61	4.39	2	54
Total units for sale in a given phase	q_t	5,522	26.33	–	20.54	1	319
Average size of the units (m^2)	size	5,522	66.59	65.35	34.92	20	807
Number of developers	–	5,522	1.21	1.13	0.45	1	4
Whether secondary market data are available	–	5,522	0.27	–	0.45	0	1
Unit price (0,000 yen)							
Primary market (age 0)	p_t^0	5,522	5,209	4,905	3,221	1,559	73,706
Secondary market (age 1)	p_t^1	5,522	4,749	4,548	2,810	1,316	70,086
Secondary market (age 2)	p_t^2	5,522	4,583	4,380	2,740	1,179	66,686
Production by an oligopolistic firm							
5 firms	q_t	35	1,475		1,033	443	4,054
10 firms	q_t	70	1,025		871	0	4,054

[a]Each observation corresponds to a group of units in one building or one development project sold at the same phase.
[b]Weights are the units in each phase.
[c]NTS stands for "nearest train station."

Table D3. Fixed Parameters.

Description	Notation	Value	Unit
Common discount rate	β	0.975	
1-period survival rate	δ	0.990	
Scrap price	$\overline{p}$	42.3	Million yen
Market size	M	3.514	Million households
Number of firms	J	5, 10	
Steady state cost	$\overline{c}_1$	24.710	Million yen
Variance of macro cost shock	σ_η^2	1	

Table D4. Parameter Estimates for the Process of x_t: The First-Step Estimation.

	Model I 5 firms	Model II 10 firms
ϑ	0.878 (0.203)***	0.897 (.1829)***
$\overline{x}$	3.846 (3.189)	3.200 (2.228)
σ_ξ^2	3.363	2.631
x_{ss}[a]	32.20 (63.30)	31.16 (75.46)
R^2	0.7692	0.7748
N	9	9

[a]The standard error are obtained by the delta method.
*=significant at 10% level, **=significant at 5% level, ***=significant at 1% level.
Standard errors are reported in parentheses. Stars refer to the significance level of a t-test.

Table D5. Demand Parameter Estimates: The Second-Step Estimation.

	OLS	GMM
α	0.016	0.328
(coefficient for ECC)	(0.002)***	(0.076)***
1(age = 0)	−11.067	−22.007
	(0.020)***	(0.426)***
1(age = 1)	−11.089	−22.636
	(0.008)***	(0.250)***
log(size)	−0.2194	2.7389
	(0.024)***	(0.673)***
$g(0)$	−11.978	−10.605
	(0.012)***	(0.181)***
$g(1)$	−11.998	−11.233
	(0.012)***	(0.102)***
Instruments		log(height) log(distance)
Observations	10,113	10,113
Anderson LR statistic		70.329
(p-val)		0.00
Hansen J		0.08
(p-val)		0.78
Endogeneity		287.56
(p-val)		0.00

Robust standard errors are in parentheses and adjusted for the noise in imputed prices by bootstrap.
*significant at 10%, **significant at 5%, ***significant at 1%.

Table D6. Cost Parameter Estimates: the Third-step Estimation.

Parameter	Explanation	Model I 5 firms	Model II 10 firms
ρ	AR(1) coefficient	0.9443***	0.9552***
		(0.0044)	(0.0012)
$\bar{c}_2$	Cost parameter	3.5812***	5.8332***
		(0.0159)	(0.0045)
σ_{λ}^2	Standard deviation of idiosyncratic production shock terminal value of $\tilde{c}$	0.1664	0.096
		(1.2056)	(1.0383)
$\tilde{c}_{2000}^{d}$		14.5151	10.4544
N		35	70

[a]Robust standard error is given in the parentheses.
[b]Stars refer to the significance level of a t-test.
[c]Standard error is obtained by the delta method.
[d]The detail for this value is described in Appendix C.
*=significant at 10% level ,**=significant at 5% level, ***=significant at 1% level.

Table D7. Responsiveness of Policy Functions to State Variables.[a]

		$\tilde{c}$ Inflation		$\tilde{c}$ Deflation
x_t Growth	s_t	0.023	s_t	0.018
	x_t	0.067	x_t	0.131
	$\tilde{c}_t$	0.037	$\tilde{c}_t$	1.034
x_t Contraction	s_t	0.025	s_t	0.010
	x_t	0.329	x_t	0.184
	$\tilde{c}_t$	0.040	$\tilde{c}_t$	0.803

[a]All figures are measured in elasticities in absolute value.

Table D8. The Model's Performance.

	5 Firms		10 Firms	
	$\sum q_{jt}$	P_t^0	$\sum q_{jt}$	P_t^0
Mean observation[a]	7.4	49.4	10.3	49.4
(Standard deviation)[a]	(1.9)	(1.9)	(2.1)	(1.9)
Mean prediction[a]	5.4	49.5	10.3	49.0
Mean deviation from observations[a,b]	3.5	7.3	3.3	7.8
Mean percentage of times that prediction[a] falls in 15percentage interval[a] from observations[a]	24.4	100.0	37.5	100.0
Markup (s.d.)[a]	0.56	(0.0005)	0.48	(0.0007)

[a]The mean is taken over time periods.
[b]Let x_t and $\hat{x}_{tm}$denote the observation in year t and the prediction for year t in m'th draw respectively. The deviation is calculated by following formula for M simulation: $D = \frac{1}{M}\sum_m(\hat{x}_{tm} - x_t)^2$.

Table D9. Decomposition of Contributors to Price Deflation.

Year	(i) Benchmark	(ii) Fix both x_t & $\tilde{c}_t$	(iii) Fix $\tilde{c}_t$	(iv) Contribution (%)	(v) Competitive price	(vi) Effect of imperfection (%)
1994	49.88	49.88	49.88	–	–	–
1995	48.97	49.88	49.48	43.63	48.919	0.098
1996	48.23	49.88	49.12	45.65	48.182	0.094
1997	48.41	49.88	49.69	12.63	48.360	0.110
1998	47.95	49.88	49.39	24.96	47.900	0.103
1999	47.10	49.88	48.50	49.74	47.064	0.082
2000	46.60	49.88	47.99	57.63	46.569	0.071
Mean	47.88	49.88	49.03	39.04	47.832	0.093

Table D10. Estimation of Imputation Equation.[a,b]

	(a) OLS	(b) Selection Model		(a) OLS	(b) Selection Model		(a) OLS	(b) Selection Model
			Height dummies:			*Transaction year dummies:*		
log(price per sq. meter in the primary market)	0.604***	0.611***	6–9 stories	−0.008	−0.008	1993	−0.138**	−0.150***
	(0.02)	(0.02)		(0.006)	(0.006)		(0.045)	(0.045)
log(total units for sale)	−0.003	0.004	10–19 stories	0.001	0.004	1994	−0.199***	−0.223***
	(0.004)	(0.005)		(0.008)	(0.008)		(0.043)	(0.044)
log(distance from NTS)	−0.013***	−0.011 ***	>20 stories	0.160***	0.161***	1995	−0.273***	−0.308***
	(0.003)	(0.003)		(0.015)	(0.015)		(0.043)	(0.045)
log(total area for sale)	0.023***	0.022***				1996	−0.258***	−0.304***
	(0.005)	(0.005)	*Age dummies*				(0.043)	(0.046)
Constant	1.893***	1.786***	Age 2	−0.035**	−0.025*	1997	−0.278***	−0.335***
	(0.119)	(0.125)		(0.011)	(0.012)		(0.044)	(0.049)
Birth cohort dummies			Age 3	−0.094***	−0.073***	1998	−0.292***	−0.360***
1993	0.051***	0.062***		(0.012)	(0.014)		(0.045)	(0.052)
	(0.01)	(0.011)	Age 4	−0.153***	−0.121***	1999	−0.273***	−0.353***
1994	0.088***	0.101***		(0.013)	(0.018)		(0.046)	(0.055)
	(0.01)	(0.011)	Age 5	−0.215***	−0.172***	2000	−0.234***	−0.325***
1995	0.093***	0.104***		(0.015)	(0.023)		(0.047)	(0.059)
	(0.012)	(0.012)	Age 6	−0.263***	−0.208***	2001	−0.197***	−0.299***
1996	0.104***	0.121***		(0.018)	(0.028)		(0.048)	(0.062)
	(0.013)	(0.014)	Age 7	−0.325***	−0.260***			

1997	0.099***	0.116***		(0.021)	(0.033)			
	(0.015)	(0.016)	Age 8	−0.398***	−0.322***	N	3,119	3,119
1998	0.056**	0.069***		(0.024)	(0.038)	ρ		0.377
	(0.017)	(0.018)	Age 9	−0.505***	−0.417***	σ		0.128
1999	0.031	0.035		(0.031)	(0.046)	λ		0.377
	(0.021)	(0.021)						(0.018)

[a]In both specification, ward dummies and railroad dummies are included.
[b]Selection equation includes distance from the nearest station, total size of area, height of the building, maximum size of unit, year dummies, floor plan dummies, ward dummies, large firm dummies, dealer dummies. Robust standard errors are in parentheses.
*** significant at 1% level, ** significant at 5% level, * significant at 10% level.

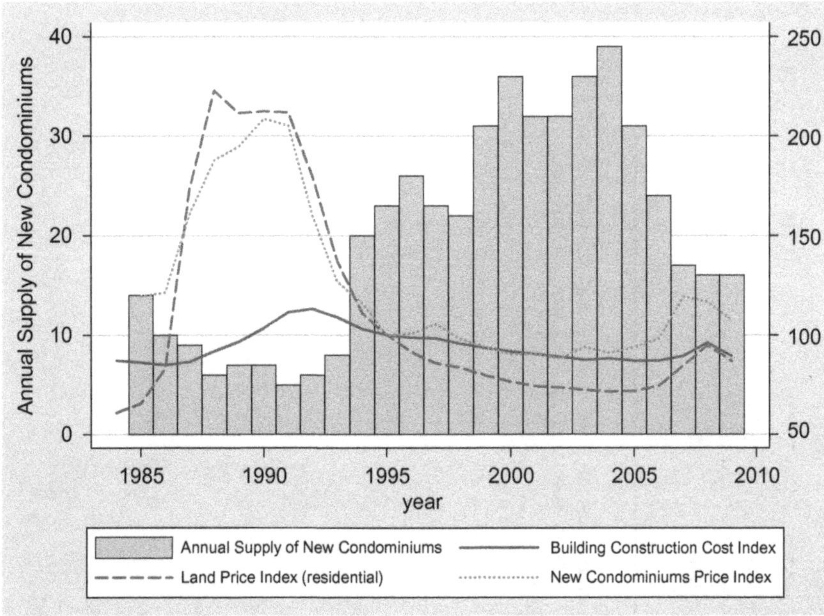

Fig. D1. Key variables in the Tokyo condominium market – 1986–2009.

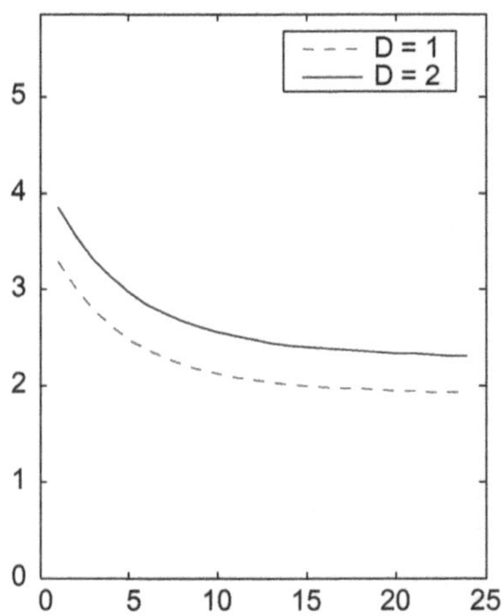

Fig. D2. Simulated production at different product lifespans.

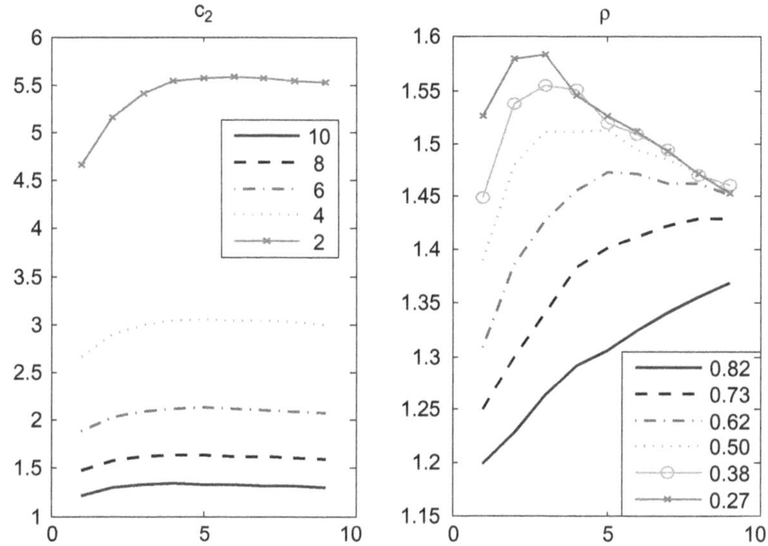

Fig. D3. Simulated production at different parameter values.

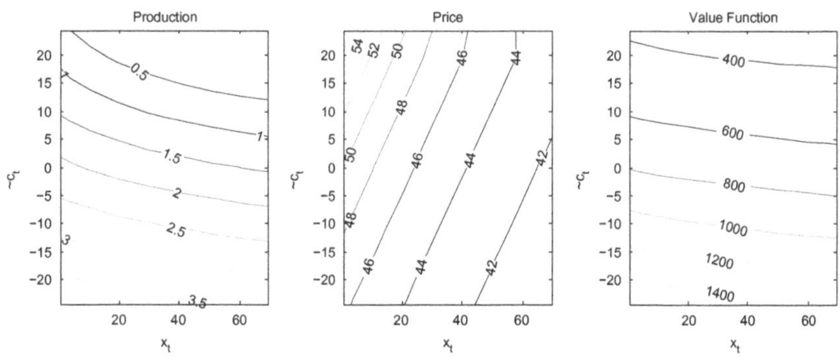

Fig. D4. The solution at $s_t = 31,160$.

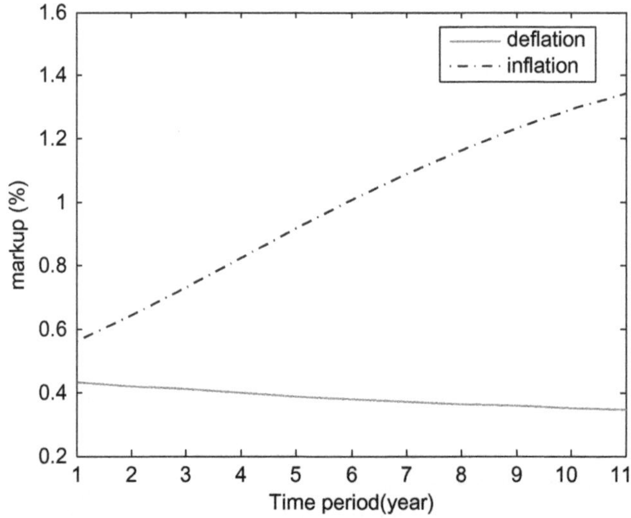

Fig. D5. Simulated markups – inflation versus deflation.

A DYNAMIC ANALYSIS OF THE U.S. CIGARETTE MARKET AND ANTISMOKING POLICIES

Wei Tan

ABSTRACT

A dynamic oligopoly model of the cigarette industry is developed to study the responses of firms to various antismoking policies and to estimate the implications for the policy efficacy. The structural parameters are estimated using a combination of micro and macro level data and firms' optimal price and advertising strategies are solved as a Markov Perfect Nash Equilibrium. The simulation results show that tobacco tax increase reduces both the overall smoking rate and the youth smoking rate, while advertising restrictions may increase the youth smoking rate. Firm's responses strengthen the impact of antismoking policies in the short run.

Keywords: Dynamic oligopoly; cigarette market; antismoking policies

JEL classification: L1

Structural Econometric Models
Advances in Econometrics, Volume 31, 387–432

ISSN: 0731-9053/doi:10.1108/S0731-9053(2013)0000032012

INTRODUCTION

Due to the potentially hazardous health consequence of cigarette smoking, the cigarette industry has been the focus of attention for many economists, public health advocates, and policymakers. Numerous antismoking policies with significant economic impacts[1] – for example, tax increases and advertising and marketing restrictions – have been proposed in order to reduce the overall smoking rate, in particular, that of young people. Many economic studies have investigated the effectiveness of these policies and have provided useful recommendations. However, such studies are potentially biased inasmuch as they fail to anticipate the reactions of cigarette manufacturers to the proposed policies. Arguably, firms could counteract some if not all of the policy effects by changing their pricing and advertising strategies. In addition, firm responses may cause such policies to have varying effects across different subpopulation groups. A policy that works well on the overall population might have perverse effects on a particular subpopulation, such as that of young smokers.

To understand firm behavior in the cigarette market, I develop an empirical dynamic oligopoly model of the U.S. cigarette industry. Firms coordinate in price and compete in advertising in a dynamic game in order to maximize their discounted future profits. The dynamic oligopoly model captures three crucial features of the cigarette market. First, due to the addictiveness of cigarettes, current demand is an important determinant of future demand. Thus, profit-maximizing firms face a fundamental tradeoff. On the one hand, firms have strong incentives to exploit current smokers since they are addicted to smoking. On the other hand, firms are aware of the importance of keeping current smokers smoking and of encouraging young people to start smoking. The dynamic incentives are critical in determining firm responses to antismoking policies, both in the short run and in the long run.

Second, young people are extremely important to the tobacco industry. As majority of the smokers form their smoking habits before age 24, young people are the chief source of new consumers to the tobacco industry. In order to survive, tobacco industry must be able to replace the loss of consumers who either quit smoking or die from smoking-related diseases. Similarly, preventing young people from start smoking is critical to the success of antismoking policies. The effectiveness of any antismoking policies depends on their ability to reduce the youth smoking rate.

Finally, I explicitly model the widely documented differences[2] between young smokers and adult smokers with respect to how they respond to price and advertising.[3] These differences may cause policy interventions to have varying effects across different subpopulations.

The dynamic model is set up in such a way that I can estimate the structural coefficients from the data. The ability to empirically estimate the model coefficients allows me to test how well the dynamic model approximates real industry behavior. To be more specific, I first estimate the structural parameters from a combination of micro-level survey data and aggregate level data. I then compute the optimal price and advertising spending for firms as a Markov Perfect Nash Equilibrium based on the estimated structural parameters. Afterwards, I compare the model's predictions with the observed price and advertising data. The comparison shows that the dynamic model predicts the industry behavior extremely well. Differences between the predicted prices and the observed prices for the study period are less than 5 cents per pack (i.e., 4% of the observed price). Likewise, differences between the predicted advertising spending for Marlboro and its observed advertising spending are less than 10% of the observed values. The model's ability to predict firm prices and advertising expenditures supports the use of the dynamic model for policy evaluation.

Two most commonly used antismoking policies – advertising restrictions and tobacco tax increases – are studied. The simulation results show that increasing the tobacco tax reduces both the overall smoking rate and the youth smoking rate. Contrarily, the results indicate that advertising restrictions could potentially back fire and actually *increase* the youth smoking rate. Though advertising restrictions have a direct effect on reducing the incentive to smoke, they would indirectly increase the smoking rate inasmuch as the advertising restrictions would lead to lower prices. As young smokers are more responsive to price, the indirect effect of advertising restrictions through the price drop is likely to be stronger than their direct effect.

Furthermore, my findings suggest that firm's responses strengthen the impact of antismoking policies in the short run. For example, the simulations of tax increases show that, in the short run, firms will raise the price of cigarettes *more* than the actual tax increases.[4] This phenomenon is due to changes in the dynamic incentives faced by the firms. When antismoking policies take effect, cigarette firms are able to anticipate that a certain percentage of current smokers are likely to quit soon, and thus have a stronger incentive to exploit current smokers by charging a higher price in the short run. In the long run, however, such incentive gradually diminishes, as the remaining smokers are less likely to quit. As a result, firms reduce prices over time and the effects of antismoking policies decrease over time. This finding also suggests that one should take into account firms' change in strategy when evaluating any antismoking policies. The short run estimates of policy effects likely will over estimate the policy efficacy.

In addition to adding to the policy debate, this article extends the existing class of dynamic oligopoly models (Ericson & Pakes, 1995, and the subsequent literature) to include demand side dynamics brought about by switching costs.[5] In the standard dynamic oligopoly model, the product market is modeled as a static price/quantity setting game and the dynamics in the model stem from firm investments. This simplification restricts the use of this model in studying markets with dynamic demand brought about by switching costs, as in these markets, price/quantity decisions are determined by dynamic incentives. The extension of dynamic oligopoly models to markets that have switching costs allows us to explore more complicated dynamics and issues facing many real industries.

The rest of the article is divided into eight sections. In the second section, I review the existing literature. The third section provides a description of the U.S. cigarette industry. In the fourth section, I specify the dynamic oligopoly model and discuss its properties. The fifth section contains a description of the data and the empirical estimation and calibration of the model. The sixth section compares the model prediction with the observed data and evaluates the fit of the model. In the seventh section, I conduct counterfactual experiments and compare the outcomes of various antismoking policies. The eighth section offers concluding remarks and discusses a plan for future research.

THE EXISTING LITERATURE

Numerous studies have examined smoking behavior (see Chaloupka & Warner, 2000 for an extensive review of the literature). The majority of the existing studies have looked at various factors that affect cigarettes demand, including price and tax (see Chaloupka & Warner, 2000 for a review), dynamic demand (Arcidiaco, Sieg, & Sloan, 2007), advertising (Baltagi & Levin, 1986; Lewit, Coate, & Grossman, 1981; Pollay et al., 1996; Seldon & Doroodian, 1989), advertising restrictions (see Saffer & Chaloupka, 2000 for an extensive literature review), smoking bans and restrictions (Evan, Farrelly, & Montgomery, 1999; Taurus & Chaloupka, 1999), counter advertising (Hu, Sung, & Keeler, 1995a), and peer effect (Powell, Tauras, & Ross, 2003). Furthermore, most of the studies have considered the effects of these factors on young smokers and adult smokers separately and have found that significant differences exist between the two. Most of the existing literature (Chaloupka & Grossman, 1997; Evans & Farrelly, 1998; Gilleski & Strumpf, 2005; Gruber & Zinman, 2001; Lewit & Coate, 1982) supports the claim that young smokers are more sensitive to price than older smokers, while some studies (Chaloupka, 1991; DeCicca, Kenkel, & Mathios, 2002; Wasserman, Manning, Newhouse, & Winkler, 1991) argue the opposite. On the other hand, a few studies have looked into the effects of advertising on cigarette demand, especially that among young smokers. Lewit et al. (1981) found that television advertising has a strong effect on youth smoking and Pollay et al. (1996) has shown that advertising has a strong influence on the market share of young adults.

However, relatively few have tried to model oligopoly firm behavior in the cigarette industry.[6] Roberts and Samuelson (1988) have empirically studied the advertising competition in the cigarette market. Showalter (1999) has considered the monopoly pricing for the addictive product and offers an alternative explanation for the observed correlation of current demand with future events. Two recent papers use dyanmic oligopoly model developed by Pakes and McGuire (1994) to study industry dynamic in the cigarette market. Tan (2006) employs a dynamic oligopoly model to study the effects of antismoking policies on the market structure of the U.S. cigarette industry. Qi (2012) estimates a dynamic model of advertising to evaluate the impact of advertising ban. Both papers do not model the addictive effect of smoking.

This article is closely related to the dynamic oligopoly model framework developed by Ericson and Pakes (1995). Many studies have extended their framework to deal with more complicated dynamics.[7] Closely related to this article, a few studies have extended the standard dynamic oligopoly model to allow for demand/cost side dynamics. Benkard (2004) studies the cost side dynamics due to learning in the aircraft industry. In his model, current output influences an experience variable, which in turns affects the cost of production in the future. Fershtman and Pakes (2000) consider the demand side dynamics caused by collusion, where the ability to collude in each period depends on a state variable describing the collusion history of the industry. Markovich (2008) looks at the demand side dynamics resulting from network externality.

Several recent papers have used dynamic oligopoly models to study advertising dynamics. These papers use the framework of Pakes and McGuire (1994) for the static product market, and the dynamics in their models stem from firm advertising investments. Doraszelski and

Markovich (2007) study the effects of both "goodwill advertising" and "awareness advertising" on industry dynamics. In addition, they examine the anticompetitive effects of advertising restrictions and how firms use advertising to affect the entry/exit decisions of opponents. Dube, Hitsch, and Manchanda (2005) use the advertising carry-over effects and the S-shape advertising response function to explain the "pulsing" behavior of advertising.

Some studies take a further step by empirically estimating the model parameters to study real industry behavior. Similar to the approach used in this article, Benkard (2004) and Dube et al. (2005)[8] estimate the demand side and cost side parameters separately without imposing an equilibrium – such as the assumption that the observed firm behavior is generated "optimally" from a particular model – in the estimation process.

THE U.S. CIGARETTE INDUSTRY

The U.S. cigarette industry is a highly concentrated industry dominated by four firms – Philip Morris, R.J. Reynolds, Brown and Williamson, and Lorillard.[9] According to the 1997 Economic Census, the four firm concentration ratio, at 98.9, is among the highest of all industries. The market is traditionally grouped into two price segments: premium brands and discount brands. Premium brands are of a higher quality, and are more expensive and more heavily advertised. Table 1 tabulates the market share and advertising spending of the top brands from 1990 to 1996.

Cigarette firms historically coordinate in price and compete in advertising. Over the last two decades, the wholesale prices of different cigarette brands within the same price segment have remained the same despite a consistent difference in their market share.[10] Recently released tobacco company documents further produce evidence of extensive cooperation of firm in pricing decisions. According to an article published in the Economist magazine,[11] the tobacco company documents revealed that "...the big tobacco multinationals colluded to fix prices in as many as 23 countries in Africa, Asia, the Middle East, Latin America and Europe."

Several features of the cigarettes industry facilitate the coordination of pricing decision among firms. First of all, the market structure of the industry is very stable over the last several decades. There is no major entry or exit in the market until the Master Settlement Agreement in 1998. In addition, the industry keeps very detailed record of any price changes in the

Table 1. U.S. Cigarettes Industry in the Early 1990s[a].

	1990	1991	1992	1993	1994	1995	1996
Smoking rate among adults (25+)	24.48%	23.99%	22.96%	22.59%	22.55%	22.09%	22.82%
Smoking rate among young adults (18–24)	22.05%	21.95%	23.69%	23.44%	24.07%	23.59%	27.16%
Total number of cigarettes (billion)	522.05	509.1	506.95	461.18	489.6	481.1	484.98
Premium brand price ($/pack)	0.954	1.027	1.106	1.097	0.961	0.962	0.958
Advertising spending ($M)							
Marlboro	132.7	118.0	135.3	79.9	143.0	148.0	141.8
Salem	37.0	30.2	22.5	10.4	7.9	4.2	7.8
Merit	25.0	13.8	60.6	23.9	29.0	27.6	26.2
Winston	21.6	44.5	46.1	58.0	16.7	24.0	14.8
Benson & Hedges	27.3	22.1	37.0	43.1	25.0	28.2	17.6
Newport	74.5	66.8	59.0	61.3	37.6	38.7	40.0
Camel	57.5	58.3	46.6	70.5	48.6	56.5	78.7
Virginia Slims	43.6	23.2	32.1	31.0	30.0	31.5	37.6
Market share							
Marlboro	26.00%	25.80%	24.40%	23.50%	28.10%	30.10%	32.30%
Salem	6.10%	5.40%	4.80%	3.90%	3.80%	3.70%	3.60%
Merit	3.50%	3.10%	3.00%	2.30%	2.40%	2.40%	2.30%
Winston	8.80%	7.50%	6.80%	6.70%	5.80%	5.80%	5.30%
Benson & Hedges	3.60%	3.20%	3.10%	2.50%	2.40%	2.40%	2.30%
Newport	4.70%	4.70%	4.80%	4.80%	5.10%	5.60%	6.10%
Camel	4.30%	4.00%	4.10%	3.90%	4.00%	4.40%	4.60%
Virginia Slims	3.10%	2.80%	2.60%	2.30%	2.40%	2.40%	2.40%
Other	39.90%	43.50%	46.40%	50.10%	46.00%	43.20%	41.10%

[a]The smoking rate among adults (25+) and that among young adults (18–24) are obtained from the Behavioral Risk Factor Surveillance System (BRFSS) survey. Total number of cigarettes consumption and market share are obtained from Maxwell's Report. The premium brand prices are obtained from USDA. Advertising spending data are obtained from The Legacy Tobacco Documents Library at the University of California, San Francisco.

market. Thus any price reduction will be easily observed by other firms. Moreover, recent law-suits against tobacco industry often allow firms to negotiate as a group to various charges. They also provide the tobacco industry protection from antitrust investigation.

The cigarette industry is one of the most heavily advertised industries. The Federal Trade Commission (2001) reported that in 2001, the five largest cigarette manufacturers collectively spent $11.22 billion on advertising and promotion in the U.S. market. Philip Morris, the largest tobacco company in the United States with an annual advertising expenditure of over $2.5 billion, was ranked second in 2000 and third in 1999 in total U.S. market advertising spending by the Ad Age 100 Leading National Advertisers Report. In addition to newspaper, magazine, and outdoor (e.g., billboards) advertising, cigarette firms promote their product by various means, such as promotion allowance, retail value added, coupons and special item distribution,[12] and so forth.

Due to the addictiveness of cigarettes and the health consequences of smoking, cigarette consumption has several unique features that differentiate it from most other products. In addition to differences between young and adult smokers in their responses to price and advertising, existing studies have found that a majority of smokers start smoking at an early age. The 1994 Surgeon General's Report finds that the majority of current smokers began to smoke by the time they were 20 years old. It is very unlikely that a person would start smoking once he passes the smoking initiation age. Thus, young people are the chief source of new consumers for the tobacco industry, an industry that each year must replace the many consumers who either quit smoking or die from smoking-related diseases. Furthermore, brand preference differs significantly across different age groups. Young smokers tend to choose from a limited number of brands. The top three brands for young smokers – Marlboro, Camel, and Newport – make up over 80% of the market. By contrast, the overall market share is much more evenly distributed.

4A MODEL OF PRICE AND ADVERTISING COMPETITION IN THE CIGARETTE INDUSTRY

This section provides the details of my dynamic oligopoly model for the cigarette industry. First, I describe the environment of the industry and the evolution of states. I then specify the firm demand function and profit function. Afterwards, I define the Markov Perfect Nash Equilibrium solution concept used in this article. This is followed by a discussion of the model's properties. In an effort to empirically estimate the model parameters, I make certain assumptions specific to the cigarette industry.

The Competition Environment and the Evolution of the State

A brand is considered as a firm and there are J major firms in the market. In the article, I use the term "brand" and "firm" interchangeably. There is no entry or exit in the market.[13] The quality levels of the firms in the industry are characterized by two vectors $\boldsymbol{\phi} = [\boldsymbol{\phi}_1, \ldots, \boldsymbol{\phi}_J]$ and $\boldsymbol{\varphi} = [\boldsymbol{\varphi}_1, \ldots, \boldsymbol{\varphi}_J]$, where $\boldsymbol{\phi}_j$ measures the quality of brand j among adult smokers and $\boldsymbol{\varphi}_j$ measures its quality among young smokers. In addition to the above top J firms, there are many smaller firms that I group into one category as "other brands" (brand $J+1$). The quality level for this category is $\boldsymbol{\phi}_{J+1}$ for adult smokers and $\boldsymbol{\varphi}_{J+1}$ for young smokers. Instead of specifying the stochastic process of change in product quality, as done by Pakes and McGuire (1994), I assume that the quality levels are time invariant for all brands. This assumption is made in order to reduce the computation burden of the model as well as to focus on the dynamics resulting from addiction.[14]

Based on the observed lack of price competition in the cigarette market, I assume that firms coordinate in price and compete in advertising. Instead of modeling the details of how they coordinate in price, I assume that there exists a cartel manager who sets the price of cigarettes,[15] and that firms simultaneously determine their advertising spending.[16] For the sake of model simplicity, I also assume that only the major firms (brand $j = 1, \ldots, J$) advertise (i.e., those in the "other brands" category do not[17]). To further simplify the model, I only consider the pricing for premium brands[18] and assume that the cartel manager sets a single price for all brands.[19]

The size of the total population is normalized at 1. To capture the differences between young smokers and adult smokers, I separate the population into two age groups – "adults" and "young adults." The relative size of young adults is assumed to be constant at γ_1; the rest are adults.[20] Young adults are in the experimental stage of smoking. For them, smoking has not yet developed into a habit. Potentially, any young adult could become a smoker. Adults can be further broken down into two groups – "nonsmokers" and "existing adult smokers." Nonsmokers will never smoke, and existing adult smokers choose whether or not to continue smoking. At the end of every period, a fraction of young adults γ_2 pass through the experimental stage of smoking and become adults. If they are no longer smoking at that point, they become "nonsmokers" and will not smoke at any point later in life. Otherwise, they join the pool of "existing adult smokers." Among those existing adult smokers who decide to discontinue smoking during this period, a fraction will quit smoking permanently and become nonsmokers. I assume a successful quitting rate of γ_3.

There are two state variables in the model. The first state variable σ_t is the share of existing smokers among adults. It measures the size of addicted smokers. Let the current period smoking rate of existing adult smokers be s_t and that of young adults be $\tilde{s}_t$. Assuming that adult smokers will eventually quit smoking before they die, the share of existing smokers among adults for the next period is

$$\sigma_{t+1} = \sigma_t s_t + \sigma_t(1-\gamma_3)(1-s_t) + \frac{\gamma_1\gamma_2}{1-\gamma_1}\tilde{s}_t$$

The share of existing smokers for the next period consists of: (1) existing adult smokers who choose to continue smoking during the period; (2) existing adult smokers who choose to discontinue smoking during the period but fail to permanently quit; and (3) young adult smokers who have become adults during the period.

The second state variable, κ_t, is the social sentiment against smoking. It measures the effects of other factors, such as antismoking campaigns and regulations, on consumers' smoking decision. It is assumed to follow the following AR(1) process.

$$\kappa_{t+1} = \rho\kappa_t + \zeta_t$$

where ζ_t is the random shock and ρ measures the autocorrelation of κ_t. To simplify the computation of the model, ζ_t is assumed to be distributed as

$$\zeta_t = \begin{cases} 0 & \text{with prob } \pi_{0\zeta} \\ \zeta_1 & \text{with prob } \pi_{1\zeta} \\ \vdots & \\ \zeta_N & \text{other wise } \pi_{N\zeta} \end{cases}$$

where $\zeta_N > \ldots > \zeta_1 > 0$ and $\sum_{n=0}^{N} \pi_{n\zeta} = 1$. This specification of the Markov process has several computational advantages. First, the sentiment against smoking is bound between the interval $[0, \zeta_N/(1-\rho)]$ as long as $\rho \neq 1$. Second, because of the discrete distribution of the shock term ζ_t, the computation of the expected value function can be easily carried out.

Product Demand and profit Function

The standard discrete choice model for differentiated products is used to model the demand for cigarettes. In addition to choosing between smoking and nonsmoking, both young adults and existing adult smokers must also decide which brand of cigarettes to smoke. There are $J+1$ brands available in the market. Thus, the total number of choices for both "existing adult smokers" and "young adults" is $J+2$.

The indirect utility function of existing adult smoker i choosing choice j is assumed to be

$$u_{ijt} = V_{jt} + \varepsilon_{ijt}$$

$$V_{jt} = \begin{cases} \boldsymbol{\phi}_j + \beta_1(p_t + T) + f_1(x_{jt}) - \kappa_t & \text{for Brand } j = 1, \ldots, J \\ \boldsymbol{\phi}_{J+1} + \beta_1(p_t + T) - \kappa_t & \text{for Other Brands (choice } J+1) \\ 0 & \text{for Quit Smoking (choice 0)} \end{cases}$$

where $\boldsymbol{\phi}_j$ is the quality parameters defined above, p_t is the before-tax price of cigarettes, and T is the tax per pack of cigarettes. x_{jt} is the total advertising spending by brand j at period t. To further simply the model, I assume that the parametric specification of the aggregate advertising response function is

$$f_1(x_{jt}) = \mu_1 \frac{\nu_1 x_{jt}}{1 + \nu_1 x_{jt}}$$

where μ_1 measures the maximum advertising response that can be generated from advertising.[21] This functional form is used by Pakes and McGuire (1994) to model the investment function. A property of this advertising response function is that $f_1(.)$ is concave if $\nu_1 > 0$. The advertising response function can therefore capture the decreasing return to scale properties of advertising spending. An implicit assumption of the model is that lagged advertising spending has no "carry-over effect." Namely, lagged advertising does not affect current demand directly. As the time period in my application is based on the calendar year, the advertising "carry-over effect" is small in this context.[22] Dube et al. (2005) discuss the implications of the advertising "carry-over effect" and the "S-shape" advertising response function. The "carry-over effect" is strong in their application, since they use weekly advertising data.

Similarly, the indirect utility of young adult i to smoke brand j is assumed to be

$$u_{ijt} = \tilde{V}_{jt} + \varepsilon_{ijt}$$

$$\tilde{V}_{jt} = \begin{cases} \varphi_j + \beta_2(p_t + T) + f_2(x_{jt}) - \kappa_t & \text{for Brand } j = 1, \ldots, J \\ \varphi_{J+1} + \beta_2(p_t + T) - \kappa_t & \text{for Other Brands (choice } J+1) \\ 0 & \text{for Quit Smoking (choice 0)} \end{cases}$$

where $\boldsymbol{\varphi}_j$ is the brand quality level for young smokers. The advertising response function of young smokers is assumed to take a similar functional form as that for existing adult smokers, but with different coefficients

$$f_2(x_{jt}) = \mu_2 \frac{\nu_2 x_{jt}}{1 + \nu_2 x_{jt}}$$

Addiction effect is captured by the differences in the existing smokers' perceived quality parameters $\boldsymbol{\phi}_j$ and that of young adult $\boldsymbol{\varphi}_j$. When $\boldsymbol{\phi}$ are greater than $\boldsymbol{\varphi}$, existing smokers will be more likely to smoke than young adult. Put it in another way, quitting smoking is harder for someone who is a current smoker than someone who has not developed smoking habit yet. Existing smoker and young adult will chooses choice j that yields the highest level of utility in the current period. That is, choice j is chosen if and only if $u_{ijt} \geq u_{iqt}$ for any $q = 0, \ldots, J+1$.

Rational addiction models have been developed since Becker and Murphy (1988). The key distinction of these models is that they not only assume the rationality of consumer behavior, but likewise that of consumer expectations. Within the context of my model, a truly "rational" consumer should not only know the pricing and advertising strategies of firms in what is, after all, a complicated dynamic game, but also be able to predict them correctly.

The rational addiction models have been empirically tested by Becker, Grossman, and Murphy (1994), Chaloupka (1991), and Arcidiacono et al. (2007). The empirical evidence in support of the "rational addiction" model is based on the observed correlation of the current consumption of cigarettes with future price. However, as Showalter (1999) points out, this phenomenon can also be caused by the forward-looking behavior of firms. As this article tries to focus on the implications of the forward-looking behavior of firms, I use a demand model can be viewed as a linear approximation to the dynamic demand model.

Given the above assumptions and assuming that ε_{ijt} is iid extreme value distributed, I derive the market share of brand j among existing adult smokers as

$$s_{jt} = \frac{\exp(V_{jt})}{1 + \sum_{q=1}^{J+1} \exp(V_{qt})}$$

and the smoking rate of existing adult smokers as $s_t = \sum_{j=1}^{J+1} s_{jt}$. Similarly, the market share of brand j among young adults can be derived as

$$\tilde{s}_{jt} = \frac{\exp(\tilde{V}_{jt})}{1 + \sum_{q=1}^{J+1} \exp(\tilde{V}_{qt})}$$

and the smoking rate of young adults as $\tilde{s}_t = \sum_{j=1}^{J+1} \tilde{s}_{jt}$.

Suppose that the market size is fixed at M. Based on the above market share for young adults and adults, I obtain the demand for firm j at period t given the current share of existing adult smokers among adults σ_t, the current sentiment against smoking κ_t, the price of cigarettes p_t, and the level of advertising spending for all firms $x_t = [x_{1t}, \ldots, x_{Jt}, x_{J+1t}]$[23]:

$$D_{j,t}(\sigma_t, \kappa_t, p_t, x_t) = M((1-\gamma_1)\sigma_t \times s_{jt} + \gamma_1 \times \tilde{s}_{jt}) \qquad \text{for } j = 1, \ldots, J+1$$

I assume that the marginal cost of brand j is constant at mc_{jt}. Thus, the profit for firm j at period t is

$$\pi_{j,t}(\sigma_t, \kappa_t, p_t, x_t) = (p_t - mc_{jt}) D_{j,t}(\sigma_t, \kappa_t, p_t, x_t) - x_{jt} \qquad \text{for } j = 1, \ldots, J+1$$

Firms' problem

The price and advertising decisions of firms are modeled as a dynamic game with $J+1$ players, one cartel manager, and J major firms. The cartel manager's objective is to maximize the weighted discounted total profit of the industry by setting the price. The value function for the cartel manager therefore must satisfy the following Bellman Equation:

$$\begin{aligned} V_m(\sigma_t, \kappa_t) &= \max_{p_t} \{\pi_{mt}(\sigma_t, \kappa_t, p_t, x_t) + \delta E[V_m(\sigma_{t+1}, \kappa_{t+1})]\} \\ &= \max_{p_t} \left\{ \sum_{j=1}^{J+1} w_j \pi_{jt}(\sigma_t, \kappa_t, p_t, x_t) + \delta E[V_m(\sigma_{t+1}, \kappa_{t+1})] \right\} \end{aligned}$$

where δ is the discount factor and w_j is the weight that the cartel manager assigns to firm j's profits. I assume that the cartel manager tries to maximize the joint profit of the industry. Thus $w_j = 1/(J+1)$ for all j.

Each major firm maximizes its discounted present value by choosing their advertising spending x_{jt}. The Bellman Equation for firm j ($j = 1, \ldots, J$) is given by

$$V_j(\sigma_t, \kappa_t) = \max_{x_{jt}} \{\pi_{jt}(\sigma_t, \kappa_t, p_t, x_t) + \delta E[V_j(\sigma_{t+1}, \kappa_t)]\}$$

The Equilibrium Concept

The solution concept used in this article is the Markov Perfect Nash Equilibrium (MPNE). The MPNE, as defined by Maskin and Tirole (1988a, 1988b), is more restrictive than the Subgame Perfect Nash Equilibrium (SPNE), as it restricts players' strategies to those dependent only on the pay-off-relevant state. As applied here, the cartel manager's pricing decision and the firm's advertising decision rely only on the share of existing adult smokers σ_t and the social sentiment against smoking κ_t.

The MPNE considered in this article may not be unique or even exist. Ericson and Pakes (1995) discuss the conditions for the existence of equilibria. For the purpose of my study, I only need to ensure that an equilibrium exists at the estimated parameter values, and that it is automatically checked by the numerical solution algorithm. Although I cannot rule out the existence of multiple equilibria, I can check for it using different starting values during the computation. For the estimated dynamic model, I find no signs of multiple equilibria.

This model differs in several ways from the majority of the dynamic oligopoly models based on the Pakes and McGuire (1994, 2001) framework. First and most importantly, demand-side dynamics due to addiction are included in the model. Since current smokers are the main source of future consumers, current demand will affect future demand. Hence, both the cartel manager's price decision and the firms' advertising decisions will take into account the decisions' effects on future profits. The demand-side dynamics make it impossible to solve the static profit function apart from the value function, as was done by Pakes and McGuire (1994).

In order to overcome the above difficulties, I use the collocation method instead.[24] The collocation method uses a series of "well behaved" basis functions to approximate the value function. Thus, the dynamic programming problem becomes a matter of finding the coefficients of the basis functions. I first approximate the value function as a linear combination of a set of known basis functions. The dynamic game is then solved at the chosen collocation states. Afterward, I interpolate the value function at the intervals between the chosen collocation states and update the coefficients for the basis functions. The dynamic game is solved by repeating the above process until the value function converges.

Solution Method

The MPNE of the dynamic game with M players can be characterized by the following set of M simultaneous Bellman Equations:

$$\begin{aligned} V_m(s_t) &= \max_{x_m}\{f_m(s_t, x_m, x_{-m}(s_t)) + \delta E[V_m(s_{t+1})]\} \\ &= \max_{x_m}\{f_m(s_t, x_m, x_{-m}(s_t)) + \delta E[V_m(g(s_t, x_m, x_{-m}(s_t), \zeta)]\} \end{aligned}$$

for $m = 1, 2, \ldots, M$, where s_t are the state variables, x_m are the control variables of player m, and $x_{-m}(s_t)$ are the controls taken by other players when the state is s_t. The state transition rule is determined by the following equations $s_{t+1} = g(s_t, x_m, x_{-m}(s_t), \zeta)$ and ζ are the random shocks. In my application, the M players are one cartel manager and J major firms. The state variables s_t include the share of existing smokers and the social sentiment against smoking. The control variables x are the price set by the cartel manager and the advertising spending by the firms.

To use collocation method, I approximate the value function for each player as a linear combination of N known basis functions $\boldsymbol{\phi}_1, \boldsymbol{\phi}_2, \ldots, \boldsymbol{\phi}_N$, whose coefficients $c_m = [c_{m1}, c_{m2}, \ldots, c_{mN}]$ are to be determined

$$V_m(s) \approx \tilde{V}_m(s) = \sum_{n=1}^{N} c_{mn} \boldsymbol{\phi}_n(s)$$

One can choose from a variety of basis function and collocation states. Which set of basis function and collocation states approximate the value functions better depends on the problems. The computation example in this article use Cubic Spline function. Other functional approximation, such as Chebechev functions, gives the same results. In addition, I choose $N = 20$, that is, I approximate the value function by a 20th order polynomials.

The numerical procedure to solve the dynamic programing problem entails the following steps.

Step 1: Start with an initial guess of $c^0 = [c_1^0, \ldots, c_M^0]$.

Step 2: At iteration t, given the basis coefficients for the M players $c^t = [c_1^t, \ldots, c_M^t]$, solve the Bellman equations for each players sequentially at the N collocation states $\sigma_1, \ldots, \sigma_N$. Namely, I solve the following equation system:

$$\sum_{n=1}^{N} c_{mn}\boldsymbol{\phi}_n(\sigma_i) = \max_{x_m}\left\{f_m(\sigma_i, x_m, x_{-m}(\sigma_i)) + \delta E\left[\sum_{n=1}^{N} c_{mn}\boldsymbol{\phi}_n(g(\sigma_i, x_m, x_{-m}(\sigma_i), \zeta))\right]\right\}$$
$$= \max_{x_m}\{f_m(\sigma_i, x_m, x_{-m}(\sigma_i))$$
$$+\delta \sum_{k=1}^{K}\sum_{n=1}^{N} c_{mn}\boldsymbol{\phi}_n(g(\sigma_i, x_m, x_{-m}(\sigma_i), \zeta_k))P(\zeta_k)\}$$

for $m = 1, 2, \ldots, M$ and $i = 1, 2, \ldots, N$. The collocation states $\sigma_1, \ldots, \sigma_N$ are chosen optimally depending on the basis functions (see Miranda & Fackler, 2004 for a detail). Let the collocation function $v_m(c_m, x_{-m})$ be the value function after solving the Bellman Equation at the collocation states for player m

$$v_m(c_m, x_{-m}) = \max_{x_m}\left\{f_m(\sigma_i, x_m, x_{-m}(\sigma_i)) + \delta \sum_{k=1}^{K}\sum_{n=1}^{N} c_{mn}\boldsymbol{\phi}_n(g(\sigma_i, x_m, x_{-m}(\sigma_i), \zeta_k))P(\zeta_k)\right\}$$

Step 3: After solving the collocation function for all the players in the game, update the coefficients of the basis function c^t by Pseudo Newton Method, which use the following iterative update rule:

$$c_m^{t+1} = c_m^t - [\Phi - v'(x^t)]^{-1}[\Phi c_m^t - v_m(c_m^t, x_{-m}^t)]$$

for $m = 1, 2, \ldots, M$. Φ is the collocation matrix and its ijth elements is the jth basis function evaluated at the ith collocation nodes.

$$\Phi_{ij} = \boldsymbol{\phi}_j(\sigma_i)$$

$v'(x^t)$ is the n by n Jocobian of the collocation function with respect to the basis coefficients c_m^t. The ijth the element of $v'(x^t)$ is computed by the Envelop Theorem

$$v'_{ij}(x^t) = \delta \sum_{k=1}^{K} \boldsymbol{\phi}_n(g(\sigma_i, x, \zeta_k))P(\zeta_k)\}$$

Step 4: Iterate the step 2 and step 3 until the convergence criterion is reached. I use three sets of convergence criterion, converge in value function, policy function or basis coefficients.

THE EMPIRICAL ESTIMATION AND THE CALIBRATION OF PARAMETERS

This section discusses in detail the estimation and calibration of the parameters in the above dynamic oligopoly model. I begin with a description of the data used in the estimation, followed by a specification of the empirical model. I then present the estimation results and explain the calibration details for the parameters that I cannot estimate directly from the data.

Data

The individual level data for my analysis comes from the California Tobacco Survey (CTS).[25] For the purpose of this study, I use the data from the 1990–1991, 1992, and 1996 adult extended surveys.[26] The main reason for using CTS data is that, to my knowledge, it is the only publicly available dataset that contains detailed information concerning consumers' cigarette brand choices during the early 1990s, a period for which I have firm advertising spending data as well. Most of the datasets used in the existing literature only ask survey respondents whether they smoke or not. As a consequence, they cannot be used together with brand level price and advertising data. The CTS surveys, on the other hand, provide information about smokers' brand choices by asking the respondents explicitly, "What brand do you usually smoke?" Given the large number of brands in the market, I focus on the top eight premium brands.[27] The remaining 46 brands are grouped into one category as "other brand."

In addition to detailed information concerning the current smoking status of respondents, the CTS surveys also collect detailed information about their smoking histories. In particular, the respondents are asked, "Did you smoke everyday or someday at this time 12 months ago?" Based on their answers, I define the sample of existing adult smokers as adults (ages 25+) who either smoke currently or smoked everyday or some days 12 months before the interview. Former smokers who had quit smoking for more than one year are considered as having quit smoking permanently.[28] Young adults in my study include all adults age 18 through 24. Due to the lack of data,[29] I do not consider adolescent (age < 18) smokers in this article. Though adolescent smoking is a central concern among public health advocates, from the point of view of tobacco companies, early adulthood (18–24) is the more critical period as far as acquiring new consumers. It is during this period that most smokers first become serious about smoking, experience symptoms of addiction, and begin considering the cost of smoking.[30]

The main limitation of the CTS data is that it is state-wide data. It lacks variation across states, and thus may not be a good representation of the U.S. population overall. To compare the smoking prevalence in California with that in the United States, I use data from the Behavioral Risk Factor Surveillance System (BRFSS) collected by the Center for Disease Control. The BRFSS survey is an annual national level telephone survey that was started in 1984. Similar to CTS data, it also collects information about respondents' smoking histories. Table 2 compares the smoking prevalence in California with that in the United States. As one can see, the smoking rate in California is lower than that in the United States overall. The smoking rate among adults (25+) in the United States was 24.48, 22.96, and 22.82% for 1990, 1992, and 1996 respectively; that in California for the same age groups and for the same years was 20.67, 20.11, and 18.10% respectively. A similar pattern exists for young adults. For the above three years, the smoking rate among young adults (18–24) in the United States was 22.05, 23.69, and 27.16% respectively; in California, it was 17.68, 20.53, and 22.16% respectively. On the other hand, although the smoking rate in California is different from that in the United States, it changes in the same way. For the above period, the smoking rate decreased among older adults (25+) and increased among young adults (18–24) in both California and the United States.

Annual advertising spending data is obtained from tobacco companies' documents released in accordance with the 1998 Master Settlement Agreement.[31] My advertising expenditure variable excludes expenditures on promotional items, coupons, and promotional allowances. To control changes in the market size, I divide the real advertising expenditure in 1982–1983 dollars by the total U.S. population age 18 and above, and use the per capita real advertising expenditure as the advertising measure in the estimation.

Due to data limitations, I am unable to measure the exact out-of-pocket cost to consumers for all available brands.[32] Hence, the price variable used in my article is the after-tax wholesale price. The wholesale prices of

Table 2. Comparison of Smoking Prevalence in California and in the United States[a].

Smoking rate	Year	California Tobacco Survey	Behavioral Risk Factor Surveillance System (BRFSS) California	Behavioral Risk Factor Surveillance System (BRFSS) U.S.
Adult (age 25+)				
	1990	21.59%	20.67%	24.48%
	1992	19.76%	20.11%	22.96%
	1996	18.36%	18.10%	22.82%
Young adult (age 18–24)				
	1990	22.44%	17.68%	22.05%
	1992	20.95%	20.53%	23.69%
	1996	21.01%	22.16%	27.16%
Share of existing adult smokers[b]				
	1990	24.15%	23.33%	27.18%
	1992	22.17%	22.35%	25.56%
	1996	20.33%	19.95%	25.20%
Quiting rate among existing adult smokers				
	1990	10.61%	11.41%	9.93%
	1992	10.85%	10.05%	10.18%
	1996	9.69%	9.28%	9.47%

[a]Sample weights are used.
[b]Existing adult smokers are adults (25+) who either smoke currently or smoked everyday or some days 12 months before the interview.

premium brands are taken from Tobacco Outlook, which is published by the U.S. Department of Agriculture. The figures contained therein already include the federal exercise tax. By adding the state tax taken from the Tobacco Institute (1998), I get the after-tax wholesale price. For every respondent, I calculate the after-tax wholesale price for all available brands in 1982–1983 dollar according to their price segment at the time of the interview.[33]

The national-level, sales-based market share data are obtained from Maxwell's Report. The data cannot be used directly in the estimation, since it does not include the share of outside alternatives (i.e., not smoking). I therefore multiply the sales-based market share by the smoking rate among existing adult smokers obtained from the BRFSS in order to calculate the market share of adult smokers used in the second step estimation. To obtain the national-level market share of young adults, I multiply the implied market share based on the CTS data by the smoking rate among young adults based on the BRFSS data.

Other variables used in the study include three dummy variables for education (some college, college, graduate), three dummy variables for ethnic group (white, black, Asian), age, a dummy variable for gender, and a set of dummy variables reflecting which income group they belong to. Table 3 presents the summary statistics for the demographic variables used in the estimation.

The Empirical Model

The objective of the empirical model is to estimate the demand side coefficients, including β_1 and β_2 for price, μ and ν for the advertising response function, and the brand quality level $\boldsymbol{\phi}$ and $\boldsymbol{\varphi}$ in a way consistent with the behavior model. Due to data limitations, the individual-level data that I use are at the state level (California). The ultimate goal of the empirical

Table 3. Demographic Variable Definitions and Summary Statistics[a].

		Young Adults (18–24)		Existing Adult Smokers (25+)	
Variable	Definition	Mean	SD	Mean	SD
Male	Male	0.53	0.50	0.55	0.50
Age	Age	20.81	2.07	42.44	13.41
edu1	Some college	0.33	0.47	0.28	0.45
edu2	College	0.05	0.23	0.09	0.29
edu3	MA or Ph.D.	0.01	0.10	0.06	0.25
White	Non-Hispanic White	0.46	0.50	0.64	0.48
Black	Black	0.07	0.25	0.08	0.27
Asian	Asian	0.10	0.30	0.06	0.23
inc1	Household income 10K–20K	0.12	0.32	0.11	0.31
inc2	Household income 20K–30K	0.12	0.33	0.12	0.33
inc3	Household income 30K–50K	0.13	0.34	0.17	0.37
inc4	Household income 50K–75K	0.08	0.27	0.11	0.31
inc5	Household income 75K+	0.07	0.25	0.08	0.27
inc6	Income missing	0.36	0.48	0.33	0.47

[a]Based on the pooled California Tobacco Survey data.

model, however, is to estimate the coefficients at the national level. Since there are significant differences across states in terms of smoking restrictions, estimates based on state level data would not be representative of the overall U.S. population.

To control for differences in smoking prevalence and brand preference across states, I assume that the coefficients of price $\{\beta_1, \beta_2\}$ and advertising $\{\mu, \nu\}$ are the same for both the U.S. population and the California population, but the brand fixed effects $\{\boldsymbol{\phi}, \boldsymbol{\varphi}\}$ are potentially different.[34] This assumption enables me to employ a two-step estimation. First, I use the individual level data from California to estimate the price coefficients $\{\beta_1, \beta_2\}$ and advertising coefficients $\{\mu, \nu\}$. I then estimate the brand quality level based on the national level data using the price and advertising coefficients estimated in the first step.

The two-step estimation method has several advantages. First, by employing individual level data, I can estimate differences in the effects of price and advertising on young adults and existing adult smokers. In addition, as the first step estimation uses the individual level data, price and advertising can be viewed as exogenous from consumers' point of view. Thus I can avoid dealing with the endogeneity problem of advertising and price commonly faced by empirical IO economists using aggregate level data.[35]

An alternative to the two-step method is to estimate the model in one step by combining micro level survey data with the aggregate level data, such as the method used by Berry, Levinsohn, and Pakes (2004). The one-step method is more efficient and less restrictive than the two-step method. However, it requires finding instruments for price and advertising to control for the endogeneity problems related to the use of aggregate-level data. In my application, due to the limitation of data, I am unable to find convincing instruments for price and advertising.

First Step estimation

Individual consumers choose whether or not to smoke and, if choosing to smoke, which brand of cigarettes to smoke. The available brands in the market are labeled $j = 1 \ldots J$. In order to reduce the computation burden, I restrict consumers' choice of brand to one of eight premium brands. In addition to the above major brands, consumer may choose other brands of cigarettes which are grouped together as a combined brand called "other brands." "Not smoking" constitutes the "outside alternative," and is labeled as choice 0. Consumers may thus choose from 10 possible choices, and $J = 9$.

To capture the difference between young smokers and existing adult smokers, consumers are grouped into two types: "existing adult smokers" and "young adults." The indirect utility function of existing adult smoker i choosing choice j ($j=0, \ldots, J$) at period t is assumed to be

$$u_{ijt} = V_{ijt} + \varepsilon_{ijt}$$

where the V_{ijt} is the deterministic part and ε_{ijt} is the iid shock term. V_{ijt} are specified as

$$V_{ijt} = \begin{cases} \xi_j^1 + \beta_1 p_{it} + \mu_1 \dfrac{\nu_1 x_{jt}}{1+\nu_1 x_{jt}} + \eta_1 Z_i + \tau_1 T_i & \text{for Brand } j=1, \ldots, J-1 \\ \xi_{Jt}^1 + \beta_1 p_{it} + \eta_1 Z_i + \tau_1 T_i & \text{for Other Brands (choice } J) \\ 0 & \text{for Quit Smoking (choice 0)} \end{cases}$$

where ξ_j^1 is the brand-specific fixed effect for existing adult smokers in California,[36] p_{it} is the after-tax wholesale price per pack of premium brand cigarettes in California at the time of individual i's interview, and x_{jt} is the real per-capita advertising spending of brand j in year t. I employ a set of demographic variables Z_i – a variable for age, three indicator variables for education (some college, college, graduate), three dummy variables for ethnic group (white, black, Asian), one dummy variable for gender, and a set of dummy variables for income – to measure for differences in the tendency to smoke across different demographic groups. T_i are the time dummies controlling for unobserved changes in sentiment toward smoking in California.

Assuming that the error terms ε_{ijt} are iid extreme value distributed, one can easily derive the probability of existing smoker i choosing choice j at period $t(y_{ijt}=1)$ as

$$\Pr(y_{ijt}=1) = \frac{\exp(V_{ijt})}{\sum_{j=0}^{J} \exp(V_{ijt})}$$

for $j=0, 1, \ldots J$. In the sample, not every smoker specifies his or her brand choice. For these smokers, $y_{ijt}=0$ for all $j=0, 1, \ldots J$. Let $\tilde{y}_{it}=1$ if existing smoker i is currently smoking but fails to report his or her brand choice. Assuming that there is no selection in missing brand choice, the probability of observing $\tilde{y}_{it}=1$ is the probability of smoking

$$\Pr(\tilde{y}_{it}=1)=\frac{\sum_{j=1}^{J}\exp(V_{ijt})}{1+\sum_{j=1}^{J}\exp(V_{ijt})}$$

Let $\Omega=\{\xi,\beta_1,\mu_1,\nu_1,\eta_1,\tau_1\}$ be the parameter space, the contribution to the likelihood function for existing smoker i is

$$l_i(\Omega)=\prod_{j=0}^{J}\Pr(y_{ijt}=1)^{y_{ijt}}\Pr(\tilde{y}_{it}=1)^{\tilde{y}_{it}}$$

Similarly the indirect utility of young adult i smoking brand j at period t is assumed to be

$$u_{ijt}=\tilde{V}_{ijt}+\varepsilon_{ijt}$$

and $\tilde{V}_{ijt}$ is specified as

$$\tilde{V}_{ijt}=\begin{cases}\xi_j^2+\beta_2 p_{it}+\mu_2\dfrac{\nu_2 x_{jt}}{1+\nu_2 x_{jt}}+\eta_2 Z_i+\tau_2 T & \text{for Brand } j=1,\ldots,J-1\\ \xi_{Jt}^2+\beta_2 p_{it}+\eta_2 Z_i+\tau_2 T & \text{for Other Brands (choice } J)\\ 0 & \text{for Quit Smoking (choice 0)}\end{cases}$$

The likelihood function for young adults can be derived in a way similar to that for existing adult smokers.

Although the assumption on the distribution of error terms imposes strong restrictions on the substituting behavior among choices, and thus makes my model subject to the problem of Independent of Irrelevant Alternatives (IIA), it allows for an easy estimation of the parameters and is consistent with the assumption made regarding the demand function used in the dynamic model. Though other discrete choice models, such as the Multinomial Probit model, are free of IIA problem, they would be computationally near impossible when attempting to solve the dynamic oligopoly model.

Second-Step estimation

The second step estimation is a "data-fitting" exercise aimed at finding the parameter value for brand quality level, $\{\phi,\varphi\}$ in the dynamic model that are consistent with the observed market share among existing adult smokers, s_{jt}, and young adults, $\tilde{s}_{jt}$, at the national level.

To correspond with the theoretical model, I assume that the aggregate market share takes the following form:

$$s_{jt} = \frac{\exp(\overline{V}_{jt})}{1 + \sum_{j=1}^{J} \exp(\overline{V}_{jt})}$$

$$\overline{V}_{jt} = \begin{cases} \boldsymbol{\phi}_j + \beta_1 p_t + \mu_1 \dfrac{\nu_1 x_{jt}}{1 + \nu_1 x_{jt}} - \kappa_t + \overline{\eta}_{jt} & \text{for Brand } j = 1, \ldots, J-1 \\ \boldsymbol{\phi}_J + \beta_1 p_t - \kappa_t + \overline{\eta}_{Jt} & \text{for Other Brands (choice } J) \\ 0 & \text{for Quit Smoking (choice 0)} \end{cases}$$

where $\boldsymbol{\phi}_j$ is the brand-specific effect among existing adult smokers, p_t is the weighted average after-tax price of premium cigarettes in the United States, x_{jt} is the per-capita advertising spending of brand j in period t, and $\overline{\eta}_{jt}$ is the unobserved deviation of brands quality level from $\boldsymbol{\phi}_j$ at period t. The latter is assumed to be mean zero and variance $\sigma^2_{\eta j}$. In a similar way, I assume that the predicted market share of brand j among young adults is

$$\tilde{s}_{jt} = \frac{\exp(\tilde{V}_{ijt})}{1 + \sum_{j=1}^{J} \exp(\tilde{V}_{ijt})}$$

$$\tilde{V}_{jt} = \begin{cases} \boldsymbol{\varphi}_j + \beta_2 p_t + \mu_2 \dfrac{\nu_2 x_{jt}}{1 + \nu_2 x_{jt}} - \kappa_t + \tilde{\eta}_{jt} & \text{for Brand } j = 1, \ldots, J-1 \\ \boldsymbol{\varphi}_{J+1} + \beta_2 p_t - \kappa_t + \tilde{\eta}_{jt} & \text{for Other Brands (choice } J) \\ 0 & \text{for Quit Smoking (choice 0)} \end{cases}$$

where $\boldsymbol{\varphi}_j$ is the brand fixed effect among young adults. To estimate the brand quality level $\boldsymbol{\phi}_j$ and $\boldsymbol{\varphi}_j$, I match the observed market share with the predicted market share. Using the transformation method developed by Berry (1994), I transform the above predicted market share equation by taking the log difference between the market share of brand j and the market share of outside alternatives (not smoking), and obtain

$$\log(s_{jt}) - \log(s_{0,t}) = \boldsymbol{\phi}_j + \beta_1 p_t + \mu_1 \frac{\nu_1 x_{jt}}{1 + \nu_1 x_{jt}} - \kappa_t + \overline{\eta}_{jt}$$

$$\log(\tilde{s}_{jt}) - \log(\tilde{s}_{0,t}) = \boldsymbol{\varphi}_j + \beta_2 p_t + \mu_2 \frac{\nu_2 x_{jt}}{1 + \nu_2 x_{jt}} - \kappa_t + \tilde{\eta}_{jt}$$

Since the price coefficients and advertising coefficients are already estimated in the first step using individual-level data, I substitute the estimated price coefficients $\{\hat{\beta}_1, \hat{\beta}_2\}$ and advertising coefficients $\{\hat{\mu}_1, \hat{\mu}_2, \hat{\nu}_1, \hat{\nu}_2\}$, into the above equations. Thus, if we let $M_{jt} = \log(s_{jt}) - \log(s_{0,t}) - \hat{\beta}_1 p_t - \hat{\mu}_1 \frac{\hat{\nu}_1 x_{jt}}{1+\hat{\nu}_1 x_{jt}}$ and $\tilde{M}_{jt} = \log(\tilde{s}_{jt}) - \log(\tilde{s}_{0,t}) - \hat{\beta}_2 p_t - \hat{\mu}_2 \frac{\hat{\nu}_2 x_{jt}}{1+\hat{\nu}_2 x_{jt}}$, the above equations become

$$M_{jt} = \boldsymbol{\phi}_j - \kappa_t + \bar{\eta}_{jt}$$

$$\tilde{M}_{jt} = \boldsymbol{\varphi}_j - \kappa_t + \tilde{\eta}_{jt}$$

Let $y = \begin{bmatrix} M \\ \tilde{M} \end{bmatrix}$, $c = [\boldsymbol{\phi}, \boldsymbol{\varphi}]$, and $\eta = \begin{bmatrix} \eta \\ \tilde{\eta} \end{bmatrix}$, I obtain

$$y = cI + \kappa T + \eta$$

where I are the brand dummy variables and T are the time dummy variables. η is distributed with mean 0, finite variance, and uncorrelated with I and T. To estimate $\boldsymbol{\phi}$ and $\boldsymbol{\varphi}$ consistently, one can treat them as fixed effect coefficients. A simple OLS regression of y on the brand dummies I and time dummies T would then give us consistent estimates for $\boldsymbol{\phi}$, $\boldsymbol{\varphi}$, and κ.

Empirical Estimates

Table 4 shows the demand estimates. Similar to the findings by Gilleskie and Strumpf (2005), young adults are more responsive to price and less responsive to advertising than existing adult smokers. The price coefficient of young adults, β_2, is estimated at –5.78, while that of existing adult smokers, β_1, equals –3.75. In addition, the estimated advertising response coefficients μ_2 and ν_2 of young adults are not significant, while the μ_1 and ν_1 of existing adult smokers are significant at 1.7 and 28.8 respectively. Moreover, the estimated coefficient for μ and ν are both positive, which supports the existence of a decreasing return to scale of advertising.

While many studies support the finding that young smokers are more responsive to price, one is surprised to find that advertising has a small and insignificant effect on them. One possible explanation is that the brand choice of young smokers is not affected by advertising, but rather by other unobserved brand characteristics. The top three brands among young smokers – Marlboro, Camel, and Newport – enjoy a consistently high market share despite their much lower share of advertising spending. This explanation is further supported by evidence that, for young adults, the estimated coefficients for the above top three brands are significantly higher

Table 4. Demand Estimates[a].

	Young Adults (18–24)		Existing Smokers (25+)		Overall Population	
Variables	Coefficient	SD	Coefficient	SD	Coefficient	SD
First step estimates[b]						
Advertising response μ	0.03	0.98	1.71	0.04		
Advertising response ν	0.54	18.99	28.8	1.54		
Price β	−5.78	0.11	−3.75	0.12		
Second step estimates						
Marlboro	4.06	24.45	2.61	12.71		
Salem	−0.63	−1.19	1.74	8.97		
Merit	−2.05	−12.16	1.04	5.64		
Winston	−0.11	−0.32	1.99	9.08		
BH	0.70	3.92	1.03	6.08		
Newport	1.81	8.65	1.29	5.36		
Camel	2.39	8.77	0.75	3.58		
Virginia Slims	−0.36	−1.21	0.89	6.55		
Other Brand	1.33	2.63	5.04	40.91		
Time effect						
T92					0.77	5.69
T96					−0.10	−0.65

[a]Sample weights are used in estimation.
[b]Other variables used in the first step estimation include age, gender, a set of dummy variables for education, race and income, brand, and time dummy variables.

than those for other brand dummies. Moreover, many other factors, such as peer pressure, may significantly affect young smokers' decisions as well. In addition, if young smokers were more responsive to advertising, one would expect the other brands to challenge the dominant position of the above top three brands by increasing their advertising spending. Yet no other brand has succeeded in overtaking the dominant position of the top brands in the young smokers market in the last two decades.

Nonetheless, one should interpret these results with caution. Due to the lack of data, advertising spending in this article is inclusive only of limited forms of advertising, such as that represented by newspapers, magazines, and billboards. The insignificant effect of traditional types of advertising on the cigarette demand of young people does not mean that other types of advertising are ineffective. During the 1990s, cigarette companies significantly increased the use of other marketing practices,[37] such as the use of promotional items, the sponsoring of sports events, the provision of free samples, and so forth. These new advertising practices may have significant effects on young people's smoking decisions.

Table 4 presents the estimates from the second-step estimation. The quality levels for existing adult smokers are quite close for all brands. For young adults, by contrast, the quality levels of the top three brands, Marlboro, Camel, and Newport, are significantly higher than those of other brands.

Other Parameters

Table 5 contains the parameters that I obtain from other sources. For the supply side parameters, the market size is set to be equal to the annual cigarette consumption per person. Since smokers on average consume one

Table 5. Other Coefficients[a].

Parameter	Explanation	Value
M	Market size	365
mc90	Marginal cost in 1990	0.22
mc92	Marginal cost in 1992	0.26
mc96	Marginal cost in 1996	0.24
γ_1	Size of young adults	0.15
γ_2	Transition rate from young adults to adults	0.14
γ_3	Successful quiting rate	0.25
δ	Discount factor	0.926
Stochastic distribution parameters		
ρ		0.730
ζ_1		0.135
ζ_2		0.270
ζ_3		0.410
ζ_4		0.540
$\pi_{0\zeta}$	Probability of $\zeta_t = \zeta_0$	0.30
$\pi_{1\zeta}$	Probability of $\zeta_t = \zeta_1$	0.25
$\pi_{2\zeta}$	Probability of $\zeta_t = \zeta_2$	0.20
$\pi_{3\zeta}$	Probability of $\zeta_t = \zeta_3$	0.15
$\pi_{4\zeta}$	Probability of $\zeta_t = \zeta_4$	0.10

[a]The calibration details are in the article.

pack of cigarettes per day, the implied market size is set at 365. According to the estimates from Bulow and Klemperer (1998), the manufacturing cost excluding marketing expenses per pack of cigarettes was 25 cents in 1997.[38] After adding the per pack promotion cost obtained from the Federal Trade Commission (2001),[39] I obtain the marginal cost of cigarettes for 1990, 1992, and 1996 at 0.22, 0.26, and 0.24 (in 1982–1983 dollar) respectively. I use these as estimates for the marginal cost of all brands.

Based on the 1990 population estimates from the U.S. Census Bureau, I set the relative size of young adults γ_1 at 0.15, which equals the percentage of adults in the age range 18–24 among all adults over the age of 18. The transition rate of young adults to adults γ_2 is set at 0.14. According to Krall et al. (2002), the smoking relapse rates for smokers trying to quit range from 60% to 90% within the first year of quitting. Thus, I set the successful quitting rate coefficient γ_3 at 0.25.

For the dynamic parameters, the discount factor δ is set at 0.926, a value commonly used in the applied IO literature (Benkard, 2004; Pakes & McGuire, 1994). The autocorrelation parameter, ρ, is calibrated at 0.73. The distribution parameters for the stochastic process of social sentiment are chosen as follows. I assume that ζ_t take the following values $\{0, 0.135, 0.27, 0.41, 0.54\}$ with probability $\{0.3, 0.25, 0.2, 0.15, 0.1\}$ respectively. Under this assumption, the state variable κ is bounded between [0,2] and the steady state level is 0.75.

THE RESULTS OF THE EQUILIBRIUM AND A COMPARISON WITH THE HISTORICAL DATA

Before using the dynamic model to study the responses of firms to various antismoking policies, I conduct a "with-in sample" test of the model. More specifically, I first solve firm price and advertising strategies based on the theoretical model using the estimated coefficients and the state variables.[40] I then compare the observed data with the model's predictions. The comparison serves to answer two questions: (1) Is the dynamic oligopoly model a good approximation of firm behavior? (2) Are the assumptions about firm behavior and the parameters used in the model reasonable? If the model's predictions match the observed data, it would serve as evidence that the model is a good approximation of firm behavior. This comparison is an important test of the model, since the model is still an abstraction of the decision making process of firms, which is much more complex in the real world. Additionally, the parameters of the model are estimated from various sources. The test would give us more confidence in using the estimated model to conduct policy simulations.

One important feature of this comparison is that I estimate the model's structural parameters without making any assumptions about firm behavior. In the empirical section, the demand estimates are based on the individual level data, brand quality levels are estimated to match the observed market share, and the other parameters are chosen on the basis of other studies. Nowhere in the empirical estimation do I assume that firms behave optimally or use any information implied by the dynamic model, such as the price-cost mark up. Therefore, the predicted pricing and advertising strategies are based solely on the equilibrium property of the model.

Table 6 compares the observed price and advertising spending with that predicted by the model. The model does a very good job predicting observed prices. Differences between the observed prices and the predicted ones are less than 4.7 cents per pack, which is about 4% of the observed prices. With respect to advertising spending, the model's predictions are reasonably close to the observed data, especially for the top brands. For example, differences between Marlboro's predicted advertising spending and the observed advertising spending are less than 10% of the observed values. In addition, the model's predictions about other key variables of interest – such as the quitting rates of existing adult smokers, the smoking rates of young adults, and the market share – all match closely with the observed data. Thus, for example, the predicted smoking rates among young adults for the years 1990, 1992, and 1996 are, respectively, 25, 29, and 24%, versus corresponding observed smoking rates of 22, 24, and 27%.

To show the importance of using the dynamic model, I also solve the static version of the dynamic game by setting the discount factor at zero ($\delta = 0$). In the static model, firms are "myopic" and maximize their current period profit without considering the effects of current strategy (price and advertising) on future profit. Table 6 shows that, in the absence of incentives to keep current smokers smoking and to attract young people to smoke, firms set prices at a much higher level than that in the dynamic model. The predicted prices are \$1.33, \$1.49, and \$1.34 per pack for 1990, 1992, and 1996 respectively. On average, the static model overpredicts the cigarette price by 38%. Furthermore, the static model drastically underpredicts the smoking rate of young adults and overpredicts the quitting rate of existing adult smokers. The predicted smoking rates of young adults based on the static model are, respectively, 3, 3, and 4% for 1990, 1992, and 1996, versus corresponding observed smoking rates of 22, 24, and

Table 6. Comparison of Model Prediction with Observed Data[a].

	1990 ($\sigma=0.271, \kappa=0.97$)			Y1992 ($\sigma=0.256, \kappa=0.2$)			Y1996 ($\sigma=0.252, \kappa=1.07$)		
	Observed	Predicted		Observed	Predicted		Observed	Predicted	
		Dynamic	Static		Dynamic	Static		Dynamic	Static
Price ($/pack)	0.950	0.919	1.325	1.110	1.063	1.489	0.960	0.992	1.338
Advertising spending ($)[b]									
Marlboro	0.548	0.530	0.662	0.511	0.565	0.694	0.461	0.494	0.594
Salem	0.153	0.331	0.425	0.085	0.356	0.448	0.025	0.307	0.378
Merit	0.103	0.219	0.286	0.229	0.237	0.303	0.085	0.201	0.252
Winston	0.089	0.382	0.487	0.174	0.410	0.513	0.048	0.356	0.435
Benson & Hedges	0.113	0.217	0.284	0.140	0.236	0.301	0.057	0.200	0.250
Newport	0.308	0.256	0.331	0.223	0.277	0.350	0.130	0.236	0.293
Camel	0.237	0.181	0.239	0.176	0.198	0.253	0.256	0.165	0.209
Virginia Slims	0.180	0.198	0.261	0.121	0.216	0.277	0.122	0.182	0.229
Smoking prevalence									
Smoking rate among young adults	22.05%	25.24%	3.14%	23.69%	28.92%	3.36%	27.16%	23.69%	4.03%
Quiting rate among existing smokers	9.93%	8.47%	29.33%	10.18%	8.33%	30.64%	9.47%	9.45%	27.34%
Market share									
Marlboro	26.00%	26.31%	19.95%	24.40%	25.38%	19.48%	32.30%	29.81%	23.89%
Salem	6.10%	6.53%	7.33%	4.80%	6.17%	7.19%	3.60%	7.18%	8.23%
Merit	3.50%	3.89%	4.55%	3.00%	2.77%	3.31%	2.30%	2.61%	3.02%
Winston	8.80%	11.22%	12.63%	6.80%	7.25%	8.39%	5.30%	8.23%	9.36%
Benson & Hedges	3.60%	3.93%	4.24%	3.10%	3.30%	3.41%	2.30%	2.94%	3.21%
Newport	4.70%	4.43%	4.19%	4.80%	4.85%	4.65%	6.10%	6.18%	6.01%
Camel	4.30%	4.13%	3.44%	4.10%	4.57%	2.71%	4.60%	4.06%	2.88%
Virginia Slims	3.10%	2.92%	3.33%	2.60%	2.78%	3.12%	2.40%	2.37%	2.72%
Other brand	39.90%	36.64%	40.34%	46.40%	42.93%	47.75%	41.10%	36.62%	40.67%

[a]The dynamic model use discount factor $\delta=0.926$, and the static model use discount factor $\delta=0$.
[b]Per capita annual real advertising spending in 1982–1983 dollar.

27%. The failure of the static model to predict industry behavior shows that it is critical to use the dynamic model when studying the cigarette industry.

There are two conclusions that I draw from the above comparison. First, I believe that the comparison provides strong support for the dynamic model. Despite all the simplifications, the model's predictions about firm behavior are very close to the observed data for all three years, which greatly boosts our confidence in using the dynamic model to perform policy simulations. Second, the comparison indicates that the model's assumptions about firm behavior and the estimated coefficients are reasonable.

POLICY SIMULATIONS

This section conducts counterfactual policy experiments and evaluates the two commonly used smoking control policies: advertising restrictions and tobacco tax increases.

Most of the advertising restrictions either reduce the advertising channels – for instance, by forbidding advertising on television and billboards – or restrict the content of advertisements – for instance, by prohibiting firms from using cartoon figures. Since cigarette companies use a wide variety of methods to promote their products, forbidding them to use one method only leads them to use other less effective methods. Put another way, advertising restrictions only serve to make advertising less effective. I choose not to model the details of how advertising restrictions affect the shape of the aggregate advertising response function. Instead, I model the effects of advertising restrictions as a decrease in the value of μ and an increase in the value of ν.[41]

For all the simulations conducted in this section, I begin with no policy intervention, and use the state variable for 1996 ($\sigma = 0.52$, $\kappa = 1.07$) as the starting value to simulate the industry for 100 periods. By doing so, the market reaches the steady state before the policy change. Therefore I avoid the potential bias caused by the initial conditions. I then implement the smoking control policy, and use the optimal price and advertising strategies under the new policy to simulate the industry for another 100 periods. In addition, in order to compare the model's predictions with those made using models that ignore firms' responses, I also simulate the industry after the policy change while holding prices and advertising spending fixed at the pre-impact level. For the above simulations, I use 1,000 random draws and record the average values of the key variables of interest, among them, the share of existing smokers, the price, total industry advertising spending, total industry profit, the smoking rate of existing adult smokers, and the smoking rate of young adults.

Both the short run effects and the long run effects of policy interventions are considered in the policy simulations. In the short run, the state variables – in particular, the share of existing adult smokers – remain the same; in the long run (after 100 period), the state variables change as a result of policy interventions. Table 7 compares the changes in key variables before the policy interventions, right after policy interventions, and in the long run. In addition, in order to capture the evolution of the market over the period of simulations, I plot in Figs. 1–3 the change in the average values of the key variables after a partial advertising ban, a complete advertising ban, and a tax increase respectively.

The Effects of Advertising Restrictions

For the partial advertising restrictions, I reduce the values of μ_1 and μ_2 to half the estimated $\hat{\mu}_1$ and $\hat{\mu}_2$, and increase the values of ν_1 and ν_2 to twice the estimated $\hat{\nu}_1$ and $\hat{\nu}_2$. These changes correspond to a reduction in the advertising channels by half.[42] As to the complete advertising ban, I reduce the values of μ_1 and μ_2 to zeros and keep the values of ν_1 and ν_2 the same.

> **Result 1a.** Both partial advertising restrictions and a complete advertising ban reduce the steady state smoking rate slightly, increase the youth smoking rate, increase the existing smokers quitting rate, reduce the price, reduce total industry advertising spending, and slightly reduce industry profit.

> **Result 1b.** The long run effects and short run effects of advertising restrictions are close.

The differences between the long run effects and the short run effects are caused by changes in the state variables, in particular, the share of existing smokers. As Table 7 shows, after partial advertising restrictions are imposed, the share of existing smokers remains almost the same (changing from 23.72% to 23.65%). Thus, the long run effects of advertising restrictions are similar to the short run effects. For this reason, I focus on discussing the long run effects of advertising restrictions.

Table 7. Comparison of the Effects of Antismoking Policies[a].

Key Variable of Interest	Before	Dynamic Model[b]		Ignore Firms' Reactions[c]	
		SR	LR	SR	LR
Partial advertising restriction					
Price ($/pack)	1.01	0.97	0.97	1.01	1.01
Total industry advertising spending ($M)	422.10	156.35	156.52	422.10	422.10
Industry profit ($b)	5.96	5.70	5.63	5.81	4.48
Share of existing smokers	23.72%	23.72%	23.65%	23.72%	17.75%
Smoking rate among young adults	23.14%	27.41%	27.60%	87.39%	87.24%
Smoking rate among existing adult smokers	90.52%	88.60%	88.72%	23.24%	23.00%
Complete advertising ban					
Price ($/pack)	1.01	0.96	0.95	1.01	1.01
Total industry advertising spending ($M)	422.10	0.00	0.00	422.10	422.10
Industry profit ($b)	5.96	5.55	5.33	5.60	3.72
Share of existing smokers	23.72%	23.72%	23.01%	23.72%	14.83%
Smoking rate among young adults	23.14%	29.41%	29.93%	84.47%	84.55%
Smoking Rate among existing adult smokers	90.52%	87.10%	87.27%	23.01%	23.01%
Tax increase of 20 cents per pack					
Price ($/pack)	1.01	1.24	1.11	1.21	1.21
Total industry advertising spending ($M)	422.10	409.01	198.99	422.12	422.12
Industry profit ($b)	5.96	4.99	1.93	4.80	0.90
Share of existing smokers	23.72%	23.72%	10.39%	23.72%	4.90%
Smoking rate among young adults	23.14%	7.69%	14.79%	8.66%	8.66%
Smoking rate among existing adult smokers	90.52%	80.53%	86.07%	81.86%	81.86%

[a]1,000 simulations are used and sample averages are reported in the table. Short run effects (SR) are based on the average of simulations in the period immediately after the policy implementation. Long run effects (LR) are based on the average of simulations at the 100 period after the policy implementatio. Use the state variables in 1996 as starting value.
[b]Use the optimal policy after the policy intervention to simulate the industry.
[c]Use the price and advertising spending before policy intervention to simulate the industry.

In the long run, other key variables are significantly affected by advertising restrictions. After partial advertising restrictions are imposed, total industry advertising spending is reduced from $422 million to $157 million. On the other hand, the decrease in consumers' advertising responses increases the demand elasticity. As a result, the cartel manager lowers the price from $1.01 per pack to $0.97 per pack. Though the reduction in

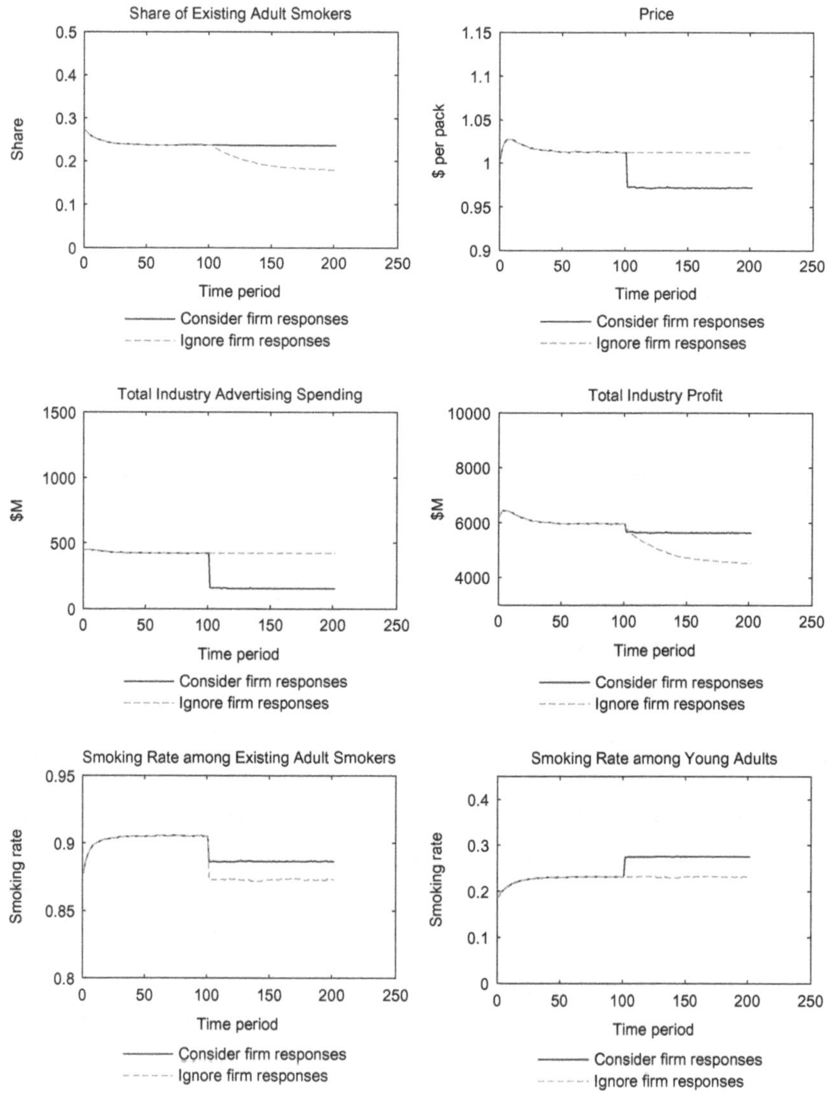

Fig. 1. Simulation of a partial advertising ban.

advertising spending and advertising effectiveness decreases consumers' incentive to smoke, the indirect effect of advertising restrictions through the price drop can offset the direct effect. As a result, advertising restrictions only lead to a small reduction in the smoking rate of existing adult

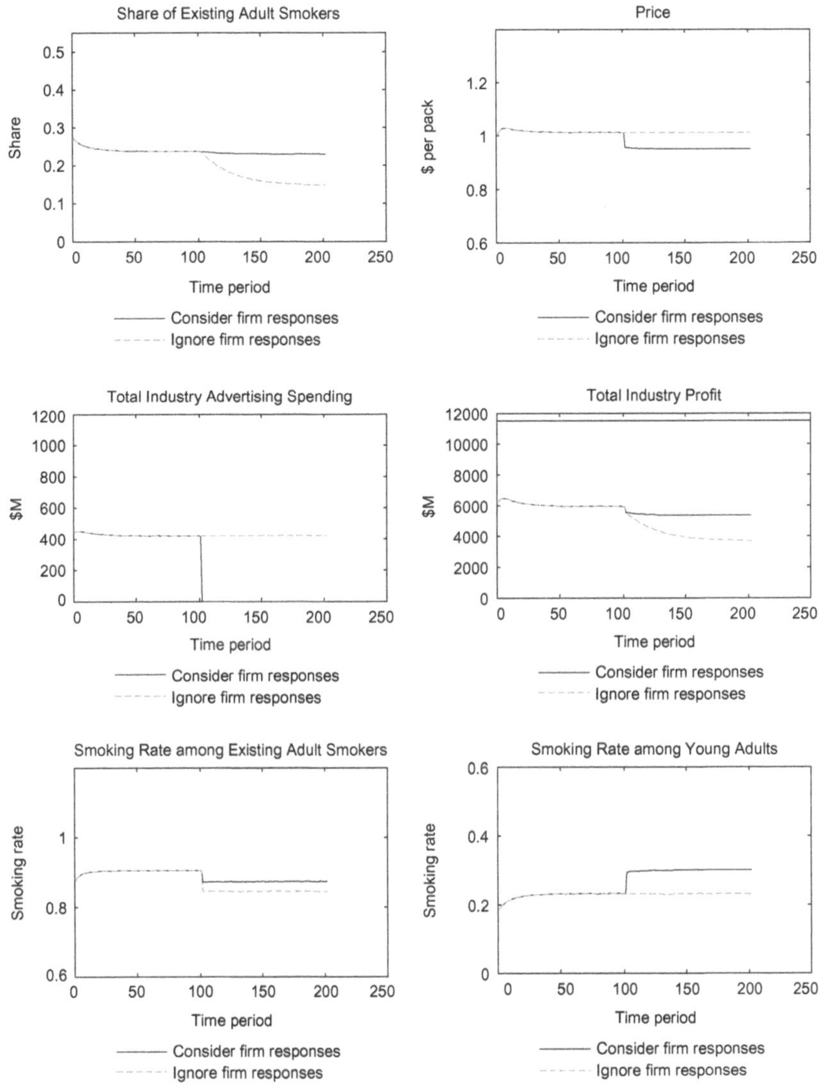

Fig. 2. Simulation of a complete advertising ban.

smokers, from 90.5% to 88.7%. Furthermore, advertising restrictions *increase* the smoking rate of young adults from 23.14% to 27.6%, as the indirect effect dominates the direct effect of advertising restrictions for young adults.

In addition, Table 7 provides the changes in key variables if we ignore the responses of firms. It shows that failing to control for firm's responses will overestimates the effects of partial advertising restrictions. It predicts a reduction in the share of smokers from 23.72% to 17.75% in the long run. Furthermore, it fails to capture the possibility of an increase in the youth smoking rate. This shows the importance of taking into account the reactions of tobacco companies to policy changes.

The results of a complete advertising ban are also presented in Table 7. Total industry advertising spending is reduced to zero, while the price of cigarettes drops from $1.01 per pack to $0.95 per pack. Similar to the findings about the partial advertising restrictions, the complete advertising ban has a negligible effect on the share of existing smokers and actually increases the smoking rate of young adults. As far as the prevention of youth smoking is concerned, a complete advertising ban is even worse than a partial advertising ban. The smoking rate of young adults increases from 23.14% to 29.93%.

The Effects of Tax Increases

For the tax increase exercise, I simulate the effects of a 20 cents per pack tax increase. Since the model parameters are estimated based on 1982–1983 dollar, the tax increase considered here equals to a 33 cents per pack tax increase in 1997 dollars. Thus the magnitude of the tax increase corresponds to that implemented in the 1998 Master Settlement Agreement. A point worth mentioning is that the simulation is based on the inflation adjusted tax increase. However, most of the existing tobacco taxes are not indexed by the inflation rate. Therefore, the real tax rate decreases over time, and the simulation here may overestimate the effects of the tax increases.

Result 2a. In the short run, a tax increase significantly increases the price of cigarettes, significantly reduces the smoking rate of young adults and existing adult smokers, and slightly reduces industry advertising spending and industry profit.

Result 2b. In the long run, a tax increase reduces the smoking rate of young adults and existing adult smokers but by a smaller magnitude than is the case in the short run. In addition, the tax increase significantly reduces the share of existing smokers, industry profit, and industry advertising spending.

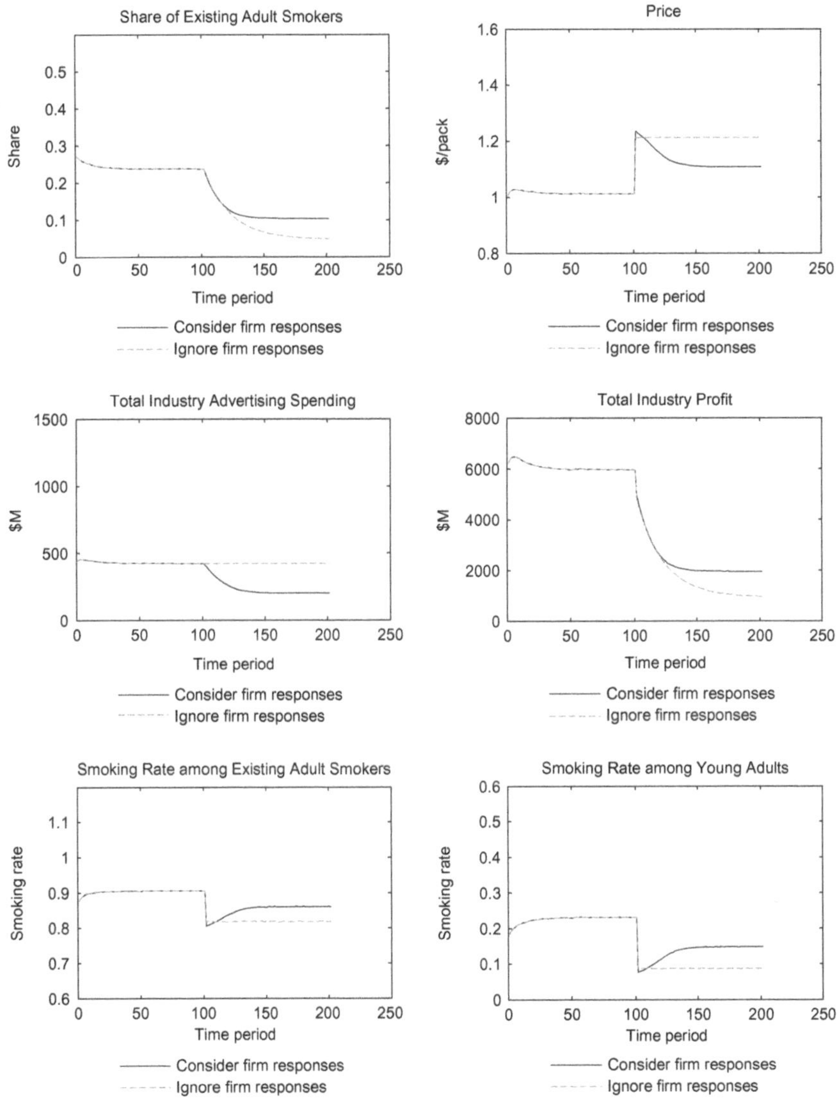

Fig. 3. Simulation of 20c/pack tax increase.

Table 7 and Fig. 3 indicate that tax increases constitute a very effective policy in the short run. Immediately after a 20 cents increase in tax, the price of cigarettes increases from $1.01 per pack to $1.23 per pack, which in turn causes a huge reduction in the smoking rate of young adults from

23.14% to 7.69%, and in that of the existing adult smokers from 90.52% to 80.53%.

An interesting result is that the price increases by 22 cents, which is more than the actual tax increase. This is because after the tax increase, the share of existing current smokers is higher than the steady state level. As a result, cigarette firms anticipate current smokers to quit soon. They thus have a stronger incentive to exploit current smokers in the short run. Therefore, this leads to a price increase greater than the actual tax increase.

However, the effects of the tax increase diminish over time. In the long run, the steady state share of existing smoker decreases from 24% to 10%. As the share of existing smokers approaches the steady state level, the incentive of firms to exploit current smokers gradually decreases, while the incentive to increase the share of existing smokers gets stronger. Hence, in the long run, the price of cigarettes decreases from $1.23 per pack, the level right after the policy intervention, to $1.10 per pack. As a result, the smoking rate of young adults increases from 7% to 15%, and that of existing smoker increases from 81% to 86%.

Furthermore, a tax increase has relatively small effects on advertising spending and industry profit in the short run. However, it would significantly reduce both in the long run due to the reduction in the number of smokers. Immediately after the tax increase, total industry advertising spending drops from $422 million to $409 million, while industry profit drops from $5.96 billion to $4.99 billion. In the long run, total industry advertising spending reduces to $199 million and industry profit reduces to $1.93 billion.

Ignoring the responses of firms to tax increases is also very problematic, especially in the long run. Simulation results show that the predicted steady state share of existing smokers is 4.9% in the long run and that the smoking rate of young adults and existing adult smokers remain 8.6% and 81.86% respectively, both in the short run and in the long run. Thus, ignoring firm response would drastically overpredict the effectiveness of tax increase in the long run, while under-predicting them in the short run.

A Discussion of the Results

This section summarizes the above simulation results.

Result 3. Ignoring firm responses to antismoking policies seriously biases the estimated policy effects.

For the antismoking policies considered above, ignoring firm responses leads to an overestimation of policy effectiveness in the long run and its underestimation in the short run. In addition, it can't capture the possible increase in the smoking rate of young adults.

Result 4. The long run effects of antismoking policies on reducing smoking rates are smaller than the short run effects.

The above simulation results show that the long run effects of antismoking policies on reducing smoking rates are smaller than the short run effects. A successful antismoking policy usually leads to a reduction in the share of existing adult smokers in the long run. In the short run, however, inasmuch as they face a higher share of existing adult smokers than that at the steady state level, cigarettes firms have a stronger incentive to exploit current smokers by raising prices. This in turn further lowers the smoking rate. However, as the share of existing smokers approaches the new steady state level, the incentive of firms to increase the share of smokers gets stronger. This causes firms to reduce prices, and as a result, the smoking rate increases.

Result 5. Reduction in youth smoking is critical for the long run success of any antismoking policies.

In order to achieve the long run reduction in smoking rate, the antismoking policy has to successfully reduce the youth smoking rate. The simulations show that despite advertising restriction reduce smoking rate among existing smoker, it fails to reduce the overall smoking prevalence in the long run. This is precisely because of the increase in the youth smoking rate.

A final point that I would like to emphasize is that, in addition to the efficacy of antismoking policies on reducing the smoking rate, the policy effects on the interested parties must be factored in, in particular, with respect to industry profits and the cost to smokers. If an antismoking policy significantly increases the cost of smoking or reduces the cigarette industry's profit, it may face greater political challenges, thus making it more difficult to implement. From this point of view, advertising restrictions are easier to implement than tax increases, as their impact on industry profits and on the cost to smokers is much less than that of tax increases. Not surprisingly, the tobacco industry fought less fiercely against advertising restrictions in recent legal cases.[43]

CONCLUSION

I use an empirical dynamic oligopoly model of the U.S. cigarette industry to study industry price and advertising strategies and to evaluate the effects of antismoking policies taking into account firms' optimal responses. The dynamic model captures three key features of the cigarette industry: (1) dynamic demand due to addiction; (2) the importance of younger people to the tobacco industry; and (3) differences between young people and adult smokers in their responses to price and advertising. The model's structural parameters are estimated using a combination of micro-level and aggregate-level data, and firms' optimal price and advertising strategies are solved as an MPNE. Using the empirically estimated coefficients, the estimated dynamic model predicts industry prices and advertising expenditures extremely well.

Several antismoking policies are evaluated and the following key findings are discussed in this article. First, increasing the tobacco tax would reduce the overall smoking rate and the youth smoking rate, while advertising restrictions might actually *increase* the youth smoking rate. Second, the effects of antismoking policies on reducing smoking rates tend to decrease over time; that is, the long run effects are smaller than the short run effects. Third, ignoring firm responses to policy changes would underestimate policy efficacy in the short run, while overestimating it in the long run.

Studying firm behavior is critical to understanding the effectiveness of antismoking policies. An important consequence of antismoking policies is the change in the market structure in the forms of entry and exit of firm. These changes in market structure has very important policy implications. For example, since the Master Settlement Agreement of 1998, many generic brands entered the market. Even though individual firms are small, together they have a significant effect on the cigarette market. It would be interesting to study how the MSA has induced the entry of generic brands into the market and what policies could be used to reduce the effects of generic brands on the smoking rate.

NOTES

1. Tobacco companies agreed to pay $206 billion to the 46 state governments in the 1998 Multistate Settlement Agreement. More recently, the U.S. federal government charged the top American cigarette producers with lying to the public about the hazards of smoking, and sought penalties of $280 billion.

2. See Chaloupka and Warner (2000) and the literature review in the section "The Existing Literature."

3. There are numerous reasons underlying those differences. One reason is the effect of nicotine use. Others include social and behavioral changes. For example, the peer effect is not that important for adult smokers. Individual heterogeneity may also explain part of the difference between long-term smokers and new smokers.

4. Interestingly, the 1998 Master Settlement Agreements (MSA) provided an example of such a case. The MSA imposed a permanent national per pack tax that started at 7.2 cents in 1997 and increased to around 38.5 cents in 2002. However, the per pack price of premium brand cigarettes increased from $1.33 in January 1998 to $2.64 in January 2002, while the per pack price of discount brand cigarettes raised from $1.14 to $2.51 during the same period.

5. A switching cost results from the consumer's desire for compatibility between his current purchase and a previous purchase. It can be caused by a variety of reasons, including the need for compatibility, the transaction cost, the cost of learning, uncertainty regarding changes, psychological costs such as "brand loyalty," and so forth. See Klemperer (1995, 1987a, 1987b), Beggs and Klemperer (1992), and Farrell and Klemperer (2007) for a discussion of industries that have switching costs.

6. See Chaloupka and Warner (2000) for an extensive review of the literature.

7. See Doraszelki and Pakes (2007) for a literature review.

8. Benkard (2004) uses data for the wide-bodied commercial aircraft industry. Dube et al. (2005) use scanner data for the frozen food product industry.

9. R.J. Reynolds merged with Brown and Williamson on July 30, 2004.

10. The retail prices for different brands of cigarettes may differ even though they are sold at the same location. Cigarette firms use a variety of marketing practices to compete at the retail level, such as promotional allowances (payments to retailers to facilitate the sale of cigarettes), retail value added (expenditures associated with offers such as "buy one, get one free"), and coupons.

11. "The Price is not Quite Right," July 5, 2001.

12. Specialty item distribution includes the practice of selling or giving consumers items such as T-shirts, caps, sunglasses, key chains, calendars, lighters, and sporting goods bearing a cigarette brand's logo.

13. Due to the huge sunk costs, such as advertising and legal costs, large scale entry and exit are rare in the cigarette industry before the Master Settlement Agreement in 1998.

14. There are nine players in the dynamic game. Keeping track of the evolution of the quality levels of all brands would require a huge amount of computation. In addition, the quality and the taste of cigarettes seldom changes and respective brand market shares in the industry are pretty stable over time.

15. Other alternatives for modeling firm behavior, such as the price leadership model or the simultaneous move non-collusive model usually do not generate the observed uniform pricing pattern with a highly asymmetric market share.

16. Based on the observed data, there is no obvious pattern of sequential decision for cigarette price and advertising.

17. There are over 50 brands in the combined category and most of them advertise very little or do not advertise at all.

18. Premium brands account for over 70% of cigarette sales and are the main source of profit for the tobacco industry.

19. The cartel manager is assumed to set the price for discount brands parallel to that for premium brands. I thus include discount brands in the "other brands" category. Following the "Marlboro Friday" event of April 2, 1993, discount brand prices stayed around 27 cents per pack lower than premium brand prices.

20. The relative size of young adults is pretty stable in the United States for the time period of the study.

21. One can justify this type of advertising response function by assuming that the total advertising spending x_{jt} is spent on K advertising channels, each with a spending x_{jt}^k, and advertising response function $f_1^k(x_{jt}^k)$ bounded by μ_k. Thus, the aggregate advertising response function $(f_1(x_{jt}) = \sum_{k=1}^{K} f_1^k(x_{jt}^k))$ is bounded by $\sum_{k=1K} \mu_k$.

22. Baltagi and Levin (1985) find that the effect of advertising on cigarette consumption decays fairly quick. Seldon and Doroodian (1989) suggest that advertising effect depreciates within one year.

23. x_{J+1t} is always zero, as I assume that brand $J+1$ (Other Brands) do not advertise.

24. Miranda and Fackler (2004) and Judd (1988) provide excellent illustrations of the use of the collocation method.

25. Tan (2004) contains a detailed description of the data.

26. The CTS data is an annual repeated cross-sectional data. As I only have information about brand level advertising spending before 1996, other waves of CTS data are not used in the study.

27. The eight premium brands are Marlboro, Salem, Merit, Winston, Benson & Hedges, Camel, Virginia Slim, and Newport.

28. Most smoking resumption occurs within one year of quitting. Former smokers who are able to avoid smoking for more than one year are unlikely to resume smoking. A recent study (Krall, Garvey, & Garcia, 2002) finds that "former cigarette smokers who remain abstinent for at least two years have a risk of relapse of 2 percent to 4 percent each year within the second through sixth years, but this risk decreases to less than 1 percent annually after 10 years of abstinence."

29. The CTS data only include adults age 18 and above.

30. Adolescent smokers cannot legally purchase cigarettes themselves and must therefore rely on other sources in order to obtain cigarettes. In addition, many adolescent smokers are only casual smokers.

31. The documents were obtained from The Legacy Tobacco Documents Library at the University of California, San Francisco.

32. The publicly available scanner dataset commonly used in the marketing literature in which actual purchase prices are recorded does not include cigarettes.

33. I do not explicitly consider the problem of cigarette smuggling in this study, since previous research has found that the smuggling effect is small in California (Hu et al., 1995a).

34. These differences may be caused by differences in tobacco control policies across states.

35. Berry, Levinsohn, and Pakes (1995) and the subsequent literature have developed techniques to deal with the above endogeneity problem.

36. The brand-specific fixed-effect for "other brands" is allowed to be time varying in order to control for changes in unobserved advertising spending for those brands.

37. See Hu, Sung, and Keeler (1995b) for a discussion of tobacco industry's responses to advertising restrictions.

38. According to Bulow and Klemperer (1998), the manufacturing costs for different brands of cigarettes are very close.

39. According to the FTC (2001), the cigarette industry spent 2.2, 3.69, and 3.46 billion on promotion spending, inclusive of promotional allowances, coupons, and retail value added, in 1990, 1992, and 1996 respectively. After dividing total spending by total sales data, I obtain promotion spending at 6, 10, and 9 cent per pack (in 1982–1983 dollar) respectively.

40. According to the BRFSS survey, the share of existing smokers σ_t is 0.271, 0.256, and 0.252 for 1990, 1992, and 1996 respectively. Since the estimated time effect for 1992 and 1996 are 0.77 and –0.09 respectively, the average estimated time effect over three years is 0.225 and the deviation from the average time effect is 0.225, –0.725, and 0.315 for 1990, 1992, and 1996 respectively. Assuming that the average sentiment against smoking for the above three years is at the steady state level, I calculate the social sentiment against smoking in 1990, 1992, and 1996 by adding the steady state social sentiments (0.75) to the deviation from the estimated average time effect – that is, κ equals 0.97, 0.20, and 1.07 for 1990, 1992, and 1996 respectively.

41. In the special case when the advertising response function in each of the K advertising channel is identical and $f^k(x_{jt}^k) = \mu \frac{\nu x_{jt}^k}{1+\nu x_{jt}^k}$, the advertising spending in any of K advertising channels is the same, that is, $x_{jt}^k = \frac{x_{jt}}{K}$. Thus the aggregate advertising response function $f(x_{jt}) = \sum_{k=1K} f^k(x_{jt}^k) = K\mu \frac{\nu x_{jt}^k}{1+\nu x_{jt}^k} = \bar{\mu}_K \frac{\bar{\nu}_K x_{jt}}{1+\bar{\nu}_K x_{jt}}$, where $\bar{\mu}_K = K\mu$ and $\bar{\nu}_K = \frac{\nu}{K}$. If K_1 number of the advertising channels are blocked, the aggregate advertising response function would be $f(x_{jt}) = \bar{\mu}_{K-K_1} \frac{\bar{\nu}_{K-K_1} x_{jt}}{1+\bar{\nu}_{K-K_1} x_{jt}}$.

42. I assume that all advertising channels have identical advertising response functions.

43. In the 1998 Multistate Settlement law-suit, the first concession made by the tobacco companies was voluntary advertising restriction. Later on, the tobacco industry agreed to use part of the settlements to fund antismoking groups. In the meantime, the Universal Tobacco Settlement Act (McCain Bill), which proposed a \$1.00 per pack cigarette tax, came under strong opposition from the tobacco industry and was defeated in the U.S. Senate.

ACKNOWLEDGMENTS

I would like to thank Joseph E. Harrington, Jr. and Matthew Shum for their advice and encouragement. I also thank Robert Moffitt, Tiemen

Woutersen, and seminar participants at Johns Hopkins University, North Carolina State University, University of Oklahoma, Arizona State University, Georgia State University, Rutgers, SUNY-Stony Brook, 2005 International Industrial Organization Society Conference, and 2006 Econometric Society Summer Meetings.

REFERENCES

Arcidiacono, P., Sieg, H., & Sloan, F. (2007). Living rationally under the volcano? An empirical analysis of heavy drinking and smoking. *International Economic Review*, *48*(1), 37–65.

Baltagi, B., & Levin, D. (1986). Estimating dynamic demand for cigarettes using panel data: The effects of bootlegging, taxation and advertising, reconsidered. *Review of Economics and Statistics*, *68*(1), 148–155.

Becker, G., Grossman, M., & Murphy, K. (1994). An empirical analysis of cigarette addiction. *The American Economic Review*, *84*(3), 396–418.

Becker, G., & Murphy, K. (1988). A theory of rational addiction. *Journal of Political Economy*, *96*(4), 675–700.

Beggs, A., & Klemperer, P. (1992). Multiperiod competition with switching costs. *Econometrica*, *60*(3), 651–666.

Benkard, L. (2004). Dynamic analysis of the market for wide-bodied commercial aircraft. *The Review of Economic Studies*, *71*(3), 148–155.

Berry, S. (1994). Estimating discrete choice models of product differentiation. *RAND Journal of Economics*, *25*(2), 242–262.

Berry, S., Levinsohn, J., & Pakes, A. (1995). Automobile prices in market equilibrium. *Econometrica*, *63*(4), 841–890.

Berry, S., Levinsohn, M., & Pakes, A. (2004). Estimating differentiated product demand systems from a combination of micro and macro data: The new car model. *Journal of Political Economy*, *112*(1), 68–105.

Bulow, J., & Klemperer, P. (1998). The tobacco deal. *Brookings Papers on Economic Activity, Microeconomics*, *1998*, 323–394.

Chaloupka, F. (1991). Rational addictive behavior and cigarette smoking. *Journal of Political Economy*, *99*(4), 722–742.

Chaloupka, F., & Grossman, M. (1997). Price, tobacco control policy and youth smoking. *Journal of Health Economics*, *16*(3), 359–373.

Chaloupka, F., & Warner, K. (2000). The economics of smoking. In J. Newhouse & A. Culyer (Eds.), *Handbook of health economics* (Vol. 1B). Amsterdam: North-Holland.

DeCicca, P., Kenkel, D., & Mathios, A. (2002). Putting out the fires: Will higher taxes reduce the onset of youth smoking?. *Journal of Political Economy*, *110*(1), 144–169.

Doraszelski, U., & Markovic, S. (2007). Advertising dynamics and competitive advantage. *Rand Journal of Economics*, *38*(3), 557–592.

Doraszelski, U., & Pakes, A. (2007). A framework for applied dynamic analysis in I.O. In M. Armstrong & R. Porter (Eds.), *Handbook of industrial organization* (Vol. 3, pp. 1887–1966). North-Holland, Amsterdam.

Dube, J., Hitsch, G., & Manchanda, P. (2005). An empirical model of advertising dynamic. *Quantitative Marketing and Economics*, *3*, 107–144.

Ericson, R., & Pakes, A. (1995). Markov perfect industry dynamics: A framework for empirical work. *Review of Economic Studies*, *62*(1), 53–82.

Evan, W., Farrelly, M., & Montgomery, E. (1999). Do workplace smoking bans reduce smoking? *The American Economic Reviews*, *89*(4), 728–747.

Evans, W., & Farrelly, M. (1998). The compensating behavior of smokers: Taxes, tar, and nicotine. *RAND Journal of Economics*, *29*(3), 578–595.

Farrell, J., & Klemperer, P. (2007). Coordination and lick-in: Competition with switching costs and network effects. In M. Armstrong & R. Porter (Eds.), *Handbook of industrial organization* (Vol. 3, pp. 1967–2072). North-Holland, Amsterdam.

Federal Trade Commission. (2001). Federal trade commission cigarette report for 2001. Washington, DC: Federal Trade Commission.

Fershtman, C., & Pakes, A. (2000). A dynamic game with collusion and price wars. *RAND Journal of Economics*, *31*(2), 207–236.

Gilleskie, D., & Strumpf, K. L. (2005). The behavioral dynamics of youth smoking. *Journal of Human Resource*, *40*, 822–866.

Gruber, J., & Zinman, J. (2001). Youth smoking in the United States: Evidence and implications. In J. Gruber (Ed.), *Risky behavior among youths: An economic analysis* (pp. 69–120). Chicago, IL: University of Chicago Press.

Hu, T. W., Sung, H., & Keeler, T. (1995a). Reducing cigarette consumption in California: Tobacco taxes vs an anti-smoking media campaign. *American Journal of Public Health*, *85*(9), 1218–1222.

Hu, T. W., Sung, H., & Keeler, T. (1995b). The state anti-smoking campaign and the industry response: The effects of advertising on cigarette consumption in California. *American Economic Review: Papers and Proceedings*, *85*(2), 85–90.

Klemperer, P. (1987a). Markets with consumer switching costs. *Quarterly Journal of Economics*, *102*(2), 375–394.

Klemperer, P. (1987b). The competitiveness of markets with switching costs. *Rand Journal of Economics*, *18*(1), 138–150.

Klemperer, P. (1995). Competition when consumers have switching costs: An overview with applications to industrial organization, macroeconomics, and international trade. *The Review of Economic Studies*, *62*(4), 515–539.

Krall, E., Garvey, A., & Garcia, R. (2002). Smoking relapse after 2 years of abstinence: Findings from the VA normative aging study. *Nicotine & Tobacco Research*, *4*, 95–100.

Lewit, E., & Coate, D. (1982). The potential for using excise taxes to reduce smoking. *Journal of Health Economics*, *1*, 121–145.

Lewit, E., Coate, D., & Grossman, M. (1981). The effects of government regulations on teenage smoking. *Journal of Law and Economics*, *24*(3), 545–569.

Marcovich, S. (2008). Snowball – A dynamic oligopoly model with indirect network effects. *Journal of Economic Dynamics and Control*, *38*, 909–938.

Maskin, E., & Tirole, J. (1988a). A theory of dynamic oligopoly, I: Overview and quantity competition with large fixed costs. *Econometrica*, *56*(3), 549–569.

Maskin, E., & Tirole, J. (1988b). A theory of dynamic oligopoly, II: Price competition, kinked demand curves, and edgeworth cycles. *Econometrica*, *56*(3), 557–599.

Miranda, M., & Fackler, P. (2004). *Applied computational economics and finance*. Cambridge, MA: MIT Press.

Pakes, A., & McGuire, P. (1994). Computing Markov perfect Nash equilibrium: Numerical implications of a dynamic differentiated product model. *RAND Journal of Economics*, *25*(4), 555–589.

Pakes, A., & McGuire, P. (2001). Stochastic algorithms, symmetric Markov perfect equilibria, and the 'curse' of dimensionality. *Econometrica*, *69*(5), 1261–1281.

Pollay, R., Siddarth, S., Siegel, M., Haddix, A., Merritt, R., Giovino, G., & Eriksen, M. (1996). The last straw? Cigarette advertising and realized market shares among youths and adults,1979–1993. *Journal of Marketing*, *60*(1), 1–16.

Powell, L., Tauras, J. and Ross, H. (2003). Peer effects, tobacco control policies, and youth smoking behavior. Mimeo, University of Illinois at Chicago.

Qi, S. (2012). The impact of advertising regulation on industry: The cigarette advertising ban of 1971. Mimeo, Florida State University.

Roberts, M., & Samuelson, L. (1988). An empirical analysis of dynamic, nonprice competition in an oligopolistic industry. *The RAND Journal of Economics*, *19*(2), 200–220.

Saffer, H., & Chaloupka, F. (2000). The effect of tobacco advertising bans on tobacco consumptions. *Journal of Health Economics*, *19*, 1117–1137.

Seldon, B. J., & Doroodian, K. (1989). A simultaneous model of cigarette advertising: Effects on demand and industry response to public policy. *Review of Economics and Statistics*, *71*(4), 673–677.

Showalter, M. (1999). Firm behavior in a market with addiction: The case of cigarettes. *Journal of Health Economics*, *18*, 409–427.

Tan, W. (2006). The effects of taxes and advertising restrictions on the market structure of the U.S. cigarette market. *Review of Industrial Organization*, *28*(3), 231–251.

Taurus, J., & Chaloupka, F. (1999) Price, clean indoor air laws, and cigarette smoking: Evidence from longitudinal data for young adults. Mimeo, University Illinois Chicago.

Tobacco Institute. (1998). The tax burden on Tobacco: Historical compilation. Washington, DC: Tobacco Institute.

Wasserman, J., Manning, W., Newhouse, J., & Winkler, J. (1991). The effects of excise taxes and regulations on cigarette smoking. *Journal of Health Economics*, *10*, 43–64.